# Management Communication

This textbook introduces students to the strategic communication methods that are crucial to master in order to develop into effective and ethical managers at all levels of business.

Effective communication skills are necessary for success in the business world, and O'Rourke has written a highly readable book filled with anecdotes and examples to engage students in the learning process. This edition includes several classic and new features:

- The strategic approach is integrated throughout the book, allowing students to understand how a communicated message impacts the business as a whole.
- Case studies throughout the book provide students with hands-on experience of scenarios they will encounter in the real world. The book includes at least three dozen fresh, classroom-tested cases.
- An ethical thread is woven through the text, demonstrating how ethical decision making can be applied in all aspects of communication.
- Separate chapters on technology (including social media), intercultural communication, nonverbal communication and conflict management provide students with the skills to building relationships and influencing stakeholders; key skills for any manager.

A companion website includes comprehensive support material to teach this class, making *Management Communication* a complete resource for students and instructors.

**James S. O'Rourke, IV** is an American rhetorician and Professor of Management at the University of Notre Dame, USA. He was founder of the Fanning Center for Business Communication and – from 1990 to 2018 – served as Arthur F. and Mary J. O'Neil Director. He is the author of 23 books on communication and is the directing editor of more than 350 business school case studies.

# Management Communication

## A Case Analysis Approach

### Sixth Edition

JAMES S. O'ROURKE, IV

Routledge
Taylor & Francis Group

NEW YORK AND LONDON

Sixth edition published 2019
by Routledge
52 Vanderbilt Avenue, New York, NY 10017

and by Routledge
2 Park Square, Milton Park, Abingdon, Oxon, OX14 4RN

*Routledge is an imprint of the Taylor & Francis Group, an informa business*

First edition published by Pearson Education 2000
Fifth edition published by Pearson 2012

*Library of Congress Cataloging-in-Publication Data*
A catalog record for this title has been requested

ISBN: 978–0-367–17811–6 (hbk)
ISBN: 978–0-367–17812–3 (pbk)
ISBN: 978–0-429–05779–3 (ebk)

Typeset in Bembo and Frutiger
by Apex CoVantage, LLC

Visit the eResources: www.routledge.com/9780367178123

MIX
Paper from
responsible sources
FSC™ C013985
FSC
www.fsc.org
Printed in the United Kingdom
by Henry Ling Limited

# Contents

Preface                                                                                          vii

Acknowledgments                                                                                   xi

**1  Management Communication in Transition**                                                       1

Case 1.1: Airbnb: Scaling Safety with Rapid Growth   12

Case 1.2: Great West Casualty Company v. Estate of G. Witherspoon (A)   23

Case 1.3: Domino's "Special" Delivery: Going Viral Through Social Media (A)   27

**2  Communication and Strategy**                                                                  35

Case 2.1: Chipotle Mexican Grill, Inc.: Supply Chain in Crisis (A)   46

Case 2.2: Gilead Sciences and Sovaldi: The Cost of a Cure (A)   56

**3  Communication Ethics**                                                                        65

Case 3.1: Excel Industries, Inc. (A)   80

Case 3.2: The National Football League: Responding to Traumatic Brain Injuries   84

Case 3.3: Target Corporation: Predictive Analytics and Customer Privacy   98

Case 3.4: Starbucks Corporation: Tax Avoidance Controversies in the United Kingdom (A)   107

**4  Speaking**                                                                                    115

Case 4.1: Old Dominion Trust Company   135

Case 4.2: Staples, Inc.: Preparing the CEO for a Press Conference   137

**5  Writing**                                                                                     141

Case 5.1: Microsoft Corporation: Communicating Layoffs to 18,000 Employees   157

Case 5.2: Carnival Cruise Lines: Wreck of the Costa Concordia   166

Case 5.3: Cerner Corporation: A Stinging Office Memo Boomerangs   176

**6  Persuasion**                                                                                  183

Case 6.1: The United States Olympic Committee: Persuading Business to Participate in the Olympic Movement   199

Case 6.2: An Invitation to Wellness at Whirlpool Corporation  202
Case 6.3: Theranos, Inc.: Managing Risk in a High-Flying Biotech Start-Up  205

7     **Technology**                                                            **217**
Case 7.1: Samsung Electronics Co., Ltd.: Galaxy Note 7 Crisis  239
Case 7.2: Johnson & Johnson's Strategy with Motrin: The Growing Pains
of Social Media  248
Case 7.3: Facebook, Inc.: Curating Moods in a Newsfeed Experiment  254

8     **Listening and Feedback**                                                **265**
Case 8.1: Earl's Family Restaurants (A): The Role of the Regional Sales Manager  282
Case 8.1: Earl's Family Restaurants (B): The Role of the Chief Buyer  285
Case 8.1: Earl's Family Restaurants (C): The Role of the Observer  288
Case 8.2: The Kroger Company (A): The Role of the Store Manager  291
Case 8.2: The Kroger Company (B): The Role of the Pepsi-Cola Sales Manager  294
Case 8.2: The Kroger Company (C): The Role of the Instructional Facilitator  296
Case 8.3: Three Feedback Exercises  298

9     **Nonverbal Communication**                                               **301**
Case 9.1: L'Oreal USA: Do Looks Really Matter in the Cosmetic Industry?  318
Case 9.2: Maria Sharapova: Banishment from WTA Tour and a Loss
of Sponsorship  323

10    **Intercultural Communication**                                           **331**
Case 10.1: Oak Brook Medical Systems, Inc.  342
Case 10.2: Barneys New York: A Case of "Shop and Frisk"  345

11    **Managing Conflict**                                                     **355**
Case 11.1: Hayward Healthcare Systems, Inc.  367
Case 11.2: Dixie Industries, Inc.  370
Case 11.3: The National Football League: Tackling Difficult Positions  376

12    **Business Meetings That Work**                                           **385**
Case 12.1: Yahoo! A Female CEO and New Mother Forbids Working from Home  399
Case 12.2: Zappos: An Experiment in Holacracy  408

13    **Dealing with the News Media**                                           **419**
Case 13.1: The United States Olympic Committee: Protecting Their Girls
or The Gold?  436
Case 13.2: Whole Foods Market, Inc.: Damage Control Over Product
Mislabeling (A)  446
Case 13.3: Mars, Incorporated: Skittles Becomes Part of a Controversial
Shooting  456

Appendix A: Analyzing a Case Study                                              463
Appendix B: Writing a Case Study                                               469
Appendix C: Sample Business Letter                                             477
Appendix D: Sample Strategy Memo                                              479
Appendix E: Documentation: Acknowledging the Sources of Your Research          483
Appendix F: Media Relations for Business Professionals: How to Prepare
for a Broadcast or Press Interview                                            491
Index                                                                          497

# Preface

Many years ago, as an Air Force officer assigned to a flight test group in the American Southwest, I had the opportunity to speak with an older (and obviously wiser) man who had been in the flying business for many years. Our conversation focused on what it would take for a young officer to succeed – to become a leader, a recognized influence among talented, trained and well-educated peers. His words were prophetic: "I can think of no skill more essential to the survival of a young officer," he said, "than effective self-expression." That was it. Not physical courage or well-honed flying skills. Not advanced degrees or specialized training, but "effective self-expression."

In the years since that conversation, I have personally been witness to what young managers call "career moments." Those moments in time are when a carefully crafted proposal, a thorough report or a deft response to criticism saved a career. I've seen young men and women offered a job as a result of an especially skillful speech introduction. I've seen others sputter and stall when they couldn't answer a direct question – one that fell well within their area of expertise – during a briefing. I've watched in horror as others simply talked their way into disfavor, trouble or oblivion.

Communication is, without question, the central skill any manager can possess. It is the link between ideas and action. It is the process that generates profit. It is the emotional glue that binds humans together in relationships, personal and professional. It is, as the English poet William Blake put it, "the chariot of genius." To be without the ability to communicate is to be isolated from others in an organization, an industry or a society. To be skilled at it is to be at the heart of what makes enterprise, private and public, function successfully.

The fundamental premise on which this book is based is simple: Communication is a skill that can be learned, taught and improved. You have the potential to be better at communicating with other people than you now are. It won't be easy, but this book can certainly help. The fact that you've gotten this far is evidence that you're determined to succeed, and what follows is a systematic yet readable review of those things you'll need to pay closer attention to in order to experience success as a manager.

## WHAT THIS BOOK IS ABOUT

This book will focus on the processes involved in management communication and concentrate on ways in which business students and entry-level managers can become more effective by becoming more knowledgeable and skilled as communicators.

The second premise on which this book is based is also simple: Writing, speaking, listening and other communication behaviors are the end-products of a process that begins with critical thinking. It is this process that managers are called on to employ every day in the workplace to earn a living. The basic task of a manager, day in and day out, is to solve managerial problems. The basic tools at a manager's disposal are mostly rhetorical.

*Management Communication* supports learning objectives that are strategic in nature, evolving as the workplace changes to meet the demands of a global economy that is changing at a ferocious pace. What you will find in these pages assumes certain basic competencies in communication, but encourages growth and development as you encounter the responsibilities and opportunities of mid-level and higher management, whether in your own business or in large and complex, publicly traded organizations.

## WHAT'S DIFFERENT ABOUT THIS BOOK

This book is aimed directly at the way most professors of management communication teach, yet in a number of important ways is different from other books in this field.

First, the process is entirely strategic. We begin with the somewhat non-traditional view that all communication processes in successful businesses in this century will be fully integrated. What happens in one part of the business affects all others. What is said to one audience has outcomes that influence others. Without an integrated, strategic perspective, managers in the twenty-first century economy will find themselves working at cross-purposes, often to the detriment of their businesses.

Second, the approach offered in *Management Communication* integrates ethics and the process of ethical decision making into each aspect of the discipline. Many instructors feel either helpless or at least slightly uncomfortable teaching ethics in a business classroom. Yet, day after day, business managers find themselves confronted with ethical dilemmas and decisions that have moral consequences for their employees, customers, shareholders and other important stakeholders.

This text doesn't moralize or preach. Instead, it offers a relatively simple framework for ethical decision making that students and faculty alike will find easy to grasp. Throughout the book, especially in case studies and role-playing exercises, you will learn to ask questions that focus on the issues that matter most to your classmates and colleagues. The answers won't come easily, but the process of confronting the issues will make you a better manager.

Third, this text includes separate chapters on Technology (Chapter 7) and Listening and Feedback (Chapter 8), as well as Nonverbal Communication (Chapter 9), Intercultural Communication (Chapter 10) and Managing Conflict (Chapter 11). These are topics that are often either ignored or shortchanged in other texts. These kinds of interpersonal communication skills are clearly central to relationship building and the personal influence all managers tell us they find indispensable to their careers. And, you'll find a newly revised chapter devoted to Persuasion (Chapter 6), which explores the science that underlies the process of influence.

Finally, *Management Communication* examines the often tenuous but unavoidable relationship that business organizations and their managers have with the news media. A step-by-step approach is presented to help you develop strategies and manage relationships, in both good news and bad news situations. Surviving a close encounter with a reporter while telling your company's story – fairly, accurately and completely – may mean the difference between a career that advances and one that does not.

## THE ADDED VALUE OF A CASE STUDY APPROACH

The sixth edition of this book contains at least three dozen original, classroom-tested case studies that will challenge you to discuss and apply the principles outlined in the chapters. Two of the chapters (8 and 13) include role-playing exercises. Appendix A, "Analyzing a Case Study," will introduce you to the reasons business students find such value in cases and will show you how to get the most from the cases included in this book. A rich, interesting case study is always an opportunity to show what you know about business and communication, to learn from your professors and classmates, and to examine the intricate processes at work when humans go into business together. Reading and analyzing a case are always useful, but the more profound insights inevitably come from listening carefully as others discuss and defend their views. Appendix B, "Writing a Case Study," will provide enough information for you and a small group of classmates to begin researching and writing an original business case on your own.

## THE REST IS UP TO YOU

What you take from this book and how you use it to become shrewder and more adept at the skills a manager needs most is really up to you. Simply reading the principles, looking through the examples, or talking about the case studies with your friends and classmates won't be enough. You'll need to look for ways to apply what you have learned, to put into practice the precepts articulated by successful executives and discussed at length in this book. The joy of developing and using those skills, however, comes in the relationships you will develop and the success you will experience throughout your business career and beyond. They aren't simply essential skills for learning how to earn a living; they're strategies for learning how to live.

James S. O'Rourke, IV
Professor of Management
Notre Dame, Indiana/USA
January 2019

# Acknowledgments

To Pam, Colleen, Molly and Kathleen. And to Jay, Cianan and Ty:
Your inspiration, patience and support have been indispensable. Thank you for making this possible.

To my colleagues:
Amanda McKendree, Sandra Collins, Eric Zimmer and Carolyn Langley. You are among many who have encouraged me, corrected me, kept me honest and held me accountable for my ideas.

To Elisa Podrasky:
Teaching and writing are so much easier with your help. I am so much better with you in the game.

To my friends in The Management Communication Association and the Arthur W. Page Society:
Thank you for the support, counsel and good ideas. My life is richer for having shared your company.

Finally, to Nicholas Gerstbauer:
This book is substantially better than it would have been without your very able research assistance.

# CHAPTER 1

# Management Communication in Transition

This book will argue that management communication is the central skill in the global workplace of the twenty-first century. An understanding of language and its inherent powers, combined with the skill to speak, write, listen and form interpersonal relationships, will determine whether you will succeed as a manager.

At the midpoint of the twentieth century, management philosopher Peter Drucker wrote,

> Managers have to learn to know language, to understand what words are and what they mean. Perhaps most important, they have to acquire respect for language as [our] most precious gift and heritage. The manager must understand the meaning of the old definition of rhetoric as "the art which draws men's hearts to the love of true knowledge."[1]

Later in the twentieth century, Harvard Business School professors Robert Eccles and Nitin Nohria reframed Drucker's view to offer a perspective of management that few others have seen. "To see management in its proper light," they write, "managers need first to take language seriously."[2] In particular, they argue, a coherent view of management must focus on three issues: the use of rhetoric to achieve a manager's goals, the shaping of a managerial identity, and taking action to achieve the goals of the organizations that employ us. Above all, they say, "the essence of what management is all about [is] the effective use of language *to get things done.*"[3]

The job of becoming a competent, effective manager thus becomes one of understanding language and action. It also involves finding ways to shape how others see and think of you in your role as a manager. A number of noted researchers have examined the important relationship between communication and action within large and complex organizations and conclude that the two are inseparable. Without the right words, used in the right way, it is unlikely that the right actions will ever occur. "Words do matter," write Eccles and Nohria, "they matter very much. Without words we have no way of expressing strategic concepts, structural forms, or designs for performance measurement systems." Language, they conclude, "is too important to managers to be taken for granted or, even worse, abused."[4]

So, if language is a manager's key to effective action, the next question is obvious: How good are you at using your language? Your ability to take action – to hire people, to restructure an organization, to launch a new product line – depends entirely on how effectively you use rhetoric, both as a speaker and as a listener. Your effectiveness as a speaker and writer will determine how well you are able to get others to do what you want. And your effectiveness as a listener will determine how well you understand others and can do things for them.

This book will examine the role language plays in the life of a manager and the central position occupied by rhetoric in the life of business organizations. In particular, though, this book will help you examine your own skills, abilities and competencies as you use language, attempt to influence others, and respond to the requirements of your superiors and the organization in which you work. If you think that landing your first really big job is mostly about the grades on your transcript, think again. Communication skills are most often cited as the primary personal attribute employers seek in college graduates, followed by a strong work ethic, teamwork skills, initiative, relating well to others, problem-solving skills, and analytic abilities.[5]

*Management Communication* is about the movement of information and the skills that facilitate it – speaking, writing, listening and processes of critical thinking – but it's more than just skill, really. It's also about understanding who you are, who others think you are, and the contributions you as an individual can make to the success of your business. It's about confidence – the knowledge that you can speak and write well, that you can listen with great skill as others speak, and that you can both seek out and provide the feedback essential to your survival as a manager and a leader.

This chapter will first look at the nature of managerial work, examining the roles managers play and the characteristics of the jobs they hold. We'll also look at what varies in a manager's position, what is different from one manager's job to another. And we'll look at the management skills you will need to succeed in the years ahead. At the heart of this chapter, though, is the notion that communication, in many ways, is the work of managers, day in and day out. This book goes on to examine the roles of writing and speaking in your life as a manager, as well as other specific applications and challenges you will face as you grow and advance on the job.

## WHAT DO MANAGERS DO ALL DAY?

If you were to consult a number of management textbooks for advice on the nature of managerial work, many – if not most – would say that managers spend their time engaged in planning, organizing, staffing, directing, coordinating, reporting and controlling. These activities, as Jane Hannaway found in her study of managers at work, "do not, in fact, describe what managers do."[6] At best they seem to describe vague objectives that managers are continually trying to accomplish. The real world, however, is far from being that simple. The world in which most managers work is a "messy and hectic stream of ongoing activity."[7]

Managers are in constant action. Virtually every study of managers in action has found that they "switch frequently from task to task, changing their focus of attention to respond to issues as they arise, and engaging in a large volume of tasks of short duration."[8] Professor Harvey Mintzberg of McGill University observed CEOs on the job to get some idea of what they do and how they spend their time. He found, for instance, that they averaged 36 written and 16 verbal contacts per day, almost every one of them dealing with a distinct or different issue. Most of these activities were brief, lasting less than nine minutes.[9]

Harvard Business School professor John Kotter studied a number of successful general managers over a five-year period and found that they spend most of their time with others, including subordinates, their bosses and numerous people from outside the organization. Kotter's study found that the average manager spent just 25 percent of his or her time working alone, and that time was spent largely at home, on airplanes or commuting. Few of them spend less than 70 percent of their time with others, and some spend up to 90 percent of their working time this way.[10]

Kotter also found that the breadth of topics in their discussions with others was extremely wide, with trivial issues taking time alongside important business matters. His study revealed that managers rarely make "big decisions" during these conversations and rarely give orders in a traditional sense. They often react to others' initiatives and spend substantial amounts of time in unplanned activities that aren't on their calendars. He found that managers will spend most of their time with others in short, disjointed conversations. "Discussions of a single question or issue rarely last more than ten minutes," he notes. "It is not at all unusual for a general manager to cover ten unrelated topics in a five-minute conversation."[11] More recently, managers studied by Lee Sproull showed similar patterns. During the course of a day, they engaged in 58 different activities with an average duration of just nine minutes.[12]

Interruptions also appear to be a natural part of the job. Rosemary Stewart found that the managers she studied could work uninterrupted for half an hour only nine times during the four weeks she studied them.[13] Managers, in fact, spend very little time by themselves. Contrary to the image offered by management textbooks, they are rarely alone drawing up plans or worrying about important decisions. Instead, they spend most of their time interacting with others – both inside and outside the organization. If you include casual interactions in hallways, phone conversations, one-on-one meetings and larger group meetings, managers spend about two-thirds of their time with other people.[14] As Mintzberg has pointed out, "Unlike other workers, the manager does not leave the telephone or the meeting to get back to work. Rather, these contacts *are* his work."[15]

The interactive nature of management means that most management work is conversational.[16] When managers are in action, they are talking and listening. Studies on the nature of managerial work indicate that managers spend about two-thirds to three-quarters of their time in verbal activity.[17] These verbal conversations, according to Eccles and Nohria, are the means by which managers gather information, stay on top of things, identify problems, negotiate shared meanings, develop plans, put things in motion, give orders, assert authority, develop relationships and spread gossip. In short, they are what the manager's daily practice is all about. "Through other forms of talk, such as speeches and presentations," they write, "managers establish definitions and meanings for their own actions and give others a sense of what the organization is about, where it is at, and what it is up to."[18]

## THE ROLES MANAGERS PLAY

In Professor Mintzberg's seminal study of managers and their jobs, he found the majority of them clustered around three core management roles.

### *Interpersonal Roles*

Managers are required to interact with a substantial number of people in the course of a workweek. They host receptions; take clients and customers to dinner; meet with business prospects and partners; conduct hiring and performance interviews; and form alliances, friendships and personal relationships with many others. Numerous studies have shown that such relationships are the richest source of information for managers because of their immediate and personal nature.[19]

Three of a manager's roles arise directly from formal authority and involve basic interpersonal relationships. First is the *figurehead* role. As the head of an organizational unit, every manager must perform some ceremonial duties. In Mintzberg's study, chief executives spent 12 percent of their contact time on ceremonial duties; 17 percent of their incoming mail dealt with acknowledgments and requests related to their status. One example is a company president who requested free merchandise for a handicapped schoolchild.[20]

Managers are also responsible for the work of the people in their unit, and their actions in this regard are directly related to their role as a *leader*. The influence of managers is most clearly seen, according to Mintzberg, in the leader role. Formal authority vests them with great potential power. Leadership determines, in large part, how much power they will realize.[21]

Does the leader's role matter? Ask the employees and investors of Intuit. "My personal first choice for ethical and meaningful . . . leadership is Brad Smith, CEO of Intuit," says *Forbes* contributing editor, David K. Williams. Intuit is one of the world's largest and most successful financial software companies. More than 95 percent of the company's revenue comes from activities within the U.S., which makes it a domestic hero. Intuit's core product is the Quick-Books accounting software ubiquitous to entrepreneurs, producing $5.2 billion in revenue in 2017, up 10 percent year-on-year. As a leader, Brad Smith has fostered a culture in which the company's 8,000 employees are allowed to take risks and to grow by learning from their failures as well as their successes.[22]

Other recent examples include the return of Starbucks founder Howard Schultz to re-energize and steer his company, Amazon CEO Jeff Bezos and his ability to innovate during a downturn in the economy, and General Motors CEO Mary Barra, who took command of a floundering automaker, guiding it through a perilous set of recalls and setting the stage for innovation, greater market share and an impressive financial recovery.[23] [24]

Popular management literature has had little to say about the *liaison* role until recently. This role, in which managers establish and maintain contacts outside the vertical chain of command, becomes especially important in view of the finding of virtually every study of managerial work that managers spend as much time with peers and other people outside of their units as they do with their own subordinates. Surprisingly, they spend little time with their own superiors. In Rosemary Stewart's study, 160 British middle and top managers spent 47 percent of their time with peers, 41 percent of their time with people inside their unit and only 12 percent of their time with superiors.[25] Robert H. Guest's study of U.S. manufacturing supervisors revealed similar findings.[26]

### Informational Roles

Managers are required to gather, collate, analyze, store, protect and disseminate many kinds of information. In doing so, they become information resource centers, often storing huge amounts of information in their own heads, moving quickly from the role of gatherer to the role of disseminator in minutes. Although many business organizations install large, expensive information technology systems to perform many of those functions, nothing can match the speed and intuitive power of a well-trained manager's brain for information processing. Not surprisingly, most managers prefer it that way.[27]

As *monitors*, managers are constantly scanning the environment for information, talking with liaison contacts and subordinates, and receiving unsolicited information, much of it as a result of their network of personal contacts. A good portion of this information arrives in oral form, often as gossip, hearsay and speculation.[28]

In the *disseminator* role, managers pass privileged information directly to subordinates, who might otherwise have no access to it. Managers must not only decide who should receive such information, but how much of it, how often and in what form. Increasingly, managers are being asked to decide whether subordinates, peers, customers, business partners and others should have direct access to information 24 hours a day without having to contact the manager directly.

In the *spokesperson* role, managers send information to people outside of their organizations: An executive makes a speech to lobby for an organizational cause, or a supervisor suggests a product modification to a supplier. Increasingly, managers are also being asked to deal with representatives of the news media, providing both factual and opinion-based responses that will be printed, broadcast or posted to vast unseen audiences, often directly or with little editing. The risks in such circumstances are enormous, but so too are the potential rewards in terms of brand recognition, public image and organizational visibility.

### Decisional Roles

Ultimately, managers are charged with the responsibility of making decisions on behalf of both the organization and the stakeholders with an interest in it. Such decisions are often made under circumstances of high ambiguity and with inadequate information. Often, the other two managerial roles – interpersonal and informational – will assist a manager in making difficult decisions in which outcomes are not clear and interests are often conflicting.

In the role of *entrepreneur*, managers seek to improve their businesses, adapt to changing market conditions and react to opportunities as they present themselves. Managers who take a longer-term view of their responsibilities are among the first to realize that they will need to reinvent themselves, their product and service lines, their marketing strategies, and their ways of doing business as older methods become obsolete and competitors gain advantage.

While the entrepreneur role describes managers who initiate change, the disturbance or *crisis handler* role depicts managers who must involuntarily react to conditions. Crises can arise because bad managers let circumstances deteriorate or spin out of control, but just as often good managers find themselves in the midst of a crisis that they could not have anticipated but must react to just the same.

The third decisional role of *resource allocator* involves managers making decisions about who gets what, how much, when and why. Resources, including funding, equipment, human labor, office or production space, and even the boss's time are all limited, and demand inevitably outstrips supply. Managers must make sensible decisions about such matters while still retaining, motivating and developing the best of their employees.

The final decisional role is that of *negotiator*. Managers spend considerable amounts of time in negotiations: over budget allocations, labor and collective bargaining agreements, and other formal dispute resolutions. In the course of a week, managers will often make dozens of decisions that are the result of brief but important negotiations between and among employees, customers and clients, suppliers, and others with whom managers must deal.[29]

# MAJOR CHARACTERISTICS OF THE MANAGER'S JOB

## Time Is Fragmented

Managers have acknowledged from antiquity that they never seem to have enough time to get all those things done that need to be done. In the early years of the twenty-first century, however, a new phenomenon arose: Demand for time from those in leadership roles increased, while the number of hours in a day remained constant. Increased work hours was one reaction to such demand, but managers quickly discovered that the day had just 24 hours and that working more of them produced diminishing marginal returns. According to one researcher, "Managers are overburdened with obligations yet cannot easily delegate their tasks. As a result, they are driven to overwork and forced to do many tasks superficially. Brevity, fragmentation, and verbal communication characterize their work."[30]

## Values Compete and the Various Roles are in Tension

Managers clearly cannot satisfy everyone. Employees want more time to do their jobs; customers want products and services delivered quickly and at high-quality levels. Supervisors want more money to spend on equipment, training and product development; shareholders want returns on investment maximized. A manager caught in the middle cannot deliver to each of these people what each most wants; decisions are often based on the urgency of the need and the proximity of the problem.

## The Job Is Overloaded

In recent years, many North American and global businesses were reorganized to make them more efficient, nimble and competitive. For the most part, this reorganization meant decentralizing many processes along with the wholesale elimination of middle management layers. Many managers who survived such downsizing found that their number of direct reports had doubled. Classical management theory suggests that seven is the maximum number of direct reports a manager can reasonably handle. Today, high-speed information technology and remarkably efficient telecommunication systems mean that many managers have as many as 20 or 30 people reporting to them directly.

## Efficiency Is a Core Skill

With less time than they need, with time fragmented into increasingly smaller units during the workday, with the workplace following many managers out the door and even on vacation, and with many more responsibilities loaded onto managers in downsized, flatter organizations, efficiency has become the core management skill of the twenty-first century.

# WHAT VARIES IN A MANAGER'S JOB? THE EMPHASIS

## The Entrepreneur Role Is Gaining Importance

Managers must increasingly be aware of threats and opportunities in their environment. Threats include technological breakthroughs on the part of competitors, obsolescence in a manager's organization, and dramatically shortened product cycles. Opportunities might include product or service niches that are underserved, out-of-cycle hiring opportunities, mergers, purchases, or upgrades in equipment, space or other assets. Managers who are carefully attuned to the marketplace and competitive environment will look for opportunities to gain an advantage.

## So Is the Leader Role

Managers must be more sophisticated as strategists and mentors. A manager's job involves much more than simple caretaking in a division of a large organization. Unless you are able to attract, train, motivate, retain and promote good people, your organization cannot possibly hope to gain advantage over the competition. Thus, as leaders, managers must constantly act as mentors to those in the organization with promise and potential. When you lose a highly capable worker, all else in your world will come to a halt until you can replace that worker. Even if you should find someone ideally suited and superbly qualified for a vacant position, you must still train, motivate and inspire that new recruit, and you must live with the knowledge that productivity levels will be lower for a while than they were with your previous employee.

### Manager's Must Create a Local Vision as They Help People Grow

The company's website, annual report and those slick-paper brochures your sales force hands to customers may articulate the vision, values and beliefs of the company. But what do those concepts really mean to workers at your location? What does a competitive global strategy mean to your staff at 8:00 a.m. on Monday? Somehow, you must create a local version of that strategy, explaining in practical and understandable terms what your organization or unit is all about and how the work of your employees fits into the larger picture.

## MANAGEMENT SKILLS REQUIRED FOR THE TWENTY-FIRST CENTURY

The twenty-first century workplace requires three types of skills, each of which will be useful at different points in your career.

### Technical Skills

These are most valuable at the entry level, but less valuable at more senior levels. Organizations hire people for their technical expertise: Can you assess the market value of a commercial office building? Can you calculate a set of net present values? Are you experienced in the use of C++ or SAP/R3 software? These skill sets, however, constantly change and can become quickly outdated. What gets you in the door of a large organization won't necessarily get you promoted.

### Relating Skills

These are valuable across the managerial career span and are more likely to help you progress and be promoted to higher levels of responsibility. These skills, which help you to form relationships, are at the heart of what management communication is about: reading, writing, speaking, listening and thinking about how you can help others and how they can help you as the demands of your job shift and increase at the same time.

### Conceptual Skills

These skills are least valuable at the entry level, but more valuable at senior levels in the organization. They permit you to look past the details of today's work assignment and see the bigger picture. Successful managers who hope to become executives in the highest levels of a business must begin, at a relatively early age, to develop the ability to see beyond the horizon and ask long-term questions. If you haven't formed the relationships that will help you get promoted, however, you may not be around long enough to have an opportunity to use your conceptual skills.

## TALK IS THE WORK

Managers across industries, according to Deirdre Borden, spend about 75 percent of their time in verbal interaction.[31] Those daily interactions include the following:

### One-on-One Conversations

Increasingly, managers find that information is passed orally, often face-to-face in offices, hallways, conference rooms, cafeterias, rest rooms, athletic facilities, parking lots and literally dozens of other venues. An enormous amount of information is exchanged, validated, confirmed and passed back and forth under highly informal circumstances.

### Telephone Conversations

Managers spend an astounding amount of time on the telephone these days. Curiously, the amount of time per tele-phone call is decreasing, but the number of calls per day is increasing. With the nearly universal availability of cellular, satellite and online telephone service, very few people are out of reach of the office for very long. The decision to switch off your cellular telephone, in fact, is now considered a decision in favor of work–life balance.

### Video Teleconferencing

Bridging time zones as well as cultures, videoconferencing facilities make direct conversations with employees, col-leagues, customers and business partners across the nation or around the world a simple matter. Carrier Corporation, the air-conditioning manufacturer, is now typical of firms using desktop videoconferencing to conduct everything from staff meetings to technical training. Engineers at Carrier's Farmington, Connecticut, headquarters can hook up with service managers in branch offices thousands of miles away to explain new product developments, demonstrate repair techniques and update field staff on matters that would, just recently, have required extensive travel or expen-sive, broadcast-quality television programming. Their exchanges are informal, conversational and not much different than they would be if both people were in the same room.[32]

### Presentations to Small Groups

Managers frequently find themselves making presentations, formal and informal, to groups of three-to-eight people for many different reasons: They pass along information given to them by executives; they review the status of proj-ects in process; they explain changes in everything from working schedules to organizational goals. Such presenta-tions are sometimes supported by PowerPoint slides or printed outlines, but they are oral in nature and retain much of the conversational character of one-to-one conversations.

### Public Speaking to Larger Audiences

Most managers are unable to escape the periodic requirement to speak to larger audiences of several dozen or, per-haps, several hundred people. Such presentations are usually more formal in structure and are frequently supported by PowerPoint or Corel software that can deliver data from text files, graphics and photos, and even motion clips from streaming video. Despite the more formal atmosphere and sophisticated audio–visual support systems, such presentations still involve one manager talking to others, framing, shaping and passing information to an audience.

## THE MAJOR CHANNELS OF MANAGEMENT COMMUNICATION ARE TALKING AND LISTENING

A series of scientific studies, beginning with Rankin in 1926,[33] and later with Nichols and Stevens (1957)[34] and Wolvin and Coakley (1982),[35] serve to confirm what each of us knows intuitively: Most managers spend the largest portion of their day talking and listening. E. K. Werner's thesis at the University of Maryland, in fact, found that North American adults spend more than 78 percent of their communication time either talking or listening to others who are talking.[36]

According to Werner and others who study the communication habits of postmodern business organizations, managers are involved in more than just speeches and presentations from the dais or teleconference podium. They spend their days in meetings, on the telephone, conducting interviews, giving tours, supervising informal visits to their facilities and at a wide variety of social events. Each of these activities may look to some managers like an obli-gation imposed by the job.

Shrewd managers see them as opportunities to hear what others are thinking, to gather information informally from the grapevine, to listen in on office gossip, to pass along viewpoints that haven't yet made their way to the more formal channels of communication, or to catch up with a colleague or friend in a more relaxed setting. No matter what the intention of each manager who engages in these activities, the information they produce and the insight that follows from them can be put to work the same day to achieve organizational and personal objectives.

"To understand why effective managers behave as they do," writes Professor John Kotter, "it is essential first to recognize two fundamental challenges and dilemmas found in most of their jobs." Managers must first figure out what to do, despite an enormous amount of potentially relevant information (along with much that is not), and then they must get things done "through a large and diverse group of people despite having little direct control over most of them."[37]

## THE ROLE OF WRITING

Writing plays an important role in the life of any organization. In some organizations, it becomes more important than in others. At Procter & Gamble, for example, brand managers cannot raise a work-related issue in a team meeting unless the ideas are first circulated in writing. For P&G managers, this approach means explaining their ideas in explicit detail in a standard one-to-three-page memo, complete with background, financial discussion, implementation details and justification for the ideas proposed.

Other organizations are more oral in their traditions – 3M Canada comes to mind as a "spoken" organization – the fact remains: The most important projects, decisions and ideas end up in writing. Writing also provides analysis, justification, documentation and analytic discipline, particularly as managers approach important decisions that will affect the profitability and strategic direction of the company.

### Writing Is a Career Sifter

If you demonstrate your inability to put ideas on paper in a clear, unambiguous fashion, you're not likely to last. Stories of bad writers who've been shown the door early in their careers are legion. Your principal objective, at least during the first few years of your own career, is to keep your name out of such stories. Remember, those who are most likely to notice the quality and skill in your written documents are the very people most likely to matter to your future.

### Managers Do Most of Their Own Writing and Editing

The days when managers could lean back and thoughtfully dictate a letter or memo to a skilled secretarial assistant are mostly gone. Some senior executives know how efficient dictation can be, especially with a top-notch administrative assistant taking shorthand, but how many managers have that advantage today? Very few, mostly because buying a computer and printer is substantially cheaper than hiring another employee. Managers at all levels of most organizations draft, review, edit and dispatch their own correspondence, reports and proposals.

### Documents Take On Lives of Their Own

Once it's gone from your desk, it isn't yours anymore. When you sign a letter and put it in the mail, it's no longer your letter – it's the property of the person or organization you sent it to. As a result, the recipient is free to do as he or she sees fit with your writing, including using it against you. If your ideas are ill-considered or not well expressed, others in the organization who are not especially sympathetic to your views may head for the copy machine with your work in hand. The advice for you is simple: Don't mail your first draft, and don't ever sign your name to a document you're not proud of.

## COMMUNICATION IS INVENTION

Without question, communication is a process of invention. Managers literally create meaning through communication. A company, for example, is not in default until a team of auditors sits down to examine the books and review the matter. Only after extended discussion do the accountants (and their bankers) come to the conclusion that the company is, in fact, in default. It is their discussion that creates the outcome. Until that point, default was simply one of many possibilities.

The fact is managers create meaning through communication. It is largely through discussion and verbal exchange – often heated and passionate – that managers decide who they wish to be: market leaders, takeover artists, innovators or defenders of the economy. It is only through communication that meaning is created for shareholders, for employees, for customers and others. Those long, detailed and intense discussions determine how much the company will declare in dividends this year, whether the company is willing to risk a strike or labor action, and how soon to roll out the new product line customers are asking for. Additionally, it is important to note that managers usually figure things out by talking about them as much as they talk about the things they have already figured out. Talk serves as a wonderful palliative: justifying, dissecting, reassuring and analyzing the events that confront managers each day.

## INFORMATION IS SOCIALLY CONSTRUCTED

If we are to understand just how important human discourse is in the life of a business, several points seem especially important.

### Information Is Created, Shared and Interpreted by People

Meaning is a truly human phenomenon. An issue is only important if people think it is. Facts are facts only if we can agree on their definition. Perceptions and assumptions are as important as truth itself in a discussion about what a manager should do next.[38]

### Information Never Speaks for Itself

It is not uncommon for a manager to rise to address a group of his colleagues and say, "Ladies and gentlemen, the numbers speak for themselves." Frankly, the numbers never speak for themselves. They almost always require some sort of interpretation, some sort of explanation or context. Don't assume that others see the facts in the same way you do and never assume that what you see is the truth. Others may see the same set of facts or evidence but may not reach the same conclusions. Few things in life are self-explanatory.

### Context Always Drives Meaning

The backdrop to a message is always of paramount importance to the listener, viewer or reader in reaching a reasonable, rational conclusion about what she sees and hears. What's in the news these days as we take up this particular subject? What moment in history do we occupy? What related or relevant information is under consideration as this new message arrives? We cannot possibly derive meaning from one message without considering everything else that surrounds it.

### A Messenger Always Accompanies a Message

It is difficult to separate a message from its messenger. We often want to react more to the source of the information than we do to the information itself. That's natural and entirely normal. People speak for a reason, and we often judge their reasons for speaking before analyzing what they have to say. Keep in mind that, in every organization, message recipients will judge the value, power, purpose, intent and outcomes of the messages they receive by the source of those messages as much as by the content and intent of the messages themselves. If the messages you send as a manager are to have the impact you hope they will, they must come from a source the receiver knows, respects and understands.

## YOUR GREATEST CHALLENGE

Every manager knows communication is vital, but every manager also seems to "know" that he or she is great at it. Your greatest challenge is to admit to flaws or shortcomings in your skill set and work tirelessly to improve them. First, you must admit to the flaws.

T. J. Larkin and Sandar Larkin, in a book entitled *Communicating Change: Winning Employee Support for New Business Goals*, write:

> Deep down, managers believe they are communicating effectively. In ten years of management consulting, we have never had a manager say to us that he or she was a poor communicator. They admit to the occasional screw-up, but overall, everyone, without exception, believes he or she is basically a good communicator.[39]

## YOUR TASK AS A PROFESSIONAL

As a professional manager, your first task is to recognize and understand your strengths and weaknesses as a communicator. Until you identify those communication tasks at which you are most and least skilled, you'll have little opportunity for improvement and advancement. Foremost among your goals should be to improve existing skills. Improve your ability to do what you do best. Be alert to opportunities, however, to develop new skills. Add to your inventory of abilities to keep yourself employable and promotable.

Two other suggestions come to mind for improving your professional standing as a manager. First, acquire a knowledge base that will work for the years ahead. That means speaking with and listening to other professionals in your company, your industry and your community. Be alert to trends that could affect your products and services, as well as your own future.

It also means reading. You should read at least one national newspaper each day, including *The Wall Street Journal*, *The New York Times* or the *Financial Times*, as well as a local newspaper. Your reading should include weekly news magazines, such as *Bloomberg BusinessWeek* and *The Economist*. Subscribe to monthly magazines such as *Forbes* and *Fortune*. And you should read at least one new hardcover title a month. A dozen books each year is the bare minimum on which you should depend for new ideas, insights and managerial guidance.

Your final challenge is to develop the confidence you will need to succeed as a manager, particularly under conditions of uncertainty, change and challenge.

## FOR FURTHER READING

Axley, S. R. *Communication at Work: Management and the Communication-Intensive Organization.* Westport, CT: Quorum Books, 1996.

Christensen, L. T., M. Morsing and G. Cheney. *Corporate Communications: Convention, Complexity, and Critique.* Thousand Oaks, CA: Sage Publications, Inc., 2008.

Clutterbuck, D. and S. Hirst. *Talking Business: Making Communication Work.* Burlington, MA: Butterworth-Heinemann, 2002.

Drucker, P. F. *Management Challenges for the 21st Century.* New York: HarperBusiness, 1999.

Ferguson, N. *The Ascent of Money: A Financial History of the World.* New York: The Penguin Press, 2008.

Hamel, G. and B. Breen. *The Future of Management.* Boston, MA: Harvard Business School Press, 2007.

Krisco, K. H. *Leadership and the Art of Conversation.* Schoolcraft, MI: Prima Publishing, 1997.

Mintzberg, H. *Managing.* San Francisco, CA: Berrett-Koehler Publishers, Inc., 2009.

Van Riel, C. B. M. and C. J. Fombrun. *Essentials of Corporate Communication.* New York: Routledge, 2008.

Wishard, W. V. D. *Between Two Ages: The 21st Century and the Crisis of Meaning.* Washington, DC: Xlibris Corporation, 2000.

## NOTES

1  Drucker, P. F. *The Practice of Management.* New York: Harper & Row, 1954.

2  Eccles, R. G. and N. Nohria. *Beyond the Hype: Rediscovering the Essence of Management.* Boston, MA: The Harvard Business School Press, 1992, p. 205.

3  Ibid., p. 211.

4   Ibid., p. 209.
5   *Job Outlook 2008.* National Association of Colleges and Employers, Chart A.
6   Hannaway, J. *Managers Managing: The Workings of an Administrative System.* New York: Oxford University Press, 1989, p. 39.
7   Eccles and Nohria. *Beyond the Hype*, p. 47.
8   Hannaway. *Managers Managing*, p. 37. See also Kotter, J. P. *The General Managers.* New York: The Free Press, 1982.
9   Mintzberg, H. *The Nature of Managerial Work.* New York: Harper & Row, 1973, p. 31. See also Mintzberg, H. *Managing.* San Francisco, CA: Berrett-Koehler Publishers, Inc., 2009.
10  Reprinted by permission of *Harvard Business Review* from Kotter, J. P. "What Effective General Managers Really Do," *Harvard Business Review*, March–April 1999, pp. 145–59. Copyright © 1999 by the Harvard Business School Publishing Corporation; all rights reserved.
11  Kotter. "What Effective General Managers Really Do," p. 148.
12  Sproull, L. S. "The Nature of Managerial Attention," in L. S. Sproull (ed.), *Advances in Information Processing in Organizations.* Greenwich, CT: JAI Press, 1984, p. 15.
13  Stewart, R. *Managers and Their Jobs.* London: Macmillan, 1967.
14  Eccles and Nohria. *Beyond the Hype*, p. 47.
15  Mintzberg. *The Nature of Managerial Work*, p. 44 (emphasis mine).
16  Pondy, L. R. "Leadership Is a Language Game," in M. W. McCall, Jr. and M. M. Lombardo (eds.), *Leadership: Where Else Can We Go?* Durham, NC: Duke University Press, 1978, pp. 87–99.
17  Mintzberg. *The Nature of Managerial Work*, p. 38.
18  Eccles and Nohria. *Beyond the Hype*, pp. 47–48.
19  Reprinted by permission of *Harvard Business Review* from Mintzberg, H. "The Manager's Job: Folklore and Fact." *Harvard Business Review*, March–April 1990, pp. 166–167. Copyright © 1990 by the Harvard Business School Publishing Corporation. All rights reserved.
20  Mintzberg. "The Manager's Job," p. 167.
21  Ibid., p. 168.
22  Williams, D. K. "10 Influential American Business Leaders Today," *Forbes*, Online at www.forbes.com/sites/davidkwilliams/2017/01/03/top-10-list-americas-most-influential-business-leaders-today/#3d0061896e67. Accessed Monday, July 2, 2018 at 1:34 p.m. EDT.
23  McGregor, J. "Bezos: How Frugality Drives Innovation," *BusinessWeek*, April 28, 2008, pp. 64–66.
24  Boudinet, J. "40 Successful Business Leaders to Follow," *Ambition*, Online at https://ambition.com/blog/entry/2016-5-12-business-team-leader-icons/. Accessed Monday, July 2, 2018 at 1:44 p.m. EDT.
25  Stewart, R. *Managers and Their Jobs.* London: Macmillan, 1967.
26  Guest, R. H. "Of Time and the Foreman," *Personnel*, May 1956, p. 478.
27  Mintzberg. "The Manager's Job," pp. 166–167.
28  Ibid., pp. 168, 170.
29  Ibid., pp. 167–171.
30  Ibid., p. 167.
31  Borden, D. *The Business of Talk: Organizations in Action.* New York: Blackwell, 1995.
32  Ziegler, B. "Video Conference Calls Change Business," *Wall Street Journal*, October 13, 1994, pp. B1, B12. Reprinted by permission of *Wall Street Journal*, Copyright © 1994 Dow Jones & Company, Inc. All rights reserved worldwide.
33  Rankin, P. T. "The Measurement of the Ability to Understand Spoken Language" (unpublished Ph.D. dissertation, University of Michigan, 1926). *Dissertation Abstracts* 12, No. 6 (1952), pp. 847–848.
34  Nichols, R. G. and L. Stevens. *Are You Listening?* New York: McGraw-Hill, 1957.
35  Wolvin, A. D. and C. G. Coakley. *Listening.* Dubuque, IA: Wm. C. Brown and Co., 1982.
36  Werner, E. K. "A Study of Communication Time" (M.S. thesis, University of Maryland, College Park, 1975), p. 26.
37  Kotter. "What Effective General Managers Really Do," pp. 145–159.
38  Searle, J. R. *The Construction of Social Reality.* New York: The Free Press, 1995. See also Berger, P. L. and T. Luckmann. *The Social Construction of Reality.* New York: Doubleday, 1967.
39  Larkin, T. J. and S. Larkin. *Communicating Change: Winning Employee Support for New Business Goals.* New York: McGraw-Hill, 1994.

# Case 1.1: Airbnb

## Scaling Safety with Rapid Growth

### THE LOPEZ INCIDENT

When 19-year-old Jacob Lopez traveled overseas to Madrid in July 2015, he anticipated an enjoyable trip and planned to stay at an Airbnb property. His decision to book an Airbnb in Madrid stemmed mainly from his great experience at an Airbnb property in Brazil just a year prior.[1,2]

Lopez arrived in Madrid on July 4 and met his host, who turned out to be transsexual, at the subway near the property. The male-transformed-to-female walked with Lopez to the apartment and, upon arrival, locked the main door to the unit. Then, according to Lopez, the woman ordered him to perform a series of sexual acts. Lopez initially refused to obey. He was scared for his life after the host began to hint that she would harm him if he did not comply. She also severed the Internet lines to hinder his ability to reach out for assistance.

Lopez texted his mother, Micaela Giles, in the U.S. Giles immediately phoned Airbnb from the family's Massachusetts home for help. However, Airbnb personnel indicated that an address to the property could not be provided as she was not the registered guest. They went on to say that Giles would need to ask the Madrid police to call Airbnb directly for the address to be released. She hung up the phone and repeatedly attempted to call the Madrid police. Each time she rang authorities, she was led through a series of prompts in Spanish only to have her calls continuously dropped. After several attempts, Giles tried to call Airbnb again, but was unable to connect to the company's emergency hotline.

Eventually, Lopez was able to escape by telling the host that he had to meet friends who knew where he was and who would call the police if he did not show up to join them. According to Lopez, the host sexually assaulted him prior to his escape. When questioned, the host maintained that the sexual actions were consensual. Lopez has undergone extensive counseling to overcome the trauma resulting from the situation.[3]

### AIRBNB COMPANY OVERVIEW

In 2007, two 20-something entrepreneurs, Brian Chesky and Joe Gebbia, saw a need in a century-old industry. These two recognized that the lodging and hospitality business had not tapped into the sharing economy. Doing so could provide convenient and economical options for consumers. So, with a website called airbedandbreakfast.com, the duo launched their idea.[4] Chesky and Gebbia decided to pair the debut of their start-up with a local San Francisco design conference in hopes of garnering more attention. For $80 a night, the friends rented air mattresses in their shared apartment and reached out to members of the city's designer population to do the same. Gaining the interest of only three guests and three hosts, the first attempt was an overall failure.[5]

But Chesky and Gebbia did not stop there. Instead, they paralleled their second attempt with an even bigger event, the 2008 Democratic National Convention in Denver, Colorado. At this time, Nathan Blecharczyk, Gebbia's former and technologically savvy roommate, joined the team. The three were able to secure a steady revenue. However, when elections came to an end, revenue dropped significantly.[6]

On the advice of an established entrepreneur, the three took their gig to New York City, an area overpopulated with tourists and desperate for economical lodging options. This environment, paired with an increasingly "open" society in which members were quickly becoming more willing to share due to social media expansion, proved to be the perfect springboard for the start-up.[7]

Not long after its debut, Air Bed and Breakfast, or more commonly referred to as Airbnb, transformed into a global billion-dollar company. The entity's transactional process is fairly straightforward. Airbnb hosts post pictures of their property on the company's website and online community members can search the site to find lodging. Property prices range from less than $50 to more than $1,000 a night and guests can choose between renting an entire home or apartment, a private room or a shared room.[8]

Airbnb prides itself in fostering a community feel amongst guests and hosts. Chesky sums it up as follows, "Airbnb is about so much more than just renting space. It's about people and experiences. At the end of the day, what we're trying to do is bring the world together. You're not getting a room, you're getting a sense of belonging."[9] Airbnb's business model provides assets to both hosts and guests. Hosts are able to earn supplemental income, sometimes enough to cover the cost of their own rent or other property-related expenses, and guests have access to relatively low-cost accommodations that they can book efficiently.

Today, a small team of Airbnb executives manages the company. These key staff members include the Chief Executive Officer, Chief Technology Officer, Chief Product Officer, Chief Financial Officer, Head of Global Hospitality, Head of Global Policy and Government Affairs, and Chief Business Affairs and Legal Officer.[10]

## AIRBNB'S BUSINESS MODEL

Airbnb is among the fastest growing accommodation companies in the world. In December 2014, Chesky shared some news via *Twitter*: "Airbnb now has 1 million homes on its platform, and is adding more than 20,000 new ones each week."[11] Equally impressive, the company's growth stemmed from a small workforce of approximately 1,600 employees globally.[12] Airbnb deliberately runs a lean operation, but what is most compelling about the company is that it does not own real estate. Unlike traditional hotel companies, which own and profit from physical real estate, Airbnb is purely in the business of connecting people with other people and, by doing so, people with places.

The company's core focus is connecting cost-focused travelers to homeowners that provide lodging solutions in desirable sections of cities that hotels traditionally underserve. Many users are repeat customers highlighting the fact that the service enables travelers to live like the locals. In essence, Airbnb provides unique travel experiences as well as quick, affordable and safe accommodation for travelers.

Airbnb's business model is straightforward. Users fall into one of two classifications: hosts or guests. Hosts represent the asset owners who list their homes and apartments on the platform. In effect, hosts provide the listings that are available to customers on the Airbnb digital platform. Guests reflect the demand on the platform, representing customers that are seeking to rent listings in cities around the world.

Airbnb's two main customer segments are personal travelers and business travelers, with personal travelers comprising the majority of its users.[13] Airbnb approaches customer acquisition through two core sales channels – online advertising and word-of-mouth.[14]

According to Kenontech.com, a blog that highlights start-ups, "Airbnb is very aggressive with its online marketing and ads can be found through an extensive network of affiliate sites and as part of search results on major search engines."[15] Kenontech.com goes on to say that the second sales channel, which emphasizes a word-of-mouth approach, stems from the founders' belief that "if they provided their users with a great experience there would be a high probability that their users would spread the word."[16]

**Example:** 4-night reservation at a listing with a nightly rate of $100 and $50 cleaning fee

**Subtotal:** (4 nights x $100) + $50 cleaning fee = $450

- Host Payout: $450 – (3% x $450) = $436.50
- $450 - $436.50 = $14
- Host Service Fee to Airbnb = $14 (*rounded up to nearest dollar amount*)[19]

**FIGURE 1.1** Sample Nightly Fee Rates

Furthermore, the company generates revenue from two main sources: commission from renters and commission from homeowners. Commission rates are maintained at a minimum to keep users from moving the transaction offline. Airbnb charges hosts a 3 percent host service fee for each booking completed on its platform. Withdrawn from the host payout, this fee covers the cost of processing guest payments.[17] Airbnb also charges a guest service fee when a customer's reservation is confirmed. The current guest service fee is a variable fee that ranges between 6–12 percent of the reservation subtotal (before fees and taxes). The higher the subtotal, the lower the percentage, allowing users to save money when booking large reservations.[18] Figure 1.1 illustrates a sample calculation that the company provides on its website to explain the host service fee structure.

## THE NATURE OF THE SHARING ECONOMY

The sharing economy offers the ability for anyone with an asset, whether a car, home or extra space in his or her driveway, to capitalize monetarily on that asset simply by renting it.[20] The nature of the sharing economy facilitates peer-to-peer business transactions. By way of a digital clearinghouse, companies such as Parking Panda allow consumers to find a parking space before they even enter a garage. Via Uber or Lyft's electronic platform, a consumer can summon a personal driver with just a couple of clicks.[21] As for finding a deal on overnight accommodations in an instant, Airbnb allows travelers to forego a call to the Holiday Inn by renting another consumer's bedroom for $50 a night or, if one prefers a more glamorous option, renting a beachside mansion for $1,000 a night by simply perusing the company's website.[22]

All members of the sharing economy share three main attributes:

1. They rely on recent technological advances to satisfy established consumer demands in innovative ways;
2. They enter a space with well-established companies and disrupt the current competitive landscape; and
3. They function in interstitial areas of the law due to the timing of emergence.[23]

## RAPID GROWTH OF AIRBNB

Since 2008, Airbnb has enjoyed unmatched growth in the accommodations industry compared to its peers. According to *The Wall Street Journal*, which reported Airbnb's most recent valuation in June of 2015, the company has a valuation of $25 billion and 2015 revenues were projected to reach $900 million.[24] By comparison, Marriott, which manages more than 4,000 hotels, is valued at $21 billion and last year reached $13.8 billion in revenue.[25] In only a few years, Airbnb grew from a small start-up to an established company with a market value larger than many of its traditional hotel competitors. Furthermore, Airbnb's valuation is approximately twice the size of rival travel site Expedia and more than five times the size of HomeAway, Airbnb's closest online competitor (see Figure 1.2).

Analysts contend Airbnb commands a premium valuation given the company's accelerated growth rate over the last few years. Airbnb's $900 million in projected revenue for 2015 was 360 percent of the company's revenue in 2013, which totaled $250 million. From 2014 to 2015, the company had an estimated revenue growth of 113 percent year-over-year.[26] Airbnb's next closest competitor for year-over-year growth was HomeAway at 24 percent and Expedia at 20 percent. Traditional hotels like Marriott continue to grow at more conservative rates hovering between 5 percent and 10 percent (see Figure 1.3).

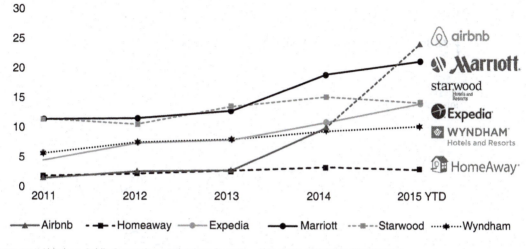

**FIGURE 1.2**  Airbnb vs. Public Competitors: Valuations Over Time ($B): 2011–2015 YTD (06/18/2015)

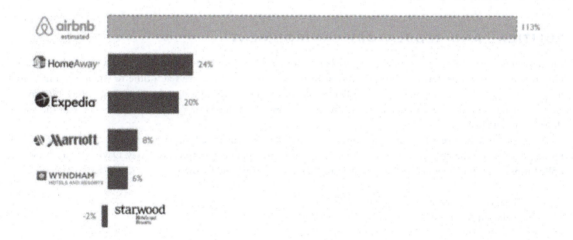

**FIGURE 1.3**  Airbnb vs. Public Competitors: Revenue Growth: 2014 vs. 2015

Beyond revenue and valuation, Airbnb is quickly becoming a mainstream lodging brand recognized among travelers. According to equity research firm CB Insights, the term "Airbnb" recently surpassed "Marriott" in Google search popularity for the first year ever in 2015.[27] Analysts remain bullish that Airbnb's online dominance will likely continue to grow, further enhancing its competitive position among its primary rivals in the lodging industry (see Figure 1.4).

With many promising growth metrics, institutional investors continue to flock to Airbnb as a seemingly secure investment opportunity with a bright future. The Dow Jones Venture Source, an online database that tracks company performance of privately held ventured-backed companies, currently ranks Airbnb as the third most valuable private start-up in the world, trailing only Uber and Xiaomi.[28] Airbnb maintains a stable roster of prominent investors. Notable companies include Sequoia Capital, Andreessen Horowitz, Tiger Global Management, TPG Growth, T. Rowe Price, and Fidelity Investments.[29] What is clear is that the company is well capitalized and positioned to grow. What remains uncertain to some is the company's ability to sustainably manage this rate of growth.

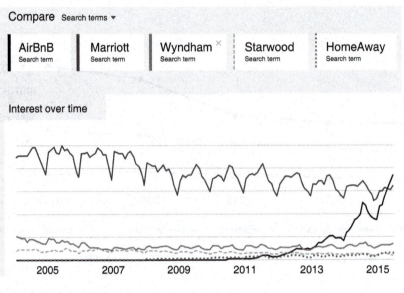

**FIGURE 1.4** Google Search Popularity (2015)

## POLITICAL AND REGULATORY ENVIRONMENT

On September 2, 2014, an independent city-wide poll from Quinnipiac University asked, "Do you think New York City residents should be permitted to rent rooms in their homes for a few days at a time to strangers, similar to a hotel, or should this practice be banned?"[30] The results of this poll showed a sound majority of voters, 56 percent, in favor of allowing short-term rentals to strangers. Only 36 percent of New York voters wanted to ban the use of short-term rentals.[31]

Approximately one year later, in November 2015, Airbnb commissioned a survey to gauge whether New York residents perceived the company and their rental service in a favorable or unfavorable way. David Binder Research polled more than 400 respondents over an 11-day period and found the following:

- 65% believed Airbnb should be legal in New York
- 22% believed Airbnb should be illegal in New York
- 05% answered they view Airbnb "very unfavorable"
- 10% answered they view Airbnb "somewhat unfavorable"
- 25% answered they view Airbnb "somewhat favorable"
- 12% answered they view Airbnb "very favorable"
- 48% of voters had "No Opinion" of Airbnb[32]

While Airbnb maintains sound consumer support in many of the cities where it operates, the company is no stranger to political and regulatory controversy. Over the last two years, the company has been embroiled in high-profile political battles with regulators in some of its most lucrative markets, including San Francisco and New York City. In November of 2015, San Francisco voters headed to the polls to vote on Proposition F, which was commonly known as the "Airbnb Initiative."

Proposition F was a ballot initiative drafted by city officials in an effort to toughen regulations on short-term rental apartments and homes in the city of San Francisco.[33] A political initiative capable of reducing short-term listings and revenue for Airbnb, Proposition F presented the first significant instance in which Airbnb faced an organized political effort to regulate the company's business model in its own backyard – San Francisco. Numerous Airbnb opponents, including hotel industry-backed opposition, affirmed Airbnb was operating under interstitial areas of law and urged regulators to codify clear rules that would regulate online rental platforms to a similar standard that traditional hotels must comply with under the law.

Proposition F attempted to enact the following key rules for Airbnb and other short-term rental platforms. If the proposition passed by a majority vote, each company, and their rental hosts, would be required to comply with the following rules:

1. A 75-day imposed limit over the course of a year on all forms of short-term rentals where the host is not present during the stay. Hosts prohibited from listing a unit if it exceeded the 75-day limit.
2. Require hosts and rental platforms to submit quarterly reports to the San Francisco Planning Department detailing which nights the unit was rented out and which nights the host occupied the unit.
3. Insert Legal Standing provisions enabling permanent residents and non-profit housing groups the right to sue hosts and rental platforms for violating the rules.

On November 4, 2015, Airbnb scored a victory as voters favored letting city residents rent out their homes.[34] Proposition F lost by a vote of 55 percent to 45 percent. Airbnb outspent its opposition by a factor of 16 to 1, spending $8 million to defeat the measure. In comparison, Unite Here, a hotel workers' union, raised only $482,000 in support of the measure. In the wake of Airbnb's victory, Christopher Nulty, a spokesman for the company, released the following statement: "Voters stood up for working families' right to share their homes and opposed an extreme, hotel-industry-backed measure."[35]

## TERMS OF SERVICE AND USER LIABILITY

As opposition groups across the country remain committed to portraying Airbnb as unsafe and preoccupied with evading sensible regulations, Brian Chesky, CEO and Co-Founder of Airbnb, provides his viewpoint as it relates to the sharing economy. Chesky asserts, "There were laws created for businesses, and there were laws for people. What the sharing economy did was create a third category: people as businesses."[36] Regulators in cities across the world, in particular where Airbnb operates, continue to grapple with the new business model that has risen from the sharing economy. While consumers continue to lend support to Airbnb and similar sharing economy services, questions still remain on where liabilities rest in this new way of doing business. Do liabilities rest with the users of the service or the company facilitating the service?

Airbnb's Terms of Service agreement clearly defines which party assumes liability and how Airbnb approaches risk management and legal strategy. Airbnb operates in hundreds of countries, territories and cities across the world. Naturally, this diverse geographical presence makes it inherently difficult to inform users of all the applicable public safety, housing and zoning laws that might apply to them as hosts or guests. Instead of opting to educate all users of the relevant housing and safety laws that apply to them in their respective territories, Airbnb chooses to place all legal responsibility on the user through their Terms of Service agreement.

Airbnb's Terms of Service state, "Please read these terms of service carefully as they contain important information regarding your legal rights, remedies, and obligation." Airbnb's Terms of Service are over 16,000 words in length.[37] In comparison, Marriott's Terms of Use for the United States and Canada are just under 2,500 words.[38] Uber's Terms are under 5,000 words,[39] and HomeAway, an Airbnb competitor which owns more than five other rental companies, has a Terms page on their website that totals just under 13,500 words.[40] As of February 14, 2016, Airbnb's Terms of Service were last edited on July 6, 2015, two days after the Lopez incident.

Airbnb says that it has no control over the conduct of its hosts, guests or any other user of the site. The company disclaims all liability in this regard to the maximum extent permitted by the law. Airbnb states that it does not control the content contained in any of its listings and the condition, legality or suitability of any accommodations. Moreover, Airbnb states that all bookings are made and accepted at the member's own risk. The Terms of Service agreement also states that Airbnb does not act as an insurer.

However, as of May 2012, Airbnb began offering a Host Protection program or Host Guarantee, in which hosts are covered up to $1 million for damage and injuries. Airbnb's website states that the Host Guarantee does not cover cash and securities, pets, personal liability or common areas.[41] Furthermore, the insurance is "secondary," meaning the Airbnb policy takes effect only after a host exhausts his or her personal insurance coverage.[42]

Members of Airbnb are sometimes listed as "verified" or "connected," which simply indicates that they went through the verification process. Per the Terms of Service, this is not a guarantee of the member's identity or whether they are trustworthy, safe or suitable. Members are encouraged to use their own judgment when accepting and selecting hosts and guests.

Airbnb's preferred strategy of informing users of their legal responsibilities through the Terms of Service agreement does not come without contention between users and the company. Many users confirm they do not read the Terms of Service agreement and the company is aware of this significant caveat.

In September 2012, Nigel Warren, a New York City resident, illegally rented out his bedroom for $100 a night while he was away in Colorado for a three-night trip. Upon his return from Colorado, Nigel was contacted by his landlord who had been cited for five violations for operating as an "illegal transient hotel."[43] The fines, if enforced, would have amounted to $40,000 in punitive damages. Fortunately for Mr. Warren and his landlord, the city dropped the sizable fines due to an administrative error of the city's buildings department.

Due to his experience, Mr. Warren posed a pressing question that many stakeholders wish the company would more thoroughly address. Acknowledging that Airbnb knows within reason that many of its hosts who live in large cities are violating rules, he wondered why Airbnb doesn't warn people about the potential for legal hassles. "By ignoring local laws, you (Airbnb) are making casualties of the very people you need to make your site a success," Warren said.[44]

## AIRBNB'S SAFETY TIPS

### Tips for Guests:

Clicking on the link "Trust and Safety" at the bottom of Airbnb's homepage directs viewers to another page with a link entitled "I'm a guest. What are some safety tips I can follow?" Airbnb suggests reading the reviews of other guests to ensure the host is reputable. If guests are skeptical about the host after reading the review, they are encouraged to use their intuition and not book their stay with that host. Guests can also ask hosts to complete "profile verifications" before booking with them. Airbnb suggests that guests talk to the host and start a conversation about the upcoming stay. It also recommends traveler's insurance and reminds guests to call the local police or emergency services immediately if personal safety is threatened.[45]

### Tips for Hosts:

Above the link for guest safety tips, customers can learn about how to stay safe as a host. Airbnb encourages hosts to read reviews of the guests and to use common sense when accepting a guest's request to stay at their listing. Hosts can require guests to complete verifications before they book, such as Verified ID. With Verified ID, guests might be asked to upload their government-issued ID, link their Airbnb account with their page on another social media site (i.e. Facebook) or upload an Airbnb profile photo. Airbnb also asks hosts to call the local police or emergency services if their personal safety is threatened. Airbnb suggests that hosts designate a safe location in case of an emergency. Hosts can also notify their neighbors that they are hosting an Airbnb guest as a precautionary measure.[46]

## OTHER INCIDENTS LEADING UP TO JULY 2015

### Incident 1:

In June of 2011, an Airbnb host who identified herself as "EJ" reported that the person who rented her apartment trashed it and stole jewelry, cash and electronics. EJ wrote about this incident on her personal blog. Airbnb initially responded by trying to persuade EJ to remove her blog post and declined to help her recover from the damages. Following the incident, Chesky stated in a blog on Airbnb's website on August 1, 2011, that he hopes:

> this can be a valuable lesson to other businesses about what not to do in a time of crisis. With regards to EJ, we let her down, and for that we are very sorry. We should have responded faster, communicated more sensitively, and taken more decisive action to make sure she felt safe and secure. But we weren't prepared for the crisis and we dropped the ball. Now we're dealing with the consequences.

Following the response Airbnb said they would provide a $50,000 insurance guarantee for any loss or damages at the property of an Airbnb host. Since the incident, the policy has increased to $1 million but is secondary to the host's personal insurance. Also, Airbnb planned to launch a 24/7 hotline for its users to report problems. Finally, Chesky offered his own e-mail address in case customers had trouble getting in contact with an Airbnb representative.[47]

## Incident 2:

A couple rented an Airbnb property in the Hamptons (New York) in June 2014. Following Airbnb's safety tips, the couple read the reviews of the host and, because of the positive nature of the reviews, decided to book the stay. Before arriving at the home and meeting with the host, the couple texted the host to let him know the timing of their arrival and asked a few questions about items in the house and where to pick up the keys. The host was reportedly friendly and responsive.

Later that night at 2:45 a.m., the male guest received a text from the host that read, "Do you want to try." Shortly after, the host let himself into the locked house with another set of keys and appeared to be inebriated. The host then asked the male guest, "The girlfriend, she's cool, right?" The male guest calmly asked the host to leave, but not before the host picked up the guest's keys and wallet. The male guest asked the host to put the items down and the host did so before departing.

Shortly afterward, the terrified couple left the home. The female guest tried to call the 24-hour emergency line, but could not reach an Airbnb representative after waiting on the line for 45 minutes. The couple then filed a complaint and received a response that Airbnb would be forwarding the case to their Trip Experience Team. The couple drove back to Manhattan where they found a hotel priced at $350 per night. That Monday, the couple called Airbnb twice by phone, but no one returned their calls.

Only after *Business Insider* reached out to Airbnb for comment on the incident did Airbnb take down the host's listing and ban him from the site permanently. They reimbursed the couple for their stay, apologized for the delay and gave them a $500 credit to try Airbnb again. A spokesperson for Airbnb commented about the incident in a *Business Insider* article, "We deeply regret that this matter was not handled properly and our response fell well short of the standards we set for ourselves. This behavior is totally unacceptable and the host has been permanently removed from Airbnb."[48]

In September 2015, the couple ventured back onto Airbnb's site and found that the same property where the incident occurred was relisted on the site under a different name. As a result, Airbnb banned the property again.

Nick Papas, an Airbnb spokesman, commented in another *Business Insider* article:

We have technological tools and procedures that help ensure bad actors don't try to come back to our community. In this case, one investigator didn't properly employ these tools. We've since addressed this issue and we are implementing procedures to ensure it doesn't happen again. We will also make it clear to the host that he is not welcome and has no place in the Airbnb community.[49]

## RESPONSE TO LOPEZ INCIDENT

The onus was left on Jacob Lopez's mother to rescue her son in Spain. At the time of the incident, Airbnb's policy was to withhold the location of the guest if anyone other than the guest were to ask and would not report a crime unless contacted by the guest. Lopez's mother called the Madrid police department, but was unsuccessful in her attempts. Even if she had been able to reach someone in Madrid, the inefficiency of Airbnb's protocol would likely not have allowed for police to reach her son in time.

Nick Papas commented in a *New York Times* article,

We realize we can learn a lot from this incident and we can do better. We are clarifying our policies so that our team will always contact law enforcement if we are made aware of an emergency situation in progress. Safety is our number one priority, and we want to get our hosts and guests as much help as possible.[50]

As reported on July 13, 2015, Belinda Johnson was promoted to Airbnb's Chief Business Affairs and Legal Officer. In this role, she is responsible for legal matters, civic partnerships, public policy, social and philanthropic initiatives, and communication. According to Airbnb CEO Brian Chesky, she'll "become more of the face and the voice of the company."[51]

## DISCUSSION QUESTIONS

1. If the press posed the following question to you as an Airbnb executive, how would you respond? "You claim that safety is your first priority, yet a teenager was sexually assaulted in one of your properties. How do you explain this?"
2. Is it Airbnb's responsibility to protect its guests? Should the company implement an automaticity plan?
3. Should Airbnb communicate all safety and policy changes to customers? How should it communicate changes?
4. Is Airbnb being proactive enough in its safety efforts? Is the business growing too fast to properly protect guests?
5. Although it would slow growth, is a more thorough vetting process for hosts and guests needed?

## WRITING ASSIGNMENT

Please respond in writing to the issues presented in this case by preparing two documents: a communication strategy memo and a professional business letter.

In preparing these documents, you may assume one of two roles: you may identify yourself as an Airbnb senior manager who has been asked to provide advice to Chip Conley, Strategic Advisor for Hospitality and Leadership, regarding the issues he and the company are facing. Or, you may identify yourself as an external management consultant who has been asked by the company to provide advice to Mr. Conley.

Either way, you must prepare a strategy memo addressed to Chip Conley, that summarizes the details of the case, identifies critical issues, discusses their implications (what they mean and why they matter), offers specific recommendations for action (assigning ownership and suspense dates for each) and shows how to communicate the solution to all who are affected by the recommendations.

You must also prepare a professional business letter for the signature of Mr. Brian Cheskey, Airbnb Chief Executive Officer. That document should be addressed to all Airbnb customers and prospective customers, explaining the actions the company is taking. That letter, which would contain no inside address or by-name salutation, would be posted to the company's website. If you have questions about either of these documents, please consult your instructor.

## ACKNOWLEDGMENTS

This case was prepared by research assistants Matthew Beck, William Foster and Claire Kenney under the direction of James S. O'Rourke, Teaching Professor of Management, as the basis for class discussion rather than to illustrate either effective or ineffective handling of an administrative situation. Information was gathered from corporate as well as public sources. Editorial assistance: Judy Bradford.

## NOTES

1 Stump, Scott. "Airbnb Horror Story Reveals Safety Issues for Lodging Site," *Today Money*. August 17, 2015. Online at www.today.com/money/airbnb-horror-story-reveals-safety-issues-lodging-site-t39091.
2 Gander, Kashmira. "Airbnb Safety: Sexual Assault Allegations Against Host in Madrid Raise Questions About Website's Responsibilities," *Independent*. August 16, 2015. Online at www.independent.co.uk/travel/news-and-advice/airbnb-safety-sexual-assault-allegations-against-host-in-madrid-raise-questions-about-websites-10457992.html. Accessed February 2016.
3 Lieber, Ron. "Airbnb Horror Story Points to Need for Precautions," *The New York Times*. August 14, 2015. Online at www.nytimes.com/2015/08/15/your-money/airbnb-horror-story-points-to-need-for-precautions.html. Accessed February 2016.
4 Helm, Burt. "Airbnb is Inc.'s 2014 Company of the Year," *Inc*. Online at www.inc.com/magazine/201412/burt-helm/airbnb-company-of-the-year-2014.html.
5 Ibid.
6 Ibid.
7 Ibid.

8    "About Us," *Airbnb*. Online at www.airbnb.com/about/about-us. Accessed February 2016.

9    Helm. "Airbnb is Inc.'s 2014 Company of the Year."

10   "Company Overview of Airbnb, Inc." *Bloomberg*. Online at www.bloomberg.com/research/stocks/private/people.asp?privcapId=115705393. Accessed February 2016.

11   Griswold, Alison. "Airbnb's Latest Milestone: 1 Million Homes, and Hardly Anyone Noticed," *Slate.com*. December 8, 2014. Online at www.slate.com/blogs/moneybox/2014/12/08/airbnb_has_1_million_homes_brian_chesky_announces_milestone_and_almost_no.html. Accessed April 2016.

12   Poletti, Therese. "What Really Keeps Airbnb CEO Up at Night," February 13, 2015. *Marketwatch*. Online at www.marketwatch.com/story/what-really-keeps-airbnbs-ceo-up-at-night-2015-02-13.

13   On, Ken. "Dissecting Airbnb's Business Model Canvas," *Kenontek*. February 9, 2014. Online at www.kenontek.com/2014/02/09/dissecting-airbnbs-business-model-canvas/.

14   Ibid.

15   Ibid.

16   Ibid.

17   "What Are Host Service Fees," *Airbnb*. Online at www.airbnb.com/help/article/63/what-are-host-service-fees. Accessed February 2016.

18   "What Are Guest Service Fees," *Airbnb*. Online at www.airbnb.com/help/article/104/what-are-guest-service-fees. Accessed February 2016.

19   "What Are Host Service Fees," *Airbnb*.

20   Kokalitcheva, Kia. "Who's Liable When an Airbnb Stay or Uber Ride Ends Badly?" *Fortune*. November 10, 2015. Online at http://fortune.com/2015/11/10/sharing-economy-safety-liability/. Accessed February 2016.

21   Geron, Tomio. "Airbnb and the Unstoppable Rise of the Share Economy," *Forbes/Tech*. February 11, 2013. Online at www.forbes.com/sites/tomiogeron/2013/01/23/airbnb-and-the-unstoppable-rise-of-the-share-economy#73ff0df56. Accessed February 2016.

22   Ibid.

23   Nadler, Michael and Roberta Kaplan. "Airbnb: A Case Study in Occupancy Regulation and Taxation," *The University of Chicago Law Review*. 2016. Online at https://lawreview.uchicago.edu/page/airbnb-case-study-occupancy-regulation-and-taxation.

24   Winkler, Rolfe and Douglas Macmillan. "The Secret Math of Airbnb's 24 Billion Valuation," *The Wall Street Journal*. June 17, 2015. Online at www.wsj.com/articles/the-secret-math-of-airbnbs-24-billion-valuation-1434568517. Accessed February 2016.

25   Ibid.

26   Krishnan, Nikhil. "Why That Crazy-High Airbnb Valuation Is Fair," *LinkedIn*. June 24, 2015. Online at www.linkedin.com/pulse/why-crazy-high-airbnb-valuation-fair-nikhil-krishnan. Accessed February 2016.

27   Ibid.

28   Austin, Scott, Chris Canipe and Sarah Slobin. "The Billion Dollar Start Up Club," *The Wall Street Journal*. February 18, 2015. Online at http://graphics.wsj.com/billion-dollar-club/. Accessed February 2016.

29   Ibid.

30   "New Yorkers Welcome Democratic Convention 3–1; Quinnipiac University Poll Finds; Voters Want Right to Rent Rooms Like a Hotel," News Release, PDF, *Quinnipiac University*, September 2, 2014. Online at www.qu.edu/news-and-events/quinnipiac-university-poll/new-york-city/release-detail?ReleaseID=2076, as cited in Fischer, Ben. "Q-Poll Doesn't Quite Say What Airbnb Wants it to Say," *Biz Journals*. September 2, 2014. Online at www.bizjournals.com/newyork/blog/techflash/2014/09/q-poll-doesnt-quite-say-what-airbnb-wants-it-to.html. Accessed February 2016.

31   Ibid.

32   Noto, Anthony. "Poll: Majority of New Yorkers View Airbnb in positive light," *Biz Journals*. November 5, 2015. Online at www.bizjournals.com/newyork/news/2015/11/05/majority-of-new-yorkers-view-airbnb-in.html. Accessed February 2016.

33   Lien, Tracey. "Everything You Need to Know About San Francisco's Airbnb Ballot Measure," *Los Angeles Times*. October 30, 2015. Online at www.latimes.com/business/technology/la-fi-tn-airbnb-prop-f-san-francisco-20151029-htmlstory.html. Accessed February 2016.

34   Said, Carolyn. "Prop F: S.F. Voters Reject Measure to Restrict Airbnb Rentals," *SF Gate*. November 4, 2015. Online at www.sfgate.com/bayarea/article/Prop-F-Measure-to-restrict-Airbnb-rentals-6609176.php. Accessed February 2016.

35   Ibid.

36   Kessler, Andy. "Brian Chesky: The 'Sharing Economy' and Its Enemies," *The Wall Street Journal*, January 17, 2014. Online at www.wsj.com/articles/SB10001424052702304049704579321001856708992.

37   Airbnb website. "Airbnb Terms of Service." Online at www.airbnb.com/terms. Accessed February 2016.

38   "Marriott Terms of Use for United States & Canada," *Marriott*. Online at www.marriott.com/about/terms-of-use.mi. Accessed February 2016.

39   "Uber Terms and Conditions," *Uber*. Online at www.uber.com/legal/usa/terms/. Accessed February 2016.

40  "HomeAway Terms and Conditions," *HomeAway*. Online at www.homeaway.com/info/about-us/legal/terms-condi
    tions. Accessed February 2016.
41  "Airbnb Host Guarantee Terms and Conditions," *Airbnb*. Online at www.airbnb.com/terms/host_guarantee. Accessed Feb-
    ruary 2016.
42  Lieber, Ron. "A Liability Risk for Airbnb Hosts," *The New York Times*. December 5, 2014. Online at www.nytimes.
    com/2014/12/06/your-money/airbnb-offers-homeowner-liability-coverage-but-hosts-still-have-risks.html. Accessed Feb-
    ruary 2016.
43  Lieber, Ron. "A Warning for Hosts of Airbnb Travelers," *The New York Times*. November 30, 2012. Online at www.nytimes.
    com/2012/12/01/your-money/a-warning-for-airbnb-hosts-who-may-be-breaking-the-law.html?_r=1. Accessed Febru-
    ary 2016.
44  Ibid.
45  "Airbnb Trust and Safety," *Airbnb*. Online at www.airbnb.com/help/article/241/i-m-a-guest—what-are-some-safety-tips-i-
    can-follow. Accessed February 2016.
46  "Airbnb Trust and Safety," *Airbnb*. Online at www.airbnb.com/help/article/231/i-m-a-host—what-are-some-safety-tips-i-
    can-follow. Accessed February 2016.
47  Olivarez-Giles, Nathan. "Airbnb Offers $50,000 Insurance Policy After User's 'Nightmare'." *Los Angeles Times*. August 1, 2011.
    Online at http://latimesblogs.latimes.com/technology/2011/08/airbnb-insurance-guarantee.html. Accessed February 2016.
48  Bort, Julie. "An Airbnb Host Got Drunk and Let Himself Into the House While a Business Insider Employee
    Was Sleeping." *Business Insider*. June 24, 2014. Online at www.businessinsider.com/bi-employee-has-airbnb-hor
    ror-story-2014-6. Accessed February 2016.
49  Bort, Julie. "Banned Airbnb Host Who Entered the House While His Guests Were Sleeping Was Back On Airbnb." *Business
    Insider*. October 6, 2014. Online at www.businessinsider.com/banned-airbnb-host-was-back-on-the-site-2014-10. Accessed
    February 2016.
50  Lieber. "Airbnb Horror Story Points to Need for Precautions."
51  Bellstrom, Kristen. "Exclusive: Meet Airbnb's highest ranking female exec ever." *Fortune*. July 13, 2015. Online at http://
    fortune.com/2015/07/13/airbnb-belinda-johnson-promotion/. Accessed February 2016.

# Case 1.2: Great West Casualty Company v. Estate of G. Witherspoon (A)

A. C. Zucaro, Chairman and CEO of Old Republic International Corporation, arrived at work on January 15, 1999, and picked up that morning's edition of *The Wall Street Journal*, as usual. As he worked deliberately through his first cup of coffee, his well-honed business instincts told him this would be a good day: interest rates were down, the market was up and the many subsidiaries of Old Republic were performing well. For the moment, Mr. Zucaro was a happy man.

As he moved to section two of the *Journal*, his optimism sank. There, on the front page of the "Marketplace" section was an article discussing a lawsuit involving a subsidiary of Old Republic, Great West Casualty Company. Nothing new for a company with $2 billion in revenues and nine operating subsidiaries. But Zucaro knew from the headline that this Friday morning would be less pleasant than most: "An Old Woman Crossed the Road, and Litigiousness Sank to New Low."

## THE EVENTS OF JULY 1, 1998

On her way to work at 4:30 a.m. on July 1, 1998, 81-year-old Gertie Witherspoon blew out a tire and careened into a roadside ditch. With her automobile disabled, Mrs. Witherspoon left her car and began walking along U.S. Route 71 near Adrian, Missouri. Still dazed from the accident, she attempted to cross the highway to reach help. At just that moment, two semi-trucks traveling almost side-by-side spotted the small figure in the road as they passed under a bridge. Traveling nearly 70 miles per hour, the truckers were unable to avoid hitting her. According to the police report, the driver of the rig slammed on his brakes and skidded more than 100 feet. Mrs. Witherspoon was pronounced dead at the scene.

Friends and relatives were stunned and saddened, particularly at Dave's Wagon Wheel Restaurant, where Mrs. Witherspoon worked 50 hours a week as a waitress. No one took the news harder than Joyce Lang, Mrs. Witherspoon's only daughter. "The family was crushed," she said, "and I was determined to find out more about what happened that morning."

## A RELATIVE CONTACTS THE INSURANCE COMPANY

In the days and weeks following the accident, Ms. Lang sought more information about the accident. She received only indifferent statements from the Missouri Highway Patrol and the truck owner, Rex Williams of Vernon County Grain & Supply. Frustrated in her attempts to learn more about her mother's death, Ms. Lang telephoned a claims adjuster at Great West Casualty Company to ask a few questions.

The adjuster at Great West Casualty explained that the police report and witness' statements showed no fault on the part of the truck driver. "Is that all you can tell me?" she asked.

"The case is closed," the adjuster responded.

"Well," said Ms. Lang, "I can open it."

Believing the family was preparing legal action against Great West Casualty Company, the claims representative moved to file suit on behalf of his company against Gertie Witherspoon's estate. "It was never my intention to sue the company." Ms. Lang said later. "I did contact an attorney, but it was only to find out what our rights were. We filed no claims or lawsuits."

About five months later – just a few days before Christmas – on December 18, 1998, Joyce Lang received notice of a legal claim filed against the Witherspoon estate for damages to the truck that struck her mother. Specifically, the claim sought $2,886 "on account of property damage caused to a vehicle due to the negligent actions of Gertie Witherspoon on July 1, 1998."

The local news media first reported this incident on September 4, 1998, when Barbara Shelly, a reporter for the *Kansas City Star* and an acquaintance of Ms. Lang, wrote a brief article elaborating on the life of Gertie Witherspoon. By coincidence, Ms. Shelly happened to be speaking with Ms. Lang on the day the claims notice arrived. "Seeing my mother's name in print like she was a criminal," said Ms. Lang, "I was devastated." Ms. Lang received the notice because she was serving as executor of her mother's estate. "I'm not paying them for killing my mom," she said. "I'll sit in jail first."

Amazed by the insurance company's actions, Ms. Shelly wrote a second article discussing the accident and the insurance company's response. Details in the second article appeared in the January 8, 1999 edition of the *Kansas City Star*. The story was then picked up by *The Wall Street Journal* and reported on January 15, 1999 (see Appendix at the end of this Case). It was at that moment that A. C. Zucaro sensed trouble. Covering the claim filed by Rex Williams was a fairly small matter. The more immediate problem for him would be the company's response to the storm of media criticism.

## OLD REPUBLIC INTERNATIONAL CORPORATION

In January of 1999, Old Republic International Corporation was a financially strong and efficient insurance enterprise with substantial interests in each segment of the insurance and reinsurance industry. Old Republic International was primarily a commercial line underwriter, serving many of America's leading industrial and financial services companies as valued customers. For the year ended 1997, the company's net income was $298 million on revenues of $1.962 billion.

Old Republic International had grown steadily as a specialty insurance business since 1923. The company was regarded as independent and innovative, which was reflected in its growth. Most Wall Street insurance analysts thought the company's performance reflected an entrepreneurial spirit, sound forward planning and an effective corporate structure that promoted and encouraged the assumption of prudent business risks. At the time, Old Republic International had nine subsidiaries across four general business lines, including a General Insurance Group, Mortgage Guaranty Group, Title Insurance Group and Life Insurance Group.

Old Republic International's corporate communication department consisted of one individual who handled investor relations. All other forms of communication were outsourced to a large public relations firm in Chicago, Illinois, that reported directly to the company's president. The work performed by the public relations firm was financially orientated, and included such tasks as preparing annual reports and earnings announcements.

## GREAT WEST CASUALTY COMPANY

Great West Casualty Company was an independent subsidiary of Old Republic. Founded in 1956, Great West Casualty served the special needs of the trucking industry. By 1999, the company served 29 states and had regional offices in Boise, Idaho (Western Region); Bloomington, Indiana (Eastern Region); Arlington, Texas (Southern Region); and Knoxville, Tennessee (Southeastern Region). The corporate headquarters in South Sioux City, Nebraska, served the Central and Northern Regions. Great West Casualty employed more than 600 professionals company-wide. Their policies included automobile liability, cargo coverage, general liability, inland marine floaters, physical damage, property coverage, umbrellas and workers compensation.

The Great West Casualty communication's department also had just one employee, Ms. Leslie Bartholomew. As Corporate Information Director, she handled all communications for the firm. Aside from an operational manual provided by Old Republic International, consisting mostly of general guidelines for handling corporate communication, Great West Casualty made virtually all communication decisions independently.

For Zucaro and his senior team at Old Republic International, the questions were direct and fairly simple: What should they do, how soon should they do it, and how should their actions be communicated? Would they need professional help from a public relations firm? And, more to the point, what did this series of events say to the company about its corporate communication strategy?

## WRITING ASSIGNMENT

Please respond in writing to the issues presented in this case by preparing two documents: a communication strategy memo and a professional business letter.

In preparing these documents, you may assume one of two roles: you may identify yourself as an Old Republic International senior manager who has been asked to provide advice to Mr. A. C. Zucaro regarding the issues he and the company are facing. Or, you may identify yourself as an external management consultant who has been asked by the company to provide advice to Mr. Zucaro.

Either way, you must prepare a strategy memo addressed to A. C. Zucaro, Chairman and Chief Executive Officer of the company, that summarizes the details of the case, rank-orders critical issues, discusses their implications (what they mean and why they matter), offers specific recommendations for action (assigning ownership and suspense dates for each) and shows how to communicate the solution to all who are affected by the recommendations.

You must also prepare a professional business letter for Mr. Zucaro's (or another officer's) signature. That document should be addressed to Ms. Joyce Lang. If you have questions about either of these documents, please consult your instructor.

## ACKNOWLEDGMENT

This case was prepared by Research Assistants Eric Gebbie, John Nemeth and Jeffrey White under the direction of James S. O'Rourke, Teaching Professor of Management, as the basis for class discussion rather than to illustrate either effective or ineffective handling of an administrative situation. Information was gathered from corporate as well as public sources. Copyright © 1999. Revised 2017.

## APPENDIX

### An Old Woman Crossed the Road, and Litigiousness Sank to New Low

**By Carl Quintanilla**

Staff Reporter of *The Wall Street Journal*

Anybody in the insurance industry could answer this one: An 81-year-old woman steps in front of a big truck on a highway and gets killed. What happens next?

A claim for damages, of course. But in this case, it isn't the woman's family that is seeking compensation. Instead, the trucker's insurance company is charging the elderly dead woman with negligence—and seeking damages from her estate.

"I'm not paying them for killing my mom," says Joyce Lang, the dead woman's daughter. "I'll sit in jail first."

The accident happened before dawn one morning last July when Gertie Witherspoon of Adrian, Mo., was on her way to work. At 81, she was vibrant and active, working 50 hours a week at a restaurant called Dave's Wagon Wheel, where regulars called her "Sammy."

Suddenly she had a blowout. Her car careened into a roadside ditch. Dazed, she climbed out and walked in front of an oncoming grain truck. According to the police report, the driver of the rig slammed on his brakes and skidded more than 100 feet. But Mrs. Witherspoon was pronounced dead at the scene.

About five months later, just before Christmas, Ms. Lang received notice of a claim from the grain truck's insurer, Great West Casualty Co., for damage incurred by the truck. The amount Great Western is seeking: $2,800.

"Seeing my mother's name in print like she was a criminal, I was devastated," says Ms. Lang, the executor of her mother's estate.

Ms. Lang, who first told her story to the *Kansas City Star*, has hired an attorney to fight the bill. "How much damage can a 5-foot, 105-pound woman do to a big truck like that?" she asks.

Great West, a unit of Chicago-based Old Republic International Corp., won't say. Citing company policy, it refuses to discuss the specifics of the case. But the company does claim that the way in which Mrs. Witherspoon crossed the road was "negligent."

Rex Williams, owner of Vernon County Grain & Supply, the company whose truck was involved in the accident, says he has no comment on the matter.

Still, Scott Rager, Great West's executive vice president, concedes that the insurance company's pursuit of $2,800 is risky from a public-relations standpoint. "It doesn't do anything to help people's impressions of us," he says.

*The Wall Street Journal*, Friday, January 15, 1999, p. B1.

# Case 1.3: Domino's "Special" Delivery

## Going Viral Through Social Media (A)

We all have our secret ingredients. . . . and in about five minutes they will be sent out on delivery where somebody will be eating these. Yes, eating 'em. And little did they know that cheese was in his nose and that there was some lethal gas that ended up on their salami. Now, that's how we roll at Domino's![1]

Mondays are never anyone's favorite day to be at work. But, for Tim McIntyre, VP of Corporate Communications at Domino's Pizza, Monday, April 13, 2009, might rank as the worst Monday he had experienced in his 25 years with the company.[2] While wrapping up his workday at the corporate office in Ann Arbor, Michigan, McIntyre received an e-mail alerting him that videos featuring company employees contaminating food in an unidentified store had been posted on the online video sharing site, YouTube. What had been a quiet day following Easter weekend suddenly turned into the first day of a full-fledged communications and marketing nightmare.

### THE NIGHTMARE BEGINS

At 4:30 p.m. on April 13, McIntyre received an e-mail from the webmaster of www.GoodAsYou.org, a GLBT advocacy blog site, alerting him of the existence of a number of damaging videos the group had discovered posted on YouTube.[3] (The GLBT site showed interest in the videos because the word "gay" could be heard several times in the narration.)

After just one viewing, McIntyre knew that the five amateur videos could seriously damage the Domino's brand, not to mention putting the company at legal risk. He said, "You know what, this is a bad one – they're in uniform, they're in the store. We need to do something about it."[4] Each video, recorded by a current female Domino's Pizza employee featured a male employee performing various acts of food contamination. To make things worse, the director and actor are in full Domino's uniforms, are at work during normal store hours and imply in the narrative that the contaminated food will soon be delivered to unsuspecting customers. It wouldn't be until much later that night that McIntyre and team would discover the identity and location of the people responsible for the videos.

Thankfully for Domino's, Good As You felt obligated to quickly notify corporate headquarters as soon as the videos were found; however, to protect the public, the bloggers also posted the video links on their own site.[5] (Refer to the Appendix at the end of this Case Study for McIntyre's response and correspondence with Good As You.) McIntyre said that this initial notification came about 15 minutes prior to his corporate social media team discovering the existence of the videos online.[6] Within that same hour, another popular consumer affairs blog site, www.consumerist.com, also posted the videos on their site. Within 24 hours, McIntyre would learn that the most popular video had received 250,000 YouTube views.[7] And that was just the beginning – the videos were going viral before McIntyre's eyes.

McIntyre scanned through the past experiences of his long tenure with Domino's to recall a situation in which he had dealt with something similar – crimes, accusations and brand problems – something to use as a reference point on how to proceed. When nothing similar came to mind, he realized that no plans, protocols or off-the-shelf solutions in a communications handbook could help remedy the situation before him.[8] It was up to him to pull his team together to face this unprecedented threat. But what should his first step be? And what kind of irreparable damage might Domino's suffer if he chose the wrong course of action?

## THE VULGAR VIDEOS

McIntyre credits two savvy readers at The Consumerist who used clues in the videos and innovative geo-mapping and investigative tools to identity the location of the videos' creators by 11:00 p.m. on Monday, just six-and-a-half hours after the videos originally surfaced.[9] The two culprits in their early 30s, Kristi Hammond and Michael Setzer, turned out to be full-time employees at a Domino's Pizza franchise location in Conover, North Carolina.

Hammond's "opus piece" is a two-minute-and-26-second video named, "Dominos Pizzas Special Ingredients" (sic) in which the two employees joke about being lazy workers and mention that their manager is in the back reading a newspaper, as usual. The video shows Setzer in vivid detail passing gas on salami and stuffing cheese for sandwiches up his nose, all while Hammond laughs and jokes in the background about this being business as usual at Domino's. The camera then pans to the overhead order screen, which Hammond says displays the name of the customer who will receive the delivery.

The other videos, called "Sneeze Sticks," "Dominos Pizza Buger" (sic) and "Domino's Part I," contain Setzer sneezing on cheesy bread, stuffing a pepper up his nose while making oven-baked sandwiches, and demonstrating how long it takes to make change for a customer due to restrictive policies. The following are a sample of quotes transcribed from one of the videos:

Kristi: *"Hello, this is Kristi back again. And here at Domino's I like to be lazy . . . You see Michael over there hard at work – yeah, not really. Did y'all see that? He just blew a booger on those sandwiches! Do you remember the time when you sneezed? [laughter] Do it again, do it again!"*

Michael: *"This is Michael's special Italian sandwich."*

Kristi: *"And on the sandwich it goes. Now, Michael, I think that these sandwiches are going to be full of protein. . . . "*

**FIGURE 1.5**   Kristi Hammond (Director/Narrator) and Michael Setzer (Actor)

**FIGURE 1.6**   Video 1: "Dominos Pizzas Special Ingrediants" (sic)

**FIGURE 1.7**   Video 2: "Sneeze Sticks"

**FIGURE 1.8**   Video 3: "Pizza Buger" (sic)

**FIGURE 1.9**   Video 4: "Dominos Pizza Part I"

## DOMINO'S PIZZA BACKGROUND

Started in 1960 by Tom Monaghan as a single store, Domino's Pizza quickly grew through a network of company-owned and franchise-owned stores. With more than 5,000 stores in the U.S. and 3,700 stores in international markets, the chain is now recognized as the world leader in pizza delivery, based on reported consumer spending.[10] Domino's employs 125,000 team members in the U.S. and more than 60 countries around the world.[11] These employees crafted and delivered well over 400 million pizzas worldwide in 2008.[12]

Domino's Pizza is a publicly traded company on the NYSE under the symbol DPZ. In 2008, the company had global revenues of $1.4 billion. Sales were split with 55 percent in the U.S. and 45 percent international. Between 2004 and 2008, Domino's experienced growth primarily from international expansion, with just 39 new stores opening in the U.S. and 977 stores opening internationally.[13]

## FRANCHISEES

While the network of Domino's stores consists of company- and franchise-owned stores, the latter remain the primary driver behind the company's growth. Over 90 percent of U.S. and 100 percent of international stores are franchise-owned. Franchise owners are required to operate their stores in compliance with written policies, standards and specifications drafted by Domino's corporate headquarters, but there are numerous cases in which franchise owners have autonomy, including setting menu prices and hiring employees. The corporate headquarters provides franchisees with training materials, comprehensive operation manuals and franchise development classes, but it is up to the franchisee to ensure operations and employees meet the standards of the Domino's brand.[14]

## CORPORATE COMMUNICATIONS TEAM

Tim McIntyre began his tenure at Domino's Pizza immediately after graduating from college. Twenty-five years later, as vice president of corporate communications, he now reports to the executive vice president of corporate communications, who reports to the company's CEO.[15] McIntyre's long, successful tenure at Domino's contributes to what he refers to as high levels of trust and "full support from the management team" on critical issues.[16]

McIntyre's internal team handles all of the company's public relations, but partners with two external agencies for advertising and new media strategy work.[17] A new team focused specifically on social media formed at Domino's about one month prior to the outbreak of the YouTube videos. This team had been planning to launch the company's presence online through several social media outlets just one week later – before Hammond beat them to it.

## THE COMPETITIVE PIZZA INDUSTRY

Domino's Pizza operates in the highly competitive food service industry in the Quick Service Restaurant (QSR) sector. The QSR pizza category is large and fragmented and, at $33.9 billion a year, is the second largest category in the $230 billion U.S. QSR sector. Competition within the QSR sector is particularly intense with regard to product quality, price, service, convenience and concept. Within the U.S. there are approximately 69,000 pizzerias serving about 3 billion pizzas annually, but the main pizza delivery and carry-out competitors are Domino's, Pizza Hut and Papa John's. Together these three comprise 47 percent of pizza delivery in the U.S. Internationally, Pizza Hut is the principal competitor to Domino's.[18]

In general, individual customers in the QSR sector do not comprise a large portion of sales. Instead, businesses rely on volume and repeat purchase. For Domino's Pizza, no customer accounts for more than 10 percent of sales.[19] If customers perceive a problem in product quality, price, service or convenience, the implications to future business success could be serious. For this reason, there is nothing more important or sacred to Domino's than the trust of its customers.[20]

## SOCIAL MEDIA PLAYERS

Due to the growth of social media websites on the Internet, individuals now have the ability to instantly share messages, images and videos with a global audience. Once a posting is made, it can also be copied by other users and uploaded to other sites, thus compounding the impact of the posting. In this case, three sites were immediately involved: www.YouTube.com had the original posting by Hammond and Setzer; and two prominent blog sites, www.GoodAsYou.org and www.consumerist.com, copied the posting and put it on their own websites within hours.

In today's technologically advanced world, the Internet instantly connects people all over the globe. In the U.S. alone, estimates of broadband Internet connection show that 84 million of the 119 million U.S. households, or 71 percent, had broadband connection to the Internet by 2010.[21] With the simple click of a mouse, Internet users can quickly access unprecedented amounts of information. Much of that information is posted by companies, news outlets or other organizations, but increasingly, information is being posted and shared by common users on social networking websites.[22]

Some of the most popular social networking and content sharing websites in the U.S. are Facebook, MySpace, Twitter and YouTube.[23] Facebook boasts a network of more than 350 million active users with an average of 50 percent logged on every day,[24] MySpace has more than 100 million active users,[25] and Twitter had the largest yearly growth of members at 1,382 percent when it hit 7 million members in February 2009.[26] YouTube started in 2005 and is now the most widely viewed video service in the U.S. ahead of Fox Interactive Media, CBS Corporation, Yahoo! sites and others.[27] By January of 2009, YouTube claimed more than 100 million unique U.S. visitors.[28] YouTube's users, according to the website, watch "hundreds of millions of videos a day" on YouTube, and every minute, an additional 20 hours of video is uploaded to YouTube by users.[29]

The uploaded content by users on many social networking sites does not go through a formal review or approval processes by the website, so the users have great authority to post information they deem as appropriate. Once a posting is made, the content can easily be copied by other users and uploaded to other sites. This compounding effect of information being shared across websites is difficult to control and contain, so information can quickly spread and reach other users. "Viral" is a term commonly used to describe Internet content that is quickly popularized through sharing by users.[30]

In this situation with Domino's Pizza, the videos posted by Hammond and Setzer went viral. Once this occurred, Hammond and Setzer, as well as Domino's, lost the ability to control where the videos were posted and who was able to view them. This trend of everyday users posting and sharing information, and the impact of information going viral, is summarized well by Tim McIntyre in a response to www.consumerist.com about the Domino's video pranks. McIntyre said:

> The "challenge" that comes with the freedom of the Internet is that any idiot with a camera and an Internet link can do stuff like this – and ruin the reputation of a brand that's nearly 50 years old, and the reputations of 125,000 hard-working men and women across the nation and in 60 countries around the world.[31]

A single Internet user, according to McIntyre, can have an immediate impact felt globally.

## PUTTING OUT THE FIRE

Tim McIntyre knows that the most valuable asset of Domino's is the unfailing trust of its customers. Because of the nature of the industry it is in – home food delivery – Domino's customers literally invite the company and its delivery drivers into their homes at the same time they hand over home addresses, credit card information, phone numbers and names as they place an order. It was this trust that McIntyre was afraid would be forever damaged if this issue was not contained quickly and quietly.[32]

Instinct was telling McIntyre that the videos were most likely a hoax – a stupid prank pulled by two bored workers – but he didn't know for sure. But, whether the videos were pranks or not, Domino's customers would soon decide for themselves if he didn't come up with a plan.

When talking about that first day, McIntyre said,

> My first reaction when I saw it was anger. I was angry because I love this place, I love this brand, I love the franchisees that I work with. And I took it personally . . . we [the immediate response team] channeled anger into action.[33]

Needless to say, Monday's events were not a practice fire-drill for McIntyre and his team; the following weeks were going to need a lot of that action to contain this rapidly spreading media fire.

## DISCUSSION QUESTIONS

1. What appears to be the business problem facing Domino's in this case?
2. Who are the key stakeholders?
3. What should Tim McIntyre and the communications team do first?
4. What should Domino's do about the employees who made the video?
5. What should Domino's do about the store where the video was made?
6. What steps should Domino's take to resolve this crisis?
   a. How should Domino's respond at the local, national and/or global level?
   b. What mediums should Domino's use to communicate its message?
7. How can Domino's ensure a similar crisis does not occur in the future?
   a. How should Domino's work with franchisees?

# WRITING ASSIGNMENT

Please respond in writing to the issues presented in this case by preparing two documents: a communication strategy memo and a professional business letter.

In preparing these documents, you may assume one of two roles: you may identify yourself as a Domino's Pizza senior manager who has been asked to provide advice to Tim McIntyre regarding the issues he and the company are facing. Or, you may identify yourself as an external management consultant who has been asked by the company to provide advice to Mr. McIntyre. Either way, you must prepare a strategy memo addressed to Tim McIntyre that summarizes the details of the case, rank-orders critical issues, discusses their implications (what they mean and why they matter), offers specific recommendations for action (assigning ownership and suspense dates for each) and shows how to communicate the solution to all who are affected by the recommendation.

You must also prepare a professional business letter for President and COO Patrick Doyle's signature. That document should be addressed, in general, to all Domino's retail customers. As an alternative, you may address a different letter to Domino's franchisees, explaining to them what they should know about the facts of the case and the company's response. If you have questions about either of these documents, please consult your instructor.

# APPENDIX

---

**\*\*UPDATE:** From Domino's corporate:

> **Thank you for bringing these to our attention. I don't have the words to say how repulsed I am by this – other than to say that these two individuals do not represent that 125,000 people in 60 countries who work hard every day to make good food and provide great customer service. I've turned this over to our security department. We will find them. There are far too many clues that will allow us to determine their location quite easily.**
>
> **Regards,**
>
> **Tim McIntyre**
>
> **Vice President, Communications Domino s Pizza, LLC**

---

**FIGURE 1.10**  Tim McIntyre's response to Good As You

# ACKNOWLEDGMENTS

This case was prepared by Research Assistants Adam Peeples and Christina Vaughn under the direction of James S. O'Rourke, Concurrent Professor of Management, as the basis for class discussion rather than to illustrate either effective or ineffective handling of an administrative situation. Information was gathered from corporate as well as public sources.

# NOTES

1  Direct quote from Kristi Hammond, narrator of Domino's prank video.
2  Personal interview with Tim McIntyre, September 25, 2009.
3  Ibid.
4  Jacques, Amy. "Domino's Delivers During Crisis," *The Strategist*, Summer 2009, p. 7.
5  "Video: Let the Domino's Appall as They May," *Good As You*. Online at www.goodasyou.org/good_as_you/2009/04/video-let-the-dominoes-appall.html.
6  Personal interview with Tim McIntyre, September 25, 2009.

7   Ibid.

8   Ibid.

9   Jacques. "Domino's Delivers During Crisis," p. 8.

10   "About Us," *Domino's Pizza*. Online at www.dominosbiz.com. Accessed October 5, 2009.

11   Domino's Investor Relations. Online at http://phx.corporate-ir.net/phoenix.zhtml?c=135383&p=irol-homePro file&t=&id=&. Accessed October 5, 2009.

12   2008 Domino's Pizza Annual Report.

13   Ibid.

14   Ibid.

15   Personal interview with Tim McIntyre, September 25, 2009.

16   Ibid.

17   Ibid.

18   Ibid.

19   Ibid.

20   Ibid.

21   "Social Networking and Connectivity in the Digital Age – US – January 2008," *Mintel Report*. Section called, "Demographics and Trends." Online at http://academic.mintel.com.proxy.library.nd.edu/sinatra/oxygen_academic/search_results/show&/display/id=294369.

22   Ibid.

23   Ibid.

24   "Press Room: Statistics," *Facebook*. Online at www.facebook.com/press/info.php?statistics. Accessed December 2009.

25   "Fact Sheet," *MySpace*Online at www.myspace.com/pressroom?url=/fact+sheet/. Accessed December 2009.

26   Carlson, Nicholas. "Twitter Traffic Grows 1,382% In a Year." BusinessInsider.com. March 19, 2009. Online at www.business insider.com/twitter-traffic-grows-1382-in-a-year-2009-3. Accessed December 2009.

27   Research by comScore. Posted by emarketer.com in the article, "YouTube Hits 100 Million." March 18, 2009. Online at www.emarketer.com/Article.aspx?R=1006981. Accessed December 2009.

28   Ibid.

29   "YouTube Fact Sheet," *YouTube*. Online at www.youtube.com/t/fact_sheet. Accessed December 2009.

30   "Viral Internet Marketing: Why Viral Content is Great," *Articlesbase*, October 22, 2009. Online at www.articlesbase.com/internet-marketing-articles/viral-internet-marketing-why-viral-content-is-great-1369574.html. Accessed December 2009.

31   Letter to Jonathon Drake by Tim McIntyre on April 14, 2009. Posted by Chris Walters. "Consumerist Sleuths Track Down Offending Domino's Store." Consumerist.com. April 14, 2009. Online at http://consumerist.com/2009/04/consumerist-sleuths-track-down-offending-dominos-store.html#comments-content. Accessed December 2009.

32   Ibid.

33   Jacques. "Domino's Delivers During Crisis," p. 7.

CHAPTER 2

# Communication and Strategy

In Chapter 1, we looked at the role communication plays in the life of a manager – we examined why managers communicate. In this chapter, we look much more closely at how managers communicate – we examine the process itself. Elsewhere in this book we will examine the products of that process: writing, speaking, listening, conflict management and group interaction.

## DEFINING COMMUNICATION

First, though, a definition may be helpful. If you read enough books on this subject, you'll find more definitions than you can understand or remember. Here's one that is both easy to understand and easy to remember: Communication is the transfer of meaning.[1]

"I sent you an e-mail," your manager asserts. "Didn't you get it?" You got 40 e-mails that day. What did his say?

"We put out a memo on that subject just last month," a junior VP claims. "Why weren't the employees complying?"

They get dozens of pieces of paper in their in-boxes each day. Are you surprised no one read it? For those of you who remember the memo, did you understand it? For those who think they understood what the vice president meant, what was your reaction? Wasn't that just a backgrounder? An update of some sort, meant to provide you with information about the development and implementation of some policy that won't really affect you? For those who received, read, understood and remembered the memo: What was your incentive for complying with the vice president's request? How does this affect you and, more importantly, what's your motivation for getting involved?

"That memo is crucial to the future of this company," your boss thunders. "It's about the vision our senior team wants to see throughout the entire organization." Gee, all that in one memo, and you just glanced through it and tossed it aside. Maybe it's still around somewhere. When you get a few minutes, you really should read it. For now, though, there's a lot more on your plate that seems much more urgent, and "vision memos" will have to wait.

Sounds familiar? It's all too familiar in many organizations because people, particularly managers, confuse the act of communicating with the process of communication. They honestly believe that a message sent is a message received. And a message received would certainly be understood and complied with, right? For them, communication is mostly, if not entirely, about sending messages.

For managers who truly understand the process, however, communication is about much more than sending messages. It's about the transfer of meaning.

When I understand a subject the way you understand it – with all of the intricacies, complexities, context and detail – then you have communicated with me. If I am aware of not only what you know about a subject but also how you feel about it, then you have communicated with me. When I comprehend just how important a subject is to you and why you think it's important to take action now, you have communicated with me. All of this may be possible in a memo to the staff, but it's certainly not easy. Because communication is a complex, ongoing process that involves the whole substance of ourselves, it would be an unusual memo that could capture all of that. The transfer of meaning may take more than just a phone call or an e-mail message.

## ELEMENTS OF COMMUNICATION

To successfully transfer meaning, you should know that every message you receive comes from a sender who encodes the details of its content and selects a medium through which to transmit what she knows or feels. That message may be impeded by noise, primarily because of the cultural context against which it will be delivered as well as the field of experience of the receiver. The effect of the message will also depend on the frame of mind or attitudinal set you bring to the situation, along with the system of ethics that governs communication in your organization, your industry and your society.

If all of this looks complex, congratulations, you now have a firm grasp on the obvious: Human communication is intricate, delicate, difficult and, above all, complex. The remarkable fact is, however, we do it every day, and, more often than not, we achieve some degree of success. Orders get placed, deliveries are made, customers are satisfied, people do what you ask of them and the business you work for runs – more or less – the way it's supposed to.

The real question here isn't whether you can communicate. You showed that you can do that when you filled out a business school admissions application. The real question is whether you can get better at it. Can you impress your clients enough to keep them? Can you encourage a reluctant employee to give the best he's got? Can you convince the boss that you are the one to take on those new responsibilities? We each have basic skills. What we need is a set of higher-level competencies that will serve the world-class organizations we will work for in the years ahead.

## PRINCIPLES OF COMMUNICATION

Communication is a process that involves several basic principles. These are concepts we know to be true about human communication across time and cultures, across organizations and professions, and across nations and economies. Above all, we know that communication is:

### Dynamic

Human communication is constantly undergoing change. One message builds on another; one experience adds to another.

### Continuous

Communication never stops. Even when you disconnect the telephone, you're communicating the message that you have nothing more to say. Silence, in fact, can be among the more powerful forms of communication. Simply said: You cannot *not* communicate.

### Circular

Communication is rarely ever entirely one-way. We each take in information from the outside world, determine what it means, and respond. The cycle we refer to as feedback is nothing more than receivers becoming senders, and vice versa. When we stop speaking to listen, we join the feedback loop.

## Unrepeatable

Heraclitus, a Greek philosopher-mathematician, once wrote that "No man can step in the same river twice." What he meant was that if you attempt to repeat an experience, the experience will be different – circumstances change and so will you. So it is with communication. Even if we say something again in precisely the same way, our listeners have heard it before. The same message delivered to two different listeners amounts to two different messages. That's also true of the same message delivered twice to the same listeners. Once we have heard or seen a message, we have some notion of what to expect. Thus, it's not the same experience as when we heard it or saw it for the first time.

## Irreversible

Some processes are reversible – we can freeze water into ice and then thaw it back into water again – but not communication. We may wish we could unsay something, but we can't. All we can do is explain, apologize and say more – but we can't ever get it back.

## Complex

Communication is complex, not only because of the various elements and principles at work in the process, but also because it involves human beings. Each of us is different in a number of important and meaningful ways, which means that each of us will assign slightly different meaning to words, react in slightly different ways because of our background, education and experience, and behave in slightly different ways around other people. Nothing is simple or entirely straightforward about the ways in which people communicate.[2]

# LEVELS OF COMMUNICATION

Human communication also occurs at various levels. The complexities of the process, particularly audience analysis and message construction, increase as the level of communication elevates.

## Intrapersonal

When we communicate within ourselves, sending messages to various parts of our bodies, thinking things over or working silently on a problem, we are communicating intrapersonally.

## Interpersonal

When we communicate between or among ourselves, sending messages from one person to another – verbally and nonverbally – we are communicating interpersonally.

## Organizational

When we communicate with one another in the context of an organization, sending and receiving messages through various layers of authority, using various message systems, discussing various topics of interest to the group we belong to or the company we work for, we are communicating organizationally.

## Mass or Public

Occasionally, when we send messages from just one person or source to many people simultaneously, as in a newspaper advertisement, television commercial or Twitter message, we are communicating publicly.[3]

## BARRIERS TO COMMUNICATION

If we each understand the principles of communication and the levels at which it can take place, and if we each use and understand the same language, why don't we succeed more often than we do? What's holding back the transfer of meaning? Broadly speaking, two barriers keep us from communicating successfully.

### Physiological Barriers

Because all the information we receive about the world must come through one or more of our five senses (sight, sound, taste, touch and smell), we depend on those senses to report accurately on what's going on around us. It is possible, though, for our senses to be impaired or for the source of the message to provide inadequate information (insufficient light to read a message, an announcement not loud enough to be audible, and so on). In sending messages to others, we must be sensitive to the fact that they may not see, hear, taste, touch or smell in the same way we do.

### Psychological Barriers

Communication is much more than simply sending and receiving messages. It's about understanding them, as well. Remember, communication is the transfer of meaning, and if I don't know what you mean – even though I may see and hear you well enough – no communication has taken place. Everything from the culture in which we live to the norms or standards of the groups we belong to can influence how we perceive and react to the messages, events and experiences of everyday life. Even individual mind-sets, including prejudice and stereotypes, can affect what we understand and how we react to others. We examine each of these barriers in greater detail in Chapter 4, "Speaking."

## COMMUNICATING STRATEGICALLY

To communicate strategically means several things. First, it means that your plans for communication, your proposed messages, the medium (or media) you select, the code you employ, the context and experience you bring to situations, and the ethics you adopt will all have a direct effect on the outcome. Remember the elements of communication we discussed earlier? Those are the keys to successful strategic communication.

You should know, however, that those are all just tools; they are means to an end. You should first ask what end you hope to reach. What are your communication goals? If you are communicating strategically, those goals will be aligned with and will directly support the goals of the organization you work for. And, at each level of your organization, the ways in which you communicate will be consistent and aimed at the same objectives. To develop a communication strategy that will help you and your organization achieve the goals you have set for yourselves, you first must ask yourself a few questions related to the elements of communication we've discussed:

### Sender

Who should communicate this message? Will your signature compel people to action? Should you ask your manager or vice president to sign this letter? Should someone closer to the intended audience send the message?

### Receiver

Who is the intended audience for this message? What do you know about them? More important, what do they know about you and your subject? What feelings do they have about it and you? What's their previous experience with this subject and this sender? What's their likely reaction?

### Message

What should your message contain? How should your message say what you intend for your audience to know? Should your message contain the bare minimum to evoke a reaction, or should you provide greater detail? Should the message focus on just one topic or should you include many issues for them to consider?

### Medium

What's the best way to send this message? Is one medium quicker than another? Will one medium offer your audience better opportunities for feedback? Will one medium carry more detail than another? Does one carry a greater sense of urgency than another? Will one cost more than another?

### Code

Encoding your message simply means selecting the right words and images. Style and tone matter as you approach readers and listeners with new information. Will they understand the words you plan to use? Will they understand the concepts you offer them? For your audience, decoding is a more complex matter of assigning meaning to the words and images you have selected. Will they mean the same thing to your receiver as they mean to you? Do these words and images have multiple meanings for you and your audience?

### Feedback

What's the reaction of your audience? How will you know if you've communicated successfully? What measure will you use to determine whether they understand this subject the same way you understand it? Will the audience response be delayed? Will it be filtered through another source? How much feedback will you need before you decide to communicate again?

### Noise

How many other senders and messages are out there? Whose message traffic are you competing with? Will others try to deflect, distort or disable your communication attempts? How can you get the attention of your intended audience with all that they have to read, see, hear and think about each day?

### Effect

To achieve the goals you've set for yourself and your organization, you must know how to motivate others. You must show them how the information or ideas you have offered are useful and worth acting upon.

## SUCCESSFUL STRATEGIC COMMUNICATION

Getting people to listen to what you say, read what you write or look at what you show them isn't easy. More often than not, people up and down the line have other interests that seem more immediate and other concerns to focus on. How, then, do you persuade them that paying attention to your message and cooperating with you is in their best interest?

Successful strategic communication usually involves the following six steps:

### Link Your Message to the Strategy and Goals of the Organization

What are the strategic objectives of your business? Chances are good that your organization has published a document outlining its vision, values and beliefs. Of course, the corporate annual report to shareholders is a good place to look for business strategy. If you can't find what you're looking for, call corporate communication and explain what you want and why you want it. Every division within a business should have a set of simple, easy-to-understand business objectives (e.g., "Increase cash flow by 10 percent during this fiscal year," or "Be number one or two in on-time take-offs this fiscal year"). All of your communication – no matter what the audience, no matter what the medium, no matter what the purpose for communicating – should be consistent with and directly supportive of those business objectives. If your writing and speaking don't fit that description, either you don't understand the company's objectives or you don't agree with them. If that is the case, you should make an effort to learn and understand them or look for work elsewhere.

## *Attract the Attention of Your Intended Audience*

Appeal to basic needs or to the fundamentals of physiology to attract the attention of your intended audience. Basic needs would include the bottom rungs of Abraham Maslow's Hierarchy of Human Needs. This hierarchy explains the frequent focus on issues related to survival, food, water, sex appeal and other needs.[4] The fundamentals of physiology are simply activities designed to appeal to the sight, hearing, taste, touch or smell capacities of the audience. Loud noises, bright lights and similar devices can attract attention; the more important issue is whether you can hold that attention once the audience knows who you are and what you want.

## *Explain Your Position in Terms They Will Understand and Accept*

If your audience is willing to spend time and effort attending to your message but cannot understand what you intend, you'll raise nothing other than their frustration level. As you will see in Chapter 5, using language they are likely to understand and accept will make comprehension and compliance that much easier. This is about knowing your audience: knowing who they are, how much they know about this subject, how they feel about it and their level of sophistication.

## *Motivate Your Audience to Accept and Act on Your Message*

Several motivational appeals are available for you to reach and move your audience. First, consider an *appeal to authority*. If you are either in a position of organizational authority or an acknowledged expert on the matter, you may legitimately ask your audience to respond to those forms of authority. It is the equivalent, to some, of hearing ". . . because I'm you're mother," but it works more often than not. And, in some instances, you may have neither the time nor the patience to explain in detail why the audience should comply. Successful appeals to authority usually involve a follow-up stage in which the authority figure provides justification for the request.

Second, you might consider *social conformity* to move your audience, which is equivalent to the "celebrity endorsement" or "millions of satisfied customers can't be wrong" approach. The vast majority of people don't like to be out of step with other members of the society in which they live; they appreciate and value conformity and what it does for society. An endorsement to your intended audience from a person they respect (it doesn't matter if *you* respect him or her) may prove helpful. If not, you can always resort to opinion polls ("Four out of five dentists who chew gum recommend our product").

Finally, you might use *rationality and consistency theory* to motivate your audience. Just as the majority of people wish to conform to what others think is proper, so too do they want rational, consistent behavior in their lives. If they see what you are advocating as irrational or inconsistent with their existing beliefs, they won't buy it. You must show them that it is consistent with what they already believe and – for those who admire logic – entirely rational.[5]

## *Inoculate Them against Contrary Messages and Positions*

Persuasion theorists have shown that beliefs persist in the face of contrary evidence if the holder of those beliefs has been inoculated against counter-persuasion at some point. Several options are available to make those actions you advocate resistant to the appeals of your competitors. First, you can ask for a tangible commitment from your audience. If that commitment is public, or at least known to other members of the target audience, so much the better. Everything from signing a pledge card to wearing a campaign button will bolster the beliefs of your audience.[6] A Los Angeles restaurateur dramatically cut the number of reservation "no-shows" by asking diners a simple question as they called for reservations: "Do you promise to call us if your dinner plans change?" The act of saying "yes" on the telephone committed them to a course of behavior that benefited the restaurant substantially.[7]

## *Manage Audience Expectations*

People are disappointed in the service or the products you deliver only if their expectations exceed the quality of what they receive. The same is true of communication. Always deliver what you promise, never less. Always meet or exceed your audience's expectations. Manage those expectations by cueing your audience about what to expect from your communications with them. If you deliver what you say you will, your audience will reward you with its attention and consideration for your message.

## WHY COMMUNICATING AS A MANAGER IS DIFFERENT

Communication is a fundamental skill central to the human experience. We each know how to do it; we've done it since birth and receive additional practice each day. So, why is it so difficult to communicate on the job? What does the workplace do to change the nature of communication?

Several factors in business life alter the way we look at communication. These factors influence the way we write and speak with others, right down to word selection and format. They influence our willingness to listen or to devote time to the concerns of others. And they influence the way we think about our daily problems, responsibilities and challenges.

### Levels of Responsibility and Accountability

The higher your level of responsibility in an organization, the more you have to think about. If you spend the majority of your day focused on just one or a few well-defined issues, your communication will tend to be much more keenly focused. If you have many problems, many challenges to address during the day, your communication style will be more fragmented and broadly focused. As you read in Chapter 1, time management and communication efficiency become core skills. Additionally, as you become more accountable, you tend to keep better records. If you know you'll be asked about particular issues, it's to your advantage to update and maintain what you know about those subjects. A phone call from your boss, posing questions you can't answer, is always a difficult experience.

### Organizational Culture

Some organizations have a very written culture. Procter & Gamble, for example, requires that every issue be written in memo form and circulated to team members before it can be raised as an agenda issue in a team meeting. Other organizations, such as 3M Canada, are more "oral" in nature, offering employees an opportunity to talk things through before writing anything down. Many companies rely on a particular culture to move day-to-day information through the organization, and to succeed in such a business, you must adapt to the existing culture rather than try to change it or ask it to adapt to you.

### Organizational Dynamics

Organizations, like the humans who populate and animate them, are in constant flux. Businesses change with the conditions of the marketplace and the lives of the managers who run them. Your communication will have to adapt to the conditions in which you find yourself.

That does not mean signing your name to a document that is false or passing along information that you know isn't true, even if the organization presses you for time or will not give you access to information you really need to do your job. It does mean adapting your style to the standards and norms of the industry. It may mean greater concision or more detail than you might personally prefer. It may mean shorter turnaround times on requests than you think are reasonable. Or it may mean sharing or withholding information from those you work with each day. Each organization has its own style that is conditionally and temporally affected by a range of issues from market share to target-status in a takeover.

### Personality Preferences

Finally, it's important to acknowledge that each of us has his or her own preference for gathering, organizing and disseminating information. Each of us also has a style for making decisions. You'll have to accommodate those you work with and work for in order to succeed in business. If the boss wants plenty of detail and plenty of time to think it over before making a decision, accommodate that. Provide an executive summary, but give her the detail in tabular or appendix form if that's what she wants. Meet or beat submission deadlines. And provide the information in the form your reader or listener most wants. If your client likes e-mail, learn to live with brief, keystroked messages and attached text files. If your client likes personal briefings, schedule the time it will take to go over the information in detail. It is counterintuitive, but if you put the information-gathering and decision-making needs of others – particularly your boss and your clients – ahead of your own preferences, you'll get what you want faster and with much less pain.

## CRISIS COMMUNICATION

Crisis can come in many shapes and forms. Some crises unfold slowly over many months or years. Others arrive quickly or explosively, without notice.

The Coca-Cola Company's mishandling of a product contamination crisis in Europe during the summer of 1999 is a case in point. A bad batch of $CO_2$ found its way into Coca-Cola products bottled in Belgium and onto grocery store shelves in the cities of Bornem, Lochristi and Kortrijk. When reports of school children feeling nauseous and seeking hospital treatment after consuming Coca-Cola products hit the local press, company executives dismissed the incidents as overblown and "hardly a health hazard."[8]

CEO Doug Ivester, in fact, was in Paris at the time of the incident, yet chose to fly back to Atlanta rather than address it directly. He not only misread local sentiment regarding the company's obligations but failed to grasp the larger cultural implications of the crisis. Belgian Prime Minister Jean-Luc Dahaene had been forced out of office because of a scandal involving contamination of the food supply, and others seized the opportunity to take cheap shots at the American soft drink giant.

Sweden's *Svenska Dagbladet* proclaimed, "200 Poisoned by Coca-Cola," and Italy's *La Stampa* declared, "Alarm across Europe for Coca-Cola Products."[9] Following a recall of the company's products that cost $103 million over a six-week period and resulted in a drop of more than 20 points in Coca-Cola's share price, the brand did recover. It took just less than a year for consumers in Europe to resume their pre-crisis consumption patterns and for the company's stock value to return to the $75 per share level. The damage to the company's reputation cost Doug Ivester his job, however, as key investors lost confidence in his ability to protect the brand.

Other crises are years in the making. On the morning of February 5, 1995, Jim Adamson arrived at the corporate offices of Flagstar Companies in Spartanburg, South Carolina. As the firm's newly appointed CEO, his task was to reshape the future of a troubled company. His predecessor, Jerry Richardson, had struggled to keep the company alive with $2.3 billion in debt from a series of restructuring attempts. Despite those efforts, the company lost money for five consecutive years from 1985 to 1990.[10]

More ominously, Adamson had to confront the issue of racial discrimination. Flagstar was the parent company of Denny's Restaurants, a chain of restaurants that had become a symbol for racism in the U.S. He also had serious questions about the company's business model as a holding firm for quick-service and convenience-dining restaurants. With few assets and no experienced management team at his disposal, Adamson was brought to Flagstar from his position as CEO at Burger King by Henry Kravis, the New York junk-bond buyout king from Kohlberg Kravis & Roberts. His instructions were clear: Turn this company around. Make money or make way for someone who can.[11]

Each of these events represents a crisis and a potential threat to the reputation, financial health and survival of the companies involved. And while each executive responded in a different way to the threats, each was faced with a moment of decision: "What am I facing, and what shall I do?"

### Crisis Defined

Let's draw a line between business problems and a genuine crisis. "Problems," according to author Lawrence Barton:

> are commonplace in business. What differentiates crisis from the routine or even extraordinary management dilemma is this: a crisis is a major, unpredictable event that has potentially negative results. The event and its aftermath may significantly damage an organization and its employees, products, services, financial condition, and reputation.[12]

Ordinary business problems can be addressed in a limited time frame without arousing public attention and draining the resources of an organization. By contrast, a crisis is more expensive and often takes considerable time to understand and react to. And, of course, a crisis is far more threatening.

## Types of Crises

Some professionals draw further distinctions within crisis management, observing that some crises are *internal* in nature. Think of the accounting scandal and misappropriations for which Tyco CEO Dennis Kozlowski was convicted. The problems were almost entirely internal, as were those created by William Aramony at United Way. By contrast, other crises are *external* or *oppositional* in nature. When People for the Ethical Treatment of Animals (PETA) attacked Procter & Gamble and its Iams Dog Food division in March of 2003, alleging mistreatment of animals in a research facility, the crisis involved one organization opposing another.

## Preparing for a Crisis

When it comes to crisis communication, British physician Thomas Fuller got it right in 1732, when he wrote, "A man surprised is half beaten."[13] Clearly, it pays to be prepared. "Preparedness planning is definitely *not* a waste of time," says J. Adaire Putnam, Director of Corporate Communications at the Kellogg Company in Battle Creek, Michigan. "Because, when a crisis strikes, it usually strikes without warning, only giving you time to react and respond to whatever it triggers. Your foresight in getting ready for a crisis," she says, "will get you 80 percent of the way at a time when – in the chaos a crisis unleashes – all you can afford is the time to go the additional 20 percent."[14]

How an organization reacts to an incident or emergency can be a defining moment that can salvage or destroy a reputation. And it is often impossible to know when an emergency will occur. Arthur Andersen's accountants, Firestone Tire's executives, the makers of Tylenol, and Wendy's restaurant officials certainly didn't anticipate a calamity happening to them. But managers with responsibility for safeguarding the reputation of a product, a brand or an organization can certainly prepare for communicating in a crisis.

Here are five rules that Adaire Putnam thinks all managers should consider as they approach crisis communication:

1. **Develop a detailed crisis management action plan that includes detailed research.** "Assess all potential issue-and-crisis vulnerabilities and plan accordingly," she says. With a system in place, you'll be less likely to waste valuable time trying to decide how to communicate. When cable-TV operator Cox Communications prepared for contract negotiations with broadcasters several years ago to carry their programs, the company asked Putnam and her former employer, public relations firm Ketchum, to help manage the issue because if the programming agreement were to fail, it would result in a "dark channel." Careful research helped the company define their message points, audiences and best position on the issue. When a crisis struck on New Year's Day and Fox Television precluded Cox subscribers from watching college bowl games and the NFL playoffs, the crisis communications plan went into effect. Cox and their partners at Ketchum continuously reviewed media treatment and customer correspondence to determine the effectiveness of their strategy and message points.[15]

2. **Set specific objectives and principles.** The Cox Communications crisis-preparedness plan established three objectives: to motivate broadcasters to provide retransmission consent, to minimize customer defections to satellite, and to minimize the damage to the company's public image. Those objectives each proved to be measurable and achievable.

3. **Establish a crisis-control team and an outline of responsibilities and authority for taking action when a crisis develops.** Decide who will comprise your crisis team, creating that team around the expertise you will need and the personalities involved. Assign at least one hands-on person, says Putnam, as the crisis-communications team leader and then choose a backup.

   Additionally, you must select your primary and secondary spokespeople. Line up the outside experts and help you will need, possibly including outside legal counsel, an environmental cleanup expert and mental health workers for trauma victims, among others. Develop a communications contact tree with everyone's phone numbers on it, including mobile phones, and make sure they're updated regularly.

Contact a local hotel or motel and inform the proprietor that a day may arise when you will need all the rooms and you'll pay what he or she wants. Establish a "war room" or conference facility where the entire team can work. Make sure there are enough phone lines there and that those in the room will have cell phone service. Also, establish a separate press room away from the "war room" so that the media won't know who is there and demand access to other potential spokespeople.[16]

4. **Speak with one voice.** Create a communications plan that ensures all of your stakeholders – employees, customers, suppliers, community, regulatory officials and others – receive the same clear, valid information. Consider making your website or even a special crisis website *the* place to get crisis-related information.

Your website can prove invaluable for responding to a crisis, explaining the company's position, or rallying public support behind an issue. In September 2004, when the pharmaceutical firm Merck & Company made the decision to pull its important pain-killing drug Vioxx from the market, company vice president Joan Wainwright realized she would have to reach millions of concerned patients, physicians, pharmacists and others. More than 100 million prescriptions had been written for the drug. Within 60 hours of the initial announcement, she and her communications team launched a website at www.vioxx.com and established a toll-free telephone number to answer questions and address concerns.[17]

During October and November 2004, Merck's public affairs efforts generated more than 4 billion media impressions on the topic. The company's Vioxx website traffic grew from about 4,000 daily visits on September 29 to 234,000 on October 1. By early December, the vioxx.com website had attracted more than 2 million visitors, and the company's merck.com website had experienced an additional 1 million visitors. The team's toll-free telephone number received more than 120,000 calls in the first six days following the announcement. Additionally, the company reported issuing more than a half-million refunds for Vioxx prescriptions worldwide. Without the Web presence and a competently staffed call center, Merck would simply not have been able to address the enormous public concern that arose literally overnight.[18]

5. **Train for a crisis.** Develop scenarios in advance and work out responses on a case-by-case basis. Anticipating what information you will need can help to ensure that you have it when a crisis occurs. Establish what-ifs, contingencies you can employ if needed and experts you can tap to work side-by-side with you. Consider holding a mock crisis, a simulation, to test your procedures and better prepare your team and its resources. Prepare background materials that will be needed, including press release templates, fact sheets, biographies and position statements that can be formatted for easy revision and updated during an actual crisis.

In May 2005, FedEx gathered its main communications forces for such a crisis simulation. It was a global exercise involving more than 75 participants from FedEx's four operating companies in offices around the U.S., Europe, Asia, Canada and Latin America. FedEx and their partners at Ketchum developed a scenario involving a terrorist attack on the FedEx system, infecting employees around the globe with a chemical warfare agent. FedEx communicators faced the threat of serious damage to the company's reputation and the possible shutdown of the entire system.

Armed with 93 scripts that advanced the storyline, facilitators in seven cities role-played a variety of FedEx personnel, media outlets and customer contacts to make the situation as real as possible for the players. After the exercise, facilitators addressed gaps that the simulation exposed and incorporated the best practices that emerged into all FedEx communicators' crisis processes. The company also made a commitment to testing its crisis preparedness annually.

"Preparation really is the key," says Adaire Putnam. "Simply expect the unexpected. The better prepared you are for the worst to happen, the more quickly and effectively you can respond. The best way to manage communications during a crisis truly is to plan for it in advance."[19]

## FOR FURTHER READING

Argenti, P. "Crisis Communications," in *Corporate Communication*, 7/e. New York: Irwin McGraw-Hill, 2015, pp. 257–283.

Austin, L. L. and Y. Jin. *Social Media and Crisis Communication.* London: Routledge, 2017.

Coombs, T. *Ongoing Crisis Communication: Planning, Managing, and Responding*, 4/e. Thousand Oaks, CA: Sage Publications, Inc., 2014.

Goodman, M. B. and P. B. Hirsch, P. B. *Corporate Communication: Strategic Adaptation for Global Practice*. New York: Peter Lang Publishing, Inc., 2010.

Hatch, M. J. and M. Schultz. *Taking Brand Initiative: How Companies Can Align Strategy, Culture, and Identity Through Corporate Branding*. San Francisco, CA: Jossey-Bass, 2008.

Mitroff, I. I., C. M. Pearson and L. K. Harrington. *The Essential Guide to Managing Corporate Crises*. New York: Oxford University Press, 1996.

O'Hair, D., G. W. Friedrich and L. D. Shaver. *Strategic Communication in Business and the Professions*, 7/e. Boston, MA: Allyn & Bacon, 2010.

## NOTES

1 Fabun, D. *Communication: The Human Experience.* New York: William Morrow, 1968.

2 See DeVito, J. A. *The Interpersonal Communication Book*, 10/e. New York: HarperCollins Publishers, 2003, pp. 23–36. See also Watzlawick, P., J. H. Beavin and J. D. Jackson. *Pragmatics of Human Communication: A Study of Interactional Patterns, Pathologies, and Paradoxes.* New York: Norton, 1967.

3 DeVito, J. A. *Human Communication: The Basic Course*, 9/e. New York: HarperCollins Publishers, 2002, p. 5.

4 Maslow, A. "A Theory of Human Motivation," *Psychological Review* 50 (1943): 370–396.

5 Bem, D. J. *Beliefs, Attitudes, and Human Affairs.* Belmont, CA: Brooks/Cole Publishing Company, 1970, pp. 24–38.

6 Cialdini, R. B. *Influence: The Psychology of Persuasion.* New York: Quill Books, 1993.

7 Grimes, W. "In War against No-Shows, Restaurants Get Tougher," *The New York Times*, October 15, 1997, pp. B1–B6. Copyright 1997 © by the New York Times Company. Reprinted with permission.

8 Smith, H. and A. Feighan. *Coca-Cola and the European Contamination Crisis (A), (B).* Notre Dame, IN: Eugene D. Fanning Center, Mendoza College of Business, 2000.

9 Ibid.

10 Adamson, J., R. NcNatt and R. B. McNatt. *The Denny's Story: How a Company in Crisis Resurrected Its Good Name.* New York: John Wiley & Sons, 2000.

11 Abes, M. J., W. B. Chism and T. F. Sheeran. *Denny's Restaurants: Creating a Diverse Corporate Culture (A), (B).* Notre Dame, IN: Eugene D. Fanning Center, Mendoza College of Business, 2000.

12 Barton, L. *Crisis in Organizations: Managing and Communicating in the Heat of Chaos.* Cincinnati, OH: South-Western Publishing Company, 1993, p. 2.

13 Fuller, T. Online at www.inspirational-quotes.org/competition-quotes.html. Accessed November 7, 2005.

14 Putnam, J. A. In a personal interview with the author, August 1, 2005, Chicago, IL.

15 Ibid.

16 Ibid.

17 Wainwright, J. Vice President for public affairs, Merck & Company, in a teleconference interview from her offices at Merck corporate headquarters, Whitehouse Station, NJ, December 9, 2004.

18 Ibid.

19 Putnam. In a personal interview with the author.

# Case 2.1: Chipotle Mexican Grill, Inc.

## Supply Chain in Crisis (A)

I trusted they were providing me with "food with integrity." We fell for their branding.[1]

~ Chris Collins; Customer of Chipotle's E. Coli infected food

### THE CRISIS

On Saturday, October 31, 2015, Oregon health officials announced that more than 20 individuals were infected by the E. Coli bacteria as a result of consuming Chipotle Mexican Grill (Chipotle) food items. Specifically, 22 people contracted the illness that included eight hospitalizations. In the coming days, it would be announced that victims were from multiple states including Washington and Oregon, and that the specific source was undetermined. As a direct result, in early November 2015, Chipotle Mexican Grill, Inc. temporarily closed 43 restaurants located throughout the Pacific Northwest.[2]

Over the next few months, the E. Coli outbreak spanned 14 states and ultimately led to 60 cases and 22 hospitalizations. The Centers for Disease Control (CDC), the U.S. Food and Drug Administration (FDA) and the U.S. Department of Agriculture (USDA), along with state public health officials, launched an investigation to better understand the situation and to identify the specific source or sources of the bacteria.[3]

Ultimately, the investigation concluded that two outbreaks occurred involving the Shiga toxin-producing Escherichia coli O26 (E. Coli) – a rare strain of the bacteria. The first outbreak reported cases from October 19, 2015 to December 1, 2015 and spanned 11 states including: California, Delaware, Illinois, Kentucky, Maryland, Minnesota, New York, Ohio, Oregon, Pennsylvania and Washington. The second, smaller outbreak, occurred from November 18–26, 2015, and spanned three states including: Kansas, North Dakota and Oklahoma.[4]

The investigation could not identify a specific source of the E. Coli as a result of Chipotle's cooking practices. Given Chipotle's method[5] of mixing of multiple ingredients and food items during preparation, the study could not conclusively determine a specific contamination source.

| Category | Initial, Larger Outbreak | Second, Smaller Outbreak |
| --- | --- | --- |
| Dates | October 19–December 1 | November 18–26 |
| Bacteria | E. Coli O26 | E. Coli O26 |
| Number of States | 11 states | 3 states |
| Number of Cases | 55 cases | 5 cases |
| Number of Hospitalizations | 21 hospitalizations | 1 hospitalization |
| Age Range of Those Affected | 1–94 years of age | 6–25 years of age |
| Percent of Those Affected –Women | 57% | 80% |
| Deaths | 0 deaths | 0 deaths |

**FIGURE 2.1**   Summary: Investigation Results[6]

# E. COLI

E. Coli is bacteria that is commonly found in the intestines of humans and animals. Most E. Coli strains, in fact, are normally harmless and requisite to the normal digestive process. However, some E. Coli strains are pathogenic and cause illness, such as diarrhea and other gastrointestinal maladies.[7] Specifically, E. Coli O26 infections present with watery and/or bloody diarrhea along with abdominal cramps. To confirm diagnosis, stool samples are captured and tested to confirm the presence of E. Coli O26.[8]

E. Coli is transmitted through contaminated water, food, or affected animals and humans. More specifically, E. Coli enters a supply chain through ingredient sourcing. The manure from an affected animal is used as fertilizer on a crop, which is then harvested and sold to suppliers of restaurants.[9] If the ingredient is not handled appropriately or treated to kill E. Coli bacteria, it is possible for the ingredient to then make it into the food at the retail locations. Government entities test and regulate crops for E. Coli to prevent affected crops from moving through the supply chain.[10]

Anyone who comes into contact with or consumes the bacteria is at risk of infection. More precisely, anyone with a suppressed immune system, young children or the elderly are especially susceptible.[11]

# CHIPOTLE MEXICAN GRILL, INC.

Chipotle Mexican Grill, Inc. (Chipotle) was founded by Steve Ells in an effort to provide high-quality food, classic cooking techniques and a distinctive interior to customers. This business model adapted features from the Quick Service Restaurant industry (QSR) and defined a new category, Fast Casual (FC).

Chipotle's value proposition is "Food with Integrity." This tagline encompasses its business operations to show that food served fast does not have to be "fast food." The menu offerings are sourced from high-quality ingredients from local and regional suppliers and prepared by hand on-site in the retail locations. Chipotle believes there is a connection between how food is raised, prepared, served and consumed by the consumer. And finally, Chipotle is engaged in corporate social responsibility initiatives (CSR) through its Chipotle Foundation.[12]

# COMPANY TIMELINE

In 1993, Steve Ells opened the first Chipotle in Denver, Colorado. Three years later, Bob and Barbara Ells – Steve's parents – raised $1.3 million from friends in Chipotle's only private offering to date. Chipotle grew to 13 stores within five years. In the same year, 1998, McDonald's offered an initial $50 million investment in Chipotle, which remained autonomous from McDonald's corporate strategy.[13] Chipotle did not adopt the drive-thru concept or the franchise business model, and created a sanitary and welcoming retail presence through its design and friendly employees.

In 2004, McDonald's moved Chipotle to its distribution center in Portland, Oregon. Here, there is a contrast between how McDonald's manages its produce and Chipotle's approach to supply chain. McDonald's procures its ingredients from a few large suppliers, which are then packaged and sealed in mass quantities and shipped to retail locations. In contrast, Chipotle ships produce to its retail locations for preparation and storage on-site.

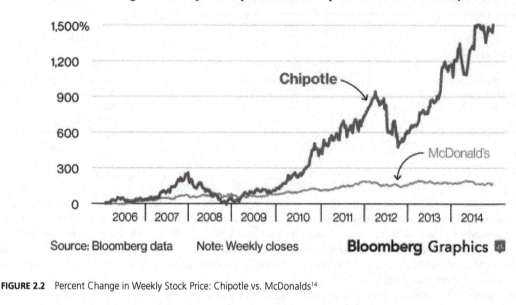

**Percent change in weekly share price since Chipotle's IPO on Jan. 26, 2006**

Source: Bloomberg data    Note: Weekly closes    **Bloomberg Graphics** 📊

**FIGURE 2.2**    Percent Change in Weekly Stock Price: Chipotle vs. McDonalds[14]

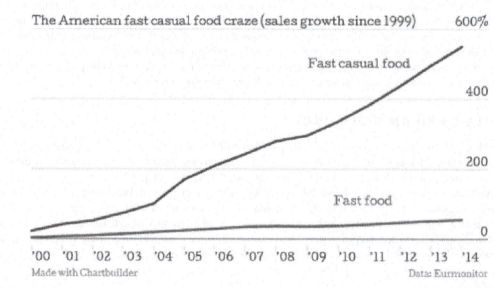

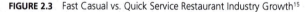

**FIGURE 2.3**    Fast Casual vs. Quick Service Restaurant Industry Growth[15]

On January 26, 2006, Chipotle issued an Initial Public Offering under the ticker, CMG, with an initial share offering of $22/share. For 90 minutes, the stock wouldn't open and effectively doubled on its first trade at $44/share.[16] Thus, McDonald's divested its majority ownership stake and the official relationship was extinguished. Chris Arnold, Communications Director at Chipotle, notes "I would think of it in terms of McDonald's being the rich uncle and Chipotle as the petulant nephew."[17] In Figure 2.2, Chipotle and McDonald's percent change in weekly share price is juxtaposed since the initial public offering to demonstrate Chipotle's exponential growth in comparison with McDonald's relative steady state.

In 2013, Chipotle was the first national restaurant chain to inform the public about the presence of GMOs in its food. In April, 2015, the company officially banned GMOs in its ingredients.[18] Currently, Chipotle operates around 2,000 stores, each averaging $2.4 million in revenue a year.[19]

Chipotle also owns ShopHouse and Pizzeria Locale, two portfolio brands attempting to capture market share in the FC sector within the QSR restaurant industry.[20]

## FAST CASUAL RESTAURANT INDUSTRY

Fast Casual (FC) is a diverging market segment of the quick service restaurant industry (QSR), which includes restaurants such as McDonald's, Taco Bell and Burger King.

The FC market emerged in the early 2000s. Panera Bread is widely recognized as the restaurant brand to revolutionize the industry and differentiate its business model from other QSR restaurants. FC restaurants traditionally appeal to adults with discretionary income to spend and to parents who are looking for a quick yet healthy meal for their children. After the financial crisis in 2008, Chipotle experienced noted growth due to a rebound of consumers' purchasing power and a shift in consumer focus to "fast food" that was fresh, healthy and sustainably sourced.[21]

Likewise, the FC market segment tends to have differentiating characteristics from its QSR counterparts. Figure 2.4 breaks down these characteristics in a comprehensive manner from farm to fork.

## GOVERNMENT REGULATION

Three principal government entities regulate food safety in restaurants in the U.S.: the Centers for Disease Control (CDC), the United States Department of Agriculture (USDA) and the United States Food and Drug Administration (USFDA).[22]

In 2011, President Obama initiated industry-wide food safety initiatives. These reforms were the most comprehensive overhaul of policy in over 70 years. The President's Food Safety Working Group (FSWG) established performance standards for poultry suppliers and required nutrition labels on single-ingredient raw protein items.

Additionally, a "test and hold" policy ensures that ingredients tested for E. Coli and other bacteria are not released until the results confirm that the produce or ingredient is safe. The Public Health Information System, a modern and comprehensive database, aggregates public health trends and compliance violations in one central system from the 6,100+ plants the Food Safety and Inspection Service (FSIS) regulates. These initiatives are communicated to the public through the Food Safe Families consumer education campaign under the auspices of the Ad Council, FDA and CDC.[23]

## GOVERNMENT INTERVENTION AT CHIPOTLE

The CDC, USDA and FDA investigated the 2015 E. Coli outbreak at Chipotle and determined that STEC O26 E. Coli was present in the food served in retail locations. These public health investigators utilized PulseNet, a national database system, to identify and connect the various country-wide outbreaks. This DNA fingerprinting is performed on E. Coli, which has been isolated from affected individuals through the process of pulsed-field gel electrophoresis (PFGE).

Investigators also used whole genome sequencing (WGS) in an effort to prove or disprove a connection among the various patients. Samples were taken from Chipotle's restaurants, distribution channels and customers, but as discussed previously, the results did not yield a specific ingredient or source that could explain the outbreak. It is important to note that once ingredients have been mixed and cooked together, bacteria cannot be traced back and isolated to determine the affected input source.[24]

| Category | FC | QSR |
|---|---|---|
| Average Check | $9.00–$13.00 | $5.00 |
| Drive Thru | No | Yes |
| Décor | First rate, technological advanced | Inexpensive |
| Ingredients | Fresh | Pre-packaged, bulk |
| Menu Offerings | Flexible | Fixed |
| Food Type | Wholesome | "fast food" |

**FIGURE 2.4** Industry Specifications[25]

## FOOD SAFETY AT CHIPOTLE

Chipotle advocates a two-pronged approach for monitoring food safety at the supplier and retail location levels.

### *Suppliers*

Unlike QSR restaurants that use multiple large-scale and bulk suppliers, Chipotle prefers to buy from local and regional suppliers, which increases the number of total suppliers. Additionally, Chipotle engages in high resolution testing, which tests a relatively large sample from a small sample of a specific ingredient. If one piece fails testing, the entire batch is removed from the supply chain. Chipotle also tests ingredients in central kitchens. A batch of tomatoes will enter, be washed, chopped, washed again and then tested. If one piece fails testing, the entire batch of tomatoes fails.[26]

### *Restaurants*

Within retail locations, prep cooks marinate chicken and steak at night in an attempt to mitigate cross-contamination of utensils and kitchen tops. Produce with skin, such as limes and onions, are blanched to kill bacteria resting on the outer shell. Additionally, each retail location follows strict sanitation practices mandated both by government entities and Chipotle corporate. Chipotle fully complies with audits and inspections. Likewise, the company offers extended sick leave and wellness initiatives to prevent ill employees from coming to work.[27]

## SUPPLY CHAIN: FOOD SOURCING

A supply chain is a network of organizations that work together to convert and move goods from the raw materials stage to the end customer.[28] In a typical supply chain, raw materials are procured and items are produced at one or more factories, shipped to warehouses for intermediate storage and then shipped to retailers or customers.[29] Food supply chains generally follow this same model, as illustrated in Figure 2.5.

Food supply chains are exposed to several particular risks due to the production methods and short shelf life associated with most foods. Fertilizers containing animal waste may expose food products to pathogens such as E. Coli, which can infect humans if the raw foods are not cleaned properly. Furthermore, many food products require special handling, refrigeration and expedited delivery due to their eventual spoilage.

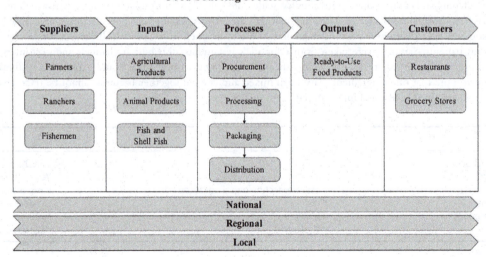

**Food Sourcing Process SIPOC**

**FIGURE 2.5** Food Sourcing Process SIPOC

The complexities of food supply chains are further compounded when companies introduce progressive food policies in response to modern consumer preference. For example, increasing freshness, removing genetically modified organisms (GMOs), and sourcing ethically raised animal products all require increased use of smaller, more specialized suppliers.

As restaurants procure food products from low-volume sources, the total number of suppliers required to meet total demand increases. Managing these large networks of suppliers exposes companies to ever-increasing risk.

## CHIPOTLE'S SUPPLY CHAIN

Chipotle's supply chain is constructed around its intent to deliver on the company's promise of providing customers "Food with Integrity."[30] As a result of these core operating principles, Chipotle has constructed a highly complex supply chain using a decentralized network of local and regional suppliers. Although this fresh, farm-to-table approach shortens the overall length of the supply chain relative to other restaurants, it also introduces considerable risk into the company's supplier quality and food production processes.

Melinda Wilkins, director of Michigan State University's Master of Science in Food Safety program, discussed Chipotle's challenges and risks at length with *Wired Magazine*. "The more complicated your supply chain is, the more opportunity you have to introduce problems," Wilkins said.[31] Wilkins also suggested that Chipotle's model of offering local ingredients through a decentralized supply chain increased its risk relative to QSR competitors, such as McDonald's and Taco Bell.[32]

Because Chipotle's business model and value proposition require it to operate a more complex supply chain, supplier quality and internal quality processes become critical to its operations.[33]

John Gray, Associate Professor of Operations Management at Ohio State University's Fisher College of Business, discussed some of these quality-related challenges on CNBC's *Power Lunch*. Gray pointed out the importance of process controls as well as supplier and employee compliance, saying, "the supply chain of Chipotle is extremely complex – thousands of stores, lots of local suppliers . . . you really need one hundred percent compliance of every individual throughout the supply chain."[34] Gray acknowledged that Chipotle has numerous internal processes already in place, but also suggested that, "a lot of these [controls] 'drift' with lack of attention."[35]

## MARKETPLACE RESPONSE

Given the magnitude of the outbreak and the Chipotle brand recognition, many interested parties reacted to the outbreak and subsequent news. An integral component to Chipotle's business viability and future sales directly results from customers visiting and purchasing meals from corporately owned restaurants.

In Chipotle's fourth quarter earnings calls, a standard review of financial and business performance held for investors, Mark Crumpacker, Chipotle's Chief Creative and Development Officer said, "Of those who are customers and who are also aware of the issues, right around 60% have indicated that it would cause them to visit less."[36] Additionally, it was apparent that consumer perception of the brand has waned drastically. According to the YouGov Brand Index, an index tracking consumer perceptions toward brands, a significant drop-off in brand perception occurred after the first news reports of E. Coli contamination.[37]

Chipotle's popularity among consumers and investors made news of the outbreak salient. The story was covered by a variety of news organizations including major television networks, news publications and digital media websites. Additionally, the issue was channeled to the public via social media. By February of 2016, coverage of the outbreak surged as events continued to unfold and create further complications for the company. Chipotle's Chief Financial Officer, Jack Hartung, described his frustration with the media in December at the Bernstein Consumer Summit where he said that "the media likes to write sensational headlines" in reference to coverage of the outbreak.[38]

Competitors in the FC space also seemed to gain from Chipotle's food quality crisis with many, such as Moe's Southwest Grill, using social media to target customers during times Chipotle was closed.[39] According to Yahoo Finance, Ticker Tags, which monitors the social media universe to showcase trends in the market, concluded that search queries for Qdoba increased in the beginning of November. The results of increased foot traffic in restaurants across the competitive landscape will reveal itself over time through Chipotle's sales and financial performance.[40]

As a result of sickness, Chipotle faces legal action from affected consumers. In November 2015, a customer who contracted E. Coli filed a lawsuit against Chipotle. That customer is seeking financial compensation due to concerns about long-term health.[41] Additionally, in January 2016, a civil lawsuit was filed in New York alleging that Chipotle did not disclose proper information necessary for investors to adequately assess the stock. Specifically, the filing discusses the lack of information about "quality controls" surrounding food safety protocols. The lawsuit claims that Chipotle investors should be awarded damages as compensation for the company's alleged violation of SEC regulations.[42]

## FINANCIAL IMPACT

Chipotle's financial performance suffered as a result of the E. Coli outbreak and the public's subsequent response. To start, sales suffered during the last quarter of 2015. Specifically, Chipotle's sales decreased by almost 7 percent over a three-month period. Steve Ells, Chipotle's Co-CEO, characterized the period by saying, "[t]he fourth quarter of 2015 was the most challenging period in Chipotle's history."[43]

Additionally, Chipotle reported a 44 percent reduction in profit during the same time period.[44] Lastly, Chipotle suffered unprecedented erosion in its stock value as the outbreak unfolded. The stock's value before the outbreak was $747 per share and declined to $480 after the investigation of the outbreak – a decline of more than 35 percent. Figure 2.6 illustrates the decline as well as key events in the outbreak to further explain the stock's performance.

## CHIPOTLE'S INITIAL RESPONSE

In November 2015, immediately following the initial reports of E. Coli outbreaks at Pacific Northwest Chipotle locations, the firm immediately announced that it would be hiring food safety consultants from IEH Laboratories and Consulting Group in Seattle, Washington.[45] Over the next 30 days Chipotle would continue to reassure the public, announcing that it completed a "deep-cleaning" of its restaurants on November 20, 2015,[46] and announcing its renewed commitment to industry leadership in food safety on December 4, 2015.[47]

Coinciding with the company's food safety announcement on December 4, it also announced through an 8K filing that it had lowered its earnings forecasts for the fourth quarter of 2015 and all of 2016.[48] Less than a week later, Chipotle CFO Jack Hartung blamed aggrandized media coverage and the reporting methods of the CDC for making Chipotle's situation worse.[49] *Fortune* magazine writer Phil Wahba criticized the CFO's comments, stating that his commentary was, "hardly the best way to handle a crisis."[50]

Even as Chipotle began to address and resolve the E. Coli outbreak, new events interrupted its efforts. In mid-December 2015, Chipotle was forced to acknowledge two new incidents. First, the ongoing E. Coli outbreak had expanded to the Midwest, sickening customers from Minnesota to Ohio.[51]

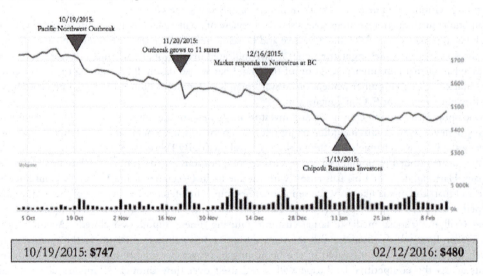

**FIGURE 2.6** Chipotle's Stock Performance: October 2015–February 2016[52]

The more damaging incident, however, was a new outbreak of Norovirus near the campus of Boston College, which sickened over 120 students.[53] This case garnered significant media attention, as it affected eight of the 14 players on the College's men's basketball team, nearly causing its game against Providence to be postponed.[54] In response, Chipotle closed its Cleveland Circle location in Boston for cleaning[55] and temporarily halted the marketing and advertising efforts it had planned to reassure customers until it could gain control of the situation.[56]

In late December 2015 and January 2016, Chipotle took additional actions to reassure its customers, announcing that it would introduce new cooking methods for some foods[57] and that it would close all of its stores for a company-wide food safety meeting on February 8, 2016.[58] Concurrently, media outlets reported that the company had planned a large marketing campaign for February aimed at winning back its previously loyal customer base.[59]

## CONCLUSION

The E. Coli STEC O26 outbreak has affected Chipotle's core operations and future financial viability. In future, it will consider how key stakeholders are affected and will be forced to assess its ability to deliver "Food with Integrity." Customers and investors will be the ultimate judge of the adequacy of Chipotle's response to the crisis.

## WRITING ASSIGNMENT

Please respond in writing to the issues presented in this case by preparing two documents: a communication strategy memo and a professional business letter.

In preparing these documents, you may assume one of two roles: you may identify yourself as a senior communications manager for Chipotle Mexican Grill, Inc. who has been asked to provide advice to Mr. Ells and Mr. Moran regarding the issues they and the company are now facing. Or, you may identify yourself as an external management consultant who has been asked by the company to provide advice to Mr. Ells and Mr. Moran.

Either way, you must prepare a strategy memo addressed to Mr. Steve Ells, Chairman and Co-Chief Executive Officer, and Mr. Montgomery F. Moran, Co-Chief Executive Officer, that summarizes the details of the case, rank-orders critical issues, discusses their implications (what they mean and why they matter), offers specific recommendations for action (assigning ownership and suspense dates for each) and shows how to communicate the solution to all who are affected by the recommended actions.

You must also prepare a professional business letter for Mr. Ells's signature. That document may be addressed to one of three groups: investors, customers or employees, knowing that this will become a public document available to nearly everyone with an interest in this case. If you have questions or concerns about either of these documents, please consult your instructor.

## ACKNOWLEDGMENTS

This case was prepared by research assistants Syvia Banda, Elizabeth Sadler and Bradley Wise under the direction of James O'Rourke, Teaching Professor of Management, as the basis for class discussion rather than to illustrate either effective or ineffective handling of an administrative situation. Information was gathered from corporate as well as public sources. Editorial assistance: Judy Bradford.

## NOTES

1  Berfield, Susan. "Inside Chipotle's Contamination Crisis," *Bloomberg Business*, December 22, 2015. Online at www.bloomberg.com/features/2015-chipotle-food-safety-crisis/. Accessed January 4, 2016.

2  "Chipotle Closes 43 Stores as Officials Investigate E. Coli Outbreak," *CBS News*, November 2, 2015. Online at www.cbsnews.com/news/43-chipotles-remain-closed-as-officials-investigate-e-coli-outbreak/. Accessed December 1, 2015.

3   "Multistate Outbreaks of Shiga Toxin-producing Escherichia Coli O26 Infections Linked to Chipotle Mexican Grill Restaurants," *Centers for Disease Control and Prevention*, February 1, 2016. Online at www.cdc.gov/ecoli/2015/o26-11-15/. Accessed February 6, 2016.

4   Ibid.

5   Ibid.

6   Ibid.

7   "E. Coli: General Information," *Centers for Disease Control and Prevention*, February 2016. Online at www.cdc.gov/ecoli/general/index.html. Accessed February 12, 2016.

8   Ibid.

9   "Teaching the Food System: Food Safety Background Reading," *A Project of the Johns Hopkins Center for a Livable Future*, February 2016. Online at www.jhsph.edu/research/centers-and-institutes/teaching-the-food-system/curriculum/_pdf/Food_Safety-Background.pdf . Accessed February 12, 2016.

10  "E. Coli: General Information," *Centers for Disease Control and Prevention*.

11  Ibid.

12  "Food with Integrity," *Chipotle*. Online at www.chipotle.com/food-with-integrity. Accessed February 3, 2016.

13  Stock, Kyle and Vanessa Wong. "Chipotle: The Definitive Oral History," *Bloomberg*, February 2, 2016. Online at www.bloomberg.com/graphics/2015-chipotle-oral-history/. Accessed February 12, 2015.

14  Ibid.

15  Ibid.

16  Ibid.

17  Ibid.

18  Masunaga, Samantha. "Chipotle Says it's the First Chain to Get Rid of GMO Ingredients," *Los Angeles Times*, April 27, 2015. Online at www.latimes.com/business/la-fi-chipotle-gmo-20150427-story.html.

19  "Investor Relations," *Chipotle Investor Relations*, February 2016. Online at http://ir.chipotle.com/phoenix.zhtml?c=194775&p=irol-newsArticle&ID=2098750. Accessed February 6, 2016.

20  Stock and Wong. "Chipotle: The Definitive Oral History."

21  Ferdman, Roberto A. "The Chipotle Effect: Why America is obsessed with fast casual food," *The Washington Post*, February 2, 2015. Online at www.washingtonpost.com/news/wonk/wp/2015/02/02/the-chipotle-effect-why-america-is-obsessed-with-fast-casual-food/. Accessed February 12, 2015.

22  "Selected Federal Agencies with a Role in Food Safety," *Foodsafety*, Online at www.foodsafety.gov/about/federal/. Accessed February 12, 2016.

23  "USDA Takes New Steps to Fight E. Coli, Protect the Food Supply," *United States Department of Agriculture*, archived 2011. Online at www.usda.gov/wps/portal/usda/usdahome?contentidonly=true&contentid=2011/09/0400.xml. Accessed February 12, 2016.

24  "FDA Investigates Multistate Outbreak of E. Coli O26 Infections Linked to Chipotle Mexican Grill Restaurants," *Federal Drug Administration*. Online at www.fda.gov/Food/RecallsOutbreaksEmergencies/Outbreaks/ucm470410.htm. Accessed February 12, 2016.

25  Ibid.

26  "Food Safety," *Chipotle*. Online at www.chipotle.com/foodsafety. Accessed February 3, 2016.

27  Ibid.

28  Boyer, Kenneth and Rohit Verma. *Operations & Supply Chain Management in the 21st Century*. Mason, OH: South-Western/Cengage Learning, 2010, p. 19.

29  Harrison, Terry P., Hau L. Lee and John J. Neal. *The Practice of Supply Chain Management: Where Theory and Application Converge*. New York: Springer Science & Business Media, Inc., 2003, p. 14.

30  "Food with Integrity," *Chipotle*.

31  Alba, Davey. "Chipotle's Health Crisis Shows Fresh Food Comes at a Price," *Wired Magazine*, January 15, 2016. Online at www.wired.com/2016/01/chipotles-health-crisis-shows-fresh-food-comes-at-a-price. Accessed February 6, 2016.

32  Ibid.

33  Balakrishnan, Anita. "Local Sourcing: Chipotle's Double-Edged Sword," *CNBC*, December 22, 2015. Online at www.cnbc.com/2015/12/22/local-sourcing-chipotles-double-edged-sword.html. Accessed February 6, 2016.

34  "Weak Links in Supply Chain," *CNBC Power Lunch*, 2015. Online at http://video.cnbc.com/gallery/?video=3000468548. Accessed February 6, 2016.

35  Ibid.

36  Krisiloff, Scott. "Chipotle 4Q15 Earnings Call Notes," *Avondale Asset Management*, February 3, 2016. Online at http://avondaleam.com/chipotle-4q15-earnings-call-notes. Accessed February 14, 2016.

37  Marzilli, Ted. "Chipotle Perception Drop Equals GM's," *YouGovBrandIndex*, December 17, 2015. Online at www.brandindex.com/article/chipotle-perception-drop-equals-gms. Accessed February 9, 2016.

38  Wahba, Phil. "Chipotle is Blaming the Government and the Media for Their E. Coli PR Nightmare," *Fortune*, December 8, 2015. Online at http://fortune.com/2015/12/08/chipotle-media-ecoli/. Accessed December 15, 2016.

39    Alesci, Cristina. "Moe's Chides Chipotle: We're Open All Day," *CNN Money*, February 8, 2016. Online at http://money.cnn.com/2016/02/08/news/companies/moes-chipotle/. Accessed February 10, 2016.

40    Duggan, Wayne. "Chipotle's E. Coli Disaster Was Qdoba's Gain, New Data Shows," *Yahoo Finance*, February 1, 2016. Online at http://finance.yahoo.com/news/chipotles-e-coli-disaster-qdobas-191130518.html. Accessed February 14, 2016.

41    Smith, Aaron. "Chipotle Sued by Customer Who Says She Got E. Coli," *CNN Money*, November 4, 2015. Online at http://money.cnn.com/2015/11/03/news/companies/chipotle-sued-e-coli/. Accessed December 1, 2016.

42    Polansek, Tom. "Chipotle Sued for Misleading Investors Over Food Safety," *Reuters*, January 8, 2016. Online at www.reuters.com/article/us-chipotle-mexican-lawsuit-idUSKBN0UM2BD20160108. Accessed January 20, 2016.

43    Stock, Kyle. "Chipotle's Sales Have Dropped by 10.3 Million Burritos," *Bloomberg Business*, February 2, 2016. Online at www.bloomberg.com/news/articles/2016-02-02/chipotle-s-sales-have-dropped-by-10-3-million-burritos. Accessed February 13, 2016.

44    Dulaney, Chelsey. "Chipotle, Stung by E. Coli Outbreak, Posts First-Ever Sales Decline," *The Wall Street Journal*, February 2, 2016. Online at www.wsj.com/articles/chipotle-stung-by-e-coli-outbreak-posts-first-ever-sales-decline-1454449916. Accessed February 13, 2016.

45    Giammona, Craig and Nick Turner. "Chipotle Hires Safety Consultants to Cope with Health Scare," *Bloomberg Business*, November 3, 2015. Online at www.bloomberg.com/news/articles/2015-11-03/chipotle-hires-food-safety-consultants-to-cope-with-health-scare. Accessed February 6, 2016.

46    Arnold, Chris (Chipotle). "Press Release: Chipotle Updates on E. Coli Investigation," *BusinessWire*, November 20, 2015. Online at www.businesswire.com/news/home/20151120005928/en. Accessed February 6, 2016.

47    Arnold, Chris (Chipotle). "Press Release: Chipotle Commits to Become Industry Leader in Food Safety," *BusinessWire*, December 4, 2015. Online at www.businesswire.com/news/home/20151204005113/en. Accessed February 6, 2016.

48    Chipotle Mexican Grill, Inc. "8K Filing E. Coli Incident Impact," *Chipotle Investor Relations*, December 4, 2015. Online at http://ir.chipotle.com/phoenix.zhtml?c=194775&p=irol-SECText&TEXT=aHR0cDovL2FwaS50ZW5rd2l6YXJkLmNvbS9maWWxpbmcueG1sP2lwYWdlPTEwNjEyNzk3Jk RTRVE9MSZTRVE9MiZTUURFU0M9U0VDV. Accessed February 6, 2016.

49    Banjo, Shelly. "It's Time for Chipotle to Eat Crow," *Bloomberg Gadfly*, December 8, 2015. Online at www.bloomberg.com/gadfly/articles/2015-12-08/chipotle-e-coli-outbreak-is-a-major-pr-problem. Accessed February 6, 2016.

50    Wahba. "Chipotle is Blaming the Government and the Media."

51    Jargon, Julie. "CDC Probes New Chipotle-Linked E. Coli Cases," *The Wall Street Journal*, December 21, 2015. Online at www.wsj.com/articles/cdc-probing-another-chipotle-linked-e-coli-outbreak-1450730153. Accessed February 6, 2016.

52    Nasdaq Interactive Price Chart, Chipotle Mexican Grill. Online at www.nasdaq.com/symbol/cmg/interactive-chart.

53    Jargon, Julie. "Norovirus Confirmed in Boston Chipotle Outbreak," *The Wall Street Journal*, December 9, 2015. Online at www.wsj.com/articles/norovirus-confirmed-in-boston-chipotle-outbreak-1449684009. Accessed February 6, 2016.

54    Katz, Andy. "All 8 BC Players Return to Practice, Game vs. Providence Still On," *ESPN*, December 9, 2015. Online at http://espn.go.com/mens-college-basketball/story/_/id/14315661/at-least-eight-boston-college-eagles-players-food-poisoning. Accessed February 6, 2016.

55    "Boston Chipotle Shut Down After 30 BC Students Get Sick," *CBS Boston*, December 7, 2015. Online at http://boston.cbslocal.com/2015/12/07/boston-college-chipotle-illness. Accessed February 6, 2016.

56    Jargon, Julie. "Why You Won't Soon See Chipotle Ads," *The Wall Street Journal*, December 25, 2015. Online at www.wsj.com/articles/why-you-wont-soon-see-chipotle-ads-1451083903. Accessed February 6, 2016.

57    "Chipotle Tweaks Cooking Methods After E. Coli Outbreak," *Chicago Sun Times*, December 23, 2015. Online at http://chicago.suntimes.com/business/7/71/1202596/chipotle-e-coli-cooking-methods. Accessed February 6, 2016.

58    Fickenscher, Lisa. "Why Chipotle Will Close Every Store for a Few Hours on Feb. 8," *MarketWatch*, January 15, 2016. Online at www.marketwatch.com/story/chipotle-to-launch-pr-blitz-to-woo-back-customers-2016-01-14. Accessed February 6, 2016.

59    Jargon, Julie. "Chipotle Plans Marketing Campaign to Win Back Customers," *The Wall Street Journal*, January 13, 2016. Online at www.wsj.com/articles/chipotle-plans-marketing-campaign-to-win-back-customers-1452726402. Accessed February 6, 2016.

# Case 2.2: Gilead Sciences and Sovaldi

## *The Cost of a Cure (A)*

### INTRODUCTION

December 6, 2013, had the makings of a good day for Gilead Sciences, Inc. The United States Food and Drug Administration (FDA) had just approved Sovaldi,[1] a hepatitis C treatment, after a wildly successful trial program that saw more than 90 percent of patients cured.[2] In addition, the cost of the treatment would be in line with less effective hepatitis C treatments, and several times lower than the cost of treating or replacing a damaged liver, a possible consequence of hepatitis C.[3]

This was not the message that traveled through the media on December 6, though. Instead, the fact that the $84,000 total cost of the treatment amounted to $1,000 per pill captured the attention of the media, the public and even government officials.

While it is not uncommon for drugs to exceed this cost, none target a disease with such a large patient population. Gilead Sciences has its work cut out for itself, but it would not be the first time the company faced such an obstacle.

### GILEAD SCIENCES, INC.

In 1979, Michael Riordan graduated with honors from Washington University with degrees in biology and chemical engineering. Upon graduation, he accepted a Luce scholarship, which allowed him to travel to several countries in Asia, including a stint with the Ministry of Health in the Philippines.[4]

While working at a malnutrition clinic in Asia, Mr. Riordan contracted dengue fever. Speaking about his experience, he said: "I was flat on my back for three weeks and nothing could be done about it. There's just not much in the medical toolkit for this virus."[5] His experiences in Asia, particularly in dealing with dengue fever, created a curiosity within him about the science of human disease.

Mr. Riordan went on to receive his M.D. from Johns Hopkins School of Medicine.[6] He was not finished with his education, though, and after finishing medical school decided to pursue an M.B.A. from Harvard. After graduation in

1986, he took the seemingly unusual step of joining Menlo Ventures, a venture capital firm.[7] One year later in 1987, Dr. Riordan founded Gilead Sciences, named after what is considered the world's first pharmaceutical product. His experience in venture capital served him well, as he raised $2 million in venture capital funding in 1988 and another $10 million in 1989.[8] Dr. Riordan's vision for Gilead was to treat and eventually eradicate viruses such as the one he faced in Asia, as well as HIV, hepatitis B and influenza.

After several more rounds of private funding, Gilead Sciences went public in January 1992. The IPO raised more than $86 million for the company, but Gilead still had no pharmaceutical products. In fact, Gilead's first product did not debut in the U.S. until the latter half of 1996.[9] The slow growth of the company did not deter Dr. Riordan from pursuing his vision. In 1998, Gilead acquired NeXstar Pharmaceuticals, a Colorado company with several products already on the market and sales that were three times that of Gilead. This led to a period of tremendous growth for Gilead, and by 2001 its sales increased by 500 percent.

Throughout the 2000s, Gilead pursued its own research and development, and continued acquiring other companies. In 2002 it acquired Triangle Pharmaceuticals for $464 million in order to gain access to Triangle's HIV and hepatitis B treatments.[10] In 2011, Gilead paid $11 billion for a company with a promising treatment for hepatitis C: Pharmasset Inc.[11]

## PHARMASSET INC.

A student at Emory University first introduced Dr. Raymond Schinazi and Dr. Dennis Liotta, professors of pediatrics and chemistry respectively, to each other. Both were interested in virology, with a particular interest in HIV treatments.[12] After working together for several years, Drs. Schinazi and Liotta formed Pharmasett in 1998. Among their medical advancements were the main anti-HIV drug used in the majority of AIDS "cocktails," and a promising treatment for hepatitis C that by 2011 was ready for FDA approval. Investors and users alike were anxiously awaiting the FDA's decision.

**FIGURE 2.7** Pharmasset (VRUS) Stock Price, 10/5/09–12/20/11

# THE DRUG DEVELOPMENT PROCESS

The process by which a drug is developed varies widely from molecule to molecule. Traditionally, new molecular compounds are sought out by screening natural products for potential drugs. Penicillin, a mold found in a soil sample, was discovered by chance in Alexander Fleming's laboratory to kill a range of bacteria.[13] In fact, the discovery of penicillin prompted pharmaceutical companies to collect massive libraries of soil samples, with the hope of discovering the next major drug. Pfizer was known to solicit traveling salesmen, missionaries, soldiers and other world travelers to bring back soil samples from their travels; the company was reported to have a library of over 20,000 soil cultures.[14]

Advances in biochemistry and genetics have greatly altered the drug discovery process. This process is still arduous and time consuming, taking an average of 10 to 15 years and costing an estimated $500 million to $2 billion per successful drug.[15] Furthermore, for every 5,000–10,000 drugs in the drug discovery process, five are estimated to enter clinical trials, and the FDA will approve just one.[16] Furthermore, patent protection for pharmaceutical products lasts for 20 years, but patents are typically filed at the time of the molecule's discovery, leaving as little as five years of patent protection once the drug has been approved for marketing.[17]

Today, the drug development process typically involves a process known as rational drug design, although screening is still used in many cases. The first step of the process is identifying a target molecule, such as a protein that allows a cancer to replicate out of control. Rational drug design uses combinatorial chemistry or biochemistry to engineer new molecules whose function is to hopefully inhibit the behavior of target molecules. The discovery stage is estimated to cost between $30 and $50 million. During the discovery stage, investigators will test molecules on cells and tissues to determine whether or not the drug candidate can influence the target molecule.

Before a drug is tested on humans, it is tested in animal models to determine the pharmacokinetics of the drug – how it moves throughout the body. In particular, scientists look for a series of characteristics known as ADMET, which stands for: Absorption (into the blood stream), Distribution (throughout the body), Metabolism (the enzymatic changes undergone by the drug), Excretion (out of the body) and Toxicity (looking for adverse effects). Estimates for the cost of preclinical studies range from $50 to $160 million,[18] and the process typically takes three to five years.

Once a drug is ready for human testing, it must undergo a rigorous series of clinical trials. In Phase I studies, the drug is tested for safety and adverse effects in healthy volunteers. Once safety is determined, investigators may also test for maximum tolerable dosage. Phase I studies typically involve 20 to 100 healthy volunteers, and may take several months to a year. Typically, 70 percent of molecules and compounds will advance to Phase II trials.

In Phase II trials, the drug candidate is tested for effectiveness, short-term side effects and risks. Phase II trials involve from 100 to 500 patients with the disease that the candidate drug is designed to treat, and may take several months to two years. Approximately 33 percent of drug candidates then advance to Phase III trials. Phase III trials are large-scale tests that seek additional evidence of efficacy. The sample size in Phase III trials typically ranges from 300 to 5,000 patients with the disease, increasing the likelihood that benefits or adverse effects found will be statistically significant.

Phase III trials can take one to four years, and approximately 65 percent of Phase III candidates advance.[19] If a Phase III trial successfully meets its goals, the sponsor company then submits a New Drug Application (NDA) to the FDA. NDAs include every detail of the drug design and trial results, can be hundreds of thousands of pages, and take as long as two years to be fully reviewed. The total cost of the clinical trials process is astronomical, and increases as drugs advance to Phase III trials, which can cost companies as much as 90 percent of the total cost of the entire development process.[20]

Recall that Phase III trials may involve ten times as many volunteer patients as Phase II trials, and may involve multiple trials testing combinations of drugs, or the same drug in different variations of a disease (for example, different variants of a genetic mutation that cause the same disease). Furthermore, the cost-per-patient increases as trials advance through phases.[21] Sovaldi, for example, was tested in 1,947 patients in six different Phase III trials, and was tested as a standalone drug, and in various combinations with ribavirin and peginterferon-alfa (more commonly known as interferon).[22]

# HEPATITIS C

"Hepatitis" is the name of a family of viral diseases that result in inflammation of the liver. Hepatitis A, B and C are the most common types of hepatitis, and are caused by three different viruses. Although they produce similar symptoms, they affect the liver in different ways, and have different modes of transmission. People infected with hepatitis A often improve without treatment. Hepatitis B and C can often appear as acute infections, but in some patients, the virus remains in the body, resulting in chronic disease and long-term liver problems. Hepatitis A and B are preventable with vaccines, while hepatitis C is not. In the U.S., there are typically 16,000-to-18,000 new cases of hepatitis C reported each year (known as incidence), and an estimated 3.2 million people living with chronic hepatitis (known as prevalence); approximately 75 percent of people infected with the virus develop chronic hepatitis C.[23] Globally, 130-to-150 million people have chronic hepatitis C, and some 300,000-to-500,000 people each year die from hepatitis C-related liver diseases.[24]

Hepatitis C is transmitted through the blood. People at increased risk of hepatitis C include those who use injectable drugs, recipients of infected blood products, children born to mothers with the virus, people with sexual partners with the virus, people who use intranasal drugs and people who have tattoos or piercings.

Symptoms of hepatitis C may vary widely, including fever, fatigue, loss of appetite, nausea, jaundice and vomiting. Symptoms typically appear six-to-seven weeks after exposure, but this can range from two weeks to six months. Many people who live with hepatitis C do not develop symptoms; however, if a person has been infected for many years they may experience liver damage. In many cases, symptoms do not appear until the patient experiences long-term health issues such as liver failure, cirrhosis of the liver, liver cancer or even death.[25] The cost burden of hepatitis C has been estimated at an average of $65,000 per patient, but the cost of liver failure is dramatically higher. The estimated average cost of a liver transplant in 2011, for example, was $577,000.[26]

The hepatitis C virus was first discovered in 1989. Prior to that year, the virus was known to be associated with blood transfusions, but was only referred to as non-A, non-B hepatitis because the virus was not yet identified; it is now known that there are four distinct genotypes of the hepatitis C virus.

Reliable blood tests for hepatitis C were not developed until 1992, and as a result, people who received blood transfusions, blood products or organ transplants before that year were at higher risk of contracting the virus.[27] As a result, the majority of hepatitis C carriers in developed countries are, on average, over the age of 40, but also since 1992, the incidence of new cases of hepatitis C has decreased dramatically.[28]

The first approved treatment for hepatitis C is a drug known as Shering's pegylated interferon alpha-2b. Interferons are proteins usually released by host cells in response to the presence of pathogens such as viruses and bacteria, which cause cells to ramp up their anti-viral defenses. The sustained viral response (the rate at which patients show an absence of the virus) of interferon treatment was 14 percent for genotype 1 (the most common type of hepatitis C), and 47 percent for genotypes 2 and 3.[29] Since the approval of Shering's Peg-Intron, and the discovery of the enormous population affected with the hepatitis C virus, pharmaceutical companies have been racing to develop the most effective cure with the fewest side effects, highest sustained viral response and easiest treatment plan.

One of the first and most successful pharmaceutical drugs approved to treat hepatitis C was Incivek (generic name telaprevir), co-developed and marketed by Vertex Pharmaceuticals and Johnson & Johnson. Incivek was approved by the FDA in April 2011 for treatment of genotype 1 hepatitis C, in combination with Peg-Intron and ribavirin. The recommended treatment was a 48-week course requiring Incivek to be taken twice daily for 12–24 weeks, and interferon and ribavirin for the entirety of the treatment period.[30] Following the FDA's approval, Incivek became one of the fastest selling drugs of all time, and was taken by an estimated 100,000 people within three years of its approval.[31] The drug was priced at $49,200 for the course of treatment upon its approval by the FDA.[32]

The potential financial rewards of developing the most effective hepatitis C cure are derived from the size of the infected population and the high cost of liver disease associated with hepatitis C. As a result, the pharmaceutical industry experienced a high level of activity in acquisitions of small drug developers with promising molecules. In addition to Gilead's $11 billion acquisition of Pharmasset, several other acquisitions of note stand out due to high acquisition cost and lack of drugs in advanced trials. In June 2014, Merck announced that the company would acquire Idenix Pharmaceuticals for approximately $4 billion, nearly triple its market value. In 2012, Bristol-Myers Squibb acquired Inhibitex Inc. for $2.5 billion, nearly four times its market value.

Of note given high costs for the various treatments for hepatitis C: the cost for treating cancer can run to tens of thousands of dollars, and can exceed $100,000 per year in some cases.[33] Treatments for extremely rare and debilitating diseases can cost hundreds of thousands of dollars *annually*. Soliris, for example, marketed by Alexion Pharmaceuticals to treat a rare blood disease called paroxysmal nocturnal hemoglobinurina, cost $440,000 per patient per year in 2012, and Vertex Pharmaceutical's cystic fibrosis treatment Kalydeco was priced at approximately $300,000 per patient per year in 2013.[34] These diseases are referred to as "orphan diseases," a designation for diseases affecting fewer than 200,000 people in the U.S. The high cost of treatment is necessary for companies to recover the cost of drug development, and incentivize future drug developers to attempt treatments and cures for other orphan diseases. Hepatitis C, by contrast, is believed to affect as many as 3 million people in the U.S., and up to 150 million globally.

## REACTION TO SOVALDI PRICING

The reaction to the news that Gilead would price Sovaldi at $1,000 per pill within the U.S. was not well received, and the company experienced significant backlash from businesses, doctors, non-governmental organizations and U.S. legislators.

Molina Healthcare, a company that operates Medicaid managed-care programs for 11 states, told state officials that it would not be able to cover the cost of the drug. CEO Mario Molina stated, "We cannot absorb this kind of a hit. It would cause us and other health plans to potentially become insolvent." Due to the price, other healthcare companies announced plans to delay access for patients. Express Scripts, the largest prescription drug benefit manager in the U.S., encouraged its doctors to delay prescribing Sovaldi to patients who were healthy enough to wait.[35] These and other warnings translated into Colorado and Pennsylvania limiting the use of Sovaldi to all but the sickest of patients.[36]

In California, a panel of medical experts from top California universities and hospitals voted to classify Sovaldi as a low-value treatment due to its extreme cost. The group, known as the California Technology Assessment Forum, helps assess the costs and benefits of new drugs for the insurance industry. The group estimated that replacing currently used hepatitis C drugs with Sovaldi would raise drug costs in California between $18 and $29 billion per year.[37]

Just three days after the FDA approved Sovaldi, a group of healthcare-focused, international non-governmental organizations including Doctors Without Borders and Doctors of the World released a statement criticizing Gilead for its pricing of Sovaldi. The groups demanded that Gilead price the drug close to the cost of production in low- and middle-income countries to ensure availability to the widest possible distribution of people within less economically fortunate nations.[38]

Gilead also received attention from the U.S. Congress. In a letter to Gilead CEO Dr. John C. Martin, Congressmen Henry Waxman, Frank Pallone and Congresswoman Diana DeGette demanded that Gilead provide a briefing to the House Committee on Energy and Commerce on Sovaldi. The letter states, "Our concern is that a treatment will not cure patients if they cannot afford it." Specifically, the letter asks for an explanation of the method used to price the drug, the availability of the drug to low-income individuals, the value Gilead received from expedited FDA review and the public health impact of insurers and public health programs refusing to cover Sovaldi for all hepatitis C patients.[39]

Investors did not react strongly in either direction to the announcement of the Sovaldi price. Over the period from the price announcement until the April 22, 2014 Q1 10-Q quarterly earnings report that included Sovaldi sales, Gilead's stock retreated approximately 3 percent.[40]

## GILEAD'S RESPONSE

Gilead's response to the various pressures it received generally included cooperation with all stakeholders, a willingness to work to lower the price within international markets, and the view that it had priced Sovaldi fairly within the U.S.

Amy Flood, Vice President of Public Affairs at Gilead, said that the company was surprised at the response it had received, and offered this statement:

> We were surprised by the disproportionate response and focus on Sovaldi, particularly given that its approval was widely anticipated within the payer community, and that we priced the medicine to be in line with the previous standard of care regimen for hepatitis C. Our conversations with payers in the U.S. indicate that the overwhelming volume (patient demand) and subsequent budget impact is driving much of the reaction. It should be noted that we have seen a more balanced conversation over time with the emergence of voices that recognize the value of curing hepatitis C and fostering innovation in healthcare.[41]

Gilead negotiated several price discounts with developing nations and non-governmental organizations following the release of Sovaldi. One such discount was negotiated with Egypt, which has one of the highest prevalence rates of hepatitis C in the world. Further, in April 2014, Gilead reached an agreement with Doctors Without Borders to provide the group with the full 12-week course of Sovaldi for $900 in several nations, including India, Myanmar, Kenya and Mozambique.[42]

Gilead showed no intention of lowering the cost of Sovaldi within the U.S. When asked how Gilead determined the price for Sovaldi, Amy Flood responded:

The final determination of the price of a new medicine is made just before, or immediately in conjunction with, its approval by the U.S. FDA. In developed countries, Gilead considers several value and market-based factors in pricing its medicines, which may change frequently – particularly in therapeutic areas that are seeing rapid advances. Sovaldi was priced based upon the attributes of the medicine as a breakthrough cure for HCV, extensive research with payer segments regarding access, and our assessment of its value in the context of an already-established market which had seen multiple successful product launches.[43]

The company responded to the Congressional letter, and stated that it had been and would continue to cooperate with lawmakers. The company then released the following statement:

We had heard the concerns raised in the letter and had reached out to a number of members of Congress prior to this letter to address those concerns. We have been working with a number of stakeholders, including federal and state officials, to share the scientific and medical evidence.[44]

## GILEAD'S FIRST QUARTER EARNINGS

The controversy surrounding Gilead's pricing of its superstar drug Sovaldi came to a head when, on April 22, 2014, the company released its 10-Q quarterly earnings report. The drug maker reported $5 billion in revenue on $4.87 billion in product sales, compared to $2.53 billion in revenue on $2.39 billion in product sales a year earlier. Diluted earnings per share were reported at $1.33 on net income of $2.23 billion, compared to $0.43 on net income of $722.2 million a year earlier. Sovaldi accounted for nearly 50 percent of the company's product sales, at $2.27 billion.[45] The company's share price jumped nearly 3.5 percent on the news.

## DECISION POINT

The news that Sovaldi had brought Gilead soaring profits was sure to further ignite public debate about the drug's pricing, both domestically and abroad. Gilead would need to carefully consider how to respond to the situation and effectively communicate to its stakeholders.

Who are the key stakeholders?
Has Gilead priced Sovaldi fairly?
Has the communication strategy thus far been sufficient?
How should Gilead adjust and communicate its strategy both domestically and internationally moving forward?

## DISCUSSION QUESTIONS

1. What is the central business problem in this case? Does that problem pose a threat to the profitability or continued existence of the company?
2. Who are the key stakeholders? What's at stake for them? Can you identify any interested observers with no genuine stake in the outcome?
3. Has Gilead priced Sovaldi fairly? If so, what's their defense? If not, what should they do?
4. Has the communication strategy thus far been sufficient? How should Ms. Flood and other corporate officers respond to public criticism, including complaints from government regulators and elected officials?
5. How should Gilead adjust and communicate its strategy both domestically and internationally?

# WRITING ASSIGNMENT

Please respond in writing to the issues presented in this case by preparing two documents: a communication strategy memo and a professional business letter.

In preparing these documents, you may assume one of two roles: you may identify yourself as a Gilead senior manager who has been asked to provide advice to Vice President Amy Flood regarding the issues they and their company are facing. Or, you may identify yourself as an external management consultant who has been asked by the company to provide advice to them.

Either way, you must prepare a strategy memo addressed to Ms. Flood that summarizes the details of the case, identifies critical issues, discusses their implications (what they mean and why they matter), offers specific recommendations for action (assigning ownership and suspense dates for each) and shows how to communicate the solution to all who are affected by the recommendations.

You must also prepare a professional business letter for the signature of John F. Milligan, Gilead Sciences Chief Executive Officer. That document should be addressed either to all Sovaldi patients or to another group of key stakeholders, explaining what happened and the actions the company is taking. If you have questions about either of these documents, please consult your instructor.

# ACKNOWLEDGMENTS

This case was prepared by research assistants Benjamin Budish, Chase Lane and Richard Zaleski under the direction of James S. O'Rourke, Teaching Professor of Management, as the basis for class discussion rather than to illustrate either effective or ineffective handling of an administrative situation. Information was gathered from corporate as well as public sources. Editorial assistance: Judy Bradford.

# NOTES

1  "U.S. Food and Drug Administration Approves Gilead's Sovaldi (Sofosbuvir) for the Treatment of Chronic Hepatitis C," *Gilead Sciences*, press release, December 6, 2013, on the Gilead Sciences website. Online at www.gilead.com/news/press-releases/2013/12/us-food-and-drug-administration-approves-gileads-sovaldi-sofosbuvir-for-the-treatment-of-chronic-hepatitis-c. Accessed September 26, 2014.

2  "High Hepatitis C Cure Rates in Trial of Sovaldi and Daclatasvir," *Hepmag.com*, January 21, 2014. Online at www.hepmag.com/articles/daclatasvir_Sovaldi_2501_25081.shtml. Accessed September 21, 2014.

3  LaMattina, John. "Forgotten in the Sovaldi Price Debate: Hep-C Patients and Healthcare Savings," *Forbes*, June 25, 2014. Online at www.forbes.com/sites/johlamattina/2014/06/25/forgotten-in-the-sovaldi-price-debate-hep-c-patients-and-healthcare-savings. Accessed September 25, 2014.

4  Brown, Kathryn. "Balms from Gilead," *Washington University Magazine*, Spring 1997. Online at www.slideshare.net/Alumni Link/binder-brown-washington-u-mag-3-pages. Accessed September 20, 2014.

5  Ibid.

6  *Gilead Sciences IPO Prospectus*, January 1992, Online at www.scribd.com/doc/176254938/Gilead-Sciences-Initial-Public-Offering-Prospectus-January-1992, p. 39.

7  Ibid.

8  "Gilead Sciences, Inc. History," *Funding Universe*. Online at www.fundinguniverse.com/company-histories/gilead-sciences-inc-history/. Accessed September 15, 2014.

9  Ibid.

10  Ibid.

11  Murphy, Tom. "Gilead Sciences to Buy Pharmasset for $11 billion," *Associated Press*, November 21, 2011, as cited in http://news.yahoo.com/gilead-sciences-buy-pharmasset-11-billion-122429720.html. Accessed September 23, 2014.

12  Loftus, Mary J. "The Dream Team," *Emory Magazine*, Spring 2005. Online at www.emory.edu/EMORY_MAGAZINE/spring_2005/aids_sidebar.htm. Accessed September 13, 2014.

13  Werth, Barry. *The Billion Dollar Molecule*. New York: Simon & Schuster, 1995, p. 125.

14  Wong, George. *The Aftermath of Penicillin*, Lecture Notes to Botany 135, University of Hawaii. Online at www.botany.hawaii. edu/faculty/wong/BOT135/Lect23.htm. Accessed September 24, 2014.

15  Feyman, Yevgeniy. "Shocking Secrets of FDA Clinical Trials Revealed," *Forbes*, January 24, 2014. Online at www.forbes.com/sites/theapothecary/2014/01/24/shocking-secrets-of-fda-clinical-trials-revealed. Accessed September 17, 2014.

16  "The Research and Development Process," *Pharmaceutical Researchers and Manufacturers of America*. Online at www.phrma.org/research-development-process. Accessed September 9, 2014.

17  "Frequently Asked Questions on Patents and Exclusivity," *Food and Drug Administration*. Online at www.fda.gov/Drugs/DevelopmentApprovalProcess/ucm079031.htm#How%20many%20years%20is%20a%20patent%20granted%20for. Accessed September 7, 2014.

18  Morgan, Steve, et al. "The Cost of Drug Development: A Systematic Review," *Health Policy*, 100, 2011. Online at http://moglen.law.columbia.edu/twiki/pub/LawNetSoc/BahradSokhansanjFirstPaper/100HealthPoly4_cost_of_drug_development_2010.pdf. Accessed September 20, 2014.

19  Keegan, Karl. *Biotechnology Valuation: An Introductory Guide*. Chichester, England: Wiley Finance, 2008, pp. 53–56.

20  Roy, Avik. "How the FDA Stifles New Cures, Part II: 90% of Clinical Trials' Costs are Incurred in Phase III," *Forbes*, April 25, 2012. Online at www.forbes.com/sites/theapothecary/2012/04/25/how-the-fda-stifles-new-cures-part-ii-90-of-clinical-trial-costs-are-incurred-in-phase-iii/. Accessed September 9, 2014.

21  "Phase 3 Clinical Trial Costs Exceed $26,000 Per Patient," *PR Newswire*. Online at www.prnewswire.com/news-releases/phase-3-clinical-trial-costs-exceed-26000-per-patient-56447427.html. Accessed September 19, 2014.

22  "FDA Approves Sovaldi for Chronic Hepatitis C," *Food and Drug Administration* Press Release, December 6, 2013. Online at www.fda.gov/NewsEvents/Newsroom/PressAnnouncements/u cm377888.htm. Accessed September 5, 2014.

23  "Hepatitis C FAQs for the Public," *Centers for Disease Control and Prevention*. Online at www.cdc.gov/hepatitis/c/cfaq.htm. Accessed October 1, 2014.

24  "Hepatitis C," *World Health Organization*, Media centre, updated April, 2014. Online at www.who.int/mediacentre/factsheets/fs164/en/. Accessed October 1, 2014.

25  Ibid.

26  "Transplant Costs," *Transplant Living*. Online at www.transplantliving.org/before-the-transplant/financing-a-transplant/the-costs. Accessed September 24, 2014.

27  "Hepatitis C," *San Francisco Department of Public Health*. Online at www.sfcdcp.org/hepatitisc.html. Accessed October 1, 2014.

28  "Hepatitis C: 25 Years of Discovery," *Centers for Disease Control and Prevention*. Online at www.cdc.gov/knowmorehepatitis/timeline.htm. Accessed September 20, 2014.

29  "A Brief History of Hepatitis C," *Hepatitis C Support Project*, HCV Advocate, January, 2006. Online at http://hcvadvocate.org/hepatitis/factsheets_pdf/Brief_History_HCV_2006.pdf. Accessed September 29, 2014.

30  Prescribing Information, Incivek, Vertex Pharmaceuticals. Online at http://pi.vrtx.com/files/uspi_telaprevir.pdf.

31  Weisman, Robert. "Vertex to Stop Selling Hepatitis C Drug Incivek," August 12, 2014. Online at www.bostonglobe.com/business/2014/08/12/vertex-stop-selling-hepatitis-drug-incivek/El0jtOpH9I1CaIgQpSUKWO/story.html. Accessed September 27, 2014.

32  McQueen, Courtney. "FDA Approves Vertex's New Drug Incivek for Treatment of Hepatitis C," *The AIDS Beacon*, May 23, 2011. Online at www.aidsbeacon.com/news/2011/05/23/fda-approves-vertexs-new-drug-incivek-telaprevir-for-treatment-of-hepatitis-c. Accessed September 20, 2014.

33  "Cancer Prevalence and Cost of Care Projections," *National Cancer Institute*, January, 2011. Online at http://costprojections.cancer.gov/annual.costs.html. Accessed September 30, 2014.

34  Nocera, Joe. "The $300,000 Drug," The Opinion Pages, *The New York Times*, July 18, 2014. Online at www.nytimes.com/2014/07/19/opinion/joe-nocera-cystic-fibrosis-drug-price.html?_r=0. Accessed September 30, 2014.

35  Somashekhar, Sandhya. "Costly Hepatitis Drug Sovaldi Rattles Industry," March 1, 2014. Online at www.washingtonpost.com/national/health-science/costly-hepatitis-drug-sovaldi-rattles-industry/2014/03/01/86cab0b4-a091-11e3-9ba6-800d1192d08b_story.html. Accessed September 30, 2014.

36  Armstrong, Drew. "Hepatitis C Drug Price Limiting State Medicaid Approvals," March 5, 2014. Online at www.bloomberg.com/news/2014-03-05/hepatitis-c-drug-price-limiting-state-medicaid-approvals.html. Accessed September 30, 2014.

37  "California Technology Assessment Forum (CTAF) Issues Final Report and Action Guides on New Treatments for Hepatitis C," *CTAF News Release*, May 20, 2014. Online at https://icer-review.org/announcements/california-technology-assessment-forum-ctaf-issues-final-report-and-action-guides-on-new-treatments-for-hepatitis-c/.

38  "Gilead's HCV Drug Sofosbuvir Approved by the FDA But Accessible for How Many?" *Doctors of the World*, et al. December 9, 2013. Online at http://doctorsoftheworld.org/wp-content/uploads/2013/07/Gileads-HCV-drug-sofosbuvir-approved-but-accessible-for-how-many-09DEC2013.pdf. Accessed September 19, 2014.

39  Waxman, Henry, Frank Pallone Jr and Dianna DeGette to John Martin, March 20, 2014, in Democrats Committee on Energy and Commerce. Online at http://democrats.energycommerce.house.gov/sites/default/files/documents/Martin-Gilead-Sciences-Hepatitis-C-Drug-Sovaldi-Pricing-2014-3-20.pdf.

40  Google Finance, Gilead Sciences Stock Chart. Online at www.google.com/finance?q=NASDAQ%3AGILD&ei=liQsVNC7G4-DrQG-n4GwCw. Accessed September 22, 2014.

41  Flood, Amy, Interview by Chase Lane, e-mail interview, October 2, 2014.

42  Kitamura, Makiko. "Developing Countries Seek Lower Price for Gilead Sovaldi," *Bloomberg*, April 11, 2014. Online at www.bloomberg.com/news/2014-04-10/emerging-markets-pay-1-of-u-s-price-for-gilead-sovaldi.html. Accessed September 28, 2014.

43  Flood, Amy, Interview by Chase Lane.

44  Armstrong, Drew. "Gilead's $84,000 Treatment Questioned by Lawmakers," *Bloomberg*, March 21, 2014. Online at www.bloomberg.com/news/2014-03-21/gilead-s-84-000-treatment-questioned-by-congress.html. Accessed September 19, 2014.

45  "Gilead Sciences Announces 2014 First Quarter Results," *Gilead Sciences*, Press Release, April 22, 2014, on the Gilead Sciences website. Online at http://investors.gilead.com/phoenix.zhtml?c=69964&p=irol-newsArticle&ID=1920785&highlight=. Accessed September 19, 2014.

# CHAPTER 3

# Communication Ethics

Never suffer a thought to be harbored in your mind which you would not avow openly. When tempted to do anything in secret, ask yourself if you would do it in public. If you would not, be sure it is wrong.

Letter from Thomas Jefferson to his grandson Francis Eppes,
age 14, Monticello, May 21, 1816

Pick up *The Wall Street Journal* or *The New York Times* any given morning and look through sections A and C. The news is not especially encouraging:

"AUCTION" BROKERS ARE CHARGED. Authorities Say Ex-Credit Suisse Employees Misled Investors. A federal grand jury in Brooklyn indicted two former Credit Suisse Group Brokers, alleging that they lied to investors about how $1 billion of their money was placed into short-term securities. The 12-page indictment describes how the brokers, Julian Tzolov and Eric Butler, allegedly misled corporate clients around the world, primarily through e-mails. The brokers made it appear as if the securities were backed by federally guaranteed student loans, when in fact they were tied to riskier mortgage products and other debt that earned the brokers higher commissions, according to the indictment.[1]

On other days, it's likely to be a story like this:

Holding up a few drops of blood, Elizabeth Holmes became a darling of Silicon Valley by promising that her company's new device would give everyday Americans unlimited control over their health with a single finger prick.

Ms. Holmes, a Stanford University dropout who founded her company, Theranos, at age 19, captivated investors and the public with her invention: a technology cheaply done at a local drugstore that could detect a range of illnesses, from diabetes to cancer.

With that carefully crafted pitch, Ms. Holmes, whose striking stage presence in a uniform of black turtlenecks drew comparisons to Steve Jobs, became an overnight celebrity, featured on magazine covers and richest-woman lists and in glowing articles.

Her fall – and the near collapse of Theranos – has been equally dramatic in the last few years. On Wednesday, the Securities and Exchange Commission charged Ms. Holmes, now 34, with widespread fraud, accusing her of exaggerating – lying – about her technology while raising $700 million from investors.[2]

While a less-recent list of convictions ranges from investment fund director Bernard Madoff to Enron and World-Com executives to Martha Stewart (good grief!), it's not always chief executives and senior corporate officers who find themselves in ethical and legal trouble. Often, it's a young college graduate, confronted with choices she wasn't required to think about in college.

AN EMPLOYEE ON WALL ST. IS ARRESTED. Said to Profit from Her Position of Trust. Prosecutors said yesterday that they had arrested a brokerage firm employee responsible for protecting market-sensitive information and charged her with using the information to profit from insider trading.

The employee . . ., an analyst in the legal department at Morgan Stanley, Dean Witter, Discover & Company, was arrested on Monday at work and charged on Tuesday with grand larceny, possession of stolen property, scheming to defraud, commercial bribe receiving, and securities fraud, the office of District Attorney Robert M. Morgenthau of Manhattan said. Investigators indicated at a news conference yesterday that they expected to make more arrests. . . .

[She] is said to have sold to other unnamed parties her advance knowledge of a revamping of Georgia Pacific, and – just last week – sold proprietary information about a Morgan Stanley analyst's forthcoming downgrade of Einstein Bagels stock. "Whenever you have a market as heated as this market is, there's a temptation for someone with inside information to trade on it," Mr. Morgenthau said.

[The employee] is a law school graduate who, according to one investigator, earned [a substantial salary] at Morgan Stanley. She lives on Manhattan's Upper East Side.[3]

A day hasn't gone by in the past year without at least one news item dealing with allegations of misstatement, misappropriation, equivocation or fraud. They're often printed alongside stories of people who have lied to their employers, to their customers and clients, to regulatory agencies and to the courts. In other instances, they have simply deceived themselves.

What's going on here? Does this behavior represent a sudden outbreak of unethical conduct or confusion over appropriate uses of proprietary information in North American businesses? Or are investigation and prosecution techniques improving? While the latter may be true in part, it's hard to believe that managers have only recently begun to display illegal or unethical tendencies. Many experts on this subject report that a surprising percentage of businesspeople seem to believe they can handle information in any way they see fit and can communicate (or fail to do so) with shareholders, clients, customers, competitors, regulatory agencies, legislative bodies and other branches of government without regard to truth, fairness, equity, justice and ethics.

The latest round of accounting scandals, executive misconduct and deception on the part of corporate financial officers only serves to underscore the need for values and integrity throughout the corporate world. According to *BusinessWeek*'s John A. Byrne:

In the post-Enron bubble world, there's a yearning for corporate values that reach higher than the size of the chief executive's paycheck or even the latest stock price. Trust, integrity, and fairness do matter, and they are crucial to the bottom line.[4]

In recent years, too many companies allowed performance to be disconnected from meaningful corporate values. "A lot of companies simply looked at performance in assessing their leaders," says Larry Johnson, CEO of Albertson's, Inc., the food retailer. "There have to be two dimensions to leadership: performance and values. You can't have one without the other."[5]

And, according to Landon Thomas of *The New York Times*, "with regulatory scrutiny heightened after the collapse of Enron and other companies, corporations and their boards are adopting zero tolerance policies. Increasingly, they are holding their employees to lofty standards of business and personal behavior." The result, he writes, "is a wave of abrupt firings as corporations move to stop perceived breaches of ethics by their employees that could result in law enforcement action or public relations disasters."[6]

## THE ETHICAL CONDUCT OF EMPLOYERS

Recent research from Eagle Hill Consulting discovered that employees care about the ethical conduct of their employers. What should be of serious concern is that employees are questioning the ethics of many of their managers today. With surveys and interviews of 1,506 members of the adult working population, Eagle Hill has found that 54 percent believe that corporate integrity is worsening. What was the most worrisome finding? More than half of the adult working population have the highest trust in their colleagues, much higher than their trust in executive leadership (11 percent) or their boss (35 percent).[7]

Other findings may be cause for concern, as well. Only a third of employees feel comfortable reporting misconduct, in part because fewer than half feel that ethical or compliance problems are dealt with fairly and completely. Case in point: 30 percent of employees know of or suspect ethical violations in their organizations in the past two years.

However, the majority of these employees – six in ten – who have seen or know about a violation have not reported it. Why not? Three primary reasons were given for not reporting actual observed misconduct.

- Employees did not feel the organization would respond.
- There was a perceived lack of anonymous and confidential means of reporting.
- Fear of retaliation from management prevented workers from reporting the misconduct they had witnessed.[8]

*Fast Company* magazine reported that 76 percent of workers in a national survey had observed violations of the law or company standards during the preceding 12 months. Nearly two-thirds of those surveyed thought their company would not discipline workers guilty of an ethical infraction, and more than half said that "management does not know what type of behavior goes on in its company." Worse, nearly 40 percent said that "management would authorize illegal or unethical conduct to meet business goals."[9]

Do any of these findings – these attitudes about ethical behavior – have any effect on you? Virtually all business leaders say they do. Business – even in a free marketplace – is governed by rules. Those rules range from complex tax laws and restrictions on exports to broad, general notions of truth in advertising and reliance on a person's word. If competitors either break the rules or behave as though no rules exist, the free marketplace is jeopardized, expectations are destroyed and trust is undermined.

If you behave in unethical ways, people will quickly realize that you cannot be trusted. Your performance will be seen as unreliable and self-centered. Aside from running afoul of the law, unethical behavior will eventually isolate you from the community of business practitioners who play by the rules and for whom trust is an important part of doing business.

## DEFINING BUSINESS ETHICS

Raymond Baumhart, a former college president and ethicist, once asked a number of business managers what the word *ethical* meant to them. Half of the managers in his interviews defined *ethical* as "what my feelings tell me is right." Yet feelings are often an inadequate basis on which to make decisions. Twenty-five percent of his respondents defined *ethical* in terms of what is "in accord with my religious beliefs" and 18 percent defined the term as what "conforms to the golden rule." Religious authority has been devastatingly criticized, along with the "golden rule," as an inadequate foundation for ethical claims.[10]

For one thing, religion often requires an act of faith to accept guidelines, norms, dogma or precepts. And the golden rule ("Do unto others, as you would have others do unto you") assumes that we each would wish for the same form of treatment. Our interests and preferences, in fact, may be substantially different. A supervisor's inquiry on behalf of an employee may be seen as a thoughtful, caring gesture by some and as intrusive snooping or prying by others. If such guides are helpful, but hardly definitive, how should we make ethical judgments? What does *ethical* mean to a business communicator?

Ethics most often refers to a field of inquiry, or discipline, in which matters of right and wrong, good and evil, virtue and vice, are systematically examined. Morality, by contrast, is most often used to refer not to a discipline but to patterns of behavior that are actually common in everyday life. In this sense, morality is what the discipline of ethics is about. And so business morality is what business ethics is about.[11]

The phrases "corporate social responsibility" and "corporate citizenship" are sometimes used as though they were synonymous with business ethics. Oil companies frequently advertise about how careful they are with the environment, and chemical companies proclaim their "good citizen" role of providing jobs, opportunity and the chance to "do good things." However, these statements can be misleading if they imply that business ethics deals exclusively with the relationships between business organizations and what have come to be called their external constituencies, such as consumers, suppliers, government agencies, community groups and host countries. Even though these relationships define a large and important part of business ethics, they do not encompass the entire field. Important internal constituencies, such as employees, stockholders, boards of directors, and managers, are also involved, as well as ethical issues that do not lend themselves to constituency or stakeholder analysis. Thus, business ethics is a much larger notion than corporate social responsibility, even though it includes that concept.[12]

## THREE LEVELS OF INQUIRY

The three most common concerns in the moral responsibilities, obligations and virtues of business decision making have been the choices and characters of persons, the policies and cultures of organizations, and the arrangements and beliefs of entire social and economic systems, such as capitalism. Business ethics, then, is multi-leveled.

### The Individual

For the individual businessperson, business ethics concerns the values by which self-interest and other motives are balanced with concern for fairness and the common good, both inside and outside of a company. The project leader who unfairly claims credit for a proposal that many of his subordinates worked on is clearly putting his own self-interest ahead of that of the organization and his fellow employees. It may not be illegal, but it's certainly unfair.

### The Organization

At the level of the organization, business ethics concerns the group conscience that every company has (even though it may be unspoken) as it pursues its economic objectives. This conscience is a reflection of both organizational culture and conduct. A real estate development firm that buys an entire city block filled with low-income housing may see only the benefits to be derived from demolishing the apartments and constructing offices, shops and a parking garage. The people occupying the low-income apartments to be demolished may have great difficulty finding another place to live that they can afford. A failure to see them as an important part of the purchase and development plans, again, would not likely be against the law, but it would certainly be unjust.

### The Business System

Finally, at the level of the entire business system, ethics concerns the pattern of social, political and economic forces that drives individuals and businesses – the values that define capitalism, for example. But even capitalism works within a system of ethical rules. For the government of one nation to decide that it will not enforce copyright laws or extend patent protection to products or intellectual property produced overseas is to invite chaos within the free market system.[13]

## THREE VIEWS OF DECISION MAKING

For business communicators and others who make business decisions, three points of view are available to assist in making those decisions. They include a moral point of view, an economic point of view and a legal point of view.

### Moral Point of View

From this perspective, businesspeople ask, "Morally, what is the best thing to do?" Such questions would be separate from inquiries about economic decisions that seek to maximize shareholder wealth or legal decisions that ask what the law requires, permits and forbids.

According to many business ethicists, a moral point of view has two important features. The first is a willingness to seek out and act on reasons. Second, a moral point of view requires the decision maker to be impartial: Decision makers must demonstrate a commitment to use reason in deliberating about what to do, constructing moral arguments that are persuasive to themselves and to others. They will also give all interests equal weight in deciding what to do. The problem with this point of view is that most ethical business issues aren't especially clear and, in many instances, decision makers don't have adequate information at the time they need it most.[14]

### Economic Point of View

An economic point of view, by contrast, employs a free market model of capitalism in which scarce resources or factors of production are used to produce goods and services. The forces of supply and demand are used to allocate resources, and the structure of the marketplace determines what is in the best interests of the organization. Economic theory, however, is not entirely value-neutral. Certain assumptions about a free market underlie all business activities including basic notions about honesty, theft, fraud and the like.

In addition, it is important for business communicators to understand that companies are not merely abstract economic entities but large-scale organizations that involve flesh-and-blood human beings. Those same firms, further, must operate in a complex environment with many constituencies to please, some of which are often in conflict with others.[15]

### Legal Point of View

A third point of view for ethical decision making in business is the legal viewpoint. Most business activity takes place within an extensive system of laws, so that all business decisions – especially those involving communication – must be made from a legal as well as an economic standpoint. Many businesspeople assume that "if it's legal, then it's morally okay." This attitude ignores a number of realities involving the law and decision making.

First, the law is inappropriate for regulating certain aspects of business activity. Not everything that is immoral is, in fact, illegal. Hiring a relative for a position that other, better qualified, applicants have applied for will certainly raise conflict-of-interest questions, but it may not be illegal. Second, the law is often slow to develop in new areas of concern. Technology, for example, not only presents new opportunities for unethical behavior but often outpaces legal restrictions.

The law often employs moral concepts that are not precisely defined, so it is often difficult to use the law to make decisions without also considering issues of morality. In addition, the law itself is often unsettled or in a state of evolution on many issues. Frequently, the notion of whether an action was legal or illegal must be decided case-by-case in the courts, with key issues often being decided higher within the appellate court system. The law cannot provide specific guidance for behavior in all possible instances. For example, the issue of whether a conversation among a few friends constitutes protected speech or is sexual harassment is one that courts must decide on the merits of the specific incident. Finally, the law is generally seen as an inefficient instrument, inviting expensive legislation and litigation where more efficient systems of decision making might do just as well in producing workable answers.[16]

## AN INTEGRATED APPROACH

Many business ethicists advocate a decision-making process that integrates these three viewpoints, considering the demands of morality, economics and the law together. Decisions, they say, can be made on the basis of morality, profit and legality together, to arrive at workable solutions that will take into account the best interests of all concerned, protect the investment of shareholders and obey the law.

A company that elects voluntarily to remove a tainted or defective product from supermarket shelves considers the safety and welfare of its customers while, at the same time, avoiding lawsuits and protecting the company's good name and market share. Such decisions, though costly in the short run, almost always prove to be beneficial in the long run.

What about those cases in which neither the issue at hand nor the outcome of the decision is entirely clear? Some ethicists focus on the value of dialogue in arriving at an ethical answer. Michael G. Bowen and F. Clark Power write, "In this regard, our definition of the moral manager is a person willing to engage in a fair and open dialogue with interested stakeholders or their representatives."[17]

Making choices based on the input and ideas of those who are most affected by the outcome of your decisions can help to produce better decisions. Becoming an ethical business communicator may involve more than a simple willingness to talk about the issues with stakeholders, though. It might also include some knowledge of moral judgments and how they are made.

## THE NATURE OF MORAL JUDGMENTS

Two basic types of judgments are normative judgments and moral judgments. Normative judgments are claims that state or imply that something is good or bad, right or wrong, better or worse, ought to be or ought not to be. Normative judgments, then, express our values. They indicate our attitudes toward some object, person, circumstance or event. Non-normative judgments, on the other hand, are value-neutral. They describe, name, define, report or make predictions.[18]

If I were to say, "These figures are mistaken," that would be normative. To say, "These figures do not match the auditor's," would be non-normative. Normative judgments are prescriptive, while non-normative judgments are descriptive. Moral judgments, then, are a special subset or category of normative judgments.

Ethics does not study all normative judgments, only those that are concerned with what is morally right and wrong or morally good and bad. When decisions are judged to be morally right or wrong, or morally good or bad, the underlying standards on which the judgment is based are moral standards. It would be immoral by such standards to short-weight a shipment of goods, for example, or to identify the contents of a package as containing "all natural ingredients," when, in fact, it does not.

Businesspeople use two types of moral standards to make decisions. Moral norms, on the one hand, are standards of behavior that require, prohibit or allow certain kinds of behavior. Moral principles, on the other hand, are much more general concepts used to evaluate both group and individual behavior. A norm, for example, might permit rounding of figures to the nearest hundred or thousand in standard accounting procedure, while principles might deal with the general notion of full disclosure to interested stakeholders.

Alfred P. West, Jr., for example, believes that transparency is a moral principle fundamental to building trust among those involved in a business. West is founder and CEO of financial-services firm SEI Investments Company, which operates back-office services for mutual funds and bank trust departments. His goal of building an open culture of integrity, ownership and accountability is a harbinger for what he believes organizations will look like in the future. "We tell our employees a lot about where the company is going," he says. "We over-communicate the vision and the strategy and continually reinforce the culture."[19]

## DISTINGUISHING CHARACTERISTICS OF MORAL PRINCIPLES

Moral standards, in many respects, are like other standards. They provide direction, guidance and counsel. They are guideposts or compass headings when decisions have to be made. They are different from other standards in several important respects, though.

### *They Have Potentially Serious Consequences to Human Well-Being*

Moral standards require distinguishing between things that matter and things that don't. Omitting small details about packaging or manufacturing from a product insert may be an important legal matter but is probably not a moral issue. Failing to reveal potential hazards of product use is certainly a moral issue.

### Their Validity Rests on the Adequacy of the Reasons That Are Used to Support and Justify Them

If the reasons you employ to support your decisions are not accepted by the society at large, or at least by a thoughtful group of people who have given the matter careful consideration, then you may wish to reassess just how adequate your standards are.

### They Override Self-Interest

Genuine moral standards transcend the interests of just one or a few people. They involve doing things for the greater good of society or people at large. Rather than asking, "How will this affect me?" you might wish to ask, "How will this decision affect the entire firm or the whole community?"

### They Are Based on Impartial Considerations

Moral standards are devised from a universal standpoint and are clearly more objective than subjective. They don't bring harm or disruption to many simply to benefit a few.[20]

## FOUR RESOURCES FOR DECISION MAKING

Four simple but powerful resources are available to every business communicator who is trying to make ethical decisions. They are observations, assumptions, value judgments and proposals. Let's examine each of them independently.

### Observations

These descriptive statements tell about the situations. "Not all of the information about pending litigation against the company is revealed in the annual report to shareholders." Such statements rely on a correct presentation of the facts and can usually be verified through more research. The usefulness of observations can also be evaluated by the degree of objectivity they contain. The more objective the statement, the more likely it is to be an observation. A statement qualifies as an observation if contrary evidence can disprove it. If I observe, for example, that "an increasing number of product liability suits is jeopardizing our industry," I could verify or refute that statement with specific evidence.

Observations sometimes look like assumptions because they both appear to describe. An important difference is that observations are usually specific and empirical in nature. "Our product package insert does not reveal all of the potential hazards associated with this product's use." This statement is an example of an observation; a related assumption might be that revealing all potential hazards would be useful or instructive to our customers. An opposing assumption might be that revealing all potential hazards would only serve to frighten our customers because many of the hazards are extremely rare.

### Assumptions

These *reflective statements* express world views and attitudes. "Our employees are honest." Statements such as this one rely on culture, religion, social and personal history. They are usually taken for granted in day-to-day conversation and business correspondence, but they have theoretical roots in our attitudinal system. They can be evaluated by such criteria as relevance, consistency and inclusiveness.

Table 3.1 summarizes the key differences among these resources. Proposals and value judgments, for example, are action oriented, telling the listener or reader what to do. Observations and assumptions, on the other hand, merely serve to describe. Proposals and observations tend to be specific in nature, focused on the action or situation at hand. Value judgments and assumptions, though, are more general in nature and provide broad guidance to a decision maker.

**TABLE 3.1** Four Resources for Decision Making

|  | Action-Orientation | Descriptive-Orientation |
|---|---|---|
| Specific | Proposals | Observations |
| General | Value Judgments | Assumptions |

*Source:* Adapted from Marvin T. Brown. *The Ethical Process: A Strategy for Making Good Decisions.* Upper Saddle River, NJ: Prentice Hall, Inc., 1996, p. 7.

### Value Judgments

These normative statements guide the actions of others. "Information that significantly affects a worker's schedule or position should be delivered in person by the supervisor." Such statements rely on assumptions and make the connection between a proposal and an observation. These statements, however, cannot be verified by empirical research. They can be evaluated by different ethical traditions.

Value judgments can also be asserted as *should statements*. Unlike proposals, which are usually specific, value judgments are general statements. "We should be fair in our dealings with customers." This statement does not indicate what we should do specifically in each instance with a customer. It is, rather, a general guideline for action.

### Proposals

These prescriptive statements suggest actions. "We should develop a child care center for our company," would be an example of a proposal. It is a statement that relies on observations, value judgments and assumptions but goes further. It suggests actions that people should take and that can be evaluated by examining supporting reasons. Proposals often reveal what people have been paying attention to (observations) and can frequently serve as a clue to their values and assumptions.

Proposals are often answers to questions. Good questions can generate good proposals. "Should we revise our performance review system?" The best questions are specific and action oriented, while the best proposals are specific responses to such questions. For example: "We should revise our performance review system to include semiannual peer feedback." The only missing element of this proposal is the underlying reasoning or the values that prompted it.[21]

## MAKING MORAL JUDGMENTS

Moral judgments seem to depend on decision makers having and using four separate capacities: ethical sensibility, ethical reasoning, ethical conduct and ethical leadership.[22]

### Ethical Sensibility

An ethical sensibility is reflected in your capacity to impose ethical order on a situation – to identify aspects of the situation that have ethical importance. A person who is insensitive to the ethically important features of a situation is vulnerable to acting in ways that are improper.

Suppose you are working as an IT software consultant, and a local charitable group asks you to serve as a member of its volunteer advisory board. Sounds noble and worthwhile, right? Well, suppose further that the charitable group decides to accept bids on an information technology system that will assist in fund-raising. You're in a position to provide expert advice. Now what happens if your employer decides to bid on that IT system? Can you remain a member of that advisory board? Not if you recognize the conflict of interest that faces you. Your interests as a commercial software consultant conflict with your interests as an advisor to the charitable group. Ethical sensibility would make you aware of that conflict.

## *Ethical Reasoning*

Recognizing the ethically important features of a situation is the first step toward dealing with them appropriately. The next step is to reason carefully about the situation to determine what kind of ethical problem you face: Is it bribery, an unfair labor practice or consumer deception? Ethical reasoning then offers opportunities for solution: What would be fairest for all concerned? Is this problem similar to one we've seen in the past? Is a rule or policy applicable in determining our conduct in this case? If not, should we consider writing one? What's the basis for the argument I'm faced with?

Sometimes simple recognition of an ethical problem will point toward a solution. Let's say your job is to review advertising copy for your company's products. As you do so, you recognize a series of misleading claims in the proposed ad copy. Your solution is easy enough: Return the copy to the writing team with specific instructions to remove or correct the misleading claims. More often, however, the solution to an ethical problem involves conflicting values.

Let's say you are a manager who discovers that the production line presents potential hazards to the reproductive health of female workers. You also recognize that removing women from the line would be unfair. Two competing values in this instance – equal employment opportunity and keeping workers from harm – require some careful ethical reasoning in order to make an appropriate moral judgment.

## *Ethical Conduct*

Recognizing ethical dilemmas and reasoning your way to an appropriate solution are simply the first two steps in living an ethical life in business. It's one thing to know what you should do and quite another to do it. Lynn Sharp Paine of the Harvard Business School says, "Hypocrisy and cowardice, both reflected in discrepancies between professed beliefs and actual conduct, are the enemies of integrity."[23]

Recognizing that it would be wrong to file an inflated travel voucher following a business trip, you remind your colleagues that the company will gladly reimburse all necessary expenses but only for the amounts actually spent. Although you encourage and expect others to comply with that reasoning, you claim expenses in excess of what you actually spent and ask for reimbursement for expenditures that were not legitimate business expenses. In such a case, hypocrisy would best describe your behavior.

If you were witness to a fellow employee stealing supplies from your company but failed to speak with either him or your supervisor, you might well be guilty of cowardice. You recognized the problem and knew what the appropriate response would be but failed to act. Such situations require a certain amount of moral courage – the ability to stand up and do what is right, even though it won't be easy, profitable or popular.

## *Ethical Leadership*

The capacity for ethical leadership, according to Professor Paine, "is associated with the highest levels of integrity." She quotes Confucius, saying "The superior person seeks to perfect the admirable qualities of others and does not seek to perfect their bad qualities. The lesser person does the opposite of this." She goes on to note that most business students will work in organizations in which they will have the power and responsibility not only to exercise their own ethical capacities but to influence the exercise of those capacities in others.[24]

Numerous researchers and commentators attribute critical importance to the ethical example provided by an organization's top officials. It seems unlikely that great integrity would emerge in an organization led by men and women lacking in basic integrity. Yet, without question, leadership is not confined to the chairman or chief executive officer of an organization. It extends directly to every organization's executives and senior managers.

Executive-search firm Russell Reynolds, along with personality-testing firm Hogan Assessment Systems, conducted psychological profiles of more than 1,400 managers in large U.S. companies. Each manager was given 28 true-or-false questions on rule compliance and interactions with others to gauge their level of integrity. The somewhat troubling result: One out of every eight responded in ways that may be seen as "high risk." According to Dean Stamoulis, an executive director at Russell Reynolds, the findings indicate that those managers are far more likely to break the rules than the others. "These are folks who believe the rules do not apply to them," he says.[25]

Ethical leadership also extends from those managers to their frontline supervisors. Day-to-day, these supervisors are responsible for setting examples and assisting those who work for them. Others in an organization will watch what you do, and if you're in a position of leadership or responsibility, an ethical obligation accompanies your management duties. If you let your employees know, directly or indirectly, that you condone industrial spying or the theft of competitive marketing data, they will assume that the company approves of this and that such acts are probably all right. The plain fact is, the moral education of those beneath you in an organization depends on your willingness to engage in and reward ethical behavior.[26]

## APPLYING ETHICAL STANDARDS TO MANAGEMENT COMMUNICATION

Ethical business practice is a noble goal to which virtually all firms aspire. Many companies, however, fail to achieve this lofty ideal for a number of reasons. Increased levels of global competition, financial pressures, lack of communication throughout organizations and the absence of moral leadership at the top levels are but a few of the most prevalent reasons.[27]

## STATEMENTS OF ETHICAL PRINCIPLES

Perhaps the most important means of establishing moral leadership in a business organization – and demonstrating that leadership to employees, customers, clients, competitors and the world at large – is through a formal statement of ethical principles. Developing and publishing a corporate statement of ethics certainly will not, by itself, make a company ethical, but it is certainly a good first step. To the question of why a company should have such a statement, Professor Patrick E. Murphy of Notre Dame offers this response:

First, and most important, ethics statements denote the seriousness with which the organization takes its ethical commitments. Words are empty without some documentation. The written statement then serves as a foundation from which ethical behavior can be built. Corporate culture is often viewed as being more important than policies in setting the ethical climate for any organization. However, written ethical principles send a strong signal that ethics matters to the firm.[28]

Once an organization's size, according to Murphy, goes beyond a handful of employees who interact regularly face-to-face, it becomes difficult to convey a sense of an organization's principles and values. An ethics statement makes expectations more concrete. Furthermore, developing such a document forces those engaged in the process, whether they be the founder or current management, to articulate their beliefs in a cohesive fashion and then set them down in writing for possible challenge by others.[29]

### Types of Ethical Statements

Although ethics statements can be classified into several types, three appear to predominate. They include values statements, corporate credos (or sets of basic beliefs) and corporate codes of ethics.

The most prevalent form in which ethical principles are stated in U.S.-based corporations is a code of ethics. More than 90 percent of large organizations have one. At least half of those same companies also have a values statement. A corporate credo appears to exist in about one-third of all large U.S.-based firms. Interestingly, while fewer firms seem to have a corporate credo, *many that do have such documents have had them in place for a long time.*[30]

A recent Conference Board survey of 124 companies in 22 countries found that more than three-quarters of all boards of directors are now setting ethical standards in those companies, up from just 41 percent a few years earlier. Executives at those companies see self-regulation as a way to avoid legislative or judicial intrusions in their business operations. The study also found that ethics codes help promote tolerance of diverse practices and customers while doing business overseas.[31]

Jacques Polet, in reviewing corporate ethical statements in both the U.S. and Europe, found that the most recurring principles are clarity, transparency, honesty, truth or objectivity (negative and unpleasant information must be communicated, as well as positive information), credibility, coherence, loyalty, and respect for human beings.[32]

In examining corporate ethical statements, the importance of communication, as well as many other behaviors, receives considerable attention. "In the same spirit," writes Polet, "communication must serve the company (its shareholders, staff, and customers) without prejudicing third parties or hurting respectable feelings. Basically, it should reflect the company project, expressing its goals, its strategy, and the corporate culture. . . . "[33] Thus, effective management communication is not only a means to an end (a way to convey the principles) but an end in itself (ethical communication is a fundamental principle guiding management behavior).

### Tension and Ethical Values

Many values, along with the roles and objectives that managers must follow, are in competition with one another, and a certain tension inevitably pulls first in one direction and then another. The value of transparency, or of not hiding from public view what the company really does and how it does it, may be in competition with the value of confidentiality. Employees expect a certain measure of privacy in the workplace, yet the demand for disclosure is ever-present. Managers must respond to these conflicts and to the tension that arises from them with caution, sensitivity and a sense of fairness to everyone concerned.[34]

Every communication activity, from annual reports to general shareholder meetings, becomes a balancing act for executives and managers. To be honest with our employees and our shareholders, what and how much must we disclose? To preserve our competitive edge, what and how much shall we hold back? Ethical philosopher Gilles Lipovetsky, in *The Dawn of Duty*, captures the dialectical debate in this way: "It is obvious: an ethics of company communication does not present itself in terms of a choice between Good and Evil (a question of Morality). In real life, there is a balance between 'various more or less contradictory imperatives.'"[35]

### The Value of Corporate Values

A new emphasis on values at the corporate level has made it fashionable for many companies to make their values explicit. That's a change – quite a significant change – from corporate practices just a few years ago. At Xerox, former CEO Anne Mulcahy says that corporate values "helped save Xerox during the worst crisis in our history" and that "living our values" has been one of Xerox's five performance objectives for the past several years. These values are "far from words on a piece of paper," she says. "They are accompanied by specific objectives and hard measures."[36]

According to market and social trend analyst Daniel Yankelovich, the public's widespread cynicism toward businesses today is the third wave of public mistrust about corporations in the past 80 years. The first, set off by the Great Depression, continued until World War II; the second, caused in part by economic stagflation and the Vietnam War, lasted from the early 1960s until the early 1980s. In each of these periods, companies tended to be reactive, blaming "a few bad apples," dismissing values as "not central to what we do," or ignoring opportunities to improve.[37]

The current wave of disapproval began in 2001 with the bursting of the dot-com bubble, the ensuing bear market and financial scandals involving Madoff Investment Securities, Enron Corporation, WorldCom, Tyco and others. This time, according to a recent survey, the response appears to be different. More and more companies are looking inward to see what has gone wrong and looking outward for answers. They are questioning the quality of their management systems and their ability to inculcate and reinforce values that benefit the firm, their stakeholders and the wider world. And they are showing little patience with executives who place their businesses at risk by crossing the line from prudent to unethical behavior.

In their survey of 365 companies in 30 nations and five regions around the world, consulting firm Booz Allen Hamilton and the Aspen Institute found that ethical behavior is a core component of company activities. Of the 89 percent of companies that have a written corporate values statement, 90 percent specify ethical conduct as a principle. Further, some 81 percent believe their management practices encourage ethical behavior among staff employees. The study found that ethics-related language in formal statements not only sets corporate expectations for employee behavior but it also serves as a shield in an increasingly complex legal and regulatory environment.[38]

### How Ethical Statements Can Help

While the presence of an ethical statement will not automatically ensure ethical behavior on the part of corporate employees, such documents certainly can raise ethical awareness, create an atmosphere in which ethical behavior is expected and rewarded, and promote a company-wide dialogue about the value of ethical behavior.

In 1982, seven people died in the U.S. after taking Tylenol capsules that had been poisoned with cyanide. Investigators eventually determined that some unknown person had tampered with the capsules after they had been placed on store shelves for sale. Even before Johnson & Johnson, which manufactures the product, had obtained all the information on the cause of the tragedy, and even before legal liability had been evaluated, the company assumed moral liability for it, immediately recalling 31 million bottles of Tylenol with a market value of $100 million. The company set up a toll-free help line to answer questions from the general public.[39] Johnson & Johnson chairman and CEO James Burke opened up the company's meetings to the news media and offered a reward of $100,000 to anyone able to supply information leading to the arrest of the culprit. According to Lipovetsky, "There is no doubt as to the ethical orientation of the operation. It was nonetheless a triumph of communication which managed to dramatize the firm's responsible action."[40]

The Tylenol crisis highlights the importance of personal ethical commitment of top management in a special way. In these periods of extreme tension, while managers may wish to do the right thing, it's not always immediately clear what the right thing to do is. Johnson & Johnson employees had worked with their credo, a broadly phrased statement of company ethics, since 1947. In the words of one Johnson & Johnson official during the crisis, "What we are doing here is not specifically mentioned in the Credo, but it is definitely generated by the Credo."[41]

Johnson & Johnson's Jim Burke had no hesitation in assuming direct responsibility for and control over the true spirit of the credo. As Laura Nash reports, "Jim Burke has often stated that the guidance of the Credo played the most important role in management's decision making during the crisis."[42] If anyone doubted that Burke and his president, David Collins, did the right thing, the proof is that 11 weeks after the start of the crisis, the Tylenol brand had recovered 80 percent of its initial market share and within two years had recovered all of it.[43]

## How to Make Ethical Statements Work

Professor Murphy offers a series of seven imperatives to follow when writing and living out the principles of a corporate ethics statement, code or credo:

- **Write it.** Writing down the guiding philosophy or values of the firm makes it possible for management to communicate those ideas to all stakeholders, especially to the employees. A written document also signals to everyone concerned that the company is serious about its ethical views.
- **Tailor it.** Tailoring a statement of ethics to an organization's industry or line of business offers managers an opportunity to place special emphasis on those issues most likely to arise in the course of ordinary business and to address those matters that it regards as especially important.
- **Communicate it.** This step may be most important in ensuring that all stakeholders, external as well as internal, are aware of and understand the behavior that the company expects of them. Many authors note that this process must be ongoing for every company.
- **Promote it.** It is not enough to simply communicate the ethics document. It should be actively promoted at every opportunity through as many publications, events and channels as possible.
- **Revise it.** Revising the document every few years will help to keep it current, reflecting changing worldwide conditions, community standards and evolving organizational practices.
- **Live it.** The litmus test for any type of ethics document, according to Murphy and others, is whether members of the organization follow it on a daily basis. Top management must make a concerted effort to reward employees who follow the principles listed in the statement.
- **Enforce/Reinforce it.** For those who refuse to live by the principles, management must exact punishment. Sanctions and penalties must be enforced in a fair and evenhanded manner so that all stakeholders understand how they will be treated and exactly what will be the consequences of their behavior.[44]

For an ethics code to work, top management must convince employees that the company is not simply using the code to sidestep recent events and – even more important – they must act on what they say they value. Linda Klebe Trevino, a professor of organizational behavior at Pennsylvania State University, said that outlining appropriate or inappropriate behavior in a code with the intention of avoiding future problems "can be a healthy response. But if you create a code, especially in response to some problem, and it's inconsistent with the culture as employees perceive it, then it appears to be only window dressing and hypocritical," she added.[45]

"When management disciplines somebody, they're sending a very powerful signal," says Professor Trevino:

Most people are going about their business trying to do the right thing. When they see somebody engage in highly inappropriate behavior that everybody agrees is inappropriate and management doesn't do much about it, it devalues the norm and, in a sense their own status.[46]

## THE "FRONT PAGE" TEST

In judging whether its policies or its actions are fundamentally sound, managers might simply apply what's come to be known as the "front page" test. Would you be pleased if the policies in your organization or the behavior of your employees were to appear in a story on the front page of *The Wall Street Journal* or, perhaps, your hometown newspaper? If not, then you might ask yourself, "Why not?" What are we doing wrong that I wouldn't want others to know about?

Do the methods and means of communication in your organization hold up to that test? Does your company deal honestly with its customers and clients, treating each of them fairly and with respect? Do you honestly and accurately disclose to regulatory agencies and governmental organizations all that they are entitled to know? Are your relations with the press and news media based on openness, honesty and candor? If not, what can you do to improve them?

Are the rituals, ceremonies and formal activities of your organization planned and conducted with a sense of inclusion, honesty and equality? Do people in your organization know how they will be evaluated, by whom and against which set of standards in their hopes for promotion or advancement?

Day in and day out, do you and others in your company speak, write, listen and act with a sense that others will appreciate and respect? Do you treat people not simply as they might treat you, but in a way they prefer to be treated? In many ways, ethics and communication are not simply inseparable but are essential to the success of any business and at the heart of how human beings interact with one another. Striving for ethical perfection, both as you communicate and as you manage your business, is probably pointless. Striving each day to observe the best of ethical principles, to demonstrate a level of conduct that others can aspire to, and to lead by example, however, is not only possible but also unquestionably worthwhile.

## FOR FURTHER READING

Allen, L. and D. Voss. *Ethics in Technical Communication: Shades of Gray.* New York: John Wiley & Sons, 1997.

Donaldson, T. and P. Werhane. *Ethical Issues in Business: A Philosophical Approach*, 8/e. Upper Saddle River, NJ: Prentice Hall, 2007.

Ferrell, O. C. and J. Fraedrich. *Business Ethics: Ethical Decision Making and Cases*, 7/e. Mason, OH: South-Western College Publishing, 2010.

Fritzsche, D. J. *Business Ethics: A Global and Managerial Perspective*, 2/e. New York: McGraw-Hill, 2004.

Gardner, H. "The Ethical Mind," *Harvard Business Review* (March 2007): 51–56.

Hartman, L. P. *Perspectives in Business Ethics.* New York: McGraw-Hill, 2001.

Lancaster, H. "You Have Your Values: How Do You Identify Your Employer's?" *The Wall Street Journal*, April 8, 1997, p. B1.

McCarthy, M. J. "Virtual Morality: A New Workplace Quandary," *The Wall Street Journal*, October 21, 1999, pp. B1, B4.

Murphy, P. E. "Creating Ethical Corporate Structures," *Sloan Management Review* (Winter 1989): 81–87.

Paine, L. S. "Managing for Organizational Integrity," *Harvard Business Review* (March–April 1994): 106–117.

Seglin, J. L. "In Ethics, It's the Thought That Counts," *The New York Times*, December 19, 1999, p. BU-4.

Thomas, L. "On Wall Street, a Rise in Dismissals Over Ethics," *The New York Times*, March 29, 2005, pp. A1, C4.

Trevino, L. K. and K. A. Nelson. *Managing Business Ethics: Straight Talk About How to Do It Right*, 4/e. New York: John Wiley & Sons, 2006.

Van Lee, R., L. Fabish and N. McGaw. "The Value of Corporate Values," *Strategy + Business* 39 (Summer 2005): 52–65.

Velasquez, M. G. *Business Ethics: Concepts and Cases*, 7/e. Upper Saddle River, NJ: Prentice Hall, 2011.

Weiss, J. *Business Ethics: A Stakeholder and Issues Management Approach*, 5/e. Cincinnati, OH: South-Western College Publishing, 2008.

**NOTES**

1   Efrait, A. and R. Smith. "Auction Brokers Are Charged," *The Wall Street Journal*, September 4, 2008, p. C1. Copyright © 2008 by Dow Jones & Company, Inc. All rights reserved worldwide. Reprinted with permission.

2   Thomas, K. and R. Abelson. "Elizabeth Holmes, Theranos C.E.O. and Silicon Valley Star, Accused of Fraud," *The New York Times*, March 14, 2018, p. A1.

3   Truell, P. "An Employee on Wall St. Is Arrested," *The New York Times*, November 7, 1997, p. C8. Copyright © 1997 by The New York Times Company. Reprinted with permission.

4   Byrne, J. A. "After Enron: The Ideal Corporation," *BusinessWeek*, August 26, 2002, p. 68.

5   Ibid., p. 70.

6   Thomas, L. "On Wall Street, a Rise in Dismissals Over Ethics," *The New York Times*, March 29, 2005, pp. A1, C4.

7   "More Than Half of Americans Say Corporate Integrity Deteriorating According to New Research from Eagle Hill Consulting," *Street Insider*, May 22, 2018. Online at www.streetinsider.com/Press+Releases/More+Than+Half+Of+Americans +Say+Corporate+Integrity+Deteriorating+According+To+New+Research+From+Eagle+Hill+Consulting/ 142244 98.html. Accessed July 13, 2018.

8   *The 2018 Global Business Ethics Survey*. Vienna, VA, The Ethics and Compliance Initiative. June 2018. Online at www.ethics. org/research/gbes. Accessed Tuesday, July 17, 2018.

9   "Conduct Unbecoming," *Fast Company*, September 2000, p. 96.

10  Baumhart, R. *An Honest Profit: What Businessmen Say About Ethics in Business*. New York: Holt, Rinehart, Winston, 1968, pp. 11–12.

11  Goodpaster, K. E. "Business Ethics," in L. C. Becker (ed.), *Encyclopedia of Ethics*. New York: Garland Publishing, Inc., 1992, p. 111.

12  Ibid., pp. 111–112.

13  Boatright, J. R. *Ethics and the Conduct of Business*, 5/e. Upper Saddle River, NJ: Prentice Hall, 2006, pp. 6–7.

14  Ibid., pp. 7–9.

15  Ibid.

16  Ibid.

17  Bowen, M. G. and F. C. Power. "The Moral Manager: Communicative Ethics and the Exxon Valdez Disaster," *Business Ethics Quarterly* (February 1993): 10.

18  Velasquez, M. G. *Business Ethics: Concepts and Cases*, 6/e. Upper Saddle River, NJ: Prentice Hall, 2005, pp. 8–16.

19  Byrne. "After Enron," p. 74.

20  Velasquez. *Business Ethics*, pp. 11–13.

21  Brown, M. T. *The Ethical Process: An Approach to Disagreements and Controversial Issues*, 3/e. Upper Saddle River, NJ: Prentice Hall, 2003, pp. 5–7.

22  Paine, L. S. "Ethics as Character Development: Reflections on the Objective of Ethics Education," in R. E. Freeman (ed.), *Business Ethics: The State of the Art*. New York: Oxford University Press, 1991, pp. 67–86.

23  Ibid., p. 81.

24  Ibid., p. 82.

25  Lavelle, L. "Another Crop of Sleazy CEOs?" *BusinessWeek*, August 26, 2002, p. 12.

26  Paine. "Ethics as Character Development," pp. 82–83.

27  Murphy, P. E. *Eighty Exemplary Ethics Statements*. Notre Dame, IN: University of Notre Dame Press, 1998, p. xiii.

28  Ibid., p. 1.

29  Ibid., p. 2.

30  "Global Ethics Codes Gain Importance as a Tool to Avoid Litigation and Fines," *The Wall Street Journal*, August 19, 1999, p. A1. Reprinted by permission of the *Wall Street Journal*, Copyright © 1999 by Dow Jones & Company, Inc. All rights reserved worldwide.

31  Ibid.

32  Polet, J. "Company Communication: From the Ethics of Communication to the Communication of Ethics," in G. Enderle (ed.), *International Business Ethics: Challenges and Approaches*. Notre Dame, IN, and Hong Kong, China: The University of Notre Dame Press and the University of Hong Kong Press, 1998.

33  Ibid., p. 6.

34  Ibid., p. 7.

35  Lipovetsky, G. *Le Crepuscule du Devoir. L'Ethique Indolore des Noveaux Temps Democratiques*. Paris: Gallimard, 1992, p. 248.

36  Mulcahy, A. M. Keynote Address, Business for Social Responsibility, Annual Conference. New York, November 11, 2004.

37  Yankelovich, D. "Making Trust a Competitive Asset: Breaking Out of Narrow Frameworks," a report of the Special Meeting of Senior Executives on the Deeper Crisis of Trust. New York, May 15–17, 2003. Available at www.view pointlearning.com.

38  For a complete description of the study, see Van Lee, R., L. Fabish and N. McGaw. "The Value of Corporate Values," *Strategy+Business* 39 (Summer 2005): 52–65.

39 Barton, L. *Crisis in Organizations: Managing and Communicating in the Heat of Chaos.* Cincinnati, OH: Southwestern Publishing Company, 1993, pp. 84–85.

40 Lipovetsky. *Le Crepuscule du Devoir*, pp. 269–270.

41 Nash, L. L. "Johnson & Johnson's Credo." In *Corporate Ethics: A Prime Business Asset.* New York: The Business Roundtable, 1988, p. 100.

42 Ibid., p. 97.

43 Lipovetsky. *Le Crepuscule du Devoir*, p. 270.

44 Murphy. *Eighty Exemplary Ethics Statements*, pp. 5–9.

45 Seglin, J. L. "An Ethics Code Can't Replace a Backbone," *The New York Times*, April 21, 2002, p. BU-4. Copyright © 2002 by The New York Times Company. Reprinted with permission.

46 Ibid.

# Case 3.1: Excel Industries, Inc. (A)

## BACKGROUND NOTE

The workforce in North America, particularly in the U.S. and Canada, is becoming increasingly female, reflecting a general trend toward two-paycheck families.

According to a recent study from The Hudson Institute, an increasing number of women are entering the North American job market. Since 2000, approximately two-thirds of all new entrants to the workforce have been women. And, by early in the 21st century, nearly two-thirds of all working-age women in the U.S. will be employed.

Other studies indicate that women in the U.S. are entering the job market more for economic than for professional reasons. While the number of women with college degrees and professional credentials is rising, so is the number of single-parent families headed by women. These families are, for the most part, well below average in income and education, and are more likely than two-parent households to require public assistance.

Employers are coming to realize that what had formerly been seen as "women's issues" – including flexible scheduling, maternity and family leave, and daycare – are really "family issues" deserving serious attention from both the public and private sectors. Some of these matters have become the object of protracted and heated negotiation during collective bargaining. And, what once was regarded as a luxury or fringe benefit in many organizations is more frequently viewed by employees as an entitlement.

In North America, and especially in the U.S., daycare for the children of working mothers is not seen as an entitlement to be provided by government. The U.S. Federal Government views itself as constitutionally excluded from issues related to management of education and child care, and state and local governments cite a lack of funding. Corporate America has increasingly come to see a social responsibility for the children of their employees, and employees have come to expect and depend on such corporate responsiveness to their needs.

This case deals with several aspects of these recently emerging family issues. While each employee has both a cost and a value to a business organization, each employer has concomitant obligations and responsibilities to those employees. This case is about balance among those obligations and management decision making when obligations are in conflict or when responsibilities pull in opposite directions.

This is also a case involving corporate communication. The executives and management of every business enterprise operate in an environment that is information-rich, yet rife with rumor, misunderstanding and misinformation.

Business leaders must understand that every action, whether intended for public discussion or not, will have an effect on the public's perception of their business.

Business leaders should also understand that, as they draft their corporate strategy and implement tactical moves in the marketplace, they will interact and communicate with a very diverse and complex audience. Those who will see and hear of management's actions will have varying backgrounds, reading abilities, knowledge of the subject, political views, prejudices and interests.

In many ways, the mass audience reached by radio, television, newspapers and magazines is many smaller audiences. It may be helpful to think of the larger audience as comprising shareholders; customers; suppliers; competitors; politicians; local, regional and national government officials; potential investors; prospective employees; neighbors; community members, and others.

In some cases, business leaders might well consider separate messages for separate audiences, designing their content for the backgrounds, needs, interests, inclinations and potential reactions of each. Shareholders, for instance, might have a greater interest in knowing how an event or announcement will affect their investment than do members of the surrounding community. Employees might have a much keener interest in how an event will affect their jobs and their lives in the organization than would others.

## A MANUFACTURER MOVES INTO CHILD CARE

Several years ago, Excel Industries, Inc., a supplier of window systems to the automotive industry, purchased Nyloncraft, Inc., a $40 million injection molding company. Both firms are headquartered in northern Indiana, in the heart of the domestic automobile supply region. At the time of the acquisition, Nyloncraft was a highly regarded firm with great promise for growth, and had exactly the sort of manufacturing capacity, equipment and labor force that Excel Industries was looking for.

At the time of the corporate takeover, Nyloncraft, Inc. operated a daycare facility that was regarded as among the most innovative in the nation. *Money* magazine, *U.S. News & World Report* and other business publications featured the facility, describing it as "one of the best equipped 24-hour-a-day learning centers in the Midwest that is operated by a corporation for the benefit of its employees."

James J. Lohman is Chairman, President and Chief Executive Officer of Excel Industries. "When the Learning Center was opened," he said:

> it suited the needs of Nyloncraft very nicely. It was expensive, but it helped us to attract and retain a reliable workforce that would help the company grow. We had a number of female workers who were of child-bearing age and it made good sense for us to assist them with their child care needs. We knew from experience . . . that a first-class, on-site learning center would reduce turnover, absenteeism, and tardiness. It was good for business, it was good for our employees, and it was good for the kids.

When he said expensive, Lohman wasn't exaggerating. "When Excel acquired Nyloncraft, we immediately invested $200,000 in the Learning Center, improving it so that it met or exceeded all recommended standards for facilities of that type." The Center's annual budget was in excess of $400,000 to provide round-the-clock care and instruction for 162 children.

## THE COST OF PROVIDING ON-SITE CHILD CARE

"Within a few years," Lohman said, "we discovered that fewer and fewer of our employees had children enrolled in the Nyloncraft Learning Center, so we expanded enrollment to the community at large." Two years ago, employees' children accounted for about 45 percent of the enrollment at the Center. "By this spring," he said, "less than seven percent of those enrolled were children of Nyloncraft employees." And by then, he added, the annual subsidy had grown to nearly $300,000. All parents with children enrolled in the Learning Center, regardless of who their employer might be, received a substantial tuition discount, each paying just a fraction of what such care and instruction would be worth on the retail market.

"We weren't just looking after these children, as a baby-sitting service might," he added:

> We provided state-certified instruction, professional pre-school development programs, and we fed them. Our insurance, reporting, and oversight problems were growing by the day. It was becoming increasingly difficult

to justify a subsidy that was well in excess of a quarter-of-a-million dollars for the children of only 10 Excel employees. The financial pressure was simply too great for us to continue the operation.

Excel tried unsuccessfully for nearly a year to find a buyer for the Learning Center. Failing that, they tried to find a management firm that would agree to take over the day-to-day operations of the facility. "No one would step forward to help us," he said, "We didn't want to close the Nyloncraft Learning Center. But, increasingly, I saw fewer alternatives open to us."

Lohman began to think carefully about the alternative decisions available to him and the audiences that would be most affected by his choice. Looking after the children of those few employees who still used the Learning Center would be neither difficult nor expensive. But how would others react to a management decision to close the facility? What other choice did the company have? What other choice did the parents have? Quality daycare was in short supply in the local area, and time was running out for Jim Lohman. The Board of Directors wanted an answer from him soon.

The two most troubling questions were deceptively simple: What should I do about the Learning Center and how should we communicate our decision?

## WRITING ASSIGNMENT

Please respond in writing to the issues presented in this case by preparing two documents: a communication strategy memo and a professional business letter.

In preparing these documents, you may assume one of two roles: you may identify yourself as an Excel Industries manager who has been asked to provide advice to Mr. Lohman regarding the issues he and the company are facing. Or, you may identify yourself as an external management consultant who has been asked by the company to provide advice to Mr. Lohman.

Either way, you must prepare a strategy memo addressed to Jim Lohman that summarizes the details of the case, rank-orders critical issues, discusses their implications (what they mean and why they matter), offers specific recommendations for action (assigning ownership and suspense dates for each) and shows how to communicate the solution to all who are affected by the recommendations.

You must also prepare a professional business letter for Mr. Lohman's signature. That document may be addressed to parents of children attending the Nyloncraft Learning Center, addressing their concerns in the case. If you wish, you may write separate letters to parents who are Excel employees and to parents who are not employees of the company. If you have questions about either of these documents, please consult your instructor.

## ACKNOWLEDGMENTS

This case was prepared from personal interviews and public sources by James S. O'Rourke, Teaching Professor of Management, as the basis for class discussion rather than to illustrate either effective or ineffective handling of an administrative situation. Copyright © 1994. Revised: 2018.

Eugene D. Fanning Center for Business Communication. All rights reserved. No part of this publication may be reproduced, stored in a retrieval system, used in a spreadsheet, or transmitted in any form or by any means – electronic, mechanical, photocopying, recording, or otherwise – without permission.

**NYLONCRAFT**
**Summary Balance Sheet**

| | |
|---|---:|
| Cash | 97 |
| Accounts Receivable | 3,207 |
| Inventory | 7,308 |
| Prepaid Expense | 93 |
| | |
| Total Current Assets | 10,705 |
| Fixed Assets, Net | 8,585 |
| Goodwill and Other Assets | 3,691 |
| | |
| Total Assets | 22,981 |
| Accounts Payable | 1,897 |
| Accrued Liabilities | 1,232 |
| Current Portion Ltd | 413 |
| Long Term Debt, Banks | 1,800 |
| Due to Parent/Equity | 17,639 |
| | |
| Total Liabilities & Equity | 22,981 |

**NYLONCRAFT**
**Income Statement**

| | |
|---|---:|
| Sales | 36,730 |
| Cost of Goods Sold | 35,332 |
| | |
| Gross Profit | 1,398 |
| | |
| Selling and Administrative Expense | 2,697 |
| Operating Income | (1,299) |
| | |
| Other Expenses | (522) |
| | |
| Loss Before Tax and Corp. Allocation | (1,821) |

Note: Figures are given in thousands of dollars (U.S.).

# Case 3.2: The National Football League

## Responding to Traumatic Brain Injuries

### THE CRISIS

On May 2, 2012, Roger Goodell received word that Junior Seau, a well-respected former player and on-air NFL analyst, committed suicide by shooting himself in the chest. Mr. Goodell, Commissioner of the National Football League (NFL), had just handed down significant suspensions to four players and four coaches and front-office personnel from the New Orleans Saints for creating an incentive system rewarding the injury of opponents, in what has been called "Bountygate."[1]

The scandal surrounding the New Orleans Saints made headline news in the preceding weeks, but was rendered "a mere footnote" by news of Seau's death, the third apparent player suicide in just over a year, due to Seau's reputation as a model football player and great teammate.[2]

In the days following Seau's suicide, information surfaced linking Seau's death with those of Ray Easterling and David Duerson. Both Duerson and Easterling had been diagnosed with a debilitating brain injury, chronic traumatic encephalopathy (CTE), and while it was too early to diagnose Seau, the method of his suicide – shooting himself in the chest – along with the request to pass his brain along for study, strongly indicated that Seau was experiencing early symptoms of CTE and planning to mirror the suicide of Duerson.

In the wake of this most recent player suicide, former players and NFL analysts took to their television programs and social media accounts to voice their frustration at the pace of change in the NFL and the lack of support mechanisms for former players.[3] Meanwhile, more than 1,500 NFL retirees became part of 50 lawsuits against the league for personal injury and wrongful death.[4]

Former NFL employees have indicated that Seau's death, in particular, marked a turning point in the way that the NFL responded to the public debate regarding concussions. NFL leadership, and Commissioner Goodell specifically, had already been arguing that the NFL needed "a change in culture," but this incident clearly accelerated efforts to address player safety.[5] In the weeks and months following the suicide, the NFL would begin to implement a number of initiatives to make the game safer, ranging from rule changes, equipment improvements and youth initiatives to increased funding for research into the long-term impact of football on the human brain.

## THE NATIONAL FOOTBALL LEAGUE AND ITS CORPORATE STRUCTURE

The National Football League (NFL) was founded in 1920 as the American Professional Football Conference. After a short series of name changes, the NFL was officially formed in 1922.[6] In 1966, the NFL agreed to merge with the American Football League (AFL) starting with the 1970 season, creating the NFL as it stands today.[7]

It is important to note that a change in the tax code, enacted in 1966 to facilitate the AFL merger, made the new NFL a 501(c)(6), non-profit organization.[8] The NFL is led by current Commissioner Roger Goodell, who took over from predecessor Paul Tagliabue in 2006. Commissioner Goodell's tenure has so far emphasized player safety (to include increased disciplinary measures for illegal hits), as well as initiatives aimed at reducing instances of head trauma.[9]

The NFL serves as a unifying and independent body that "governs and promotes the game of football, sets and enforces rules, and regulates team ownership," in cooperation with team owners and executive staff.[10] In addition, the NFL is typically considered a trade association serving to present a unified front in promoting football and its constituent members. Its corporate structure represents all 32 professional football teams that make up the league, and as a result, the NFL receives an antitrust exemption from Congress.[11]

The league office itself holds a number of positions found in a typical corporation (e.g., Public Relations, Marketing, and Finance), but also supports functions such as Player Health and Safety, Player Engagement, and Player Operations. The vast majority of league-wide decisions are made by the Commissioner's office without the need for approval from team owners. However, the 32 team owners act much like a company's board of directors, and are typically consulted on any significant issues to ensure maximum buy-in and cooperation.

In many cases, the Commissioner will work directly with specific committees (e.g., Competition Committee) comprising a small number of owners (or front-office staff; Rich McKay, President of the Falcons, leads the Competition Committee) acting as representatives for team owners, as a whole.

For major, controversial decisions, the Commissioner will likely seek approval from all 32 team owners, individually, at their annual Owners' Meeting held in the spring (typically May). Though technically all teams receive an equal vote, certain owners are considered more influential than others in shaping NFL policy, strategy and negotiations. These owners include Dan and Art Rooney (Pittsburgh Steelers), Robert Kraft (New England Patriots), John Mara and Steve Tisch (New York Giants), the Green Bay Packer's Executive Committee (publicly owned, ownership staff elected) and Jerry Jones (Dallas Cowboys). Individual owners can oftentimes have a disproportionate influence on league activity (e.g., the Rooney rule regarding minority hiring).[12]

The NFL's response to the issue of traumatic brain injuries originates from a number of different offices within the Corporate Headquarters. The Communications and Public Affairs office (currently led by Vice President Paul Hicks), is key to the league's interaction with the public. Greg Aiello, Senior Vice President of Communications, currently acts as the NFL's primary spokesperson. Likewise, Player Operations (led by Troy Vincent) and Player Engagement (led by Ray Anderson) deal with the execution of league policy, as well as communication with individual players.

With respect to ongoing litigation, the NFL is represented by its Law and Labor Policy office (led by Senior Vice President Adolpho Birch) and the office of the General Counsel (currently Jeff Pash).[13] In light of the uptick in efforts to address player safety, the NFL has formed a small task force of personnel in the corporate office whose sole function is to deal with player health and safety. This small task force is led by Jeff Miller (Vice President of Health and Safety Policy). Miller and his staff initially worked within the Communications & Public Affairs office, but in practice report to Commissioner Goodell.[14]

## THE NATIONAL FOOTBALL LEAGUE PLAYERS' ASSOCIATION

The National Football League Players' Association (NFLPA) is the labor organization representing professional football players in the NFL. It was founded in 1956 and officially recognized by the NFL and team owners in 1968. Team owners were initially reluctant to allow a union to engage in collective borrowing on behalf of individual players, but eventually relented due to persistent strikes and lockouts. The NFLPA is currently led by DeMaurice Smith, who took over in March 2009.[15]

The NFLPA typically represents the players in contract negotiations, as well as disputes between players and their respective teams. The NFL and NFLPA by the nature of their respective missions do not typically cooperate, but it is widely believed that Executive Director DeMaurice Smith and NFL Commissioner Goodell have a particularly negative relationship, as demonstrated by outspoken opposition to suspensions to New Orleans Saints players and staff, as well as the NFL's execution of concussion protocols.[16,17]

At the time of Junior Seau's suicide, many believed that the NFLPA would itself be the subject of lawsuits due to perceived culpability in lack of communication regarding the effects of head trauma.[18]

## DIFFERING OPINIONS

Public reaction to the broader concussion debate has fluctuated over time to coincide with major events. A Google Trends chart including the terms "NFL" and "concussion" indicates that unique searches on the subject were almost non-existent until Greg Aiello's interview with *The New York Times*, in which he said that "it's quite obvious from the medical research that's been done that concussions can lead to long-term problems."[19]

Interest surged again with the national story of 21-year-old college football player Owen Thomas, who was diagnosed with CTE (the first for a college player) without ever suffering from a reported concussion. In May 2012, following Junior Seau's suicide, interest would spike for a third time, and begin a persistent upward trend peaking shortly after the NFL's $765 million settlement in August 2013.

Increased public consciousness has led to a number of different viewpoints regarding the impact of concussions in football. For fans, increased publicity regarding the impact of head trauma on current and former players led some to change the way they viewed the game, but the vast majority of fans state that they will continue to watch the game and believe that the NFL is taking significant measures to make the game safer. Opinions regarding the head trauma debate include:

It changed the perspective a little bit, but we love football. We're a football family.

If I had a son, I would look at the way they play football. But as far as watching a game, that's what you pay for. They're kind of like gladiators.[20]

[The NFL's reaction] is kind of stifling the game because all of the rules and new penalties that players are getting is kind of changing the way we watch football.[21]

Current and former players are likewise conflicted regarding player safety. Seattle Seahawks cornerback Richard Sherman believes that players know the risk associated with playing football, saying ". . . and the next time I get hit in the head and I can't see straight, if I can, I'll get back up and pretend like nothing happened. Maybe I'll even get another pick in the process."[22]

Furthermore, an ESPN NFL Survey indicated that "of the 320 NFL players polled on whether they would play in the Super Bowl with a concussion 85 percent said they would do it."[23] Many even believe the NFL is making a good faith effort to make the game safer. On the other hand, as will later be discussed, thousands of players are currently suing the NFL for "glorifying" violence and "spreading misinformation" about the risk of long-term neurological damage caused by playing football.[24]

The NFL itself has taken the position that there are undoubtedly "unanswered questions" regarding concussions. Commissioner Goodell has acknowledged that football causes damage, but will not admit to any guilt, specifically as it relates to the ongoing lawsuit. Commissioner Goodell believes that the NFL's response has been "very responsible," and that the NFL's key mission is to help the players and make the game safer.

An interview with NFL Spokesperson Greg Aiello reinforced the NFL's position that its response to the issue of head trauma has evolved with time, as medical understanding regarding the brain has progressed. This interview supported statements from Commissioner Goodell, made in the public record, indicating that the NFL is not ready to definitely support the idea that player concussions directly lead to long-term neurological issues.[25,26]

Individual owners have remained in line with the Commissioner. Robert Kraft (New England Patriots) exemplifies this viewpoint, stating "I think we've seen great leadership from (NFL Commissioner) Roger Goodell and (NFL executive) Jeff Pash on this issue. . . . We're devoting a lot of research, energy, and this is still the greatest game on earth."[27]

The NFLPA occupies a precarious position in the ongoing head trauma debate due to its complicity in delaying constructive dialogue regarding the impact of concussive and subconcussive hits.[28]

As such, it has yet to take a firm stance in the public domain. The NFLPA has opted instead to focus its efforts on enforcement (by pushing for "neuro-trauma consultants") and research, providing $100 million in funding for

Harvard Medical School to assess the effects of football on current and former players.[29] Head trauma is included in the study, but also includes heart problems and skeletal injuries.

## TYPICAL PLAYER INJURIES

Football is, by its very nature, subject to a wide spectrum of injuries. Nearly half of retired players experienced zero-to-two major injuries while playing, and 22 percent of players experienced five or more major injuries. Furthermore, nine out of ten former players claim to have suffered at least one concussion while playing, and six out of ten reported experiencing three or more. Two out of three of those experiencing concussions report that they continue to suffer from occasional concussion-like symptoms. Former players report constantly feeling "like hell every morning" and like they are "40 going on 65." Nine out of ten former players report feeling aches and pains on a daily basis.[30]

Statistics indicate that across all levels of football, approximately 40 percent of injuries are strains and sprains, 25 percent are bruises, 15 percent are dislocations, 10 percent are fractures and 5 percent are concussions.[31] Of these, orthopaedic injuries (e.g., torn anterior cruciate ligament) are the most common in occurrence given the pace and style of the game (36 percent of all injuries occur to athletes' knees), but head injuries are becoming increasingly prominent given the number of recent player suicides, enhanced quality of detection reporting and safety protocols, as well as increased awareness of the potential long-term effects of brain trauma.

Even milder instances of brain trauma can lead to significant long-term damage. A growing number of former players are developing or have developed chronic traumatic encephalopathy (CTE) and amyotrophic lateral sclerosis (ALS), progressive neurodegenerative diseases that cause significant decreases in quality of life and can lead to dementia (in the case of CTE) and death (in the case of ALS, also known as Lou Gehrig's disease).[32,33]

The prevalence of specific types of injuries depends heavily on the position of the player in question. Quarterbacks, for instance, are prone to shoulder injuries, while all other positions tend to receive knee, foot and ankle injuries.[34] Head injuries occur across positions, but skill position players – primarily in the defensive secondary and wide receiver corps – gain the most publicity due to the sheer force of the concussive hits they receive.[35]

However, offensive and defensive linemen typically face the largest number of concussions as the result of sustained, sub-concussive trauma experienced over the course of an entire season. In fact, the number of concussions reported for linemen spikes dramatically toward the end of the season.[36] Dealing with these issues, though, requires cooperation from the players themselves. It is widely believed that many players fail to report concussions in an effort to stay on the field.[37]

The total number of injuries in the NFL has steadily risen from 2,640 in 2000 to 4,473 in 2011 (though some of that increase can be attributed to enhanced reporting standards).[38] Some proponents believe the decrease in practice during the off-season has had an adverse effect on injuries, while others believe new helmet-to-helmet regulations are increasing leg injuries.[39]

At the youth level, the number of annual injuries rose from 274,094 in 1990 to 346,772 in 2007.[40] Of note, while rare, 468 non-fatal injuries resulting in permanent neurological damage (directly attributable to high school football) occurred between 1982 and 2011.[41]

Additionally, a 2013 study on fatalities in high school and college football indicated that there are typically four fatalities directly related to football (e.g., head trauma, cervical injury and intra-abdominal issues) on an annual basis and 8.2 indirectly related to football (e.g., heat stroke, cardiac arrest).[42]

## LEAGUE REVENUE AND MEDIA RIGHTS

The league has historically had a collective-thinking attitude that has allowed them to maximize revenue by employing a revenue-sharing model that provides a 60/40 split (after standard 15 percent deduction for game expenses).

This attitude has been challenged lately with the emergence of luxury seats which are not counted in the shared revenue model. A split has occurred within the league between teams that have upgraded their stadiums to include luxury seating and those that cannot afford to do the same. As a result, revenue sharing has dropped to 75 percent of national revenue in 1993 to 63 percent in 2010.[43]

Media rights represent the largest percentage of total NFL revenue (50 percent compared to gate revenue of 21 percent). Media rights have grown at a compound rate of 12 percent since the merger, increasing from $47 million in 1970 to $4 billion in 2013.[44] In December of 2011, the NFL renewed contracts with FOX, CBS and NBC. In September of the same year, it renewed its contract with ESPN through 2022. That brings total media revenue each year to $6.1 billion (including DirecTV), representing a 52 percent increase over the previous contract.[45]

## YOUTH PARTICIPATION

### Pop Warner

On a national news broadcast on June 12, 2012, Dr. Julian Bailes, a neurosurgeon with NorthShore Medical Group and Chief Medical Officer for Pop Warner stated that ". . . (youth) players who get a second, a third, and a fourth concussion really can have detrimental effects and have a degradation in their function."[46]

The very next day, the Pop Warner National Office announced that it would make two rule changes to help reduce the potential for concussions in youths.[47] The first requires that no player spend more than one-third of practice in contact drills. The second states that no full-speed head-on-head drills may take place where players start more than 3 yards apart.

Publicity over the dangers of football, especially in youth, continued. ESPN's "Outside the Lines" featured over ten stories on football-related concussions in 2012 alone. In an episode aired on August 28, a poll by ESPN revealed that 57 percent of parents who are fans of the NFL say they are less likely to encourage their children to play due to stories about concussions.

Additional polling data revealed that 69 percent of parents that are NFL fans have children that have played, are playing or will play football while 67 percent of parents who are not NFL fans say their children will not play football before the age of 12. These statistics indicate a strong correlation between NFL fandom and youth participation in football.

In 2013, ESPN announced that the Pop Warner leagues saw an overall reduction of almost 24,000 players between 2010 and 2012, representing roughly 10 percent of total participants. Officials from Pop Warner cited other factors in the decline such as the trend of youngsters focusing on one sport; however, Dr. Bailes was adamant that head injuries were the main reason for the drop. "Unless we deal with these truths, we're not going to get past the dropping popularity of the sport and people dropping out of the sport," said Bailes.[48]

### High School

High school participation may also be affected by concussion reports in the media. Given football's immense popularity, it may be difficult to imagine that football wouldn't exist at the high school level. It is worthy of note, however, that at the turn of the last century, baseball, boxing and horse racing were the three most popular sports. It is more unlikely for a sport to continue to dominate in popularity than it is for it to be passed up.

In the case of high school football, it may be lawsuits that present the most challenging obstacle to its survival. As ex-players continue to pursue litigation and win large settlements, insurance carriers may require cost-prohibitive premiums from high schools to offset the risk of long-term medical costs. In parts of the country that do not have an entrenched football culture, high schools may opt to disband their football program rather than float this cost.

Outside of lawsuits, schools may eventually be prohibited from fielding football teams directly through government regulation. Research into CTE is growing, and if direct links are found between CTE and football, then pressure could mount from the general public for Congress to intercede directly.

The NFL has responded with initiatives such as Play 60 and Heads Up Football. Play 60 is designed to tackle childhood obesity by getting kids active through in-school, after-school and team-based programs, online child-targeted outreach on NFLRUSH.com, and many partnerships with like-minded organizations. Heads Up Football is USA Football's national initiative to help make the sport of football better and safer. They accomplish this by teaching proper tackling techniques that minimize injuries.

## POTENTIAL CHANGES TO THE GAME

In 2010, Commissioner Goodell and several league owners began a push to increase the 16-game regular-season schedule to 18 games.[49] This increase would mark the first time since 1978 that the NFL has lengthened its season.

The NFLPA rejected Roger Goodell's proposal, citing player safety as the largest deterrent, and through a collective bargaining agreement during the NFL lockout prior to the 2011 season, traded percentages of player revenue for a less rigorous offseason and training camp.[50] The reasoning was that team rosters would not have depth enough to accommodate the extra games, and the tight salary cap would mean having to field players who may be vulnerable to injury as the season progresses.

By September of 2013, NFL owners had again resumed their push to persuade the NFLPA to expand the regular season, this time proposing that no one player may play more than 16 games whereas a team would play 18 games.[51]

Over the past few years, the NFL has implemented several rule changes aimed to improve safety. The reworded rules now prohibit a player from launching himself off the ground and using his helmet to strike a player in a defenseless posture in the head or neck. Additionally, when a player with the ball loses his helmet, the play is immediately whistled dead.

Since May 2012, additional rules have been added. Ball carriers and players are banned from initiating contact with the crown of their helmets in the open field. During field-goal and extra-point attempts, the defense cannot position any player on the line directly across from the snapper, who's considered to be in a defenseless position.

In addition to the previous conduct rules, equipment rules have also been improved; all players besides kickers and punters are now required to wear thigh and knee pads.[52] The rules are still open for modification, and Commissioner Goodell has mentioned the possibility of ending the three-point stance in an effort to reduce concussions.[53]

A change passed by team owners (voting 26 to 6) moved kickoffs from the 30-yard line to the 35-yard line and required the coverage unit to start closer to the ball. This change has seen positive results in limiting violent collisions. According to the Elias Sports Bureau, 16.4 percent of kickoffs led to touchbacks in 2010; in 2011 that figure rose to 43.5 percent. Subsequently, the NFL found that players suffered 40 percent fewer concussions on kickoffs in 2011. Despite this improvement, Commissioner Goodell and then Tampa Bay Buccaneers coach Greg Schiano had discussed the possibility of eliminating kickoffs entirely.[54]

Though the National Operating Committee on Standards for Athletic Equipment (the committee responsible for certifying and approving helmets for the NFL, NCAA and high school football) recently stated that the primary focus should be to minimize unnecessary hits, the committee does recognize that equipment changes would make a difference to the safety of the game.

Currently no studies exist to prove that extra helmet padding would reduce concussions. Rather, manufacturers of the extra padding say the material helps reduce impact. In an effort to reduce injuries, the NFL is requiring players to wear more padding and will penalize running backs who lead with the crown of their helmets.[55]

The issue with rule changes discouraging hits to the head is that now players are aiming lower to tackle opponents. According to Brandon Merriweather, the Washington Redskins safety who served a one-game suspension for repeated helmet-to-helmet collisions, "To be honest man you just gotta go low now, man. You gotta end people's careers. You gotta tear people's ACL and mess up people's knees. You can't hit them high anymore. You just gotta go low."[56]

## DETECTION REPORTING PROTOCOL AND STANDARDS

According to the NFL Head, Neck and Spine Committee's Protocols Regarding Diagnosis and Management of Concussion, the NFL Sideline Concussion Assessment is the evaluation developed by the NFL's Head Neck and Spine Committee based on the Standardized Concussion Assessment Tool (SCAT2) published by the Concussion in Sport Group (McCrory '09). It is used to aide in the diagnosis of concussion, even in the event of a delayed onset of symptoms.[57] The document details signs to look for, emergency medical action planning, concussion management and the return-to-participation process (which can take weeks to finish).

This impressive list of protocols, however, is perceived more as a set of guidelines rather than a rule. The Madden Rule, which states that a player diagnosed with a concussion must vacate the field until a qualified specialist clears him to return, was violated by New Orleans Saints cornerback Keenan Lewis and Green Bay Packers' left tackle to David Bakhtiari during the wild-card round of playoffs in January 2014.

According to blogger and sports consultant Chad Walters, "what the NFL should look to implement is higher-level poka-yoke measures to better ensure that players leave the field in a timely manner."[58] NFL spokesman Greg Aiello proposed that players who violate the NFL's concussion protocol could be subject to fines. This crackdown is an effort to prevent dangerous events such as San Diego Chargers offensive guard Kris Dielman receiving a concussion during the October 2011 game against the New York Jets but continuing to play, only to later suffer a grand mal seizure on his flight home.[59]

## MTBI AND HEAD, NECK AND SPINE COMMITTEE

In 1994, the NFL created the Mild Traumatic Brain Injury committee to study the short- and long-term effects of head trauma on the lives of football players. Dr. Elliot Pellman was appointed chair although he was a rheumatologist and lacked any experience in brain science. At this time, Dr. Pellman cited drugs, knee injuries and drinking as far more critical problems to player safety than head trauma. Later that year, the NFL Commissioner, Paul Tagliabue, referred to the concussion problem as a "pack journalism issue" citing that concussions are an uncommon occurrence and have not grown from year to year.

In March of 1997, the American Academy of Neurology published a report indicating that repetitive concussions can cause brain damage, and suggested that players be removed from the game if they lose consciousness or exhibit any concussion symptoms 15 minutes post-injury. The report goes on to warn that "repeated concussions can cause cumulative brain injury in an individual over months or years." The MTBI committee responded publicly to this report in May of 2000. The committee cited lack of research backing up the report with committee member and neurologist Dr. Mark R. Lovell stating, "We don't know whether being knocked out briefly is any more dangerous than having amnesia and not being knocked out."

Dr. Kevin Guskiewicz, a sports medicine researcher at the University of North Carolina, published a paper in November of 2003 suggesting that repeat concussions may lead to slower recovery of neurological functioning:

Our study suggests that players with a history of previous concussions are more likely to have future concussive injuries than those with no history; 1 in 15 players with a concussion may have additional concussions in the same playing season; and previous concussions may be associated with slower recovery of neurological function.

The MTBI committee would dispute Dr. Guskiewicz's research in October of 2004, saying:

They [Guskiewicz et al.] concluded that there may be an increased risk of repeat concussive injuries and there may be a slower recovery of neurological function after repeat concussions in those who have a history of previous concussions. The results of this present NFL study do not support those conclusions.[60]

In January of 2004, the MTBI committee published a paper in *Neurosurgery* that concludes that most concussed players recover quickly citing:

A total of 92% of concussed players returned to practice in less than seven days. . . . More than one-half of the players returned to play within one day, and symptoms resolved in a short time in the vast majority of cases.[61]

Later that year, the committee published its fifth and most controversial paper in *Neurosurgery* by suggesting that the brains of NFL players were less susceptible to MTBI due to the players having gone through a winnowing process whereby self-selected players had a type of artificial skeleton around their brains.

In January of 2005, the MTBI committee published yet another paper in *Neurosurgery* stating that there is no further risk of injury for a player to return to play in a game in which he was concussed:

Players who are concussed and return to the same game have fewer initial signs and symptoms than those removed from play. Return to play does not involve a significant risk of a second injury either in the same game or during the season.

The committee further states that these findings may have relevance for youth participants:

Under the right circumstances, specifically with regard to final decision making on return to play being solely at the clinical discretion of a knowledgeable team physician, it might be safe for college/high school football players to be cleared to return to play on the same day as their injury. The authors suggest that, rather than blindly adhering to arbitrary, rigid guidelines, physicians keep an open mind to the possibility that the present analysis of professional football players may have relevance to college and high school players.[62]

In June of 2005, Terry Long, a previous football player with the Pittsburgh Steelers, committed suicide. Dr. Omalu later examined his brain and found CTE. An MTBI committee member would later state in January of 2006 that Dr. Omalu's findings had "fallacious reasoning," stating "to go back and say that he was depressed from playing in the NFL and that led to his death 14 years later, I think is purely speculative." He added, "He could have had a head injury that wasn't reported before football. He could have had a fight, he could have had a head injury. . . . And that's why I'm saying it's so speculative." Dr. Omalu would also publish his findings on Mike Webster's brain that year. In May of 2006, the MTBI committee would call for the retraction of his article stating "Omalu et al's description of chronic traumatic encephalopathy is completely wrong," they write. "The diagnosis of a chronic condition requires a medical history indicating a long-standing nature of the illness. . . . Such a history is completely lacking in the Omalu et al report." In November of 2006, Dr. Omalu would follow up in *Neurosurgery* that he also found CTE in Terry Long's brain stating, "Our first and second cases both had long careers without multiple recorded concussions. Both manifested Major Depressive Disorder after retirement."[63] In that same month, Andre Waters, a former Philadelphia Eagles player, committed suicide at age 44. Dr. Omalu examined his brain, as well, and found evidence of CTE.

In January of 2009, a team of scientists including Dr. Ann McKee held a press conference in Tampa Bay, Florida, while the media was gathered for the Super Bowl to announce several new cases of CTE, including the brain of an 18-year-old high school student who died ten days after suffering his fourth concussion. Dr. McKee went on further to meet with the MTBI committee in May of 2009; however, she told *Frontline* that the committee was dismissive of her since the research did not reveal a specific cause for CTE.

Dr. McKee's research would wind up in front of a congressional hearing in October of 2009 where Rep. Linda Sanchez (D-Calif.) told Commissioner Goodell that the league's response to the problem reminds her of the tobacco industry's handling of the link between smoking and health problems in the 1990s. Likely in response to the congresswoman's remarks, the co-chairs of the MTBI committee resigned shortly after. In their place, the league installed neurological surgeons Dr. H. Hunt Batjer and Dr. Richard G. Ellenbogen as co-chairs of the renamed "Head, Neck and Spine Committee" and appointed Dr. Kevin Guskiewicz as a member.

In December of 2009, NFL spokesman Greg Aiello was quoted as saying "it's quite obvious from the medical research that's been done that concussions can lead to long-term problems." This was the first time the NFL officially recognized concussions as having long-term effects. In the same month, new return-to-play guidelines were established which restrict any player who suffers symptoms of concussions from returning to play. In January of 2010, the NFL also designated Dr. McKee's Center for the Study of Traumatic Encephalopathy at Boston University as its "preferred" brain bank while donating $1 million dollars for research.[64]

Due to statements from the MTBI committee that often appeared to favor league interests and contradict statements from independent medical experts, the NFL established a new committee in 2010 named the Head, Neck and Spine Medical Committee. Dr. H. Hunt Batjer and Dr. Richard G. Ellenbogen were chosen to lead the new committee. This committee has since taken a more proactive approach to researching head trauma, to include publication of a new sideline concussion protocol and symptoms checklist.[65]

## CLASS-ACTION LAWSUIT AND SETTLEMENT

On August 17, 2011, former Atlanta Falcons safety Ray Easterling, his attorney Larry Coben and seven other former players filed a lawsuit against the NFL and football helmet manufacturer Riddell, claiming that the NFL:

continuously and vehemently denied that it knew, should have known or believed that there is any relationship between NFL players suffering concussions while playing . . . and long-term problems such as headaches, dizziness, dementia and/or Alzheimer's disease that many retired players have experienced.[66]

Additionally, former players have also brought claims against Riddell for strict liability "for design defect, manufacturing defects, failure to warn, and negligence."[67] Shortly thereafter, other former players followed suit. By early March of 2012, 854 ex-players had filed different lawsuits, and by April that figure rose to 1,200.[68]

After the tragic suicide of Ray Easterling on April 19, 2012, Boston University discovered that he suffered from CTE.[69] By December 2012, 34 out of 35 brains of former NFL players donated to the Boston University Center for the Study of Traumatic Encephalopathy were found to have CTE.[70]

On June 7, 2012, some 80 separate concussion-related lawsuits combined to create a unified lawsuit filed in federal court in Philadelphia on behalf of over 2,000 NFL players. In the Multi-district Litigation Case No. 2323, players accused the NFL of negligence and failing to notify players of the link between concussions and brain injuries. By early September 2012, the NFL filed a motion to dismiss the concussion-related lawsuits filed by former players. The federal judge in Philadelphia instead ordered mediation between both parties, and insisted that they refrain from discussing the details of the mediation. In September 2012, The Foundation for the National Institutes of Health announced that the NFL would donate $30 million to fund research on medical conditions experienced by athletes.[71]

In August 2013, more than 4,000 former players and families suing the league over head trauma reached a settlement with the NFL that amounted to $765 million plus legal fees to be paid over 20 years.[72] The money would be used toward medical exams, concussion-related compensation and medical research. Plaintiffs included Hall of Famer Tony Dorsett, Super Bowl-winning quarterback Jim McMahon and the family of Pro Bowl linebacker Junior Seau, who committed suicide on May 2, 2012.[73] Former players diagnosed with head trauma-related illnesses are eligible for different tiers of monetary awards from the settlement. For instance, players suffering from Lou Gehrig's disease (ALS) are eligible for $5 million, estates for players who died with CTE are eligible for $4 million, players with either Alzheimer's disease or Parkinson's disease are eligible for $3.5 million, while players with neurocognitive impairment are eligible for $3 million and $1.5 million for Level 2 and Level 1, respectively.[74]

## JUDGE BRODY DENIES APPROVAL OF THE SETTLEMENT

On January 14, 2014, less than six months after the settlement, Judge Anita Brody denied approval of the settlement. According to Audibles, she denied the preliminary motion on grounds that "she was concerned with a lack of documentation regarding the fairness of the final monetary figure, and whether the players involved would be diagnosed and paid properly based on their claims."[75] Furthermore, she stated that ". . . it is difficult to see how the Monetary Award Fund would have the funds available over its lifespan to pay all claimants at these significant award levels."[76] Should Judge Brody ultimately rule that the settlement is insufficient, both sides will have to continue efforts to bridge the gap between the NFL's original offer and the players' initial demand of $2 billion.[77]

Brody's motion to deny approval presents Commissioner Goodell and his staff with a number of additional challenges. Without the framework of a settlement, the NFL now faces an unknown, but potentially much higher, level of financial liability. Commissioner Goodell remained positive, maintaining that "The No. 1 thing for us right now is to get the money in place so that we can help the players and their families if they need it, and that is our priority," and is continuing to lobby for approval of the original $765 million settlement.[78] Likewise, if a compromise cannot be reached, additional litigation may ensue, taking several more years, potentially raising the NFL's financial liability, and ensuring that the NFL faces an embarrassing discovery phase during the trial.[79,80]

## DISCUSSION QUESTIONS

1. How can the NFL improve communication with the NFLPA, team owners, players and fans to improve its response to concern regarding head trauma?
2. How should the NFL, as a non-profit representing the teams and the sport, weigh financial stability with the health of its players?
3. What can the NFL do to address issues at the high school and Pop Warner level?
4. How should Goodell, Birch and Pash approach renewed negotiations regarding the settlement? What impact might that have on public opinion?
5. How should the NFL compensate players with brain injuries resulting from football? What is their responsibility as an organization?
6. What types of rule changes and initiatives should Goodell introduce to improve player safety? What impact will that have on the integrity of the sport and its popularity?

## WRITING ASSIGNMENT

Please respond in writing to the issues presented in this case by preparing two documents: a communication strategy memo and a professional business letter.

In preparing these documents, you may assume one of two roles: you may identify yourself as an NFL senior manager who has been asked to provide advice to NFL Spokesman Greg Aiello regarding the issues he and the league are facing. Or, you may identify yourself as an external management consultant who has been asked by the league to provide advice to them.

Either way, you must prepare a strategy memo addressed to Mr. Aiello that summarizes the details of the case, identifies critical issues, discusses their implications (what they mean and why they matter), offers specific recommendations for action (assigning ownership and suspense dates for each) and shows how to communicate the solution to all who are affected by the recommendations.

You must also prepare a professional business letter for the signature of Roger S. Godell, Chief Executive Officer, National Football League. That document should be addressed either to the public as a published document, or to another group of key stakeholders, explaining what has happened, the league's position and the actions the league is taking. If you have questions about either of these documents, please consult your instructor.

## ACKNOWLEDGMENTS

This case was prepared by research assistants David Hall, Robert Meara and Joseph Nachio under the direction of James S. O'Rourke, Teaching Professor of Management, as the basis for class discussion rather than to illustrate either effective or ineffective handling of an administrative situation. Information was gathered from corporate as well as public sources.

## APPENDIX

| Term | Years | Clubs | Total Rights | Annual Rights | Broadcast ABC | CBS | NBC | FOX | Cable ESPN | TBS | Satellite DirecTV |
|---|---|---|---|---|---|---|---|---|---|---|---|
| **American Football League** | | | | | | | | | | | |
| 1960–1964 | 5.0 | 8.0 | 10.6 | 2.1 | 2.1 | – | – | – | – | – | – |
| 1965–1969 | 5.0 | 10.0 | 42.5 | 8.5 | – | – | 8.5 | – | – | – | – |
| **National Football League** | | | | | | | | | | | |
| 1960–1961 | 2.0 | 14.0 | 0.6 | 0.3 | – | 0.3 | – | – | – | – | – |
| 1962–1963 | 2.0 | 14.0 | 10.5 | 5.3 | – | 4.7 | 0.6 | – | – | – | – |
| 1964–1965 | 2.0 | 14.0 | 32 | 16 | – | 16 | – | – | – | – | – |
| 1966–1969 | 4.0 | 16.0 | 98 | 24.5 | – | 25 | – | – | – | – | – |
| 1970–1973 | 4.0 | 26.0 | 188 | 47 | 8 | 22 | 17 | – | – | – | – |
| 1974–1977 | 4.0 | 28.0 | 218 | 54.5 | 13 | 24 | 18 | – | – | – | – |
| 1978–1981 | 4.0 | 28.0 | 646 | 161.5 | 60 | 54 | 48 | – | – | – | – |
| 1982–1986 | 5 | 28 | 2,100 | 420 | 115 | 120 | 107 | – | – | – | – |
| 1987–1989 | 3 | 28 | 1,428 | 476 | 125 | 165 | 135 | – | 51 | – | – |
| 1990–1993 | 4 | 28 | 3,600 | 900 | 225 | 265 | 188 | – | 111 | 111 | – |
| 1994–1997 | 4 | 30 | 4,388 | 1,097 | 230 | – | 217 | 395 | 131 | 124 | – |
| 1998–2005 | 8 | 31 | 19,600 | 2,450 | 550 | 500 | – | 550 | 600 | – | 400 |
| 2006–2011 | 6 | 32 | 22,410 | 3,735 | – | 623 | 600 | 713 | 1,100 | – | 700 |
| 2012–2013 | 2 | 32 | 8,130 | 4,065 | – | 613 | 600 | 743 | 1,100 | – | 1,000 |
| 2014–2022 | 9 | 32 | 55,620 | 6,180 | – | 1,080 | 1,050 | 1,150 | 1,900 | – | 1,000 |

**FIGURE 3.1** The Economic Structure of the NFL

Source: Table 2.1, Vrooman, J. *The Economic Structure of the NFL*. New York: Springer.

# NOTES

1   "Line of Scrimmage: Seau's Death Clouds Goodell's Statement," *Fox News*. FOX News Network, May 3, 2012. Online at www.foxnews.com/sports/2012/05/03/line-scrimmage-seau-death-clouds-goodell-statement/. Accessed February 21, 2014.

2   Ibid.

3   Lopresti, Mike. "Is Junior Seau Death Part of Bigger Problem?" *USA Today*, May 3, 2012. Online at http://usatoday30.usatoday.com/sports/columnist/lopresti/story/2012-05-02/lopresti-junior-seau-dave-duerson/54709254/1. Accessed February 21, 2014.

4   Saffir, Douglas. "Junior Seau's Death Shows Continued Negligence from Roger Goodell, NFL," *NESN*, May 3, 2012. Online at http://nesn.com/2012/05/junior-seaus-death-shows-ongoing-negligence-from-roger-goodell-nfl/. Accessed February 21, 2014.

5   Lopresti. "Is Junior Seau Death Part of Bigger Problem?"

6   "History Release," *History of Football*. Pro Football Hall of Fame, n.d. Online at www.profootballhof.com/history/. Accessed February 25, 2014.

7   Cross, Duane. "The AFL: A Football Legacy – Merging into History," *CNNSI*, January 22, 2001. Online at http://sportsillustrated.cnn.com/football/news/2001/01/22/afl_history_2/. Accessed February 25, 2014.

8   Watson, Tom. "The Real Super Bowl Question: Should The NFL Be A Nonprofit?" *Forbes Magazine*, January 30, 2014. Online at www.forbes.com/sites/tomwatson/2014/01/30/the-real-super-bowl-question-should-the-nfl-be-a-nonprofit/. Accessed February 24, 2014.

9   Taylor, Jean-Jacques. "Roger Goodell's Authority Takes a Hit," *ESPN Internet Ventures*, December 13, 2012. Online at http://espn.go.com/dallas/nfl/story/_/id/8741639/nfl-commissioner-roger-goodell-invulnerable-authority-takes-hit-over-turned-suspensions. Accessed February 26, 2014.

10  "National Football League Company Information," *Hoovers*, n.d. Web. 21 Feb. 2014.

11  Boudway, Ira. "A Republican Senator's Lonely Mission to Make the NFL Pay Taxes," *Bloomberg Business Week*, September 19, 2013. Online at www.businessweek.com/articles/2013-09-19/a-republican-senator-s-lonely-mission-to-make-the-nfl-pay-taxes. Accessed February 21, 2014.

12  Graham, Tim. "Power Rankings: Top 10 NFL Owners." *ESPN Internet Ventures*, May 10, 2011. Online at http://espn.go.com/blog/afceast/post/_/id/28755/power-rankings-top-10-nfl-owners. Accessed February 21, 2014.

13  National Football League. *Black Book: 2012 Media Directory*. New York: National Football League, 2012.

14  Garriott, Khalil. "NFL Says Concussions, ACL Injuries Decreased this Season," *National Football League*, January 30, 2014. Online at www.nfl.com/news/story/0ap2000000320373/article/nfl-says-concussions-acl-injuries-decreased-this-season. Accessed February 20, 2014.

15  "About-Us – NFLPlayers.com," *NFLPA*, n.d. Online at www.nflplayers.com/about-us/. Accessed February 25, 2014.

16  Breer, Albert. "NFLPA Could Challenge Commissioner Roger Goodell's Power," *National Football League*, January 31, 2013. Online at www.nfl.com/news/story/0ap1000000133566/article/nflpa-could-challenge-commissioner-roger-goodells-power. Accessed February 21, 2014.

17  Mortensen, Chris. "NFLPA Wants Concussion Experts," *ESPN Internet Ventures*, November 13, 2012. Online at http://espn.go.com/nfl/story/_/id/8626328/nfl-players-association-wants-concussion-specialists. Accessed February 21, 2014.

18  Florio, Mike. "Absence of NFLPA Looms over Concussion Lawsuits." *ProFootballTalk, NBC Sports*, May 13, 2012. Online at http://profootballtalk.nbcsports.com/2012/05/13/absence-of-nflpa-looms-over-concussion-lawsuits/. Accessed February 21, 2014.

19  Schwarz, Alan. "N.F.L. Acknowledges Long-Term Concussion Effects," *The New York Times*, December 20, 2009. Online at www.nytimes.com/2009/12/21/sports/football/21concussions.html?pagewanted=all&_r=0.

20  Vevea, Becky. "Bears Fans React to Debate over Concussions," *WBEZ 91.5 Chicago*, October 11, 2013. Online at www.wbez.org/news/bears-fans-react-debate-over-concussions-108905. Accessed February 25, 2014.

21  Quinones, Todd. "Former Players, Fans Weigh In on NFL Concussion Lawsuit Settlement," *CBS Philly*, August 29, 2013. Online at http://philadelphia.cbslocal.com/2013/08/29/former-players-fans-weigh-in-on-nfl-concussion-lawsuit-settlement/. Accessed February 25, 2014.

22  Sherman, Richard. "We Chose This Profession," MMQB In This Corner with Peter King, March 9, 2014. Online at http://mmqb.si.com/2013/10/23/richard-sherman-seahawks-concussions-in-the-nfl/.

23  Brown, Scott. "NFLN Survey/Player Safety: Steelers." *ESPN Internet Ventures*, January 27, 2014. Online at http://espn.go.com/blog/pittsburgh-steelers/post/_/id/4478/nfln-surveyplayer-safety-steelers. Accessed February 25, 2014.

24  "NFL Brain-Injury Panel a 'Sham,' Former Players Say," *CBSNews*, April 9, 2013. Online at www.cbsnews.com/news/nfl-brain-injury-panel-a-sham-former-players-say/. Accessed February 25, 2014.

25  "Reaction to Concussions by Goodell, NFL Featured in *Time* Cover Story," *SportsBusiness Daily*. Street & Smiths, December 6, 2012. Online at http://m.sportsbusinessdaily.com/Daily/Issues/2012/12/06/Leagues-and-Governing-Bodies/Goodell-NFL.aspx. Accessed February 25, 2014.

26  "Source: Both Parties in NFL Concussion Suit Could Have Been Hurt by Proceeding to Trial," *SportsBusiness Daily*. Street & Smiths, September 4, 2013. Online at www.sportsbusinessdaily.com/Daily/Issues/2013/09/04/Leagues-and-Governing-Bodies/NFL-Concussions.aspx. Accessed February 25, 2014.

27  Hanzus, Dan. "Robert Kraft's Take on NFL Concussion Suit Settlement," *National Football League*, August 29, 2013. Online at www.nfl.com/news/story/0ap1000000235715/article/robert-krafts-take-on-nfl-concussion-suit-settlement. Accessed February 25, 2014.

28  Florio, Mike. "Absence of NFLPA Looms over Concussion Lawsuits," *ProFootballTalk*. NBC Sports, May 13, 2012. Online at http://profootballtalk.nbcsports.com/2012/05/13/absence-of-nflpa-looms-over-concussion-lawsuits/. Accessed February 25, 2014.

29  Ezell, Lauren. "Timeline: The NFL's Concussion Crisis," *PBS*, October 8, 2013. Online at www.pbs.org/wgbh/pages/frontline/sports/league-of-denial/timeline-the-nfls-concussion-crisis/. Accessed February 21, 2014.

30  Jenkins, Sally, Rick Maese and Scott Clement. "Do No Harm: Retired NFL Players Endure a Lifetime of Hurt," *The Washington Post*, May 16, 2013. Online at www.washingtonpost.com/sf/feature/wp/2013/05/16/do-no-harm-retired-nfl-players-endure-a-lifetime-of-hurt. Accessed February 21, 2014.

31  Saal, J. A. "Common American Football Injuries," *Sports Medicine* (Daly City, California: San Francisco Spine Institute at Seton Medical Center), August 12, 1991, 2: 132–147. PMID 1947533.

32  Prettyman, Kaitlin. "Chronic Traumatic Encephalopathy (CTE) Can Be a Consequence of a Football Career," *Deseret News*, May 3, 2011. Online at www.deseretnews.com/article/700132298/Chronic-traumatic-encephalopathy-CTE-can-be-a-consequence-of-a-football-career.html?pg=all. Accessed February 21, 2014.

33  "What Is ALS and How Does It Affect the Body?" *PBS*, April 3, 2007. Online at www.pbs.org/wgbh/pages/frontline/somuchsofast/etc/faqs.html. Accessed February 20, 2014.

34  Andrews, Wilson, Bonnie Berkowitz and Alberto Cuadra. "NFL Injuries: Where Does It Hurt?" *The Washington Post*, May 17, 2013. Online at www.washingtonpost.com/wp-srv/special/sports/nfl-injuries/. Accessed February 21, 2014.

35  "NFL Injuries Increasing," *The Washington Post*, April 13, 2013. Online at www.washingtonpost.com/sports/nfl-injuries-increasing/2013/03/16/8d14a18e-8eac-11e2-b63f-f53fb9f2fcb4_graphic.html. Accessed February 21, 2014.

36  "2011 Concussion Report – End of Regular Season," *The Concussion Blog*, January 10, 2011. Online at http://theconcussionblog.com/2012/01/10/2011-concussion-report-end-of-regular-season/. Accessed February 21, 2014.

37  Saffir, Douglas. "Junior Seau's Death Shows Continued Negligence from Roger Goodell, NFL," *NESN*, May 3, 2012. Online at http://nesn.com/2012/05/junior-seaus-death-shows-ongoing-negligence-from-roger-goodell-nfl/. Accessed February 21, 2014.

38  "NFL Injuries Increasing," *The Washington Post*, April 13, 2013. Online at www.washingtonpost.com/sports/nfl-injuries-increasing/2013/03/16/8d14a18e-8eac-11e2-b63f-f53fb9f2fcb4_graphic.html. Accessed February 21, 2014.

39  Knoblauch, Max. "NFL Players Had More than 1,300 Injuries This Season," *Mashable*, February 1, 2014. Online at http://mashable.com/2014/02/01/nfl-injuries-infographic/. Accessed February 27, 2014.

40  "Increase in Football-Related Injuries Among Youth Found in New U.S. Study," *ScienceDaily*, April 12, 2011. Online at www.sciencedaily.com/releases/2011/04/110412065807.htm. Accessed February 21, 2014.

41  Smith, Corbett. "Special Report: Some Texas Schools Fail to Provide Catastrophic Care for Injuries (Part 1)," *The Dallas Morning News*, November 9, 2013. Online at www.dallasnews.com/sports/high-schools/headlines/20131109-catastrophic-insurace-part-1-cost-for-care-can-be-staggering-not-all-student-athletes-covered-for-catastrophic-injuries.ece. Accessed February 21, 2014.

42  Boden, B. P., I. Breit, J. A. Beachler, A. Williams and F. O. Mueller. "Fatalities in High School and College Football Players," *The American Journal of Sports Medicine* 41.5 (2013): 1108–1116. Online at www.ncbi.nlm.nih.gov/pubmed/23477766.

43  Vrooman, John. "Chapter 2," in *The Economic Structure of the NFL*. New York: Springer, pp. 7–31.

44  Ibid.

45  Crupi, Anthony. "The NFL Hammers Out Nine-Year Rights Renewals with NBC, CBS, Fox | Adweek," *AdWeek*, December 14, 2011. Online at www.adweek.com/news/television/nfl-hammers-out-nine-year-rights-renewals-nbc-cbs-fox-137128. Accessed February 27, 2014.

46  "Pop Warner Issues New Safety Regulations," *Nightly News*, NBC, June 12, 2012. Online at www.nbcnews.com/video/nightly-news/47789555#47789555. Accessed February 21, 2014.

47  "Pop Warner News: Rule Changes Regarding Practice & Concussion Prevention," *Pop Warner National Office*, June 13, 2012. Online at www.popwarner.com/About_Us/Pop_Warner_News/Rule_Changes_Regarding_Practice___Concussion_Prevention_s1_p3977.htm. Accessed February 21, 2014.

48  Fainaru, Steve and Mark Fainaru-Wada. "Youth Football Participation Drops," *ESPN OutsideTheLines*, ESPN Internet Ventures, November 14, 2013. Online at http://espn.go.com/espn/otl/story/_/page/popwarner/pop-warner-youth-football-participation-drops-nfl-concussion-crisis-seen-causal-factor?src=mobile. Accessed February 26, 2014.

49  Hill, Jemele. "Injuries Warn Against 18 NFL Games," *ESPN Commentary*, ESPN.com, October 18, 2010. Online at http://sports.espn.go.com/espn/commentary/news/story?id=5700242. Accessed February 15, 2014.

50   Clayton, John. "Pump the Brakes on 18-Game Season," *ESPN*, ESPN Internet Ventures, September 25, 2013. Online at http://espn.go.com/nfl/story/_/id/9721935/nfl-injuries-complicate-18-game-proposal-john-clayton-mailbag. Accessed February 22, 2014.

51   Michael, Patrick. "New NFL 18-Game Season Rumor a Nightmare for New Orleans Saints Fans," *Yahoo Sports*, September 29, 2013. Online at http://sports.yahoo.com/news/nfl-18-game-season-rumor-nightmare-orleans-saints-221200402—nfl.html. Accessed February 15, 2014.

52   Berkes, Peter. "NFL Announces Rule Changes for 2013 Season – SBNation.com," *SBNation.com*, August 8, 2013. Online at www.sbnation.com/nfl/2013/8/8/4594316/nfl-rule-changes-2013. Accessed February 18, 2014.

53   "New NFL Rules Designed to Limit Head Injuries," *NFL.com*, August 6, 2010. Online at www.nfl.com/news/story/09000d5d81990bdf/article/new-nfl-rules-designed-to-limit-head-injuries. Accessed February 26, 2014.

54   "NFL Will Consider Ending Kickoffs," *ESPN*, ESPN Internet Ventures, December 6, 2012. Online at http://espn.go.com/nfl/story/_/id/8720551/roger-goodell-says-nfl-competition-committee-consider-eliminating-kickoffs. Accessed February 18, 2014.

55   Mihoces, Gary. "More Padding the Issue of Concussions and Better Helmets," *USA Today*, Gannett, August 23, 2013. Online at www.usatoday.com/story/sports/ncaaf/2013/07/30/concussions-college-football-nfl-guardian-caps/2601063/. Accessed February 19, 2014.

56   "Meriweather: You Gotta Go Low, Tear ACLs and End Careers," *CBS DC.*, October 28, 2013. Online at http://washington.cbslocal.com/2013/10/28/meriweather-you-gotta-go-low-and-end-careers/. Accessed February 27, 2014.

57   NFL. Head, Neck, and Spine Committee. *NFL Head, Neck and Spine Committee's Protocols Regarding Diagnosis and Management of Concussion.* N.p.: n.p., n.d.

58   Walters, Chad. "Mark Graban's Blog about Lean in Hospitals, Business, and Our World," *Lean Blog Standardized Work Why Are NFL Concussion Guidelines Not Always Followed Comments*, n.p., January 11, 2014. Online at www.leanblog.org/2014/01/standardized-work-why-are-nfl-concussion-guidelines-not-always-followed/. Accessed February 27, 2014.

59   Farrar, Doug. "NFL Could Fine Players for Violating Concussion Protocol," *Audibles SIcom RSS*, January 16, 2014. Online at http://nfl.si.com/2014/01/16/nfl-concussion-protocol/. Accessed February 27, 2014.

60   Guskiewicz, Kevin M., Michael McCrea, Stephen W. Marshall, et al. "Cumulative Effects Associated with Recurrent Concussion in Collegiate Football Players: The NCAA Concussion Study," *Journal of the American Medical Association*, 290.19 (2003): 2549–2555. Online at http://jama.ama-assn.org/cgi/content/full/290/19/2549.

61   Pellman, E. J., J. W. Powell, D. C. Viano, I. R. Casson, A. M. Tucker, H. Feuer, M. Lovell, J. F. Waeckerle, and D. W. Robertson. "Concussion in Professional Football: Epidemiological features of game injuries and review of the literature," Part 3. *Neurosurgery*. 2004, January. 54 (1): 81–94. Discussion, 94–96. Online at www.ncbi.nlm.nih.gov/pubmed/14683544. Accessed December 7, 2018.

62   Ezell, Lauren. "Timeline: The NFL's Concussion Crisis," *Frontline*, October 8, 2013.

63   Ibid.

64   Ezell, Lauren. "Timeline: The NFL's Concussion Crisis," *PBS*, October 8, 2013. Online at www.pbs.org/wgbh/pages/frontline/sports/league-of-denial/timeline-the-nfls-concussion-crisis/. Accessed February 22, 2014.

65   Schwarz, Alan. "N.F.L. Overhauls Concussion Committee," *The New York Times*, March 16, 2010. Available through Lexis Nexis Academic. Accessed February 27, 2014.

66   Farrar, Doug. "Ray Easterling, Lead Plaintiff in NFL Concussion Lawsuit, Commits Suicide," Shutdown Corner, *Yahoo Sports*, April 21, 2012. Online at http://sports.yahoo.com/blogs/nfl-shutdown-corner/ray-easterling-lead-plaintiff-nfl-concussion-lawsuits-commits-025009388.html. Accessed February 27, 2014.

67   Amended Master Complaint at 77–81, In Re National Football League Players' Concussion Injury Litigation, No. 2:12-md-02323-AB (E.D. PA 2012) (MDL No. 2323). "Helmet to Helmet: Riddell's Role in the NFL's Concussion Litigation." Online at http://nflconcussionlitigation.com/wp-content/uploads/2012/08/Helmet-to-Helmet-copy.pdf.

68   Farrar, Doug. "Mark Rypien, 14 Other Former Redskins Added to Enormous List of Concussion Plaintiffs," Shutdown Corner. *Yahoo Sports*, March 27, 2012. Online at http://sports.yahoo.com/blogs/nfl-shutdown-corner/mark-rypien-14-other-former-redskins-added-enormous-224221572.html. Accessed February 27, 2014. See also Lisk, Jason. "Breaking Down the NFL Head Injury Litigation Situation," thebiglead, *USA Today Sports*, April 16, 2012. Online at http://thebiglead.com/2012/04/16/breaking-down-the-nfl-head-injury-litigation-situation/.

69   Ezell, Lauren. "Timeline: The NFL's Concussion Crisis," *PBS*, October 8, 2013. Online at www.pbs.org/wgbh/pages/frontline/sports/league-of-denial/timeline-the-nfls-concussion-crisis/. Accessed February 22, 2014.

70   Lupkin, Sydney. "CTE, a Degenerative Brain Disease, Found in 34 Pro Football Players," *abcNEWS*, December 3, 2012. Online at http://abcnews.go.com/Health/cte-degenerative-brain-disease-found-34-pro-football/story?id=17869457. Accessed February 27, 2014.

71   CNN Library. "NFL Concussions Fast Facts," *CNN*, January 14, 2014. Online at www.cnn.com/2013/08/30/us/nfl-concussions-fast-facts/. Accessed February 26, 2014.

72   Farrar, Doug. "Report: Ex-NFL Players Wanted $2 billion in Concussion Lawsuit Settlement," *Audibles SIcom RSS*, September 1, 2013. Online at http://nfl.si.com/2013/09/01/report-former-players-wanted-2-billion-in-concussion-settlements-nfl-offered-a-pittance-in-return/. Accessed February 27, 2014.

73   Associated Press, as cited in "NFL, Ex-Players Agree to $765M Settlement in Concussions Suit," *NFL.com*, August 29, 2013. Online at www.nfl.com/news/story/0ap1000000235494/article/nfl-explayers-agree-to-765m-settlement-in-concussions-suit. Accessed February 25, 2014.

74   Farrar, Doug. "Judge Anita Brody Denies Preliminary Approval for NFL Concussion Settlement," *Audibles SIcom RSS*. NFL SI, January 14, 2014. Online at http://nfl.si.com/2014/01/14/nfl-concussion-lawsuit-settlement-2/. Accessed February 27, 2014.

75   Ibid.

76   Judge Brody, Anita B. "In Re: National Football League Players' Concussion Injury Litigation," MDL No. 2323; 12-md-2323. Denial of Preliminary Approval of NFL Concussion Settlement. U.S. District Court for Eastern District of Pennsylvania. January 14, 2014. Online at www.scribd.com/doc/199648447/Denial-of-Preliminary-Approval-of-NFL-Concussion-Settlement.

77   Farrar. "Judge Anita Brody Denies Preliminary Approval."

78   Klein, Gary and Sam Farmer. "Roger Goodell Says NFL Is Trying to Get Approval for Settlement," *Los Angeles Times*, January 31, 2014. Online at http://articles.latimes.com/2014/jan/31/sports/la-sp-super-bowl-notes-20140201. Accessed February 21, 2014.

79   McCann, Michael. "What Rejection of Settlement Means to Concussion Case Against NFL," SI.com, *Sports Illustrated*, February 14, 2014. Online at http://sportsillustrated.cnn.com/nfl/news/20140114/judge-rejects-proposed-nfl-concussion-settlement/. Accessed February 21, 2014.

80   Breslow, James M. "Judge Rejects $765 Million NFL Concussion Settlement," *PBS*, January 14, 2014. Online at www.pbs.org/wgbh/pages/frontline/sports/league-of-denial/judge-rejects-765-million-nfl-concussion-settlement/. Accessed February 19, 2014.

# Case 3.3: Target Corporation

## Predictive Analytics and Customer Privacy

### THE STORY

An enraged father walks into a Target store outside of Minneapolis, demanding to see the manager. In his hand, he has coupons for baby clothes and cribs. When the manager approaches him, the man angrily explains that his teenage daughter received the coupons. He then lectures the manager on how wrong it is that Target is encouraging his daughter to become pregnant by sending her the advertisements. The manager immediately apologizes and takes a look at the mail. He finds that the father's claims are true. His daughter had received Target advertisements exclusively for baby products.

The manager called the father a few days later to apologize again. Before he can apologize, however, he receives an apology. The previously irate father says, "It turns out there's been some activities in my house I haven't been completely aware of. She's due in August. I owe you an apology."[1]

### PREDICTIVE ANALYTICS

Predictive analytics, also referred to as analytics, big data, business intelligence, data science and data mining,[2] has infiltrated and shaped many facets of contemporary life. Experiences such as driving, shopping, studying, voting, watching TV and seeing the doctor have been affected by predictive technology.[3] Major corporations began using predictive analytics as early as the mid-1990s, when Chase Bank made transactional decisions in its mortgage portfolio using predictive technology developed by Dan Steinberg.[4]

The current state of predictive analytics is a derivation of basic machine learning, the trial and error process by which computers generate new knowledge and capabilities "by furiously feeding on modern society's greatest and most potent *unnatural* resource: data."[5] In the words of European Consumer Commissioner Meglena Kuneva, "Data is the new oil."[6]

An estimated 2.5 quintillion bytes of data are encoded and warehoused from decisions ranging from consumer transactions, medical procedures and Facebook posts every day.[7] The machine learning process begins with encoding data about things that have already happened, and then attempting to uncover the patterns that either caused or explain the outcome.[8] Predictive analytics is "technology that learns from experience (data) to predict the future behavior of individuals in order to drive better decisions."[9] Predictive analytics is used to create a predictive model, the actual mechanism that predicts individual behavior.[10]

Predictive analytics is different from forecasting. Forecasting makes predictions on a macroscopic level focusing on aggregate behaviors, while predictive technology delivers insights about individual behavior.[11] Traditionally, analytics was used to evaluate past decisions and events to determine what went right or wrong without direct bearing on future decision making.[12] Predictive analytics is different in that it is used to determine the probable outcome of future events to guide current decisions.[13] The core element of predictive analytics is the selection of the predictor, the variable that is measured to predict future outcomes.[14] Selecting multiple predictors leads to the creation of a predictive model.[15] Such models are revised and adjusted as new data becomes available. The selection of multiple predictive variables and the formation of a model allows analysts to predict what, when and how to perform an action for optimal probable results.

Another distinction between predictive analytics and other analytical business methods is the method of input. Using traditional business insight tools, analysts first make assumptions, and then test to verify the accuracy of those assumptions based on statistical patterns. In contrast, predictive analytics looks for previously unknown patterns in seemingly disparate information to deliver something more useful than assumptions: predictions.[16] Another important aspect of predictive analytics is the distinction between data mining and data extraction. Data extraction is the process of pulling data from one database and placing it into another.[17] By contrast, data mining actually pulls out hidden predictive information from a database, and is also referred to as knowledge-discovery.[18] Among the major players in the production of predictive analytics technology are SAS, SPSS Inc and IBM. SPSS was founded in 1968 and began by developing programs for statistical analysis in social sciences. Over time, SPSS has transformed into one of the leaders in the emergence of predictive analytics as part of business intelligence software packages.[19] More recently, the big innovation in predictive technology is its application to consumer behavior. Dunnhumby Ltd, based in the U.K., and its partnership with Kroger in the U.S., called dunnhumbyUSA, revolutionized retail membership rewards programs with the development of hyper-individualized marketing capabilities, driven by predictive analytics, for Kroger and other "customer focused" companies in 2003.[20]

One distinction between Kroger's use of the methods created by dunnhumbyUSA and other retailers is the open advertisement of the individualized rewards program. Kroger explicitly advertises the advantage on its promotions website with this directive to customers: "Be sure to use your Shopper's Card every time you shop to become eligible for special personalized coupons based on your favorite items!"[21] However, Kroger does not reveal the details of the methods they use to process consumer data. One of the applications of this technology is the implementation of individualized pricing, allowing retailers like Kroger to reward loyalty through lower prices to individuals who consistently purchase a specific brand of product. On the flip side, this same technology can be used to employ price discrimination based on individual customer loyalty, allowing retailers to charge higher than average prices when it appears that price is not a factor in an individual's choice of brand.[22] On the other end of the consumer information and consumer privacy spectrum are organizations such as the Electronic Privacy Information Center (EPIC) and Consumers Against Supermarket Privacy Invasion (CASPIAN). These and similar organizations actively fight against the exploitation of consumer data and personally identifiable information for commercial purposes and the methods by which such data is collected. EPIC is a public interest research center established "to focus public attention on emerging civil liberties issues and to protect privacy, the First amendment, and constitutional values."[23] Privacy and consumer profiling are among the issues addressed by EPIC. On its website, EPIC offers information about the methods that businesses use to collect, analyze and trade personal data, and offers advice and direction on how to protect your privacy.[24] Similarly, CASPIAN acts as a defender for individual rights to privacy, but focuses specifically on supermarkets. Its website also offers advice on defending one's privacy and encourages collective action to remove programs such as membership rewards cards from supermarkets. CASPIAN also highlights the success of supermarkets that do not employ loyalty cards and the success of activists in convincing supermarkets to voluntarily drop their rewards programs.[25]

## HABIT FORMATION

As a field of research, the science of habit formation has grown substantially over the past two decades. Understanding the role of habits in daily life carries enormous medical potential in treating anxiety, depression and addictions. It also holds the promise of financial gains for companies that are able to capitalize on this "golden age" of behavioral research. A shrewd understanding of the core behavioral elements underlying habit formation is essential if companies are to benefit from the large pool of consumer behavioral data available to them.[26] The habit formation process may be described as a three-step loop: cue, routine and reward. The cue tells the brain to go on autopilot. It is an indication that the required behavior for that specific scenario has been performed many times before, and that the individual need not devote any extra brainpower to processing the situation. The routine is the actual physical, mental or emotional action or behavior. One example is the process of a driver backing a car out of a driveway. At first, there are many sensory inputs and a complicated series of necessary actions that require a great amount of mental concentration. But as the behavior is repeated over time and becomes routine, the driver does not need to concentrate as hard because the brain has "chunked" large portions of the routine together, permitting the brain to focus on other matters. The reward indicates to the brain whether or not this particular routine is worth remembering in the future. Cues can be obvious, like the sugar rush from a doughnut, or more subtle, like the barely perceptible sense of relief issued after successfully backing out of a driveway.[27]

Habits can be changed, but not very easily. In most cases, to change a habit, an individual has to deliberately, consciously fight an existing habit. This requires replacing old cues and rewards with new ones. But habits are never completely extinguished. Introducing the old cue could lead to an immediate re-emergence of the old habit. For retailers and other businesses looking to exploit human behavioral tendencies, understanding habits may enable them to control habits in their customers.[28]

There is a small set of circumstances during which habits are more susceptible to change. These circumstances usually occur as a result of major life changes, such as marriage, pregnancy, childbirth, divorce, starting or leaving a job, entering or graduating from school, and moving. During these periods of vulnerability, many of the usual cues and rewards that surrounded a person are no longer available or visible. In the case of pregnancy and childbirth, expectant mothers and couples begin shopping for completely new categories of merchandise which may or may not be found at the retailers they are accustomed to visiting. This sudden change in environmental circumstances, coupled with psychological and emotional changes, causes these individuals to be more open to different cues and rewards offered by retailers. As expectant parents begin to stock up on unscented laundry detergent, diapers and other baby essentials, retailers like Target bait such customers with coupons and special deals for unscented laundry detergent, diapers and other baby essentials.

The motive for Target is that while the expectant parents are in the store to buy new and unusual items, they also purchase products that had previously been purchased at competing retailers. In this case, the cue is the baby-related coupon, the routine is to purchase baby-related and non-baby-related items simultaneously at Target, and the reward is the satisfaction of obtaining all of their merchandise at one store: Target. The process of generating a "pregnancy prediction" score to identify prospective parents so that Target can focus their marketing efforts relies on predictive analytics.[29]

## PRIVACY CONCERNS

There are many issues to consider regarding the infringement on individual rights to privacy and predictive analytics. One concern is the ability for a company to predict with tremendous accuracy the occurrence of a significant life change before the individual's family, or even the individual, may be aware of it. While some customers may appreciate the extra savings, what is the motive of the retailer and what happens when the prediction is wrong? The anecdote regarding the father who stormed into his local Target store illuminates the undesired repercussions when major corporations reveal personal truths instead of a family member. In that case, the information turned out to be accurate. But what happens if the once true personal circumstances change before the retailer catches on? "What if a woman miscarries in the first trimester only to receive coupons for baby products in the mail? Will Target know to stop sending coupons, or will it continue to market to her through her probable due date?"[30]

In addition to the use of customer data to enhance a company's own bottom line, some privacy policies include language which authorizes a companies such as Target to sell the data and its associated predictions to other companies.[31] Such practices are not unlawful for retailers, as they are not legally limited in sharing the information they collect. Such information is especially potent, because individual consumption habits are directly linked to personally identifiable information.[32] Many retailers require customers to show state-issued identification upon enrolling in store membership or loyalty rewards clubs.[33] Companies in various sectors of the economy, from credit institutions, to retailers, to healthcare providers purchase data culled from the other sectors to bolster their own analytical models. Overlaying these diverse sets of data provides companies the opportunity to create better profiles of individuals' lifestyle behaviors.[34]

## CONSUMER PRIVACY BILL OF RIGHTS

In addition to the moral and business considerations of employing potentially invasive tactics using predictive analytics, companies must operate within legal parameters. Are the methods of data extraction and analysis employed by Target legal? The answer is yes.[35] However, as consumers are becoming increasingly aware of how their private data are being used by corporations, advocacy groups and the White House have stepped forward to defend the privacy rights of individuals. On February 23, 2012, the White House released its proposal for a Consumer Privacy Bill of Rights, just four days after Charles Duhigg's *New York Times* article sent a shockwave through the media detailing the extent of private information available to businesses. In his introductory letter to the proposal, President Barack Obama connected America's affection for privacy to the foundation of the republic, citing protections against unlawful intrusion into the home and the invasion of the privacy of mails. He emphasized that as new forms of communication technology were developed, Congress applied extended privacy protections because "Citizens who feel protected from misuse of personal information feel free to engage in commerce, to participate in the political process, or to seek needed health care." He also characterized the need for privacy as essential to the heart of American democracy.[36] According to the Foreword of the proposal, there is already a strong framework of consumer data privacy protection but it lacks a clear statement of privacy principles and a commitment from all stakeholders. While the Consumer Privacy Bill of Rights was a starting point and not legally binding, the White House encouraged Congress to pass legislation applying the Consumer Privacy Bill of Rights to commercial sectors that are currently exempt from Federal data privacy laws.[37] The following excerpt summarizes the provisions of the Consumer Privacy Bill of Rights:

### *A Consumer Privacy Bill of Rights*[38]

This document sets forth a Consumer Privacy Bill of Rights that, in the Administration's view, provides a baseline of clear protections for consumers and greater certainty for companies. The Administration will encourage stakeholders to implement the Consumer Privacy Bill of Rights through codes of conduct and will work with Congress to enact these rights through legislation. The Consumer Privacy Bill of Rights applies comprehensive, globally recognized Fair Information Practice Principles (FIPPs) to the interactive and highly interconnected environment in which we live and work today. Specifically, it provides for:

Individual Control: Consumers have a right to exercise control over what personal data companies collect from them and how they use it.

Transparency: Consumers have a right to easily understandable and accessible information about privacy and security practices.

Respect for Context: Consumers have a right to expect that companies will collect, use and disclose personal data in ways that are consistent with the context in which consumers provide the data.

Security: Consumers have a right to secure and responsible handling of personal data.

Access and Accuracy: Consumers have a right to access and correct personal data in usable formats, in a manner that is appropriate to the sensitivity of the data and the risk of adverse consequences to consumers if the data is inaccurate.

Focused Collection: Consumers have a right to reasonable limits on the personal data that companies collect and retain.

Accountability: Consumers have a right to have personal data handled by companies with appropriate measures in place to assure they adhere to the Consumer Privacy Bill of Rights.

# TARGET CORPORATION

George D. Dayton, a banker and real estate investor, formed the Dayton Dry Goods Company – today known as Target Corporation – in 1902 in Minneapolis, Minnesota. The Dayton Dry Goods Company grew from being the fourth largest retailer in Minneapolis to a regional department store company to a national retailer, giving its Initial Public Offering on October 18, 1967.[39] Target Corporation is now the nation's #2 discount chain (behind Wal-Mart). The company operates about 1,765 Target and SuperTarget stores in 49 states, as well as an online business at target.com. Target and its larger grocery-carrying incarnation, SuperTarget, offer more upscale, trend-driven merchandise than rivals Wal-Mart and Kmart. Target also distributes a proprietary Target credit card, good only at Target.[40] In 2011, Target Corporation generated $69.87 billion in total revenues, $68.5 billion coming directly from its retail sales. The company's sales mix during this period was composed of household essentials (25 percent), hardlines (19 percent), apparel and accessories (19 percent), food and pet supplies (19 percent), and home furnishings and décor (18 percent).[41] The company employed 365,000 full-time, part-time and seasonal employees in 2011. During its peak sales period from Thanksgiving to the end of December, employment levels peaked to about 414,000 employees.[42]

# TARGET'S PRIVACY POLICIES

Target Corporation's website, target.com, has a section devoted to its privacy policies. If a customer goes to the website and scrolls down to the end of the page, she will see a small gray link titled "privacy policy." Upon entering this section of the website, the customer can see what information about her is collected, and how this information is collected, used, shared and protected. She is also given the opportunity to opt out of certain Target services. For example, she can opt out of receiving promotional postal mail, e-mail and phone calls. She also receives instructions about how she can request that Target not share her information with other companies, how she can disable Target and third-party cookies, and how to opt out of receiving enhanced marketing and analytics in connection with her use of in-store WiFi services. Target also promises that it will not knowingly disclose information about children aged 13 years or younger, and that if a child of that age has provided Target with personally identifiable information, they provide instructions for the parent or guardian to contact Target.[43]

# ANDREW POLE AND TARGET

Andrew Pole was hired as a statistician for Target in 2002. He worked as part of Target's Guest Marketing Analytics Department. His job was to efficiently gather data and to link that data to customers. This meant that he had to create algorithms that would identify customer trends and habits using predictive analytics. Predictive analytics is Pole's area of specialty, as he holds a master's degree in both statistics and economics.[44]

At Target he was tasked with identifying pregnant women by their shopping habits. Most large retailers, including Target, get their information on birth dates from public records that are available only through birth certificates. Retailers use this information to send advertisements and coupons for baby-related products to families. If Target is able to determine the due dates of pregnant women before other retailers, it would have a significant competitive advantage. Pole embarked on this task with his team of analysts, using a sample of women whom he knew to be pregnant and tracked their habits through their use of baby registries. The team managed to identify 25 products that were bought more frequently and in greater quantities when women were pregnant. Their conclusions led to what Target calls the Pregnancy Prediction Score, which identifies, with 87 percent accuracy, whether women are pregnant or not. The analytics can also tell what the due date is within a short period.[45]

# GUEST ID SYSTEMS

Like many retailers, Target employs a data collection system tied to a Guest ID unique to each shopper. Every purchase is recorded each time a consumer uses his or her credit or debit card, visits the store website or interacts with the company in other ways.[46] The information extracted from these transactions is then sorted and warehoused for use by analysts. In conjunction with behavioral experts, the analysts use the data to classify the consumer according to buying patterns which serve as predictors of future purchase behavior.[47] Abrupt changes in spending habits and buying choices for a shopper may indicate that the individual just went through a major life disruption, which makes them especially vulnerable to targeted marketing by retailers to form the customer's new buying habits.[48] In addition to identifying potential target consumers, companies also benefit by removing non-responders from their marketing efforts, cutting costs and conserving resources.[49]

## DATA COLLECTION

Target has a somewhat fixed customer base, and works on creative ways to expand its market share. In the large retailer space, once people find "their store" it is hard to change their loyalty. Retailers understand this phenomenon, and Target has identified the segments which are most likely to change their shopping habits. People who are most vulnerable to giving up their loyalty are those who experience a major event in their lives. Examples of those events include, but are not limited to, pregnancy, graduating from college, moving, new job or divorce. Using predictive analytics, Target can identify those people by the data they collect on them.

Target assigns a Guest ID number to as many customers as possible.[50] All the information collected on a customer is linked to their Guest ID. Target records every time a customer uses a credit card or a coupon, fills out a survey, mails in a refund, calls customer service, opens an e-mail from them or visits their website. They also buy demographic information on their customers such as age, marital status, the area in which a customer lives, salary, credit cards, education and preferred brands. The information collected builds a profile for each customer, and through the algorithms produced by the analytics team, the needs of the customers are identified.

## RESPONSES

The Target story broke on February 16, 2012 by Charles Duhigg in the *New York Times*. The article, entitled "How Companies Learn Your Secrets"[51] focused heavily on analytics and its uses by Target. However, the story about the pregnant girl was the main focus of many other media outlets. *Forbes*, for example, titled their article, "How Target Figured Out a Teen Girl Was Pregnant Before Her Father Did."[52] Extensive public outrage followed the *New York Times* article, which is to be expected, as Target's methods seem invasive to many people, especially because those being studied are not aware of it. The blogosphere was active in distributing the pregnancy story, capitalizing on the paranoia felt by blog readers and commenters. The public is uncomfortable with the fact that large corporations are able to collect vast amounts of data on people. At the same time people are not aware of the extent of information corporations have on them. An example of a blog post article is, "Is There a Target on Your Back?"[53] In popular media, Stephen Colbert dedicated his "The Word" segment to add a comedic spin to the Target story. The segment subtitle was "Surrender to a Buyer Power." Colbert managed to summarize the *New York Times* articles and spiced it with some humor.

Target Corporation first declined to respond to inquiries from the *New York Times* reporter.[54] Instead, they issued a statement: "We've developed a number of research tools that allow us to gain insights into trends and preferences within different demographic segments of our guest population."[55] They also confirmed that Target "is in compliance with all federal and state laws, including those related to protected health information."[56] It is clear how important predictive analytics is to the company. Target decided to change how they sent their advertisements and targeted their customers following negative feedback from customers who complained that the ads they received were invasive. Thereafter, the company began mixing its baby-related advertisements with random and irrelevant products such as lawnmowers and wineglasses to divert their customers' attention from Target's very specific knowledge of them.

## DISCUSSION QUESTIONS

1. As the communications director for the company, what course of action would you take after you hear of the enraged father visiting one of Target's stores?
2. At the time of the incident, headlines about Target, consumer privacy, predictive analytics and teen pregnancy were not yet racing through media outlets. But, such a sensational story is ripe for media attention. What will

happen if a major, trusted news outlet learns about the incident and publicizes trade secrets? Will the company itself become a target for media and consumer backlash?

3. How much do consumers actually know and understand about how their data is used by Target? Is knowledge power for Target's customers, or is it better that they remain unaware?

4. How much should store-level employees know and understand about Target's data collection policies?

5. How much should a company reveal about its data collection practices to the public? Would disclosure neutralize Target's competitive advantage?

6. Should warning labels or informative signage be displayed at the point of purchase to warn/educate customers about the ramifications of using rewards/member cards programs and credit/debit cards?

7. The decision point in this case occurs just after the pregnant teenager incident. As the communications director for Target, how would you respond after the *New York Times* article was published?

8. Given the financial potential from using data mining and predictive analytics, should Target fight against legislation that would limit the use of such data?

## WRITING ASSIGNMENT

Please respond in writing to the issues presented in this case by preparing two documents: a communication strategy memo and a professional business letter.

In preparing these documents, you may assume one of two roles: you may identify yourself as an external communication consultant who has been asked to provide advice to Ms. Susan Kahn, Senior Vice President, Communications and Reputation Management, or you may identify yourself as a communication manager within Target Corporation headquarters. Either way, you must prepare a strategy memo addressed to Ms. Kahn.

You must also prepare a professional business letter for the signature of Mr. Gregg W. Steinhafel, President, Chairman, and CEO of Target Corporation. That document should be directed to a key Target stakeholder group: investors, customers or employees. The choice of specific audience is yours, but the content must reflect the strategy you've recommend in your memo and must address the specific concerns of that particular stakeholder group.

Your strategy memo should provide analysis of the business problem, the relevant background details, critical issues, audience factors, options for action and specific recommendations. Think broadly and provide comprehensive advice for Ms. Kahn to take to the senior team.

## ACKNOWLEDGMENTS

This case was prepared by research assistants Brett Belock, Firas Fasheh and Anna McKeever under the direction of James S. O'Rourke, Teaching Professor of Management, as the basis for class discussion rather than to illustrate either effective or ineffective handling of an administrative situation. Information was gathered from corporate as well as public sources.

## NOTES

1 Duhigg, Charles. "How Companies Learn Your Secrets," *The New York Times Magazine*, February 16, 2012. Online at www.nytimes.com/2012/02/19/magazine/shopping-habits.html?pagewanted=all&_r=3&.

2 Siegel, Eric. *Predictive Analytics: The Power to Predict Who Will Click, Buy, Lie, or Die.* Wiley, 2013, p. 12.

3 Ibid., p. 2.

4 Ibid., p. 2.

5 Ibid., p. 3.

6 Ibid., p. 3.

7   Ibid., p. 3.

8   Ibid., p. 31.

9   Ibid., p. 11.

10  Ibid., p. 26.

11  Ibid., p. 12.

12  Zaman, Mukhles. "Predictive Analytics: The Future of Business Intelligence." *Technology Evaluation Centers*, 2005. Online at www.ism.co.at/analyses/Business_Intelligence/Predictive_Analytics.html.

13  Ibid.

14  Ibid.

15  Ibid.

16  Ibid.

17  Ibid.

18  Ibid.

19  Ibid.

20  Pichler, Josh. "dunnhumby: Retailer's Secret Weapon," Cincinnati.com, January 31, 2013. Online at http://news.cincinnati.com/article/20130130/BIZ/301190100/dunnhumby-Retailers-secret-weapon? nclick_check=1.

21  "Promotions," Kroger website. Online at www.kroger.com/promotions/Pages/default.aspx.

22  Clifford, Stephanie. "Shopper Alert: Price May Drop for You Alone," *The New York Times*, August 10, 2012. LexisNexix Academic.

23  "About EPIC," Electronic Privacy Information Center (EPIC). Online at http://epic.org/epic/about.html.

24  "Privacy and Consumer Profiling," Electronic Privacy Information Center (EPIC). Online at http://epic.org/privacy/pro filing/.

25  "News," Consumers Against Supermarket Privacy Invasion and Numbering. Online at www.nocards.org/news/index.shtml#pub2.

26  Duhigg. "How Companies Learn Your Secrets."

27  Ibid.

28  Ibid.

29  Ibid.

30  Ramasastry, Anita. "Should Target Tell Your Loved Ones You Are Pregnant, Or Should You?" Justia.com, Verdict, Consumer Law, February 28, 2012. Online at http://verdict.justia.com/2012/02/28/should-target-tell-your-loved-ones-you-are-pregnant-or-should-you.

31  "Privacy and Consumer Profiling," EPIC.

32  Ibid.

33  Ibid.

34  Ibid.

35  Ramasastry. "Should Target Tell Your Loved Ones You Are Pregnant, Or Should You?"

36  Consumer Data Privacy in a Networked World: A Framework for Protecting Privacy and Promoting Innovation in the Global Digital Economy. The White House, Washington. Online at www.whitehouse.gov/sites/default/files/privacy-final.pdf.

37  Ibid.

38  Ibid.

39  "About Target, Target Through the Years," Target. Online at https://corporate.target.com/about/history/Target-through-the-years.

40  Target corporation. 2013. Hoover's Company Records, Austin, United States, Austin: Dun and Bradstreet, Inc. Online at http://search.proquest.com/docview/230625353?accountid=12874.

41  "Target 2011 Annual Report," pp. 38 and 27 respectively. Online at https://corporate.target.com/annual-reports/2011/images/company/annual_report_2011/documents/Target_2011_ Annual_Report.pdf.

42  Ibid., p. 27.

43  "Privacy Policy," Target website. Online at www.target.com/spot/privacy-policy.

44  Duhigg. "How Companies Learn Your Secrets."

45  Ibid.

46  Ramasastry. "Should Target Tell Your Loved Ones You Are Pregnant, Or Should You?"

47  Ibid.

48  Ibid.

49  Siegel. *Predictive Analytics*, p. 10.

50  Duhigg. "How Companies Learn Your Secrets."

51  Ibid.

52  Hill, Kashmir. "How Target Figured Out a Teen Girl Was Pregnant Before Her Father Did," Forbes.com, February 16, 2012. Online at www.forbes.com/sites/kashmirhill/2012/02/16/how-target-figured-out-a-teen-girl-was-pregnant-be-fore-her-father-did/.

53  Colbert Nation, Comedy Central, February 22, 2012. Online at www.colbertnation.com/the-colbert-report-videos/408981/february-22-2012/the-word---surrender-to-a-buyer-power.

54  Duhigg. "How Companies Learn Your Secrets."

55  Ibid.

56  Ibid.

# Case 3.4: Starbucks Corporation

## Tax Avoidance Controversies in the United Kingdom (A)

> Starbucks' coffee menu famously baffles some people. In Britain, it's their accounts that are confusing. Starbucks has been telling investors the business was profitable, even as it consistently reported losses.[1]

## INTRODUCTION

On October 15, 2012, Reuters released a special report titled "*How Starbucks avoids UK Taxes.*" The investigative reporters at Reuters compared legal filings in the English company register, *Companies House*, with Starbucks' own group reports and 46 transcripts of conference calls with investors and analysts over a 12-year period. What they turned up were stark differences in how Starbucks viewed its U.K. subsidiary internally and how it was portrayed to the U.K. government, specifically the tax authority, Her Majesty's Revenue and Customs.

Starbucks officials internally gushed praise on their U.K. business unit. On multiple occasions it was referred to as "profitable" and a model for other regions to follow. In November 2007, the Chief Operating Officer Martin Coles told analysts that the U.K. unit's profits were funding Starbucks' expansion in other overseas markets. However, the unit's accounts showed a tenth consecutive annual loss. The Reuters report went on to cite multiple instances when Starbucks provided positive news to analysts yet showed operating losses to the U.K. government:

> For 2008, Starbucks filed a 26 million pounds loss in the UK. Yet CEO Schultz told an analysts' call that the UK business had been so successful he planned to take the lessons he had learnt there and apply them to the company's largest market – the United States. He also promoted Cliff Burrows, former head of the UK and Europe, to head the U.S. business.[2]

As soon as the newspaper hits newsstands and the Reuters website, there was an immediate public and political outcry. UK Uncut, an activist organization, planned boycotts and sit-ins. Several Members of Parliament (MPs) voiced outrage and quickly summoned Starbucks Chief Financial Officer Troy Alstead to testify before committee.

# STARBUCKS HISTORY AND IMAGE

## Starbucks Corporation

In 1971, Starbucks was founded in Seattle as a coffee bean roaster and retailer. The location sold high-quality coffee beans and equipment. The company started serving espresso coffee, the first drink that Starbucks sold, in 1986. The next year, the original owners sold the fledgling chain to former employee and current CEO Howard Schultz, who began an aggressive expansion campaign. Since 1986, the company has opened, on average, two stores per day.

Starbucks issued its Initial Public Offering in June 1992. At the time the company owned or licensed 140 outlets and booked annual revenue of $75 million. In 2012, the total number of stores in operation numbered more than 18,000 and were spread over 60 countries. For the fiscal year, Starbucks' consolidated revenues reached a record $13.3 billion. Company-operated stores accounted for 79 percent of total net revenues during the 2012 fiscal year.[3]

Coffee is no longer the only item sold through Starbucks locations. This excerpt from the 2012 10-K filing with the United States Securities and Exchange Commission summarizes the extent of their offerings:

> Starbucks stores offer a choice of coffee and tea beverages, distinctively packaged roasted whole bean and ground coffees, a variety of premium single serve products, juices and bottled water. Starbucks stores also offer an assortment of fresh food offerings, including selections focusing on high-quality ingredients, nutritional value and great flavor. A focused selection of beverage-making equipment and accessories are also sold in our stores.[4]

Starbucks has also spun off a unique tea bar concept called Teavana Fine Teas and Tea Bar. They are also expanding their juice line, Evolution Fresh, with an aggressive growth strategy with the goal of further increasing their market share in the super-premium juice category. The company has also begun exploring handcrafted carbonated beverages to offer for sale in its existing locations.

## Howard Schultz

Howard Schultz is the Chairman, President and Chief Executive Officer of Starbucks. Before joining the company he was the general manager for a Swedish drip coffee maker manufacturer called Hammarplast.[5] Starbucks was a client of Hammarplast and Schultz was impressed by the company's knowledge of coffee and the amount of business that they were conducting, even as a small outfit. A couple of years after his first encounter with Starbucks, Schultz joined the company in 1983 as the Director of Marketing.

While visiting Milan on a buying trip, Schultz was struck by the presence of a coffee bar on virtually every street corner. Not only were they serving countless espresso drinks, they also acted as meeting places or public squares, providing a sense of community and belongingness. He took this newfound knowledge back with him and tried to convince the owners to start offering hot brewed beverages in addition to the coffee beans and leaf teas that they already offered. The owners resisted and, after a brief stint trying to start his own coffee company, Schultz bought the retail unit of Starbucks for $3.8 million.[6]

## Social Responsibility

Howard Schultz is considered the "soul" of the company. His passion and business savvy have made the company into what it is today. He also brought to the company "a distinctive set of values that has and continually shapes how the company engages their customers, their employees, and the communities where they do business."[7] The company continually monitors its adherence to the norms of social responsibility, noting in a CRS report:

> We have been building a company with a conscience for more than four decades, intent on the fair and humane treatment of our people as well as the communities where we do business, and the global environment we all share.[8]

Starbucks provides full benefits for all of its employees, which it refers to as "partners." They also established a business practices goal: All of their coffee would be "ethically sourced" by 2015. The cornerstone of this approach is their Coffee and Farmer Equity (C.A.F.E.) Practices, "a comprehensive coffee buying program that ensures coffee quality while promoting social, economic and environmental standards." Through 2012, the company purchased 93 percent of their coffee in this manner.[9]

# INTERNATIONAL TAXATION

## Typical International Tax Methods

Most governments tax individuals and/or corporations on income or profits, respectively. These taxes are used to pay for everything from national defense and transportation infrastructure to food stamps and farm subsidies. These taxation systems vary widely by government and there are few broad, general rules. However, it is possible to understand the general corporate tax environment by understanding a few choices that each government must make when it comes to their corporate tax policy.

Countries usually pick between two systems: territorial or residential. In a territorial system, only the income from a source inside the country is taxed. For example, an American company with locations in Canada would only have to pay Canadian taxes on the portion of sales that are within Canadian borders. In a residential system, the residents of a country are taxed on their worldwide income, not just local income. The residential system is geared more toward personal income tax and does not affect corporations.

Corporate tax rates also vary widely by country. Every country has different funding needs based on their size, the extent to which the government operates social welfare programs and numerous other factors. Those looking to increase investment within their borders may offer lower tax rates and those with large infrastructures to maintain may have higher tax rates. These varied tax rates provide an unintended incentive for companies to attempt to transfer revenues and profits from countries with higher tax rates to those with lower tax rates, thereby retaining more net income for shareholders and managers.

Several tax avoidance strategies exist. Some companies charge subsidiaries for the use of "intellectual property" such as the brand name and their business practices. These types of arrangements typically charge 4 percent of revenue. Other companies that are vertically integrated upstream and downstream charge units in high tax jurisdictions higher prices in order to move money to lower-taxed countries. Transfer-pricing regulations allow this practice and companies can then allocate profits to high-charging subsidiaries in low tax rate areas.

## Starbucks Money Trail

Starbucks employs various legal methods in order to minimize their tax liability within the U.K. The corporate tax rate in the U.K. in 2011 was 26 percent. Each step along the money trail is designed so that in the end, the Starbucks subsidiary in the U.K. shows no profits on paper. This effectively reduces their tax bill in that jurisdiction to zero even though that market may be very profitable for them.

The Starbucks subsidiary in the U.K. is heavily debt-financed. Even for a company with positive net cash flows, the U.K. subsidiary still has large amounts of debt and large interest bills. All of these loans are from the Starbucks headquarters in Seattle. The interest on these loans is higher than the interest rate on the average Starbucks bond, at the LIBOR rate plus 4 percent versus the LIBOR rate plus 1.3 percent. While this moves profits to the U.S. where there is a relatively high tax rate, the interest stays within the company instead of being paid out to banks or investors who purchase their bonds.

Starbucks also charges the U.K. unit a royalty and licensing fee of 6 percent. This is higher than the 4 percent that a typical arrangement of this sort would charge. Starbucks claims that it has some independent licensees who also pay 6 percent, so they are within their legal right to charge their own subsidiary the higher rate, as well.[10]

The final method that Starbucks employs is how it pays for its main product and largest source of revenue: coffee. A Starbucks entity is set up in Switzerland which is responsible for all coffee bean purchases. The Switzerland location then has those beans sent to roasters throughout Europe, which turn the raw beans into product suitable for making coffee products. The beans are then sold to the U.K. Starbucks with a 20 percent markup. The beans never physically enter Switzerland. Switzerland has an approximate 5 percent corporate tax rate on profits tied to international trade in commodities, a category under which coffee falls.[11]

## COFFEE SHOP MARKET

Starbucks' growth plan and business model have been widely successful, allowing it to become the second largest restaurant chain globally after McDonald's with a market capitalization of $40 billion.[12] Starbucks' 2012 SEC annual filings reports revenues of $13.3 billion, with revenues in the EMEA region, including the U.K., of $1.14 billion. The EMEA revenues represent a 9 percent growth over the previous fiscal year. Within the U.K. specifically, the coffee shop market has remained strong despite a recession. A 2009 study from Allegra Strategies shows that the coffee shop market in the U.K. has seen 15 consecutive years of either flat sales or growth, with the market reaching £2 billion in consumer spending in 2012.[13]

Within the U.K., Starbucks faces a fierce competitor in Costa Coffee. Founded in London in 1971, Costa Coffee has grown from a wholesale roasted coffee supplier to become the U.K.'s largest coffee chain, supplanting Starbucks in 2010.[14] In 2012, Costa saw an increase in profits of nearly 30 percent, reaching £90.1 million. In contrast to Starbucks, Costa paid a tax bill of £15 million during the 2011–2012 reporting period. While the U.K. coffee shop market appears strong and close competitor Costa Coffee reports growing profits, Starbucks claims that it is not generating profits within the U.K. Global CFO Troy Alstead reports that Starbucks has recorded profits in only three years since they entered the U.K. in 1998 and that 25 percent of their U.K. stores run at a loss.[15]

High rents and space costs within U.K. cities were proposed as reasons for Starbucks' failure to generate profits; however, Costa Coffee has been able to achieve an operating margin of 14.3 percent with a similar retail footprint and comparable labor costs.[16] Chief executive of Costa Coffee, Andy Harrison, appeared to enjoy Starbucks' tax avoidance controversy, commenting "Costa has been the UK's favourite coffee shop for quite some time and we remain the taxman's favourite coffee shop, too."[17]

## HMRC, PARLIAMENT AND PUBLIC OPINION

The taxman within the U.K. is Her Majesty's Revenue and Customs (HMRC), which is responsible for the collection of both personal and corporate income taxes, among other duties. Formed in 2005 as a merger of two previous tax entities, the HMRC outlined its purpose and vision by stating "We make sure that the money is available to fund the UK's public services" and "We will close the tax gap, our customers will feel that the tax system is simple for them and even-handed, and we will be seen as a highly professional organisation."[18] In the HMRC charter, it is further laid out that the public can expect the HMRC to "tackle people who deliberately break the rules and challenge those who bend the rules."[19]

The HMRC received help in their mission from Reuters in publishing their special report on Starbucks, as well as from several other media investigations in 2012. A *Guardian* report on Amazon showed the online retail giant paid no corporation tax on more than £3 billion in sales within the U.K.,[20] while *The Telegraph* reported that Google paid just £6 million in tax on £395 million of U.K. turnover.[21] Following these reports, representatives from all of the firms were summoned to Parliament to speak to the Publics Account Committee. Corporate tax avoidance had become a hot button issue for both the media and government, with Michael Meacher, an MP for the Labour Party, stating specifically that Starbucks' tax behavior "is certainly profoundly against the interests of the countries where they operate and is extremely unfair. . . . they are trying to play the taxman, game him. It is disgraceful."[22]

While several corporations were the subject of media tax avoidance investigations and summoned to Parliament, Starbucks faced the brunt of the public uproar. According to the YouGov BrandIndex, which measures the strength of a company's brand perception, Starbucks dropped to a record low score of −28.6 following the release of the Reuters special report. In the month leading up to the Parliament summons, Starbucks' score remained around −16.7, which is in sharp contrast to its score from 2011 of +3.1.[23] In contrast, the BrandIndex scores for Google and Amazon barely dropped due to their media reports and Parliament summons. The U.K. director for BrandIndex, Sarah Murphy, commented:

A brand's buzz score typically recovers following a spate of bad press, but we aren't seeing that with Starbucks, which is quite unusual. Its scores started to level out around the end of last month, but whatever modest recovery Starbucks has made could well be in jeopardy if this story flares up again in the media.[24]

## UK UNCUT

The continued negative public backlash against Starbucks could have something to do with the actions of the organization UK Uncut. While it started as a simple hashtag, UK Uncut grew during the recession into an organized movement with protests and boycotts in over 50 U.K. cities.[25]

UK Uncut campaigned against the government's austerity plans to cut public services and reduce the deficit, claiming the deficit could be reduced and welfare services maintained if the government collected all the tax revenue it was due. A UK Uncut FAQ says, "It is estimated that £25bn a year is lost through tax avoidance – money that could fund the refuges, rape crisis centres, sure start centres and child benefit payments that are currently being axed by the government."[26]

One of the first UK Uncut targets, Vodafone, was forced to close nearly 30 stores around the country due to protests and sit-ins.[27] Since 2010, banks such as Barclays, RBS and HSBC, and retailers like Boots and Tesco have come under fire from UK Uncut.

Following the release of the Reuters report in October 2012, UK Uncut began to target Starbucks with protests and boycotts. On November 11, 2012, the date that Starbucks CFO Troy Alstead was scheduled to meet with Parliament, UK Uncut announced a new campaign against Starbucks, titled "Refuge from the Cuts." The intent of the campaign was to turn dozens of Starbucks' locations on a Saturday in December 2012 into services that were being cut by the government, such as refuges, homeless shelters and crèches.[28] A UK Uncut activist was quoted as saying "Starbucks is a really great target because it is on every high street across the country and that's what UK Uncut finds really important: people can take action in their local areas."[29]

## WHAT NEXT?

In November 2012, Starbucks finds itself in an untenable situation with the British government summoning CFO Troy Alstead to hearings in Parliament, and public protests and demonstrations against the company escalating. Starbucks has not been accused of illegal activities, but has followed common international tax procedures to minimize payments within the U.K.

1. How should CFO Troy Alstead testify at the Parliament hearings? Should he continue Starbucks claims of an unprofitable U.K. market, or admit to tax avoidance practices?
2. What actions, if any, should Starbucks take in order to minimize the impact of the public outcry and actions planned by UK Uncut?
3. Does Starbucks have a responsibility to the community to obey the spirit of corporate tax laws, or an obligation to shareholders to legally minimize tax expenses?
4. How can Starbucks, or other companies, avoid such situations in the future?

## WRITING ASSIGNMENT

Please respond in writing to the issues presented in this case by preparing two documents: a communication strategy memo and a professional business letter.

In preparing these documents, you may assume one of two roles: you may identify yourself as an NFL senior manager who has been asked to provide advice to Starbucks Vice President for Global Communications, Corey Dubrowa, regarding the issues he and the company are facing. Or, you may identify yourself as an external management consultant who has been asked by the league to provide advice to him.

Either way, you must prepare a strategy memo addressed to Mr. Dubrowa that summarizes the details of the case, identifies critical issues, discusses their implications (what they mean and why they matter), offers specific recommendations for action (assigning ownership and suspense dates for each) and shows how to communicate the solution to all who are affected by the recommendations.

You must also prepare a professional business letter for the signature of Starbucks Chairman and Chief Executive Officer, Howard Schultz. That document should be addressed either to the public as a published document, or to another key stakeholder, such as the Chancellor of the Exchequer, explaining what has happened, the company's position and the actions the company is taking. If you have questions about either of these documents, please consult your instructor.

## ACKNOWLEDGMENTS

This case was prepared by research assistants Jack Gay and Scott Manwaring under the direction of James S. O'Rourke, Teaching Professor of Management, as the basis for class discussion rather than to illustrate either effective or ineffective handling of an administrative situation. Information was gathered from corporate as well as public sources. Editorial assistance: Judy Bradford.

## NOTES

1   Bergin, Tom. "Special Report: How Starbucks avoids UK Taxes," Reuters, October 15, 2012. Online at http://uk.re uters.com/article/2012/10/15/us-britain-starbucks-tax-idUKBRE89E0EX20121015.

2   Ibid.

3   "Starbucks 2012 Form 10-K," United States Securities and Exchange Commission. Online at www.sec.gov/Archives/edgar/data/829224/000082922412000007/sbux-9302012x10k.htm.

4   Ibid.

5   "Starbucks' Howard Schultz on How He Became Coffee King," Mirror News, August 5, 2010. Online at www.mirror.co.uk/news/uk-news/starbucks-howard-schultz-on-how-he-became-239790.

6   Ibid.

7   "2012 Global Responsibility Report Message from Howard Schultz," Starbucks.com. Online at www.starbucks.com/responsibility/global-report/leadership-letter.

8   Ibid.

9   "Ethically Sourced Coffee Goals and Progress," Starbucks.com. Online at www.starbucks.com/responsibility/sourc ing/coffee.

10  Pollock, Lisa. "How Starbucks Stirs Things Up to Pay No UK Tax," Financial Times, December 15, 2012.

11  Bergin. "Special Report: How Starbucks avoids UK taxes."

12  Ibid.

13  Ibid.

14  Poulter, Sean. "Costa, The Coffee Chain That Keeps on Growing: Brand to Open Hundreds More Stores Across the UK and Around the World," Daily Mail, April 30, 2013. Online at www.dailymail.co.uk/news/article-2317419/Costa-coffee-chain-keeps-growing-Chain-open-hundreds-stores-UK-world.html.

15  Houlder, Vanessa, Barney Jopson and Louise Lucas. "Starbucks Ground Down: Taxation; Public Anger Over Tax Avoidance by Corporate Giants is Spreading Around the Globe, as the US Coffee Chain Found to its Cost," Financial Times, December 8, 2012.

16  Ibid.

17  Poulter. "Costa, The Coffee Chain That Keeps on Growing."

18  "HM Revenue & Customs: The HMRC Vision," Her Majesty's Revenue and Customs, The National Archives. Online at http://webarchive.nationalarchives.gov.uk/+/http://www.hmrc.gov.uk/governance/vision.htm.

19  "Your Charter," Her Majesty's Revenue and Customs. Online at www.gov.uk/government/uploads/system/uploads/attachment_data/file/91888/charter.pdf.

20  Griffiths, Ian. "Amazon: £7bn Sales, No Corporation Tax," The Guardian, April 4, 2012. Online at www.theguardian.com/technology/2012/apr/04/amazon-british-operation-corporation-tax.

21  Warman, Matt. "Google Pays Just £6m UK Tax," The Telegraph, August 8, 2012. Online at www.telegraph.co.uk/tech nology/google/9460950/Google-pays-just-6m-UK-tax.html.

22  Bergin. "Special Report: How Starbucks avoids UK taxes."

23  Neville, Simon and Shiv Malik. "Starbucks Wakes Up and Smells the Stench of Tax Avoidance and Controversy," *The Guardian*, November 11, 2012. Online at www.theguardian.com/business/2012/nov/12/starbucks-tax-avoidance-controversy.
24  Ibid.
25  "About," UK Uncut. Online at www.ukuncut.org.uk/about/ukuncut.
26  "Starbucks Tax Dodging FAQs," UK Uncut. Online at www.ukuncut.org.uk/media/W1siZiIsIjUxM2NiZmJhYjAx OTFmMDAwMzAwMDE1MyJdXQ/starbucks-tax-dodging-faqs.pdf.
27  "About," UK Uncut.
28  Neville and Malik. "Starbucks Wakes Up and Smells the Stench of Tax Avoidance and Controversy."
29  Ibid.

# CHAPTER 4

# Speaking

Your stomach is in a knot, you're sweating, turning, tossing, anxious. The room seems hot. How can that be? You got up ten minutes ago to turn down the thermostat. A glance at the clock reveals that it's 2:00 a.m. At this rate, you'll never get to sleep.

What's going on here? Is a bad meal keeping you up? Has a lumpy hotel mattress worked its magic on your back once again? Has a case of jet lag thrown your circadian rhythms off? While any of these maladies is possible, it's much more likely that your sleeplessness and anxiety are caused by the greatest among human fears: the knowledge that you have a speech to give.

CBS News journalist Charles Osgood posed the question this way: "Have you ever been driving at night and come upon a deer frozen in the beam of your headlights? Here's my theory," says Osgood. "The deer thinks the lights are spotlights, and what has it paralyzed is stage fright. It imagines the worst: It has to give a speech."[1]

According to an often-cited study by market researchers, speaking before a group came in first among "worst human fears." Death was number 6, elevators number 12.[2] The reason, according to Osgood, is that we're all afraid of making fools of ourselves. The more important the speech, the more frightened we become.[3]

Those fears are not entirely unreasonable, either. Peter Shea, a plant controller for Imperial Chemical Industries, was asked to make a five-minute presentation on his value to the company. Shea wanted to capture the imagination of the 18 senior executives in the room, so he opened with a metaphor: His factory was like a race car and he wanted to keep it running fast. Bad idea. The executives cut him off after four sentences and asked him to leave the room. "I lost it," he said. "I wilted and died."[4]

He's not alone. Others have tried to be clever with a business presentation and flopped. Dave Jensen is an executive recruiter with Search Masters International, a search firm focused on the biotechnology industry. He was giving a presentation in San Diego to the Society for Industrial Microbiology and wanted to charge up the crowd. So he opened with a joke from a book of speaking tips. Bad idea. "It just died," he recalls. "It wasn't very funny. And industrial microbiologists aren't a funny group to begin with. When you lose something in the first two minutes of a talk, you just can't get it back."[5]

Darryl Gordon, an advertising manager from La Jolla, California, was invited to demonstrate the power of digital technology to 60 advertising agency presidents. So he decided to run his presentation on his laptop computer, complete with colorful slides, bright graphics, and sound. The one thing he hadn't checked before he began was the battery in his computer. Bad idea. When he pushed the power button, nothing happened. It took 15 minutes to load the presentation onto a spare machine. "Every second of that 15 minutes felt like a lifetime," he said. "I'll never forget it."[6]

The advice for people about to give a speech is simple: Preparation will help you overcome fear, whether that fear is reasonable or not. Really thorough preparation can set you up for success, help you achieve the goals you've set for yourself, and get the audience you fear so much to do exactly what you want them to do.

## WHY SPEAK?

Often, we don't have a choice. As a manager, you'll find yourself preparing to speak to an audience you'd rather not meet on a topic you'd rather not talk about. Addressing the corporate executive committee on the subject of a quarterly budget shortfall is no one's idea of a good time, but you will do it because it's part of your management responsibility. Many speaking assignments are directive in nature. You do it because you're told to, or you do it because you must. These occasions are not easy, but they are certainly nothing to be afraid of.

Many speaking opportunities, however, are voluntary in nature. You give the talk because you choose to do so. You drop in on a group of employees to share the good news that the company has just landed a big contract they had worked hard to secure. You could have shared that information in an e-mail, but you'd rather see their faces, hear them cheer and watch "high fives" around the room.

It might be another occasion, explaining to your daughter's elementary school class what you do for a living (come to think of it, that might be tougher than the employee meeting). You might also accept the invitation of a local Kiwanis Club to speak at their weekly luncheon. Each speaking opportunity you accept, each speech you give will increase your self-assurance and reinforce the idea that you are competent, confident and capable of speaking in public (and speaking well).

Every speaking opportunity, even if it's involuntary, becomes an occasion for you to show what you know and to demonstrate your skills. Joan Finnessy, now vice president for finance at Fisher Scientific International in Pittsburgh, Pennsylvania, found that out firsthand in a prior job:

> A few years ago, I was working as a division controller for a company that held a worldwide conference for its controllers. All the controllers in the company were required to make a presentation at this conference. Our company had recently purchased another organization, but we were not aware that the company was planning to reorganize itself and reduce the number of controllers.
>
> Senior finance managers were, of course, in attendance. We all had our few minutes "in the spotlight." Some controllers did a very good job at displaying strong delivery skills and solid content. Others did not do as well. The assumed purpose of the presentations was to communicate information about our divisions for the benefit of others at the conference.
>
> Approximately a month later, however, those controllers who did not display good presentation skills found themselves in negotiations for severance packages. While nothing was ever said about a connection between poor presentations and terminations, only those individuals who did not present well were terminated.[7]

Even if you haven't been expressly told that you're being evaluated during a speech, one thing seems clear: You're being evaluated. Two keys to successful evaluation present themselves time and again in public speaking: taking control of the situation and preparing yourself to succeed.

## YOUR VOICE IS OFTEN MORE POWERFUL THAN YOUR WRITING

"When you're trying to convey the quality of your mind to your boss, or to a company that's considering you for a job, your best ally may be your own voice." That's the claim of Behavioral Science professors Juliana Schroeder of the University of California, Berkeley, and Nicholas Epley of the University of Chicago Booth School of Business.[8]

While many people assume that their ideas and intellect will come across much better in written form, it turns out that using your voice can actually make you sound smarter. That insight comes from Schroeder and Epley's research investigating how people figure out what's going on in other people's minds, despite out inability to observe others' thoughts, beliefs or motivations. Research has shown that spoken language is a highly effective tool for this. It's the communication form that most clearly reveals not only what people are thinking but also their thinking ability.[9]

Shroeder and Epley asked MBA students to prepare a spoken pitch to recruiters from the companies they most wanted to work for, along with a separate written pitch. Recruiters from firms such as Microsoft and Goldman Sachs evaluated video versions of the students' appeals, as well as audio versions and a written transcript of the talk (with "um's" and "ah's" cleaned up). The evaluators considered qualities such as competence, thoughtfulness and intelligence and reported how much they liked them and how positive an impression they had made. They were also asked how interested they would be in hiring the candidates if they were considering them for employment.

The evaluators who heard audio pitches or who watched video versions judged the candidates to have greater intellect (to be more rational, thoughtful and intelligent) than those who read the written transcripts. They also liked the individual more, had a more positive overall impression and were more interested in hiring the candidates. "Although there may be some advantages to putting thoughts in writing," say Schroeder and Epley, "written passages lack critical *paralinguistic* cues that provide information about a speaker's intelligence and thoughtfulness." Most important, they say, "Written text may not convey the same impression as your voice, because it lacks a critical feature: the sound of intellect."[10]

## HOW TO PREPARE A SUCCESSFUL MANAGEMENT SPEECH

Here are 15 ideas to prepare you for any speech, large or small, important or impromptu. Focus on these points, one at a time, and you're unlikely ever to develop sweaty palms on the podium again.

- Develop a strategy.
- Get to know your audience.
- Determine your reason for speaking.
- Learn what you can about the occasion for your talk.
- Know what makes people listen.
- Understand the questions listeners bring to any listening situation.
- Recognize common obstacles to successful communication.
- Support your ideas with credible evidence.
- Organize your thoughts.
- Keep your audience interested.
- Select a delivery approach.
- Develop your visual support.
- Rehearse your speech.
- Develop confidence in your message and in yourself.
- Deliver your message.

## DEVELOP A STRATEGY

If you have no strategy, you probably shouldn't give a speech. So, what exactly is a strategy for public speaking? Simply put, it's a reason for speaking, a knowledge of who will hear your speech, and some sense of the context in which it will occur.

More than 2,300 years ago, Aristotle told his students they would have a greater chance of success as they prepared to deliver a speech if they would first consider three basic elements: audience, purpose and occasion.[11]

## GET TO KNOW YOUR AUDIENCE

Who are these people? What do you know about them? What do they know about you or your subject? How do they feel about it? Before you go any further in your preparation, perform a simple audience analysis that involves just two steps: (1) knowing something about the people you'll speak to and (2) knowing why people listen.

What should you know about your audience? Here are a few categories of information that might prove useful as you prepare your remarks.

## Age

How old are your audience members? Will they be familiar with the concepts you plan to speak about? What's their vocabulary range? What sort of life experiences have they had? Remember, if you're speaking to a group of 20-year-olds, you should know that they were born just at the turn of the century during the latter years of the Clinton administration. They have no direct memory of the Hubble Space Telescope being launched. The Persian Gulf War began before they were born, and the Internet has been available for their entire lives.

And, just for the record, they have never "rolled down" a car window; they've grown up with bottled water; being "lame" has to do with being dumb or inarticulate, not disabled; and "off the hook" has never had anything to do with a telephone.[12] Make certain your references to events and ideas are both known to them and relevant to their concerns. Similarly, an older audience might have been around for certain events, but references to WhatsApp, freeware cross-platform messaging, or social video livestream on Snapchat may well be lost on them.

## Education

Knowing the age of the audience will tell you something about how much education they have had but perhaps not as much as you would like to know. Speech content, including central themes and vocabulary, will certainly be influenced by the level and type of education of your audience.

## Personal Beliefs

What this group believes may well be more important than how old or how well educated they are. The reason is simple: What you believe defines who you are. Are these folks liberal or conservative? What's their political affiliation? Are they committed to a particular religious or social point of view? Do they have certain biases favoring or opposing such issues as red meat, cigar smoking, gun ownership or parallel parking?

## Occupation

What do these people do for a living? Are they students? As such, many of them may not do anything for a living but might hope to have occupations someday soon. Are they managers, professionals or colleagues of yours? Knowing how people earn their living will tell you something about their educational background and their daily routines, as well as their motivations and interests.

## Income

Knowing how much money an audience makes may be of some help as you formulate your remarks. By knowing their income levels, you will have some idea of what their concerns are: The less they make, the more fundamental and basic are their concerns. Abraham Maslow nicely documented the Hierarchy of Human Needs, noting that it's difficult to sell people on self-actualization if they haven't enough to eat.

## Socioeconomic Status

This term describes where in the social/economic spectrum your audience is located. It is, of course, a direct function of other factors, such as income, education, occupation, neighborhood, friends, family and more. Think of this as a single descriptor that explains just how much prestige your audience has in the eyes of others in society.[13]

### *Ethnic Origin*

This information may be worthwhile to know, but its value is limited. Its utility may lie in knowing which issues and positions are of greatest concern to members of a particular ethnic group. The limitation lies in knowing that you cannot reasonably stereotype the views of all members of such a group. Sensitivity to ethnic causes and issues, as well as language, should be sufficient as you prepare a speech.

### *Sex/Gender*

Sex refers to the biological differences between males and females. Gender refers to the social and psychological expectations, roles, norms and views of men and women. Considerable evidence now indicates that sex/gender may be among the least useful pieces of information you might want to know about your audience. Why? Because study after study has shown no statistically significant difference in the responses of professional men and women to a wide range of stimuli. Clearly, knowing that your audience might be composed exclusively of one sex or another might alter your approach somewhat, but you would be unwise to assume that you would write one speech for men and another for women. Treat them as intelligent humans and you will get the response you're seeking.

### *Knowledge of the Subject*

This category of information (along with the next) may be one for which you would be willing to pay in order to know more. A thorough knowledge of what your audience already knows about your speaking subject is useful in a number of ways. First, this would tell you where to begin. Don't speak down to them by explaining fundamentals they already understand. Similarly, don't start above their heads. Begin at a point they're comfortable with and move on from there.

### *Attitude Toward the Subject*

Even more important than what they know about your subject is how they feel about it. What I know about the federal tax code is far less relevant than how I feel about it when I listen to a talk about tax reform. My emotions are not irrelevant as I approach a subject. Neither are yours. You certainly should know what the emotional response of your audience will be to the content and direction of your talk. The greater the degree of ego involvement (or emotional response) in a given topic, the narrower will be the range of acceptable positions. In other words, people are much more open-minded on topics they are indifferent about than they are on topics they care about passionately. What you don't know in this regard can hurt you.

## DETERMINE YOUR REASON FOR SPEAKING

Knowing why you are speaking is almost as important as knowing to whom you will speak. Aristotle told his pupils that people rise to speak for three basic reasons: to inform, to persuade or to inspire.[14] Some authors have argued that all speaking is persuasive: You have chosen this topic as opposed to any other; you've selected this evidence, excluding all else. I'll accept that. However, it's especially important to know whether your audience expects you to take a position regarding the subject of your speech.

Let's say, for example, that your boss is thinking about purchasing a new color copying and printing system for the office and she has asked you to gather information about equipment available for sale or lease. She would also like you to present that information to members of the executive committee. You can find and organize such data easily. But should you take a position regarding which system to lease or buy? Should you become an advocate on behalf of one system or another? If the audience (your boss, in particular) expects information that will help her or the committee make such a decision, your views may be unwelcome. On the other hand, if you have been specifically asked to make your recommendations known, your speech would be seriously incomplete without them.

All public speaking should inform (without telling people what they already know). It should also inspire when appropriate to the occasion. Still, managers – young managers, in particular – should be careful to make certain they know the role that is expected of them as they rise to speak. Too often, young managers get into trouble with senior members of their organization by offering opinions on the topic at hand when the demand for such opinions is not especially brisk.

Keep in mind that you've been asked to speak to this audience for a particular reason: You know something they'd like to know more about. On the other hand, you can't simply step onto the platform and begin dumping data on your audience. Think about your speech in the form of a question: "If these people had money to invest, what would they want to know about this company?" Or, "If they were seeking employment in this industry, what would they want to know about this company?" Then, think of what you know as the answer to that question. You'll need to spend the first few minutes of your speech asking that question – more if the question is not well understood by the audience, less if it is. You're there to share what you know and to help them understand it from their own perspective. [15]

## LEARN WHAT YOU CAN ABOUT THE OCCASION

In addition to knowing who will hear your talk and the reasons for which you will speak, it may also be useful for you to know something about the occasion. Many occasions simply call for a polite, informative presentation. Others, however, will ask that you incorporate some theme into your speech that arises from the moment. Certain holidays lend a clear and useful tone to your talk, such as Christmas ("Peace on Earth, goodwill toward all"), Thanksgiving ("We are grateful for what we have been given and mindful of those who have less") or Independence Day ("The price of freedom is eternal vigilance").

Other occasions call for different themes. Graduations, commencements or rites-of-passage events call for a focus on the future and the responsibilities and opportunities that lie ahead. As a manager, you know you will have the opportunity to welcome new employees into the organization or, perhaps, the sad task of saying farewell to them. Your audience will pay close attention to your words, to the tone of your speech and to your approach to the subject. You are in charge and they expect you to say the right thing. It won't always be immediately clear what the right thing to say is, but your audience will know it when they hear it.

## KNOW WHAT MAKES PEOPLE LISTEN

Consultant and speech critic Sonya Hamlin says that people listen to speeches for three basic reasons: their own self-interest, who is telling the story and how it is told. [16] If you know your audience, you will know what their interests are. You can't have much effect on their views about you, at least before you speak, but you certainly can have some influence on how the speech is delivered. In terms of control, two of the three reasons people listen are well within your grasp.

### Positive Speaking Styles

Numerous studies of public speaking have shown that people react positively to speaking styles they regard as positive. Read the following list of words and see whether you can think of a public speaker whose style fits many, if not most of them:

| | |
|---|---|
| Warm | Honest |
| Friendly | Exciting |
| Interesting | Knowledgeable |
| Organized | Creative |
| Confident | Inspiring |
| Open | Authentic |

### Negative Speaking Styles

Not surprisingly, audiences react negatively to speakers whose style is the opposite of those words you just read. Consider this list of words and think of your reaction to certain speakers you heard (or were forced to listen to). What was your reaction?

| | |
|---|---|
| Pompous | Vague |
| Unenergized | Complex |
| Patronizing | Unsure |
| Formal | Irrelevant |
| Stuffy | Monotonous |
| Closed | Nervous |

The advice in response to these research findings is simple: Make your speaking style positive, embracing all those attributes described as positive. And, do what you can to eliminate or avoid those speaking styles described as negative.[17]

## THE QUESTIONS LISTENERS BRING TO ANY LISTENING SITUATION

As the members of your audience take a seat in the auditorium or conference room, each has questions about you, your message, the situation and the consequences of this speech for them.

Here are seven basic questions you should be prepared to answer, either directly or in the course of your talk to them:

### Do You Know Something I need to Know?

No matter who you are, people will listen if you know something they need to know. Obviously, the more you know about them, the better prepared you will be to answer this question. The more you can do for them, personally and professionally, the more they will reward you with their attention.

### Can I Trust You?

Trust is not simply given or demanded. It's earned. You must show your audience that you are trustworthy by providing accurate information, useful points of view and reliable evidence. It may well prove to be the most important question any audience has about a speaker.

### Am I Comfortable With You?

Audiences feel more comfortable with people who are like them, or who have experiences similar to their own, or whose values and beliefs parallel their own. What can you do to show them who you are, to raise their comfort level?

### How Can You Affect Me?

More sophisticated audiences think about outcomes. How can you influence my decisions, my career, my life? What can you do for me? If you can show them, in concrete or tangible terms, what you can do for them, they will tune in directly to what you say.

### What's My Experience With You?

If your audience has no experience with you, they may not trust you. Similarly, if they have had an unfortunate experience with you, they may not trust you. What you can do is to put them at ease, assure them that you are here to speak for their benefit.

### Are You Reasonable?

The question of how you *affect* people deals with their feelings. This question, on the other hand, deals with *reason* or *logic*. Does the content of your speech reveal that you are a reasonable person? Does your argument make sense? Are you open-minded at all, particularly to viewpoints that may be shared by members of the audience?

## *Whom Do You Represent?*

This question is often tricky and difficult, especially when you are speaking on behalf of an organization or other people. If the audience knows that you represent a particular cause or point of view, it may be difficult for them to see you as open-minded, reasonable or unbiased. Declaring your interests early in a speech may be one way to assure them of your purpose. Acknowledging their interests may be another.[18]

# RECOGNIZE COMMON OBSTACLES TO SUCCESSFUL COMMUNICATION

Every manager faces barriers to success as a speaking occasion arises. Some barriers are fairly mundane: Am I available that evening? Can I reschedule another obligation? Will I be able to gather the information I need to answer their questions? Other barriers, though, are more serious and can present great difficulty for a speaker. Obstacles to success appear to fall broadly into the following five categories.

## *Stereotypes*

Stereotyping ascribes to all members of a group or class those characteristics or behaviors observed in just one or a few. The word was coined by social scientist Walter Lippmann in 1921 when he wrote about why people so readily imagine how other people are, or why they behave as they do, even in the face of ready evidence to the contrary.[19]

The fact is people are comfortable with stereotypes. They help to explain the world around us, don't require much effort to construct and give us ready categories into which we can insert new experiences, new people and new ideas. Treating each one as unique or different is much more difficult and requires a great deal more reasoning and work on our part. Stereotypes may be useful as a starting point from which to understand groups and their members, but they can be damaging when we fail to acknowledge differences within those groups or when we fail to admit that not all people act or think in the same ways.

To succeed as a speaker, you must put aside whatever stereotypical views you may hold of your audience and try with an open mind to treat them as individuals. If you are both successful and fortunate, they may do the same for you.

## *Prejudice*

The word *prejudice*, derived from Latin, means "to judge before knowing." We do it all the time. In fact, it's not necessarily bad. We have little prejudices that serve us well: the food we eat, the stores we shop in, our taste in clothing. Often, as managers, we are forced to judge before we have all the facts. We simply don't have the time or the resources to gather more information. We must act now.

As we speak to others, though, it's best that we acknowledge we are working with incomplete data. It's useful to admit that we don't know as much as we might like or, perhaps, that we simply didn't have time to gather information that might have been easily available to us. We don't want others making judgments about us too quickly. The best way to encourage that sort of careful thinking in others is to lead by example and admit to our prejudicial thinking whenever possible.[20]

## *Feelings*

Keep your emotions in check. Control your anger. Don't display your contempt for others and their ideas in public. Good advice, but it's all easier said than done. Our emotions and those of our audience can easily get in the way of an objective look at the facts. They can blur the important distinctions that exist between factual data and our affective interpretation of what they mean. The best advice is simply to acknowledge that we have feelings and then use them to advance our cause. We must also recognize, however, that the people in our audience will have feelings – about us, our subject and our evidence – and those feelings may be at odds with our own. Acknowledge that, and then move on to make your case as best you can.[21]

## Language

You probably know from a basic communication course that words don't have meaning; people do. People assign meaning to the words they hear and read, and you should know that people with different backgrounds, different education and different life experiences will assign much different meanings to the words you speak. This will happen during the course of a single speech. Various audience members will hear the same words at precisely the same moment, spoken by the same person, yet they will assign different meaning to those words and leave the speech with different impressions of what the speaker meant.

Work around the difficulties inherent in language by offering multiple examples to illustrate your key points. Often a graph, table or visual display can convey more meaning than whole paragraphs. Give your audience several ways to understand what you mean: repeat yourself, rephrase your intentions, tell stories and give examples.[22]

## Culture

No two of us are the same, not only because of genetic individual differences, but also because we each have been enculturated in different ways. We tend to think of culture as an expression of entire nations or civilizations, but it's really much more specific than that. If culture is everything we have, say, think or do as a people, then folks who live in the country are different in important ways from those who live in the city. Those who live in one state are culturally different from those who live in another.

We have other experiences as we grow up, become educated, find our life's work and live out our lives. The experiences of one generation are not the same as those of another. Customs, habits and preferences in food and music are different from one ethnic group to another. If you look carefully, you can also see the cultural differences that exist among various corporations and business organizations. Some show a preference for informality, while others prefer more structure. Various habits from the use of titles to the use of time distinguish us from one another. Your response to the cultural habits and preferences of others is a mark of your respect for them and an acknowledgment that they are not only different but that those differences are important.[23]

### Communication Obstacles can Provoke Negative Reactions

When people feel threatened, intimidated, lost or confused, a number of things can happen. During a speech, people may stop listening. They may discover how much they don't know, which can lead to frustration, anger and hostility toward the speaker and the ideas being discussed. If the speaker has made them feel sufficiently dumb, they may withdraw entirely.

Begin with the familiar and move to the unfamiliar. Start with what the audience already knows and then move on to ideas that are a logical extension or outcome of those they are familiar with. Don't intimidate or confuse your audience; do everything you can to make them feel that they are just as smart as you are. The reward, once again, is their attention and their willingness to think about your ideas.

## SUPPORT YOUR IDEAS WITH CREDIBLE EVIDENCE

Even though your reputation or the subject you are planning to speak about may keep an audience with you for a while, you have a much better chance of convincing them of the value in your ideas if you support your talk with current, believable, easy-to-understand evidence.

Where to begin? Well, it's probably best to begin with your own experience, knowledge and interests. If you are genuinely interested in the ideas you plan to present, your audience will pick up on that and respond accordingly. You will also know where to look for the most interesting, most believable support. If you like a particular subject, chances are good that you know which publications to read, know which experts are cited most often and know a great deal about the latest developments. The confidence that comes with all of this will not be lost on your audience.

Secondly, consider new ideas, information and techniques. You and your audience may together know a great deal about the subject of your talk, but they may not know about the latest information. Here is where your interests can help them. Bring them up-to-date on the subject; share the latest innovations and developments.

Next, as you consider how to support your speech, think about the availability and quality of support material. You may have a special interest that you simply can't support because you will not have access to the right information by the time you must speak.

Talk to some experts. Not all credible evidence is found in books, magazines, journals, newspapers or on the Internet. Some of the most interesting, compelling evidence comes in the form of direct testimony from people who are genuine experts on the subject. Where can you find them? They're all around you. A punch-press operator working on a factory shop floor may not seem especially expert, but if he's been at his job for a number of years, chances are good that he knows a great deal about the machinery, the materials and the processes involved in the job. Ask him a few questions. You might be surprised how much you can learn if you listen carefully.

Know how much time is available. You can't include large amounts of detail if you have only a few minutes to speak. Because you know you must respect the time limits imposed on your talk, consider carefully how much information, and in what level of detail, you'll be able to include. You'll have some idea of whether you need more or less information once you rehearse the speech. As you begin, of course, it's always better to have too much than too little. You can easily edit a speech later on; it's much tougher to go back and begin your research again as the speaking date approaches.

## ORGANIZE YOUR THOUGHTS

Based on a number of public speeches you've already listened to, you know that a well-organized talk is easy to follow, sensible in its patterns and has a feeling of coherence. In other words, the parts fit together and flow along nicely. At the risk of dwelling on the obvious, you should know that each speech has an introduction, a main body and a conclusion. If the talk is especially well written and delivered, you may not even be aware of these separate parts, but they each exist to serve a number of important purposes.

### Your Introduction

A well-crafted introduction will help you to get the audience's attention and allow them to settle in and focus on your topic and your reason for speaking to them. Unless you have a good reason for not doing so (several good reasons do exist), you should disclose your purpose right up front. Telling an audience what your objectives are will build both credibility and interest. When should you withhold your real purpose in speaking to them? The research in this area tells us that you may safely delay stating your intentions if doing so would confuse your audience, if you plan to ask them for money or if you know the audience initially disagrees with your position. A good introduction will also recognize and involve the audience in some way. A reference to the occasion or to people who are likely to be known to the audience may help.

### How Should You Begin?

Many proven methods are available to you as you begin a speech. Consider the following approaches:

- *An anecdote.* Tell a story. People have loved listening to stories since they were kids, waiting for bedtime. Ronald Reagan's success as a speaker, in part, was due to his ability to "spin a yarn." Even those who disagreed with his politics acknowledged the importance storytelling played in his political life.
- *Humor.* People love to laugh, but be careful. Humor works really well, unless you're not funny. Foremost among the occasions when you are likely not to be funny is when the joke is on the audience or someone they hold in high regard. Spontaneous, contemporary humor tends to work best. Stay away from set-piece jokes and "amusing" stories you have heard recently.
- *A prediction.* Can you offer, based on the evidence you have gathered, a prediction that is likely to interest, amuse, frighten or arouse your audience? Make sure you can support your contentions. Also make sure the evidence on which they are based is readily available and easily understood.
- *A dramatic forecast.* This is similar to a prediction but longer-range in nature and usually involving extended or more complex events.

- *A striking example.* This is just one form of an illustration or brief anecdote. If you can make your point by citing an example, do so. Just make sure you are not citing a notable exception to prove your point.
- *A climactic moment.* Interesting speeches often base their central premise on an event or a particular moment in time. Audiences often find such examples powerful and easy to understand.
- *A suitable quotation.* You can find quotes everywhere. Rather than look in the usual sources (*Bartlett's Familiar Quotations*, *The Oxford Dictionary of Quotations* or some similar volume or website), why not pick up the phone and talk with someone close to the subject? Get a reaction from a friend, family member, participant or person who knows the events you are trying to describe. Internet search engines will turn up quotes for you by topic or by source. *Norvig's Unfamiliar Quotations* is available on the Internet by typing: http://norvig.com/quotations.html [24]
- *A reference to the occasion.* A brief explanation about why you are glad to be there or why the occasion is special might generate interest in your talk while helping to humanize you to the audience.
- *A provocative question.* If you cannot predict the future with any measure of certainty, perhaps you can pose the issue in the form of a rhetorical question. If you are actually hoping for answers from the audience, remember that you must be prepared for any response, including no response at all.
- *A description.* One effective way to introduce a topic to an audience is to describe in vivid, even lurid, detail exactly what you mean. Get the audience to visualize objects or events they cannot see. Use imagery and imaginative language to involve them in the process.
- *A statement of opinion.* This method may work, although it is important that you reveal the source of the opinion and that the source be both well known to and respected by the audience. An opinion from someone they hold in low repute will do little to bolster your cause; it may actually damage your own credibility.
- *Current or recent events.* Audiences usually respond well to information that is fresh out of the newspaper or right off the Internet. An anecdote or detail taken from a breaking news story or from a conversation with a well-respected person gives an audience a feeling that they are receiving current, inside information that others don't have or won't receive. [25]

## How Should You Structure Your Speech?

Regardless of which pattern you select for your speech, research indicates that your strongest or most important point should be placed either first or last for emphasis. Don't bury your best ideas. For an overall pattern of organization, consider one (or more) of the following:

- *Chronological order.* Time is the controlling pattern here. Start at the beginning and move to the end. Start with a particular event and move backward in time. Be consistent, giving your listeners plenty of timing cues so they will stay with you.
- *Topical organization.* When one issue is no more important than any other, you may want to organize them by topics, one after another.
- *Cause and effect.* This pattern is good if you hope to establish a likely outcome from a particular known cause or if you hope to trace the cause of a known event or effect.
- *Problem solution.* This pattern examines the nature of a problem, poses alternative solutions and then weighs those solutions according to a set of values the speaker provides. Speeches using this pattern usually offer the listener a particular solution favored by the speaker.
- *Geographic.* Compass points are the controlling motif here. The talk moves from east to west, north to south, or in some other readily identifiable direction.
- *Spatial.* Where compass points are inappropriate, you may wish to organize a talk from a front-to-back, left-to-right, top-to-bottom, inside-to-outside, stem-to-stern, or other non-geographic pattern.

## Any Advice Beyond Structure?

Yes, several bits of forensic wisdom may be helpful to you.

- *Keep it simple.* After a long church service, or so the story goes, President Calvin Coolidge's wife asked him what the sermon had been about. "Sin," said Coolidge. "What did the preacher say about it?" she wanted to know. "He was against it," Coolidge replied. [26]

Your audience is going to come away with one or two of your main ideas – one or two – not ten or fifteen. If you can't express in a sentence or two what you intend to get across, then your speech isn't focused well enough. If you don't have a clear idea of what you want to say, you can be sure your audience won't.

- **Keep it brief.** President Bill Clinton's State of the Union addresses were notoriously long, some of them more than 80 minutes. According to *The Wall Street Journal*, Congress was "begging for mercy" after an hour. "If you can do it in 20 minutes, you have the best shot at the minds of the people present," says Kevin R. Daley, the president and CEO of Communispond, Inc. "Sixty minutes is suicide. You should commit it – or they will."

At New York's Union League Club a few years ago, a prominent steel company chief ended a 90-minute presentation before 400 of his executives and managers by striding from the stage and down the middle aisle. No one applauded until he was halfway out of the room. "They didn't know he was finished," a critic recalls. "They hadn't been attentive enough to recognize that."

Offering some free advice to speakers, former New York Governor Mario Cuomo says, "When you can hear them coughing, stop whatever you are doing and get out." During his unsuccessful reelection effort a few years ago, Mr. Cuomo was losing a crowd at a late-night event but won them back when he suddenly broke into the song, "Boulevard of Broken Dreams."[27] Clever, but he'd have been better off with a shorter speech.

- **Talk, don't read.** Scripted speeches, particularly those written by someone other than the speaker, almost never sound authentic or convincing. I once wrote to a number of *Fortune 500* executives asking for video samples of speeches they had given in the previous year. A friend who is a senior executive at PepsiCo said, "I hope you don't intend to use those speeches as teaching examples. Most chief executives," he said, "are terrible speakers simply because they won't give up the script." They bury their heads in the text, ignore the audience and hope for the best. It rarely comes off the way they hope it will.
- **Relax.** Comedian Robert Klein, in his routine about the Lamaze method of natural childbirth, points out that the husband's principal role seems to be to remind the wife to breathe.[28] That's good advice, actually. Breathing steadily and naturally will help you focus, relax and deliver a convincing, entertaining and interesting speech. If you fall into a pattern of rapid, shallow breathing and can't seem to finish a sentence or a paragraph, just stop for a moment. Breathe deeply, then exhale. Bring your breathing under control once more and then continue.

## How Should You Conclude?

Conclusions are among the more important (and most welcome) portions of a public speech. Why are they important? Well, to begin, they represent one more opportunity to put your best evidence or most important ideas before your audience. They represent one last chance to say what you really mean, to reinforce your purpose for speaking and to ask for their support or compliance.

Be certain you clue people in to the fact that your speech is coming to an end. Don't leave them wondering whether there's more to come. Cue them both verbally and nonverbally to the fact that you're just about done speaking. Above all else, leave them with a clear, simple, unambiguous message. Don't let them leave the room wondering what this speech was all about.

## KEEP YOUR AUDIENCE INTERESTED

If you are worried about keeping your audience involved as you speak, think about these ideas as you prepare your remarks:

## Provide Order, Structure

If your audience is forced to work in order to follow your argument, they may lose interest. Make it easy for people to follow what you are saying: Provide a structure for them to follow, an easy-to-understand structure that will carry them from one point to another.

### Give Them Something They Can Use

Even the most charitable and altruistic among us is, from time to time, selfish. We ask ourselves, "What's in it for me?" Often, if we think a speech or a conversation holds nothing of interest for us, we'll excuse ourselves and go do something else. Your audience may be polite enough to stay in their seats, but they may not pay close attention to your talk if they cannot see their self-interests being served. Give them something they can take to the bank, some ideas or information they can put to work as soon as they leave the room.

### Make It Logical

Not everyone is influenced by logic. Many of us, in fact, can be convinced by an entirely illogical argument that contains just the right type and amount of emotion. For most of your audience members, however, logic and rationality are particularly important considerations. The more logically sound your arguments are, the greater the chance your listeners will understand and adopt your viewpoint.

### Make It Reasonable

A number of important psychological studies have shown that adults will not routinely engage in behavior that they regard as unreasonable. Now, what's reasonable to one person may seem totally unreasonable to another, but the vast majority of people will remain consistent in their definitions of what is and is not reasonable. If you know your audience well and can determine how they would characterize "reasonable behavior," you have a much better chance of convincing them to adopt your viewpoint, as long as what you ask of them falls within the limits they establish for themselves.

### Make It Clear

One reason many managerial speeches fail is that the audience simply has no idea what the speaker wants. The main point may be unclear, the supporting evidence may not be well understood, or the conclusion may be incomprehensible. Even when ambiguity may be a deliberate communication goal in some instances, consider this statement from a chief executive officer: "This firm will take all measures afforded by the law to seek the objectives we have outlined." What does that mean? Well, not only is the listener uncertain, so is the speaker. The speaker has deliberately chosen to be ambiguous, perhaps because he doesn't really know what he intends to do. Unless ambiguity is a deliberate part of your communication strategy, do what you can to make your message, your evidence and your intentions clear to your listeners.

### Use Words They Understand

Plain English will go a long way toward winning friends and influencing people. Former U.S. Securities and Exchange Commission Chairman Arthur Levitt, in speaking to people who write financial disclosure documents, said the following:

> The benefits of plain English abound. Investors will be more likely to understand what they are buying and to make informed judgments about whether they should hold or sell their investments. Brokers and investment advisors can make better recommendations to their clients if they can read and understand these documents quickly and easily.
>
> Companies that communicate successfully with their investors form stronger relationships with them. These companies save the costs of explaining legalese and dealing with confused and sometimes angry investors. Lawyers reviewing plain English documents catch and correct mistakes more easily. Many companies have switched to plain English because it's a good business decision. They see the value of communicating with their investors rather than sending them impenetrable documents. And as we depend more and more on the Internet and electronic delivery of documents, plain English versions will be easier to read electronically than legalese.[29]

Chairman Levitt was speaking specifically about the language used in written documents given to potential investors. But, if plain English works for written financial disclosure documents and has the support of a large and complex government agency like the Securities and Exchange Commission, it will probably work for you and your employer. Frankly, unless you are writing or speaking with the hope that no one will understand you, plain English is the only sensible approach.

### Keep It Moving

Your audience will be patient with you for just so long. Don't try their patience and good nature by dragging the pace of your speech or dawdling on minor points. If your talk moves along briskly, chances are good that you'll maintain audience interest.

### Answer Their Questions

Every audience has questions. Your task is to determine what they are and to answer them to their complete satisfaction. (See the section earlier in this chapter, entitled "The Questions Listeners Bring to Any Listening Situation.") If you are unwilling to address those questions, your audience may be unwilling to pay attention to or buy into your argument.

### Allay Their Fears

Everyone in your audience is afraid of something. Find out what it is. Some may be afraid that you will be asking things of them that they'll be unwilling to do. Others may be afraid they won't understand the implications of your request. If you cannot deal with their fears, no audience will accept your point of view. Fear is a powerful emotion, and when people feel frightened, they are usually unwilling to take risk or to try something new. Social psychologist Robert Cialdini suggested that persuasive speakers deal with emotions by channeling fear into excitement. Rather than simply asking an audience to calm down or not to worry, he suggests redirecting the energy inherent in audience fear into excitement for the speaker's proposals.[30]

### Respect Their Needs

Everyone in your audience has specific psychological needs. Each of them gathers and organizes information in slightly different ways, and each of them takes a slightly different approach to decision making. If you understand and respect their needs, they'll reward you.

Some may have a need for details – show them the numbers. Others may have a need to understand where this idea fits in the larger scheme of things – show them the big picture. Still others may have a need to know who else has tried or approves of this idea – show them the celebrity endorsements. If I have a specific need – say, a strong desire to know the source of your information – and you don't deal directly with my need, I'm unlikely to adopt your viewpoint or do as you ask.

## SELECT A DELIVERY APPROACH

You have four options for delivering a speech. You probably shouldn't depend on more than just one or two of them:

*Memorized* speeches are delivered verbatim, word-for-word just as the authors wrote them. The problem with memorized speeches is that, unless you are a trained actor, you cannot deliver them with any level of conviction. They sound wooden, contrived and artificial. Worse yet, you may forget where you are and have to start over. Unless you're doing Shakespeare from the stage, forget about memorized talks.

*Manuscripted* speeches are far more common among managerial and executive speaking events. The problem with speaking from a manuscript is that it sounds *read*. The impression from the audience is almost always negative:

"Why am I here? He could have e-mailed this to me." Reading a fully scripted speech ensures that you will include each key point and resist the temptation to ad lib, but without a teleprompter, you lose eye contact with the audience and seem distant or remote to them. Unless you have no other choice, don't work with a verbatim manuscript. If you must, rehearse carefully and try looking up frequently, making regular contact with the audience.

*Extemporaneous* speeches are, perhaps, the best among your alternatives. These speeches are thoroughly researched, tightly and sensibly organized, well rehearsed, and delivered either without notes or with visual aids to prompt your memory. They are especially convincing to an audience because you make and maintain eye contact, you look at them rather than at a script, and you speak (seemingly) from the heart and not from a set of prepared notes. This is really the effect you are striving for.

*Impromptu* speeches are delivered without any preparation at all. Someone in charge usually asks you to stand up and "offer a few remarks." This is not the best approach to public speaking, obviously, because you prepared no evidence and have not rehearsed. You may not even have a topic or an idea worth hearing. The good news is that the audience's expectations are low. They will applaud for nearly anything as long as it's brief and not insulting to them.

What do you do when someone asks you to stand up and "offer a few remarks"? Modesty usually dictates that you say little, but protocol usually demands that you say something. Here are a few ideas that may help.

### Maintain Your Poise

Just smile, thank your host for the opportunity to speak, and take advantage of the moment.

### Decide On Your Topic and Approach

Speak briefly about something that you understand and that will be of interest to those listening. Select a pattern of organization: past, present, future; advantages, disadvantages; risks, benefits; reasons favoring an idea, reasons opposing. Once you have your pattern, stick to it. Don't get inventive as you go along.

### Do Not Apologize

People know you didn't prepare a speech. Just talk to them.

### Summarize Your Point and Position

In one sentence, or two at the most, underscore your key points and reiterate why they are important or worthwhile.

### Be Sincere, Honest and Direct

Nothing impresses an audience more profoundly than an honest person. Convey the impression that you have nothing to hide and nothing ulterior in your motives for speaking. They will reward you by considering your ideas and applauding your delivery.

## DEVELOP YOUR VISUAL SUPPORT

In preparing a speech, managers will often ask if they even need visual support. To answer this question properly, you should consider whether visual support will help to explain, reinforce or clarify your position or your evidence. If you can't *say* it easily, you may be able to *show* it. Graphs, charts, tables and photographs are usually helpful, but not always. If you clutter the screen with unreadable or unnecessary detail, you may confuse your audience. On the other hand, if your graphics are crisp, clear and uncluttered, your audience may gain insights they might otherwise miss.

Some people are visual-attenders, while others are aural-attenders. Give each group an opportunity to hear and see your key points. One should reinforce the other. Don't show them something you don't plan to talk about. Similarly, if you choose to use visual support, don't talk at length about things you can't show or reinforce visually.[31]

Other research shows that 30 to 40 percent of people are *visual learners*, and about 20 to 30 percent are *auditory learners*, but a substantial number of others learn best through physical activity. This group, sometimes referred to as *kinesthetic learners*, is often overlooked in business presentations. The key here, according to Harvard's Nick Morgan, is to get your listeners doing something. "Get them involved early and often," he says, "through role-playing, games, working with models, even creating charts and physical representations of what you want them to learn."[32]

## When Do Visuals Work Best?

Visual information is often at its best when you are working with new data, complex or technical information, or a new context. Visual aids can help you with numbers, facts, quotes and lists. They are also frequently good for side-by-side comparisons, emphasizing similarities or differences. Geographical or spatial patterns will also frequently benefit from some form of visual illustration.[33]

Good visuals will . . .

- be simple in nature,
- explain relationships,
- use color effectively,
- be easy to set up, display and transport,
- reinforce the spoken message.

## Can I Speak Without Visuals?

Yes, of course. That's the basic difference between a narrator and a public speaker. Some speaking situations call for visual aids and you want to make certain you've done your best to illustrate the content of your speech appropriately. Other speaking occasions either don't require visual support or would be better served without it. I can't imagine John F. Kennedy, Martin Luther King, Jr. or Winston Churchill using PowerPoint to illustrate a talk. They were, of course, political orators, not businessmen. But the point is the same: Don't overdo the visual aids.

Some executives have been known to ban PowerPoint entirely from their company presentations. That may seem like an overreaction, but it's easy to understand how those feelings came about. A colleague showed me some written critiques of a presentation he gave to a supervisory development course not long ago, and they weren't encouraging: "Overhead avalanche," read one. "Death by PowerPoint," said another. My advice to him was simple: Use fewer slides, make sure they reinforce only key points, and make certain you do not overdo the basics, including color, transitions, type fonts, motion or sound effects. It can pretty quickly get to be too much for the audience.

Keep in mind that you may be the best visual of all. "Good leaders understand that *they* are the best visual," says Judith Humphrey, the president of The Humphrey Group, a Toronto-based firm that specializes in executive speech training. "They instinctively know that their message will come through best if the audience looks at them and listens to them – with no distractions."

Her recommendations include stepping out from behind the podium and making yourself a focal point of the speech. "If you are committed and engaged, the audience can see it in your face, in your gestures, in the way you walk, in the way you stand, in the way you hold your head high."[34]

"Here's the key," says Humphrey. "Great speaking is really about great thinking. People can be persuaded by the passion you have for your ideas, but only if they can see you." In a darkened room, she says, the audience is focused on the slides and not on you. "But, if you're willing to step forward, look them in the eyes, and show your conviction for those ideas, people will be more inclined to believe you." You could e-mail those slides to your audience, but when you speak to them in person, you become an important part of the speech itself. "If so much information is processed visually," she adds, "that's all the more reason to make yourself visual."[35]

That may mean inserting an occasional blank slide in your PowerPoint deck, just to create an opportunity for you to explain the main point of your talk or show why it might be particularly important for your audience to act on what you've just told them. It may mean stepping forward, out of the shadows, so that your audience can see you. At a basic level, it means taking advantage of the opportunity to create a personal bond between you and at least a few selected members of the audience who can act as proxies for the rest. The more personal and human that bond, the greater the chance your audience will understand your commitment to the ideas in the speech and respond in the way you hoped they would.

## REHEARSE YOUR SPEECH

### Should You Practice?

Absolutely! Don't even consider giving a speech you haven't rehearsed – several times. Why should you practice? Rehearsal will do at least three things for your speech.

First, it will limit timing. You will know after a run-through or two whether you have too much, too little or just enough to say. Second, rehearsal will improve your transitions. As you practice your speech, you will have an opportunity to identify the rough spots and work on movement from one main point to another and from one part of the speech to another. Finally, rehearsal will polish your delivery and build confidence. When the day to deliver the speech finally comes, you will step to the podium with the knowledge that you know this stuff inside and out. A well-rehearsed speech contains no surprises.

Not convinced? Apple CEO Steve Jobs was considered to be among the most masterful, persuasive speakers in business. How did he get that way? According to *Fortune* magazine's Adam Lashinsky:

> A key Jobs business tool was his mastery of the message. He rehearsed over and over every line he and others would utter in public about Apple, which authorizes only a small number of executives to speak publicly on a given topic. Key to the Jobs approach was careful consideration of what he and Apple would say – and wouldn't say.[36]

### Should You Use Notes?

The best speakers seem to deliver their speeches extemporaneously, or "from the heart." Such speeches aren't really memorized word-for-word, but rather are thoroughly researched, well rehearsed and professionally supported. Many extemporaneous speakers will use their visual support to prompt their memories, as if giant notecards had been placed on the wall for them and their audience to see.

If you do choose to use notecards, here are some suggestions. At a minimum, they should be:

- simple,
- compact,
- easy to follow,
- easy to handle,
- numbered,
- readable.

Having put your notecards together in this way, reconsider once again why you need them. Speech coaches and public speaking experts in the U.S. are nearly unanimous in their disapproval of notecards. Instead, use your projected visuals to prompt your memory.

## DEVELOP CONFIDENCE IN YOUR MESSAGE AND IN YOURSELF

It's one thing to know your material. It's another matter entirely to believe that you can get up on stage and speak with confidence to a group of strangers. Understanding your message and knowing that you have both quality support and a well-organized speech are important to your success, but so is self-confidence.

Rehearsal will help. Simply knowing that you've been through the contents of your speech more than once is reassuring. The knowledge that you personally arranged and rehearsed the talk will give you confidence. And, as you work on your self-assurance, consider this thought: You're the expert. This audience asked for you to speak on this subject because they want to hear what you have to say. They are interested in your expertise and your viewpoint. Chances are good that you know more about your subject than anyone else in the room (though you can never be completely certain). Use your interest, your expertise and your background to your advantage.

The more confident you are, the more credible you are. If you seem uncertain, the audience may be reluctant to believe you. Just approach this speech as you would any other managerial task, knowing that you have the ability, the intelligence and the confidence to get it done. The more professional, sincere and capable you seem, the more likely the audience is to believe you and buy into your message.

## DELIVER YOUR MESSAGE

### *Beforehand*

Before you begin your talk, make certain you've checked on all of the most important details:

- **Date, time and location.** Where are you supposed to be? When is your talk scheduled to begin? If you are unfamiliar with the location, do your best to find out all about it in advance.
- **Room layout.** It's never wise to walk into the room with no idea of how it will be organized. Don't depend on others to do it to your satisfaction, either. If you can arrange it, be there in advance and set things up the way you'd like them to be. It's your speech; take charge of the room.
- **Microphone and acoustics.** Try out the sound system in advance. If you will be wearing a wireless mike, find out exactly what you need to do to make it work. Decide in advance whether you are willing to speak without a sound system if it fails or wait for someone to repair it.
- **Visual aids.** Check out the screen, the placement of your projector and the system you plan to use to support your talk. Make sure it's focused, centered and visible to the people in the back row.
- **Stage.** Take a moment to find out how to get on and off the stage, where the sound projection limits are, and where the trapdoors, cables and high-risk footing might be.
- **Time limits.** Double-check with your host on the time limits for your talk and then abide by them. Don't disappoint by saying less than you had promised, and don't disappoint by speaking beyond your allotted time.
- **Lectern.** Find out where you will speak and, if possible, whether you'll be able to move beyond a lectern and walk around the front of the room.
- **Notes.** Don't trust anyone else with your speech. If you're working from a script or detailed notes, hang onto them personally. Review them beforehand, but don't make a point of poring over them just as your host is about to introduce you.
- **Lights.** Determine whether the overhead lighting will wash out a projected image on the screen. Are the lights bright enough for people to see you and whatever handouts you provide for them? Are they dim enough to allow them to see your visual aids?

### *Try It Out*

Use the microphone, check out the projector, walk across the stage, examine the effect of your visual aids from the back of the room. See if you can be seen and heard in all parts of the room. Gain some confidence by knowing where you'll be and what it feels like before you actually begin.

### *As You Speak*

Consider these ideas to keep your audience interested:

- Step up to the lectern, breathe deeply, smile, think positively and speak.
- Do your best to be one of them (unless it's obvious you are really not).
- Use humor where it may be appropriate (unless you are not funny).

- Share your own experiences, values, background, goals and fears.
- Focus on current local events and other issues known to the audience.
- Begin by moving from the familiar to the unfamiliar.
- Talk process first, then detail.
- Blueprint the speech: Tell them where this talk is going.
- Visualize and demonstrate.
- Use interim summaries, transitions.
- Give examples.
- Humanize and personalize.
- Tell stories, dramatize your central theme.
- Use yourself, involve them.

As you approach the challenge of becoming a speaking professional (as opposed to a professional speaker), keep in mind a few basic ideas. No one is born with great public speaking ability. Language is the habit of a lifetime, and your ability to speak with conviction and sincerity is a function of your willingness to work at it. If you work, one speech at a time, to improve your skills, chances are quite good that others in a position of influence will notice and reward you for your effort.

## FOR FURTHER READING

Arredondo, L. *Business Presentations: The McGraw-Hill 36-Hour Course*. New York: McGraw-Hill, 1994.

Booth, D., D. Shames and P. Desberg. *Own the Room: Business Presentations that Persuade, Engage, and Get Results*. New York: McGraw-Hill, 2009.

Hauer, N. and E. Martley. *The Practical Speech Handbook*. Burr Ridge, IL: Irwin Mirror Press, 1993.

Hindle, T. *Making Presentations*. New York: DK Publications, 1998.

Hofmann, T. M., D. F. Womack and J. Shubert. *Effective Business Presentations*. Cambridge, MA: Harvard Business School Publications, 1990. HBS Note 9–391–011.

Koegel, T. J. *The Exceptional Presenter: A Proven Formula to Open Up and Own the Room*. Austin, TX: Greenleaf Book Group Press, 2007.

O'Rourke, J. S. *The Truth About Confident Presenting*, 2/e. London: Anthem Press, 2018.

## NOTES

1  Osgood, C. *Osgood on Speaking*. New York: William Morrow and Company, 1989.

2  Suskind, R. and J. S. Lublin. "Critics Are Succinct: Long Speeches Tend to Get Short Interest," *The Wall Street Journal*, January 26, 1995, pp. A1, A8. Reprinted by permission of the *Wall Street Journal*, Copyright © 1995 Dow Jones & Company, Inc. All rights reserved worldwide.

3  Osgood, *Osgood on Speaking*.

4  Matson, E. "Now That We Have Your Complete Attention . . . ," *Fast Company*, February 1997, pp. 124–126.

5  Ibid.

6  Ibid.

7  Finnessy, J. M. Personal communication with the author, June 16, 2000.

8  Schroeder, J. and N. Epley. "The Science of Sounding Smart," *Harvard Business Review*, October 7, 2015. Online at https://hbr.org/2015/10/the-science-of-sounding-smart. Accessed Wednesday, July 4, 2018 at 2:57 p.m. EST.

9  Ibid.

10 Ibid.

11 Cooper, L. (ed.) *The Rhetoric of Aristotle*. Upper Saddle River, NJ: Prentice Hall, 1960, pp. 141–142.

12 For a selected list of people, concepts and ideas that have never been part of young people's lives, see the Beloit College Mindset List at www.beloit.edu/mindset/. Accessed June 22, 2018 at 1:30 p.m.

13 National Center for Education Statistics, Institute of Education Sciences, U.S. Department of Education. Retrieved from http://nces.ed.gov/programs/coe/glossary/s.asp. Accessed Wednesday, July 9, 2008, at 11:15 a.m.

14 Cooper. *The Rhetoric of Aristotle*, pp. 16–17.

15 For a thorough review of preparation for public speaking, see "The Basic Presentation Checklist," *Harvard Management Communication Letter*, October 2000, pp. 4–5.

16  Hamlin, S. *How to Talk So People Will Listen.* New York: Harper and Row, 1989, p. 23.

17  Ibid., pp. 26–29.

18  Ibid., p. 30.

19  Lippmann, W. *Public Opinion.* New York: The Free Press, 1965, pp. 53–68.

20  For an excellent discussion of the emotional foundations of prejudice and prejudicial thinking, see Bem, D. J. *Beliefs, Attitudes, and Human Affairs.* Belmont, CA: Brooks/Cole Publishing, 1970, pp. 40–44.

21  For a thorough review of current research on human emotion and the management of human feelings, see Goleman, D. *Emotional Intelligence: Why It Can Matter More Than IQ.* New York: Bantam Books, 1995.

22  Borden, G. A. *An Introduction to Human Communication Theory.* Dubuque, IA: William C. Brown, 1971, pp. 81–87.

23  Hoecklin, L. *Managing Cultural Differences: Strategies for Competitive Advantage.* Reading, MA: Addison-Wesley, 1995, pp. 23–49.

24  *Norvig's Unfamiliar Quotations.* http://norvig.com/quotations.html. Accessed Friday, June 22, 2018, 1:44 p.m. EST.

25  This remarkable list was given to me by the great *Los Angeles Times* sportswriter, Jim Murray, who often used a version of it to determine how he would lead a difficult story. A particularly moving example was his obituary tribute to California Angels center fielder, Lyman Bostock, in September 1978.

26  Osgood. *Osgood on Speaking.*

27  Suskind and Lublin. "Critics Are Succinct."

28  Osgood. *Osgood on Speaking.*

29  Smith, N. (ed.). *A Plain English Handbook: How to Create Clear SEC Disclosure Documents.* Office of Investor Education and Assistance, U.S. Securities and Exchange Commission, August 1998, p. 4.

30  Cialdini, R. B. *Influence: The Psychology of Persuasion,* rev. ed. New York: Quill/William Morrow, 1993.

31  Ingersoll, G. M. *The Effects of Presentation Modalities and Modality Preferences on Learning and Recall.* Doctoral dissertation, Pennsylvania State University. Ann Arbor, MI: University Microfilms, 1970. No. 71–16615.

32  Morgan, N. "Presentations That Appeal to All Your Listeners," *Harvard Management Communication Letter,* June 2000, pp. 4–5.

33  For a thorough and useful discussion of visual support for business presentations, see Bailey, E. P. *A Practical Guide for Business Speaking.* New York: Oxford University Press, 1992, pp. 36–78, 111–125.

34  Humphrey, J. Telephone interview with the author, July 29, 2002.

35  Ibid.

36  Lashinsky, A. "The Decade of Steve," *Fortune,* November 23, 2009, p. 98

# Case 4.1: Old Dominion Trust Company

"It was a quarter to four on Friday afternoon," said Rob Leonard.

I was just closing out my accounts and trying to clear up a few more issues before the end of the business day. Then along came my division vice president. Since my desk is in the center of the mortgage banking division, I could tell long before he got to me that I was the one he was looking for. And, frankly, the folder he dropped on my desk was the last thing in the world I expected to see.

Rob Leonard is a 26-year-old assistant broker in the mortgage banking division of Old Dominion Trust, a relatively small interstate bank located in the mid-Atlantic region. Rob's branch has regional responsibility for home mortgages in Northern Virginia and the Washington, DC area. Although he had joined Old Dominion Trust following graduation four years earlier, he was still among the more junior people in his branch.

The boss went directly to Leonard's desk and asked if he had a minute. "Of course I have a minute," said Leonard, "Who hasn't got a minute for the Branch V.P.?" Brian Lorigan was Senior Vice President, Mortgage Banking for Old Dominion and Executive Vice President for the Annandale branch office. He was not only Leonard's supervisor, but his mentor and partner in several important projects.

Leonard and Lorigan had been working on a new, federally funded mortgage program that would permit low-to-middle-income, first-time home buyers to obtain financing at very low rates. It was an important project that would require both thorough explanation to the community and careful screening of each of the applicants. The program had been in development for more than six months and would require the cooperation of state and local officials if it were to work. It was an impressive attempt, Leonard thought, on the bank's part to provide mortgage financing to people who would otherwise never qualify for a home loan.

"I thought he would want to review the screening procedures we'd been working on, or perhaps talk about the software I planned to use to help set up the program," said Leonard. What he had in mind frightened Leonard a lot more. Lorigan said that Dick Gidley, his principal assistant, had been scheduled to speak to a Capitol Hill neighborhood group about the federally assisted home loan program. Unfortunately, Gidley was in Philadelphia and had just been "bumped" from his return flight to Washington.

Lorigan asked if Leonard would fill in for Gidley at the neighborhood group meeting that evening and speak about the new loan program. "The details are all in this package," he said. He got a phone number, a set of street directions to a renovated fire station on Rhode Island Avenue, and the name of the woman who would introduce Leonard. The rest of the information would have to come from documents he had prepared for the bank and for the Select Committee that had drafted the legislation.

Leonard was philosophical about the request:

It wasn't that I minded canceling dinner plans I had for that evening. It was just that I wasn't sure I was ready to stand up in public and explain a bank loan program that I wasn't in charge of. After Mr. Lorigan shook my hand and said thanks, I looked at my watch. It was five minutes to four, and this thing in Washington was scheduled for seven o'clock.

## DISCUSSION QUESTIONS

1. Assuming you're in Rob Leonard's position, what would you do? Would it be a good idea to tell Mr. Lorigan you're just not ready (or willing) to give that speech?
2. What would you want to know about the audience that you don't already know? Where could you find that information?
3. What would you want to know about the occasion and speaking situation that you don't already know?
4. Is there anything you think you should know about the physical layout of the room or the arrangements in the fire station that you'll be speaking in?
5. How would you go about preparing your notes for this speech?
6. What else would you bring with you for this event? Do you have time to get visual aids or flipcharts made? Is that a good idea?
7. How should you dress for this occasion?
8. What do you think your principal message should be for these people?

## ACKNOWLEDGMENTS

This case was prepared from field interviews by James S. O'Rourke, Teaching Professor of Management, as the basis for class discussion rather than to illustrate either effective or ineffective handling of an administrative situation. Personal and corporate identities have been disguised.

# Case 4.2: Staples, Inc.

## *Preparing the CEO for a Press Conference*

As Elizabeth Allen pulled into her parking spot at Staples, Inc. headquarters in Framingham, Massachusetts, she knew the next three days would be a challenge. "This is a huge opportunity," she thought to herself. It would be visible, risky and filled with snares. "On the other hand," she thought, "this really should be fun." Ms. Allen was thinking about a speech manuscript she had been preparing for her Chairman and Chief Executive Officer. Less than 72 hours from now, he would give the most important talk in his professional career across the country in California.

"Technology and the Internet are clearly the most powerful communication media available to any company today," says Elizabeth Allen. "But on some occasions, there is just no substitute for face-to-face interaction and a personal statement from a senior official of the company." The statement Allen envisioned would be powerful, important to shareholders and the community, and would be seen by literally millions of people on television, both as it happened and later on news programs nation-wide.

Elizabeth Heller Allen was Vice President for Corporate Communication at Staples, Inc. and had primary responsibility – among her many other duties – for preparing members of the Staples senior team for press conferences, speeches and public appearances. The ten most senior people in the company were known as the "Point Team," and Allen's Corporate Communication staff worked very hard to prepare them for a wide range of public appearances, including the one her CEO would make the day after tomorrow.

Staples, Inc. is the #2 office supply superstore company in the U.S., with market capitalization of $13.5 billion and annual revenues of $8.3 billion. They sell office products, furniture, computers, and photocopying services at more than 1,000 stores, primarily in the U.S. and Canada, but also in Germany, the U.K., The Netherlands and Portugal. With more than 21,500 employees, the company sells some 8,000 different office products to small- and medium-sized businesses through their retail stores, a catalogue and an e-commerce site.

"Speaking opportunities are important at any business," says Allen:

> but they are especially important at a company like Staples because the current CEO, Thomas G. Stemberg, is the company founder. Like Herb Kelleher at Southwest Airlines, Bill Gates at Microsoft, or Jim Barksdale at Netscape, the founder of a company has special visibility in the marketplace and it's very important for shareholders, employees, and other stakeholders that we take best advantage of that.

According to Allen, speaking styles and preparation for speeches will vary greatly:

Some members of the Point Team will ask that every single word of a speech be written out in advance. They rehearse, they work from a manuscript, and – if one were available – they'd ask for a teleprompter. Others will say, 'Send me an outline 24 hours in advance. I'll wing it.'

For each of her senior executives, Allen found a different challenge as they prepared for a public speech.

The more important the venue or the audience, the more important the text, rehearsal and detailed preparation become. "If a lot of people are going to see and hear this speech – even fragments of it on videotape – it's all the more important that we spend time and energy in getting the speaker ready." Frequently, that means a complete manuscript, even though most executives would prefer to speak extemporaneously.

"Most of the Point Team would rather have a few key points, some supporting detail, and a couple of closing thoughts to work from," says Allen. "These are important people – supremely confident – who got to their current positions by being comfortable in front of a crowd." Her preference is to prepare such people with information about who will be in the room, the occasion on which they'll be speaking and the business objective of the talk itself. Beyond that, delivery and rehearsal are up to the individual speaker.

"There is a value to a complete manuscript, though," she says:

We not only like to know what someone said to a particular audience on a given occasion, but my staff can get substantially greater mileage out of a speech if I can share a copy of the script with the press.

Advance copies of a speech may induce a journalist to attend the talk, or inspire a reporter who couldn't attend to include direct quotes in a news story. Either way, the company and the message in the executive's speech receive greater exposure.

That morning, Elizabeth Allen had just such an opportunity as her CEO prepared for a speech on the west coast. "Staples had an agreement to purchase the naming rights for a new basketball and hockey arena in Los Angeles," she said. "A press conference was scheduled to reveal the identity of the naming-rights company." According to Allen, the event was preceded by considerable advance media coverage and speculation throughout the L.A. basin. "Many people thought the name would be a local, California company. And, of course, we did nothing to discourage the attention given to the event." It was a closely guarded secret. And Staples was about to pay $100 million for the privilege – the highest sum ever paid for the right to name an athletic venue.

"I know several things about this event," said Allen. "First, I know that it's being covered not by the business press, but the sports press. From the news media's point-of-view, this isn't a business story. It's a sports story." She also knew who would be in the room. "Dave Taylor of the Los Angeles Kings and Jerry West of the LA Lakers – both general managers – will be there." Civic officials, investors, reporters and many others would be watching and listening. "This five-minute speech of Tom Stemberg's will have huge marquee value," said Allen.

Elizabeth Allen also knew that this was more than just another corporate investment in professional sports. "This is a Boston company putting its name on a Los Angeles landmark. I know there are cultural factors at work here, and political factors as well as business factors." For Allen, this speech – brief as it would be – had to be flawless. "No faux pas," she said. "This has got to be perfect."

## DISCUSSION QUESTIONS

1. If you were assisting Ms. Allen with this event, what would you want to know that you don't already know?
2. As she drafts Mr. Stemberg's remarks, what issues should Ms. Allen pay especially careful attention to?
3. Can you think of any references, issues or remarks that Ms. Allen might want her CEO to avoid?
4. What sort of pre-event information would you want to brief Mr. Stemberg about? What sort of detail does he need about the event, the audience and the occasion?
5. Others will certainly speak on this occasion. Would it be helpful for Ms. Allen to know who they are? Would it be important for her to know what they intend to say? Why? How can she go about obtaining that information?

6. What do you imagine Mr. Stemberg's business goals are for this speech? What specific outcomes would he and Ms. Allen want to achieve as a result of his remarks to the press and the community?

7. What shadow audiences might be watching and listening to what Mr. Stemberg has to say? How should he prepare for them?

8. Would you suggest to Mr. Stemberg that he rehearse his speech? If so, how would you go about that? What kind of advice would you give to him as he prepares for this event?

## ACKNOWLEDGMENTS

This case was prepared by James S. O'Rourke, Teaching Professor of Management, as the basis for class discussion rather than to illustrate either effective or ineffective handling of an administrative situation.

# CHAPTER 5

# Writing

Business writing isn't simply a way to move information from one office to another. Nor is it just another storage mechanism for business decisions. Business writing, at its best and at its worst, is an expression of the values and beliefs of an organization. A peek inside the file drawers and outbaskets of any business will reveal a great deal about what's important to an organization, as well as how the people in that organization think about their work, their customers and clients, and themselves.

Business writing is important because, as you saw in Chapter 1, the most important projects and decisions in the life of a business end up in writing. Writing is a way of thinking about business, a way of organizing. It provides analysis of and justification for our best ideas. It also provides documentation and discipline for an organization.

Writing is also a career sifter. Managers do most of their own writing and editing, relying on the assistance and advice of others only on occasion. If you can't write at a minimally effective level, others in positions of influence will notice and you'll be looking for work elsewhere. At the very least, an inability to express yourself effectively on paper can stop a career dead in its tracks.

Why is most business writing so bad and what makes it that way? Well, most business writing isn't terrible – some is, of course – but much of it is just badly organized, passive, not parallel in structure, littered with jargon and obscure terminology. Some business writers pay little attention to the conventions of spelling and punctuation. Others just keep writing until they've told their readers *everything* they know about the subject. Sentences run on and paragraphs take up entire pages.

Most business writing isn't bad for just one reason. It's often a series of reasons, and heading the list is this: Writers simply are not writing for the benefit of their readers. They don't craft a memo, a proposal, a report or a letter with the needs and interests of their readers in mind. If they did, we would see fewer documents written like this mutual fund prospectus paragraph:

Maturity and duration management decisions are made in the context of an intermediate maturity orientation. The maturity structure of the portfolio is adjusted in the anticipation of cyclical interest rate changes.

Such adjustments are not made in an effort to capture short-term, day-to-day movements in the market, but instead are implemented in anticipation of longer term, secular shifts in the levels of interest rates (i.e., shifts transcending and/or not inherent to the business cycle). Adjustments made to shorten portfolio maturity and duration are made to limit capital losses during periods when interest rates are expected to rise.

Conversely, adjustments made to lengthen maturity for the portfolio's maturity and duration strategy lie in analysis of the U.S. and global economies, focusing on levels of real interest rates, monetary and fiscal policy actions, and cyclical indicators.[1]

Ordinary human beings who read that paragraph will recognize that it's grammatically correct and syntactically sound. Each sentence has a verb. The capital letters are used correctly. For the most part, people will recognize the words, but when words are put together like that, we read and feel confused. What can this mean? What's the writer trying to say here?

When Berkshire Hathaway Chairman Warren Buffett saw that paragraph, he got out a yellow legal pad, a ballpoint pen, and drafted another version:

We will try to profit by correctly predicting future interest rates. When we have no strong opinion, we will generally hold intermediate-term bonds. But when we expect a major and sustained increase in rates, we will concentrate on short-term issues. And, conversely, if we expect a major shift to lower rates, we will buy long bonds. We will focus on the big picture and won't make moves based on short-term considerations.[2]

The first paragraph was written by a mutual fund manager with one of several ideas in mind. He may have been insecure and eager to show his boss and the customers how many big words and important business phrases he knew. Or he may have been deliberately trying to disguise the mutual fund's lack of an investment strategy. If the prospectus isn't entirely clear, how can the fund manager be held accountable for failing to live up to the aims of his strategy?

I have another suggestion about that paragraph you just read: The fund manager who wrote it was probably modeling his writing on thousands of other mutual fund prospectus documents he's seen in his career. He's following a well-trodden path to obscurity, hoping his writing will look just like that of so many other successful managers.

Let's give him the benefit of the doubt and assume that his intentions were good but his mentors were not. Times are changing, though, and that fund manager will never again be able to write dense, impenetrable prose and get away with it. Former U.S. Securities and Exchange Commission Chairman Arthur Levitt struck a blow in favor of plain English:

Whether you work at a company, a law firm, or the U.S. Securities and Exchange Commission, the shift to plain English requires a new style of thinking and writing. We must question whether the documents we are used to writing highlight the important information investors need to make informed decisions. The legalese and jargon of the past must give way to everyday words that communicate complex information clearly.[3]

Warren Buffett responded by saying:

Chairman Levitt's whole drive to encourage "plain English" . . . [is] good news for me. For more than forty years, I've studied the documents that public companies file. Too often, I've been unable to decipher just what is being said or, worse yet, had to conclude that nothing was being said.

One unoriginal but useful tip: write with a specific person in mind. When writing Berkshire Hathaway's annual report, I pretend that I'm writing to my sisters. I have no trouble picturing them: though highly intelligent, they are not experts in accounting or finance. They will understand plain English but jargon may puzzle them. My goal is simply to give them the information I would wish them to supply me if our positions were reversed. To succeed, I don't need to be Shakespeare; I must, though, have a sincere desire to inform. No sisters to write to? Borrow mine: Just begin with "Dear Doris and Bertie."[4]

---

## Workplace Writing Is a "Threshold Skill"

A recent survey of 120 American corporations employing nearly 8 million people concludes that in today's workplace writing is a "threshold skill" for hiring and promotion among salaried (i.e., professional) employees. Survey results indicate that writing is a ticket to professional opportunity, while poorly written job applications are a figurative kiss of death.

People who cannot write and communicate clearly, the study found, will not be hired and are unlikely to last long enough to be considered for promotion. The National Commission on Writing, a panel established by the College Board, concluded that two-thirds of salaried employees in large American companies have some writing responsibility, and 80 percent or more of the companies in the service and finance, insurance, and real estate sectors now assess writing during hiring.

A similar dynamic is at work during promotions. Half of all companies take writing into account when making promotion decisions. "You can't move up without writing skills," said one respondent.

More than half of all responding companies report that they "frequently" or "almost always" produce technical reports (59%), formal reports (62%), and memos and correspondence (70%).

Communication through e-mail and PowerPoint presentations is almost universal. "Because of e-mail," said one executive, "more employees have to write more often. Also a lot more has to be documented."

The study also found that more than 40 percent of firms offer or require training for salaried employees with writing deficiencies, and it appears that such training now costs American companies as much as $3.1 billion annually.

*Source:* "Writing: A Ticket to Work . . . Or a Ticket Out," Report of The National Commission on Writing, September 2004. Available in PDF form at www.writingcommission.org/report.html

---

## AN INTRODUCTION TO GOOD BUSINESS WRITING

Good business writing is simple, clear and concise. It's virtually "transparent." By not calling attention to itself, good writing helps the reader focus on the idea you are trying to communicate rather than on the words that describe it.

Good writing, in business and elsewhere, is a pleasure to read. Ideas become clear, the writer's intentions are undisguised, and the evidence used to support those ideas is readily understandable. No one I know thinks writing is easy. Good writing – that is, writing with power, grace, dignity and impact – takes time, careful thought and revision. Such writing is often the product of many years of training and practice. And, to be sure, the language we bring to the task is the product of a lifetime of use. Even though writing seems like hard work to many of us, I know for sure that you can learn to do it well.

No teacher of writing can lay much claim to original thinking on this subject. Instead, we each have built on the good ideas given to us by those who have written, taught and observed organizational and business writing before us. If you can put some of this advice to work in your own writing, your reward will be the approval of your readers.

## FIFTEEN WAYS TO BECOME A BETTER BUSINESS WRITER

Here are 15 guidelines for better writing – a supplement, if you will, to the rules of grammar, syntax and punctuation you learned in school. These were crafted by writing consultant Jean Paul Plumez and will help you bring simplicity and clarity to your writing and power and vitality to your ideas:[5]

- **Keep in mind that your reader doesn't have much time.** Memos often travel to senior managers who have tight schedules and much to read. Your memo must be clear on first reading. The shorter it is, the better chance it has of being read and considered.

- **Know where you are going before you start writing.** Start with a list of the important points you want to cover, then put them into an outline. If you are composing a memo, write the Overview section first. It should contain your purpose for writing and the keys to understanding the rest of what follows. Then, write the most important paragraphs before you get to details and supplementary material.
- **Don't make any spelling or grammatical errors.** Readers who find bad grammar and misspelled words will perceive the writer to be careless or uneducated. They will not put much stock in the writer's ideas.
- **Be responsive to the needs of the reader.** Let no one accuse you of missing the point. Before you write, find out what the reader expects, wants and needs. If you must deviate from these guidelines, let the reader know why early in the memo.
- **Be clear and specific.** Use simple, down-to-earth words. Avoid needless words and wordy expressions. Avoid vague modifiers like *very* and *slightly*. Simple words and expressions are clearer and easier to understand. They show confidence and add power to your ideas.
- **Try to use the present tense.** Be careful not to slip from the present to the past tense and back again. Select one tense and stick to it. Use the present tense when possible to add immediacy to your writing.
- **Make your writing vigorous and direct.** Use active sentences and avoid the passive voice. Be more positive and definite by limiting the use of the word "not." Avoid long strings of modifiers.
- **Use short sentences and paragraphs.** Send bulletins not essays! Vary length to avoid monotonous-looking pages, but remember that short sentences and paragraphs are more inviting and more likely to get read.
- **Use personal pronouns.** Don't hesitate to use *I*, *we* and *you*, even in formal writing. The institutional references can be cold and sterile, while personal pronouns make your writing warm, inviting and more natural.
- **Avoid clichés and jargon.** Tired, hackneyed words and expressions make your writing appear superficial. Find your own words and use them.
- **Separate fact from opinion.** The reader should *never* be in doubt as to what is fact and what is opinion. Determine what you *know* and what you *think* before you start writing. Be consistent about facts and opinions throughout the memo.
- **Use numbers with restraint.** A paragraph filled with numbers is difficult to read, and difficult to write. Use a few numbers selectively to make your point. Put the rest in tables and exhibits.
- **Write the way you talk.** Avoid pompous, bureaucratic and legalistic words and expressions. Use informal, personal human language. Write to others the way you would talk to them. Read your memo out loud – if you wouldn't talk that way, change it.
- **Never be content with your first effort.** Revising and editing are critical to good writing. Putting some time between writing and editing will help you be more objective. Revise your memo with the intent to simplify, clarify and trim excess words.
- **Make it excellent!** Seek out and eliminate factual errors, typos, misspellings, bad grammar and incorrect punctuation. Remember, if one detail in your memo is recognized as incorrect, your entire line of thinking may be suspect.

## WRITING A BUSINESS MEMO

Memos are, for the most part, *internal* documents. We use them to pass information, ideas and recommendations to other people in the same organization. They have the advantage of not requiring an inside address, a salutation line and perfunctory opening lines that greet the reader, inquiring about matters unrelated to the subject of the document.

Good memos get to the point, focus on just one issue and support the writer's central ideas with coherent, relevant, convincing evidence.

The best of business memos are concise, written in plain English and sensibly organized. That's true of business letters as well, but it's especially true of memos. They say what they must without using any more words than necessary. They present your ideas at something less than the upper reaches of bureaucratic formality, and they are organized with headings, subheadings and parallel structure so that they are easy to read, easy to follow and easy to understand.

Your ability to write a crisp, clean, no-nonsense memo will mark you as someone who contributes to the organization – someone worth keeping, watching and promoting. Will a good memo get you promoted? That's unlikely.

A series of bad memos – poorly crafted, disorganized and densely expressed – however, may stop your career in its tracks. Writing, after all, is a career sifter. Good writers move up; bad writers get left behind.

## THE SIX COMMUNICATION STRATEGIES

Before you begin writing, begin thinking. Give some careful thought to your reader, to your objectives and to the strategy you will employ to achieve your objectives. The content and pattern of organization will follow from those. When you are sure you know what you want to achieve and what you want your reader to learn from your writing, you will need a communication strategy.

Here are six basic strategies, three designed to convey information and three designed to promote action:[6]

| Information Strategies | Action Strategies |
|---|---|
| To confirm agreement | To request assistance |
| To provide facts | To give direction |
| To provide a point of view | To seek agreement |

## WRITING AN OVERVIEW PARAGRAPH

The opening or Overview paragraph of any memo should reveal a communication strategy for the entire document. By writing it first, you will identify your purpose and main ideas. This approach will give you perspective and direction that will guide the development of the memo, letter or report.

Your reader will benefit as well. That Overview paragraph provides perspective on what's coming and what's important, much like the topic sentence of a well-constructed paragraph.

An Overview paragraph should simply and clearly tell the reader:

- **Purpose:** Why are you writing the memo?
- **Main idea:** What do you want to tell the reader? Or what do you want the reader to do?
- **Opinion:** What is your point of view on the subject?

In addition, the Overview should begin to establish the tone of the document for your reader. As the first paragraph a reader will see and, without question, one of the most important elements of a memo, the Overview should display a number of important basic qualities.[7] It should:

- **Be clear and simple.** Remember that the reader is trying to get oriented. The Overview provides perspective on what is coming. Keep the words simple and the sentences short. Think about your audience and what the various readers know. Anyone who receives the document should be able to understand it.
- **Be brief.** The Overview paragraph acts as an executive summary of the memo that follows. This summary is not the entire memo packed into a paragraph or two. Stick to the main ideas.
- **Deal with the what, not with the how.** *What* is the recommended course of action in a proposal or the main conclusion in an information memo? Avoid *how*, or implementation, at the early point in your memo. Readers have trouble dealing with implementation until they understand and agree with what should be done.
- **Include and identify the writer's point of view.** Go beyond the facts – interpret, conclude and recommend. Then take responsibility up front for what you believe by stating your point of view in the Overview. This helps convey confidence and a sense of leadership.
- **Reflect the needs of the reader.** The Overview is geared to the knowledge and skill level of the reader. It takes into account what the reader needs and wants to know.
- **Be thorough and complete.** Although brief, the Overview should be able to stand on its own. It does not tell the reader everything in the memo; it contains key highlights. The best test of a good Overview: Can the reader say "yes" without reading further?

## SAMPLE OVERVIEWS

Here are several Overview paragraphs that will help the reader to better understand what the writer is saying and what the writer wants from the reader. Pay careful attention to the length and structure of these Overviews. Note how compact and cogent each of them is.

1. This memo recommends the establishment of an on-site exercise and health club facility in the corporate headquarters complex. An initial investment of $675K in remodeling an existing, little-used storage facility will provide significant health insurance claim savings and will result in measurably greater employee productivity and morale.
2. This memo provides a summary of the GrillMaster II's market performance in each sales region for the first quarter of FY2019.
3. This memo *urgently* recommends a product design review for the DiceOmatic Plus. Warranty claims, field reports, and customer complaints about this product indicate a possible defect in the blade shield. Failure to review the design may result in significant liability exposure for the firm and may irreparably damage the brand reputation.
4. This memo recommends a 30-day continuation of the Pria Classic customer rebate program in Region 5. Initial response to the rebate coupons at retail level has exceeded market projections by 135 percent.
5. This memo recommends the addition of a Level-3 administrative assistant in the Information Technology Division. Launch of the company's new intranet and our new wireless PDA system have increased technician workloads and created a 25-day backlog in customer assistance requests. An additional administrative assistant would help solve this and other related problems.
6. This memo provides guidance and instructions for complying with the company's new Conflict-of-Interest Disclosure policy. Step-by-step instructions and frequently asked questions are included, along with contact information if you encounter difficulty.

## THE INFORMATIVE MEMO

Inter-office memos have two purposes: to inform or to persuade. If your purpose is to document, record or inform, here are some things to think about as you write.

- **Make your reasons for writing clear to the readers.** Explain, right up front, in the Overview paragraph, why you're writing. Use boldface headings and subheadings to label and describe the information you're providing.
- **Write about just one subject.** Don't confuse your readers with information about more than one subject in a memo. If you must write about several subjects, either give your memo a more general, abstract subject line or (preferably) write several memos.
- **Begin with the big picture first, then move to the details.** Don't simply download data on your readers and expect them to figure out what it means. Show your readers where this information fits into the big picture and then organize it in a way that makes sense to them.
- **Provide just as much detail as you think your reader will need.** The problem, of course, is that some readers want all sorts of detail. Others just want the bottom line or main point. There's nothing wrong with either of those groups; that's just the way they like to process information. In order to satisfy the needs of as many readers as possible, you should provide the most important information first, explaining what it is, what it means and why it's important. You might then direct those who want additional detail to a paper appendix attached to your memo or, perhaps, to an intranet or website where they can read or download what they want.
- **Group similar information together.** Read through your first draft and look for similar bits of information that appear in multiple paragraphs. Eliminate redundant sentences or paragraphs in which you've become repetitious.
- **Provide a point-of-contact for your readers.** If the people reading your memo have questions or concerns about the information you have provided, whom should they contact? Helpful informative memos will include not only a return address but telephone numbers, e-mail addresses and (if you're willing) the name of a person who can assist with questions.

- **Avoid gratuitous use of the first-person singular.** Address the reader as "you" or write in the third person. By doing so, you will reduce the temptation to include your own opinion with such phrases as "I think . . . ," "In my opinion . . . ," or "It is clear to me that. . . ."

    If you must write in the first person, use the plural form. It should be clear to the readers that we're all in this together.
- **Stick to the facts.** Distinguish clearly between fact and opinion and omit those things about which you are not sure. If you must include assumptions, please label them as such: "Assuming that interest rates do not rise by more than 25 basis points during the next six months . . . " Finally, ask yourself how you know that this information is current and accurate. What's the source of your confidence for all of this?

## THE PERSUASIVE MEMO

Writing a persuasive memo is much like constructing a winning argument. The document must provide a complete, logical argument with which the reader cannot disagree. It must anticipate all questions and responses – and deal with them. Procter & Gamble Vice President G. Gibson Carey offers this advice on persuading others by memo.[8]

- **Consider your objective against the reader's attitudes, perceptions and knowledge of the subject.** Be sure you know exactly what you want to accomplish with your memo. Do a careful assessment of the reader's mind-set at the beginning. What will it take to get the reader to say "yes"?
- **Outline on paper, focusing on the Situation Analysis and Rationale sections.** This will help you construct a complete, logical argument. An outline also helps identify missing information.
- **Include a plan of action.** A well-thought-out implementation section adds credibility and practicality to your ideas. It gives the busy reader added incentive to consider your proposal. Even if you are awaiting approval to develop a detailed plan, include an outline of the plan to demonstrate that your concept can be accomplished.
- **Don't lose your argument in the Situation Analysis.** Your proposal should flow naturally from the problem or opportunity described in the Situation Analysis. The reader who disagrees with anything in this section of the memo cannot buy your proposal. Avoid controversial issues, opinions and unsupported assertions in the Situation Analysis. Stick to the facts.
- **Use the direct approach.** Present your Recommendation and Rationale before you discuss other options that you have considered and rejected.
- **Always lead from strength.** Start your proposal with a strong, confident Overview paragraph. Bring the important ideas to the beginning of each section. In the Rationale section, always present your arguments in order of importance.
- **Use precedent to make your proposal appear less speculative.** Managers seek to avoid risk and error. Relevant precedent is the most effective way to reduce the perceived risk in a recommended action.
- **Gear your argument to the reader's decision criteria.** Know how your reader's mind works. Ask yourself if your argument is persuasive given the reader's interests and motivations.

## STANDARD FORMATS FOR MEMOS

Putting your ideas on paper helps you evaluate them. It forces you, the writer, to think through the issues carefully. Good ideas are invariably strengthened on paper and weak ideas are exposed for what they are.

Having a format in mind for the memo or report as you move forward with any project can eliminate one of the common stumbling blocks to sound thinking and good communication. The format becomes an organization plan for your ideas. It ensures that you think logically and that you don't overlook anything relevant to the project.

A standard format helps you organize information and concepts quickly. You don't have to think about where to put everything each time you start writing. If something is missing, it is immediately evident.

A standard format helps readers, too. They don't have to figure out how your mind was working each time they get a document from you. They know immediately where to find the pieces and how they fit together, which saves time and promotes understanding.

A document can be organized or put together in a variety of ways. Always be certain your case is developed in a logical and persuasive manner. Consider using a format with which your readers are familiar, to increase their comfort level. However, don't compromise on clarity, simplicity and logical flow to do so.

You'll find a suggested format for a business strategy memo in Appendix D at the end of this book. The format suggested there is appropriate for just about any memo, regardless of how long or complex. Many companies have adopted this format (or variations of it) because it works particularly well when communication is moving up to senior management. A sample business letter format appears in Appendix C. You'll also find a suggested communication strategy memo format in Appendix D.

If you work for an organization that has a detailed correspondence manual, you need only to follow the directions it provides. If your employer doesn't provide such guidance, your task is simple: Find a writing format that best suits your reasons for writing, the needs of your readers and the organization that you work for.

Note that the format suggested here separates the contents of a memo into six or seven sections, each no more than a paragraph or two, and each clearly marked with an all-caps, boldface heading.

## MEETING AND CONFERENCE REPORTS

The purpose of a conference or meeting report is to record decisions made at the meeting. Avoid long descriptions of what was discussed or presented, restatements of arguments, praise or blame. Use a standard format that includes the name of the group, persons attending and subjects covered.

Report briefly on:

- what was discussed or presented,
- what was decided and why.

Focus your report on:

- what action is required,
- who is responsible,
- what the timing will be.

## PROJECT LISTS

Many businesses keep track of current and proposed activities with project lists. These lists are nothing more than simple descriptions of what the organization is doing to achieve its goals or serve its customers. Project lists usually take more time to prepare than they are worth, so try to keep them simple. Simplicity will save time and actually make them more usable documents. Separate each project by category, then list projects in order of priority or importance. Each project on your list should include a title and brief description, status, next steps, responsible parties and due dates.

If your project list is long, consider adding a cover page to highlight key projects that require management attention.

Projects should never just disappear. Completed or terminated projects should be shown as such the following month, with a brief notation about why the project will not appear on future project lists.

## MAKE YOUR MEMOS INVITING AND ATTRACTIVE

A good document is both inviting and easy to read or easy to use as a reference.[9] Here are some ideas on how to write a good memo:

- **Grab attention up front.** A strong Overview section gives the reader perspective on what's coming and makes any memo easier to read and understand. Don't open the memo with unimportant details or information the reader already knows.

- **Vary sentence and paragraph length, but keep them short.** Short paragraphs and short sentences are inviting because they are easier to deal with. If all your sentences or paragraphs are the same length, however, the memo will seem monotonous.
- **Use headings.** The reader will understand your organization plan for the memo. Headings also make it a better reference document.
- **Use bullets and numbers to identify groupings.** This approach helps break up long paragraphs and is another way to indicate how the memo is organized.
- **Use parallel structure for lists (as this one does).** Keep things with things, actions with actions, do's with do's, don't's with don't's, and so on.
- **Underline or use boldface type to focus on topic sentences, key words and phrases.** Don't overdo it though; too much underlining makes a document look cluttered and busy.
- **Leave adequate margins.** Lots of white space makes any document more inviting. Use tables, charts and exhibits. Paragraphs full of numbers are difficult to read. Presenting the same information in a table or chart makes it easier to understand and easier to refer to.
- **Don't settle for sloppy or illegible duplication.** Make it a quality document.

## EDITING YOUR MEMOS

Good writing requires rewriting. The overall purpose of editing is to trim, clarify and simplify. Put the document aside for a while – overnight if possible – before revising. This break helps you step back, look at the memo through the eyes of the reader and be more objective.

Before revising your memo, quickly review the guidelines provided in the opening section. Then put yourself in the reader's place and go through the document several times, each time asking yourself these seven basic questions:

- **Is it clear?** Is the flow of the memo logical? Will the reader understand the development of your thesis? Are the words simple and concrete? Will the reader understand technical terms? Is every sentence clear, unambiguous, easy to read?
- **Is it complete?** Will the reader understand your purpose? Does the Situation Analysis have all the background information the reader needs to know? Are all the key numbers in the body of the memo? Have all necessary agreements been spelled out?
- **Is it persuasive?** Does your Rationale section lead from strength? Are your arguments in order of importance? Have you anticipated potential responses and questions, and dealt with them? Have you avoided exaggeration and provided a balanced, rational argument?
- **Is it accurate?** Are opinions and facts separated and clearly labeled? Is every number correct?
- **Is it concise?** Do you have too many arguments? Did you waste words telling readers what they already know? Do you have unnecessary words, phrases or sentences?
- **Is it inviting to read?** Should any large blocks of type be broken up? Did you leave adequate margins? Is the memo neat, clear and legible?
- **Is it perfect?** Or, as close to perfect as you can make it? Does the memo contain any typos, misspellings or grammatical errors that could cast doubt on the quality of your thinking?

## WRITING GOOD BUSINESS LETTERS

Business letters, unlike memos, are primarily external documents, though managers will occasionally use a letter format to correspond with subordinates and executives. Like memos, good letters are crisp, concise, spoken in tone and organized so that readers can follow and understand with a minimum of effort. They are easy to follow and don't read like a mystery story.

Nearly 50 years ago, writing consultant Rudolph Flesch offered a set of basic precepts for writing good business letters. They are as useful today as they were back then.[10]

- **Answer promptly.** Answer the mail within three business days. If you don't have an answer, must speak with someone else before you can formulate a reply, or need additional information, drop your reader a note to say

"I'll have a more complete reply in a few days, but for now please understand that I am working on a solution to the problem."

- **Show that you are genuinely interested.** The person writing to you obviously thought the issue was important enough to write about; you should think so, too. The problem or matter at hand may seem trivial in your world, but in theirs it is not. Show by your words and actions that you care about them and the issue they have written about.
- **Don't be too short, brief or curt.** We preach brevity, but you can overdo it. Make sure your reader has enough information to understand the subject. Make certain you include each issue relevant to the subject, and that you explain the process, the outcome or the decision to the satisfaction of the reader. If you were receiving the letter, would it contain enough information for you to act on? Are you satisfied that the writer (and his or her employer) has taken you seriously?
- **If it's bad news, say you are sorry.** With bad news, use phrases such as, "I am sorry to tell you that . . . " or "I regret to say that we'll be unable to refund your money because. . . ."

  You can soften the blow that accompanies bad news by saying that you're sorry it happened, you regret the outcome or some similar selection of words. If it's bad news and your reader thinks you don't care (or, worse, that you are amused by it all), you may be in for further trouble.
- **If it's good news, say you are glad.** With good news, use phrases such as, "I am delighted to tell you that . . ." or "You will be pleased to learn that. . . . " Now and again, the word *congratulations* may be in order. Go ahead and share in your reader's good fortune and joy.
- **Give everyone the benefit of the doubt.** Don't automatically assume that the person corresponding with you is doing so for the purpose of fleecing or cheating you (or your company). If it's not clear whether product failure or customer misuse is to blame, for example, give the other person the benefit of whatever doubt may exist. In the vast majority of instances, you will have done the right thing.
- **Never send off an angry letter.** Venting your spleen in an angry, hostile reply to someone may feel good, but it's almost *never* a good idea to mail such a letter. One real danger with e-mail is that you may compose a vicious reply to someone and click the send button well ahead of the arrival of rational thought. Cool down before you compose a letter and, if you have written something you are not sure about, wait until tomorrow before re-reading it. Chances are, you will think twice about posting that letter.
- **Watch out for cranks.** Occasionally, a certifiable goofball will cross your path. The advice is simple: Be polite, do your job and they will usually go away. If they persist, be firm but professional in responding. After the second letter, if you really are dealing with a whacko, you may be able to ignore their correspondence. If the tone is threatening, turn it over to security.
- **Appreciate humor.** If someone makes (or attempts) a joke, play along. Show that you have a sense of humor. Racist, sexist or profane humor is never appropriate, but ordinary self-deprecating or directionless humor can often lighten or improve a difficult situation.
- **Be careful with form letters.** A one-size-fits-all approach to writing with many recipients is a real recipe for disaster. Make sure your letter answers all (or virtually all) of the questions your audience is likely to have; respond to their fears, doubts and concerns. Once you have written a form letter and had an opportunity to edit it, why not test-market the document? Show it to several people who are (or have been) members of the audience you are writing for. Ask them to suggest improvements. Think about maps, diagrams, lists, references and ways your readers might learn more about the subject you are writing to them about.

## WHEN YOU ARE REQUIRED TO EXPLAIN SOMETHING

If you find yourself in the position of explaining something in writing to someone else, a few bits of common sense seem appropriate.[11]

- **Nothing is self-explanatory.** This may all seem self-evident to you, but that's because you've been thinking about and working on the subject for some time. Explain in simple, ordinary English what you want your reader to know. Don't assume anything.

- **Translate technical terms.** It's perfectly all right for you to use scientific or technical terminology. You just have to explain or define it first. Writing to one person you know quite well is much easier than writing to many people whom you don't know because you cannot be sure your readers will share your vocabulary.
- **Go step-by-step.** Be sequential in your explanations, moving step-by-step through processes that are complex. Don't skip anything, even steps in the process that seem absolutely self-evident to you. Your readers may be seeing this subject for the first time.
- **Don't say too little.** Your reader probably doesn't know as much about this subject as you do (that's why you are writing). Make certain you provide enough information to answer questions, allay fears and quell doubts.
- **Don't say too much.** Don't overdo it. You can bury your readers in details that will eventually confuse, frighten, anger or bore them. Provide enough detail to satisfy their curiosity but not so much that you put them off.
- **Illustrate.** If you can't explain it, perhaps you can show it. Illustrations can take the form of examples, anecdotes or explanations. Additionally, you may wish to include drawings, maps, schematics or a process flow chart.
- **Answer expected questions.** Put yourself in your reader's position. What would you most want to know? What questions are likely to arise? Which areas of this subject are likely to raise the greatest doubt, confusion or misunderstanding?
- **Warn against common mistakes.** If it's easy to misunderstand, misread or get this subject wrong, caution your readers. Explain the pitfalls, snares and traps they can easily fall into by not reading your words carefully.

## WHEN YOU ARE REQUIRED TO APOLOGIZE

If your job requires that you apologize to someone – most likely a customer or a client – for something that you or the company has done wrong (or not done at all), here are four basic guidelines to consider:

- **Take the complaint seriously.** Once again, you may not see the issue at hand as serious or important, but it's important to the person with the complaint. The sooner you act as if it's a big deal, the sooner you will satisfy the frustration or hostility that prompted the complaint in the first place.
- **Explain what happened and why.** People with complaints often seem irrational; some really are. For the most part, though, people will calm down and adopt a more understanding attitude if you can simply explain what happened and tell them why. For one thing, they will feel that they have more control over the circumstance. When you explain what's happened, they will be more likely to accept your answer.
- **Don't shift the blame.** Blaming everything on someone else is generally a bad idea. Even if someone else is at fault, your readers don't want to hear about it. Just accept responsibility for what's happened and offer a solution. Shifting the blame to "the computer system" or "those geniuses over in shipping" is simply unacceptable.
- **Don't just write, do something.** All your soothing, sympathetic words will do little to make your reader feel better if you don't offer to fix the problem. "Thanks for your input" is not enough. Telling your reader that you'll share the information with management is a good first step, but they may want more. Most people who have taken the time and effort to write to you will expect some sort of action. Don't disappoint them.[12]

## A FEW WORDS ABOUT STYLE

Your success as a business writer depends, in large measure, on your ability to convince others that what you have written is worth their attention. A considerable amount of research on this subject has shown that your writing will be better received if it meets three basic criteria: It ought to be *compact*, it should be *informal* and it absolutely must be *organized*.

Why compact, informal and organized writing? Three things seem to depend on writing that meets those criteria: organizational efficiency, personal productivity and your career. Large and complex organizations have shown time and again that the less time their employees spend at the keyboard composing correspondence, the more time they have to think about and accomplish other (presumably important) things.

If you spend less time both *writing* and *reading* what's been written for all employees in your organization, you become more personally productive. And, of course, important people – those in a position to influence your career – will notice. They will notice whether you are someone who can be counted on to draft, edit and improve written communication, or someone who struggles with the written word. In other words, they will know whether you are part of the problem or part of the solution.

## MAKE YOUR WRITING EFFICIENT

You must somehow find a way to deal with a number of different problems that appear consistently in letters, memos, reports, proposals, staff studies and other business documents. In addition to those memo-writing issues we discussed earlier, here are a dozen of the most common problems:

- **Big words.** If you want a few laughs from readers sensitive to language, use pompous substitutes for small words. Don't *start* things; *initiate* them. Don't *end* a program; *terminate* it. Readers know that *utilize* means *use* and *optimum* means *best*, but why force them to translate? You sell yourself and your ideas through your writing. Come across as a sensible person, someone who knows that good writing begins with plain English.
- **[       ]-wise.** Another no-no: words ending in -*wise*. Rather than write, "Marketwise, this firm should engage in sustained efforts to effect an improvement in our understanding of events and forces," you might consider "We need to know much more than we do about market forces."
- **Doublings.** Words that have the same or nearly the same meaning are known as *synonyms*. Select the one which most closely approximates what you really intend for your reader to know. Why write about a project's "importance and significance" when *importance* will do?
- **Noun modifiers.** Some writers insist on using one noun to modify another, when just one would do. "She is now in an important leadership position with the company" could be rewritten as "She is now a leader in this company." Look through your correspondence. You will see these noun-pairs everywhere: *management capability, market situation, habit patterns*.
- **It is.** Few words do more damage than the innocent-looking *it is*. These words stretch sentences, delay your point, encourage passives and hide responsibility. Unless *it* refers to something definite mentioned earlier, try to write around *it is*. "It is recommended that you revise . . . " becomes "We recommend that you revise," or "You should revise."
- **Legalese.** Avoid legal-sounding language like *hereto* and *aforesaid*. Such pompous and wordy language doesn't give a writer any added authority; it simply shows that his or her writing style – and perhaps his or her thinking – is outdated. Why say "Attached *herewith* is the report"? Instead, say, "Here's the report. " And rather than write, "It is incumbent upon supervisors . . . ," just say "Supervisors must. . . . " If your writing reads like a fire-and-casualty policy or a mutual fund prospectus, you may want to think twice about your style.
- **Missing hyphens.** Two-word modifiers may need hyphens when the two words act as one. Don't hyphenate if the first word ends in -*ly*: "*Fairly* recent change." Otherwise, consider it. "Three day trips" (three trips, each for a day) differs from "three-day trips" (trips, each for three days). If you are sensitive to how hyphens work, you will see what happens when they are left out of a sentence: "We're looking for a *short term accountant*. . . . " A CPA under 5'4", perhaps?
- **Smothered verbs.** Express ideas involving action with specific verbs. Weak writing relies on general verbs, which take extra words to complete their meaning. When you write general verbs such as *is, give* and *hold*, see if you can replace them by turning nearby words into specific verbs. Don't *make a choice; choose*. Don't *provide guidance; guide*. I have loaded the next two sentences with common smothered verbs: "The committee members *held a meeting* (*met*) to *give consideration to* (*consider*) the plan. They *made the decision* (*decided*) to *give their approval to* (*approve*) the product launch." Get the idea? *Make use of* (*use*) specific verbs!
- **Specialized terms.** Try to avoid specialized terms with outsiders and use them no more than you must with insiders. Acronyms, jargon and verbal shorthand unique to your organization can really confuse people who don't share the vocabulary. Are technical or specialized terms forbidden? Not at all. If you must use a technical term and you are reasonably sure that some of your readers won't understand, define it – tell them what it means and how it's used. They will show their appreciation by reading (and understanding) what you have written.

- **That and which.** More often than not, *that* and *which* don't help the meaning or flow of a sentence so use them sparingly. Sometimes you can just leave out these words; sometimes you will have to rewrite slightly. Consider this sentence: "We think (*that*) the changes (*which*) they have asked for will cost too much." Rather than writing "A system *which* is unreliable," you could say "An unreliable system." Read the sentence aloud and ask if you need *that* or *which* for meaning or flow. If not, try a revised sentence without those words.
- **The ——— ion of . . .** Shorten this ponderous *-ion* construction whenever the context permits. Instead of saying "I recommend *the adoption of* the plan," say "I recommend *adopting* the plan." And, instead of saying "We want *the participation of* all concerned," say "We want all concerned *to participate*." You add life to your writing by favoring the verb (action) form over the noun (static) form.
- **Wordy expressions.** Wordy expressions don't give writing impressive bulk; they litter it by getting in the way of the words that carry meaning. So, simplify these sentence stretchers. The longer it takes you to say something, the weaker you come across. *In order to* means *to*. *For the purpose of* usually means *to*. *In the near future* could be rephrased as *soon*. *In the event that* can be rewritten as *if*.[13]

## SPEAK WHEN YOU WRITE

To escape from outdated, excessively formal writing styles, try to make your writing more like your speaking. I'm not suggesting that you include snorts, grunts and rambling stream-of-consciousness monologues in your correspondence. We all know people who speak no better than they can write.

Still, the basic principle holds: Because people "hear" writing, the most readable writing sounds like one person talking to another. Begin by imagining your reader is in front of you and then use these ideas to guide you:

- **Write with personal pronouns.** Use *we*, *us* and *our* when speaking for the company. Use *I*, *me* and *my* when speaking for yourself. Either way, be generous with *you*.

  Avoiding these natural references to people is false modesty. Besides, the alternatives to personal pronouns are awkwardness ("Your support is appreciated," which doesn't work as well as "We appreciate your support") and hedging ("It was decided" in place of "I decided"). Stamp out "untouched by human hands" writing.
- **Use contractions (occasionally).** Write with the ones we speak with, such as *I'm, we're, you'd, they've, can't, don't* and *let's.* Not all your writing has to sound like a telephone conversation, but it certainly won't hurt if some of it does. If contractions come easily to you, then you've mastered spoken writing. If contractions seem out of place, don't remove them; deflate the rest of what you say. Also, don't overlook the advantages of negative contractions for instructions; they soften direct orders and keep readers from skipping over the word *not*.
- **Reach out to your reader occasionally by asking questions.** A request gains emphasis when it ends with a question mark. In a long report, a question can be a welcome change. Do you hear how spoken this next sentence is? Rather than write, "Please advise this office as to whether the conference is still scheduled for February 21," you might simply ask, "Is the conference still scheduled for February 21?"
- **Prefer short, spoken transitions over long, bookish ones.** Use *but* more than *however*, *also* more than *in addition*, *still* more than *nevertheless*, *so* more than *consequently* or *therefore*. Use formal transitions only for variety. And, yes, you can start a sentence with words like *and*, *but*, *so*, *yet* and *or*.
- **A preposition is a word you can end a sentence with.** Don't rework a sentence just to shift a preposition from the end. You'll lengthen, tangle and stiffen the sentence. Common prepositions include *after, at, by, from, of, to, up, with*.
- **Keep sentences short, about 20 words on average.** Use some longer and shorter sentences for variety. Short ones won't guarantee clarity, but they will prevent many of the confusions common to longer ones. Try the eye test: Average about two typed lines a sentence. Or try the ear test: Read your writing aloud and break apart any sentence you can't finish in one breath.[14]

## HOW TO MAKE PASSIVE VERBS ACTIVE

Passive sentences are deadly in business memos and letters for several reasons. First, they obscure responsibility by omitting a subject or human actor from the sentence. Second, they are almost always longer – one-quarter to one-third longer than active sentences. Finally, they delay discussion of the subject. The real action in a passive sentence or paragraph comes at the end.

The best advice: Use as few passives as possible. They're not grammatically wrong, but they are really overworked in most business writing. To write actively, remember this simple rule: *Put the doer before the verb.* By leading with the doer, you'll automatically avoid a passive verb. Consider these examples:

**Passive:** "It has been determined that more purchase decisions should be made by local managers."
**Active:** "The director decided that local managers should make more purchase decisions."

The passive version of that sentence (double passive, actually) contains 14 words. The active version contains just 11. Better yet, the active version tells the reader who made that decision – an important element missing from the passive sentence.

You can spot passive sentences by checking for these characteristics:

- The receiver of the verb's action comes before the verb. In the passive example, *it* is the receiver.
- The verb has these two parts: any form of *to be*, either simple (such as *are* or *was*) or compound (such as *is being*, *have been*, *will be* or *must be*), plus the past participle of a main verb (most end in -en or -ed). In our example, *has been decided* is the verb.
- If the doer appears at all, it follows the verb and usually has *by* just before it. But unlike active sentences, passive ones are complete without doers: *It has been determined* (by whom?).

Passive sentences may be useful in one of three circumstances:

- *When the doer is obvious:* "Donald J. Trump was elected President of the United States in November of 2016." How did *that* happen, you ask? Well . . . the explanation is complex, and you may not have time for the answer. Just leave it in the passive.
- *When the doer is unknown:* "My uncle was mugged in the park." Who mugged him? We don't really know; the mugger didn't leave a business card.
- *When the doer is unimportant:* "The parts were shipped on January 8." We don't really care who shipped them; we just know that they were sent on the eighth of January.

If you use passive sentences when you might just as easily write sentences with active verbs, your writing will be wordy, roundabout and (as the word *passive* implies) a bit sluggish. Worse, because passive sentences don't always show who is doing the action, you may forget to include important information. The result may be confusing to the reader.

- "All requests must be approved beforehand." By whom? It doesn't say because it's a passive sentence. The active version: "The regional manager must approve all requests beforehand."
- "The figures were lost." Who lost them? Again, we don't know because it's cast in the passive. The active version: "We lost the figures."

The best advice: Write actively whenever you can. If you decide to cast a sentence in the passive voice, do so only after considering what the active version would look like.[15]

## MAKE YOUR BOTTOM LINE YOUR TOP LINE

Open with your main point, the one sentence you'd keep if you could keep just one. You can often put that sentence in its own paragraph for added clarity. Give directions before reasons, requests before justifications, answers before explanations, conclusions before details, and solutions before problems.

A poorly organized letter reads like a mystery story. Clue by clue, it unfolds details that make sense only toward the end. Try the approach used in newspaper articles. They start with the most important information and taper off to the least important.

You might delay the main point to soften bad news or to remind your reader of an old conversation, for example, but avoid delaying for long. Readers, like listeners, are put off by people who take forever to get to the point. They need to know the main point at the start so they can appreciate the relevance of whatever else you may say.

If no single sentence stands out, you probably need to create one to keep from drifting aimlessly. Occasionally, as in a set of instructions or a reply to a series of questions, all your points may be equally important. In this case, create a starting sentence that tells your readers what to expect: "Here's the information you asked for."

To end most letters, just stop. When writing to persuade rather than to routinely inform, you may want to end strongly, perhaps with a forecast, appeal or implication. When feelings are involved, you may want to exit gracefully with some expression of goodwill. When in doubt, offer your help and encourage the reader to call or write back to you.[16]

Here are three ideas that will help you to better organize your letters:

- **Use headings and subheadings.** Boldface headings or italicized subheadings can help to organize your writing. When topics vary widely in one document, they let readers follow at a glance. Use them in recurring reports, proposals and even short business letters when you need to catch a reader's eye or break up long, complex paragraphs.
- **Keep paragraphs short.** Average roughly four or five sentences in each paragraph. For lists and instructions, try using subparagraphs. You make reading easier by adding white space.
- **Don't clutter up the first paragraph.** It's the most important paragraph in your letter; don't waste the prime space and impact of that paragraph with endless references to letters you've exchanged, previous reports, regulatory documents or other pieces of paper. Put your reason for writing – your most important point – right up front.

## HOW TO ENCOURAGE AND DEVELOP GOOD WRITERS

Every manager has a responsibility – in some respects, a moral obligation – to improve the skills of his or her subordinates. Writing skills are no exception. Too often, people get frustrated because assignments are given with careless direction, and comments about writing are vague and difficult to understand.

Working effectively with subordinates is not easy. It takes knowledge, experience and patience. Surprisingly, it doesn't take much time. It does take a willingness to sit down and review your expectations and their performance in specific terms. Here are some ideas to consider as you work with your people on improving communication:

- **Show your people you want clear, concise writing by example.** Give them samples of good writing and explain why it works. Sit down with new people and discuss your writing guidelines.
- **Know what you want before giving assignments.** Discuss projects with subordinates before they head off in the wrong direction. Be as specific as you can.
- **When projects are difficult or complex, break up the assignment into manageable parts.** Start with an Overview section to identify purpose and main ideas. Then have the writer prepare an outline of the document. Review this work before the writer tackles a first draft. This approach will save time and eliminate the frustration of trying to deal with a disaster.
- **Read and review before discussing a memo.** When a memo is submitted for your review, spend some time reviewing it before meeting with the writer. Be sure you understand what's wrong and how it can be fixed.
- **Try to see the big picture first.** When you review a memo, start with big issues such as strategy, logic flow and conclusions versus facts. Then move to smaller issues like grammar and appearance. Do not rewrite the memo, but be specific about areas that need work. And do remember to be positive.
- **Be certain the writer understands – and agrees with – your comments.** Make sure your writer can repeat, in his or her own words, what you want so that you're sure you are both on the same page.
- **Don't force writers to parrot your style and expressions.** Give your people flexibility and freedom to develop their own style.[17]

## FOR FURTHER READING

Alred, G. J., C. T. Brusaw and W. E. Oliu. *The Business Writer's Companion*, 7/e. Boston, MA: Bedford/St. Martin's Press, 2017.

Flintoff, J. P. "Companies Seek Help from a Man of Letters," *The Financial Times*, June 7, 2002, p. 12.

Hall, D. and S. Birkets. *Writing Well: Longman Classics Edition*, 9/e. Boston, MA: Addison- Wesley-Longman, 2006.

Holcombe, M. *Writing for Decision Makers: Memos and Reports with a Competitive Edge.* New York: Lifetime Learning, 1997.

Oliu, W. E., C. T. Brusaw and G. J. Alred. *Writing That Works: Communicating Effectively on the Job*, 12/e. Boston, MA: Bedford/St. Martin's Press, 2016.

Roman, K. and J. Raphaelson. *Writing That Works: How to Improve Your Memos, Letters, Reports, Speeches, Resumes, Plans, and Other Business Papers.* New York: Collins Reference, 2000.

Smith, N. *A Plain English Handbook: How to Create Clear SEC Disclosure Documents.* Washington, DC: The U.S. Securities and Exchange Commission, August 1998. You can obtain a copy of this document by calling the Office of Investor Education and Assistance toll-free information service at 1–800-SEC-0330, or download a PDF from www.sec.gov.

Stott, B. *Write to the Point: And Feel Better About Your Writing*, 3/e. New York: Courage, 2016.

Strunk, W. *The Elements of Style.* Charleston, SC: CreateSpace Independent Publishing, 2018.

Williams, J. M. and J. Bizup. *Style: Ten Lessons in Clarity and Grace*, 11/e. New York: Pearson, 2013.

Zinsser, W. *On Writing Well: The Classic Guide to Writing Nonfiction.* New York: Harper Perennial, 2016.

## NOTES

1   *USA Today*, October 14, 1994, p. C1. Reprinted with permission.
2   Ibid.
3   Smith, N. *A Plain English Handbook: How to Create Clear SEC Disclosure Documents.* Washington, DC: Government Printing Office, 1998, pp. 5–6.
4   Ibid., p. 4.
5   Plumez, J. P. *Leadership on Paper*, 1996, pp. 1–2. Personal communication with the author, August 8, 2002, from Larchmont, NY. Used by permission.
6   Ibid.
7   Ibid., pp. 4–5.
8   Carey, G. G. Personal communication with the author, August 20, 2002, from Cincinnati, OH. Used by permission.
9   Ruch, W. V. and M. L. Crawford. *Business Reports: Written and Oral.* Boston, MA: PWS-Kent, 1999, p. 203.
10  Flesch, R. *On Business Communication: How to Say What You Mean in Plain English.* New York: Harper & Row, 1974, pp. 100–112.
11  Ibid., pp. 113–126.
12  Ibid., pp. 139–151.
13  Murawski, T., P. Luckett, J. Mace and J. Shuttleworth. *The United States Air Force Academy Executive Writing Course.* Colorado Springs, CO: HQ USAFA, Department of English, 1983.
14  Ibid.
15  Bailey, E. *The Plain English Approach to Business Writing.* New York: Oxford University Press, 1993, pp. 93–101.
16  Murawski, et al. *The United States Air Force Academy Executive Writing Course.*
17  Plumez, *Leadership on Paper*, p. 16.

# Case 5.1: Microsoft Corporation

## *Communicating Layoffs to 18,000 Employees*

### THE ANNOUNCEMENT

On Thursday, July 17, 2014, 150 Microsoft employees gathered in a corporate headquarters conference room. Rumors of layoffs had been circulating for weeks, so it caught few by surprise when senior managers informed them that Microsoft would be moving in a new direction, thus making their roles either redundant or unnecessary. The company's human resources managers described severance packages and explained that key cards would cease to work in a few days. Employees were instructed to clean out their desks as soon as possible.[1,2]

On that same day, Stephen Elop, former CEO of the recently acquired Nokia division and current Executive Vice President for Devices and Services, circulated a lengthy, rambling memo that began with a position on productivity and helping people "get things done." After a number of jargon-filled paragraphs, the first reference to layoffs appeared in the 11th paragraph saying, "We plan that this would result in an estimated reduction of 12,500 factory direct and professional employees over the next year" (see the Appendix at the end of this case study). Approximately 14 percent of Microsoft's workforce – some 18,000 employees with 12,500 of them from the new Nokia division – are involved, in addition to limitations placed on contractors and vendors.[3]

### HISTORY OF MICROSOFT

Microsoft Corporation is a multinational computer technology firm. It is the collaborative, creative product of childhood friends Bill Gates and Paul Allen, who have been writing and testing computer programs since they were 14 years old. In 1974, personal computers increased processing power, and Gates, Allen and another friend – while attending Harvard at the time – wrote the program that began "Micro-soft," the name originating from a portmanteau of microcomputer and software.[4]

As the market for personal computers rapidly expanded, Micro-soft began selling to larger corporations. They renamed the company Microsoft, which soon began "setting the industry standards for microprocessor programming."[5] In 1980, IBM licensed Microsoft to develop operating software for the IBM-PC, which generated a great deal of revenue for the company. Founders Allen and Gates expanded company leadership when they hired Steve

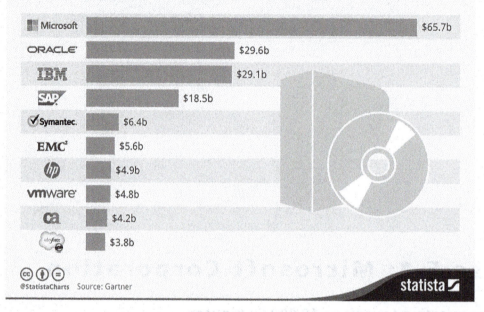

## Microsoft Remains the World's No. 1 Software Maker

Worldwide revenue of the world's largest software vendors in 2013

- Microsoft — $65.7b
- ORACLE — $29.6b
- IBM — $29.1b
- SAP — $18.5b
- Symantec. — $6.4b
- EMC² — $5.6b
- hp — $4.9b
- vmware — $4.8b
- ca — $4.2b
- salesforce — $3.8b

@StatistaCharts    Source: Gartner

statista

**FIGURE 5.1**  Microsoft Remains the World's No. 1 Software Maker

*Source:* Statista (2014, April 1), www.statista.com/chart/2078/top-10-software-vendors-2013.

Ballmer, an old college classmate, because they needed a more experienced business manager. He was a Mathematics and Economics major who enrolled in and then dropped out of the Stanford Graduate School of Business to be part of Microsoft.[6]

The company continued to grow quickly, doubling or tripling in size yearly and making millions for those fortunate (and wise) enough to take advantage of employee stock options. Microsoft operating systems continued to increase in sophistication, running on 86.3 percent of the PCs in the U.S. by 1997.[7]

With annual revenues of more than $65 billion, Microsoft Corporation is currently the largest software company in the world.[8] Microsoft runs at least one piece of software on the vast majority of personal computers worldwide. Core businesses within Microsoft include the development and production of software, including operating systems as well as Internet and productivity software. The brands generating the most revenue include Office and Windows.

## A STRUGGLE TO INNOVATE

Despite a dominant market position in computing software, the company had trouble adapting to new market conditions.[9] Although Microsoft was among the first e-book technology developers, corporate strategists decided that it was not an important product category to pursue. Other companies, however, including Amazon, capitalized on this innovative technology even though Microsoft had begun research and development much earlier.[10] In 2001, Apple introduced the iPod with Microsoft responding five years later with their Zune. By that point, Microsoft was simply unable to compete because Apple commanded 71 percent of the market.[11] Furthermore, as a response to Google, Microsoft developed MSN Search, which later became Bing in 2009. Bing "lost around $6 billion for Microsoft," while Google continued to grow market share.[12]

In 2011, Microsoft chose to focus product development in the "touch first" arena. Specifically, Windows 8 was meant to be a "really new kind of device, one that scales from touch-only small screens through to large screens, with or without a keyboard and mouse," wrote then-Corporate Vice President for Windows Experience, Julie

Larson-Green.[13] Later, the Surface RT was introduced, which Microsoft hoped would steal market share from Apple's iPad and other "traditional" tablets. Unfortunately, laptops with touch screens or hybrid laptop/tablets did not seem to impress consumers more than individual tablets and laptops. *TechCrunch* writer, Frederic Lardinois, wrote, "'Touch first'– which begat Windows 8 and the Surface – was the wrong move."[14]

Further exacerbating the situation was the downturn in the PC market. By July 2013, Gartner, an information technology research and advisory firm, reported that global PC sales had dropped 11 percent in the most recent quarter. Other PC-focused firms, such as Intel, were also feeling the pressure, as more and more of the market turned to tablets, phones and other mobile devices.[15]

## CULTURE WARS

After the dot-com bust in the late 1990s, Microsoft's culture changed dramatically. No longer the source of an easy way to make a million through stock options, employees worked to outperform their peers and get promotions in order to advance. Additional managerial positions were created, and heightened bureaucracy slowed down the process of product creation and improvement.[16]

To further complicate the situation, Microsoft put into place what it called a "stack ranking," a performance review that forces managers to place some employees in the bottom quartile of performers, regardless of their quality of work or ability to meet goals. The inevitable result was withholding of information, infighting and, at times, outright sabotage in order to keep ahead of other employees and departments.[17] Top performers were disincentivized to work with each other and innovation suffered. As a result, Microsoft fell further and further behind as companies such as Apple and Google recruited talent and introduced new features and products.

## ONE MICROSOFT

In July 2013, Ballmer took the first step in restructuring and reviving a struggling Microsoft. Ballmer replaced all department managers in order to better focus on the operating system, entertainment and mobile divisions. He expressed the need for Microsoft to better align across all teams in order to "have more integrated and rapid development cycles for [their] offerings."[18]

Although this restructuring was the first in Microsoft's history, it was widely anticipated due to Microsoft's earlier mistakes in mobile devices. Following Apple's lead, Ballmer hoped that changing department managers would allow Microsoft to offer a more competitive suite of products, similar to Apple's iPhones, iPads and Mac's strategic offerings. He stated:

> No technology company has of yet delivered a definitive family of devices useful all day for work and for play, connected with every bit of a person's information available through one cloud. We see tremendous room for innovation in software, services, and hardware to bring the consumer this new, more complete and enveloping experience.[19]

Microsoft hoped to offer a family of products to consumers including phones, tablets, PCs, 2-in-1s, TV attached devices and others, all of which would be connected to Microsoft's cloud service, Windows Azure.

A week after the restructuring announcement, Microsoft reported earning below analysts' expectations with a $900 million write-down "related to Surface RT inventory adjustments."[20] Although earnings were lackluster, then-CFO Amy Hood expressed long-term hope at opportunities in cloud services.[21]

## ACQUISITION OF NOKIA

On September 3, 2013, Microsoft announced the company would acquire Nokia. Specifically, they would purchase Nokia's Devices and Services business, license Nokia's patents, and license and use Nokia's mapping services. Microsoft paid $5.44 billion for the acquisition in cash.[22]

The acquisition brought an additional 25,000 employees to an already sizable Microsoft payroll. In 2004, Microsoft consisted of 57,000 employees, which grew to 99,000 by 2013. Post-acquisition, Microsoft reported a workforce of 127,000.[23]

The acquisition did not come as a surprise to investors. Microsoft and Nokia had established a partnership in 2011 aimed at benefiting both firms in the smart phone and mobile industry. However, the agreement had yet to help either company become a leader in that industry. Although the two companies collaborated in their efforts prior to the acquisition, both firms had separate development processes. This meant that each company had its own resources, teams, methods and trade secrets that created inefficiencies for both Microsoft and Nokia.[24]

Ballmer expressed his hope for the acquisition in a statement to the press:

It's a bold step into the future – a win-win for employees, shareholders, and consumers of both companies. Bringing these great teams together will accelerate Microsoft's share and profits in phones and strengthen the overall opportunities for both Microsoft and our partners across our entire family of devices and services. In addition to their innovation and strength in phones at all price points, Nokia brings proven capability and talent in critical areas such as hardware design and engineering, supply chain and manufacturing management, and hardware sales, marketing and distribution.[25]

Some analysts responded positively to the announcement of the acquisition. "It could help them respond more rapidly to the dynamic mobile industry," wrote Gartner analyst, Carolina Milanesi, in a *New York Times* article.[26] However, there were still questions to be answered regarding the aftermath of the acquisition. Interested parties speculated on how this acquisition would change the structure of both Microsoft and Nokia, and they questioned whether additional layoffs would come as integration ensued.

## TIME FOR A CHANGE

With declining relevance in the mobile space and activist investors clamoring for progress, Microsoft was under increasing pressure to make major changes. Steve Ballmer simply was not moving fast enough. In fact, John Thompson, longtime board member and former CEO of Symantec, bluntly told Ballmer on a conference call, "Hey, dude, let's get on with it."[27] Finally, Ballmer announced in August of 2013 that he would step down as CEO within 12 months. That same month, activist investor group ValueAct Capital Management LP placed a representative on the board at Microsoft.[28]

As CEOs, Ballmer and Gates were both aggressive personalities fiercely loyal to the Microsoft brand. Gates, the company's Founder and first CEO, was widely known as incredibly intelligent, but lacking in more personable qualities. Gates led the company to dominance in the software industry with the Windows operating system and Microsoft Office suite during his time as CEO. Under Ballmer's direction from 2000 to 2013, Microsoft revenues nearly tripled to $21.8 billion.[29] While Gates was a product and engineering genius, Ballmer has often been described as the marketing guy who was "emotionally volatile," which, coupled with his large stature, can be seen as intimidating to those who disagree or challenge him.[30] Both men remained on the board after retiring as CEO.

Finding a replacement for Ballmer proved to be a long and difficult process. In addition to taking on Microsoft's challenges, the position also required an ability to manage aggressive personalities on the board, including Gates, Ballmer and Thompson. Several names were circulated internally and leaked to the press. Media reported on the various possible challenges facing the new CEO.[31]

Shortly after Ballmer's departure, the company announced that Microsoft would abandon the now-infamous stack rankings. Tech-sector and financial media, which had long criticized the review process for destroying Microsoft's edge, rejoiced. Lisa Brummell, the executive vice president for human resources at Microsoft who announced abandonment of the system, commented at a dinner party, "I hope I never have to read another article about our review system ever again."[32]

Finally, after more than six months of speculation, one name – Satya Nadella – rose to the top. Nadella shared Gates's engineering background and generally connected well with people.[33] Born in India, Nadella started with Microsoft in 1992 and had most recently been in charge of Azure, the cloud division of Microsoft.[34]

## A NEW APPROACH

Notable about Nadella's tenure at Microsoft was his willingness to open up the insular and often fractional culture of Microsoft, seeking out feedback from outside companies and at least partially embracing open-source coding. One of Nadella's first moves as CEO was to make Microsoft Office available on iPad. Speculation abounded as to whether or not this was the beginning of a new era for a more "agnostic" Microsoft, less tied to the Windows operating system that had been the source of all its previous successes. Nadella promised, "This is only the beginning."[35]

Under Nadella's guidance, Microsoft began to expand beyond Windows and focus on cloud services and apps. Nokia became fully integrated with Microsoft in April of 2014, which resulted in 12,500 layoffs in the Nokia division. Nadella said that Microsoft would "work toward synergies and strategic alignment on Nokia Devices and Services. . . . "This meant that hardware designed in Finland and Hungary would eventually cease in order to keep those processes "in-house."[36]

## WHAT'S NEXT?

Microsoft experienced continued financial success, despite late introduction of products and lack of agility in management to keep up with the changing technological landscape. Surprisingly, in the wake of the layoff announcements, share price rose by 5 percent.[37] However, there was an outcry in Europe as the majority of cuts happened to Finnish-based Nokia. Political leaders in Finland felt betrayed, and EU commissioner Laszlo Anodr criticized the layoff announcement saying, "Company restructuring is a fact of life, but it should be done in a socially responsible way, based on social dialogue and with due respect for applicable legislation on the information and consultation of workers and collective redundancies."[38]

## QUESTIONS

1. Who are the major stakeholders in this case? What's at stake for each of them?
2. How would you describe the business problem in this case? Why is it a problem?
3. What changes, if any, would you make to Microsoft's approach to regaining relevance and market share?
4. Were these layoffs necessary and were they handled correctly?
5. If you were to advise the Microsoft senior team, what would you have suggested regarding message construction, channel selection and audience analysis for the announcement of the layoffs?
6. What are Mr. Nadella's biggest challenges and what actions should he take in the coming months to address them?
7. How can Mr. Nadella best implement change in Microsoft and what role should communication play in implementing that change?

## WRITING ASSIGNMENT

Please respond in writing to the issues presented in this case by preparing two documents: a communication strategy memo and a professional business letter.

In preparing these documents, you may assume one of two roles: you may identify yourself as a Microsoft Corporation senior manager who has been asked to provide advice to Mr. Satya Nadella regarding the issues he and the company are facing. Or, you may identify yourself as an external management consultant who has been asked by the company to provide advice to Mr. Nadella.

Either way, you must prepare a strategy memo addressed to Satya Nadella, Chief Executive Officer, Microsoft Corporation, that summarizes the details of the case, rank-orders the critical issues, discusses their implications (what they mean and why they matter), offers specific recommendations for action (assigning ownership and suspense dates for each) and shows how to communicate the solution to all who are affected by the recommendations.

You must also prepare a professional business letter for Mr. Nadella's signature. That document should be addressed to all Microsoft employees who are concerned about the events described in the case.

## APPENDIX: STEPHEN ELOP'S E-MAIL TO MICROSOFT EMPLOYEES

■ Microsoft

# News Center

Our Company ⌄     Our Products ⌄     Blogs & Communities ⌄     Press Tools ⌄

# Stephen Elop's email to employees

Posted July 17, 2014 By Microsoft News Center          f  7     ▾  1     in  378     ✉

Hello there,

Microsoft's strategy is focused on productivity and our desire to help people "do more," As the Microsoft Devices Group, our role is to light up this strategy for people, We are the team creating the hardware that showcases the finest of Microsoft's digital work and digital life experiences, and we will be the confluence of the best of Microsoft's applications, operating systems and cloud services.

To align with Microsoft's strategy, we plan to focus our efforts. Given the wide range of device experiences, we must concentrate on the areas where we can add the most value. The roots of this company and our future are in productivity and helping people get things done. Our fundamental focus — for phones, Surface, for meetings with devices like PPI, Xbox hardware and new areas of innovation — is to build on that strength. While our direction in the majority of our teams is largely unchanging, we have had an opportunity to plan carefully about the alignment of phones within Microsoft as the transferring Nokia team continues with its integration process.

It is particularly important to recognize that the role of phones within Microsoft is different than it was within Nokia, Whereas the hardware business of phones within Nokia was an end unto itself, within Microsoft all our devices are intended to embody the finest of Microsoft's digital work and digital life experiences, while accruing value to Microsoft's overall strategy. Our device strategy must reflect Microsoft's strategy and must be accomplished within an appropriate financial envelope. Therefore, we plan to make some changes,

We will be particularly focused on making the market for Windows Phone. In the near term, we plan to drive Windows Phone volume by targeting the more affordable smartphone segments, which are the fastest growing segments of the market with Lumia. In addition to the portfolio already planned, we plan to deliver additional lower-cost Lumia devices by shifting select future Nokia X designs and products to Windows Phone devices. We expect to make this shift immediately while continuing to sell and support existing Nokia X products.

To win in the higher price segments, we will focus on delivering great breakthrough products in alignment with major milestones ahead from both the Windows team and the Applications and Services Group. We will ensure that the very best experiences and scenarios from across the company will be showcased on our products. We plan to take advantage of innovation from the Windows team, like Universal Windows Apps, to continue to enrich the Windows application ecosystem. And in the very lowest price ranges, we plan to run our first phones business for maximum efficiency with a smaller team.

We expect these changes to have an impact to our team structure. With our focus, we plan to consolidate the former Smart Devices and Mobile Phones business units into one phone business unit that is responsible for all of our phone efforts. Under the plan, the phone business unit will be led by Jo Harlow with key members from both the Smart Devices and Mobile Phones teams in the management team.

This team will be responsible for the success of our Lumia products, the transition of select future Nokia X products to Lumia and for the ongoing operation of the first phone business,

As part of the effort, we plan to select the appropriate business model approach for our sales markets while continuing to offer our products in all markets with a strong focus on maintaining business continuity, We will determine each market approach based on local market dynamics, our ability to profitably deliver local variants, current Lumia momentum and the strategic importance of the market to Microsoft. This will all be balanced with our overall capability to invest.

Our phone engineering efforts are expected to be concentrated in Salo, Finland (for future, high-end Lumia products) and Tampere, Finland (for more affordable devices). We plan to develop the supporting technologies in both locations. We plan to ramp down engineering work in Oulu. While we plan to reduce the engineering in Beijing and San Diego, both sites will continue to have supporting roles, including affordable devices in Beijing and supporting specific US requirements in San Diego. Espoo and Lund are planned to continue to be focused on application software development.

We plan to right-size our manufacturing operations to align to the new strategy and take advantage of integration opportunities. We expect to focus phone production mainly in Hanoi, with some production to continue in Beijing and Dongguan. We plan to shift other Microsoft manufacturing and repair operations to Manaus and Reynosa respectively, and start a phased exit from Komaron, Hungary.

In short, we will focus on driving Lumia volume in the areas where we are already successful today in order to make the market for Windows Phone. With more speed, we will build on our success in the affordable smartphone space with new products offering more differentiation. We'll focus on acquiring new customers in the markets where Microsoft's services and products are most concentrated. And, we'll continue building momentum around applications.

We plan that this would result in an estimated reduction of 12,500 factory direct and professional employees over the next year. These decisions are difficult for the team, and we plan to support departing team members with severance benefits.

More broadly across the Devices team, we will continue our efforts to bring iconic tablets to market in ways that complement our OEM partners, power the next generation of meetings & collaboration devices and thoughtfully expand Windows with new interaction models. With a set of changes already implemented earlier this year in these teams, this means there will be limited change for the Surface, Xbox hardware, PPI/meetings or next generation teams.

We recognize these planned changes are broad and have very difficult implications for many of our team members. We will work to provide as much clarity and information as possible. Today and over the coming weeks leaders across the organization will hold town halls, host information sharing sessions and provide more details on the intranet.

The team transferring from Nokia and the teams that have been part of Microsoft have each experienced a number of remarkable changes these last few years. We operate in a competitive industry that moves rapidly, and change is necessary. As difficult as some of our changes are today, this direction deliberately aligns our work with the cross company efforts that Satya has described in his recent emails. Collectively, the clarity, focus and alignment across the company, and the opportunity to deliver the results of that work into the hands of people, will allow us to increase our success in the future.

Regards,

Stephen

Tags    press releases    uncategorized

## ACKNOWLEDGMENTS

This case was prepared by research assistants Janelle Jacka, Jackson Taffe and Leila Whitley under the direction of James S. O'Rourke IV, Teaching Professor of Management, as the basis for class discussion rather than to illustrate either effective or ineffective handling of an administrative situation. Information was gathered from corporate as well as public sources. Editorial assistance: Judy Bradford and Jennifer Cronin.

## NOTES

1   Borison, Rebecca. "Microsoft Veteran Describes Losing His Job in a Shock Mass Layoff," *Business Insider*, July 25, 2014. Online at www.businessinsider.com/former-microsoft-employee-talks-about-getting-fired-2014-7. Accessed February 17, 2015.

2   Berg, Jerry. "Microsoft Laid Me Off After 15 Years of Service. Life After Microsoft?" *Barnacules Nerdgasm*, July 21, 2014. Online at www.youtube.com/watch?v=lRV6PXB6QLk. Accessed February 17, 2015.

3   "Stephen Elop's Email to Employees," *Microsoft News Center*, July 17, 2014. Online at http://news.microsoft.com/2014/07/17/stephen-elops-email-to-employees/. Accessed February 18, 2015.

4   Gates, Bill. "Bill Gates and Paul Allen Talk," *Fortune Magazine*, Time Inc. October 2, 1995. Online at http://archive.fortune.com/magazines/fortune/fortune_archive/1995/10/02/206528/index.htm. Accessed February 18, 2015.

5   Eichenwald, Kurt. "Microsoft's Lost Decade," *Vanity Fair*, August 1, 2012. Online at www.vanityfair.com/news/business/2012/08/microsoft-lost-mojo-steve-ballmer. Accessed February 15, 2015.

6   Ibid.

7   Ibid.

8   Infographic. "Microsoft Remains the World's No. 1 Software Maker," *Statista*, April 1, 2012. Online at www.statista.com/chart/2078/top-10-software-vendors-2013/. Accessed February 23, 2015.

9   Eichenwald. "Microsoft's Lost Decade."

10  Ibid.

11  Ibid.

12  Ibid.

13  Lardinois, Frederic. "Touch: Where Microsoft Went Wrong," *TechCrunch*, July 21, 2013. Online at http://techcrunch.com/2013/07/21/touch-where-microsoft-went-wrong/. Accessed February 12, 2015.

14  Ibid.

15  Lardinois, Frederic. "Microsoft's Q4 Earnings Miss With $19.9B In Revenue, EPS of $0.59, Takes $900M Charge Against Surface RT Inventory Adjustments," *TechCrunch*, July 18, 2013. Online at http://techcrunch.com/2013/07/18/microsofts-q4-earnings-miss-estimates-with-19-9b-in-revenue-eps-of-0-59-takes-900m-charge-against-surface-rt-inventory-adjustments/. Accessed February 12, 2015.

16  Eichenwald. "Microsoft's Lost Decade."

17  Ibid.

18  Biggs, John, Natasha Lomas, Alex Williams and Frederic Lardinois. "Microsoft Realigns to Focus on Hardware and Better Compete Against the Apples and Samsungs of the World," *TechCrunch*, July 11 2013. Online at http://techcrunch.com/2013/07/11/microsoft-reorganization/. Accessed February 12, 2015.

19  Ibid.

20  Tyson, Mark. "Microsoft Financials Show Surface RT Write-Down of $900 Million," *Hexus*, July 19, 2013. Online at http://hexus.net/business/news/general-business/58013-microsoft-financials-show-surface-rt-write-down-900-million/. Accessed February 12, 2015.

21  Lardinois. "Microsoft's Q4 Earnings Miss With $19.9B In Revenue."

22  "Microsoft to Acquire Nokia's Devices & Services Business, License Nokia's Patents and Mapping Services," *Microsoft News Center*, September 3, 2013. Online at http://news.microsoft.com/2013/09/03/microsoft-to-acquire-nokias-devices-services-business-license-nokias-patents-and-mapping-services/. Accessed February 18, 2015.

23  Wilhelm, Alex. "Microsoft May Axe One-Fifth of Its Nokia-Sourced Finnish Workforce," *TechCrunch*, July 16, 2014. Online at http://techcrunch.com/2014/07/16/microsoft-may-axe-one-fifth-of-its-nokia-sourced-finnish-workforce/. Accessed February 18, 2015.

24  Molen, Brad. "What You Need to Know about Microsoft's Acquisition of Nokia." *Engadget*. April 25, 2014. Online at www.engadget.com/2014/04/25/microsoft-nokia-merger-details/. Accessed February 18, 2015.

25  "Microsoft to Acquire Nokia's Devices & Services Business," *Microsoft News Center*.

26  Wingfield, Nick. "Microsoft to Buy Nokia Units and Acquire Executive," *The New York Times*, September 3, 2013. Online at www.nytimes.com/2013/09/04/technology/microsoft-acquires-nokia-units-and-leader.html?_r=0. Accessed February 18, 2015.

27  Colvin, Geoff and Adam Lashinsky. "Inside the Microsoft CEO Search," *Fortune*, February 3, 2014. Online at http://fortune.com/2014/02/03/inside-the-microsoft-ceo-search/. Accessed February 17, 2015.

28  Ovide, Shira. "Activist Storms Microsoft's Board," *The Wall Street Journal,* August 30, 2013. Online at www.wsj.com/articles/SB10001424127887323324904579045373716627460. Accessed February 17, 2015.

29  McLean, Bethany. "The Empire Reboots," *Vanity Fair*, November 2014. Online at www.vanityfair.com/news/business/2014/11/satya-nadella-bill-gates-steve-ballmer-microsoft. Accessed February 17, 2015.

30  Ibid.

31  Tu, Janet I. "Advantages, Challenges for New CEO at Microsoft," *The Seattle Times*, August 24, 2013. Online at www.seattletimes.com/business/advantages-challenges-for-new-ceo-at-microsoft/. Accessed February 17, 2015.

32  Wingfield. "Microsoft to Buy Nokia Units and Acquire Executive."

33  Sharf, Samantha. "It's Official: Microsoft Names Satya Nadella Its Third CEO," *Forbes*, February 4, 2014. Online at www.forbes.com/sites/samanthasharf/2014/02/04/its-official-microsoft-names-satya-nadella-its-third-ceo/. Accessed February 18, 2015.

34  Ibid.

35  Brennan, Morgan. "Microsoft Unveils Office for Apple's iPad," *CNBC, Reuters*, March 7, 2014. Online at www.cnbc.com/id/101531596#. Accessed February 17, 2015.

36  Etherington, Darrell. "Microsoft to Cut Workforce By 18,000 This Year, 'Moving Now' to Cut First 13,000," *TechCrunch*, July 17, 2014. Online at http://techcrunch.com/2014/07/17/microsoft-to-cut-workforce-by-18000-this-year-moving-now-to-cut-first-13000/. Accessed February 18, 2015.

37  Interactive Stock Chart | Yahoo! Inc. Stock - Yahoo! Finance. *Microsoft Corporation (MSFT)*. Online at http://finance.yahoo.com/echarts. Accessed February 23, 2015.

38  Loeb, Steven. "EU and Finland Blast Microsoft's Huge Nokia Cuts," *vatornews*, July 21, 2014. Online at http://vator.tv/news/2014-07-21-eu-and-finland-blast-microsofts-huge-nokia-cuts. Accessed February 23, 2015.

# Case 5.2: Carnival Cruise Lines

## Wreck of the Costa Concordia

The boat started shaking. The noise – there was panic, like in a film, dishes crashing to the floor, people running, people falling down the stairs.

– survivor Fulvio Rocci[1]

## THE CRISIS

At 4:00 p.m. on the evening of January 13, 2012, the Costa Concordia set sail from Rome, Italy for a seven-day cruise as it did every week. The ship was due to arrive in Savona, Italy the next day. Around 9:15 p.m., the ship took a five-mile detour to pass closer to the picturesque Tuscan Island of Giglio (see Figure 5.2).[2] Captain Schettino appears to have misjudged the maneuver, and at 9:30 p.m., the ship collided with a rocky reef known as Le Scole. The collision ripped a 160-foot-long gash in the hull of the ship, and the Concordia lost power.

The captain is said to have performed the sail-by as a spectacle for head waiter Antonello Tievoli who was a native of Giglio, and as a salute to former Costa captain Mario Palombo, who retired in 2006. Tievoli had been invited to join the captain on the bridge as the vessel was steered by the island. Palombo is reported to have not even been on the island to see the spectacle on the night of the incident.[3] In response to the incident, Palombo is reported to have said: "I cannot understand what could have happened, what passed through my colleague's head. The captain sets the course – on board the ship, he's king. But I don't want to be dragged into this argument, for any reason."[4]

Within 15 minutes of the collision, the ship started to take on water and began to list. At this point, Captain Francesco Schettino likely realized his ship was in trouble and turned the ship back toward shore in what appeared to be an effort to make it easier to evacuate.[5] Shortly following the collision, at 10:30 p.m., according to one of the ship's cooks, Captain Schettino ordered dinner for himself and a woman.[6]

At 10:35 p.m., the crew directed the passengers to report to their muster stations, saying that the issue was an electrical problem, and technicians were working on it. At 10:58 p.m., Captain Francesco Schettino ordered abandon ship (see Figure 5.3).

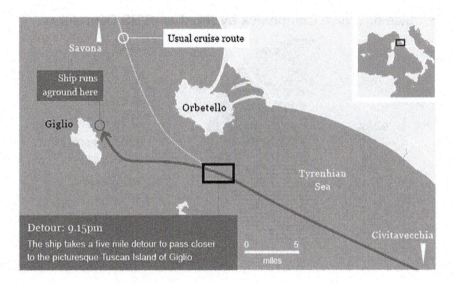

**FIGURE 5.2** Costa Concordia Route

*Source*: Agar, Michael and Andrew Blenkinso. "Concordia: How the Disaster Unfolded," *The Telegraph*, January 16, 2012. Online at www.telegraph.co.uk/news/interactive-graphics/9018076/Concordia-How-the-disaster-unfolded.html.

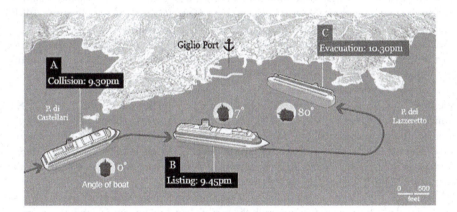

**FIGURE 5.3** Impact

*Source*: Agar, Michael and Andrew Blenkinso. "Concordia: How the Disaster Unfolded," *The Telegraph*, January 16, 2012. Online at www.telegraph.co.uk/news/interactive-graphics/9018076/Concordia-How-the-disaster-unfolded.html.

What followed can only be described as chaos. Many passengers did not know the emergency procedure, or where their muster station was, as there had been no lifeboat drill yet for the 600 passengers who boarded the ship on January 13.[7]

# BACKGROUND

## *Carnival Cruise Lines*

In 1972, entrepreneur Ted Arison formed Carnival Cruise Lines with one second-hand ship, and only enough fuel to sail from Miami to San Juan. Through determination and hard work, Mr. Arison built Carnival into a popular and

## Size of Cruise Companies by Number of US Departures

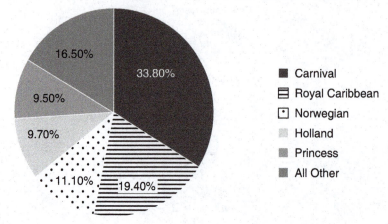

- Carnival
- Royal Caribbean
- Norwegian
- Holland
- Princess
- All Other

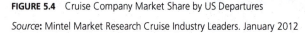

**FIGURE 5.4** Cruise Company Market Share by US Departures

*Source*: Mintel Market Research Cruise Industry Leaders. January 2012

profitable cruise line. In 1987, Carnival made an initial public offering, which provided capital to allow the company to begin expanding through acquisitions. Over the next few decades, Carnival acquired several well-known cruise companies throughout the world, including Costa Cruises in 1997 (see Figure 5.4).[8]

In 2003, Carnival Corporation merged with P&O Princess Cruises plc to create one of the largest leisure travel companies in the world. This merger added such cruise brands as P&O Cruises, P&O Cruises Australia, AIDA Cruises, Ocean Village, and Swan Hellenic, resulting in a global cruise company operating 12 different brands. Each of these brands continues to operate separately, maintaining separate sales and reservation operations.

At the time of the case, Carnival Corporation plc is currently headquartered in Miami, Florida, U.S. and London, England. Carnival operates a fleet of 101 ships, and has another ten ships scheduled for delivery by March 2016. Carnival Corporation & plc brands include: Carnival Cruise Lines, Holland America Line, Princess Cruises and Seabourn in North America; P&O Cruises and Cunard Line in the U.K.; AIDA in Germany; Costa Cruises in Southern Europe; Iberocruceros in Spain; and P&O Cruises in Australia.[9] With so many well-known brands, at any given time, there are more than 270,000 people sailing aboard the Carnival fleet.

Carnival Corporation & plc is one of the largest vacation companies in the world, in accordance with its mission: "To deliver exceptional vacation experiences through the world's best-known cruise brands that cater to a variety of different lifestyles and budgets, all at an outstanding value unrivaled on land or at sea."[10]

### Costa Cruises

Costa Cruises is based in Genoa, Italy, and currently operates a fleet of 15 ships. Costa distinguishes itself by what it calls "Cruising Italian Style," an experience which is meant to combine sophistication and fun.[11]

Costa Cruises was established in 1854, as a fleet of trading vessels. It wasn't until 1948 that Costa Cruises began operating passenger voyages. True to its entrepreneurial roots, on its first passenger voyage in 1948, the "Anna C" was the first transatlantic ship to cross the Southern Atlantic Ocean since World War II, and the first ship to offer cabins with air conditioning to its passengers.[12]

In 1997, Carnival and another firm, Airtours, jointly acquired Costa Cruises. Carnival became the sole shareholder of Costa Cruises after purchasing all Airtours shares in 2000, which was also the year Costa saw the Italian flag return to its ships. In 2004, Costa Cruises became the first company to receive BEST 4 recognition, acknowledging their effort in quality, safety, environmental protection and social responsibility. In 2005, Costa began providing training, education and economic support to help the World Wildlife Fund protect the Mediterranean Sea, the Greater Antilles and North-Eastern Brazil. As further recognition of their commitment to the environment, Costa Cruises fleet was awarded a voluntary Green Star rating by the Registro Italiano Navale, certifying that their ships comply with the highest standards in environmental protection.[13]

Costa Cruises commissioned the Costa Concordia 2004, and at the time of its launch, the Costa Concordia was the largest Italian cruise ship in history. The ship was 952 feet in length with a beam of 116 feet. At full capacity, the ship could carry up to 1,013 crew members with 3,780 passengers occupying the 1,502 staterooms.[14]

## CRUISE INDUSTRY

By 2012, the U.S. cruise market size was roughly $26.2 billion and projected to grow by an additional $10 billion over the next four years. The largest competitors in the industry are Carnival, Royal Caribbean, and Norwegian Cruise Lines.

It's unclear what impact this event will have on the industry at large. Analysts at Zack's Equity Research expect a rather modest 3 percent dip in revenues,[15] though cruise bookings in the weeks after the event showed prices and bookings for the industry as a whole remained similar to pre-incident levels. Carnival, however, saw sales drop about 15 percent below expectations in the week that followed the shipwreck, but they claimed that the slump would likely be short-lived.[16]

## SAFETY AT SEA

At the time of the incident, the Maritime and Coastguard Agency required that "On any ship carrying passengers where the passengers are scheduled to be on board for more than 24 hours, a muster of the passengers must take place within 24 hours of their embarkation."[17] During this drill, passengers are given instructions on how to properly fasten their life-jackets and what actions they are to take when they hear the emergency signal. This includes what muster station they are to report to.

## PREVIOUS PROBLEMS AT SEA

This isn't the company's first experience with trouble at sea. In the previous three years, Carnival had given consumers many reasons[18] to reconsider booking:

- In July 2011, Carnival ships Fantasy and Imagination collided while in port in Florida; no one was hurt.
- May 2011, Costa ship Deliziosa pulled 50 feet of pier from a Bergen port in Norway because it failed to disengage its moorings.[19]
- In November 2010, Carnival ship Splendor had an engine room fire, causing the ship to lose power off the coast of Mexico.
- In June 2010, Carnival ship Fascination malfunctioned and drifted for hours without power before eventually recovering.
- February 2010, Costa ship Europa collided with a pier in Egypt, killing three crew members and injuring three passengers.[20]

## THE AFTERMATH

In the chaos that followed Captain Schettino's order to abandon ship, passengers looked for leadership that simply was not available. Under maritime safety regulations, the captain of a ship is obligated to assist passengers and crew members in times of distress. However, Captain Schettino is reported to have left his command and was sailing to safety in a lifeboat before the evacuation of his ship was complete. In the course of the ship sinking, Captain Schettino had a heated exchange with the Coast Guard who ordered him to get back on board the ship and oversee the evacuation[21] (see Exhibit 5.1 at the end of this case study).

Following his arrest, Captain Francesco Schettino was recorded telling a friend that management put pressure on him to pass by Giglio in order to provide a spectacle for passengers and a salute to Captain Palombo, a veteran Costa Captain. Schettino was recorded saying:

> Management was always saying "pass by there, pass by there." Someone else in my position might not have been so amenable to pass so close but they busted my balls: "pass by there, pass by there," and now I'm paying for it.[22]

Captain Schettino was held under house arrest at his home in Meta di Sorrento, facing charges of causing a ship-wreck, abandoning ship and multiple counts of manslaughter.[23]

The Italian Civil Protection Agency led the frantic search efforts for survivors. Five days after the incident, on Wednesday January 18, 2012, with more than 20 people still missing, the search operations had to be suspended due to a shift in the vessel's position that rendered the area unsafe. Operations were resumed the next day.[24] As of January 22, 2012, of the 3,216 passengers and 1,013 crew members aboard the Costa Concordia, 13 bodies had been recovered and another 19 were still missing and presumed lost.[25] On January 31, 2012, Italian divers ended their underwater search of the wreck, as the conditions inside had become too risky. The Italian Civil Protection Agency did add that they would continue their above-water search, using special equipment to search for bodies underwater.[26]

Because the Concordia sailed under an Italian flag and their port of origin was Civitavecchia, the laws under which the Captain, Costa and Carnival will be judged are Italian. Passenger tickets indicated that any causes of law arising from problems at sea must be brought before Italian courts[27] and likely contain class-action protection for the cruise line and its employees. Notwithstanding, two lawsuits, one filed in Illinois and the other in Florida, name Carnival Corporation as defendant in a class-action case from passengers injured by the Concordia. Combined, they sought damages of more than $500 million.

## ENVIRONMENTAL EFFECTS

Concerns about the damage the accident caused to the environment were raised by the residents of Giglio, many of whom depended upon tourism. Fortunately, the environmental effects to date have been minor. While some oil spilled, the vast majority of it remained in the Concordia's fuel tanks, which stored nearly half a million gallons. There was a risk these tanks would leak if action was not taken to remove them from the wreckage. Costa would work to remove the tanks from the wreckage, but it would take at least another month to complete. It may take another two years to move or salvage the Costa Concordia. Meanwhile, the ship sits off the island of Giglio as a dramatic reminder of the cost in lives, money and Costa Cruises's reputation.[28]

## CARNIVAL'S INITIAL RESPONSE

Immediately following the incident, little was heard from Carnival as they left Costa to handle the situation. CEO Micky Arison failed to appear at the scene of the incident, instead expressing his condolences from Miami. It took five days after the incident before Arison tweeted the brief sentiment, "I gave my personal assurance that we will take care of each & every one of our guests, crew and their families" and included a link to a press release issued by Carnival on January 18 (see Exhibit 5.2).[29] It was not until a week after the crisis began that Howard Frank, a Carnival senior executive, was sent to Italy. However, it should be noted that he appeared to be only at Costa's headquarters in Genoa with no intention of making an appearance at the scene of the incident itself.

Shortly after the crisis, Costa CEO Luigi Foschi offered an initial compensation consisting of a refund and discount on future bookings. A spokesman for the cruise line stated, "The company is not only going to refund everybody, but they will offer a 30% discount on future cruises if they want to stay loyal to the company." In response to this offer, passengers were quoted as stating it was "ridiculous and insulting."[30] Costa Cruises later clarified the offer by releasing the statement:

> Costa Cruises will refund the full cost of the cruise, either directly or through their travel agency. The company will reimburse all travel expenses incurred both reaching the port of embarkation and on the homeward jour-

ney, including any independent arrangements made for transfers. Any on-board expenses also will be refunded, and any credit card charges will be credited to the account and any cash deposits will be refunded.

Costa Cruises also will reimburse any medical expenses incurred as a result of the accident. Every effort will be made to return the valuables left in the cabin safe. Information on the return of personal belongings and other forms of compensation will be communicated. The 30 percent future cruise discount, in addition to a full refund, is intended for people scheduled to sail on Costa Concordia from Jan. 14 onward.[31]

## FINANCIAL IMPLICATIONS

Moody's estimates that total costs including the vessel, environmental and passenger liability costs could reach $1 billion, but many of those costs were offset by the Concordia's insurance. Costa Cruises's insurance deductible on the vessel itself was $40 billion. The reduction in Carnival's market cap greatly exceeds the direct costs to Concordia, suggesting that there were long-term concerns about the effect of the crisis on the industry in general and Carnival specifically.

Carnival Corporation's stock appears to have weathered the crisis relatively well, though the market has priced in a greater reduction in market capitalization than the direct effect of current financial liabilities warrants. As of mid-February, 2012, the stock had stabilized down roughly 13 percent from its value prior to the crisis (see Figure 5.5). The timing of the crash may have helped mitigate the impact on share price, as the Concordia capsized Friday after the market had closed, and the market was closed the following Monday, which may have reduced downward momentum selling. Nevertheless, the reductions in stock price still translate to a market cap reduction of $2.7 billion.

## DISCUSSION QUESTIONS

1. Should Carnival distance themselves from Costa Cruises during this crisis or support the subsidiary, and how?
2. What actions, if any, should Carnival take to minimize the impact of the crisis on future cruise purchases for the industry as a whole and Carnival specifically?
3. How should Carnival compensate passengers?
4. What messages should Carnival communicate and to which audiences?
5. What long-term changes, if any, should Carnival make in its corporate structure to improve crisis management and communication?

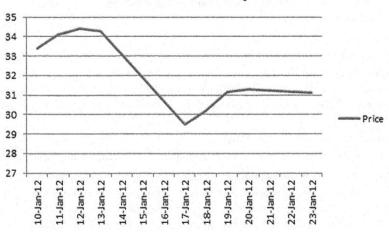

**FIGURE 5.5** Carnival Corporation's Share Price

*Source: Yahoo! Finance*, January 24, 2012.

## WRITING ASSIGNMENT

Please respond in writing to the issues presented in this case by preparing two documents: a communication strategy memo and a professional business letter.

In preparing these documents, you may assume one of two roles: you may identify yourself as a Carnival Corporation senior manager who has been asked to provide advice to Mr. Micky Arison regarding the issues he and his company are facing. Or, you may identify yourself as an external management consultant who has been asked by the company to provide advice to Mr. Arison.

Either way, you must prepare a strategy memo addressed to Mr. Arison, President and CEO, Carnival Cruise Lines, that summarizes the details of the case, rank-orders the critical issues, discusses their implications (what they mean and why they matter), offers specific recommendations for action (assigning ownership and suspense dates for each) and shows how to communicate the solution to all who are affected by the recommendations.

You must also prepare a professional business letter for Mr. Arison's signature. That document should be addressed to all passengers and families of passengers who were aboard Costa Concordia at the time of the wreck.

## ACKNOWLEDGMENTS

This case was prepared by Research Assistants Jeremy Foster, Mary Jo Sorrentino and Charles Florance under the direction of James S. O'Rourke, Teaching Professor of Management, as the basis for class discussion rather than to illustrate either effective or ineffective handling of an administrative situation. Information was gathered from corporate as well as public sources.

## APPENDIX

### Exhibit 5.1: Transcript of the Conversation between Captain Francesco Schettino and Captain Gregorio De Falco of the Coast Guard

Captain De Falco repeatedly orders Schettino to return to the ship to oversee the evacuation, while Schettino resists, making excuses that it is dark and that the ship is listing.

**De Falco**: "This is De Falco speaking from Livorno. Am I speaking with the commander?"

**Schettino**: "Yes. Good evening, Cmdr. De Falco."

**De Falco**: "Please tell me your name."

**Schettino**: "I'm Cmdr. Schettino, commander."

**De Falco**: "Schettino? Listen Schettino. There are people trapped on board. Now you go with your boat under the prow on the starboard side. There is a pilot ladder. You will climb that ladder and go on board. You go on board and then you will tell me how many people there are. Is that clear? I'm recording this conversation, Cmdr. Schettino . . . "

**Schettino**: "Commander, let me tell you one thing . . . "

**De Falco**: "Speak up! Put your hand in front of the microphone and speak more loudly, is that clear?"

**Schettino**: "In this moment, the boat is tipping . . . "

**De Falco**: "I understand that, listen, there are people that are coming down the pilot ladder of the prow. You go up that pilot ladder, get on that ship and tell me how many people are still on board. And what they need. Is that clear? You need to tell me if there are children, women or people in need of assistance. And tell me the exact number of each of these categories. Is that clear? Listen Schettino, that you saved yourself from the sea, but I am going to . . . I'm going to make sure you get in trouble. . . . I am going to make you pay for this. Go on board, (expletive)!"

**Schettino**: "Commander, please . . ."

**De Falco**: "No, please. You now get up and go on board. They are telling me that on board there are still . . ."

**Schettino**: "I am here with the rescue boats, I am here, I am not going anywhere, I am here . . ."

**De Falco**: "What are you doing, commander?"

**Schettino**: "I am here to coordinate the rescue . . ."

**De Falco**: "What are you coordinating there? Go on board! Coordinate the rescue from aboard the ship. Are you refusing?"

**Schettino**: "No, I am not refusing."

**De Falco**: "Are you refusing to go aboard commander? Can you tell me the reason why you are not going?"

**Schettino**: "I am not going because the other lifeboat is stopped."

**De Falco**: "You go aboard. It is an order. Don't make any more excuses. You have declared 'abandon ship.' Now I am in charge. You go on board! Is that clear? Do you hear me? Go, and call me when you are aboard. My air rescue crew is there."

**Schettino**: "Where are your rescuers?"

**De Falco**: "My air rescue is on the prow. Go. There are already bodies, Schettino."

**Schettino**: "How many bodies are there?"

**De Falco**: "I don't know. I have heard of one. You are the one who has to tell me how many there are. Christ."

**Schettino**: "But do you realise it is dark and here we can't see anything . . ."

**De Falco**: "And so what? You want to go home, Schettino? It is dark and you want to go home? Get on that prow of the boat using the pilot ladder and tell me what can be done, how many people there are and what their needs are. Now!"

**Schettino**: " . . . I am with my second in command."

**De Falco**: "So both of you go up then . . . You and your second go on board now. Is that clear?"

**Schettino**: "Commander, I want to go on board, but it is simply that the other boat here . . . there are other rescuers. It has stopped and is waiting . . ."

**De Falco**: "It has been an hour that you have been telling me the same thing. Now, go on board. Go on board! And then tell me immediately how many people there are there."

**Schettino**: "OK, commander"

**De Falco**: "Go, immediately!"

*Source*: "Transcript: The Costa Concordia Captain in His Own Words," *The Independent*, January 17, 2012. Online at www.independent.co.uk/news/world/europe/transcript-the-costa-concordia-captain-in-his-own-words-6290924.html

### Exhibit 5.2: Carnival Corporation's Press Release of January 18, 2012

Costa Cruises and Carnival Corporation & plc Reiterate Commitment to Support Costa Concordia Passengers and Crew

Genoa, Italy and MIAMI – January 18, 2012 – Costa Cruise Lines and its parent company, Carnival Corporation & plc, today confirmed their commitment to provide full support to those passengers, crew and families of the victims of the Costa Concordia grounding.

"I give my personal assurance that we will take care of each and every one of our guests, crew and their families affected by this tragic event. Our company was founded on this principle and it will remain our focus," said Micky Arison, chairman and CEO of Carnival Corporation & plc. "In this spirit, Costa has been arranging lodging and transportation for affected passengers and crew members to return home. Every passenger and crew member or their family is being contacted and the company has offered its assistance and counseling as needed, and will be addressing personal possessions lost on board. Costa has also begun the process of refunding all voyage costs including both passenger cruise fares and all costs incurred while on board. Our senior management teams are working together to determine additional support."

"During this time of tragedy, we are doing our very best to provide the needed support to the Costa Concordia passengers, crew and their families," said Pier Luigi Foschi, chairman and CEO of Costa Cruises.

# # #

Media Contacts:

Costa Cruises: Buck Banks/NewmanPR, +1-305-461-3300, buck@newmanpr.com

Carnival Corporation & plc: Jennifer de la Cruz, +1-305-599-2600, ext. 16000

*Source*: "Press Release," *Carnival Corporation*, January 18, 2012. Online at http://phx.corporate-ir.net/phoenix.zhtml?c=200767&p=irol-newsArticle&ID=1650164&highlight=.

## *Exhibit 5.3: Carnival Acquisitions & Mergers*

1989    Premium operator Holland America Line (this purchase included niche operator Winstar Cruises and Alaskan/Canadian tour operator Holland America Tours)

1992    Luxury brand Seabourn Cruise Line

1997    Genoa, Italy-based contemporary brand Costa Cruises, Europe's number one cruise operator

1998    Premium/luxury operator Cunard line, which built the 150,000-ton Queen Mary 2

2003    Merge with P&O Princess Cruises, adding to their fleet:

Premium brand Princess Cruises

Esteemed British operator P&O Cruises

P&O Cruises Australia

Germany's AIDA Cruises

United Kingdom operator Ocean Village, catering to a younger active clientele

Premium United Kingdom brand Swan Hellenic

Source: "Mission & History," *Carnival Corporation & PLC*. Online at http://phx.corporate-ir.net/phoenix.zhtml?c=200767&p=irol-history.

## NOTES

1   Akwagyiram, Alexis. "Italy Cruise Ship Costa Concordia Accident Eyewitness Accounts," *BBC News*, January 14, 2012. Online at www.bbc.co.uk/news/world-europe-16561382.

2   Agar, Michael and Andrew Blenkinsop. "Concordia: How the Disaster Unfolded," *The Telegraph*, January 16, 2012. Online at www.telegraph.co.uk/news/interactive-graphics/9018076/Concordia-How-the-disaster-unfolded.html.

3   Squires, Nick and Vicky Ward. "Cruise Disaster: Captain Was Bringing Crew Member Close to His Island Home," *The Telegraph*, January 16, 2012. Online at www.telegraph.co.uk/news/worldnews/europe/italy/9017767/Cruise-disaster-captain-was-bringing-crew-member-close-to-his-island-home.html.

4   Ibid.

5   Agar and Blenkinsop. "Concordia: How the Disaster Unfolded."

6   "Cruise Ship's Cook Says Captain Ordered Dinner After Crash," *CNN Europe*, January 20, 2012. Online at http://edition.cnn.com/2012/01/19/world/europe/italy-cruise-cook/index.html.

7   Beyette, Beverly. "Costa Concordia Capsizing Spotlights Cruise Ship Safety," *Los Angeles Times*, January 19, 2012. Online at www.latimes.com/travel/la-tr-insider-20120122,0,4033122.story.

8   "Mission & History," *Carnival Corporation & PLC*. Online at http://phx.corporate-ir.net/phoenix.zhtml?c=200767&p=irol-history.

9   "Corporate Information," *Carnival Corporation & PLC*. Online at http://phx.corporate-ir.net/phoenix.zhtml?c=200767&p=irol-prlanding.

10  "Mission & History," *Carnival Corporation & PLC*.

11   "Costa Cruises," *Carnival Corporation & PLC.* Online at http://phx.corporate-ir.net/phoenix.zhtml?c=200767&p=irol-prod ucts#costa.

12   "The Company History," *Costa Cruises.* Online at www.costacruise.com/contents/corporate/STORIA_COMPLETA_ USA.pdf.

13   "History of Costa Cruises," *Costa Cruise.* Online at www.costacruise.com/B2C/USA/Corporate/history/thehistory.htm.

14   Dake, Shawn. "A Short History of the Costa Concordia," *Maritime Matters,* January 22, 2012. Online at http://maritimemat ters.com/2012/01/a-short-history-of-the-costa-concordia/.

15   Zacks Equity Research, "Carnival Tops, Trims Guidance," March 9, 2012. Online at www.zacks.com/stock/news/71068/ carnival-tops-trims-guidance.

16   Sloan, Gene. "Cruise Bookings Noticeably Down After Costa Incident," *USA Today,* January 30, 2012. Online at http://travel. usatoday.com/cruises/post/2012/01/carnival-bookings-costa-concordia-accident/616043/1.

17   "Musters, Drills, On-board Training and Instructions, and Decision Support System," *Maritime and Coastguard Agency., MGN 71 (M),* page 5, Section 5.3. Online at www.dft.gov.uk/mca/mgn71.pdf.

18   Carter, Adam. "5 Troubles on Carnival Cruises," *CBC News,* February 28, 2012. Online at www.cbc.ca/news/world/sto ry/2012/02/28/f-carnival-cruise-ship-incidents.html.

19   "Cruise Ship Damages Quay," *Shipwreck Log,* May 21, 2011. Online at www.shipwrecklog.com/log/tag/costa-deliziosa/.

20   "Brits Hurt in Egyptian Boat Crash," *The Sun,* February 26, 2010. Online at www.thesun.co.uk/sol/homepage/ news/2869843/Brits-hurt-in-Egyptian-boat-crash.html.

21   Dake. "A Short History of the Costa Concordia."

22   Squires, Nick. "Costa Concordia Captain Francesco Schettino 'Under Intense Pressure to Sail Close to Giglio,'" *The Telegraph,* January 25, 2012. Online at www.telegraph.co.uk/news/worldnews/europe/italy/9037602/Costa-Concor dia-captain-Francesco-Schettino-under-intense-pressure-to-sail-close-to-Giglio.html.

23   Ibid.

24   "Costa Concordia: Search Resumes for Ship Survivors," *BBC News,* January 19, 2012. Online at www.bbc.co.uk/news/ world-europe-16626640.

25   Dake. "A Short History of the Costa Concordia."

26   "Divers Abandon Search on Costa Concordia," *RTE News,* February 1, 2012. Online at www.rte.ie/news/2012/0131/italy. html.

27   Bodzin, Robert and Burnham Brown. "Will Class-Action Law Protect Costa Concordia Passengers and Crew Members?" *Thomson Reuters News & Insight,* February 13, 2012. Online at http://newsandinsight.thomsonreuters.com/Legal/Insight/2012/02_-_ February/Will_class-action_law_protect_Costa_Concordia_passengers_and_crew_members_/.

28   "Giglio Islanders Threaten to Sue if Costa Ship Damages Coast," *Mail Online,* January 31, 2012. Online at www.dailymail. co.uk/travel/article-2094330/Costa-Concordia-Giglio-islanders-threaten-sue-cruise-shhttp://www.dailymail.co.uk/travel/ article-2094330/Costa-Concordia-Giglio-islanders-threaten-sue-cruise-ship-damages-coast.htmlip-damages-coast.html.

29   Walker, Jim. "Cruise Crisis Management FAIL – How Carnival is Ruining its Reputation Following the Costa Concordia Disaster," *Cruise Law News,* January 22, 2012. Online at www.cruiselawnews.com/2012/01/articles/social-media-1/ cruise-crisis-management-fail-how-carnival-is-ruining-its-reputation-following-the-costa-concordia-disaster/.

30   Russell, Mark. "Costa Offers Survivors 30% Off . . . A New Cruise," *Newser,* January 23, 2012. Online at www.newser.com/ story/138046/cruise-survivors-offered-30-off-future-costa-cruises.html.

31   Huber, David. "Carnival to Costa Concordia Survivors: Get 30% Off Your Next Cruise," *IRA.com,* January 24, 2012. Online at www.ira.com/carnival-offers-survivors-30-percent-discount.

# Case 5.3: Cerner Corporation

## A Stinging Office Memo Boomerangs

We are getting less than 40 hours of work from a large number of our KC-based EMPLOYEES. The parking lot is sparsely used at 8 a.m.; likewise at 5 p.m. As managers – you either do not know what your EMPLOYEES are doing; or YOU do not CARE.

I will hold you accountable. You have allowed this to get to this state. You have two weeks. Tick, tock.

Neal L. Patterson, CEO Cerner Corporation

**April 5, 2001:** *The New York Times* **by Edward Wong.** The only things missing from the office memo were expletives. It had everything else. There were lines berating employees for not caring about the company. There were words in all capital letters like "SICK" and "NO LONGER." There were threats of layoffs and hiring freezes and a shutdown of the employee gym.

The memo was sent by e-mail on March 13 by the chief executive of the Cerner Corporation, a healthcare software development company based in Kansas City, Missouri, with 3,100 employees worldwide. Originally intended only for 400 or so company managers, it quickly took on a life of its own.

The e-mail message was leaked and posted on Yahoo. Its belligerent tone surprised thousands of readers, including analysts and investors. In the stock market, the valuation of the company, which was $1.5 billion on March 20, plummeted 22 percent in three days. Now, Neal L. Patterson, the 51-year-old chief executive, a man variously described by people who know him as "arrogant," "candid," "passionate," says he wishes he had never hit the send button.

"I was trying to start a fire," he said. "I lit a match, and I started a firestorm."

That is not hard to do in the Internet age, when all kinds of messages in cyberspace are capable of stirring reactions and moving markets. In the autumn of 2000, for example, a young California investor pleaded guilty to criminal charges that he made $240,000 by sending out a fake news release that resulted in a sharp drop in the stock of Emulex, a communications equipment manufacturer.

In Mr. Patterson's case, this is what the world saw:

We are getting less than 40 hours of work from a large number of our K.C.-based EMPLOYEES. The parking lot is sparsely used at 8:00 a.m.; likewise at 5:00 p.m. As managers – either you do not know what your EMPLOYEES are doing; or YOU do not CARE. You have created expectations on the work effort which allowed this to happen inside Cerner, creating a very unhealthy environment. In either case, you have a problem and you will fix it or I will replace you. NEVER in my career have I allowed a team which worked for me to think they had a 40-hour job. I have allowed YOU to create a culture which is permitting this. NO LONGER.

Mr. Patterson went on to list six potential punishments, including laying off 5 percent of the staff in Kansas City. "Hell will freeze over," he vowed, before he would dole out more employee benefits. The parking lot would be his yardstick of success, he said; it should be "substantially full" at 7:30 a.m. and 6:30 p.m. on weekdays and half full on Saturdays.

"You have two weeks," he said. "Tick, tock."

On March 21, Patterson's memo was leaked to the public on Yahoo's message boards. Shortly thereafter, Cerner's stock (NASDAQ: CERN) plummeted, from $5.45 on March 20, the day before the leak, to a low point of $4.13 four days later on March 26. Trading skyrocketed as volume reached 32.61 million and 23.62 million shares on March 25 and 26 respectively, figures that were five to six times the average volume on any given day over the prior year. All of this resulted in Cerner's market capitalization falling from $1.51 billion on March 20 to $1.14 billion on March 26, representing a 24.5 percent drop in shareholder value.

Some analysts say that other factors could have contributed to the drop in the stock price. The overall market was shaky, and Cerner's share price had been on a decline since mid-February. In fact, by March 20, prior to the leak, Cerner's stock had already experienced a 27.5 percent drop in value since February 15. There were investors who wanted to sell the stock short, betting that it was ready for a fall, after it had been trading at 70 to 75 times forward earnings expectations at the beginning of the year. One analyst was especially bearish about the company. But even Mr. Patterson acknowledged that his memo "added noise" to what was already out there.

"While the memo provided some much-needed laughter on Wall Street after a tough week, it probably got overblown as an issue," said Stephen D. Savas, an analyst with Goldman, Sachs who rates the stock a market performer, which is relatively low. "But it did raise two real questions for investors. One: Has anything potentially changed at Cerner to cause such a seemingly violent reaction? And two: Is this a CEO that investors are comfortable with?"

Mr. Patterson said that the memo was taken out of context and that most employees at Cerner understood that he was exaggerating to make a point. He said he was not carrying out any of the punishments he listed. Instead, he said, he wanted to promote discussion. He apparently succeeded, receiving more than 300 e-mail responses from employees.

Glenn Tobin, chief operating officer at Cerner, said he had read several. "Some people said, 'The tone's too harsh, you've really fouled this one up,'" he said. "Some people said, 'I agree with your point.'" Mr. Patterson, who holds an MBA from Oklahoma State University and worked as a consultant at Arthur Andersen before starting Cerner with two partners in 1979, attributes his management style to his upbringing on a 4,000-acre family wheat farm in northern Oklahoma. He spent day after day riding a tractor in the limitless expanse of the fields with only his thoughts for company, he said, and came to the conclusion that life was about building things in your head, then going out and acting on them. "You can take the boy off the farm," he said, "but you can't take the farm out of the boy."

And his directness with subordinates is not necessarily a management liability. Cerner is a fast-growing company that had $404.5 million in revenue in 2000 and met earnings projections for the first three quarters of 2001. The company made *Fortune* magazine's lists in 1998 and 2000 of the "100 Best Companies to Work for in America."

"He has opinions," Mr. Tobin, Cerner's No. 2 executive, said. "He gives his opinions. He can have a blunt style with people who he thinks don't get it, don't understand the challenges they're facing."

March 13 began like any other day. Mr. Patterson said he woke up at 5:00 a.m. and did some work at home. Then he drove the 30 miles to Cerner's corporate campus, seven brick-and-glass buildings, surrounded by 1,900 parking spaces atop a hill in northern Kansas City. In the elevator, he spoke with the receptionist, a woman who had been

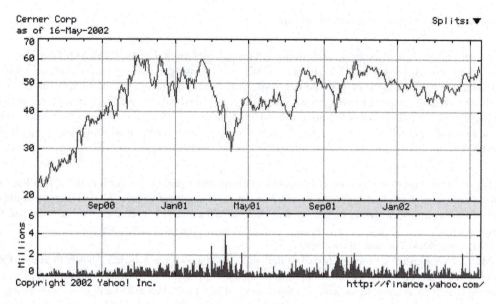

Cerner Corp
as of 16-May-2002

Splits: ▼

**FIGURE 5.6** Cerner Corporation Stock Performance. June 2000 to May 2002.

*Source*: Yahoo Finance. Used by permission.

with the company for 18 years. She remarked that the work ethic had been declining at the company, he said, reinforcing his own fears.

At 7:45 a.m., he walked into his sixth-floor office and typed up a draft of the memo. He met with a client downstairs, then had two managers and his assistant read over the memo. At 11:48, he sent it. The memo went up on the Yahoo message board a week later. Analysts began getting calls from investors. They, in turn, called Cerner to verify the authenticity of the memo, then exchanged a flurry of phone calls and e-mail messages, trying to divine the tea leaves of Mr. Patterson's writings.

"The perception was that they have to work overtime to meet their quarter," said Stacey Gibson, an analyst with Fahnestock & Company, who rated the company's stock a "buy" and was among the first to post a warning on Thomson Financial/First Call about the memo. "Whether that's true or not, I don't know," she said. "This is how it was taken on the Street."

Some analysts say that other factors could have contributed to the drop in stock price. The overall market was shaky. There were investors who wanted to sell the stock short, betting that it was ready for a fall. One analyst was especially bearish about the company. But even Mr. Patterson acknowledged that his memo "added noise" to what was already out there.

At the end of the week, as the stock fell, Mr. Patterson sent out another e-mail message to his troops. Unlike the first memo, it was not called a Management Directive, but rather a Neal Note. It began this way: "Please treat this memo with the utmost confidentiality. It is for internal dissemination only. Do not copy or e-mail to anyone else."

## QUESTIONS

1. What's the principal business problem here?
2. From the company's perspective, what would an optimal outcome look like?
3. Who are the key stakeholders in this case?
4. If Mr. Patterson were to ask for your counsel on this matter, what would you advise?
5. Which actions would you encourage him to take first? What measure would you use to determine success in resolving the business problem identified in question number one?
6. What sort of problems did Mr. Patterson create for himself when he chose e-mail as his communication medium? How should discussions of this sort be conducted?

## WRITING ASSIGNMENT

Please respond in writing to the issues presented in this case by preparing two documents: a communication strategy memo and a professional business letter.

In preparing these documents, you may assume one of two roles: you may identify yourself as a Cerner Corporation senior manager who has been asked to provide advice to Mr. Neal Patterson regarding the issues he and his company are facing. Or, you may identify yourself as an external management consultant who has been asked by the company to provide advice to Mr. Patterson.

Either way, you must prepare a strategy memo addressed to Neal Patterson, Chairman and Chief Executive Officer of the company, that summarizes the details of the case, rank-orders the critical issues, discusses their implications (what they mean and why they matter), offers specific recommendations for action (assigning ownership and suspense dates for each) and shows how to communicate the solution to all who are affected by the recommendations.

You must also prepare a professional business letter for Mr. Patterson's signature. That document should be addressed to all Cerner Corporation employees. If you have questions about either of these documents, please consult your instructor.

## ACKNOWLEDGMENTS

This case was prepared by James S. O'Rourke, Teaching Professor of Management, as the basis for class discussion rather than to illustrate either effective or ineffective handling of an administrative situation. Information was gathered from corporate as well as public sources. Copyright © 2002. Revised: 2017.

Eugene D. Fanning Center for Business Communication. All rights reserved. No part of this publication may be reproduced, stored in a retrieval system, used in a spreadsheet, or transmitted in any form by any means – electronic, mechanical, photocopying, recording, or otherwise – without permission.

## APPENDIX

—— Original Message ——

From: Patterson, Neal.

To: DL_ALL_Managers.

Subject: MANAGEMENT DIRECTIVE: Week #10_01: Fix it or changes will be made.

Importance: High.

To the KC-based managers:

I have gone over the top. I have been making this point for over one year. We are getting less than 40 hours of work from a large number of our KC-based EMPLOYEES. The parking lot is sparsely used at 8 AM; likewise at 5PM. As managers – you either do not know what your EMPLOYEES are doing; or YOU do not CARE. You have created expectations on the work effort which allowed this to happen inside Cerner, creating a very unhealthy environment. In either case, you have a problem and you will fix it or I will replace you.

NEVER in my career have I allowed a team which worked for me to think they had a 40-hour job. I have allowed YOU to create a culture which is permitting this. NO LONGER. At the end of next week, I am planning to implement the following:

1.    Closing of Associate Center to EMPLOYEES from 7:30 AM to 6:30 PM.

2.    Implementing a hiring freeze for all KC-based positions. It will require Cabinet approval to hire someone into a KC-based team. I chair our Cabinet.

3.    Implementing a time clock system, requiring EMPLOYEES to "punch in" and "punch out" to work. Any unapproved absences will be charged to the EMPLOYEES vacation.

4.    We passed a Stock Purchase Program, allowing for the EMPLOYEE to purchase Cerner stock at a 15% discount, at Friday's BOD meeting. Hell will freeze over before this CEO implements ANOTHER EMPLOYEE benefit in this Culture.

5.    Implement a 5% reduction of staff in KC.

6.    I am tabling the promotions until I am convinced that the ones being promoted are the solution, not the problem. If you are the problem, pack your bags.

      I think this parental-type action SUCKS. However, what you are doing, as managers, with this company makes me SICK. It makes me sick to have to write this directive. I know I am painting with a broad brush and the majority of the KC-based associates are hard-working, committed to Cerner success and committed to transforming health care. I know the parking lot is not a great measurement for "effort." I know that "results" is what counts, not "effort." But I am through with the debate.

We have a big vision. It will require a big effort. Too many in KC are not making the effort.

I want to hear from you. If you think I am wrong with any of this, please state your case. If you have some ideas on how to fix this problem, let me hear those. I am very curious how you think we got here. If you know team members who are the problem, let me know. Please include (copy) Kynda in all of your replies.

I STRONGLY suggest that you call some 7AM, 6PM and Saturday AM team meetings with the EMPLOYEES who work directly for you. Discuss this serious issue with your team. I suggest that you call your first meeting – tonight. Something is going to change.

I am giving you two weeks to fix this. My measurement will be the parking lot. It should be substantially full at 7:30 AM and 6:30 PM. The pizza man should show up at 7:30 p.m. to feed the starving teams working late. The lot should be half full on Saturday mornings. We have a lot of work to do. If you do not have enough to keep your teams busy, let me know immediately.

Folks this is a management problem, not an EMPLOYEE problem. Congratulations, you are management. You have the responsibility for our EMPLOYEES. I will hold you accountable. You have allowed this to get to this state. You have two weeks. Tick, tock.

Neal

Chairman & Chief Executive Officer

Cerner Corporation www.cerner.com

2800 Rockcreek Parkway, Kansas City, Missouri 64117

"We Make Health Care Smarter"

—— End of Original Message ——

## SOURCES

"Boss's E-Mail Bites Back," *BBC News Online*. Online at www.news.bbc.co.uk/hi/english/world/americas/news id_1263000/1263917.stm. Accessed May 17, 2002 at 2:38 p.m.

Burton, T. M. "Irate CEO's E-Mail Puts Him in Hot Water," *WSJ.com: Career Journal*. Online at www.careerjournal. com/myc/killers/20010427-burton.htm. Accessed May 17, 2002 at 2:44 p.m.

Clancy, J. "Weekend Work Piles Up for Execs," *CNN.com*. Online at wysiwyg://17http://www.cnn.com/2001/ world/europe//04/06/executive.stress. Accessed May 17, 2002 at 2:47 p.m.

From Cerner Corp to Employees. Online at www.clas.ufl.edu/users/creed/Business/Professional/Communication/ Assignments3.

Gillis, W. C. "Think Twice Before Hitting Send," *Small Business Computing*. Online at www.smallbusinesscomput ing.com/biztools/. Accessed May 17, 2002 at 3:04 p.m.

Korzeniowski, P. "Firms Try to Stamp Out 'Bad' E-mail Disclosures," *Omniva Policy Systems. Investors Business Daily*. Online at www.disappearing.com/ann/investorsbusinessdaily_inthenews.htm. Accessed May 17, 2002 at 2:43 p.m.

Wendland, M. "Masses of Sloppy E-Mail Are Holding Workers Back," *The Detroit Free Press*, May 3, 2001. Online at www.freep.com/money/tech/mwend3_20010503.htm. Accessed May 17, 2002 at 2:42 p.m.

Wong, E. "A Stinging Office Memo Boomerangs: Chief Executive is Criticized After Upbraiding Workers by E-Mail," *The New York Times*, Thursday, April 5, 2001, pp. C1, C13. Reprinted with permission.

# CHAPTER 6

# Persuasion

"A baseline of trust must exist in order to effectively persuade people to accept a different point of view or participate in an activity that may vary from the status quo. People need to be informed and engaged," said Susan Hoff, "before you can change their behavior." Ms. Hoff is senior vice president and chief communications officer for Best Buy Company, a *Fortune* 500 retailer based in Richfield, Minnesota. "At Best Buy," she said, "we use a variety of communication techniques to move people to the desired outcome."[1]

Every communications plan developed and implemented at Best Buy includes a set of key messages, as well as elements focused on what Ms. Hoff calls "the head, the heart, and the hands of the stakeholders we are trying to reach." The head refers to the facts: "Our actions must be based on research." The heart assures that the company's messages resonate in a personal, emotive way with the audience. And the hands are the direction to "specific actions that we want the stakeholder to take." This head/heart/hands approach is used in the company's employee communications activities, as well as those with external stakeholders.[2]

"As a retailer, we must persuade customers to come into our stores each day," said Hoff: As an employer, we must persuade potential employees that Best Buy is a great place to work, and work to retain them. As a publicly traded entity, we must persuade shareholders that Best Buy is a viable growth company that merits their continued investment. As a newcomer into a community, we must persuade our neighbors that we will be a good and thoughtful corporate citizen. And, every time we interact with a member of the news media, we must persuade them to take the time to listen to our point of view.

Persuasion, she says, is not about selling or spinning. It's about building a level of trust so that people will be open to a new perspective.[3]

Virtually all elements of organizational communication include some element of persuasion. It might be an interpersonal communication, such as a manager approaching an employee with a stretch goal or the opportunity to work on a new project. Or it could be a much larger, more structured communication related to a major corporate initiative.

For example, Best Buy recently decided to outsource its information systems function to Accenture. The challenge for Ms. Hoff and her communications team was to persuade 600 Best Buy employees to transition their employment to Accenture. "This was a significant cultural shift that required trust," she noted, "as well as frequent and transparent communications that were grounded in our company values."[4] Using the head/heart/hands approach, they employed a variety of two-way communications to move employees along the change curve – including everything from information sessions and department meetings to brown bag seminars, employee roundtables, and a special transition website – all to ensure that they acknowledged employees' questions and concerns.

> "It was essential," said Hoff, that our key messages (what we said) matched our actions and behaviors (what we did). With that baseline of trust and credibility, we were able to successfully persuade our employees to transition to Accenture, with a higher-than-expected retention rate of 98%.[5]

What Susan Hoff and her team faced was the daunting task of convincing others – many different people in this instance – that an important portion of their business had changed and why restructuring would be inevitable. It amounted to persuading them that cooperating with her was really in their own best interest.

What we believe defines, in so many important ways, *who* we are. Yet what we believe – or hold to be true – is not simply a function of what we know. It is a product of how we were raised, who educated us and the lives we led when we were young. We were each raised by different people, in different places, at different times. We were educated, coached and enculturated by many different people, each of whom had some influence on who we would ultimately become. Our potential, combined with our personality preferences and our life experiences, results in unique individuals. No two of us believe exactly the same things. And no two of us have precisely the same interests, attitudes or feelings about life and the world around us. We are, in so many ways, different from one another.

The human attitudinal system – that collection of beliefs, attitudes and opinions that makes us who we are – is a rich and interesting mixture of education, experience and inventiveness. Our attitudinal systems constantly undergo re-evaluation and change. We add new information each day; we reinforce existing beliefs; we remove old ideas and concepts; and we frequently challenge new assumptions.

## TWO SCHOOLS OF THOUGHT

For as long as people have been trying to influence others, the focus has been squarely on human behavior. Two old aphorisms have it that "actions speak louder than words" and that "talk is cheap, but action has value." What conventional wisdom has been telling us for thousands of years is that we cannot often tell what people are thinking, but we can certainly observe their behavior. And, such wisdom tells us, behavior is a much surer measure of a person's real intentions.

### Behaviorism

One school of thought, behaviorism, contends that human behavior will most clearly reveal what a person is thinking and that persuasion is most effectively exercised at the behavioral level. Learning theory that dominated educational psychology during the first half of the twentieth century was mainly behaviorist in nature and represented an approach to psychology that emphasized observable, measurable behavior and discounted the role or value of mental activity. Learners were viewed by behaviorists as passively adapting to their environment, and instruction focused on conditioning a learner's behavior. Learning, thus, is indicated by a measurable change in the frequency of observable events. These changes are the result of a strengthening of the relationship between cue and behavior, driven by a pattern of consequences, called reinforcement (which may come in the form of rewards or punishment). This shaping of behavior, with enough practice, can create a link so strong that the time between cue and behavior gets very small.[6]

John B. Watson published an early paper promoting the view that psychology should be concerned only with the objective data of behavior.[7] Professors B. F. Skinner of Harvard and Stanley Milgram of Yale later underscored what Ivan P. Pavlov had so famously demonstrated a generation earlier: Behavior is conditioned by its consequences. If human behavior can be conditioned to respond to external influences, an internal change in attitudes and beliefs *may* result.

## *Cognitivism*

On the other hand, cognitivism, which emerged in the 1950s and 1960s, represents a different view of learning. Many theorists disagreed with the strict focus on observable behavior, arguing that it was entirely possible to learn something without changing the learner's behavior. The cognitivist school basically went inside the head of the learner to see what mental processes were activated and changed during the course of learning. In cognitive theories, knowledge is viewed as symbolic mental constructs in the learner's mind, and the learning process is the means by which the symbolic representations are committed to memory.[8]

Changes in behavior are observed, but only as an indicator to what is going on inside the learner's head. Even though our actions may be informed and motivated by our beliefs, cognitive psychologists have come to see the human attitudinal system in a different way. They look at what psychologist Howard Gardner calls "the contents of what we think about – concepts, theories, stories, and skills – and the formats in which our mind/brain does that thinking."[9]

Among the early cognitivists, the work of Milton Rokeach at Michigan State University stands out as particularly important to our understanding of how human beings think and behave. In a landmark work entitled *Beliefs, Attitudes, and Values: A Theory of Organization and Change*, Rokeach explored the human attitudinal system. Among other things, he examined the relationship among the elements that comprise our beliefs and the factors associated with attitudinal assimilation and behavioral change. His work also includes a description of the basic ways in which we each organize and structure what we know and what we believe. Figure 6.1 is a simplistic adaptation of Rokeach's work, but it may help us to understand the relationship between those constructs that are fundamental to our beliefs and that, in so many important ways, help to define who we are, and less important, less central attitudes that may, nonetheless, guide or inform our behavior.[10]

In Rokeach's view of the human attitudinal system, three components help to define what we believe, how we organize those beliefs and how they influence our day-to-day behavior.

## *Beliefs*

At the core of the system and acquired early in life, beliefs are the most fundamental component of our values. They come to us from highly trusted sources, including our parents, close relatives, teachers, coaches, religious instructors and other authority figures. Because young children are generally unable to form what psychologists call higher cognitive structures, they are not able to reason in the way that adults are able to.[11] They tend to respond to emotional needs and direct instruction from their elders. We come to believe the world is a particular way because that's what we've been told by those who feed, house, instruct and care for us. Pre-adolescent children, thus, form a view of the

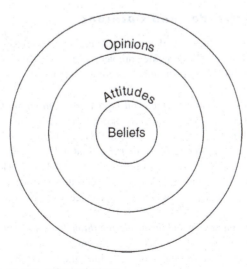

**FIGURE 6.1** A Conceptual View of the Human Attitudinal System

world around them largely because they have few other choices.[12] These basic beliefs encompass everything from an understanding of God, to our relationship with nature, or our views about health and nutrition.

Our most basic beliefs don't necessarily follow, one from another, nor are they carefully aligned. They generally represent some sense of balance and consistency, though, even if some beliefs contradict others. A basic belief about nutrition, for example, might be that "eating healthy is good for me, and the occasional consumption of red meat is fine." Others (particularly vegetarians) might disagree with you or try to convince you to give up eating meat, but for now let's assume you're comfortable with your position.

## Attitudes

As outgrowths of our beliefs, our attitudes are dependent on them and tend to be consistent with them. The term *attitude* is really a navigational term describing your position relative to the rest of the world. Thus, our attitudes about a particular topic will influence not only how we perceive the world around us but how we are perceived by others. One belief may give rise to literally dozens of attitudes, each of which may have an important role to play in how we organize and live out our lives.[13]

Your views about meat, for example, might give rise to the idea that an occasional steak or beef burrito would be a nice addition to your diet. That attitude doesn't say much about why you believe it's good or about where to eat, just that you enjoy an occasional beef dish for dinner. (By way of disclosure: I am the grandson of a Montana cattle rancher, so it's easy to see how I came by my own beliefs about the role of beef in my diet.)

## Opinions

At the very fringes of our belief system, our opinions are among the least stable. Rokeach and others believe that opinions, in fact, are the structures in our belief system most susceptible to persuasion. They are the outgrowths of many different attitudes (themselves not as stable and central to our view of the world as our core beliefs); they are dependent on little more than preference, and can easily be shifted, modified, created or done away with entirely.

My views about what to have for dinner, as we have just seen, are guided by my fundamental belief that it's okay for me to occasionally include meat in my diet (even though others whom I respect and admire don't agree with me), and that one attitude (among many) tells me that an occasional beef burrito might be just fine. My opinion about where to eat or who makes the best burritos in town may be less stable, less enduring, and more quickly and easily subject to change than those attitudes and beliefs that support it. A bad experience at one particular Mexican restaurant might easily cause me to switch my preference for where I dine. Similarly, a good experience at a new restaurant might establish a new loyalty – all based on the underlying, positive attitude about beef burritos.

## The Role of Beliefs, Attitudes and Opinions

As we noted, beliefs change slowly – if at all – over the course of a lifetime, while attitudes are more easily shaped by life experience, education and current events. Opinions are completely ephemeral; they come and go, seemingly with the next piece of evidence that arrives. The human attitudinal system is governed by a number of other principles, as well.

- *Change in one layer may expose a more fundamental layer to reexamination, but will require no change in the more basic layer.* If I have a bad fish dinner at one restaurant, it may cause me to rethink the wisdom of ordering fish in Indiana, though it will not require that I change my views about the role of seafood in my diet.
- *Change in a basic layer will require change in all higher attitudinal layers.* If I should decide to stop smoking because it's bad for my health (and those around me), the attitudes I've developed about when and where to smoke, along with the opinions about brand selection, are all out the window. My basic change in belief (from "smoking is cool" to "smoking is harmful") will mandate changes in all attitudinal structures dependent on that belief.
- *The more basic the change, the more profound the reordering throughout the system.* G. K. Chesterton once wrote, "When a man stops believing in God, he doesn't start believing in nothing. He starts believing in anything."[14] Our beliefs are among the most basic and stable of our values, and to alter or cast aside any of them is to invite confusion and instability in our belief system.

- *The less rational the basis for adoption, the more difficult is the basis for change in a given belief or attitude group.* Emotionally charged attitudes are especially difficult to change because they were not rationally acquired. As such, they are particularly resistant to rational attempts or the use of logic to change them. I may see the merit or value in what the Chicago White Sox do each summer, but I'll never be a fan, even if you tell me they're doing great things for the neighborhood and the city of Chicago. I'm a Cub fan. And, of course, that loyalty involves enough emotion to fill the rest of this book.
- *The closer a structure is to the center of one's belief system, the more central it becomes to one's self-concept.* Such beliefs, thus, become self-defining.[15] If you are a committed environmentalist, you will most likely identify yourself as such, describing your beliefs, views and actions in personal terms. These beliefs can define who you are and how you live your life each day.

## THE OBJECTIVES OF PERSUASION

In seeking to influence the views of others, most psychologists tell us that we have three general aims in mind: to reinforce positive opinion, to crystallize latent or unformed opinion and to neutralize hostile opinion.

### *Reinforcing Positive Opinion*

A particularly useful and productive approach to persuasion is to reinforce positive opinion because it offers the speaker or writer the advantage of addressing people who already think the same way, believe the same things and who are likely to respond in a positive, enthusiastic way to the messages they receive. The second, often hidden, advantage of "preaching to the choir" is that people who are already on your side, who believe as you do, will offer their reinforced views to others who may not yet have formed an opinion. Reinforcing positive opinion not only helps to prevent backsliding on the part of those who agree with you; it may also help to influence those who are not yet informed or convinced on this topic.

### *Crystallizing Latent Opinion*

Some instruction and, perhaps, some extensive explanation are required for this purpose. To convince someone with no background on the subject at hand, and no emotional link to either the topic or your position, often requires an extended effort. For most purposes, you don't really need to convince everyone in town of your views, you only need to reach the few who matter – those in a position to influence the outcome of a debate or controversy. Often, though, if we ignore the vast, uninformed masses, we risk allowing someone hostile to our position to reach them first. In the absence of accurate information about your position or views, the uninformed may make up their minds with the first bit of useful information that comes along.

### *Neutralizing Hostile Opinion*

The task of neutralizing hostile opinion is never easy and never-ending. Those whose views are diametrically opposed to your own are likely never to be convinced that you're actually correct, that you're right about a particular issue or idea. The point is not to convert these people; you can't. Who they are is often the polar opposite of who you are. The best you can hope for is to prevent them from reaching the uninformed before you or your allies do. Your best weapons are the truth; a solid, rational argument; an emotional connection to the topic; and speed. The sooner you reach those who have yet to form an opinion, the sooner you'll have an opportunity to change their minds. Don't worry about converting those who disagree.

## OUTCOMES OF THE ATTITUDINAL FORMATION PROCESS

Any attempt at persuasion must first consider the goals and objectives of the persuader: Why are you communicating with this particular group or person? What do you hope to achieve as a result? Is your purpose to raise awareness or to influence behavior? Any persuasive attempt must also consider the goals and objectives of the audience: Why would they agree to read, listen or pay attention to this communication? Do they want information? Are they seeking encouragement for a decision? What do they hope for as a result of this interaction? In general, the outcomes of persuasion – or the attitudinal formation process – include the following:

- *Reinforcement of existing attitudes.* As you've already seen, your first task in persuasion is to reinforce the views of those who agree with you. This reinforcement not only helps to prevent backsliding but will expand the number of people who can help you reach the uninformed.
- *Modification or shifting of existing attitudes.* This outcome is a bit more difficult but certainly possible. Attitudes will move in one direction or another with the arrival of new evidence from credible sources, but this process happens slowly. New evidence that doesn't fit our frame of reference is likely to be rejected, but over time, enough new evidence from sources we trust might tip the balance and cause us to rethink our position.
- *Creation of new attitudes.* Perhaps the most difficult goal of persuasion is the creation of entirely new attitude sets. This task is best done by linking the position we hope to create to an existing belief (or beliefs) in our audience. Advertisers often try to get consumers to switch brands by showing how a new product is more economical, cleaner and kinder to the environment, or safer than existing brands. An extended instructional task may be involved as you attempt to construct new attitudes, but if done properly, the result may be a useful, enduring viewpoint.

## THE SCIENCE OF PERSUASION

"A lucky few have it," says Professor Robert Cialdini, "most of us do not. A handful of gifted 'naturals' simply know how to capture an audience, sway the undecided, and convert the opposition."[16] How is it that such masters of persuasion are able to work their magic on an audience? What techniques or principles do they apply that others do not? Is some science at work here, or is it all high artistry beyond the grasp of ordinary mortals? As it happens, and as Cialdini has shown, managers and executives can improve their abilities to persuade by turning to science.

"For the past five decades, behavioral scientists have conducted experiments that shed considerable light on the way certain interactions lead people to concede, comply, or change. This research," he writes:

shows that persuasion works by appealing to a limited set of deeply rooted human drives and needs, and it does so in predictable ways. Persuasion, in other words, is governed by basic principles that can be taught, learned, and applied.[17]

Cialdini has identified six scientific principles that ordinary business writers and speakers can apply each day to win concessions, cut deals or secure consensus:

- *Liking.* We tend to like those who like us, but we also tend to like those who *are* like us. Making friends with others may help us to influence them. Uncovering real similarities and offering genuine praise can help us to persuade others.
- *Reciprocity.* The Japanese call this principle *giri*, a kind of mutual indebtedness. It means that people repay in kind and expect to receive what they give. If what you want from your colleagues and coworkers is their time and help with your problems, then you must be prepared to share your time and help with them.
- *Social proof.* People follow the lead of similar others when they're asked to do something. If you can show that you have the support of neighbors, friends, colleagues and others known to those you hope to influence, you'll have a better chance of success. Testimonials from satisfied customers, surveys and opinion polls can all have a powerful effect on a person's decision, particularly if that support comes from key opinion leaders admired by your audience.
- *Consistency.* If nothing else, people genuinely enjoy being consistent. They do what they say they will and they appreciate staying within their own "comfort zone." People align with their clear commitments, particularly if those are both public and voluntary. That campaign button on your lapel is not intended to get me to vote for your candidate. It's designed to prevent you from voting for someone else. If you've publicly said you're voting for a candidate, you're unlikely to back away from that position or do something else.

- **Authority.** If you can't convince people that their friends and neighbors support your position, then perhaps you can show them an expert who does. People readily defer to experts, and you can use this ready inclination in two ways. You can explain your own expertise (people often don't recognize or appreciate your experience), or you can find someone whose expertise they do understand.
- **Scarcity.** The value of an object often rises as fewer of them become available. The odd thing is that people often want something simply because it *is* scarce. To claim something is rare, unavailable, or in short supply when it's actually not would be unethical. "This deal is only good until 5:00 o'clock," says the salesman. Chances are, he'll have a similar deal tomorrow or next week. To apply this principal ethically, you should highlight unique benefits of what you advocate or offer exclusive information unavailable elsewhere.[18]

## SUCCESSFUL ATTEMPTS AT PERSUASION

Most successful attempts at persuasion involve four separate yet related steps. Following these steps won't guarantee success with any particular audience, but they will set the conditions for attitudinal assimilation and behavioral change to follow.

### Gaining the Attention of Your Audience

The marketplace is crowded. The in-box is full. People are clamoring for your attention in the media, on the phone and in the workplace. Attention serves as a human gate-keeping function. Each day we are exposed to so many stimuli — sight, sound, taste, touch and smell — that our senses would quickly be overloaded if we were not selective in what we pay attention to. Psychologists refer to this ability as *selective perception*. In other words, we select — often subconsciously — what we will pay attention to, take in, think about and act on. And we selectively ignore virtually everything else.[19]

It's clear that a stimulus we choose to pay attention to has an advantage over one that we ignore. Whatever controls our attention tends to produce action. What we choose to pay attention to is hardly accidental. Two factors are at work in our selections: First, people pay attention to stimuli that contain inherent attention-getting factors (bright lights, noise, motion, color and so on). And, second, people respond to stimuli that relate to their needs and goals. Restaurant signs seem more obvious to us when we're hungry and, by contrast, we are less likely to notice "help wanted" ads unless we're looking for work.

### Providing the Appropriate Motivation for Your Audience

The persuasive writer or speaker is one who can lead an audience to believe in what he or she is advocating and to encourage some form of behavior that is consistent with that belief. This approach amounts to giving good reasons for what you believe. Rhetorician Karl R. Wallace goes even further to say that these shouldn't simply be reasons that *you* think are good. They must be reasons that your audience will think are good. Of course, that means you must know your audience well, long before you write or speak to them.[20]

Research in behavioral psychology has shown six broad, general categories of motivators for human behavior:

- **Human needs as motivation.** Psychologist Abraham Maslow offered a theory, widely known as the Hierarchy of Needs, in which he describes a set of five needs, the most basic of which must be satisfied first, followed by the need to feel secure, a need to belong, a need to be loved or admired and finally, self-actualization needs. He observed that people have various kinds of needs that emerge, subside and emerge again as they are met or not met. For example, the need for food and water emerges and then recedes as we eat or drink. Maslow argued that these needs have a *prepotency* — that is, they are linked together so that weaker, higher needs emerge only after stronger, more basic needs have been met and satisfied.

    Figure 6.2 is only a model and the divisions between the various levels are not as distinct as the lines might suggest. Also, it's important to note that higher needs are not necessarily superior to or more important than lower ones. They're simply weaker and less likely to emerge until our basic needs have been met.
- **Basic needs** include the most fundamental of physiological requirements for human life: air, food, water, sleep and elimination of waste. Until these needs are met, we cannot concern ourselves with other, higher needs. The basic needs are simply too strong to be forgotten in favor of other needs.

**FIGURE 6.2**  Maslow's Hierarchy of Human Needs

- *Security needs* are on the second level of Maslow's hierarchy, and they deal with our feelings of well-being and confidence. Our insecurities may range from fears of becoming a crime victim to fears about our jobs, our families' well-being and our future. This need is relatively constant, and even when it is satisfied, it frequently redefines itself and is, thus, present to some extent in our lives.

- *Belonging needs* follow those related to security. Once we feel secure, we become aware of needs at a third level. Humans have a relatively strong desire for association or affiliation with other humans. We are social animals who continue to form relationships and associate with other humans in groups. Belonging, being a part of the group, being accepted by others is a powerful motivation for most people, even for those who say they don't care what others think about them. Deep inside, we each long for the company of others.

- *Love or esteem needs* are one step up from belonging, in level four of Maslow's hierarchy. We each want to feel loved, wanted and admired by other people, especially those closest to us. Humans frequently are disappointed with themselves when they encounter failure, not so much because their own self-image has suffered, but because they have disappointed or "let down" a close friend or member of the family. If we find that we are loved and needed by our family, the need for esteem does not disappear; it is a reemerging need. We seek approval and acceptance from others, including friends and coworkers. The more of this need we satisfy, the less powerful it becomes, but it is never fully satisfied.

- *Self-actualization needs'* position at the top of Maslow's hierarchy suggests that each person cannot really become all that he or she could be unless each of the four lower needs is first satisfied. Only with satisfaction of all lower needs, said Maslow, can people then truly begin to live up to their full potential. Later in life, Maslow rethought some of his earlier writing on this subject and amended his thinking to include the idea that people can self-actualize early in life, long before they have met and satisfied all four levels of their needs. He described "peak experiences" in which people learn to be self-reliant, perform to the maximum of their ability and live up to their potential at various stages of their lives. Maslow's later thinking does not contradict any of his earlier writing but amends it to demonstrate that we needn't live out our lives entirely or be promoted to president of the company before we can begin to self-actualize.[21]

## ERG Theory of Motivation

Yale University Psychologist Clayton Alderfer developed another need-based approach called *ERG theory*. It involves a streamlining of Maslow's classifications and some different assumptions about the relationship between needs and motivation. The name *ERG* comes from Alderfer's compression of Maslow's five-category system into three categories: existence, relatedness and growth:

- *Existence needs* are satisfied by some material substance or condition and might include the need for such things as food, shelter, pay and safe working conditions.

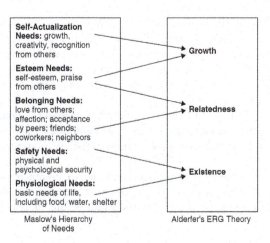

**FIGURE 6.3** The Relationship between Maslow's Hierarchy of Human Needs and ERG Theory

- *Relatedness needs* are satisfied by open communication and the exchange of thoughts and feelings with other human beings, including friends, family members and coworkers.
- *Growth needs* are fulfilled by strong involvement in work, education and personal development. They often involve not only the full use of a person's skills and abilities but the development of new ones.

In many ways, Alderfer's theory is similar to Maslow's, with three broad classifications substituting for five in Maslow's Hierarchy of Human Needs. According to Alderfer, an apparently satisfied need can act as a motivator by substituting for an unsatisfied need. ERG theory's contribution to our understanding of human motivation rests on two basic premises: First, as more lower-level needs are satisfied, more higher-level need satisfaction is desired. And, second, the less higher-level needs are satisfied, the more lower-level need satisfaction is desired. The value of this theory, along with Maslow's work, for a business communicator is that both can tell us something about what motivates people. Knowing which needs have been satisfied in a particular target audience will help in formulating messages to prompt further behavior.[22]

Figure 6.3 shows how the theories of Abraham Maslow and Clayton Alderfer are closely related and provide similar insights into human motivation.

### Eight Hidden Needs

In the late 1950s, author and critic Vance Packard gathered and published motivational research done on behalf of advertisers in a book called *The Hidden Persuaders*. In the results of a series of complex psychological tests measuring the motivation for consumer goods purchases of a large number of people, Packard found eight "compelling needs" that were frequently used in selling products with a motivational research approach. More than 60 years later, many advertisers still rely on these findings, though in a more sophisticated way:

- *Need for emotional security.* We need to be reassured that everything will be okay, that we will be secure and safe. Everything from disease to terrorists can threaten our sense of well-being.
- *Need for reassurance of worth.* No matter who we are or what we do for a living, we need reassurance that we have personal value, that we're worth something as an individual. We like to know that people understand and appreciate us.
- *Need for ego gratification.* We need to be told that we're not only worth something but that we are actually special or – in some ways – better than other people at certain things. Compliments, public recognition and awards confirm this worth.
- *Need for creative outlets.* We each feel the need to assemble, craft, configure or create on our own. When a mom adds an egg to her boxed cake mix, she's "creating" dessert for her family. Powdered eggs in the cake mix would leave the housewife with nothing to add and no sense of creative accomplishment.

- *Need for love objects.* In addition to being loved, we have a strong need to love others. Everyone (and everything) from movie stars, royalty and celebrities to family pets can fulfill our need to extend love.
- *Need for a sense of power.* A feeling of power can come in different ways for different people. For a young man, the roar of a motorcycle engine that responds to his command will convey a sense of power. For women, power can mean something entirely different: They may look for financial independence, control or decision authority as a source of power satisfaction in their lives.
- *Need for roots.* In a society that moves frequently and often over vast distances, the need for roots can be powerful. Reminders of home, family experiences, "old-fashioned" products and middle-class values are often used to motivate consumer purchases ranging from over-the-counter medication to convenience dining comfort food.
- *Need for immortality.* We often like to think we can exert influence on others even after we're dead. Life insurance policies, trust funds and other products appeal to this need. A continuing emphasis on youth in advertising appeals to our fears about growing old. Immortality and youth, we are told, can be bought from a jar.[23]

## Relating Needs Theory to Persuasive Messages

In an affirmative appeal, a writer might argue that if the reader accepts his or her proposal, a need not now being satisfied will be met or a need being met will be satisfied more fully, more efficiently or quickly. The human resources group in your company might argue, for example, that opening an on-site exercise center will help to improve employee fitness and health, boost morale and give the firm an edge in recruiting new employees.

In a threat or fear appeal, a writer might pose a threat to the continued satisfaction of a need and then argue that if the reader follows the advice, the threat will be neutralized or avoided. A group of industrial tenants might argue, for instance, that building management must increase security in their facilities. If management doesn't comply, the tenants say, they will relocate their businesses at the end of their lease agreements.

A substantial amount of research on fear appeals shows that:

- A highly credible source gets a good response from a fear appeal. If the audience knows and trusts the message source, they're much more likely to comply.
- If a strong fear appeal threatens the welfare of a loved one, it tends to be more effective than if it threatens the members of the audience themselves.
- A strong fear appeal may be related to personality characteristics of the audience; that is, uneducated people and those with poor self-esteem may be easily influenced by a direct threat.
- The arousal of fear in an audience seems to depend on the speaker's ability to convince the audience of the probability that the threat will materialize and the magnitude of the consequences. It's much easier to sell home fire insurance or automobile accident coverage than it is to sell asteroid collision insurance to a home owner. Even if the probability of an event is fairly high (say, bad breath in the morning), the writer must still convince the reader that the consequences of such an event are serious.[24]

## Motivating by Appeal to Rationality and Consistency

In addition to being motivated by their fulfillment needs, people are also motivated to be reasonable in their behavior by the traditions of society. We are constantly urged to be rational, to behave consistently. Thus, consistency theories assume that people try to avoid incongruent or inconsistent beliefs, attitudes and actions.

These theories all say that the greater the dissonance or imbalance in our inner mental states, the greater the motivation to resolve it. Dissonance is nothing more than inner tension created when we come into contact with information that is at odds with what we already know and believe. Because we are uncomfortable with that tension, we're highly motivated to resolve the problem and relieve the tension. For example, let's assume you have done business with a supplier for a number of years and enjoy a good working relationship. Now you discover that he's been implicated in a corruption scandal involving illegal kickbacks and bribes in his business dealings. How do you respond to that news? Most likely, you'll dismiss the information as untrue or the work of your supplier's competitors.

If you should discover highly credible evidence from reliable sources that the charges are true, however, it's likely that you'll resolve the dissonance by buying supplies from someone else.[25]

As you attempt to apply such theories, you must first show your audience how the position you advocate – along with its subsequent actions and behavior – is consistent with their existing beliefs. Or you must show them how alternative positions, advocated by your competitors or opponents, are inconsistent with their current beliefs.

## Social Conformity as Motivation

A number of important social forces shape each of us as human beings, including the following:

- *Admired individuals:* Parents, teachers, entertainers, politicians, professional athletes, friends, relatives, teachers, coaches, religious leaders and many others.
- *Peer groups:* Early in life, people identify most closely with those of their own age, race, ethnic group, social status and common interests. Pressure from such groups to conform can be powerful.
- *Societal norms:* Standards of behavior are imposed by our social groupings and social interactions with other people, even if we are not conscious of group affiliation with them. These norms are so widely accepted by society as a whole that they tend to become invisible prescriptions for behavior. They include everything from language use to how we dress to the food we eat to personal mannerisms.[26]

As managers, we must look for ways to motivate those whom we're trying to communicate with. Human needs, rational and consistent behavior, and social conformity can be powerful tools to persuade others to think and act as we would like them to. Whether they are customers, suppliers, shareholders, employees, supervisors or people we work with, each will react in separate ways to our attempts to motivate them. The key is to know your audience.

## Channeling the Motivation of Your Audience to Take Action

Once your audience has begun to pay attention to your message and has been given some appropriate and powerful motivation to believe in the message, you must provide them with a channel or an outlet for action. This motivation comes in two basic forms:

- *Recommend a specific proposition or proposal.* A specific proposal allows your audience to adopt it in order to attain the satisfaction you've promised. In other words, tell them specifically what you want them to do, as well as when and how they're to do it. "Sign up for ride-sharing Monday through Friday of this week at the main reception desk or in the first-floor cafeteria and receive close-in parking for the next 12 months."
- *Show the high probability that the satisfactions will be forthcoming.* Your audience is looking for some assurance that what you've promised will actually come true if they do as you've asked. "If you are not completely satisfied, we will refund your money anytime within 30 days of purchase."

## Inducing Resistance in the Audience to Counter-persuasion

Information decays quickly. So do the positions assumed by your audience in response to your persuasive message. Emotional appeals, in particular, are ephemeral or transitory. If you've convinced someone to donate money to your cause based on an emotional appeal, you must find a way to collect the donations quickly, before the fervor of the moment passes. Much impulse buying is dependent on actions taken before the buyer's motivation changes.

To help assure that those who are persuaded by your message will remain believers, you must induce in each of them a resistance to counter-persuasion and counter-arguments. Several ways are available to you:

- *By stating opposing arguments and refuting them.* If you know your audience will hear the arguments of your competitors, it might not be a bad idea to present at least part of their argument to the audience and then explain what's wrong with it, refute it or show where it's flawed.

- *By encouraging audience commitment in some tangible or visible way.* As we explained a few pages ago, it's much more difficult to back away from a position or an idea for which we've publicly proclaimed our support. George Bush the elder greatly regretted using the phrase, "Read my lips. No new taxes." Just 18 months after that public declaration, he was maneuvered by his political opposition into raising taxes and was then roundly criticized for it.
- *By warning the audience that others will attempt to get them to change their minds.* If you know your audience will be exposed to your competitor's message, it's not a bad idea to warn them that others are out for their money, their votes or their commitment. Some popular advertisements warn against look-alikes: "Accept no substitutes, ask for the real thing when you place your order."

## SHOULD YOU USE A ONE- OR TWO-SIDED ARGUMENT?

People often wonder if they should even mention the other side (or sides) of an argument, or whether it's best to simply leave it alone. Will the discussion of another point of view make it easier for your opponent to influence the audience, or would it be better for you to raise and refute that argument? When is a two-sided argument most effective, and when is it best to simply leave the opposition's ideas alone? Again, behavioral scientists looked at this question, conducted experiments, and here's what their evidence suggests:

**One-sided arguments work best when:**

- *The audience initially agrees with your position and your aim is simply to intensify agreement.* If you know they're already on your side, there's no need for a complicated, multifaceted argument. Simply tell them what you believe and why you think it's important, and boost their confidence in your position.
- *The audience is not well educated or has relatively low self-esteem.* In some instances, people may not have the education or background to fully understand an issue. Young children, the elderly and others may respond best to a persuasive presentation that offers just one side of the issue.
- *The audience will not later be exposed to any form of counter-persuasion.* If you know that this argument is the only one your audience will be exposed to and you're asking for the equivalent of a one-time purchase, a one-sided argument may work best.

**Two-sided arguments work best when:**

- *The audience initially disagrees with your proposal.* For example, if you intend to explain why it's unwise for employees to bring food into the company computer lab – and most of your audience already agrees with you – a simple, one-sided presentation of the factors and your reasons for the decision will suffice. If you advocate eliminating all food and refreshments from the building – and most of your audience disagrees with you – it may be more effective to present both sides of the story: reasons for having food in the workplace and reasons for eliminating it.
- *You know the audience will be exposed to subsequent counter-persuasion or propaganda.* Regardless of the audience's initial attitude, a two-sided presentation is usually best when you are certain your audience will hear the other side of the argument. If you are selling products or services to a customer who will receive sales calls from your competitors, it may be a good idea to present all the facts – including those your competition will raise – before making the case for why your products or services are best.
- *The audience has a low level of knowledge or personal involvement with the topic.* If your intended audience doesn't know much about the subject at hand, or when the position you take is widely different from their views, a two-sided presentation is usually most effective. A neighbor rang our doorbell recently with a petition to prevent the construction of a 24-hour convenience store in a nearby residential neighborhood. Because most of the people he spoke with had little involvement in or information about the subject, our neighbor constructed a brief but careful two-sided argument, for and against the new store, concluding with the reasons why it shouldn't be built in our neighborhood.
- *You hope to produce more enduring results.* A two-sided presentation seems to ensure that any change in attitude provided by your message will endure longer than if the attitude change is secured by a one-sided message. If

you want long-term commitment from the people you communicate with, they will want to know the underlying arguments and reasons for your position. Give them both sides of the argument before presenting your persuasive position.[27]

Keep in mind that you may face an ethical need to disclose both sides of an argument. If you have an agreeable, yet poorly educated, audience that is not likely to learn about possible counter-arguments – but who might possibly benefit from knowing them – you should consider disclosing all aspects as you underscore the value of your own position.

One of the great traditions of Jesuit education may be summarized in a simple mantra: "A man cannot understand his own argument until he has visited the position of a man who disagrees." If you can show why and how others might disagree with your position, and then demonstrate why your position is superior (or others are flawed), you'll have a much better chance of convincing your audience to learn about, adopt and act on your position.[28]

Finally, remember that you have an obligation to be honest with your audience. If you misrepresent the facts or if you don't tell the truth, you will eventually be found out – perhaps not immediately, but eventually. Your credibility can and will be harmed. Be logical, organize your material carefully and use evidence that is consistent, believable and up-to-date.

## NOT ALL THAT WE REMEMBER IS ACTUALLY TRUE

What we believe to be true often simply isn't so. During the early stages of the U.S. War in Iraq (2003–2011), numerous press accounts offered conflicting reports, some of which were later proven to be untrue and subsequently retracted by various news organizations. But new research suggests that even with a public correction of the record, readers of the original report may continue to believe the now discredited story. The research, published in *Psychological Science*, a journal of the American Psychological Society, suggests that once you've seen a news report, you may go on believing it even if later information shows it to have been false.[29]

"People build mental models," explains Stephan Lewandowsky, a psychology professor at the University of Western Australia, who led the study. "By the time they receive a retraction, the original misinformation has already become an integral part of that mental model, or world view, and disregarding it would leave the world view a shambles." He concludes that "people continue to rely on misinformation, even if they demonstrably remember and understand a subsequent retraction."[30]

This finding comes as no surprise to memory researchers. Time and again, lab studies show that people have an astonishing propensity to recall things that never happened. If you read a list of words such as *pillow*, *bed* and *pajamas*, and later asked whether the word *sleep* was there, a remarkable number of people would recall that word as having been on the list.[31] The task of changing minds under such circumstances can be daunting. Influencing what people believe to be true, even when it's not, is a difficult but manageable task. It amounts to showing people why change is both possible and desirable and then offering incentives to make the change, first in attitude and then in behavior.

## MANAGING HEADS AND HEARTS TO CHANGE BEHAVIORAL HABITS

Managing change in a business organization is never easy. Most people will say they're eager for change, but they're not really. They're simply trying to look cooperative, like team players helping the organization along. The vast majority of us prefer things the way they are: It's easier, simpler, more familiar and less stressful to continue doing business just as we always have. The status quo has powerful support.

However, as a well-known business educator once said, "There is no status in the status quo."[32] The pressure for businesses to change is enormous and inexorable, mostly because the competition is changing, and so is the marketplace. Most management strategists agree that there is no such thing as a permanent strategic advantage. If that's true, then virtually all advantage in business is temporary and subject to change. So how can you compete when all about you are changing? The answer, of course, is change itself. To set the stage for change in the attitudes and behaviors of those responsible for an organization's success, three conditions must be present:

- *You must create a new frame of reference through which information and messages are interpreted.* We don't operate on facts, figures or data as much as we work with stories, narratives and ideas that help us to see and understand the world we live in. These frames of reference are the touchpoints for any new information or persuasive messages that we receive. When new employees start at W. L. Gore & Associates, the maker of Gore-Tex fabrics, they often refuse to believe that the company doesn't have a hierarchy with job titles and bosses. It just doesn't fit their frame of reference. It often takes several months for new hires to begin to understand Gore's reframed notion of the workplace, which relies on self-directed employees making their own choices about joining one another in egalitarian small teams.[33]
- *You must manage the emotions and expectations of your audience.* To convince others of the value of your viewpoint, you must evoke the appropriate emotion both in them and in yourself. As author and psychologist Daniel Goleman has shown in *Emotional Intelligence*, "The goal is balance, not emotional suppression: every feeling has its value and significance. A life without passion would be a dull wasteland of neutrality, cut off and isolated from the richness of life itself. But," says Goleman, "as Aristotle observed, what is wanted is *appropriate* emotion, feeling proportionate to circumstance."[34]
- *You must provide constant reinforcement to prevent backsliding.* The opinions that motivate behavior are ephemeral, fleeting and subject to change on a moment's notice. Even though attitudes are a bit more enduring, they too can shift, modify or vanish with enough evidence and motivation. To prevent such losses in your audience, continual reinforcement of the position you advocate is often necessary. Harvard Business School professors David Garvin and Michael Roberto describe the problem this way:

Without a doubt, the toughest challenge faced by leaders during a turnaround is to avoid backsliding into dysfunctional routines – habitual patterns of negative behavior by individuals and groups that are triggered automatically and unconsciously by familiar circumstances or stimuli. In our studies of successful turnarounds . . . we've found that effective leaders explicitly reinforce organizational values on a constant basis, using actions to back up their words. Their goal is to change behavior, not just ways of thinking.[35]

## BEING PERSUASIVE

Ultimately, your ability to persuade people that your point of view is correct, moral, optimal, desirable, just or simply preferable may come down to a few, simple precepts about how other people feel, think and react to you and your argument:

- *Know your audience.* Aristotle was right; it's really *all* about them. The more you know, the greater your chance of success. You have little incentive and almost no excuse for failing to do your homework on what the audience knows and how it feels about the subject on which you're trying to persuade them.
- *Know what you want and what they want.* Part of knowing your audience means an understanding of their goals and objectives. The extent to which you know what they want is the degree to which you can offer ideas and evidence that will help you to get what you want. If you can't give them something they want or can use, you have little hope of persuading them to change behaviors.
- *Select your evidence carefully.* Not all evidence is equally persuasive, and not all audiences will approach the same argument in the same way. Make sure you understand the sources your audience will respect and the frame of reference through which they will interpret what you say. Logic and rationality may work for some, but emotion or source credibility may appeal more to others.
- *Keep the argument simple.* The more complex your argument, the lower the probability it will be acknowledged, understood, internalized and acted on. Simplicity, underscored by a cogent, brief presentation, will carry the day far more often than not.
- *Listen before you speak.* It is frequently difficult to know what they're thinking, what they want or what they're afraid of if you won't listen. You must listen carefully for content, emotion and intention. If you can tune into their thoughts and feelings before you speak – and convince them that you've done so – your chances for success are greater.

- *Manage your emotions as well as theirs.* Keep your own emotions under control and you'll have a greater opportunity to manage those of your audience. If you let their hopes and fears run away with the discussion, an "emotional hijacking" can ruin your chances at persuading them of your position.
- *Connect with your audience on a personal level.* Finally, although your audience cares in a general sense about the nature of your evidence and the organization of your argument, they care a lot more about how it will affect them. Answer their basic questions: "Can I trust you?" "What do I know about you?" "Do you know something I need to know?" "Can you help me?" and you'll find yourself rewarded with their attention and their agreement with your ideas.

## NOTES

1 Hoff, S., Senior Vice President and Chief Communications Officer, Best Buy Company, Richfield, MN. Personal interview, May 27, 2005.

2 Ibid.

3 Ibid.

4 Ibid.

5 Ibid.

6 Buell, C. *Behaviorism.* Available online at web.cocc.edu/cbuell/theories/behaviorism. Retrieved July 4, 2005.

7 Watson, J. B. *Psychology as the Behaviorist Views It.* Available online from York University of Canada at psychclassics.yorku.ca/Watson/views.htm. Accessed July 10, 2008 at 2:20 p.m.

8 For an extensive description of cognitivism, see Wikipedia's online discussion at: en.wikipedia.org/wiki/Cognitivism_(psychology).

9 Gardner, H. *Changing Minds: The Art and Science of Changing Our Own and Other People's Minds.* Boston, MA: Harvard Business School Press, 2004, p. 42.

10 Rokeach, M. *Beliefs, Attitudes, and Values: A Theory of Organization and Change.* San Francisco, CA: Jossey-Bass, 1968. See also Rokeach, M. *The Open and Closed Mind: Investigations into the Nature of Belief Systems and Personality Systems.* New York: Basic Books, 1960, pp. 3–27.

11 Travers, R. M. W. "Piaget's Approach to Learning and the Development of the Intellect," in *Essentials of Learning,* 4/e. New York: Macmillan Publishing, 1977, pp. 147–203.

12 Bem, D. "The Cognitive Foundations of Beliefs," in *Beliefs, Attitudes, and Human Affairs.* Belmont, CA: Brooks/Cole Publishing, 1970, pp. 4–13.

13 Ibid., pp. 14–23.

14 Chesterton, G. K. *The American Chesterton Society.* An extended discussion of the origins of this quote is available online at www.firstthings.com/onthesquare/2005/12/rjn-123005-one-more-word.

15 Daryl Bem writes:

Our most fundamental primitive beliefs are so taken for granted that we are not apt to notice that we hold them at all; we remain unaware of them until they are called to our attention or are brought into question by some bizarre circumstance in which they appear to be violated. For example, we believe that an object continues to exist even when we are not looking at it; we believe that objects remain the same size and shape as we move away from them even though their visual images change; and, more generally, we believe that our perceptual and conceptual worlds have a degree of orderliness and stability over time. These are among the first beliefs that a child learns as he interacts with his environment, and in a psychological sense, they are continuously validated by experience. As a result, we are usually unaware of the fact that alternatives to these beliefs *could* exist, and it is precisely for this reason that we remain unaware of the beliefs themselves. We shall call primitive beliefs of this fundamental kind "zero-order" beliefs. They are the "nonconscious" axioms upon which our other beliefs are built

Bem. *Beliefs, Attitudes, and Human Affairs,* pp. 5–6.

16 Reprinted by permission of *Harvard Business Review* from Cialdini, R. B. "Harnessing the Science of Persuasion," *Harvard Business Review,* October 2001, pp. 72–79. Copyright © 2001 by the Harvard Business School Publishing Corporation; all rights reserved.

17 Ibid., p. 74.

18 Cialdini, R. B. *Influence: Science and Practice,* 4/e. Boston, MA: Allyn & Bacon, 2000.

19 Ross, R. S. *Understanding Persuasion,* 3/e. Englewood Cliffs, NJ: Prentice Hall, 1990, pp. 79–80.

20 Wallace, K. R. "The Substance of Rhetoric: Good Reasons," in R. Johannesen (ed.), *Contemporary Theories of Rhetoric: Selected Readings.* New York: Harper and Row, 1971, pp. 357–370.

21 Larson, C. U. *Persuasion: Reception and Responsibility,* 6/e. Belmont, CA: Wadsworth, 1992, pp. 159–163.

22   Johns, G. *Organizational Behavior*, 2/e. Glenview, IL: Scott, Foresman, 1988, pp. 158–159. See also Alderfer, C. P. "An Intergroup Perspective on Group Dynamics," in J. W. Lorch (ed.), *Handbook of Organizational Behavior*. Englewood Cliffs, NJ: Prentice Hall, 1987, p. 211.

23   Packard, V. *The Hidden Persuaders*. New York: Pocket Books, 1964.

24   Cho, H. and White, K. "A Review of Fear-Appeal Effects," In J. S. Seiter and R. H. Gass (eds.), *Perspectives on Persuasion, Social Influence, and Compliance Gaining*. Boston, MA: Allyn & Bacon, 2004, pp. 223–235.

25   Larson. *Persuasion*, pp. 71–73.

26   Ibid., pp. 71–73.

27   Minnick, W. C. *The Art of Persuasion*, 2/e. Boston, MA: Houghton Mifflin, 1968, pp. 263–264.

28   O'Malley, J. W., S. J. Personal communication with the author, July 8, 2018. Fr. O'Malley is an American historian and University Professor of Theology, Georgetown University, Washington, DC. Fr. O'Malley agrees that this quotation, as offered: is part of the Jesuit rhetorical tradition, in that being familiar with "the adversaries" was part of Jesuit training in both philosophy and theology, and it was an essential part of the classical tradition of so-called forensic oratory, with which most Jesuits would be familiar.

29   Lewandowsky, S., W. G. K. Stritzke, K. Oberauer and M. Morales. "Memory for Fact, Fiction, and Misinformation," *Psychological Science* 16.3 (2005): 190–195.

30   "People Believe a 'Fact' That Fits Their Views Even If It's Clearly False," *The Wall Street Journal*, February 4, 2005, p. B-1. Reprinted by permission of Dow Jones & Company, Inc. Copyright © 2005 Dow Jones & Company, Inc. All rights reserved worldwide. License number 1280830699090.

31   Roediger, H. L., III, and K. B. McDermott. "Creating False Memories: Remembering Words Not Presented in Lists," *Journal of Experimental Psychology: Learning, Memory, and Cognition*, 21 (1995): 803–814. See also Roediger, H. L., III. "Memory Illusions," *Journal of Memory and Language* 35 (1996): 76–100.

32   Keane, J. G., former dean, Mendoza College of Business, University of Notre Dame. Personal interview, June 21, 2005.

33   Deutschman, A. "Making Change," *Fast Company*, May 2005, pp. 54–62.

34   Goleman, D. *Emotional Intelligence*. New York: Bantam Books, 1995, p. 56.

35   Garvin, D. A. and M. A. Roberto. "Change Through Persuasion," *Harvard Business Review*, February 2005, p. 111.

# Case 6.1: The United States Olympic Committee

## Persuading Business to Participate in the Olympic Movement

"We don't receive government funds," said Lynne Cribari: "so corporate funds and private donations provide the bulk of our support. And, in asking for corporate sponsorship, we walk a very fine line between encouraging enthusiasm for and participation in the Olympic spirit on the one hand, and crass over-commercialization on the other."

Lynne Cribari is Manager of Corporate Participation for the United States Olympic Committee, and works in the USOC's Headquarters in Colorado Springs, Colorado. She received a political science degree from The Colorado College and, following a brief career in media relations and local television, joined the USOC as assistant director of broadcasting. Today, her task is to assist the Director of Marketing and the Executive Director of the USOC in securing corporate sponsorship for U.S. athletes training for and participating in the Olympic Games.

"Asking for corporate sponsorship is a difficult task," she said, "because we maintain exclusivity in each product category and we must negotiate separately with each corporation for the rights to use our marks and logos." Exclusivity, she explained, means that only one sponsor will be permitted to use the USOC's logotypes, including the universally recognized five-ring Olympic symbol. Current sponsors include such corporate giants as IBM, Bausch & Lomb, Eastman Kodak, VISA Cards International, and Anheuser-Busch Brewing.

"Our task is to create an environment in which the marks are used appropriately," Cribari said, "and that means that we're directly involved in what's known as 'cause-related marketing.' If you use your VISA card to make a purchase, for example, VISA will contribute a certain amount to the U.S. Olympic Committee."

Cribari said the persuasive challenge in her job is to create a partnership in which both the Olympic Movement and the corporate sponsor will benefit:

We have a $600 million budget for the current four-year period and, as you can imagine, the costs involved in training and preparing an Olympic team for the coming games are enormous. We're proud of the fact that 85 cents from every dollar contributed will go directly to our primary purpose: training athletes.

"We usually ask our sponsors for cash," she explained, "but some provide us with 'value in kind.'" For example, 97 percent of the food fed to athletes in the Colorado Springs Training Center is "value in kind" and comes from corporate sponsors in the food business. These contributions are not trivial, though. "On average," she said:

we receive about $60 million from each sponsor. As you can see, this represents a huge investment for these companies, because they'll probably spend twice that amount on advertising and promotion in order to use our trade marks and logos.

How does the USOC approach a potential sponsor and ask for that much money? "Well," said Cribari, "we look at these partnerships from a value-added viewpoint. Altruism only goes so far; at a certain point, we must show them how their sponsorship of Olympic athletes will pay off in greater sales and increased corporate revenues."

"We usually begin with some historical data about the Olympic movement," she explained:

and then demonstrate how association with the movement has helped drive sales for other firms. Once a potential sponsor understands how the association works, we'll help them develop a marketing plan that will make the most effective use of our marks.

Cribari cited the case of Kraft General Foods as an example. "We helped them develop a fully-integrated persuasive campaign," she said:

Kraft wanted to change the public perception of processed cheese. The public impression was that their products weren't in sync with a health-conscious diet, so they began using the phrase, "Kraft sets the U.S. Olympic training table." We worked with Kraft to develop their campaign, because we insist in truth in advertising, accuracy, and the use of actual athletes in their commercials. It's been a successful partnership for both of us.

The campaign involves more than just the use of the Olympic rings, however. "A typical arrangement with a corporate sponsor will include help with advertising, promotions, product packaging, and such things as point-of-purchase giveaways." In the case of Kraft, the USOC helped produce a number of Olympic training table recipes using Kraft products, a cookbook that consumers could receive by mail, and a number of in-store appearances by Olympic athletes.

"As we formulate persuasive messages," Cribari said:

we must keep in mind that we're accountable to the public, to our sponsors, and to the Congress of the United States. As a result, we insist on truthfulness and accuracy and we work very hard to establish and maintain long-term relationships with prestigious, reliable sponsors.

Coca-Cola, for example, has been an Olympic partner for more than 75 years.

"Our persuasive task doesn't end with a signed agreement for corporate sponsorship," Cribari explained:

After we've convinced a sponsor that association with the Olympic movement will help them sell products, we must convince them to use the logos and marks appropriately, and to remain both ethical and true to the spirit of the Olympic movement. Our relationship is unique to each sponsor . . . and it's an on-going, evolving matter for us.

What's the single greatest challenge in all of this for the USOC? "No question about it," Cribari replied:

We're competing for corporate sponsorship in a market that includes the NFL, the NHL, the NBA, and Major League Baseball. We're after limited sponsorship dollars and it's up to us to show how the Olympic movement is useful, productive and worthwhile for a corporate sponsor. If we succeed . . . it's a win-win situation for all of us: for the sponsor, for the USOC and the Olympic movement, and for U.S. athletes who'll compete for the gold in the Olympic games.

## DISCUSSION QUESTIONS

1.  Are Ms. Cribari and her colleagues at the USOC following the basic theories of persuasion in any way? Can you identify in their work any of the steps discussed earlier in this chapter?
2.  What sort of attention-getting device is she employing?
3.  What's the principal motivation for corporate sponsors to pay such large sums of money for the use of the Olympic name and logos?
4.  Do you see resistance to counter-persuasion in any of their work?
5.  Who are Ms. Cribari's main competitors?
6.  What do you suppose is the reason for exclusivity in each product category?
7.  Can you imagine some product categories the USOC would not be interested in securing sponsorship for?

## WRITING ASSIGNMENT

Please respond in writing to the issues presented in this case by preparing two documents: a communication strategy memo and a professional business letter.

In preparing these documents, you may assume one of two roles: you may identify yourself as a an external marketing consultant who has been asked to provide advice to the USOC, or you may assume the role of Ms. Lynne Cribari, Manager of Corporate Participation for the USOC.

Either way, you must prepare a strategy memo addressed to Dr. Harvey Schiller, Executive Director of the USOC, that identifies a corporate sponsorship prospect and suggests ways in which the USOC might convince that firm to participate in the Olympic movement, either with sponsorship in cash or sponsorship in kind (goods and/or services).

Your memo should explain something about the company you have chosen as a prospect, what industry they compete in, their size, as well as their business model. Your discussion of the company should identify the principle(s) of persuasion which you think will be most effective in convincing the company's leadership to become an Olympic sponsor, in addition to the reasons why such an arrangement would be in their best interest.

You must also prepare a professional business letter for Dr. Schiller's signature. That document should be addressed to an officer of the corporation you have selected and must offer to open a dialogue on the advantages of participation in the Olympic movement. If you have questions about either of these documents, please consult your instructor.

## ACKNOWLEDGMENTS

This case was prepared from personal interviews by James S. O'Rourke, Concurrent Professor of Management, as the basis for class discussion rather than to illustrate either effective or ineffective handling of an administrative situation.

# Case 6.2: An Invitation to Wellness at Whirlpool Corporation

We know there is a direct correlation between employee wellness and the use of insurance benefit dollars. Employees who are well spend less of the company's money. They feel better. They're more productive. And, of course, they lead healthier, happier lives.

Dana Donnley is Director of Employee Communication for Whirlpool Corporation, a $12.1 billion appliance manufacturer and marketer with assets placing it 140th on *Fortune* magazine's list of 500 largest business organizations. With corporate headquarters in Benton Harbor, Michigan, Whirlpool has more than 92,000 employees in the U.S. and 30 foreign nations.

"During the month of his or her birthday," Donnley said, "we offer each employee in the headquarters a free mini-physical. Our company health nurse sends a letter to each employee sometime toward the end of the month before their birthday, inviting that person to participate." Is this letter persuasive or directive in tone? "Oh, it's persuasive," Donnley replied:

The program is entirely voluntary. We pick up the cost and certainly encourage each employee to participate, but we can't make them do it. We've got to persuade them that it's in their best interest to have a physical at least once a year.

"The biggest objection," said Donnley,

usually revolves around confidentiality. People are concerned about that and sometimes have questions regarding how the information will be used. We do our best in that letter, and in personal conversations, to convince them that the results of these physicals are entirely confidential. The company doctor will see the results and then mail them to the employee. We don't keep any records – the employee gets the original and no copies are made.

What's involved in the physical? "Well, it's fairly comprehensive. The nurse records each employee's height, weight, blood pressure, and vital signs. A routine exam is performed, testing various functions and reflexes, providing each employee with a relatively complete work-up."

What's the doctor looking for?

This is a screening program designed to let our employees know the general condition of their health. A number of different illnesses and diseases can develop without any outward symptoms. And, of course, if he catches something early – before it has a chance to progress very far – it's all to the employee's benefit. In such cases . . . we'll recommend that the employee contact his or her family physician and seek appropriate treatment.

Does Whirlpool have trouble getting people to participate? "Not really," said Donnley:

Most people are eager to be involved. That hasn't always been the case, though, and it's taken a concerted effort on our part to persuade them that this wellness program benefits them at least as much as it benefits the company. This year, in fact, we've opened the program to spouses of our employees, as well.

The task of convincing a husband or wife to participate, according to Donnley, is really a two-step process. "First, we've got to sell each employee on the idea. Then, they've got to go home and convince their wife or husband to get involved." Is that important to Whirlpool? "Listen," she replied, "an employee with a healthy spouse is more likely to have healthy diet and exercise habits. They're certainly more conscious of what's involved in a personal wellness program. And that," she added, "is good for all of us."

## DISCUSSION QUESTIONS

1. Why do you suppose employees at Whirlpool Corporation might be concerned about confidentiality in these physical examinations?
2. What could Ms. Donnley do to reassure Whirlpool employees that exam findings and test results would be kept confidential?
3. Could you draft a letter for Ms. Donnley's signature that persuades Whirlpool employees to sign up for a physical examination during their birth month?
4. What would you choose to say first to those employees in your letter? How long should the letter be?
5. What's the value to an employee of the company's offer? What's the value of such a program to the company?
6. What means of persuasion are available to Ms. Donnley, other than a letter to each employee? What else would you choose to do?

## WRITING ASSIGNMENT

Please respond in writing to the issues presented in this case by preparing two documents: a communication strategy memo and a professional business letter.

In preparing these documents, you should identify yourself as an Employee Communication Manager at Whirlpool Corporation who has been asked to provide advice to Ms. Donnley. Your strategy memo should be directed to her, providing analysis of the business problem, the relevant background details, critical issues, audience factors, options for action and your specific recommendations. Think broadly and provide comprehensive advice for Ms. Donnley regarding the Whirlpool Corporation Employee Wellness Program.

You must also prepare a professional business letter for Ms. Donnley's signature. That document should explain directly to Whirlpool employees the purposes of the program, the reasons for their participation and the benefits you expect them to derive from doing so. If you have questions about either of these documents, please consult your instructor.

## ACKNOWLEDGMENTS

This case was prepared by James S. O'Rourke, Concurrent Professor of Management, as the basis for class discussion rather than to illustrate either effective or ineffective handling of an administrative situation.

# Case 6.3: Theranos, Inc.

## Managing Risk in a High-Flying Biotech Start-Up

The minute you have a back-up plan, you've admitted you're not going to succeed.

~Theranos, Inc. CEO and founder Elizabeth Holmes

## INTRODUCTION

Theranos, Inc. (Theranos), a consumer healthcare company in Palo Alto, CA, had it all: a young, compelling CEO in Elizabeth Holmes; a mission to produce a potentially life-saving technology; over $400 million in venture capital; and the respect of Silicon Valley's tech bros.[1] However, in early October of 2015, *The Wall Street Journal* issued a damning report: the marquee technology, Edison, was only capable of a mere fraction of the promised tests.[2]

Ms. Holmes's initial response was to confidently reassert Theranos's capabilities. Two days after *The Wall Street Journal* report, she told Jim Cramer on CNBC, "First they think you're crazy, then they fight you, and then, all of a sudden, you change the world."[3]

However, the damage was done. Reports began emerging from various outlets about fraudulent tests and incomplete data. Lawsuits with former partners, like Walgreens, followed shortly thereafter.[4] The company, previously valued at $9 billion, is now worth next to nothing.[5]

## THE COMPANY

Silicon Valley start-ups have become synonymous with nerdy, plucky intelligence and the "coolness" of successful college dropout entrepreneurs such as Bill Gates, Steve Jobs and Mark Zuckerberg.[6] Theranos seemed perfectly poised to join the ranks of hits with its exciting technology bearing names such as "nanotainer"[7] and "Edison machines."[8] In addition to the technology, the company has a lofty mission: to transform the healthcare industry to allow people to better afford and manage their healthcare, describing it as Elizabeth Holmes's "life's work."[9]

The company began in 2003[10] under the name, "Real-Time Cures."[11] The company was later renamed Theranos, "an amalgam of the words 'therapy' and 'diagnosis.'"[12] Its technology is aimed at alleviating people's pain and discomfort with blood tests. Their initial funding came from various sources including: Tim Draper, ATA Ventures, Continental Properties, and Donald L. Lucas.[13] From its inception, the company has prompted intense scrutiny and mixed responses. They have been described by outside sources as everything from, "a complicated, secretive company,"[14] to "revolutionary"[15] and "transformational."[16]

The company describes itself with the following statement on its website: "at Theranos, we are developing technologies that will enable us to make it possible for more people, in more places, to get the laboratory tests they need."[17] Its goal is to "mak[e] actionable information accessible to everyone in the world at the time it matters most, we are working to facilitate the early detection and prevention of disease, and empower people everywhere to live their best possible lives."[18] In other words, if blood tests are simpler and easier to attain, people will be better able to monitor their own health and lead better lives.

## POWER PLAYERS

Elizabeth Holmes was born in 1984. From an early age, Ms. Holmes wanted to dedicate herself to the public good. As a child, she opened a letter to her father with the following: "What I really want out of life is to discover something new, something mankind didn't know was possible to do."[19] She also displayed her business acumen early, beginning her first international business in high school.

In the fall of 2003, Ms. Holmes was deciding whether or not to start her sophomore year at Stanford University. She met with her chemical engineering professor to discuss her first patent application – a wearable patch that would deliver medication and monitor the patient's blood to allow for automatic dosage adjustments. Channing Robertson, the professor in question, "knew she was different" but also pressed her for why she was considering leaving Stanford to pursue this.[20] Her answer stunned him:

> Because systems like this could completely revolutionize how effective healthcare is delivered. And this is what I want to do. . . . I want to create a whole new technology, and one that is aimed at helping humanity at all levels regardless of geography or ethnicity or age or gender.

With that, he agreed to help her and eventually became a full-time employee of Theranos. "This is the mission that she started Theranos with – to provide patients with the tools to control their own healthcare: the ability to 'access actionable information at the time it matters,'" says Robertson. "In our conversations over the next two months, she comes back to that phrase frequently. It is the theme that unifies what had seemed to me, at first, a succession of diverse, disparate aspects of her vision."[21]

In her mission for greatness, she modeled herself in many ways on Steve Jobs, the divisive but brilliant head of Apple's revitalization. This included a daily uniform: "black jacket; black mock turtleneck; black slacks with a wide, pale pinstripe; and black low-heel shoes."[22] Like Jobs, she also maintains a strict vegan diet, does not drink alcohol or caffeine, and works every day of the week. The most significant characteristic borrowed from Jobs, however, is her insistence on secrecy. Like Apple, project teams were not permitted to speak to one another and extensive non-disclosure agreements were required. She believes that this is the best way to protect their proprietary information.[23]

Others saw the parallel as well. Henry Kissinger, a former member of the company's Board of Counselors, said:

> I haven't seen anyone with her special attributes. She has iron will, strong determination. . . . I have seen no sign that financial gain is of any interest to her. She's like a monk. She isn't flashy. She wouldn't walk into a room and take it over. But she would once the subject gets to her field.[24]

Ms. Holmes was joined in her mission by President and COO, Sunny Balwani. He received his undergraduate degree from UT Austin.[25] The two met in Beijing the summer after Ms. Holmes graduated from high school in the early 2000s. He was pursuing his MBA from UC Berkeley at the time.[26] Shortly after, he began pursuing graduate studies in Machine Learning at Stanford but also dropped out to pursue Theranos in 2009.[27] He was previously employed at Microsoft and Lotus.[28] At Theranos, Mr. Balwani gained the reputation for being Ms. Holmes's pugnacious enforcer. If someone needed to be taken to task, Mr. Balwani would step up to the task with glee, sometimes levelling personal attacks on employees who had seemingly stepped out of line.[29]

Despite the large volumes of information about Ms. Holmes, Mr. Balwani is somewhat of an enigma. He has a very minimal Internet presence with most Google searches resulting in rumors. He has a seemingly personal Twitter account that has routinely posted articles about Theranos. That account has been essentially inactive since October 2015.[30] He departed the company on good terms in May 2016, prompting *Fortune* to remark, "If there should prove to be any skeletons in Theranos' closets, no one would know better where to find them than Balwani."[31]

Theranos initially pursued a non-traditional oversight structure, establishing a Board of Counselors as opposed to a Board of Directors. This board was a list of luminaries, including two former secretaries of state: Henry Kissinger, former Secretary of State for President Richard Nixon and President Gerald Ford, and George P. Shultz, "Secretary of State for President Ronald Reagan."[32] Many of these individuals were drawn to the board by Ms. Holmes's magnetic vision: "She really does want to make a dent in the universe – one that is positive," says retired U.S. Marine Corps General James Mattis, explaining why he signed up last fall as another of Theranos's strikingly illustrious outside directors.[33] The list of names is impressive but is also notable for its lack of expertise in the field of healthcare.[34]

In 2017, this structure would be retired and a Board of Directors would be installed. General Mattis remained on the board for some time and was joined by industry experts such as William H. Foege, formerly a director of the Centers for Disease Control and Prevention, and Fabrizio Bonanni, formerly an executive vice president at Amgen, a biopharmaceutical company.[35]

## THE INDUSTRY

Companies in the analytical laboratory instrument manufacturing industry produce instruments that are used primarily for laboratory analysis of chemical, physical, molecular and elemental properties. Major companies in the U.S. include Mettler-Toledo International, PerkinElmer and Thermo Fisher Scientific. International players include Eppendorf (Germany), Oxford Instruments (U.K.) and JEOL and Shimadzu (Japan).[36]

According to Technavio, a market research company headquartered in London, U.K., the global market for scientific instruments is forecast to grow 4 percent per year through 2019. Governments of emerging markets, including Brazil, China, India and Taiwan, are investing in scientific instruments to increase R&D activity in university, government and corporate laboratories.[37]

The U.S. is home to about 600 analytical instrument manufacturing companies with a combined annual revenue of about $17 billion.[38] The industry is highly concentrated, with the largest 50 companies accounting for about 80 percent of revenue.[39] The environment is extremely competitive and difficult for smaller players, as merger and acquisition activity in the analytical laboratory instrument market has further consolidated an industry already dominated by large companies. To illustrate the fierce competition, industry giant Thermo Fisher Scientific acquired Life Technologies, itself a major industry player, in 2014 for $13.6 billion.[40]

The analytical laboratory instrument manufacturing industry serves two main types of customers. The first customer base comprises end-users who use their instruments in order to develop and test their own new products themselves. For example, pharmaceutical companies use them to test the potency of their latest drug by measuring target analyte levels in the blood of clinical trial patients. Food engineering companies employ analytical instruments to isolate the incriminating protein that confers genetic superiority, such as pest resistance. Academic institutions and research divisions of hospitals need such instruments to test the efficacy of a key step in their experimental setup, such as primer design for specific DNA sequence amplification.

The other set of customers is in non-R&D settings, such as clinical laboratories and consumer health services like 23andMe. For such customers, analytical instruments are used for the analysis of bodily fluids for detection, therapeutic and diagnostic purposes. Particularly in the healthcare space, annual costs of running laboratory tests amount to $60 billion a year, most of them conducted in either hospitals' own clinical laboratories or outsourced to specialist testing firms.[41] Of interest, 70 percent of physicians' decisions with regard to monitoring patient care are informed by clinical laboratory testing.[42]

## INDUSTRY REGULATION

Not all analytical laboratory instrumentation requires approval from the U.S. Food & Drug Administration (FDA). However, instruments classified as in vitro diagnostic (IVD) products by manufacturers do need to undergo FDA approval. Such IVD products are considered "medical devices," whose reagents, instruments and systems are intended for use in diagnosis of disease or other conditions, including a determination of the state of health, in order to cure, mitigate, treat or prevent disease or its aftermath. To further elaborate on FDA code 21 CFR 809.3, such products are intended for use in the collection, preparation and examination of specimens taken from the human body.[43] The FDA approval requirement is extended to the tests that will be run on these instruments as well, in addition to the in-house evaluations to be performed by individual laboratories such as those in hospitals. Laboratories must demonstrate that they can perform a test with the same precision and accuracy as specified by the manufacturer of the test.[44]

In an effort to ensure quality laboratory testing on human specimens whose results determine the course of action in patient healthcare, three federal agencies, under the umbrella of the U.S. Department of Health and Human Services, established and uphold the Clinical Laboratory Improvement Amendments of 1988 (CLIA): the Food and Drug Administration (FDA), the Centers for Medicare and Medicaid Services (CMS) and the Centers for Disease Control and Prevention (CDC). CLIA regulations apply to approximately 254,000 laboratory entities in the U.S.[45] Each of the three agencies plays a unique role in ensuring quality standards for laboratory testing.[46]

The FDA is responsible for categorizing laboratory tests based on complexity. Technical complexities of testing processes vary, and so do their associated risk of harm if erroneous results were reported. The FDA thus established three categories of testing under CLIA on the basis of the complexity of the testing methodology: waived tests, tests of moderate complexity and tests of high complexity, all of which are in a searchable database on its website.[47] This categorization step is applicable to both clinical laboratory tests as well as to IVD manufacturers, who need to apply for CLIA categorization during the premarket process.[48] Laboratories performing only waived tests are subject to minimal regulation; such tests are simple, easy to use and have low risk for incorrect results. Examples of waived tests are pregnancy, fecal occult blood tests and some types of urine tests.[49]

Conversely, moderate to high complexity tests require some degree of personnel education and/or specialization, training and experience. Such tests, which are held to a higher standard than waived tests, are also subject to standards governing certification, proficiency testing (PT, which will be further explained in the next paragraph), patient test management, quality assurance (QA), quality control (QC) and inspections.[50] Moderate to high complexity testing includes tests such as the complete blood count (CBC), comprehensive metabolic panel (commonly known as "Chem 14") and molecular-based tests such as histocompatibility typing. Tests offered by the Edison include those in the moderate complexity category, such as low-density lipoprotein (LDL) cholesterol and C-reactive protein (CRP).[51]

CMS ensures quality clinical laboratory testing by properly certifying clinical laboratories, in order for the labs to receive Medicare or Medicaid payments.[52] In addition to issuing laboratory certificates, CMS's responsibilities include collecting user fees, conducting inspections and enforcing regulatory compliance, and approving private accreditation organizations for performing inspections. CMS is also responsible for publishing CLIA rules and regulations.[53] One major responsibility of CMS that is pertinent to this case study is their monitoring of laboratory performance on Proficiency Testing (PT). PT is the testing of unknown samples sent to a clinical laboratory by a CMS-approved PT program, the most commonly known one being that of the College of American Pathologists (CAP). Typically, PT samples are sent as sets to participating laboratories three times per year, although this number may be higher due to a particular lab's breadth of testing offered. Participating laboratories are to test the PT samples in the same manner as they would their patient specimens. Sample results are then reported back to the PT program, where they are checked for concordance among all laboratories that received the same set of unknown samples.

The PT program grades the results using CLIA grading criteria, before sending its score report to a participating laboratory to inform it of its performance. PT is crucial in allowing a laboratory to verify the accuracy and reliability of its testing. Routine reviews of PT reports by the laboratory staff and director will alert them to areas of testing that are not performing as expected and indicate subtle shifts and trends that, over time, would affect their patient results.[54] An October 2015 report in *The Wall Street Journal* alleges that Theranos's PT samples were tested and its results reported using instruments bought from other companies, instead of using the Edison.[55] Such practices inherently invalidate the efficacy of the Edison, as CMS dictates that a lab must handle "proficiency testing samples . . . in the same manner as it tests patient specimens" and by "using the laboratory's routine methods."[56]

The CDC supports CLIA in a number of ways. These responsibilities include but are not limited to: analysis, research and technical assistance; developing technical standards and laboratory practice guidelines, including standards and guidelines for cytology; conducting laboratory quality improvement studies; and monitoring proficiency testing practices. In addition, the CDC develops and distributes professional information and educational resources, as well as manages the Clinical Laboratory Improvement Advisory Committee (CLIAC).[57]

## THE TECHNOLOGY

The technology behind analytical laboratory instruments is a combination of principles rooted in the physical and life sciences, robotics, and software used for data collection and analysis. For example, spectrophotometric measurements, both manual and automated, are used extensively in the clinical chemistry laboratory.[58] Spectrophotometry is the quantitative measurement of the reflection or transmission properties of a material as a function of wavelength.[59] The measurement of analytes such as enzymes, toxicologically significant substances, and biological by-products such as bilirubin and uric acid are just a few examples performed via spectrophotometry.[60] For determining a patient's complete blood count (CBC), one of the common technologies employed by analytical laboratory instruments is flow cytometry. Sophisticated instruments are capable of measuring cell morphology and can detect small cell populations to diagnose rare blood conditions.

Briefly, a single-cell stream passes through a laser beam. The absorbance is measured, and the scattered light is measured at multiple angles to determine the cell's granularity, diameter and inner complexity. These are the same cell morphology characteristics that can be determined manually from a slide.[61] In the field of molecular diagnostics, multiple tools not limited to centrifuges, thermocyclers and fluorescence-based detection systems are used to perform methods such as DNA extraction and DNA amplification in order to detect DNA sequences of interest.

In the case of Theranos, details of the Edison technology have not been disclosed to scientific journals, so the quality of its results is unknown, nor are they able to be compared with conventional technologies.[62] A *Business Insider* report, however, stated that the Edison uses microfluidic technology.[63] In general, the technology involves a fingerstick, to draw a few microliters of blood into a disposable cartridge, which is then loaded into a "reader" for analysis.[64]

The blood collection in itself is a unique Theranos technology. Blood is drawn from a lanced fingertip via capillary action using a Sample Collection Device (SCD), whose other end houses a pair of nanotainer tubes.[65] Blood is drawn into each nanotainer when needles puncture its caps, sliding plungers downward, akin to a syringe. The nanotainers are then removed from the SCD, ready to be tested.[66]

Test results are subsequently transmitted wirelessly from the Edison reader to a secure database, and then to the patient or patient's physician. The reader can be at the same or different location from the site of blood collection. The perceived benefits include fast results and capability to analyze panels of tests (e.g., up to 30 blood tests can be performed on a single sample), thus reducing the cost per test.[67] The feature of transmitting results to doctors and patients through a secure database circles back to Theranos's mission to "make actionable information accessible to everyone at the time it matters."[68]

## INDUSTRY EXPERTS REACT TO TECHNOLOGY

An exclusive interview with Dr. Paul Pattengale, Medical Director of the Department of Pathology and Laboratory Medicine's Core Laboratory at Children's Hospital Los Angeles, as well as author of the medical thriller *Orchestrator*, raised a major concern regarding the level of QA/QC of the Theranos instrumentation used in point-of-care settings at multiple off-site Walgreens locations. To quote Dr. Pattengale:

> In a heightened culture of patient safety and accurate lab reporting, point-of-care, off-site lab testing for critically important lab values such as those generated for the blood thinner Coumadin (which are then used to determine subsequent dosing levels), *must* be scientifically controlled with a rigorous QA/QC plan. If not, significant patient harm (e.g., bleeding or stroke) can occur. CMS objectively determined that the Theranos detection instrument did not meet those rigorous standards, and was therefore a major and immediate threat to patient care and safety. As a result, CMS issued a "cease and desist" order, which resulted in the suspension of Theranos's CLIA license and their ability to perform further testing in these off-site locations. All credible labs

*must* adhere to these standards – Theranos was only one of the thousands of labs that undergo close scrutiny by CMS. All labs must comply with these standards in order to keep their doors open. It is the "standard of practice" for laboratory medicine.[69]

The authors of this case study were also granted an interview with Dr. Jesse Hsieh, a practicing physician and former president of multi-specialty physician group The South Bend Clinic. Dr. Hsieh was initially enthusiastic upon hearing the news of what Theranos could deliver. "That would have been awesome," said Dr. Hsieh, "to know of a testing method that is lower in cost, easier, convenient and accurate – it would have changed the way physicians do things." Having observed the sequence of events that unfolded for Theranos, however, Dr. Hsieh expressed several concerns. In his position as a physician: "The ability of patients to get themselves tested at a Walgreens without any background information, let alone a physician's order, would inundate the patient's doctor with lab data lacking context and a supporting background," said Dr. Hsieh. "What is a physician to do with all that data? What are its indications? The doctor will have no context, yet is liable for all that data."

From a healthcare administrator's standpoint, Dr. Hsieh pointed out that Theranos's technology would pose a threat to physician groups, whose income support can be dependent on ancillary services' tests such as those for specialties like rheumatology and endocrinology. Nonetheless, Dr. Hsieh reiterates:

Intervariability of test results, from different instruments housed in different labs, makes it hard for doctors to monitor patient care. For certain patients, we make a lot of critical decisions based on very small changes in lab results. Doctors would have been accepting of the Theranos technology if it delivered what it promised; we would have adapted readily. Unfortunately, there is no comparative data.[70]

An anonymous source in the pharmaceutical industry gave their opinion on Theranos's technology. Ultimately, they link Theranos's current state with the fact that Theranos has been acting like a tech company rather than a healthcare company. This behavior has resulted in incorrect media coverage: "tech media are not trained to understand how the healthcare system works." In addition, given that the company is private, Theranos has greater freedom to share or not share information, resulting in more narrative control. However, in healthcare, sharing information is necessary as the key concern with any healthcare product is the patients' safety and well-being. This "scientific rigor" is accomplished in part by peer reviews that focus on the implications for patients. This is integral to the healthcare industry's requirement for quality in its products. Tangible data are also important and should be available for review and discussion. Given that Theranos held its own patents, the source was confused by the company's unwillingness to share these data. Openness can help to "legitimize" products and the efficacy of technology by involving the scientific community's expertise. In conclusion, healthcare companies are unique and sensitive with regard to their requirements success. Their need to be successful is all the more important, considering the implications of their work.[71]

Theranos has also been clear about its opinion and has defended itself against these claims. The company website contains articles that include headlines such as these: "Theranos Statement on Walgreens Suit,"[72] "Company Statement Regarding Investor Lawsuit"[73] and "An Open Letter from Elizabeth Holmes."[74] Theranos responded to the Walgreens suit by saying, "We will respond vigorously to Walgreens' unfounded allegations, and will seek to hold Walgreens responsible for the damage it has caused to Theranos and its investors."[75] In her letter, Ms. Holmes stated, "Our ultimate goal is to commercialize miniaturized, automated laboratories capable of small-volume sample testing, with an emphasis on vulnerable patient populations, including oncology, pediatrics, and intensive care."[76] She ended the letter on a positive and hopeful note with, "I look forward to sharing more with you as we progress along the way."[77] Theranos has also publicly said, "Quality and safety are our top priorities and we are working closely with government officials to ensure that we not only comply with all federal regulations but exceed them."[78]

## THE FALLOUT

Accuracy is absolutely critical in the medical industry. The initial concept around Theranos is an exciting one: less painful, quicker, cheaper, less intimidating medical testing.[79] The idea that this procedure could become simple and more approachable is very enticing. However, when news articles began to reveal information that Theranos's testing might not be accurate, the fallout was quick and intense. The first publication to call attention to the issues inside the company is the now infamous article written in *The Wall Street Journal* by John Carreyrou, published October 15, 2015.[80] Following publication of that article, 2016 was a year of loss and lawsuits for the company.

Because Theranos is a privately held company, it is not possible to track damage to the stock price, an obvious indicator of company health.[81] However, a number of public changes to the board as well as partnerships occurred. The most high profile of these changes was with Walgreens. As of June 12, 2016, the relationship between Walgreens and Theranos ended: "June 12, 2016 – Walgreens today announced that it has informed Theranos that it will be terminating its relationship and closing operations at all 40 Theranos Wellness Centers at its stores in Arizona, effective immediately."[82] Walgreens is also suing the company.[83]

Other changes have occurred within the company, including multiple new hires as well as the opposite, "Theranos laid off over 500 employees."[84] However, it is not simply a loss of funds that has been surprising, but rather the healthcare implications. In 2016, the company was subject to a "federal investigation that it misled investors and partners about the readiness of its industry-disrupting technology."[85] Lawsuits and negative media attention continued throughout the year.

The most critical aspect of the fallout, however, remains the loss of credibility within the healthcare industry. *Fortune* writer Roomy Kahn, observed that "bad tests could have resulted in possible misdiagnoses and ensuing incorrect treatments of patients by medical practitioners, thus exposing people to health risks."[86] The Centers for Medicare and Medicaid Services (CMS) "revoked the license of its California blood-testing facility and banned founder Elizabeth Holmes from owning or operating a laboratory for two years."[87] As a result, "Theranos says it will shut down its clinical labs and wellness centers and lay off more than 40 percent of its full-time employees."[88]

The opinion of the company's health and prospects appears to be dependent upon the source. A *Forbes* magazine article written in June 2016 by Peter Cohan discussed the financial implications of the fallout. He commented, "On June 13, I interviewed experts who believe that Theranos is now worth between nothing and whatever value might result from an independent audit of its intellectual property."[89] He also cited Michael Greeley who felt that Theranos was "unfinanceable."[90] However, the article itself was more forgiving in its own estimate:

> [the $800 million estimate] gives the company credit for its intellectual property and the $724 million that it has raised, according to VC Experts, a venture capital research firm. It also represents a generous multiple of the company's sales, which *Forbes* learned about from a person familiar with Theranos' finances.[91]

As a result of the fallout, Ms. Holmes said, "I've learned the point about communication,"[92] during an interview with Fortune Global Forum with Alan Murray. Ms. Holmes also noted that, "the first time we ever were in the press, ever, in terms of communicating externally was in the Fall of 2013."[93] However, as of early 2017, Ms. Holmes's point about the necessity for greater communication stands in direct contrast with the company's website. The Theranos's "About Us" page on its website offers a total of just three sentences.[94]

## A FINAL TWIST AND A FAMILY RIFT

While the initial *The Wall Street Journal* report mentioned a former employee as one of its sources, no names were given. More than a year later, in November of 2016, the initial whistleblower was revealed to be Tyler Shultz, grandson of George Shultz, a director at Theranos.[95] The younger Mr. Shultz had been a member of Theranos's product team that monitored quality control. As part of that team, he noticed that the Edison machine often "flunked Theranos' quality control standards."[96] Employees were encouraged to ignore these results by Mr. Balwani.[97] In early 2014, he met with Ms. Holmes and another employee, Daniel Young, a "vice president in charge of biostatistics" about his concerns.[98]

When that course of action did not yield results, he anonymously contacted New York State's public health lab to allege that Theranos had manipulated its proficiency testing, in what was the first regulatory report against the company.[99] Shortly after this, he left his job and various regulators began investigating Theranos in earnest. As noted previously, sanctions against the company have since been put in place.

In 2015, Mr. Shultz began to speak to Mr. John Carreyrou of *The Wall Street Journal*. Almost immediately, Theranos identified him as the source of the leak. Mr. Schultz's grandfather leveraged his friendship with Ms. Holmes and initially brokered a deal with Theranos, with both parties signing a confidentiality agreement. The situation devolved quickly when lawyers surprised Mr. Shultz with a restraining order and pressed him to sign paperwork that did not protect him from legal action. Mr. Shultz resisted and Theranos sued. Mr. Shultz and his family, by their own account, have spent more than $400,000 in legal fees. He stands firm in his decision to blow the whistle: "Fraud," he said, "is not a trade secret."[100]

## ACKNOWLEDGMENTS

This case was prepared by research assistants Caitlin Kelley, Shareen Lee and Virginia Shields under the direction of James O'Rourke, Teaching Professor of Management, as the basis for class discussion rather than to illustrate either effective or ineffective handling of an administrative situation. Information was gathered from corporate as well as public sources.

## NOTES

1   Bilton, Nick. "Exclusive: How Elizabeth Holmes's House of Cards Came Tumbling Down," *Vanity Fair*. October 2016. Online at www.vanityfair.com/news/2016/09/elizabeth-holmes-theranos-exclusive. Accessed January 24, 2017.

2   Carreyrou, John. "Hot Startup Theranos Has Struggled With Its Blood-Test Technology," *The Wall Street Journal*. October 16, 2015. Online at www.vanityfair.com/news/2016/09/elizabeth-holmes-theranos-exclusive. Accessed February 13, 2017.

3   Herper, Matthew. "Bad Blood: The Decline and Fall of Elizabeth Holmes and Theranos," *Forbes*, October 8, 2016. Online at www.forbes.com/sites/matthewherper/2016/10/08/bad-blood-the-decline-and-fall-of-elizabeth-holmes-and-theranos/#6826039f7400. Accessed February 25, 2017.

4   Bilton. "Exclusive."

5   Ibid.

6   Khan, Roomy. "Theranos' $9 Billion Evaporated: Stanford Expert Whose Questions Ignited the Unicorn's Trouble," *Forbes*, February 17, 2017. Online at www.forbes.com/sites/roomykhan/2017/02/17/theranos-9-billion-evaporatedstanford-expert-whose-questions-ignited-the-unicorn-trouble/#3b68a8606692. Accessed February 20 2017.

7   Loria, Kevin. "What We Know About How Theranos' 'Revolutionary' Technology Works," *Business Insider*, October 19, 2015. Online at www.businessinsider.com/how-theranos-revolutionary-technology-works-2015-10. Accessed February 25, 2017.

8   Ibid.

9   Holmes, Elizabeth and Alan Murray. "Elizabeth Holmes Defends Theranos," *Fortune Global Forum*, January 17, 2017. Online at www.youtube.com/watch?v=eqYHwI87cDQ. Accessed February 25, 2017.

10  Weisul, Kimberly. "How Playing the Long Game Made Elizabeth Holmes a Billionaire," *Inc.* October, 2015. Online at www.inc.com/magazine/201510/kimberly-weisul/the-longest-game.html. Accessed February 21, 2017.

11  Parloff, Roger. "This CEO is Out for Blood," *Fortune*, June 12, 2014. Online at http://fortune.com/2014/06/12/theranos-blood-holmes/. Accessed February 25, 2017.

12  Ibid.

13  Stross, Randall. "Don't Blame Silicon Valley for Theranos," *The New York Times*. April 27, 2016. Online at www.nytimes.com/2016/04/27/opinion/dont-blame-silicon-valley-for-theranos.html?_r=0. Accessed February 20, 2017.

14  Stockton, Nick. "Everything You Need to Know About the Theranos Saga So Far," *Wired.com*, May 4, 2017. Online at www.wired.com/2016/05/everything-need-know-theranos-saga-far/. Accessed February 21, 2017.

15  Weisul. "How Playing the Long Game Made Elizabeth Holmes a Billionaire."

16  Ibid.

17  "Homepage," Theranos.com. Online at www.theranos.com/. Accessed February 19, 2017.

18  "About Us," Theranos.com. Online at www.theranos.com/company. Accessed February 21, 2017.

19  Parloff. "This CEO is Out for Blood."

20  Ibid.

21  Ibid.

22  Ibid.

23    Bilton. "Exclusive."

24    Parloff. "This CEO is Out for Blood."

25    "Sunny Balwani," *Crunchbase.com*. Online at www.crunchbase.com/person/sunny-balwani#/entity. Accessed February 9, 2017.

26    Kim, Larry. "21 Surprising Facts about Billionaire Entrepreneur Elizabeth Holmes," *Inc.*, July 1, 2015. Online at www.inc.com/larry-kim/21-surprising-facts-about-the-world-s-youngest-female-billionaire.html. Accessed February 9, 2017.

27    Parloff, Roger. "Theranos Resignation is a Major Bid for Atonement," *Fortune*, May 12, 2016. Online at http://fortune.com/2016/05/12/presidents-departure-atonement/. Accessed February 9, 2017.

28    "Sunny Balwani."

29    Carreyrou, John. "Theranos Whistleblower Shook the Company—and His Family," *The Wall Street Journal*, November 18, 2016. Online at www.wsj.com/articles/theranos-whistleblower-shook-the-companyand-his-family-1479335963. Accessed January 17, 2017.

30    Sunny Balwani's Twitter account. Online at https://twitter.com/sunnybalwani?lang=en. Accessed February 9, 2017.

31    Parloff. "Theranos Resignation is a Major Bid for Atonement."

32    Carreyrou. "Theranos Whistleblower Shook the Company—and His Family."

33    Parloff. "This CEO is Out for Blood."

34    Reingold, Jennifer. "Theranos' Board: Plenty of Political Connections, Little Relevant Expertise," *Fortune*, October 15, 2015. Online at http://fortune.com/2015/10/15/theranos-board-leadership/. Accessed February 9, 2017.

35    Ramsey, Lydia. "Theranos Is Getting Rid of High-Profile Board Members Including Henry Kissinger and George Shultz," *Business Insider*, December 1, 2016. Online at www.businessinsider.com/theranos-retires-board-of-counselors-and-adds-to-board-of-directors-2016–12. Accessed February 9, 2017.

36    First Research. *Scientific & Technical Instruments Manufacturing*, November 21, 2016. Mergent Intellect database. University of Notre Dame Mahaffey Business Library, Notre Dame, IN. February 13, 2017.

37    Ibid.

38    Ibid.

39    Ibid.

40    Ibid.

41    "Young Blood," *The Economist*, June 25, 2015. Online at www.economist.com/news/business/21656196-theranos-ambitious-silicon-valley-firm-wants-shake-up-market-medical. Accessed February 13, 2017.

42    ASCP.org. Contact Congress to Support the Prohibition of Self-Referrals for Anatomic Pathology Services. September 30, 2013. Online at www.ascp.org/content/Advocacy/contact-congress-to-support-the-prohibition-of-self-referrals-for-anatomic-pathology-services.

43    U.S. Food & Drug Administration. Overview of IVD Regulation. Online at www.fda.gov/MedicalDevices/DeviceRegulationandGuidance/IVDRegulatoryAssistance/ucm123682.htm#1. Accessed February 16, 2017.

44    Lab Tests Online. Commercial Laboratory Tests and FDA Approval. Online at https://labtestsonline.org/understanding/features/practice/commercial-fda/start/2. Accessed February 16, 2017.

45    CMS.gov. Clinical Laboratory Improvement Amendments (CLIA). Online at www.cms.gov/Regulations-and-Guidance/Legislation/CLIA/index.html. Accessed February 19, 2017.

46    U.S. Food & Drug Administration. Clinical Laboratory Improvement Amendments (CLIA). Online at www.fda.gov/MedicalDevices/DeviceRegulationandGuidance/IVDRegulatoryAssistance/ucm124105.htm. Accessed February 16, 2017.

47    U.S. Food & Drug Administration. CLIA – Clinical Laboratory Improvement Amendments. Online at www.accessdata.fda.gov/scripts/cdrh/cfdocs/cfCLIA/search.cfm. Accessed February 23, 2017.

48    U.S. Food & Drug Administration. Overview of IVD Regulation.

49    Lab Tests Online. Commercial Laboratory Tests and FDA Approval.

50    U.S. Food & Drug Administration. Overview of IVD Regulation.

51    Loria, Kevin. "A Top Medical Institution Ran a Secret Study on Theranos – Here's What It Found," *Business Insider*, March 28, 2016. Online at www.businessinsider.com/theranos-study-compares-blood-tests-to-quest-and-labcorp. Accessed February 13, 2017.

52    CMS.gov. Clinical Laboratory Improvement Amendments (CLIA).

53    U.S. Food & Drug Administration. Clinical Laboratory Improvement Amendments (CLIA).

54    CMS.gov. Clinical Laboratory Improvement Amendments (CLIA) Proficiency Testing. Online at www.cms.gov/Regulations-and-Guidance/Legislation/CLIA/downloads/cliabrochure8.pdf. Accessed February 19, 2017.

55    Carreyrou. "Hot Startup Theranos Has Struggled With Its Blood-Test Technology."

56    CMS.gov. Clinical Laboratory Improvement Amendments (CLIA) Proficiency Testing.

57    CDC.gov. Clinical Laboratory Improvement Amendments (CLIA). Online at wwwn.cdc.gov/clia/. Accessed February 19, 2017.

58    Rand, Royden N. "The Role of Spectrophotometric Standards in the Clinical Chemistry Laboratory," *Journal of Research of the National Bureau of Standards – A. Physics and Chemistry*, 76A.5 (September–October 1972): 499–508.

59    NIST.gov. Spectrophotometry. Online at www.nist.gov/programs-projects/spectrophotometry. Accessed February 19, 2017.

60   Rand. "The Role of Spectrophotometric Standards in the Clinical Chemistry Laboratory."

61   "Hematology Analyzers – From Complete Blood Counts to Cell Morphology," *Labcompare.com*, May 23, 2014. Online at www.labcompare.com/10-Featured-Articles/162042-Hematology-Analyzers-From-Complete-Blood-Counts-to-Cell-Mor phology/. Accessed February 19, 2017.

62   Diamandis, Eleftherios P. "Theranos Phenomenon: Promises and Fallacies," *Clinical Chemistry and Laboratory Medicine (CCLM)*, 53.7 (June 2015): 989–993.

63   Loria. "A Top Medical Institution Ran a Secret Study on Theranos."

64   Diamandis. "Theranos Phenomenon: Promises and Fallacies."

65   "A New Way to Collect Blood," *Theranos.com*. Online at www.theranos.com/. Accessed February 21, 2017.

66   Holmes, Elizabeth. *Theranos Science & Technology: The Miniaturization of Laboratory Testing*. Presentation at the 68th AACC Annual Scientific Meeting & Clinical Lab Expo, Philadelphia, PA. August 1, 2016. Online at www.youtube.com/watch?v=n 6JRG733ReQ. Accessed January 18, 2017.

67   Diamandis. "Theranos Phenomenon: Promises and Fallacies."

68   "About Theranos," *Theranos*. Online at www.theranos.com/company. Accessed February 21, 2017.

69   Telephone interview with Paul Pattengale, MD, Medical Director Core Laboratory, Department of Pathology and Laboratory Medicine, Children's Hospital Los Angeles. February 17, 2017. Interviewers: Caitlin Kelley, Shareen Lee and Virginia Shields.

70   Personal interview with Jesse Hsieh, MD, Physician, The South Bend Clinic, Adjunct Faculty, University of Notre Dame. February 21, 2017. Interviewers: Caitlin Kelley, Shareen Lee and Virginia Shields.

71   Telephone and e-mail interview with Anonymous, Mendoza College of Business, University of Notre Dame, Notre Dame, Indiana, U.S. February 21, 2017. Interviewers: Caitlin Kelley, Shareen Lee and Virginia Shields.

72   "Theranos Statement on Walgreens Suit," *Theranos*, November 8, 2016. Online at https://news.theranos.com/2016/11/08/ theranos-statement-walgreens-suit/. Accessed February 20, 2017.

73   "Company Statement Regarding Investor Lawsuit," *Theranos*, October 11, 2016. Online at https://news.theranos. com/2016/10/11/company-statement-regarding-investor-lawsuit/. Accessed February 20, 2017.

74   "An Open Letter from Elizabeth Holmes," *Theranos*, October 5, 2016. Online at https://news.theranos.com/2016/10/05/ an-open-letter-elizabeth-holmes/. Accessed February 20, 2017.

75   "Theranos Statement on Walgreens Suit," *Theranos*.

76   "An Open Letter from Elizabeth Holmes," *Theranos*.

77   Ibid.

78   Cohan, Peter. "Beyond Movie Material, Is Theranos Worth Anything?" *Forbes*, June 14, 2016. Online at www.forbes.com/ sites/petercohan/2016/06/14/beyond-movie-material-is-theranos-worth-anything/#33f7da1e3d2a. Accessed February 21, 2017.

79   Diamandis. "Theranos Phenomenon: Promises and Fallacies."

80   Stockton. "Everything You Need to Know About the Theranos Saga So Far."

81   "What Is the Stock Symbol for Theranos?" *Reference.com*. Online at www.reference.com/business-finance/stock-sym bol-theranos-59f187558fd1b3aa. Accessed February 22, 2017.

82   "Walgreens Terminates Relationship with Theranos; Will be Closing Operations at All 40 Theranos Wellness Centers in Arizona," *Walgreens.com*, June 12, 2016. Online at http://news.walgreens.com/press-releases/general-news/wal greens-terminates-relationship-with-theranos-will-be-closing-operations-at-all-40-theranos-wellness-centers-in-ari zona.htm. Accessed 18 February, 2017.

83   "Theranos Statement on Walgreens Suit," *Theranos*.

84   Khan. "Theranos' $9 Billion Evaporated."

85   Della Cava, Marco. "Blood Lab Theranos Under Federal Investigation," *USA Today*, April 18, 2016. Online at www.usatoday. com/story/tech/news/2016/04/18/blood-lab-theranos-under-investigation-report/83211074/. Accessed February 21, 2017.

86   Khan. "Theranos' $9 Billion Evaporated."

87   Riley, Charles. "Theranos Founder Elizabeth Holmes Banned for Two Years," *CNN Tech*, July 8, 2016. Online at http:// money.cnn.com/2016/07/08/technology/theranos-elizabth-holmes-banned/. Accessed February 20, 2017.

88   "Theranos Closing Labs, Laying off 340 Following Sanctions," *The Seattle Times*, The Associated Press, October 6, 2016. Online at www.seattletimes.com/business/theranos-closing-labs-laying-off-340-following-sanctions/. Accessed February 20, 2017.

89   Cohan, Peter. "Beyond Movie Material, Is Theranos Worth Anything?" *Forbes*, June 14, 2016. Online at www.forbes.com/sites/ petercohan/2016/06/14/beyond-movie-material-is-theranos-worth-anything/#33f7da1e3d2a. Accessed February 21, 2017.

90   Ibid.

91   Ibid.

92   Holmes and Murray. "Elizabeth Holmes Defends Theranos."

93   Ibid.

94   "About Us," Theranos.com.

95   Carreyrou. "Theranos Whistleblower Shook the Company – and His Family."
96   Ibid.
97   Ibid.
98   Ibid.
99   Ibid.
100  Ibid.

# CHAPTER 7

# Technology

One tweet is all it takes to ruin a career. For Justine Sacco, the senior director of corporate communications at IAC, this experience is all too familiar. Despite having fewer than 200 followers, she sent a simple, inappropriate tweet, prompting a hashtag that found its way to the top of Twitter's trending conversations. Strangers relentlessly shamed her and called for her termination. The ordeal not only cost Sacco her dream job, it also resulted in lasting psychological damage.[1]

She's not alone. Similar situations play out daily across the globe, demonstrating the fragility of relative anonymity on social media.

Social networking is far from the only source of trouble, however. A few years ago, an insurance company manager, working with an internal mailing list devoted to his customers, replied to an office e-mail. His response focused on the company's strategy for selling a particular policy, but the message wasn't sent to just one person – it was sent to the entire listserv. He had clicked "Reply All" and, buried in that huge list was the address of the customer they were working with. That manager's crass language and arrogant approach went directly to his customer and, not surprisingly, he didn't make the sale.

How can such wonderful technology be the source of so much frustration? Shouldn't information technology (IT) – including e-mail, voice mail, social media, video conferencing, desktop computing, instant messaging, text messaging, cell phones and handheld wireless devices – make our lives easier? Aren't we all more productive as a result? Even though the inventors and manufacturers of all this technology can fairly claim great things for us personally and professionally, the new world in which we live is not without its dark side. Every opportunity has its risks, and communication technology is no exception.

## LIFE IN THE DIGITAL AGE

When MIT media technology professor Nicholas Negroponte told us that "being digital" is not simply a way of communicating but a new way of living, only the propeller-heads, IT gurus and technology buffs were enthusiastic. But nearly two decades later, just about everyone realizes that he was right. It's quicker, cheaper and easier to ship electrons (as in e-mail attachments) than it is to ship atoms and molecules (as in FedEx overnight packages). Some things still must move around physically, but so much more can move electronically.[2]

We can create files anywhere, store them in the cloud (online), access them from an iPad or wireless Android device, insert graphics and hyperlinks, and pass them on to someone else. Or with the use of shareware and collaborative software platforms, multiple authors can work on the same document at once from different locations, edit the content, discuss the changes and assure themselves of document version control.

The way we work and live has changed. We can find information quickly, check the nannycam at our children's daycare center on the Internet, manage inventory, control cash flow and follow the stock market simultaneously. We can find just about anyone with a smart phone or personal computer in a matter of seconds. Since the advent of PCs over 35 years ago, more than 2 billion have been sold worldwide. According to the Gartner Group, the industry shipped more than 300 million units in 2009, up more than 5 percent from the year before, as the price of desktop computing has dropped steadily to less than $1,000 apiece.[3,4]

By 2014, more than 84 percent of all U.S. households had access to at least one personal computer, and 73 percent had in-home access to broadband connections.[5] It will take a few more years before literally everyone has access to computerized word processing, spreadsheet technology, e-mail, social media and the Internet, but that day is coming. And as Professor Negroponte told us in the mid-1990s, it is changing the way we live.

## COMMUNICATING DIGITALLY

Professor Carolyn Boulger, in *e-Technology and the Fourth Economy*, shows how the movement from hunting and gathering to an economy based on agriculture and then industrial production made civilization possible. But a fourth economy, based entirely on mindwork – an exchange of ideas – creates possibilities previously undreamt of. No longer must we follow the herds, depend on the growing seasons or own the means of production in order to create a life for ourselves. The means of production are now in our minds, in our hands and on our desktops.[6]

Along with all of the advantages that this new technology brings to our homes, our businesses, and our personal and professional lives, it also brings complications. More than 25 million households in the U.S. do not have access to the Internet.[7] Even more surprising, perhaps: nearly 15 percent of U.S. households have never used a computer to create a document.[8] Those who do have access to computing and the Internet tell us they're not necessarily better off. "I see these people on airplanes, in building lobbies, and in restaurants," says a friend, "and they're all pounding away on their laptops, entering data in a tablet, or making client calls on a cell phone. There is absolutely no distinction anymore between work and home." Another put it more succinctly: "If I drag my notebook computer on the road with me, I feel as if I'm on the wrong end of some sort of electronic dog-leash."

Technology, it seems, is a double-edged sword with the potential to make us more productive or to drain away our time. A typical information worker who sits at a computer all day turns to his e-mail program more than 50 times and uses instant messaging 77 times, according to RescueTime, a company that analyzes computer habits. The company, which draws its data from 40,000 people who have tracking software on their computers, found that an average worker also stops at 40 websites over the course of the day. The fractured attention comes at a cost. In the U.S., more than $650 billion a year in productivity is lost because of interruptions and inattention.[9] Forbes reports that 71 percent of people experience frequent interruptions while working.[10] Vault.com reports that an astonishing 37 percent of the employees it surveyed say they constantly surf the Web at work for personal reasons.[11] And, according to SexTracker, a service that monitors Internet traffic, "On most pornographic Web sites, nearly 70 percent of traffic takes place during work hours."[12]

A recent survey in the U.K. revealed that nearly a third of all workers in Britain use e-mail at work to gossip about rivals and flirt with colleagues.[13] E-mail has already created multiple problems for businesses in this country and abroad, including legal liability, confidentiality breaches, damage to reputation, lost productivity, network congestion, downtime, and court orders demanding that e-mail records be turned over to trial judges.[14]

Any thoughtful person will tell you those aren't the only problems technology brings in the door with it. Managers must now rely on fewer nonverbal and visual cues to gather meaning. They work across time zones and with geographically dispersed groups and teams. Often, they're asked to work electronically with people they've never met and don't really know. People say they're virtually buried in e-mail some days. "If you get 35 messages a day," says a colleague, "it means that when you return from a three-day trip, you have more than a hundred messages to deal with." For some, it's voice mail ping-pong that drives them crazy. For others, it's the loss of privacy and the sense that they're no longer in control of their lives.

This chapter examines e-technology, workplace behaviors and the policies that guide them, as well as workplace privacy and employer monitoring. We also look at how companies use telecommuting and virtual workgroups to increase productivity. You will find some new rules of etiquette, along with an examination of social media and three case studies that focus directly on how these issues affect you.

## THE INTERNET AND ONLINE BEHAVIOR

Andy Perez uses the library at Rice University in Houston for the quiet, not the books. He does his research online. Edell Fiedler taps into the Internet to register for classes and check grades at Minnesota State University, Mankato, sometimes saving her the 60-mile drive to school. And Rakesh Patel regularly uses e-mail to ask his professors at Chicago's DePaul University questions about assignments.[15]

These stories are increasingly common, as the generation that grew up with the personal computer is now connected on campus and relies on the Internet in almost every dimension of college life. The findings of a large-scale survey by the Pew Internet and American Life Project confirm what many have suspected for some time: The Internet has become an integral part of college life, and not just for studying. The survey of college students across the country found that 94 percent use the Internet multiple times each day, compared with just 74 percent of the overall U.S. population.[16]

"Today's college students were born long after the first PCs were introduced to the public and they have grown up with these technologies," said Professor Steve Jones, lead author of the study and head of the department of communication at the University of Illinois at Chicago. "To them, the Internet and e-mail are as commonplace as telephones and television – and equally as indispensable."[17]

If it's true that more than 90 percent of all college students surveyed say they use the Internet more than the library for research, and if 86 percent check their e-mail each day, wouldn't you expect those behaviors to continue once they've graduated? Two-thirds say they think the Internet has improved their relationships with classmates, and more than half think e-mail has enhanced their relationships with professors. These habits are clearly likely to continue once students enter the workforce and begin communicating in a professional setting.

The Internet has become central to the way college students conduct research for their courses; communicate with their professors, friends and family; post updates to social networking sites; gather information about everything from sports to the stock market and the weather; and, finally, make important short-notice purchases of gifts, clothing and airline tickets. The trend is clear: When college students enter the workforce, online retrieval and storage of information and continual communication with others who are important to them will already have become daily and lifelong habits. The workplace of the twenty-first century will adjust to accommodate those habits and, in many ways, become more productive and interesting. The news is not all good, however, because technology and social behavior are often at odds with business goals.

## SOCIAL MEDIA

Social media is a term widely used to include a number of Internet-based platforms for connecting with other people as individuals and as members of a social community. Some writers have referred to such media as "Web 2.0," meaning an online source that not only provides information but interacts with users, as well.

Several important categories of social media are worth noting:

- **Social networking**. (Facebook, Twitter, Google+, Tumblr, LinkedIn, Foursquare, Last.FM). These sites interact by adding friends, commenting on profiles, joining groups and holding discussions.
- **Social photo and video sharing**. (YouTube, Instagram, Snapchat, Pinterest, 4chan, Flickr, DeviantArt, Imgur). These interact by sharing photos or videos and/or commenting on user submissions.
- **Social news**. (Digg, Propeller, Reddit). These interact by voting for articles by most popular, most read and most e-mailed, and commenting on them.
- **Social bookmarking**. (Del.icio.us, Blinklist, Simpy). These sites interact by tagging websites and searching through websites bookmarked by other people.
- **Wikis**. (Wikipedia, Wikia). And, finally, these interact by adding articles and allowing users to edit existing articles online.[18]

Facebook now has more than 2.13 billion active users worldwide.[19] Twitter has nearly 330 million active users per month, generating 500 million tweets a day.[20] YouTube and Instagram have 1.5 billion and 800 million monthly users respectively, and more than 187 million use Snapchat each day.[21,22,23] Dozens of minor players in the social media market are vying for your time and attention, as well, offering messaging services, connection with people you know (and might like to know), photo sharing, music downloads, shopping and a rapidly growing set of reasons to spend much of your time online, connected with other people.

Businesses are beginning to figure out how to use social media, not only for marketing purposes, but for reputation management and corporate communication, as well. There is, in fact, no shortage of public relations counselors ready and eager to provide business advice on the most profitable use of social media.

On your own time, though, social media can be helpful for boosting your career and, of course, connecting with friends. Be careful how much you log on at work, as some office computers can track how much time you spend on different sites and even what you type online. It's best to log on from a private computer or smart phone (iPhone, Android), and if you do use your desktop computer, do it during break times.

Remember that there is still a risk when you post on publicly accessible sites such as Facebook or Twitter. Don't trash your boss or coworkers, complain too severely about your work, or post photos on your profile of yourself doing something illegal or scandalous. Make sure that only the friends you approve of can see photos or more private information, and don't be reluctant to adjust privacy settings so that your boss or anyone who isn't your friend can't just click through your profile to see what you're up to on weekends.[24]

Here are some general recommendations to avoid jeopardizing your career:

- *Relax, but be vigilant.* Writing online is a lot less formal, and that's okay. The best way to avoid misinterpretation is to match the typical tone of online communication specific to the platform. For instance, LinkedIn is more formal than Facebook, but the tones of both are inappropriate for writing a sufficiently concise Tweet. If you are unsure of the tone proper to a platform, lurk a little and get a feel for it. Simultaneously, on any network with a larger audience, it is important to write with a professionalism similar to that which you would share with trusted colleagues – relaxed but respectful.
- *Discipline your message.* To improve your tone, be nicer online than you are offline (we are often poor judges of our own writing). Be respectful and considerate; there is never an excuse for offensive behavior or harassment. Make sure your posts add value to the conversation; do not respond to offensive or negative posts; avoid commenting on matters outside of your area of expertise, and steer clear of contentious topics unless in (respectful) jest. Further, keep bragging and complaining to a minimum.
- *Monitor yourself.* Each month, scroll through your posts to ascertain the overall tone of your profile. You never know when someone important will scrutinize your page.
- *Follow policy.* Following the policies of your employer and social media sites is vital, especially when discussing your company or its products and services. Do not discuss financial information, sales trends, strategies, forecasts, legal issues, future promotions or any other confidential information. Do not give out personal information about customers, clients or employees. If you are not sure if something is confidential, contact your employer first. If you make a mistake, correct it immediately and take responsibility for your actions.
- *When in doubt, don't send, forward or share it!* This should be a no-brainer. The Internet is forever, and there is no such thing as "delete."[25,26]

## ELECTRONIC MAIL

What began as a method for sharing scientific and technical information among Defense Department and university researchers more than 35 years ago is now an everyday fact of life. Electronic mail, or e-mail to most people, is a global means of staying in touch, passing data and graphics, and managing the moment-to-moment flow of information needed to run a business. It's also a gateway for the unwanted: unsolicited spam and mass advertising, scam artists, grifters, predators, pornographers, viruses, hackers and thieves. E-mail is an unlatched doorway into your computer and into the innermost secrets of your personal and professional life.

Properly managed, though, e-mail can become a productivity booster, a link to distant markets, and an essential tool for managing everything from employee communication to customer relations. It requires some forethought, discipline and planning, though. Let's begin with some personal issues and then move to the policies and procedures you should think about as you try to make e-mail work for you.

For a growing number of people, just keeping up with e-mail is a battle they can't seem to win. Consider these statistics:

- **74 trillion** e-mail messages sent annually worldwide.[27]
- **49 minutes** spent managing e-mails each day by the average office worker.
- **4 hours** spent managing e-mails by senior management workers.
- **80:** the percentage of e-mails sent which are actually "spam" – unsolicited advertisements, many of which are fraudulent or otherwise illegal.
- **62:** the percentage of workers in industrialized nations who check business e-mails while at home or on vacation.
- **10:** the point-fall in IQ experienced by workers distracted by e-mail (more than twice that found in cannabis studies).
- **20:** the percentage of workers who are stressed.[28]

Another study from the Gartner Group reveals that nearly half of all American e-mail users (more than 100 million of us) check e-mail on vacation. Nearly one in four looks for messages every weekend.[29] "I was addicted to e-mail," says Sabrina Horn, CEO of Horn Group in San Francisco. "I lived for the little bell that would go *ding*! when a new message arrived. I got sucked into using e-mail to try to figure out where in the organization I could best focus my attention," she said. As a result, "I had this nagging feeling that I was never getting anything done at the office. I went home every day completely frustrated. I knew what was going on at work, but I didn't actually *do* anything."[30]

To manage the growing problem of e-mail in your life, here are a few suggestions you can act on now.

### *Admit You Have a Problem*

Mark Elwood, author of *Cut the Glut of E-Mail*, calculates that white collar workers waste an average of three hours a week just sorting through junk mail. If you spend more time than that, you have a problem.[31]

### Send Less, Get Less

If you send less e-mail, you'll reduce the volume of return mail in your in-box. Think carefully about whether you really need to draft new messages or respond to those you've received. Misty Young of KPS3 Advertising in Reno, Nevada, says, "Unless I get an error message, I assume it got through. I don't need someone to send a 'Thank you for keeping me in the loop' or 'Is there anything else you need?' or 'Have a really great day.'"[32]

### Escape the Endless Reply Loop

Silence in response to an e-mail message is often thought of as rude. "It's like walking out on someone who is still talking to you," says Kaitlin Sherwood, who writes about the problem at overcomeemailoverload.com. She suggests that you finish a message with "No reply needed" or follow a request with "Thanks in advance." If you're fulfilling a request, you might conclude with "Hope this helped." Even though it may be helpful to anticipate questions that could arise, you should avoid asking questions you really don't want the answers to.[33]

### Check the "To" Field Before You Click "Send"

Make sure you're sending this message to the address you intend. Double-check to make absolutely certain you haven't clicked "Reply All" or are sending it to people and places you shouldn't.

### Don't Copy the World

Think twice about the people you put on your CC list. If they all respond, then how bad will your message backlog be? Mailing lists can also create problems for you and for all those family members, school chums and business contacts included on them. When you reply to mailing list messages, make sure you reply only to the sender, not the whole list. A colleague of mine (unnamed) sent an e-mail message to a list of folks on campus about a faculty meeting. Minutes later, another colleague (also unnamed) replied to the entire list, thinking she was corresponding only with the sender: "Thanks for the update. By the way, you left your keys on the kitchen counter when you left this morning. I'll drop them at your office this afternoon." Uh-oh. Who knew they were an item? Well . . . now the whole campus does.

### Pick a Subject (Almost) Any Subject

Some people leave the subject line of their e-mails blank. This is baffling because it will take more than curiosity to get me to open a message from someone I don't know. Crafting a relevant subject line will prompt people to open your messages and act on them quickly. Capital One, where employees average 40 to 50 e-mail messages a day, is trying to make their existing system better by teaching employees to write better messages. "It turns out that stronger subject lines help recipients better understand why they received an e-mail" and it also makes it easier to find the message later, if they decide to store it. Instead of writing, "here's what you asked for," as the subject line, it would be more effective to say "here's the 2019 staffing model." Using bullet points and underlining or bolding major points also makes the text more effective.[34]

### Think Before Replying

If you respond to e-mail messages immediately, you establish the expectation in your readers' minds that you will always respond quickly. The old rule about responding was simple: Return phone calls the same day; respond to postal service mail within three working days. If people expect an instant response, they'll be upset when you take longer to reply. Tell them to call if it's really urgent.

### Think Again Before Replying

If you're angry, upset or irritated at something you've just read in an e-mail message, give yourself a day – or at least a few hours – to cool down before responding. You may end up saying something you'll regret. The same goes for dumb jokes, criticism of supervisors or coworkers, off-color remarks or any other smart-aleck responses you probably wouldn't offer up in person.

### Be Careful with Criticism

E-mail – even with those clever emoticons and smiley faces that clutter up the message – eliminates virtually all of the important nonverbal cues we're accustomed to seeing and hearing as we judge a message sender's intent. E-mail can seem especially cold and inhumane if you're delivering criticism. The mother who puts her arm around you and smiles before saying, "The Thanksgiving turkey was a bit dry" probably won't cause many hurt feelings. But the mother who writes an e-mail that says, "Too bad about that overcooked turkey" may set off a family feud that lasts until next year.[35]

### Handle Each Message Just Once

If it's unimportant or irrelevant, hit the delete key. If it's something you'll need to respond to, decide whether to do it now or later, when you have the time and information you need. If you can discipline yourself to check e-mail folders, you may wish to file each message as it comes in and keep your in-box clean.

### Don't Check Your E-Mail Constantly

Have the self-discipline to check it at regular intervals, such as first thing in the morning, once after lunch and again before going home. If you leave your e-mail system open and running constantly, at least turn off the chime.

## Don't Ignore the Conventions of Correspondence

Even though e-mail seems more like a conversation than a letter, you should not write to people in all lower case letters, ignore punctuation or abandon conventional spelling. The same goes for sentence and paragraph structure. The more organizational structure and cues you include in your writing, the easier it will be for your recipients to read.

## Avoid Abbreviations and Cyberjargon

PC users have their own shorthand language that uses expressions designed to save typing, such as IMHO (in my humble opinion) or TTYL (talk to you later). Most business professionals, however, find these abbreviations unintelligible and annoying. *PCWorld's* Laurianne McLaughlin says, "You can't assume everyone is familiar with the endless acronyms circulating out there. WIDLTO: When in doubt, leave them out."[36]

## Brevity is the Soul of Wit and Wisdom

If your messages go much beyond one screen, perhaps you need to have a conversation on the phone or in person. If that's not possible, consider drafting your remarks separately as a text file and attaching them to a one-sentence cover message. Send them in as many forms (MS Word, Adobe PDF and Corel WordPerfect) as you think your readers will need. If you're sending a one-line response, consider using the subject line to carry the whole message, if it fits. That way, the recipient doesn't have to open your e-mail. For example: "Got your package today, everything fine. Thanks (no msg)."

## Make URLs Useful

When you refer people to a website, include the complete address on a line of its own. For example:

You'll find more information about our organization at this website: www.nd.edu/~fanning

Don't put any punctuation before or after the URL (universal resource locator). If you do, it may prevent your recipients from simply clicking on the URL and having the Web page open in their browser window.

## Be Cautious About Attachments

Sending unsolicited attachments can quickly turn you into an e-mail outcast. Don't attach documents, pictures or spreadsheets to your messages unless you're certain the recipient wants or needs to see them. Business journalist Scott Kirsner suggests it may be more convenient for your readers if you simply post documents to an easily accessible intranet site and send an e-mail with a pointer to their location. And if you're sending out three or more large attachments, you may want to send each as a separate message, using the subject line to alert the recipient to the contents of the file you're attaching.[37] If you're still keen on sending a large attachment, consider compressing the file with WinZip or another file compression program.

## Include a Signature File

Your outgoing e-mail should automatically include a signature file. This feature is available on virtually all e-mail software and will append your name and contact data to every message you send. Many people like to include an inspirational phrase or humorous quote with their signature file. Resist. Such things will not win you any friends.

## Check Your Time/Date Stamp

Make sure your computer – and your company's e-mail server – are set to the correct time and date. Messages with an incorrect time or date can show up in the wrong place in a recipient's e-mail in-box and can be misfiled or overlooked.

### Get Help When You Need It

Senior managers should allow administrative assistants to wade through their in-boxes. An assistant can open, read and organize e-mail messages before you respond. You may also wish to manage the flow of e-mail with an auto-response that informs those sending e-mail to you that you are out of the office or on vacation. That way, they won't expect a response until you return.

Despite the fact that e-mail is part of a new technology that has changed the ways in which we communicate, many of the old rules still apply. According to Bob Rozakis of the Alpha Development Group:

A business communication is business, period. As a result, a certain degree of formality is required. Just because e-mail tends to be more immediate and personable, it can't be casual. Business e-mail must be businesslike. You'll be judged by the quality of your writing, so spelling and grammar do count.

He goes on to say:

All forms of business communication you send reflect on you, affecting your chances for advancement. Sending e-mail riddled with misspellings is the same as wearing a shirt spattered with catsup. Sloppy e-mail gets tongues wagging about the writer's literal failings.[38]

## TEXT MESSAGING

For anyone who doubts that the texting revolution is upon us, consider this: The number of text messages the average 13-to-17-year-old sent and received peaked around 2010 at 3,339 texts a month – more than 100 per day, according to the Nielsen Co., the media research firm.[39] Though text messaging through mobile carriers has declined in recent years, the amount of messaging through third-party applications such as Facebook Messenger, WhatsApp and LINE has increased dramatically to compensate. Still, excluding messaging apps, 15.2 million texts are sent per minute around the world. Adults contribute significantly, too, spending on average 23 hours per week texting.[40] This is unsurprising as studies show that teenagers' messaging habits remain consistent as they reach adulthood.[41]

Behind the texting explosion is a fundamental shift in how we view our mobile devices.

Nielsen recently analyzed the cell phone bills of 60,000 mobile subscribers and found that adults made and received an average of 188 mobile phone calls a month during 2010, down 25 percent from three years earlier. Average "talk minutes" fell 5 percent compared with 2009; among 18-to-24-year-olds, the decline was 17 percent.[42]

Text messages – also known as SMS (Short Message Service) – take up less bandwidth than phone calls and cost less. A text message's content is so condensed that it routinely fails, even more than e-mail, according to *The Wall Street Journal* writer Katherine Rossman, to convey the writer's tone and affect. The more we text, the greater the opportunity for misunderstanding.

A recent survey of 2,000 college students asked about their attitudes toward phone calls and text-messaging and found the students' predominant goal was to pass along information in as little time, with as little small talk, as possible. "What they like most about their mobile devices is that they can reach other people," says Naomi Baron, a professor of linguistics at American University in Washington, DC, who conducted the survey. "What they like least is that other people can reach them."[43]

Part of what's driving the texting surge among adults is the popularity of social media. Sites like Twitter, with postings of no more than 140 characters, have created and reinforced the habit of communicating in micro-bursts. And these sites are also pumping up the sheer volume. Many Twitter and Facebook users create settings that alert them, via text message, every time a tweet or message is earmarked for them.[44]

Texting's rise over conversation is changing the way we interact, social scientists say. We default to text to relay difficult information. We stare at our phone when we want to avoid eye contact. Rather than make plans in advance, we engage in what Rich Ling, a professor at IT University in Copenhagen, Denmark, calls micro-coordination: "I'll txt u in 10mins when I know wh/restrnt."

Of course, phone conversations will never be completely obsolete. Deal makers and other professionals still spend much of the day on the phone. Researchers say people are more likely to use text-based communications at the preliminary stages of projects. The phone comes into play when there are multiple options to consider or binding decisions to be made.[45]

## PRIVACY AND WORKPLACE MONITORING

If you draft a quick e-mail message to a friend on your computer at work, that's your own private property, isn't it? What about the websites you visit online at the office? As long as you do it on your lunch hour, that's okay, isn't it? And those Instant Messenger notes flying around the office among friends and coworkers? Those are private, too, aren't they?

"Privacy is dead," says Sun MicroSystems CEO Scott McNealy. "Deal with it."[46] Even though your e-mail account may be password-protected, it isn't private. If your account is provided by your employer, it isn't even yours. E-mail and other forms of electronic communication, as so many people have discovered, are vulnerable to invasion and snooping. And although some of it is plainly illegal, many of those folks looking through your in-box and sent files are perfectly within their rights to do so.

J. D. Biersdorfer of *The New York Times* says, "You would probably do well to abide by an old rule of thumb when it comes to the privacy of e-mail: never put anything in an e-mail message that you wouldn't write on a postcard."[47] Between the time you click the send button and it arrives in the in-box of the recipient, a typical e-mail message travels through at least a couple of mail servers, routers and other computers. Hackers don't often target mail servers, but that's no guarantee that someone won't open, read and save what you've written.

It's much more likely, in fact, that the person reading your e-mail will be your employer.

About 55 percent of companies retain and review e-mail, according to a recent survey by the American Management Association and the e-Policy Institute, up from 47 percent four years earlier. About a quarter of them have fired workers for e-mail abuse.[48]

More than one-third of companies with 1,000 or more employees now employ staff to read or otherwise analyze outbound e-mail, according to a study by Proofpoint, an e-mail security firm. The main concern is leakage of trade secrets. Here are a few more of the company's findings in a survey of e-mail decision makers at large companies:

- Leaks of proprietary information and valuable intellectual property are the top e-mail concerns of large companies.
- Almost one in four outgoing e-mails contains content that poses a legal, financial or regulatory risk.
- More than one in four companies have terminated employees for violating e-mail policies in the past 12 months.
- More than one in three companies have investigated a suspected e-mail leak of confidential or proprietary information in the same time frame.
- More than 10 percent of companies were ordered by a court or regulatory body to produce employee e-mail in the past year.
- Seventy percent of companies say they are "concerned" or "very concerned" about Web-based e-mail as a conduit for exposure of confidential information.[49]

Just about all workplace communication experts agree: There is no such thing as private e-mail on a company-owned system. "Legally, they're not required to tell you if they're monitoring the e-mail," says Shari Steele of the Electronic Frontier Foundation. "The equipment you're using when at work belongs to the employer. And, therefore, the employer can do anything [it wants to] with the equipment."[50]

Businesses can customize the software to identify senders and scan for keywords that send up a red flag. They can also choose from a set of keywords associated with viruses or unsolicited e-mail, or spam. Once a policy is established, your employer can choose what happens next: to save the e-mail for review, divert it or send it to the trash.

### Why Do Employers Monitor?

Reasons for tracking everything from e-mail to Internet use are often justified by four basic considerations:

*Security.* Every business, no matter what industry or which part of the marketplace it competes in, has information that it wants kept confidential. Pre-release information, research and development efforts, patented or copyrighted items, bid or proposal data, or contractual negotiations are just a few of the categories that every business hopes to protect.

*Productivity.* Employees who spend a substantial portion of their workday surfing the Net, sending e-mail to family and friends, or abusing the technology on their desktops are a drain on productivity and profits. More than one-third of all lost productivity is attributed to Internet abuse at work.[51]

*Protection.* Many companies faced with costly lawsuits are monitoring e-mail, voice mail, Twitter and other communication systems to uncover and discipline workers who harass, demean, threaten or intimidate others in the workplace. In a recent survey of large firms, almost 10 percent report having received a subpoena for employee e-mail. "Almost every workplace lawsuit today, especially a sexual harassment case, has an e-mail component," says Nancy Flynn, executive director of the ePolicy Institute. Some records may be kept on file indefinitely.[52]

*Industry regulation.* State and federal regulatory agencies have published numerous rules requiring businesses of many sorts to hang onto all of their e-mail, just as they would retain their paper-based correspondence. The U.S. Securities and Exchange Commission, for example, has extensive and strict requirements for e-mail retention in the financial services industry. Brokerages and trading firms have been fined for failing to keep the electronic exchanges between brokers and their clients and between brokers and the back-office staff who execute trades.

## Does an Employee Have a Right to Privacy?

The answer to this question is yes, but it's not as extensive as you might imagine (or wish for). Several considerations are important in examining any concerns about privacy in the workplace. First, no federal law covers all aspects of an employee's right to privacy on the job. Instead, a patchwork of federal and state laws regulates everything from electronic monitoring to visual surveillance, drug testing and locker searches. Employees really do not have a right of privacy in e-mail communication on their employer's system unless the employer consistently acts in a manner giving rise to a reasonable expectation of privacy.

Such expectations may be created deliberately or inadvertently. For example, an employer can possibly create an expectation of privacy if he or she is aware of the use of the company's e-mail system for personal communications among employees and allows the system to be used for that purpose.

The Electronic Communication Privacy Act of 1986 (last amended in 2006) protects e-mail messages from interception by and disclosure to *third parties*.[53] Electronically stored communications are also protected, but the law does not prohibit employers from monitoring e-mail system activities and message content. Your boss can open your messages, read them, store them and use them to make an employment decision about you. She just can't give them to someone else unless ordered by a court to do so.[54]

Congress clearly intended to provide broad privacy protection to the individual, both inside and outside of our homes. What is less clear is the extent to which, or even whether, Congress intended to protect individuals in their capacity as employees from privacy invasions by their employers. When employers access stored data for reasons other than system maintenance, corporate security or suspicion of illegal conduct, they may become vulnerable to invasion of privacy claims. And data captured for a legally permissible purpose, such as system maintenance or monitoring against theft, may not necessarily be used for other purposes.[55]

Even though employees do have limited privacy rights in the workplace – mostly related to issues concerning modesty and non-business matters – employers clearly have the upper hand in this struggle. Employers have both rights and expectations regarding the use of company-owned systems. Here are a few basic considerations:

*Employer rights.* An employer has the right to:

- intercept and review e-mail messages generated, transmitted, stored or received on a company-owned or leased system;
- conduct an e-mail audit to determine how the system is being used, when, and under what conditions, for what purposes and by whom;
- disclose certain e-mail content to third parties if an appropriate authority (postmaster or system administrator) suspects or discovers illegal or unauthorized use;
- require employee training in e-mail system use;
- receive employee acknowledgment of training and understanding of e-mail system policy guidelines, restrictions and limitations.[56]

*Employer expectations.* An employer may reasonably expect that:

- company-owned e-mail systems will be used principally or exclusively for official business purposes;
- employees will not use company-owned e-mail systems for profit, private gain or personally owned businesses;
- employees will not use company-owned systems for illegal purposes;
- employees will not use company-owned systems for unauthorized disclosure of proprietary data or confidential information;
- employees will not use company-owned systems to send inappropriate messages, including rude or discourteous messages, sexually harassing messages, sexist or racist language, profane language, obscene language or graphic images, or correspond with unauthorized addresses.[57]

Here are a few common questions most employees have regarding workplace monitoring and their rights to privacy:

**Can my employer listen to my phone calls at work?** In most instances, yes. For example, employers may monitor calls with clients or customers for training purposes to assure quality control. Federal law, however, which regulates phone calls with people outside the state, does not allow unannounced monitoring for business-related calls.

An important exception is made for personal calls. Under federal case law, when an employer realizes the call is personal, he or she must immediately stop monitoring the call. However, when employees are told not to make personal calls from specified business phones, the employee then takes the risk that calls on those phones may be monitored.[58]

**Can my employer obtain a record of my phone calls?** This type of monitoring is easy. Telephone numbers dialed from phone extensions can be recorded by a device called a pen register. It allows an employer to see a list of phone numbers dialed by your extension and the length of each call. Cellular service providers now routinely offer calling logs for a small monthly fee.

A programming concept called "presence awareness" is able to determine whether a PC, cell phone or wireless device is turned on or in use. A new system now permits tracking technology such as global positioning systems (GPS) to detect the location of a person whose cell phone or PDA is turned on or in use. Parents may see this technology as extremely valuable, while teenagers or employees who'd like to spend the day at the ballpark may be less enthusiastic.[59]

**Can my employer watch my computer terminal while I work?** Generally, yes. Because your employer owns the computer network and terminals, he or she is free to use them to monitor employees. Most employees are given some protection from electronic monitoring under certain circumstances. Union contracts, for example, may limit an employer's right to monitor. If employers state in a written document that they do not monitor their employees, they are bound by the agreement, with just a few limited exceptions.[60]

**What sort of things can an employer monitor?** All kinds of stuff. Inexpensive software and easy-to-operate hardware make it possible for almost any employer to know who has company-provided Internet access, who's online, what they're watching, how often and for how long. Most firms keep a Top 10 "Hit Parade" of most popular sites frequented by their employees. New software will now permit an employer to follow what's happening on each employee's computer screen as it happens. It's a useful technology when you need technical support: An IT specialist can simply "reach out" to your screen, control your mouse movements and address the problem you've encountered. The software permits an employer to follow literally everything you do, keystroke-by-keystroke, and keep a record of it even if you never save it or send it anywhere. Many employers see that capability as a valuable security feature. Many employees think it's just creepy.

**How can I tell if I am being monitored?** You can't. Most computer monitoring equipment allows employers to monitor without an employee's knowledge. Some employers, however, do notify their workers that monitoring takes place. That sort of information may be contained in memos, employee handbooks, union contracts, on a user information screen that appears when your computer boots up or on a sticker attached to your computer. Look carefully. Even though they are not legally required to do so, most employers will tell you if they are monitoring your work. The reason? If you know they're watching, you're more likely to behave yourself.

**Is my voice mail private?** Not really. Voice mail and e-mail are regarded as being nearly the same in the eyes of the law (and your employer). The telephones, switching equipment and the computer hard drives on which the voice mail is stored are the property of the company that employs you and the company can access, store and listen to anyone's voice mail. A Cincinnati, Ohio, newspaper got into big trouble a few years ago when one of its reporters hacked into the voice mail system of Chiquita Brands, the banana importer. Many folks were surprised at how easily an outsider could listen to other people's passcode-protected voice messages.

**Is there any way I can keep my e-mail and other work private?** Yes, but your employer may not like it. He may, in fact, forbid it. You could encrypt personal e-mail messages before you send them. Most encryption programs will translate your message into gibberish and require the same program and a password to decipher the text on the other end. You can purchase commercial encryption software to work with your e-mail program or download a copy of the freeware version of the Pretty Good Privacy program from the link at www.openpgp.org.[61] Other companies, including ziplip.com, offer similar programs.[62] Liquid Machines of San Francisco now makes the equivalent of an e-mail shredder that automatically destroys e-mail in 30 minutes or 30 days. When the detonation time is reached, the encryption key inserted into the messages is voided, making all copies of the e-mail permanently unreadable, including forwarded copies.[63]

**What about text messages? There's no way they can monitor those . . . is there?** By now, you should have figured out that your employer can monitor just about anything, and that includes SMS texts and AOL Instant Messenger. At the annual meeting of Sonalysts, a software and consulting company in Waterford, Connecticut, systems analyst Randy Dickson recently drove home the point that even a few quick remarks flying among instant messages could be picked up by the company's computer surveillance. He displayed a document that showed a conversation between two employees whose names were blacked out. With only a few lines of text, the gist was clear. Here were the words of two employees using what Mr. Dickson called "less than professional" language to talk about a colleague. "Instant messaging is very loose and chatty, almost like a conversation," he said. Those exchanges were evidence that people divulge more than they should – and that without persistent monitoring, the company could be at risk. Secret projects could be leaked and offensive language could be forwarded inside and outside the office.[64]

Instant messaging (IM) is invading and changing the workplace. Employees started to sneak instant messaging into the office in the late 1990s, but now companies are endorsing it. Faster and more casual than e-mail, IM can foster broader collaboration among employees even as it further blurs the boundaries between work and life. About 43 percent of U.S. employees use instant messaging at work.[65] Tech consultant Gartner Inc. projects that IM will be the "de facto tool for voice, video and text chat" for 95 percent of employees in big companies within five years.[66] As any corporate IM user will tell you, however, IM has its trade-offs. If people know you're in the office or working from home and logged-on, maintaining privacy and avoiding distractions becomes much more difficult. In many workplaces, failing to respond quickly to an IM is considered rude, so workers have an incentive to sign out when they leave the office or show themselves as "busy" when they know they can't reply for a while.

With most systems, others must agree to be on your buddy list. "Presence," says Microsoft product manager Chris Niehaus, "has to be managed." At some companies, though, anyone on IM can be added to the buddy list. At IBM, for example, some 220,000 employees worldwide are registered for IM. Users can search for in-house experts on subjects such as database integration or designing Web ads and see which of them are available for a quick IM question.[67]

One other by-product of IM is beginning to appear in the nation's elementary and secondary schools. Do you recognize this list: *u, r, ur, b4, wuz, cuz, 2*? These TM/IM shortcuts are creeping into student papers and, to say the least, teachers are not impressed. "Kids should know the difference," says Jacqueline Harding, an eighth-grade English teacher at Viking Middle School in Gurnee, Illinois. "They should know where to draw the line between formal writing and conversational writing."[68] The conventions of IM are an important part of how students communicate and – in that context – nearly everyone agrees it's not wrong, it's just part of how IM works. The important issue students and others who use IM regularly must understand is that the expectations of the reader will govern which style to use. For paper-based inter-office memos, an informal style will work, but readers still expect conventional punctuation, spelling and paragraph organization. For business letters sent outside the organization, the standard is even higher because business relationships are won and lost on the impressions that readers gather from the documents they receive.

## ETIQUETTE AND OFFICE ELECTRONICS

The distinction between home and office has virtually disappeared. And so have many of the instincts that govern our behavior when we work, relax and socialize. Communication behaviors somehow seem to top the list of issues that puzzle, irritate and (yes) aggravate everyone from members of our family to coworkers and clients. Here are a few suggestions for managing new technology and the expectations of those around us:

### Cell Phones

They are an astounding invention, but one with the power to enrage as well as reassure. The basic problem with cellular telephones is that so many people have them and many of them feel compelled to use them literally everywhere. According to industry analysts, more people own cell phones than computers, and today more than 5 billion mobile phones are in use around the globe.[69] In the U.S., more than 311 million adults owned or used cellular telephones by 2018.[70,71]

That translates to about 95 percent of Americans owning a mobile phone.[72] What guidelines might govern their appropriate use? With some important exceptions, the following rules apply:

- Unless it's an absolute emergency, turn your phone off while you're driving. It's not simply a distraction, it's downright dangerous. In many states, it's now illegal to text and drive or use a handheld set to speak while you drive.
- Unless you're a doctor or employee-on-call, turn it off when you're in a restaurant, theater, concert, religious service or any other location where people expect some measure of privacy and quiet. If you must leave it on, switch your phone to vibrate and leave the immediate area before you answer or return the call.
- Don't assume everyone else within 500 meters is interested in hearing your half of the conversation. Lower your voice and respect other people's need for peace and quiet.
- Don't assume that because your employees own a cell phone they are available (or eager) to talk business 24 hours a day, seven days a week. They have lives outside of the office and would like to live them without talking to you.

A scientific poll commissioned by online wireless retailer LetsTalk found that, in the past five years, the percentage of Americans who are willing to use their cell phones in public places, including movies, restaurants and public transportation, decreased significantly. The study, conducted by Wirthlin Worldwide, also found that less than half of Americans find it acceptable to use their cell phones while in a car and only 10 percent find it appropriate to use a cell phone while at school. Surprisingly, 28 percent said it was acceptable to take a call while in a restaurant.[73]

"Despite an overall increase in cell phone usage," said Delly Tamer, President and CEO of LetsTalk:

Americans appear to be much more cognizant of their cell phone etiquette. It's important to recognize that Americans are beginning to self-police their wireless etiquette, especially as leaders evaluate the pros and cons of banning cell phone usage in public places.[74]

### Voice Mail

If you do not have an administrative assistant or someone to answer the phone for you while you're out, voice mail can be especially helpful. It's most helpful when you learn to use it properly:

- Keep your outgoing message brief: "This is Jim O'Rourke in the Fanning Center. Please leave a message and I'll get back to you soon." Note the somewhat vague use of the word *soon*. If people are required to listen to more than 10 to 15 seconds of greeting, or are required to listen to more than three "press 1 now" options, they'll grow frustrated and may simply hang up.
- Related to the overly long greeting is the new-greeting-everyday approach:

    Today is Monday, September 9th. I'll be in the office today, but have meetings at nine thirty, eleven fifteen, and three o'clock. I appreciate your business and am very sorry I'm not here to take your call. However, if you leave your name, number and a message, I'll return your call just as quickly as I can.

    Those five sentences are not much more helpful than just saying, "Leave a message and I'll call you back." One outgoing message will do the trick, unless you plan to be gone for a week.
- Tell people how to get past the outgoing message. Every voice mail system has a command that lets callers bypass the message. If your outgoing message has a number of options for listeners, just say, "You can skip this message by pressing the pound key" or whatever command your system uses for that purpose.

- If you're leaving a voice mail message, identify yourself, give your callback number, and explain *briefly* why you're calling. Don't leave a five-minute message when you can leave a 30-second message. And before you hang up, give the listener your number one more time.
- Unless you can shut the door to your office, don't listen to your voice mail messages on the speaker phone. Pick up the receiver, download your messages and give others in the office a chance to concentrate on their own work.

### E-mail

We already spoke at length about the risks and responsibilities involved in using electronic mail. Here are a few suggestions for making the system more civilized:

- Don't send e-mails that make angry demands. "I must have an answer by 2 p.m. tomorrow. Repeat, by 2 p.m." You have no idea what's happening in the life of the message recipient and can only guess at how he'll react to your demands. Such demands are better if they are toned down and written in the conditional: "Unless I hear from you by tomorrow, we may not be able to ship your order on time. If it's convenient, could you let me know of your selections?"
- Don't waste our time with the latest "jokes du jour," sent to hundreds of e-mail addresses, including mine. In fact, if that's all you send, please rethink the value of an e-mail address book.
- Please don't order people to visit your Web page or "like" you on Facebook. Ask nicely and your readers may think about it. Tell them about the interesting and useful information they'll find there, and they may see the logic in your request.
- Please don't write to anyone in all-lower case letters, or SHOUT AT YOUR READERS IN ALL-CAPITAL LETTERS. Please include proper punctuation, conventional spelling and customary paragraph and document structure, which may include headings and subheads, bulleted items or numbered lists. Make your message brief, clean and inviting to read.
- Do not ever insult, malign, harass or demean your readers or anyone else in the e-mail messages you write. Please don't spread rumors or say things that you know to be untrue. You just never know who's going to save your message and later use it to your detriment.
- Please include a salutation, complimentary close and – in the first paragraph or two – a statement of purpose. Tell your readers why you've written to them. Be polite and treat them with respect.[75]

## WORKING VIRTUALLY

"I can't figure out how people could operate a business today without virtual teams," says Elizabeth Allen, vice president for corporate communication at Dell Computer. From the corporate headquarters in Round Rock, Texas, Ms. Allen talks with her global communication team by teleconference every working day. On others, they will schedule a videoconference. Her e-mail is open constantly, providing a link to employees, clients, journalists, colleagues and other executives in the firm.[76]

Everyone uses e-mail, the telephone and many of us participate in the occasional videoconference. So what makes Dell different from other organizations? For one thing, the company actively discourages the possession and storage of paper. "I have a lovely office," said Ms. Allen, "but it has no filing cabinets, no lateral files, and not much of anywhere to put paper. We do just about everything electronically here, and we have plenty of storage space for that – online and on disk." She also mentioned that postal service mail gets delivered once a week at Dell. "If you're expecting something, you'll have to walk down to the mail room and pick it up. The incentives here to use e-mail and electronic storage are huge."[77]

Many firms are working in different ways today for obvious reasons. "When we talk, 'virtual organizations,'" says Dana Meade, retired chairman and CEO of Tenneco, "we are really talking about dramatically different ways of organizing capital, technology, information, people, and other assets than we utilized in the past."[78] Professor Sandra Collins documents the trend in her book, *Communication in a Virtual Organization*, noting that organizations, groups and teams have moved from a physical environment to a virtual environment to save money, increase efficiency, raise productivity and span everything from organizational boundaries to international time zones.[79]

Managing work with virtual tools is growing rapidly in popularity. An estimated 3.7 million Americans telecommuted, or worked away from the office more than half the time, in 2017. Between 2013 and 2014, the percentage of employees who telecommuted grew by 5.6 percent while the employee population only increased by 1.9 percent[80] According to Gallup, 43 percent of employed Americans spent at least some time working remotely.[81] Some were in the next cubicle as they connected with virtual teammates around the world. Others stayed home and logged on to a company server to do their work. Still others drove to a nearby telework center to avoid a long or costly trip into a central metropolitan area.[82]

## Advantages

The advantages of working virtually may be grouped into three basic categories: cost, productivity and access.

## Cost

Paying less for office space and employee support is certainly among the most obvious of cost advantages. Jack Heacock is a member of the International Telework Association and Council's executive committee. "At 10:45 a.m. on any particular day, 40 to 60 percent of employees are somewhere other than their offices. Walk around and see for yourself," he says.

"Then ask yourself why you are investing in real estate space you don't need." [83]

## Productivity

Efficiency and productivity can easily increase when people are offered the opportunity to work from home, to contact the office when they're traveling, or to work whenever or wherever they may have the opportunity. Professor Collins documented reduced absenteeism and increased employee retention as results of telecommuting.[84] Merrill Lynch implemented telecommuting nearly 20 years ago and today has more than 3,500 employees who work from home one to four days a week. Managers at Merrill report that they saw an average of 3.5 fewer sick days per year and a 6 percent decrease in turnover among the telecommuters during the first year of the program.[85] Merrill Lynch also saw a 10 to 50 percent increase in productivity with its telecommuters, while other organizations, including IBM, AT&T and American Express, have reported similar gains.[86]

## Access

Among the most important benefits to a company can be access, not only to its own employees at unusual times and places but to others as well. The ability to delegate work to part-time employees or free agents who can assist in project management or work against specified deadlines means that regular employees can be free to work on issues that may require face-to-face contact with coworkers. John Byrne of *Bloomberg Business Week* magazine says that the emergence of a virtual workforce means that "many outfits will depend on free agents and outside contractors to develop products faster than ever."[87]

## Disadvantages

If telecommuting, Web-based organizations, and virtual teams provide so many obvious advantages, why aren't more people taking part in them? The answers vary, but generally touch on one of several issues: costs, technology, culture and people.

## Costs

The initial outlay to purchase equipment can be significant. Equipping each worker with a laptop, printer, phone lines and software can easily exceed several thousand dollars.[88] "When everyone works from a centralized location," says Professor Collins, "all of the most expensive equipment can be shared. Not so with off-site workers."[89]

## Technology

Managers have concerns about providing technical support to remote workers and, as you very likely already know, there are only so many problems that an IT specialist can help you with over the phone. When the printer jams, you either fix it yourself or work on something else.

## Culture

In many organizations, telecommuting is appreciated, valued and rewarded. In others, it is not. "Out of sight, out of mind," may mean that telecommuters aren't given the same opportunities for training, advancement or promotion. In still other organizations, managers may be reluctant (or forbidden) to let an employee leave the building with sensitive or confidential data. Client records, government research or products-in-development may require that they and the people working on them remain in the office.

## People

Finally, it's easy to see why some people just wouldn't want to work from home. Many people develop a sense of their own self-worth from the location in which they work. They take pride in their office, enjoy socializing and interacting with their coworkers and colleagues, and find the climate in their work locations energizing and inspiring. Sitting at home in your bathrobe, thinking of all the housework (or other things) you could be doing may not prove either inspirational or productive. Issues ranging from frequency of communication to the development of trust may depend on having a workforce located in the same place.[90]

## TELECONFERENCING AND WEBINARS

The idea of teleconferencing, or using the basics of telephone and television technology to conduct a meeting with people in distant locations, has been around for many years. Educators have used low-cost video cameras and codec (coder-decoder) systems since the 1960s to link people to courses distributed from a central location. Businesses with geographically separated offices and production facilities have used teleconference systems to share everything from marketing plans to high-tech expertise across time zones and oceans.

The problem for so long with teleconferencing, however, was twofold: high cost and low quality. Fuzzy, streaky images flipped across the screens of hideously expensive two-way telecom systems. Speakers sounded as if they were trapped in a barrel, and visual aids such as flipcharts, 35-mm slides and overhead transparencies were risky at best. During the flush years of a good economy in the 1980s and 1990s, flying people here and there didn't seem expensive or difficult.

After 2001, many firms began to rethink the value of teleconference meetings. Recently, prices for relatively high-quality visual images have come down dramatically, and telecom providers have begun to develop both expertise and marketing approaches that have made teleconferencing remarkably easier and much less expensive. With the advent of Internet Webcasting, many firms have discovered that they can push images from a central location that employees can access from anywhere on earth. According to 3M Corporation's Michael Begeman, "The only ones who could afford videoconferencing a few years ago were really big companies." Begeman manages 3M's meeting network and now thinks that declining costs have "suddenly put videoconferencing into the price range of small companies."[91]

Inexpensive desktop cameras and easy-to-use software now make the average manager a potential teleconference participant in a matter of minutes. Cisco's TelePresence, the top-tier teleconferencing software and hardware for business, is redefining the playing field for immersiveness and clarity in virtual meetings. (It's almost as if you're there.)[92] As the technology has proliferated, several free alternatives (such as Skype, Viber and Google Hangouts) are reliable enough to fulfill the needs of companies that prioritize affordability.

The technology isn't foolproof, though. It's still difficult to get everyone you hope to include in a meeting on the same page at the same time of day. And while the technology is already quite robust and sophisticated, it is still common to lose your connection with one or more of the locations in a conference. The day when we can all connect with direct network line, simply by tapping a teleconference icon, isn't far off (think: FaceTime on your iPhone). To make the teleconference meetings, interviews and training sessions you are almost certain to participate in during the next few years as productive as possible, consider the following suggestions.

First, plan carefully. As you will read in Chapter 12 of this book, business meetings are time consuming, troublesome to plan and execute, and a lot more expensive than you might imagine. That includes teleconference meetings, as well. The most basic rule of meetings is simple: Don't ever schedule a meeting if you can achieve your communication goals in some other way. If e-mail or paper will work better, do it. If a voice mail message will convey your thoughts less expensively and more effectively, don't ask people to take an hour of their day to sit and listen to you speak.

That said, on some occasions meetings are unavoidable. If a teleconference will assist in achieving your goals, please think about the following ideas before you make the arrangements to conduct a virtual video meeting:

- *Identify the purpose of your teleconference meeting.* Explain to people what they will be doing and why. Be clear about your objectives in asking for their time.
- *Identify the person who will chair the meeting.* A leaderless teleconference will often end in confusion and disaster. Name one person who will be responsible for starting, stopping and running the conference. That person should be someone known to all or most of the participants and someone who can follow the agenda and keep things moving.
- *Plan the agenda.* Meetings frequently veer off-course when the organizer decides to "wing it" or just gather the participants and see what happens. A specific agenda with easy-to-accomplish items listed first will always help, as long as the conference leader can keep the group focused on those issues.
- *Distribute the agenda.* Give participants a chance to plan for the meeting by telling them in advance what you plan to discuss. They may wish to gather information or share key documents with others before the meeting.
- *Schedule the teleconference.* Select a time and date when you know for sure that all (or the majority) of your participants can dial in or show up at a conference center. Make certain that all of your indispensable participants are aware of the schedule and have agreed to be available.
- *Confirm the teleconference with the participants.* Planning for meetings of this sort often takes place days or weeks in advance of the event. It's easy for participants to forget when it will take place, where they should be or what the access codes are. Send more than one reminder as the day and time approach.
- *Share important resource materials with participants.* Send another copy of the agenda along with materials you think are important for everyone to have before the meeting begins. Don't waste teleconference airtime as people read through key documents or learn for the first time what the data mean and why they matter. Posting such information on a company intranet and sending a Web link in your reminder e-mail may be helpful.

Planning a teleconference and actually conducting one are two separate issues. No one can guarantee that your participants will all show up, will have read the materials you sent or will be in agreement with the agenda, or will even care about the subjects you plan to discuss, even if you have planned meticulously. In order to give your teleconference a better chance of success, consider these ideas:

- *Get to the conference site early.* If you're in charge of a teleconference, make sure you have an opportunity to check out the setting, meet the support technician (if you have one on site) and learn what your responsibilities for the equipment will involve. Once you walk into a room for a videoconference, avoid idle talk or unguarded comments. Assume that someone is watching and listening.
- *Watch what you wear.* Avoid lots of white, red or black. White reflects too much light, causing your face to appear dark. Black clothing causes the face to appear overexposed, and red tends to smear. Consider a light blue shirt instead of white, and choose solid colors over complex patterns. Mr. Begeman of 3M advises people to stay away from small prints, thin stripes, and plaids. Bulky or baggy clothing can make you look heavier on screen, and tinted eyeglasses give you raccoon eyes. Glittery or dangling jewelry is distracting.[93]
- *Act as if people are watching you.* Quirky mannerisms that may go unnoticed in a face-to-face meeting are magnified in a videoconference and can detract from the image you are trying to project. Avoid playing with your hair, your eyeglasses, a pencil or your nose. Rocking back and forth in your chair can be equally distracting. If you behave as though you are on stage, you're more likely to project the professional image you're hoping others will see.

- *Start on time.* Make a promise to your participants about time and keep it. If you begin on time, every time, you will encourage others to be there precisely as you begin. Reward those who are there at the start of the meeting with important or useful information. Explain to latecomers that they can catch up on what they've missed by accessing the intranet site devoted to the group's activities or by downloading an e-mail attachment you will send as a follow-up to the conference.

- *Take control of the conference.* Being in control does not mean talking all the time. It merely means providing others with an opportunity, at appropriate moments, to share what they know, ask questions and make comments. Your goals for the meeting should include widespread participation from all of those invited to join you.

- *Ask participants to introduce themselves as you begin.* Give each participant an opportunity to explain who and where they are. And as you do, be careful to mention anyone who may be in the room but out of camera range. Knowing that your boss is watching, unseen from the back of the room, could be useful information for people in other locations.

- *Jot down people's names and locations.* Knowing who is participating in the teleconference by name, title and location will be helpful as you call on them or ask for their participation.

- *Ask participants to identify themselves when they speak for the first time.* Even with high-resolution video cameras, not everyone will recognize or know everyone else. A simple introduction ("This is John Kamp in Washington") will let everyone know who is speaking.

- *Speak a bit more slowly to ensure that everyone can understand you.* Videoconferencing systems are not as sophisticated as television broadcast studios, and many people are tempted to speak at once. As you develop a little more confidence and know that people are paying attention, you can resume a more conversational pace.

- *Avoid side conversations.* Conversations among two or three participants at one location can be distracting. First, not all participants are aware that everyone can hear what they say (or see what they do), and second, mute buttons are provided for occasions when you must speak to someone else privately.

- *Be patient if the system includes a slight delay.* Some videoconferencing systems feature a slight delay in the transmission of voice and picture images. Check out the system before your meeting begins, and if you discover that it has such a delay, explain its effect to the participants as you begin. Be prepared for overlapping dialogue and long pauses. Speak more slowly, let people know when you are finished talking so they can have their turn, and try not to interrupt.

- *Use the camera properly.* You should do your best to look at the camera lens at least half (or more) of the time you are speaking. If you are responding to a difficult or sensitive question, you'll enhance your credibility dramatically if you focus squarely on the camera. Participants at other locations will feel more comfortable if it appears you are addressing them directly. Further, be mindful of visual aesthetics. Ensure the backdrop is professional and avoid presenting in front of a window.

- *Don't read a speech or prepared statement.* Such statements are something you can share with people in advance unless the information is confidential or embargoed for release at a specific time.

- *Summarize key issues as you move along.* Interim summaries can serve as transitional devices. Refer to the agenda and remind people of elapsed time as you move from point to point.

- *Establish what's next for the group.* Tell participants if you expect them to be a part of your next teleconference. Ask them to make a note of the time and date if you have already established those. Summarize the issues discussed and remind the group of any actions they may have agreed to.

- *Stop on time.* If you specified a one-hour meeting, don't let it run for 75 minutes. Keep this promise, just as you kept your promise to start on time. Time is clearly among the most valuable (and limited) commodities your colleagues have. Be respectful of how you use it.

- *Prepare and distribute minutes of the teleconference.* Ask or appoint someone (yourself, perhaps) to take notes and provide a brief summary of what happened and what the participants agreed to. Share those notes with all participants promptly – within a few days – of the meeting, if only as a reminder of the business goals you hoped to achieve by gathering everyone together.[94]

## FOR FURTHER READING

Argenti, P. and C. M. Barnes. *Digital Strategies for Powerful Corporate Communications*. New York, NY: Mc-Graw-Hill, 2009.

Belson, K. "Four Score and . . . Mind If I Take This?" *The New York Times*, Sunday September 30, 2007, p. WK-5.

Byron, K. "Carrying Too Heavy a Load? The Communication and Miscommunication of Emotion by E-mail," *Academy of Management Review*, January 2008.

"Facebook, Instant Messaging and Twitter Are Most Popular Social Media Tools," *PR Newswire*. August 4, 2010.

Lohr, S. "Slow Down, Multitaskers; Don't Read in Traffic," *The New York Times*, March 25, 2007. Online at www.nytimes.com. Accessed March 25, 2007 at 10:25 p.m.

Mamberto, C. "Instant Messaging Invades the Office," *The Wall Street Journal*, July 24, 2007, pp. B1–B2.

Mindlin, A. "You've Got Someone Reading Your E-Mail," *The New York Times*, June 12, 2006. Online at www.nytimes.com. Accessed June 12, 2006 at 8:35 p.m.

Richtel, M. "Digital Devices Deprive Brain of Needed Downtime," *The New York Times*, August 25, 2010, p. B1.

Robinson, J. "Blunt the E-Mail Interruption Assault," *Entrepreneur.com*, March 12, 2010. Online at www.msnbc.msn.com/id/35689822.

Sharma, A. and J. E. Vascellaro. "Those IMs Aren't as Private as You Think," *The Wall Street Journal*, October 4, 2006, p. D1.

Shellenbarger, S. "A Day Without Email Is Like . . . ," *The Wall Street Journal*, October 11, 2007, pp. D1–D2.

Shipley, D. and W. Schwalbe. *Send: The Essential Guide to Email for Office and Home*. New York: Alfred A. Knopf, 2007.

Villano, M. "E-Mail in Haste, Panic at Leisure," *The New York Times*, September 3, 2006, p. BU-10.

Weber, Larry. *Sticks & Stones: How Digital Business Reputations Are Created Over Time and Lost in a Click*. Hoboken, NJ: John Wiley & Sons, 2009.

Wortham, J. "Everyone Is Using Cellphones, but not so Many Are Talking," *The New York Times*, May 14, 2010, pp. A1, B4.

## NOTES

1 Ronson, Jon. "How One Stupid Tweet Blew Up Justine Sacco's Life," *The New York Times Magazine*, February 12, 2015.

2 Negroponte, N. *Being Digital*. New York: Alfred A. Knopf, 1995.

3 Number of Computers Sold Worldwide in 2009 Rose—Gartner. Online at www.fortune500global.com/news/number-of-computers-sold-worldwide-in-2009-rose-gartner/. Accessed January 3, 2011 at 1:05 p.m.

4 "Computers Sold This Year," IDC. Online at www.worldometers.info/computers/. Accessed June 19, 2018 at 9:46 a.m.

5 *Census: Computer Ownership, Internet Connection Varies Widely Across U.S.*. Pew Research Center. Full report available online at www.pewresearch.org/fact-tank/2014/09/19/census-computer-ownership-internet-connection-varies-widely-across-u-s/.

6 Boulger, C. A. *e-Technology and the Fourth Economy*. Cincinnati, OH: Thomson South-Western, 2003.

7 *Census*. Pew Research Center.

8 Percentage of Households in the United States with a Computer at Home from 1984 to 2015. Statista. Online at www.statista.com/statistics/214641/household-adoption-rate-of-computer-in-the-us-since-1997/. Accessed December 1, 2018 at 7:48 p.m. EST.

9 Richtel, M. "Lost in E-Mail, Tech Firms Face Self-Made Beast," *The New York Times*, June 14, 2008, pp. A1, A14.

10 Murphy, Mark. "Interruptions at Work Are Killing Your Productivity," *Forbes*, October 30, 2016.

11 Richtel. "Lost in E-Mail, Tech Firms Face Self-Made Beast," p. 29.

12 SexTracker.com. Online at http://links.sextracker.com/search.amp?q=Busiest+times+of+day&SUBMIT=Search. Accessed December 1, 2018 at 7:56 p.m. EST.

13 "New Study Says E-Mail May Cost British Companies Worktime," Reuters News Service. Online at www.msnbc.com/news/614783.asp. Accessed August 20, 2001.

14 "E-mail Policy: Why Your Company Needs One," Email-policy.com. Online at www.email-policy.com. Accessed August 29, 2002.

15 "Pew Survey: College Net Use at 86%," Associated Press. Online at www.msnbc.com/news/8708450.asp. Accessed September 15, 2002.

16 Kvavik, R. B. "Convenience, Communications, and Control: How Students Use Technology," EDUCAUSE Center for Applied Research and University of Minnesota, Twin Cities. Online at www.educause.edu/Resources/EducatingtheNetGeneration/Convenience CommunicationsandCo/6070. Accessed Saturday, August 27, 2011 at 2:17 p.m. (EST).

17 Ibid.

18 Nations, Daniel. "What is Social Media?" About.com. Online at http://webtrends.about.com/od/web20/a/social-media.htm. Accessed January 3, 2011 at 3:40 p.m.

19 Facebook Newsroom. Online at https://newsroom.fb.com/company-info/. Accessed June 29, 2018 at 10:04 a.m.

20   Aslam, Salman. "Twitter by the Numbers: Stats, Demographics & Fun Facts," *Omnicore.* Online at www.omnicoreagency. com/twitter-statistics/. Accessed June 19, 2018 at 10:07 a.m.

21   YouTube for Press. Online at www.youtube.com/yt/about/press/. Accessed June 19, 2018 at 10:19 a.m.

22   "Number of Monthly Active Instagram Users from January 2013 to September 2017 (in Millions)," Statista. Online at www. statista.com/statistics/253577/number-of-monthly-active-instagram-users/. Accessed June 19, 2018 at 10:23 a.m.

23   Sloane, Garett. "Oh Snap! Shares Soar as Snapchat Reports 9 Million More Daily Users and an Ad Surge," *AdAge.* February 6, 2018.

24   "Social Media and Internet." Online at www.onlineuniversities.com/careercounselor/office-etiquette/social-me dia-andinternet. Accessed January 3, 2011 at 3:59 p.m.

25   "OMG You Will Never Guess What Happened at Work Today!!: Social Media Guidelines," *Gap, Inc.*

26   Samuel, Alexandra. "Using Social Media Without Jeopardizing Your Career," *Harvard Business Review,* July 20, 2015.

27   "How Many Email are Sent Every Day? And Other Top Email Statistics Your Business Needs to Know," *Templafy,* September 1, 2017.

28   Campbell, Denis. "Email Stress—The New Office Workers' Plague," *Guardian.co.uk/The Observer.* Online at www.guardian. co.uk/technology/2007/aug/12/news/print. Accessed Monday, January 3, 2011 at 1:54 p.m.

29   Taylor, C. "12 Steps for E-Mail Addicts," Time.com. Online at: www.time.com/time/columnist/printout/ 0,8816,257188,00.html. Accessed June 3, 2002.

30   Canabou, C. "A Message About Managing E-Mail," *Fast Company,* 49 (August 2001), p. 38.

31   Taylor. "12 Steps for E-Mail Addicts," p. 2.

32   Cohen, J. "An E-Mail Affliction: The Long Goodbye," *The New York Times,* May 9, 2002, p. C5. Copyright © 2002 by The New York Times Company. Reprinted with permission.

33   Ibid.

34   Brown, Paul B. "After E-Mail," *The New York Times,* August 18, 2007, p. B5.

35   McLaughlin, L. "Essentials of E-Mail Etiquette," PCWorld.com. Online at www.pcworld.com/article/80624/essen tials_of_email_etiquette.html. Accessed August 11, 2002.

36   Ibid.

37   Kirsner, S. "The Elements of E-Mail Style," October 2001. Online at www.darwinmag.com, p. 22.

38   Rozakis, B., L. Rozakis and R. Maniscalco. *The Complete Idiot's Guide to Office Politics.* New York: Pearson/MacMillan Distribution, 1998.

39   Rossman, Katherine. "YU Luv Texts, H8 Calls," *The Wall Street Journal,* October 14, 2010, pp. D1–D2.

40   Cohen-Sheffer, Nathalie. "Text Message Response Times and What They Really Mean," *Rakuten Viber,* November 6, 2017.

41   Twenge, Jean M. *iGen: Why Today's Super-Connected Kids Are Growing Up Less Rebellious, More Tolerant, Less Happy—and Completely Unprepared for Adulthood (and What That Means for the Rest of Us).* Simon & Schuster, 2017.

42   Rossman. "YU Luv Texts, H8 Calls."

43   Ibid.

44   Ibid.

45   Ibid. See also Wortham, Jenna. "Everyone is Using Cellphones but not so Many Are Talking," *The New York Times,* May 14, 2010, pp. A1, B4.

46   Meeks, B. "Is Privacy Possible in the Digital Age?" MSNBC.com. Online at www.msnbc.com/news/498514.asp. Accessed January 22, 2002.

47   Biersdorfer, J. D. "Privacy Can Be Elusive in the World of E-Mail," *The New York Times,* July 27, 2000, p. D4. Copyright © 2000 by The New York Times Company. Reprinted with permission.

48   "2005 Electronic Monitoring and Surveillance Survey," *American Management Association and the e-Policy Institute.* Online at www.amanet.org/research/index.htm.

49   "Outbound e-Mail Security and Content Compliance in Today's Enterprise, 2005." Results from a survey by Proofpoint, Inc., fielded by Forrester Consulting on outbound e-mail content issues, May 2005. Reprinted by permission. Online at www. proofpoint.com/outbound. Accessed August 4–5, 2005. See also "Many Firms Snooping on Work-Related E-mail," *MSNBC,* June 2, 2006. Online at www.msnbc.msn.com. Accessed July 6, 2006 at 3:35 p.m.

50   Hattori, J. "Workplace E-Mail is not Your Own," *CNN.com.* Online at www.cnn.com/2002/TECH/internet/06/03/e.mail. monitoring/index.html. Accessed June 3, 2002 and August 4–5, 2005.

51   Conlin, M. "Workers, Surf at Your Own Risk," *BusinessWeek,* June 12, 2000, p. 105.

52   Hawkins, D. "Lawsuits Spur Rise in Employee Monitoring," *U.S. News & World Report,* August 13, 2001, p. 53.

53   The Electronic Communications Privacy Act of 1986 has been amended by the Communications Assistance for Law Enforcement Act of 1994, the USA PATRIOT Act of 2001, The USA PATRIOT reauthorization acts of 2006, and the FISA Amendments Act of 2008.

54   Hartman, D. B. and K. S. Nantz. *The 3 Rs of E-Mail: Rights, Risks, and Responsibilities.* Beverly Hills, CA: Crisp Publications, 1996, pp. 68–79.

55   Ibid.

56  For a more thorough discussion of employer rights and corporate-owned electronic mail systems, see Hartman and Nantz, *The 3 Rs of E-Mail*, pp. 51–79.

57  For a more thorough discussion of employer rights and corporate-owned electronic mail systems, see Hartman and Nantz, *The 3 Rs of E-Mail*, pp. 51–79.

58  "How Much Snooping Can the Boss Really Do?" *MSNBC.com*. Online at www.msnbc.com/news/498495.asp. Accessed January 22, 2002. Used by permission. See also the Privacy Rights Clearinghouse at www.privacyrights.org.

59  Guernsey, L. "You Can Surf, but You Can't Hide," *The New York Times*, February 7, 2002, p. D1. Copyright © 2002 by The New York Times Company. Reprinted with permission.

60  Ibid.

61  Biersdorfer. "Privacy Can Be Elusive in the World of E-Mail," p. D4.

62  Guernsey, L. "Free Service Is a Way to Keep Prying Eyes Off Your E-Mail," *The New York Times*, July 15, 1999, p. D3. Copyright © 1999 by The New York Times Company. Reprinted with permission.

63  Byron, E. "Omniva Lets E-Mail Disappear Without a Trace," *The Wall Street Journal*, September 6, 2001, p. B7. Reprinted by permission of *The Wall Street Journal*, Copyright © 2001 Dow Jones & Company, Inc. All rights reserved worldwide.

64  Guernsey, L. "Keeping Watch Over Instant Messages," *The New York Times*, April 15, 2002, p. C4. Copyright © 2002 by The New York Times Company. Reprinted with permission.

65  Golden, Ryan. "Poll: 42% of Employees Use Instant Messaging Tools on the Job," *HR Drive*, June 9, 2017.

66  Mamberto, C. "Instant Messaging Invades the Office," *The Wall Street Journal*, July 24, 2007, pp. B1, B2. Reprinted by permission of *The Wall Street Journal*, Copyright © 2007 Dow Jones & Company, Inc. All rights reserved worldwide.

67  Bulkeley, W. M. "Instant Message Goes Corporate: 'You Can't Hide,'" *The Wall Street Journal*, September 4, 2002, pp. B1, B4. Reprinted by permission of *The Wall Street Journal*, Copyright © 2002 Dow Jones & Company, Inc. All rights reserved worldwide.

68  Lee, J. S. "I Think, Therefore IM. Text Shortcuts Invade Schoolwork, and Teachers Are not Amused," *The New York Times*, September 19, 2002, pp. E1, E4. Copyright © 2002 by The New York Times Company. Reprinted with permission.

69  "Number of Cell Phones Worldwide Hits 4.6 B," Associated Press. Retrieved from www.cbsnews.com/stories/2010/02/15/business/main6209772.shtml. Accessed January 4, 2011 at 12:29 p.m.

70  *Mobile Fact Sheet*. Pew Research Center. February 5, 2018. Full report available online at www.pewinternet.org/fact-sheet/mobile/. See also "Cell Phones," Center on Media and Health, Children's Hospital Boston. Online at www.cmch.tv. Accessed Friday, July 11, 2008 at 4:00 p.m.

71  "U.S. Population by Month," *U.S. Census Bureau*. Online at www.multpl.com/united-states-population/table?f=m. Accessed June 22, 2018 at 10:37 a.m.

72  *Mobile Fact Sheet*. Pew Research Center.

73  "Research Updates Americans' View on Cell Phone Etiquette," press release, September 3, 2002. Online at www.letstalk.com/company/release_090302.htm. Accessed October 3, 2002. Quotation used by permission.

74  Ibid. See also Leland, J. "Just a Minute Boss. My Cellphone Is Ringing: The Workplace Is the Last Frontier for Cell Etiquette. Expect Hang-Ups," *The New York Times*, July 7, 2005, pp. E1, E2. Copyright © 2005 by The New York Times Company. Reprinted by permission.

75  Baldrige, L. "E-Etiquette," *The New York Times*, December 6, 1999, p. A29. Copyright © 1999 by The New York Times Company. Reprinted by permission.

76  Allen, E. In personal communication by telephone with Professor Sandra D. Collins, June 24, 2002.

77  Allen, E. In personal communication with the author, May 6, 2002, Armonk, New York.

78  Mead, D. G. "Retooling for the Cyber Age," *CEO Series 42*, September 2000. Online at csab.wustl.edu/csab/. August 4, 2005.

79  Collins, S. D. *Communication in a Virtual Organization*. Cincinnati, OH: South-Western College Publishing, 2003.

80  "Latest Telecommuting Statistics – As of June 2017," *Global Workplace Analytics*. Online at http://globalworkplaceanalytics.com/telecommuting-statistics. Accessed Friday, June 29, 2018 at 9:21 a.m.

81  "State of the American Workplace," *Gallup*. Online at https://news.gallup.com/reports/199961/7.aspx. Accessed June 29, 2018 at 9:25 a.m. See also: Chokshi, Niraj. "Out of the Office: More People Are Working Remotely, Survey Finds," *The New York Times*. February 15, 2017. Online at www.nytimes.com/2017/02/15/us/remote-workers-work-from-home.html. Accessed June 29, 2018 at 9:57 a.m.

82  Hafner, K. "Working at Home Today?" *The New York Times*, November 2, 2001, p. D1. Copyright © 2001 by The New York Times Company. Reprinted by permission.

83  Verespej, M. A. "The Compelling Case for Telework," *Industry Week*, September 2001, p. 23.

84  Collins. *Communication in a Virtual Organization*, pp. 9–11.

85  Wells, S. J. "Making Telecommuting Work," *HR Magazine*, 46 (2001), pp. 34–46.

86  Lovelace, G. "The Nuts and Bolts of Telework: Growth in Telework," *Telework and the New Workplace of the 21st Century*. 2000. Online at www.dol.gov/asp/telework/p1_2.html. Accessed August 5, 2005.

87  Byrne, J. A. "Management by Web," *Business Week*, August 28, 2000, p. 92.

88  Cascio, W. "Managing a Virtual Workplace," *Academy of Management Executive*, March 2000, pp. 81–90.

89    Collins. *Communication in a Virtual Organization*, p. 12.

90    Jarvenpaa, S. and D. Leidner. "Communication and Trust in Global Virtual Teams," *Organization Science: A Journal of the Institute of Management Sciences*, 10 (1999), pp. 791–846.

91    Lawlor, J. "Videoconferencing: From Stage Fright to Stage Presence," *The New York Times*, August 27, 1998, p. D6. Copyright © 1998 by The New York Times Company. Reprinted by permission.

92    "Immersive TelePresence," *Cisco*. Online at www.cisco.com/c/en/us/products/collaboration-endpoints/immersive-telePresence/index.html. Accessed June 25, 2018 at 12:47 p.m.

93    Lawlor. "Videoconferencing: From Stage Fright to Stage Presence."

94    Clark, Dorie. "How to Give a Webinar Presentation," *Harvard Business Review*, June 11, 2018.

# Case 7.1: Samsung Electronics Co., Ltd.

## *Galaxy Note 7 Crisis*

I pulled the phone out and threw it on the ground, because I didn't want it to explode in my hand. I didn't know what else to do with it.

~ Brian Green, Southwest Airlines Flight Passenger

On August 19, 2016, Samsung released its newest and most innovative smart phone: the Galaxy Note 7.[1] The unveiling of the Galaxy Note 7 created headlines and broke pre-order records.[2] The enthusiasm for and admiration of the Galaxy Note 7 were short-lived, however, because of one vital issue: the phones were catching fire (see Figure 7.1).

On September 2, 2016, Samsung suspended sales of the Galaxy Note 7 after a product design review found a manufacturing defect causing lithium-ion batteries to catch fire. Samsung announced a global recall of 2.5 million Galaxy Note 7 phones.[3]

Labor Day weekend, 2016, Nathan Dornacher, of St. Petersburg, Florida, had his Samsung Galaxy Note 7 charging in the center console of his Jeep Grand Cherokee. While his family was unloading the Jeep, however, Nathan looked outside and his Jeep was consumed in flames.[4] Nathan's Jeep caught fire, because his four-day-old Samsung phone contained a defective lithium-ion battery that generated excessive heat and exploded. Luckily, no one was injured.[5]

On September 15, 2016, the U.S. Consumer Product Safety Commission formally announced a recall of more than 1 million Galaxy Note 7 phones in the U.S.[6] Samsung exchanged the defective phones for units with batteries from a different supplier.[7] This recall, however, did not solve the problem.

On October 6, 2016, Brian Green was powering down his Galaxy Note 7 on a Southwest Airlines flight when he heard a pop and noticed smoke billowing out of his clothes. When he pulled the phone out of his pocket, he threw it on the ground, and about two rows of seats were enveloped in smoke.[8] The Southwest Airlines flight was evacuated and no one was injured. Brian Green's Galaxy Note 7, however, was a replacement phone from the first recall in September 2016, yet it still caught fire.[9] Samsung had not fixed the lithium-ion battery defect in the first recall and, instead, exchanged defective phones for defective phones.

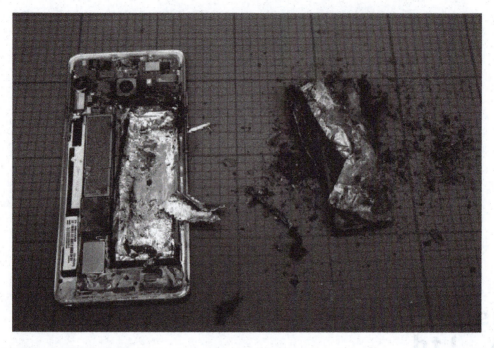

**FIGURE 7.1** Galaxy Note 7 After Battery Fire

*Source*: Mozur, Paul. "Galaxy Note 7 Fires Caused by Battery and Design Flaws, Samsung Says," *The New York Times*, January 22, 2017. Online at www.nytimes.com/2017/01/22/business/samsung-galaxy-note-7-battery-fires-report.html

As of October 11, 2016, Samsung received at least 92 reports of the Galaxy Note 7 overheating in the U.S., 25 reports of burns and 55 reports of property damage.[10] Samsung stopped production of the Galaxy Note 7 altogether, and issued a final recall, refund and exchange program on October 13, 2016.[11]

## SAMSUNG ELECTRONICS CO., LTD.

Byung-Chull Lee founded Samsung, today known as Samsung Group, in 1938 in Taegu, Korea. At the start, his business focused primarily on trade exports, selling dried Korean fish, vegetables and fruit to Manchuria and Beijing. Over the next three decades, the group diversified into other businesses including insurance, textiles, specialty chemicals, securities and trading, construction, and home appliances. Today, Samsung Group is recognized for its wide spectrum of innovative and top quality products and processes.[12]

Samsung Group's flagship company, Samsung Electronics Co., Ltd., was founded in 1969 and today leads the global market in high-end electronics manufacturing and digital media.[13] The company is structured around three business divisions: Consumer Electronics, Device Solutions, and Information Technology & Mobile Communications. The Consumer Electronics business unit provides cable television, monitors, printers, air-conditioners, medical devices, washing machines and refrigerators. The Device Solutions arm comprises flash memory and large-scale integrated circuits, while the Information Technology & Mobile Communications division offers handheld devices, computers, communication systems and digital cameras.[14] In 2013, Samsung became the world's largest manufacturer of smart phones, fueled by the popularity of its Android-powered Samsung Galaxy product line.[15] Samsung Electronics is also regarded as pioneering tablet computers with its Samsung Galaxy Note family of products.[16]

In 2015, Samsung Electronics Co., Ltd. generated $26.34 billion in operating profit and $177.33 in cumulative net sales, 51.6 percent coming directly from its Information Technology & Mobile Communications business division.[17] In that same year, the company employed 325,000 regular and contract-based employees across 80 countries. *Forbes* ranked Samsung Electronics as the #15 world's most reputable company in 2015.[18]

## LITHIUM-ION BATTERIES

Lithium-ion batteries contain two electrodes that are separated by an electrolyte (see Figure 7.2).[19] An electrolyte is a highly flammable chemical liquid between the electrodes that conducts electricity.[20] Since the electrolyte is shuttling lithium, however, it must be in a non-aqueous solution, and cannot use acid, an alkaline solution or water. Therefore, the organic liquid that lithium-ion batteries use dissolved lithium salt, allowing the lithium to shuttle back and forth between the positive and negative electrodes. The formula is effective but highly volatile and flammable.[21]

The critical component in lithium-ion batteries is the thin separator that sits between the two electrodes. If this barrier breaks down or is damaged by any outside pressure, this can trigger excessive heat and could cause a battery fire. Additionally, if this barrier breaks down to the point where the two electrodes touch, short-circuiting and over-heating will result, potentially leading to a battery fire.[22]

Samsung rushed the production and design of the Galaxy Note 7 in order to beat the release of Apple's iPhone 7, and in the process designed an exceptionally thin separator in the batteries that could increase the likelihood of fires or explosions. Battery scientists say that Samsung's aggressive design decisions made problems more likely, and that their choice to push the limits of battery technology left little safety margin in the event of a problem.[23]

Despite the design flaws of the Galaxy Note 7, Samsung engineers and other outside experts said that the Galaxy Note 7 lithium-ion battery crisis could also be blamed on manufacturing problems. During the first recall of the Galaxy Note 7, Samsung initially blamed Samsung SDI, the company's in-house battery supplier, for manufacturing faulty batteries. The initial fires in these batteries were caused, in part, by pressure damage, in which a container pinched the top corner of the battery.[24]

After preliminary reports of the batteries catching fire, Samsung ceased production of lithium-ion batteries from Samsung SDI for the Galaxy Note 7, and continued distributing Galaxy Note 7s with batteries from China's Amperex Technology Limited, or ATL, offering these phones as safe replacements. The batteries that came from this supplier, however, were also catching fire, and were found to have defects in welding, with some lacking protective tape.[25]

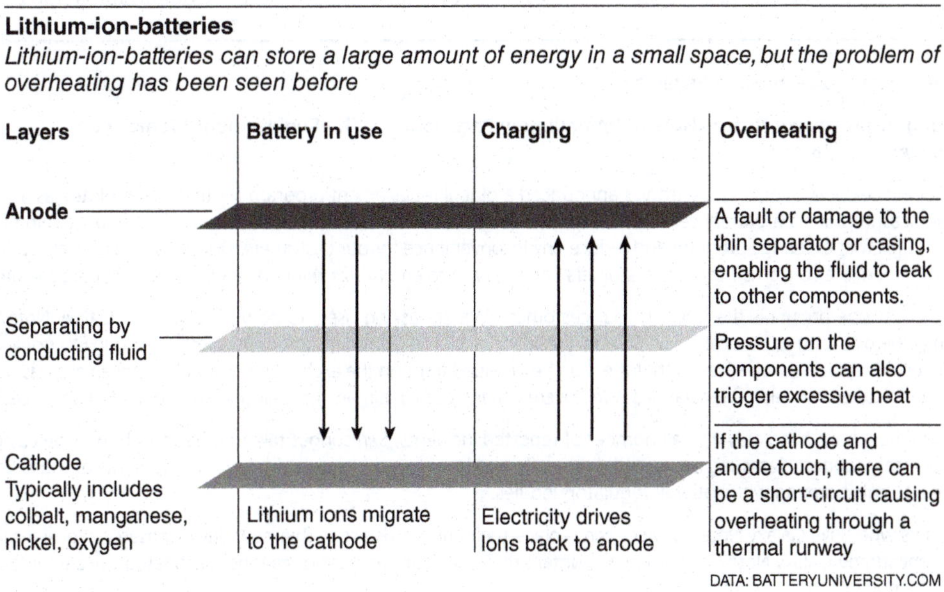

**Lithium-ion-batteries**

*Lithium-ion-batteries can store a large amount of energy in a small space, but the problem of overheating has been seen before*

| Layers | Battery in use | Charging | Overheating |
|---|---|---|---|
| **Anode** | | | A fault or damage to the thin separator or casing, enabling the fluid to leak to other components. |
| Separating by conducting fluid | | | Pressure on the components can also trigger excessive heat |
| Cathode Typically includes colbalt, manganese, nickel, oxygen | Lithium ions migrate to the cathode | Electricity drives Ions back to anode | If the cathode and anode touch, there can be a short-circuit causing overheating through a thermal runway |

DATA: BATTERYUNIVERSITY.COM

**FIGURE 7.2** Lithium-Ion Battery

*Source*: Criddle, Cristina. "Why is the Samsung Galaxy Note 7 Catching Fire? The Lithium-Ion Battery Explained," *The Telegraph Technology*, October 11, 2016. Online at www.telegraph.co.uk/technology/2016/10/11/why-is-the-samsung-galaxy-note-7-catching-fire-the-lithium-ion-b/.

## SMART PHONE INDUSTRY

The smart phone industry began to gain popularity with the release of Apple's iPhone in 2007. It wasn't until late 2008 that the first smart phone running on Android was sold to the consumer market. The smart phone industry has since grown steadily in number of suppliers, different smart phone models and market size. Industry analysts projected that by the end of 2017, over one-third of the world's population would own a smart phone, an estimated 2.6 billion users.[26]

While Samsung has the largest market share in the industry, Apple is the second largest smart phone vendor worldwide. Other key players in the industry are Huawei, Lenovo and Xiamoi.[27]

In response to the Galaxy Note 7s catching fire, Samsung's biggest competitor, Apple, did nothing in response. Apple instead focused on the launch of their iPhone 7 and iPhone 7 Plus in September 2016. Instead of referencing the Galaxy Note 7's battery issue when presenting the battery improvements of the iPhone 7 and iPhone 7 Plus, Apple did not acknowledge any Samsung recall disaster, whatsoever.[28] Despite Apple not capitalizing on Samsung's missteps, they captured the first position in global smart phone market share in the fourth quarter of 2016.[29]

Motorola, however, did take advantage of the Galaxy Note 7 crisis and Samsung's vulnerability. Some of their marketing materials were clearly aimed at Samsung's battery errors, and included "At Moto, our priority is safety first. Unlike some manufacturers, we adhere to the highest standards in quality and testing of all our batteries."[30]

## SAMSUNG'S RESPONSE

On September 2, 2016 – a few days after initial customer allegations emerged – Samsung issued a statement that it would replace 2.5 million units of the Galaxy Note 7 device as a "precautionary measure to the battery cell issue." The company socialized the statement through its own website, where it urged Note 7 users to contact their point of purchase or a call center to request a replacement phone (see Figure 7.3). On September 15, 2016, the message was posted on the Samsung Mobile U.S. Twitter and Facebook accounts[31] (see Figure 7.4). On September 23, 2016, the company also launched a software update that helped customers determine if their phone was part of the recall.

Players in the mobile industry initially praised Samsung for its decisiveness and swiftness in handling the matter. The general sentiment later turned into outrage and disappointment when it was learned that the multinational electronics company had acted without required coordination with the Consumer Product Safety Commission in the U.S., which

---

Press Resources > Issues&Facts > Statements

**Samsung Urges Galaxy Note7 Users to Immediately Participate in The Replacement Program on September 10,2016**

Just over a week ago, Samsung Electronics announced a global replacement program for the Galaxy Note7 as a precautionary measure due to a battery cell issue. Since then, we have been working hard to expedite product shipments in order to fulfill that exchange program and reduce any inconvenience for our customers. During the past week, we understand that there are concerns from our customers and we wish to emphasize the importance of exchanging the product.

"Our number one priority is the safety of our customers. We are asking users to power down their Galaxy Note7s and exchange them as soon as possible," says DJ Koh, President of Mobile Communications Business, Samsung Electronics. "We are expediting replacement devices so that they can be provided through the exchange program as conveniently as possible and in compliance with related regulations. We sincerely thank our customers for their understanding and patience."

Although there have been only a small number of reported incidents, Samsung is taking great care to provide customers with necessary support. Samsung has identified the affected inventory and stopped sales and shipments of those devices. We are also collaborating with national regulatory bodies.

Customers who have Galaxy Note7 devices can replace their current device with a new device based on local availability. We encourage Galaxy Note7 customers to contact their place of purchase or call the designated call center locally as soon as possible.

---

**FIGURE 7.3**   Samsung's Statement of September 10, 2016

*Source*: Samsung News Website. September 10, 2016. Online at https://news.samsung.com/global/samsung-urges-galaxy-note7-users-to-immediately-participate-in-the-replacement-program. Accessed February 25, 2017.

**FIGURE 7.4**   Samsung Mobile USA Twitter Post of September 15, 2016

*Source*: Maheshwari, Sapna. "Samsung's Response to Galaxy Note 7 Draws Criticism," *The New York Times*, October 11, 2016. Online at www.nytimes.com/2016/10/12/business/media/samsungs-passive-response-to-note-7s-overheating-problem-draws-criticism.html. Accessed February 25, 2017.

# Samsung Expands Recall to All Galaxy Note7 Devices

Updated – Jan. 22 2017

Samsung has announced an expanded voluntary recall on all original and replacement Galaxy Note7 devices sold or exchanged in the United States in cooperation with the U.S. Consumer Product Safety Commission and in partnership with carriers and retailers. Since the affected devices can overheat and pose a safety risk, we are asking consumers with a Galaxy Note7 to power it down and contact the carrier or retail outlet where they purchased their device.

Consumers who have a Galaxy Note7 device can exchange their phone for another Samsung smartphone, or receive a refund, under the terms of the expanded U.S. Note7 Refund and Exchange Program.

If you bought your Galaxy Note7 from Samsung.com you should click here to process your refund or exchange. If you have questions, you should contact us at 1-844-365-6197 and we can help you.

**FIGURE 7.5**   Samsung's Statement of October 11, 2016

*Source*: Samsung Website. October 11, 2016. Online at www.samsung.com/us/note7recall/. Accessed February 25, 2017.

demands that companies notify it of defects and work collaboratively to arrange public notification of recalls. At a news conference, the commission's chairman, Elliot F. Kaye, alluded to the regulator's dissatisfaction with Samsung and condemned the company for going out on its own.[32] Samsung was also called out for telling Hong Kong consumers that models there would be unaffected due to the use of a different battery, only to retract that action the following day.[33]

Just a few weeks later, on October 11, 2016, Samsung Electronics officially announced that it was halting all sales and production of the Galaxy Note 7, after reports that the replacement phones were also catching fire emerged across multiple media outlets. The South Korean conglomerate posted a statement on its website instructing owners of the phone to power it down and contact the carrier or retail outlet where they purchased the device to obtain a refund or exchange.[34] To access the statement, customers had to click a link at the top of Samsung's home page where the passive label "Updated Consumer Guidance for the Galaxy Note 7" would take them to the statement and information on the Refund and Exchange Program[35] (see Figure 7.5). On October 14, 2016, the content was cross-pollinated on the company's Facebook account (see Figure 7.6).

**Samsung Mobile USA**
October 14, 2016 · ✏

U.S. #GalaxyNote7 Safety Recall Expansion:
Important safety announcement. We are launching an
expanded recall of all Galaxy Note7 phones in
collaboration with the U.S. Consumer Product Safety
Commission. There is also a ban on carrying the
Galaxy Note7 on flights. Stop using your Note7 and
contact your carrier, retailer or Samsung immediately
for a full refund, or exchange with incentive.
smsng.us/N7Recall

### Galaxy Note7 Recall Expansion:

We are committed to your safety and
to finding the right solution for you.

We've expanded the Galaxy Note7 recall and ceased all sales and production
of the device.

If you own an original or replacement Galaxy Note7, we ask that you power it
down and contact your carrier or retailer about exchanging it for a Galaxy
device or full refund. If you bought your Galaxy Note7 from Samsung.com or
have questions, you should contact us at 1-844-365-6197.

SAMSUNG

👍😮😢 2.9K          4.6K Comments  1.9K Shares

**FIGURE 7.6**   Samsung Mobile USA Facebook Post of October 14, 2016

*Source*: Samsung Mobile USA Facebook Page. October 14, 2016.

## IMPLICATIONS

The decision to pull the plug on the Galaxy Note 7 cost Samsung an estimated $6.2 billion.[36] Even before the company announced it was discontinuing the product, its South Korea-traded shares fell by more than 8 percent, the biggest daily drop since 2008.[37] The sharp slip knocked approximately $17 billion off the company's market value.[38] Killing production of the high-end smart phone, however, did not curtail all of the questions that beset the company. An editorial in South Korea's leading newspaper, *The Chosun Ilbo*, pointed to even greater costs beyond the immediate and substantial financial blow, including the loss of public trust and the tarnishing of the brand's reputation. The article read: "You cannot calculate the loss of consumer trust in money."[39] Additionally, the publication questions the efficacy of the business model that has brought Samsung success after success in the past.

## BACKLASH

In addition to the large amount of news coverage that the Galaxy Note 7 crisis was getting from its recalls, the fires spurred unwanted media attention for Samsung in the form of tweets, Facebook posts and YouTube videos (see Figure 7.7).

As the public's frustration began to uncoil, Samsung began losing the trust of many of their customers, as evidenced by one consumer's tweet to Sprint, saying "Hey @sprint, what if I don't trust @SamsungMobile devices anymore?" The carrier responded, "Greetings, you still can trust Apple, HTC, LG or Alcatel."[40]

Additionally, the U.S. Department of Transportation, with the Federal Aviation Administration and the Pipeline and Hazardous Materials Safety Administration issued an emergency order banning Samsung Galaxy Note 7s from air transportation in the U.S. Effective October 15, 2016, the devices were not allowed to be carried on board, packed in checked bags or shipped as air cargo on flights to and from the U.S. or within the country.[41]

News of the danger of the Galaxy Note 7 devices was further emphasized when Transportation Secretary Anthony Foxx stated, "We are taking this additional step because even one fire incident inflight poses a high risk of severe personal injury and puts many lives at risk."[42]

## ADDITIONAL ISSUES

Samsung Electronics' safety problems do not end with the Galaxy Note 7. The manufacturer announced in November 2016 a recall of 2.8 million defective top-load washing machines in the U.S., exceeding the number of smart

**FIGURE 7.7**  Reaction Posts on Twitter

*Source:* Twitter.com

phones the company had recalled a month earlier. The Consumer Product and Safety Commission claimed the laundry machines were prone to detaching from the washing machine chassis during use, "posing a risk of injury from impact."[43] Samsung received 733 different reports of washing machines vibrating excessively or the tops pulling off. Additionally, the safety commission indicated there had been nine reports of related injuries, including a broken jaw and shoulder.[44]

In addition to the safety issues already plaguing Samsung, the company is also facing a graft scandal after its vice chairman and heir Jay Y. Lee was arrested on charges of corruption on February 16, 2017. Lee was accused of paying bribes to an advisor of South Korean President Park Geun-hye in exchange for political favors. The bribes are alleged to include support for a merger between two Samsung subsidiaries that allowed him to inherit corporate control from his incapacitated father, Lee Khun-hee, the chairman.[45]

## DISCUSSION QUESTIONS

1. As the communication director for the company, what course of action would you take after the initial consumer reports of the phone's defect emerged?
2. How can Samsung regain the trust of its consumers once more?
3. What processes or structures should Samsung establish to make sure it does not encounter these issues again?
4. What kind of crisis management plan, if any, should Samsung develop to address similar situations in the future?

## ACKNOWLEDGMENTS

This case was prepared by research assistants Emily Thomas and Alejandra Zeron under the direction of James S. O'Rourke, Teaching Professor of Management, as the basis for class discussion rather than to illustrate either effective or ineffective handling of an administrative situation. Information was gathered from corporate as well as public sources.

## NOTES

1  Wattles, Jackie. "Samsung Galaxy Note 7 Replacement Phone Reportedly Catches Fire on Plane," *CNN Tech*, October 6, 2016. Online at http://money.cnn.com/2016/10/05/technology/samsung-galaxy-note-7-explodes-airplane/.

2  Triggs, Robert. "Galaxy Note 7 breaks South Korean Pre-Order Record," *Android Authority*, August 11, 2016. Online at www.androidauthority.com/galaxy-note-7-breaks-pre-order-records-708863/.

3  "Here's the Timeline of Samsung's Galaxy Note 7 Recall Crisis," *Fortune Tech*, October 10, 2016. Online at http://fortune.com/2016/10/10/timeline-samsun-galaxy-note-recall-crisis/.

4  "Florida Man's Vehicle Catches Fire after Charging Galaxy Note 7 Explodes," *Fox News Tech*, September 9, 2016. Online at www.foxnews.com/tech/2016/09/09/florida-mans-vehicle-catches-fire-after-charging-galaxy-note-7-explodes.html.

5  Ibid.

6  "Here's the Timeline of Samsung's Galaxy Note 7 Recall Crisis," *Fortune Tech*.

7  Chen, Brian X. and Choe Sang-Hun. "Why Samsung Abandoned Its Galaxy Note 7 Flagship Phone," *The New York Times*, October 11, 2016. Online at www.nytimes.com/2016/10/12/business/international/samsung-galaxy-note7-terminated.html?_r=0.

8  Wattles. "Samsung Galaxy Note 7 Replacement Phone Reportedly Catches Fire on Plane."

9  Ibid.

10  Chen and Sang-Hun. "Why Samsung Abandoned Its Galaxy Note 7 Flagship Phone."

11  "Samsung Expands Recall of Galaxy Note7 Smartphones Based on Additional Incidents with Replacement Phones; Serious Fire and Burn Hazards," *United States Consumer Product Safety Commission*, October 13, 2016. Online at www.cpsc.gov/Recalls/2016/samsung-expands-recall-of-galaxy-note7-smartphones-based-on-additional-incidents-with.

12  "About Samsung," *Samsung*. Online at www.samsung.com/us/aboutsamsung/corporateprofile/history05.html.

13  Ibid.

14  "Canada's Best Employers 2017," *Forbes Magazine*. Online at www.forbes.com/companies/samsung-electronics/.

15  Garside, Juliette. "Samsung Overtakes Apple as World's Most Valuable Profitable Phone Market," *The Guardian*, July 26, 2013. Online at www.theguardian.com/technology/2013/jul/26/samsung-apple-profitable-mobile-phone.

16  "Samsung Gains Tablet Market Share as Apple Lead Narrows," *BBC News*, February 1, 2013. Online at www.bbc.com/news/business-21288852.

17  "2015 Annual Report," *Samsung Electronics Co., Ltd*. Online at www.samsung.com/us/aboutsamsung/investor_relations/financial_information/downloads/2015/2015_business_quarter04.pdf.

18  "About Us, Fast Facts" *Samsung Newsroom*. Online at https://news.samsung.com/global/fast-facts.

19  Fitzpatrick, Alex. "We Asked a Battery Expert Why Samsung's Phones Are Catching Fire," *Time Tech*, September 9, 2016. Online at http://time.com/4485396/samsung-note-7-battery-fire-why/.

20  Criddle, Cristina. "Why is the Samsung Galaxy Note 7 Catching Fire? The Lithium-Ion Battery Explained," *The Telegraph Technology*, October 11, 2016. Online at www.telegraph.co.uk/technology/2016/10/11/why-is-the-samsung-galaxy-note-7-catching-fire-the-lithium-ion-b/.

21  Fitzpatrick. "We Asked a Battery Expert Why Samsung's Phones Are Catching Fire."

22  Mozur, Paul. "Galaxy Note 7 Fires Caused by Battery and Design Flaws, Samsung Says," *The New York Times*, January 22, 2017. Online at www.nytimes.com/2017/01/22/business/samsung-galaxy-note-7-battery-fires-report.html.

23  Ibid.

24  Ibid.

25  Ibid.

26  "Statistics and Facts About Smartphones," *Statista*. Online at www.statista.com/topics/840/smartphones/.

27  Ibid.

28  Smith, Chris. "Apple's Reaction to the Galaxy Note 7 Recall was Brilliant, and We All Missed It," *Yahoo Tech*, September 13, 2016. Online at www.yahoo.com/tech/apple-reaction-galaxy-note-7-recall-brilliant-missed-184431973.html.

29  "Strategy Analytics: Global Smartphone Shipments Hit a Record 1.5 Billion Units in 2016," *Business Wire*, January 31, 2017. Online at www.businesswire.com/news/home/20170131006472/en/Strategy-Analytics-Global-Smartphone-Shipments-Hit-Record.

30  Smith. "Apple's Reaction to the Galaxy Note 7 Recall was Brilliant, and We All Missed It."

31  Maheshwari, Sapna. "Samsung's Response to Galaxy Note 7," *The New York Times*, October 11, 2016. Online at www.nytimes.com/2016/10/12/business/media/samsungs-passive-response-to-note-7s-overheating-problem-draws-criticism.html.

32  Su-Hyun, Lee and Paul Mozur. "Samsung Stumbles in Race to Recall Troubled Phones," *The New York Times*, September 15, 2016. Online at www.nytimes.com/2016/09/16/business/samsung-galaxy-note-recall.html.

33  Maheshwari. "Samsung's Response to Galaxy Note 7."

34  Ibid.

35  Ibid.

36  Ibid.

37  Chen and Sang-Hun. "Why Samsung Abandoned Its Galaxy Note 7 Flagship Phone."

38  Ibid.

39  Ibid.

40  Maheshwari. "Samsung's Response to Galaxy Note 7."

41   "DOT Bans All Samsung Galaxy Note7 Phones From Airplanes," *U.S. Department of Transportation*, October 14, 2016. Online at www.transportation.gov/briefing-room/dot-bans-all-samsung-galaxy-note7-phones-airplanes.

42   Ibid.

43   "Samsung Recalls Top-Load Washing Machines Due to Risk of Impact Injuries," *United States Consumer Product Safety Commission*, November 4, 2016. Online at www.cpsc.gov/Recalls/2016/samsung-recalls-top-load-washing-machines.

44   Ibid.

45   Russel, Jon. "Samsung Vice Chairman Arrested on Bribery Charges," *TechCrunch*, February 16, 2017. Online at https://techcrunch.com/2017/02/16/samsung-vice-chairman-arrested-on-bribery-charges/.

# Case 7.2: Johnson & Johnson's Strategy with Motrin

## The Growing Pains of Social Media

> Wearing your baby seems to be in fashion ... plus it totally makes me look like an official mom. And so if I look tired and crazy, people will understand why. Motrin® We feel your pain.

An online ad created by Taxi Advertising and Design, an advertising agency headquartered in Toronto, Ontario, with these words appeared on the Motrin website as an effort to target mothers who developed pain from carrying their babies around in slings. On Friday, November 14, 2008, 45 days after the ad was posted to the site, an influential mommy blogger with a significant Twitter following noticed the ad and began tweeting about her offense to the suggestion that moms use baby slings as fashion statements.[1] Other influential mommy bloggers picked up on the thread, and from Friday into Saturday, the Motrin ad became one of the most tweeted about topics on Twitter, even amidst the highly publicized 2008 presidential election of Barack Obama.[2]

On Saturday and Sunday, continual negative reactions appeared on Twitter. The conversation was tracked on Twitter by utilizing the hashtag "motrinmoms" that helped interested groups to closely follow the conversation.[3] The message moved into the blogosphere where several bloggers called for a boycott of Motrin, and harsh comments flooded message boards. Some angry consumers even created counter ads that they posted on YouTube.[4] The messaging of the tweets and outcry was strong, and stated that the Motrin ad "trivialized women's pain and the method of carrying babies."[5] As uproar spread through the various social media channels, the messaging shifted from *"shame on" Johnson & Johnson* to *"where is a response" from Johnson & Johnson?*[6]

## THE OPPORTUNITIES OF SOCIAL MEDIA

Global brands have continually been increasing their social media activation in advertising and marketing, as companies recognize social media's cost effectiveness and their ability to generate deep customer engagement as the consumer dictates on his or her own terms. Companies continue to realize that customer advocates are the most powerful marketing channel available, as people trust and listen to what others say most of all. The most difficult challenge for brands to succeed at this is to recruit the appropriate and influential advocates and leverage these associations; this has been notoriously difficult to achieve through traditional media. Social media provide a vehicle for a brand to learn and understand the way that customers respond and interact with a company's products and services. Social media also provide forums, such as chat rooms, for customer communities to develop.[7]

Social media outreach also provides the opportunity to learn more about the company's customer. As consumers continue to become more deeply involved with multiple social media channels, customer-volunteered information begins to further flesh out the consumer profile for the company. With more complete information, marketers are better able to facilitate messaging and placement toward a target customer group. Social media provide companies with the opportunity to better and more effectively engage customers on a meaningful basis.[8]

## JOHNSON & JOHNSON HISTORY

Johnson & Johnson was founded in 1885 by two brothers, James and Edward Mead Johnson, as a medical products company in New Brunswick, New Jersey. One year later, their brother, Robert, joined the company to make the antiseptic surgical dressing that he had developed. In 1921, Johnson & Johnson introduced two of its classic products that still exist today, the Band-Aid and Johnson's Baby Cream.[9]

J&J purchased McNeil Labs in 1959, which launched Tylenol in 1960 as an over-the-counter drug. Throughout the 1970s, the company continued to focus on consumer products, with Tylenol becoming the top-selling painkiller. In 1982, crisis struck when Tylenol capsules were laced with cyanide, killing eight people. The company immediately recalled 31 million bottles and redesigned the packaging to prohibit tampering – a response that cost the company $240 million but ultimately saved the Tylenol brand. J&J's response has become well-known and is often used as a model for proper damage control and corporate best practices. In the 1990s, J&J continued its acquisition and diversification strategy and acquired Neutrogena in 1994 to further bolster its consumer product lines. The company bought the over-the-counter rights to Motrin in 1997 from Pharmacia, which is now Pfizer. In 2006, the company acquired Pfizer's consumer products business for $16.6 billion, which added approximately 40 brands to J&J's portfolio. The company announced a major restructuring in 2007, trimming costs and executing job cuts mainly within its Pharmaceuticals segment and reinvesting in other areas.[10]

Johnson & Johnson now operates within three segments through more than 250 operating companies in approximately 60 countries. J&J's Pharmaceuticals division produces drugs for a variety of ailments including autoimmune diseases, neurological conditions, blood disorders and pain. Its Medical Devices and Diagnostics division offers monitoring devices, surgical equipment, orthopedic products, contact lenses and a variety of other products. The third division, J&J's Consumer segment, makes over-the-counter drugs and assorted products for skin, baby and oral care, and first aid and women's health. In 2009, Johnson & Johnson was ranked #33 in the Fortune 500 and reported nearly $62 billion in sales and 115,500 employees.[11]

The company is renowned for its decentralized operating structure, with management teams having wide latitude in their decision making. Johnson & Johnson has a strong drug development pipeline to address the competitive challenge of patent expiration, which is increasingly relevant as some of the company's major products have recently lost patent protection. While the company's Pharmaceuticals and Medical Devices segments each account for more than 35 percent of company sales, challenges within these segments led to recent restructuring efforts by the company. Additionally, Johnson & Johnson's Consumer segment has been growing through acquisitions, and offerings include brands such as Neutrogena, Tylenol, Listerine, Benadryl, Lubriderm, Rolaids, Sudafed and Splenda.[12]

## A SHORT HISTORY IN SOCIAL MEDIA AT JOHNSON & JOHNSON

Johnson & Johnson has always set the standard for communication in the corporate world, so it should be no surprise that it has an extensive social media network in place to reach its many customers. With the onslaught of new social media platforms, Johnson & Johnson has kept up to speed on all interfaces.

Ray Jordan joined Johnson & Johnson in 2003 as Vice President of Public Affairs and Corporate Communication. Responsible for corporate communications and public affairs for the company, Jordan oversees the Public Affairs responsibilities and activities of the entire family of Johnson & Johnson operating companies.[13] Jordan recognized that there were new groups in social media that were influencing online dialogue and Johnson & Johnson needed to develop relationships with these bloggers. Jordan created an environment where the Corporate Communication team could explore the various social media networks.[14]

## KILMER HOUSE

Johnson & Johnson's first attempt to enter the social media market was through the creation of Kilmer House. Created in 2006 by Corporate Communication team member Margaret Gurowitz, Kilmer House was Johnson & Johnson's first attempt at a blog. Named after Dr. Fredrick Kilmer, the company's first scientific director, Kilmer House serves as a history blog for the Johnson & Johnson Company.[15] This was a safe and conservative way to enter the blogosphere without causing any controversy.

Gurowitz still runs the blog as the company historian and she tries to reach out to groups interested in the history of Johnson & Johnson who want to better understand the company. Within four years of posts, the blog summarizes: "One of the best ways to understand Johnson & Johnson is to know the Company's history and the things that make it unique."[16] Gurowitz has covered topics over a wide spectrum including: the people who established Johnson & Johnson, some of its unusual products, early science and technology, the Johnson & Johnson community, anniversaries, advertising, iconic products, innovations and trivia. At the bottom of every blog, readers are able to interact with the company by leaving comments which J&J can respond to in order to clarify questions that readers might pose.

Kilmer House allowed Johnson & Johnson to develop a comfort level with its own legal and regulatory department on how to manage new issues that could arise in the blogosphere.[17] This blog set the stage for all of J&J's social media platforms by developing ways to manage content created by J&J, as well as content created by its readers.

## JNJ BTW

Kilmer House had allowed Johnson & Johnson to experiment with the voice it could establish online in addition to the development of a two-way dialogue with its customers. In early 2007, approximately six months after Kilmer House had launched, Marc Monseau, Director, Corporate Communication, Social Media, created a new blog called Johnson & Johnson By The Way, or JNJ BTW. The blog summarizes its purpose by stating:

Everyone else is talking about our company, so why can't we? There are more than 120,000 people who work for Johnson & Johnson and its operating companies. I'm one of them, and through JNJ BTW, I will try to find a voice that often gets lost in formal communications.

This is a big step for us as a company. Anyone working for a large corporation will appreciate that there are many internal limitations on what we say and how we say it.

I've been reading blogs for only a few months now, but already it's clear to me how important it is not just to watch, but to join in productively. Doing that will take some unlearning of old habits and traditional approaches to communicating — and I will have to find my own voice.

On JNJ BTW, there will be talk about Johnson & Johnson — what we are doing, how we are doing it and why. There will be comment on the news about our company and the industry — occasionally correcting any mistakes (not that that ever happens!) or simply providing more context. I hope and expect that some of my colleagues will eventually join me on this blog.[18]

Johnson & Johnson needed a way to engage these bloggers and respond with its own story. JNJ BTW was purposely designed to allow J&J to discuss corporate topics, company strategy, emerging issues and good works happening within the company in a slightly more informal manner.[19]

An example of this was when Jordan posted on JNJ BTW about Johnson & Johnson's decision to sue the American Red Cross. Being well aware that suing the American Red Cross could backfire and cause injury to the company, Jordan used JNJ BTW as a platform to discuss why J&J came to this final decision. Jordan explained how the company tried almost every other remedy before pursuing legal action. His blog post not only tempered the anger in the blogosphere, but also created advocates that posted positive reactions on JNJ BTW and went as far as re-posting Jordan's comments on their own blogs. Jordan's post changed the entire attitude of the discussion online and worked exactly how Johnson & Johnson had hoped.[20]

## JNJ YOUTUBE HEALTH CHANNEL

A few months after Monseau launched the JNJ BTW blog, Rob Halper, Director of Video Communication, launched the Johnson & Johnson health channel on YouTube. With the concept of "videos to promote a better understanding of health,"[21] the J&J health channel posts videos that provide context and information about health issues and health topics. These videos do not deal with specific J&J products or brands. They offer general information on popular health topics, such as the long-term effects of obesity, how to live with diabetes, bipolar disorder family support and Alzheimer's disease.

## FACEBOOK AND TWITTER

Following the relatively quick launches of two blogs and a YouTube channel, Johnson & Johnson opened a Facebook account in 2008. The Facebook account provided yet another channel of communication between J&J and its stakeholders. In 2009, J&J created a Twitter account to provide up-to-date information to consumers as well as to gather information. J&J now has three corporate Twitter accounts to its name. Monseau tweets for the JNJCOMM twitter account. Monseau will post on topics he finds interesting and topics that are being discussed on J&J's other social media platforms.[22]

## JOHNSON & JOHNSON USES SOCIAL MEDIA

The Motrin case of 2008 prompted Johnson & Johnson to think about becoming more involved with Twitter. The company noticed a large group of Twitter users were of interest to the company, due to the consumers' buying power and influence. J&J wanted to use Twitter as a medium not only to engage its online stakeholders, but also to gather information from them, share thoughts with them and give the stakeholders an informal way to talk with the company. As Monseau tried to figure out what kind of Twitter account to create, he grouped all Twitter accounts into five different categories:

- **Customer Service:** The company viewed the JetBlue Twitter account as a perfect example of a customer service account. JetBlue uses Twitter to keep customers up-to-date on flight delays and cancellations and allows passengers to file complaints about lost luggage.
- **Expert Source:** The accounts can provide information and key insights by an official who is knowledgeable both from within the company and out in public.
- **News Gatherer:** The account can take information about one's business and the industry the company is a part of, gather the information and provide it to customers as a news source.
- **Suggestion Box:** The account can solicit input and ideas from Twitter followers that can be redistributed to all interested parties.
- **Special Offers:** The account can be a location to distribute coupons and provide special offers.

Monseau and the social media team at J&J wanted to use Twitter to provide information as an Expert Source and News Gatherer.[23]

Johnson & Johnson wanted to increase its ability to listen, respond and engage with its customers through the use of Twitter. In order to do this effectively, Monseau and his team had to ensure there was a system of processes in place that would enable the right people in the company to speak to each of their areas of expertise. In order to allow these subject matter experts to respond quickly, J&J had to grant its employees a degree of flexibility and trust to answer questions in a timely manner with the understanding that the responders knew their limitations of what can and cannot be posted. Monseau likes to refer to these understood limitations as guardrails:

> We have specific guardrails that have been set up where we are allowed to drive all over the road and say certain things and publish different topics. If there is a topic that goes beyond those guardrails, we have to get approval for it, go through an approval process, and get sign off for it. We all have to keep in mind and be aware of where those limits are, where those guardrails fit, and if we go outside of them we have to make sure the company understands what direction we are going in.[24]

Without this flexibility and trust, J&J would not be able to post information fast enough to meet consumer needs. This would pose a challenge for the company because customers would look elsewhere for their information, and J&J would no longer be the information provider.

## JOHNSON & JOHNSON RESPONDS

On Sunday, November 16, 2008, Johnson & Johnson became aware of the outraged discussion regarding the Motrin online advertisement. The company was well aware that a significant number of mommy bloggers had worked in the areas of advertising and media, and the possibility for a media firestorm was sizable.[25] Monseau and the social media team at J&J knew that a response was in order.

Additionally, Monseau and his team would need to assess the expectations and plans for Johnson & Johnson's social media outreach. The team must also evaluate what opportunities to pursue in the future and how its social media strategy aligns with the company's business objectives as a whole. Finally, as social media continues to grow in its applications and consumer involvement, Monseau must gauge if the size and the composition of his corporate social media team is sufficient.

## DISCUSSION QUESTIONS: JOHNSON & JOHNSON RESPONDS TO THE MOTRIN CASE

1. How should Johnson & Johnson respond to the crisis?
2. What audience should the company reach out to?
3. What member(s) of the company should engage the audience?
4. What does the company offer to those offended by the ad?
5. How does J&J track the success of its response?

## DISCUSSION QUESTIONS: JOHNSON & JOHNSON ASSESSES SOCIAL MEDIA STRATEGY

1. What will Johnson & Johnson's social media strategy be moving forward?
2. What other social media platforms should J&J utilize?
3. Is the social media team big enough or should J&J grow it?
4. What metrics should the social media team utilize to measure the success of its social media outreach?
5. How can J&J link the social media objectives to the overall company's business objectives?

## ACKNOWLEDGMENTS

This case was prepared by Research Assistants Kathryn Eisele and Patrick Fishburne under the direction of James S. O'Rourke, Teaching Professor of Management, as the basis for class discussion rather than to illustrate either effective or ineffective handling of an administrative situation. Information was gathered from corporate as well as public sources.

## NOTES

1 Wheaton, K. "Middle Road in Motrin-Gate was Right Choice for J&J," *Advertising Age*, 79.44 (December 2008): 12. Retrieved September 20, 2010, from ABI/INFORM Global (Document ID: 1611223211).
2 Telephone conference with Marc Monseau, Johnson & Johnson, New Brunswick, New Jersey, 21 September 2010.
3 Anonymous, "All Companies Simply Must Get Up to Speed On Twitter," *PRweek*, 11.46 (November 2008): 6. Retrieved September 20, 2010, from ABI/INFORM Trade & Industry (Document ID: 1665581141).
4 Zerillo, N. "J&J Reaches Out to Mothers to Apologize for its Motrin Ad," *PRweek*, 11.46 (November 2008): 1. Retrieved September 20, 2010, from ABI/INFORM Trade & Industry (Document ID: 1665581021).
5 Shirley S. Wang. "J&J Pulls Online Motrin Ad After Social-Media Backlash," *The Wall Street Journal* (Eastern Edition), November 18, 2008, p. B.4. Retrieved September 20, 2010, from ABI/INFORM Global (Document ID: 1596949231).
6 Telephone conference with Marc Monseau, Johnson & Johnson, New Brunswick, New Jersey, 21 September 2010.

7   Plimsoll, S. and A. Thorpe. "Find and Target Customers in the Social Media Maze," *Marketing: Road to Recovery*, July 2010, pp. 10–11. Retrieved from ABI/INFORM Global (Document ID: 2109794771).

8   Ibid.

9   Johnson & Johnson Medical Ltd. *Hoover's Company Records*, 135526, September 15. Retrieved September 26, 2010, from Hoover's Company Records. (Document ID: 769857951).

10  Ibid.

11  Ibid.

12  Ibid.

13  "Contributing Authors," *JNJ BTW blog*. Online at http://jnjbtw.com/jnj-btw-authors/.

14  Telephone conference with Marc Monseau, Johnson & Johnson, New Brunswick, New Jersey, 21 September 2010.

15  "About Kilmer House," *Kilmer House blog*. Online at www.kilmerhouse.com/about/.

16  Ibid.

17  Telephone conference with Marc Monseau, Johnson & Johnson, New Brunswick, New Jersey, 21 September 2010.

18  "About JNJ BTW," *JNJ BTW Our People and Perspectives blog*. Online at http://jnjbtw.com/about-jnj-btw/.

19  Telephone conference with Marc Monseau, Johnson & Johnson, New Brunswick, New Jersey, 21 September 2010.

20  Ibid.

21  Johnson & Johnson Health Channel. Online at www.youtube.com/user/jnjhealth.

22  Telephone conference with Marc Monseau, Johnson & Johnson, New Brunswick, New Jersey, 21 September 2010.

23  "How J&J Joined the Twittersphere," *e-Patient Connections Conference*. Presentation by Marc Monseau, October 27, 2009.

24  Telephone conference with Marc Monseau, Johnson & Johnson, New Brunswick, New Jersey, 21 September 2010.

25  Wheaton, K. "Middle Road in Motrin-Gate Was Right Choice for J&J," *Advertising Age*, 79.44 (2008, December): 12. Retrieved September 20, 2010, from ABI/INFORM Global. (Document ID: 1611223211).

# Case 7.3: Facebook, Inc.

## *Curating Moods in a Newsfeed Experiment*

The greatest discovery of my generation is that human beings can alter their lives by altering their attitudes of mind.[1]

~ William James, American psychologist and philosopher (1842–1910)

## FACEBOOK CONDUCTS A SOCIAL EXPERIMENT

Every day people share emotions with one another through human interaction. For example, in ordinary interpersonal exchanges, people indicate through vocal tone, facial expression and eye contact just how they're feeling, conveying emotions ranging from joy to sorrow to anger. Numerous studies in social psychology have shown that affective states can easily be transferred to others via emotional contagion,[2] and people can unconsciously mimic another individual's expression of emotion.

Facebook, Inc. sought to expand on these findings and hoped to demonstrate that emotional contagion can occur just as easily through networked social media as it can through dyadic, interpersonal exchanges.[3]

In March of 2014, Facebook released a study entitled "Experimental evidence of massive-scale emotional contagion through social networks." It was published in the *Proceedings of the National Academy of Sciences (PNAS)*, a prestigious, peer-reviewed scientific journal.[4] The paper explains how social media can readily transfer emotional states from person to person through Facebook's News Feed platform. Facebook conducted an experiment on members to see how people would respond to changes in a percentage of both positive and negative posts. The results suggest that emotional contagion does occur online and that users' positive expressions can generate positive reaction, while, in turn, negative expression can generate negative reaction.[5]

## HISTORY

In 2003, Mark Zuckerberg began FaceMash[6] along with Chris Hughes and Dustin Moskovitz out of their Harvard University dorm room. The site was a matchmaking engine that rated the attractiveness of fellow Harvard students.[7]

Zuckerberg wanted a site where people could create a profile, post pictures, talk about likes and link with friends – in essence, a social networking service. After some beta bumps and bruises, Zuckerberg launched Theface-book.com the following February[8] and promoted the site among his friends. By September of 2004, Thefacebook.com had more than a quarter of a million members[9] and quickly lined up investors. By April 2005, Zuckerberg's site was valued at $100 million.[10]

Facebook began to turn a profit in 2009[11] after sourcing several streams of revenue. The single most important piece of Facebook's revenue has come from advertising.[12] Facebook's advertisements (sidebar and banner) constituted 84 percent of Facebook's revenue in 2012, and 88 percent in 2013,[13] and have become more valuable to companies with the decline of print media and broadcast media audiences.

Facebook leverages the personal information of its users to connect companies with their target audiences. For example, Facebook will enable companies like Coca-Cola to have access to users who express a preference for that beverage.[14] The remainder of Facebook's revenue comes from virtual games, although that source is rapidly drying up. In 2011, Facebook generated 12 percent of its revenue from games such as Farmville and Cityville. Today, it realizes only about 5 percent from those games because people are using their cell phones and mobile devices more, and don't play those games on their cell phones the way they once played them on their desktop computers.[15] Facebook dominates the social media advertising landscape, having earned $12.4 billion in 2014.[16]

## FACEBOOK'S VALUE PROPOSITION

Facebook has two separate value propositions aimed at two different markets with entirely different goals.[17]

Originally, Facebook's main market was its end users – people looking to connect with family and friends. At first, it was aimed only at college students at a handful of elite schools. The site is now open to anyone with an Internet connection.[18] Users can share status updates and photographs with friends and family. And all of this comes at no cost to the users.

Facebook's other major market is advertisers who buy information about Facebook's users. The company regularly gathers data about page views and browsing behavior of users in order to display targeted advertisements to users for the benefit of its advertising partners.[19]

The value proposition of the Facebook Newsfeed Experiment was to determine whether emotional manipulation would be possible through the use of social networks. This clearly could be of great value to one of Facebook's target audiences – its advertisers.

## THE EXPERIMENT

In January of 2012, from the 11th through the 18th, Facebook conducted a study on emotional contagion by manipulating the extent that a group of Facebook users were exposed to emotional expression in their News Feed.[20] The design of the experiment was such that 698,003 users were randomly selected by their User ID and separated into one of four groups.[21]

The four groups included: (1) a control group that experienced no change in their News Feed, (2) an experimental group that experienced more positive posts in their News Feed, (3) an experimental group that experienced more negative posts in their News Feed and (4) an experimental group with neutral emotional influences in their News Feed (see Figure 7.8). The test analyzed more than 3 million posts to determine the results of the experiment.[22]

To create a positivity-reduction or negativity-reduction group, Facebook changed the algorithm for selecting News Feed items. The algorithm was modified so that posts that contained emotional content, as determined by Linguistic Inquiry and Word Count software (LIWC2007), would have a 10–90 percent chance of being omitted from a user's News Feed. This content was not completely removed from user access as it was still available for direct viewing. By reducing the exposure to either positive or negative emotions Facebook theorized that users would respond by posting either more negative posts, positivity-reduced, or more positive posts, negativity-reduced.[23]

The results of the research showed that when positive words were reduced from a person's News Feed, the percentage of positive words in a person's status update was reduced by 0.1 percent compared to the corresponding control group.[24]

## Facebook Test Finds Exposure to 'Emotional Content' Leads to Small Changes in Users' Expressed Emotions

*Users exposed to different levels of positive or negative words in their 'news feed' provokes minimal changes in the emotional content of their own posts*

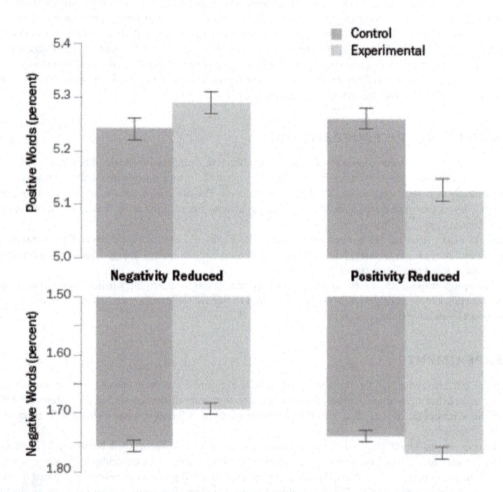

**FIGURE 7.8** Facebook Test Finds Exposure to "Emotional Content" Leads to Small Changes in Users' Expressed Emotions

Additionally, the percentage of negative words in the same person's News Feed increased by 0.04 percent.[25] For the negativity-reduced group, the percentage of negative words was reduced by 0.07 percent and the percentage of positive words increased by 0.06 percent.[26]

The results suggest that the emotions of friends on social networks influence our own emotions, thereby demonstrating emotional contagion via social networks.[27] Emotional contagion is the tendency to feel and express emotions similar to and influenced by those of others.[28] Originally, it was studied by psychologists as the transference of emotions between two people.

In "The Ripple Effect: Emotional Contagion and Its Influence on Group Behavior,"[29] Dr. Sigal Barsade found that emotional contagion has a significant effect on group behavior. This study used 94 undergraduate business school students in small groups to demonstrate that a single actor ("confederate") could influence the overall mood of a group.

Adam D. I. Kramer, a member of Facebook's Core Data Science Team and writer/designer of Facebook's experiment, said that Facebook simply wanted to investigate the effects of both positive and negative statements on users: "The reason we did this research is because we care about the emotional impact of Facebook and the people that use our product," Kramer wrote on Facebook, June 29, 2014:

> We felt that it was important to investigate the common worry that seeing friends post positive content leads to people feeling negative or left out. At the same time, we were concerned that exposure to friends' negativity might lead people to avoid visiting Facebook. We didn't clearly state our motivations in the paper.[30] (See Figure 7.9 for full text.)

**Adam D. I. Kramer** in 📍 Floyd, Virginia.
June 29, 2014 ·

OK so. A lot of people have asked me about my and Jamie and Jeff's recent study published in PNAS, and I wanted to give a brief public explanation. The reason we did this research is because we care about the emotional impact of Facebook and the people that use our product. We felt that it was important to investigate the common worry that seeing friends post positive content leads to people feeling negative or left out. At the same time, we were concerned that exposure to friends' negativity might lead people to avoid visiting Facebook. We didn't clearly state our motivations in the paper.

Regarding methodology, our research sought to investigate the above claim by very minimally deprioritizing a small percentage of content in News Feed (based on whether there was an emotional word in the post) for a group of people (about 0.04% of users, or 1 in 2500) for a short period (one week, in early 2012). Nobody's posts were "hidden," they just didn't show up on some loads of Feed. Those posts were always visible on friends' timelines, and could have shown up on subsequent News Feed loads. And we found the exact opposite to what was then the conventional wisdom: Seeing a certain kind of emotion (positive) encourages it rather than suppresses is.

And at the end of the day, the actual impact on people in the experiment was the minimal amount to statistically detect it -- the result was that people produced an average of one fewer emotional word, per thousand words, over the following week.

The goal of all of our research at Facebook is to learn how to provide a better service. Having written and designed this experiment myself, I can tell you that our goal was never to upset anyone. I can understand why some people have concerns about it, and my coauthors and I are very sorry for the way the paper described the research and any anxiety it caused. In hindsight, the research benefits of the paper may not have justified all of this anxiety.

While we've always considered what research we do carefully, we (not just me, several other researchers at Facebook) have been working on improving our internal review practices. The experiment in question was run in early 2012, and we have come a long way since then. Those review practices will also incorporate what we've learned from the reaction to this paper.

**FIGURE 7.9** Facebook Post

## ETHICAL PSYCHOLOGICAL PRACTICE

According to Dr. Sandra Collins, a social psychologist and University of Notre Dame professor of management, it is clearly unethical to conduct psychological experiments without the informed consent of the test subjects. While tests do not always measure what the people conducting the test claim, the subjects need to at least know that they are, indeed, part of a test.

The subjects of this test on Facebook were not explicitly informed that they were participating in an emotional contagion experiment. Facebook did not obtain "informed consent" as it is generally defined by researchers, nor did it allow participants to opt out.

In late June, the *PNAS* – which had published the original study – released an Editorial Expression of Concern stating that Facebook was under no obligation to tell users what it was doing because it is a private company. But, the *PNAS* Editor-in-Chief added: "It is nevertheless a matter of concern that the collection of the data by Facebook may have involved practices that were not fully consistent with the principles of obtaining informed consent and allowing participants to opt out."[31]

Two Cornell University researchers helped design the experiment and analyze the results.[32] But the Cornell University Institutional Review Board said the project didn't fall under its own Human Research Protection Program because Facebook had conducted the experiment solely for its own purposes.[33] Furthermore, the Cornell University researchers collected no data and didn't directly engage in human research.[34]

But challenges to Cornell's statement quickly emerged. Chris Chambers, a U.K. journalist with *The Guardian*, wrote:

> How is it acceptable for an ethics committee to decide that the same authors who assisted Facebook in designing an interventional study to change the emotional state of more than 600,000 people did, somehow, "not directly engage in human research?"[35]

Chambers concluded the article with the words:

> Once the brouhaha dies down, the researchers in this case may well be left with one nagging question. How did a major online company, a prestigious scientific journal, and an Ivy League university all fail to see this coming? Were it not so amateurish, one might be tempted to think this is all a ruse – that the real experiment is watching how the world reacts to revelations that Facebook conducts covert experiments on its customers.[36]

## TERMS OF SERVICE AND THE WORD "RESEARCH"

Amanda Scherker of the *Huffington Post* was quick to point out that users had agreed to be part of this experiment, whether they realized it or not. She quotes their terms of service at the time, which note that users' information may be used for "research" and that Facebook "may use all of the information we receive about you."[37] In essence, Facebook's terms of service gave it ownership of everything a user did on its website, including the ability to conduct experiments on them without their knowledge.

However, *Forbes* writer Kashmir Hill reported that the word "research" was not part of Facebook's terms of service at the time of the experiment. That word, in fact, was added months later, without public notice. In her article, published June 30, 2014, Hill writes:

> In January 2012, the policy did not say anything about users potentially being guinea pigs made to have a crappy day for science, nor that "research" is something that might happen on the platform. Four months after this study happened, in May 2012, Facebook made changes to its data use policy....[38]

The *Forbes* article also published a "red-line" version, provided by Facebook, to show how the word "research" was inserted in May, 2013 (see Figure 7.10).

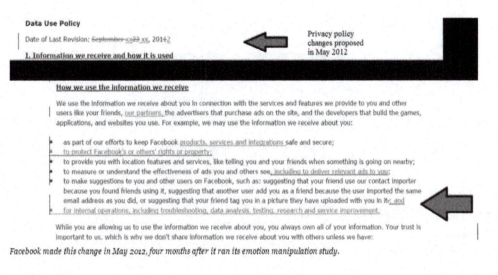

**FIGURE 7.10**  Facebook Data Use Policy

*Source*: Facebook, via *Forbes*, June 30, 2014. Online at www.forbes.com/sites/kashmirhill/2014/06/30/facebook-only-got-permission-to-do-research-on-users-after-emotion-manipulation-study/#3aa8430b10c1.

## MEDIA BACKLASH

When information about the experiment was released, the media response was overwhelmingly critical. Tech blogs reacted quickly. Sophie Weiner wrote in a blog post: "What many of us feared is already a reality: Facebook is using us as lab rats, and not just to figure out which ads we'll respond to but actually change our emotions."[39]

Josh Constine of *TechCrunch* wrote:

> . . . there is some material danger to experiments that depress people. "Some people who are at risk of depression were almost surely part of Facebook's study group that were shown a more depressing feed, which could be considered dangerous. Facebook will endure a whole new level of backlash if any of those participants were found to have committed suicide or had other depression-related outcomes after the study."[40]

"Come on Facebook, why the hell didn't you just ask for volunteers?" wrote Steven J. Vaughan-Nichols for *ZDNet* on June 30, 2014. "With over a billion users, I think you could easily get a few hundred thousand real volunteers for your study." He ended his column that day with "Stop it, Facebook. Stop it now. And never, ever do anything like this again."[41]

Mainstream media, such as *The Atlantic*, questioned Facebook's ethics and published at least two Twitter posts, one from Clay Johnson and another from Erin Kissane, who had reacted dramatically to news of the Facebook experiment.[42] (See Figure 7.11.)

*The New York Times* quoted Brian Blau, a technology analyst with the research firm Gartner, "Facebook didn't do anything illegal, but they didn't do right by their customers. Doing psychological testing on people crosses the line." Facebook should have informed its users, he said. "They keep on pushing the boundaries, and this is one of the reasons people are upset."[43]

## FACEBOOK'S RESPONSE

While some of the researchers have since expressed some regret about the experiment, Facebook as a company was unapologetic about the experiment. The company maintained that it received consent from its users through

> **Clay Johnson** @cjoh  🔲 Follow
>
> In the wake of both the Snowden stuff and the Cuba twitter stuff, the Facebook "transmission of anger" experiment is terrifying.
> 9:43 AM · 28 Jun 2014
>
> ↩  ♺ 152   ♥ 65

> **Erin Kissane** @kissane  🔲 Follow
>
> Get off Facebook. Get your family off Facebook. If you work there, quit. They're fucking awful.
> 11:33 PM · 27 Jun 2014
>
> ↩  ♺ 507   ♥ 530

**FIGURE 7.11**   Facebook User Reaction Posts on Twitter

*Source*: Twitter.com

its terms of service. A Facebook spokesman defended the research, saying "We do research to improve our services and make the content people see on Facebook as relevant and engaging as possible. . . . We carefully consider what research we do and have a strong internal review process."[44]

While Facebook is notorious for its constantly evolving terms of service, even now the Terms of Service imply – though do not state outright – that this sort of behavior may happen again. According to Facebook's Data Policy page:

> We also collect information about how you use our Services, such as the types of content you view or engage with or the frequency and duration of your activities. . . . We collect information about the people and groups you are connected to and how you interact with them, such as the people you communicate with the most or the groups you like to share with. We also collect contact information you provide if you upload, sync or import this information (such as an address book) from a device.
>
> If you use our Services for purchases or financial transactions (like when you buy something on Facebook, make a purchase in a game, or make a donation), we collect information about the purchase or transaction. This includes your payment information, such as your credit or debit card number and other card information, and other account and authentication information, as well as billing, shipping and contact details.
>
> We collect information from or about the computers, phones, or other devices where you install or access our Services, depending on the permissions you've granted. We may associate the information we collect from your different devices, which helps us provide consistent Services across your devices.[45]

Further into the Facebook Data Policy, the word "research" is used thusly: "We conduct surveys and research, test features in development, and analyze the information we have to evaluate and improve products and services, develop new products or features, and conduct audits and troubleshooting activities."[46]

To this day, Facebook still collects an enormous amount of information about its users and can use that information to manipulate what users see. Additionally, these items are not listed on Facebook's main terms of service page. Users must click on a link inside a different set of terms to arrive at the Data Policy page, making these terms onerous to find. This positioning raises questions about how Facebook will employ its users' behaviors in the future.

## DISCUSSION QUESTIONS

1.  How should Facebook respond to this situation? How can the company regain the trust of its users once more?
2.  Should the company promise to never again conduct a survey of this sort? Should it go even further and explicitly ban research intended to manipulate the responses of its users?

3. How can Facebook balance the concerns of its users with the necessity of generating revenue through advertising?
4. What processes or structures should Facebook establish to make sure it does not encounter these issues again?

## WRITING ASSIGNMENT

Please respond in writing to the issues presented in this case by preparing two documents: a communication strategy memo and a professional business letter.

In preparing these documents, you may assume one of two roles: you may identify yourself as a Facebook senior manager who has been asked to provide advice to Chief Operating Officer Sheryl Sandberg and Chief Product Officer Chris Cox regarding the issues they and their company are facing. Or, you may identify yourself as an external management consultant who has been asked by the company to provide advice to them.

Either way, you must prepare a strategy memo addressed jointly to Ms. Sandberg and Mr. Cox that summarizes the details of the case, identifies critical issues, discusses their implications (what they mean and why they matter), offers specific recommendations for action (assigning ownership and suspense dates for each), and shows how to communicate the solution to all who are affected by the recommendations.

You must also prepare a professional business letter for the signature of Mark Zuckerberg, Facebook Chief Executive Officer. That document should be addressed to all Facebook users, explaining what happened and the actions the company is taking, and will be posted to Mr. Zuckerberg's Facebook blog. If you have questions about either of these documents, please consult your instructor.

## ACKNOWLEDGMENTS

This case was prepared by research assistants Kyle Ferguson, Javier Hernandez and Mark Weber under the direction of James O'Rourke, Teaching Professor of Management, as the basis for class discussion rather than to illustrate either effective or ineffective handling of an administrative situation. Information was gathered from corporate as well as public sources. Editorial assistance: Judy Bradford.

Copyright © 2015. Eugene D. Fanning Center for Business Communication. All rights reserved. No part of this publication may be reproduced, stored in a retrieval system, used in a spreadsheet, or transmitted in any form by any means – electronic, mechanical, photocopying, recording, or otherwise – without permission.

## NOTES

1. Mindbloom life game. Online at www.mindbloom.com/apps/inspiration/detail/quote/21bcf4e2-a31b-4144-a1d0-149357b ba7bd/.
2. Carter, Sherrie Bourg. "Emotions Are Contagious – Choose Your Company Wisely," *Psychology Today*, October 20, 2012. Online at www.psychologytoday.com/blog/high-octane-women/201210/emotions-are-contagious-choose-your-company-wisely.
3. Kramer, Adam, Jamie Guillory and Jeffrey Hancock. "Experimental Evidence of Massive Scale Emotional Contagion Through Social Networks," *PNAS (Proceedings of the National Academy of Sciences of the United States of America)*. March 25, 2014. Online at www.pnas.org/content/111/24/8788.full.
4. Ibid.
5. Ibid.
6. Kaplan, Katharine. "Facemash Creator Survives Ad Board," *The Harvard Crimson*, November 19, 2003. Online at www.thecrimson.com/article/2003/11/19/facemash-creator-survives-ad-board-the/.
7. Cassidy, John. "ME MEDIA; How Hanging Out On the Internet Became Big Business," *The New Yorker*, May 15, 2006. Online at www.newyorker.com/magazine/2006/05/15/me-media. Accessed October 4, 2015.
8. Ibid.
9. Ibid.
10. "Tracking *Facebook's* Valuation," DealBook Tracking Facebook's Valuation Comments, *The New York Times*, February 1, 2012. Online at http://dealbook.nytimes.com/2012/02/01/tracking-facebooks-valuation/. Accessed October 4, 2015.
11. Macmillan, Douglas. "Facebook Climbs Toward Profitability," *The Tech Beat*, September 15, 2009. Online at www.businessweek.com/the_thread/techbeat/archives/2009/09/facebook_climbs_toward_profitability.html.

12    O'Neill, Nick. "The Secret to How Facebook Makes Money," *AdWeek*, January 19, 2010. Online at www.adweek.com/socialtimes/facebook-makes-money/313120.

13    Nair, Smita. "Must-Know: Assessing Facebook's Revenue Sources," *Yahoo! Finance*, January 15, 2014. Online at http://finance.yahoo.com/news/must-know-assessing-facebook-revenue-170009607.html.

14    Patwari, Yogesh. "What are Facebook's Main Revenue Sources?" *Quora*, December 14, 2015. Online at www.quora.com/What-are-Facebooks-main-revenue-sources.

15    D'Onfo, Gillian. "Facebook is Losing One of its Revenue Streams Because Everyone is Glued to Their Phones," *Business Insider*, August 1, 2015. Online at www.businessinsider.com/facebook-payments-revenue-declining-2015-7.

16    For 10-k, United States Securities & Exchange Commission, Facebook, Inc., page 30. Online at http://investor.fb.com/secfiling.cfm?filingID=1326801-15-6.

17    Laja, Peep. "Useful Value Proposition Examples (and How to Create a Good One), *ConversionXL*, 2015. Online at http://conversionxl.com/value-proposition-examples-how-to-create/.

18    Yadav, Sid. "Facebook – The Complete Biography," Mashable, August 25, 2006. Online at http://mashable.com/2006/08/25/facebook-profile/#orb9TmeYHiqK.

19    Felix, Samantha. "This Is How Facebook Is Tracking Your Internet Activity," *Business Insider*, September 9, 2012. Online at www.businessinsider.com/this-is-how-facebook-is-tracking-your-internet-activity-2012-9.

20    Kramer, Guillory and Hancock. "Experimental Evidence of Massive Scale Emotional Contagion Through Social Networks."

21    Morin, Rich. "Facebook's Experiment Causes a Lot of Fuss For Little Result," *Pew Research Center Fact Tank*, July 12, 2014. Online at www.pewresearch.org/fact-tank/2014/07/02/facebooks-experiment-is-just-the-latest-to-manipulate-you-in-the-name-of-research/.

22    Kramer, Guillory and Hancock. "Experimental Evidence of Massive Scale Emotional Contagion Through Social Networks."

23    Ibid.

24    Ibid.

25    Ibid.

26    Ibid.

27    Ibid.

28    "Emotional Contagion," *Dictionary.com*. Online at http://dictionary.reference.com/browse/emotional-contagion.

29    Barsade, Sigal. "The Ripple Effect: Emotional Contagion and its Influence on Group Behavior," Yale University and EBSCO Publishing, 2003.

30    Strange, Adario. "Facebook Responds to Negative Reactions to Its Experiment on Users," June 29, 2014.
      Online at http://mashable.com/2014/06/29/facebook-responds-to-negative-reactions-to-its-emotion-contagion-study/#CDwT98JcgsqS. See also Facebook, Adam. D. I. Kramer, June 29, 2014. Online at www.facebook.com/akramer/posts/10152987150867796.

31    Verman, Inder M. "Editorial Expression of Concern," *PNAS*, July 22, 2014. Online at www.pnas.org/content/111/29/10779.1.full.

32    Boesel, Whitney. "Facebook's Controversial Experiment: Big Tech Is the New Big Pharma," *Time*, July 3, 2014. Online at http://time.com/2951726/facebook-emotion-contagion-experiment/.

33    Verman. "Editorial Expression of Concern."

34    Boesel. "Facebook's Controversial Experiment: Big Tech Is the New Big Pharma."

35    Chambers, Chris. "Facebook Fiasco: Was Cornell's Study of 'Emotional Contagion' an Ethics Breach?" *The Guardian*, July 1, 2014. Online at www.theguardian.com/science/head-quarters/2014/jul/01/facebook-cornell-study-emotional-contagion-ethics-breach.

36    Ibid.

37    Scherker, Amanda. "Didn't Read Facebook's Fine Print? Here's Exactly What It Says," *Huffington Post*, July 21, 2014. Online at www.huffingtonpost.com/2014/07/21/facebook-terms-condition_n_5551965.html.

38    Hill, Kashmir. "Facebook Added 'Research' to User Agreement 4 Months After Emotion Manipulation Study," *Forbes*, June 30, 2014. Online at www.forbes.com/sites/kashmirhill/2014/06/30/facebook-only-got-permission-to-do-research-on-users-after-emotion-manipulation-study/#3aa8430b10c1.

39    Weiner, Sophie. "Facebook Experiment Manipulates Emotions of 600,000 Users," *Animal New York*, June 27, 2014. Online at http://animalnewyork.com/2014/facebook-experiment-manipulates-emotions-600000-users/.

40    Constine, Josh. "The Morality of A/B Testing," *TechCrunch*, June 29, 2014. Online at http://techcrunch.com/2014/06/29/ethics-in-a-data-driven-world/.

41    Vaughan-Nichols, Steven J. "We're All Just Lab Rats in Facebook's Laboratory," *ZDNet Between the Lines*, June 30, 2014. Online at www.zdnet.com/article/were-all-just-lab-rats-in-facebooks-laboratory/.

42    Meyer, Robinson. "Everything We Know About Facebook's Secret Mood Manipulation Experiment," *The Atlantic*, June 28, 2014. Online at www.theatlantic.com/technology/archive/2014/06/everything-we-know-about-facebooks-secret-mood-manipulation-experiment/373648/.

43   Goel, Vindu. "Facebook Tinkers With Users' Emotions in News Feed Experiment, Stirring Outcry," *The New York Times, Technology*, June 29, 2014. Online at www.nytimes.com/2014/06/30/technology/facebook-tinkers-with-users-emotions-in-news-feed-experiment-stirring-outcry.html?_r=0.

44   Sullivan, Gail. "Facebook Responds to Criticism of Its Experiment on Users," *The Washington Post*, June 30, 2014. Online at www.washingtonpost.com/news/morning-mix/wp/2014/06/30/facebook-responds-to-criticism-of-study-that-manipulated-users-news-feeds/.

45   "What Kinds of Information Do We Collect?" *Facebook, Data Policy*. Online at www.facebook.com/about/privacy/. Accessed January 29, 2016.

46   "How Do We Use This Information?" *Facebook, Data Policy*. Online at www.facebook.com/about/privacy/. Accessed January 29, 2016.

CHAPTER 8

# Listening and Feedback

Two highly accomplished lawyers are sitting at the bar at Sparks Steakhouse in New York. One is a fellow named Tom, the other is Tom's law partner, Kevin. They're having a leisurely drink, waiting for their table to open up. Sparks is a landmark steakhouse where a handful of New York's rich, powerful and glamorous are in attendance most nights. This particular night includes superstar attorney David Boies, who argued the U.S. government's antitrust case against Microsoft. He makes a beeline to the bar to say hello to Kevin, whom he knows from previous cases, and joins Tom and Kevin for a drink. A few minutes later, Kevin gets up to make a phone call outside.

Mr. Boies remains at the bar, talking to Tom for 30 minutes. "I'd never met Boies before," Tom said:

> He didn't have to hang around the bar talking to me. And I have to tell you, I wasn't bowled over by his intelligence, or his piercing questions, or his anecdotes. What impressed me was that when he asked a question, he waited for the answer. He not only listened, he made me feel like I was the only person in the room.[1]

In showing interest, asking questions and listening for the answers without distraction, Boies was simply practicing the one skill that has made him inarguably great at relating to people. "The only difference between us and the super-successful among us," says business journalist Marshall Goldsmith, "is that the greats do this all the time. It's automatic. There's no on-off switch for caring, empathy, and showing respect. It's always on." [2]

## AN ESSENTIAL SKILL

We have all grown to understand how valuable communication is to the success of any business. And few of us would argue with the value of being skilled as a communicator on a personal level. We make friends, establish relationships, pass ideas and accomplish the work that earns our living each day. Yet, strangely, the communication skill most central to our success – personally and professionally – is the one we're least likely to study in a formal way.

According to Professors Ralph Nichols and Leonard Stevens of the University of Minnesota, the average person spends about 70 percent of each day engaged in some type of communication. More specifically, researchers report that of all the time we spend communicating each day, 45 percent is spent listening, 30 percent speaking, 16 percent reading and only 9 percent writing.[3]

More recent studies show that adults now spend more than half their daily communication listening to someone else speak. Even though it's clearly a crucial skill, few people, according to Professor James Floyd, know how to do so efficiently and effectively.[4] Nichols warns, however, that "listening is hard work. It is characterized by faster heart action, quicker circulation of the blood, a small rise in bodily temperature." The implication is simple: If you are not motivated to work at listening, you are not likely to improve.[5]

Studies of listening skill repeatedly show that the average North American adult listens at an efficiency rate of just 25 percent. Your mother was right: For most of us, literally three-quarters of what we hear goes in one ear and out the other. We retain and understand just a fraction of what's going on around us.[6]

The difference between hearing and listening is substantial. Hearing is merely an involuntary physical response to the environment. Listening, on the other hand, is a process that includes hearing, attending to, understanding, evaluating and responding to spoken messages. It's a sophisticated communication skill that can be mastered only with considerable practice. It is fair to emphasize, however, that while improving one's listening skills is difficult, demanding and challenging, it can be immensely rewarding.[7]

Why have most of us become so resistant to careful listening? "It's because of our fast-paced world," says Kathy Thompson of Alverno College. "We're always in a hurry. Mentally we're saying, 'Get to the point.' We don't have time to hear the whole story. We're running from house to job to store to church. Good listening takes time."[8]

That's part of it, according to Wick Chambers, a partner in Speechworks, an Atlanta communications-training firm. "But also, people think listening is boring; it's more fun to talk."

Still others blame TV, radio and the Internet, which allow people to combine listening with so many other activities that simply listening – to music, for example – seems like a waste of time.[9]

"When you watch television," says Sheila Bentley, a Memphis, Tennessee, communications consultant:

you're listening in a way that doesn't require you to retain anything and doesn't object if you leave the room. And because it's interrupted by commercials, you don't have to develop sustained attending skills. With people spending six hours a day doing that kind of listening, it's no wonder there's concern that we're becoming a nation of poor listeners.[10]

## WHY LISTEN?

Poor listening can cause disasters, as it did in the 1977 runway collision at Tenerife Airport in the Canary Islands, when misunderstood instructions caused 583 deaths. But more often, poor listening results in millions of little time-wasting mistakes a day – the wrong coffee order, credit card charge or telephone number. Ms. Bentley spends hours with medical managers because of the massive liability awards doctors and hospitals can pay in response to poor listening. "People are realizing," she says, "that a lot of mistakes we attributed to other things are actually listening problems."[11]

At Starbucks Coffee Company stores, where a customer can order a "double-shot decaf grande iced half-skim vanilla dry cappuccino," employees are taught a procedure for hearing and calling orders developed by the company some years ago. It systematizes the sequence of words describing the drink – size, flavoring, milk, decaf – with automatic defaults. Then the person making the drink echoes the order aloud. "We expect our employees to listen," says Alan Gulick, a Starbucks spokesperson. "It's an important component of customer service."[12] Realizing just how difficult listening is, many Starbucks baristas simply prefer to write the order on the cup. Easy, if it's paper; not so easy with a ceramic mug.

Listening is the central skill in the establishment and maintenance of interpersonal relationships. No matter what type of relationship – professional, personal, neighborly, romantic – listening is the skill that forms the bond and keeps the relationship moving forward. Harvard psychologist Daniel Goleman says:

Listening is a skill that keeps couples together. Even in the heat of an argument, when both are seized by emotional hijacking, one or the other, and sometimes both, can manage to listen past the anger, and hear and respond to a partner's reparative gesture.[13]

# THE BENEFITS OF BETTER LISTENING

James J. Floyd, who has taught and written on this subject for many years, offers four specific benefits you'll obtain from becoming a better listener: increased knowledge, job success, improved interpersonal relations and self-protection.[14]

Scholars of human behavior have shown a steady tendency during the past 75 years in the U.S. toward more passive learning techniques and more passive leisure activities. As a society, we spend more time watching television, movies, videos and the Internet and less time reading. Coincidentally, we also spend more time these days listening to CDs, tapes, radio and MP3s. A study conducted by UNISYS Corporation reported that students spend 60 to 70 percent of their time in a classroom listening.[15] Professors Nichols and Stevens found in their studies at the University of Minnesota that every group of students receiving instruction in listening improved by at least 25 percent, while some groups improved by as much as 40 percent.[16] Without some instruction in listening improvement, however, it appears that the listening abilities of most people actually decline from elementary school onward.[17]

A number of other good reasons exist for you to improve your listening:

- **Listening demonstrates acceptance.** The very act of listening to another person demonstrates that you value him or her and care about what he or she is saying. If you show that you *don't care* about others, they'll quit talking to you. Good, perhaps, in the short run, but disastrous in the long term.
- **Listening promotes problem-solving abilities.** Good managers are often asked to do what bartenders, cab drivers and counselors have done for years: allow someone the time and attention to talk through a problem. Rather than providing advice and solutions right away, most successful managers encourage employees to arrive at solutions on their own. By listening carefully and reflectively, a supervisor can guide a subordinate to a solution that has a greater chance of success and substantially greater levels of employee buy-in.
- **Listening increases the speaker's receptiveness to the thoughts and ideas of others.** The best ideas don't always come from yourself or your immediate staff and colleagues. Often, you'll find great ideas where you least expect them. They may come from your customers, your employees, your suppliers and business partners, and (interestingly) from people who refuse to do business with you. You might be genuinely surprised at what your competitor's customers are saying about you, if only you'd take the time to listen to them.
- **Listening increases the self-esteem of the other person.** You are not personally responsible for the self-esteem of everyone in your organization, but think about it for a moment. Isn't it easier to come to work, concentrate on the tasks at hand, and compete successfully if you feel good about yourself? Sales managers have known intuitively for years that self-esteem is crucial to a sales representative's ability to succeed. They hear "no" so often that they come to accept failure as an inevitable part of the job. Having a manager who'll listen to them willingly and uncritically can be enormously helpful.
- **Listening helps you overcome self-consciousness and self-centeredness.** A little instruction and some practice in active listening can help talkers to shut up and the self-consciously shy to open up. Working more toward the center of the "listening–talking" continuum can be especially helpful to junior managers who are inclined to offer opinions when the demand for them is not especially brisk.
- **Listening can help to prevent head-on emotional collisions.** If you concentrate on your own needs to the exclusion of other people's needs and interests, you will find that others will return the favor: They will focus on their own interests and not yours. The key to preventing the sort of emotional train wrecks that are destructive to any organization is to put other people's needs ahead of your own. Find out what their concerns and interests are first – by listening carefully to them – and you will likely get what you want sooner and with substantially less angst.

By taking responsibility for successful communication through active and reflective listening, you can become more successful at those activities that depend on communication, including your personal and professional life. You can learn more, improve your relationships with others around you and increase your chances for success. Careful listening is no guarantee, of course, but it's a wonderful place to start.

# THE ROLE OF INEFFECTIVE LISTENING HABITS

Ralph Nichols, followed by a number of other researchers, was early to discover that many of us employ listening habits that are ineffective and may interfere with learning. The problem is not that we *can't* listen or *don't* listen. It's far more likely that we've learned to listen *haphazardly* and in ways that are simply counterproductive.[18]

The first step in becoming a more effective listener, both in the workplace and in our personal lives, is to identify the poor listening habits we've developed over a lifetime and replace them with effective, productive habits.

## AN INVENTORY OF POOR LISTENING HABITS

Here, then, are a few habits that hinder rather than help as we try to listen to what others are telling us:

### Being Preoccupied with Talking, Not Listening

The most successful CEOs, board chairs, military admirals and generals, university presidents – that handful of enormously talented high achievers who run large and complex organizations – without exception are far more interested in listening to what others have to say than they are in talking. When they talk, they invariably ask questions – to gather information, to solicit opinions, to "take the pulse" of the organization. When they speak, the sentences tend to be brief, cogent and terse. They succeed by gathering up what others know and sharing what they know selectively.

### Calling the Subject Uninteresting

We've all done it. You can probably recall doing it in algebra class or, perhaps, during a lecture on a subject you had little interest in knowing anything about. Many have paid dearly for this error by declaring that everything from cost accounting to microeconomics just "isn't especially interesting." If you declare a subject to be dull, you virtually guarantee that you'll learn nothing about it. Some subjects may be a bit duller than others, but in order to learn anything at all, you'll have to be somewhat selfish and tell yourself, "This may not be fascinating, but there's something in here that's important for me to know." Taking an interest in the subject is the first step.

### Letting Bias or Prejudice Distort the Messages You Hear

We all have biases. They are an important, almost inescapable part of who we are and the kind of lives we've led. By filtering incoming messages through these biases, stereotypes or prejudices, however, we put another speaker's intentions at risk. We hear what our biases tell us to hear and not what's being said. The best advice is not to rid yourself of your preferences but simply to know what they are. Don't let your views on a particular subject or about a particular speaker interfere with what you're hearing.

### Oversimplifying Answers or Explanations

This form of uncritical listening comes from an all-too-understandable desire to reduce the complex to something simpler, to eliminate detail, to tighten up arguments that depend on important detail. Listen carefully to what's being said and later examine those parts of the explanation or answer that may be eliminated, keeping what's most valuable or useful.

### Yielding to External Distractions

It's certainly easy to be distracted. If you work in a cubicle rather than a private office, you may be exposed to a half-dozen or more conversations at once. Carol Hymowitz of *The Wall Street Journal* says, "In this open-space era, aimed at flattening hierarchies and promoting teamwork, managers . . . have to adapt to less privacy and more contact, to being constantly seen and heard as they make decisions and deals." Learning to focus on the task at hand, whether it's a phone conversation or a face-to-face meeting with an employee, is crucial to success as a listener.[19]

### Yielding to Internal Distractions

These can come from anywhere, even (or especially) when you're isolated and trying to concentrate. Put aside your personal concerns – everything from car payments to your next appointment – and devote just a few minutes to the listening task at hand, and you will find far fewer problems in your life. A few minutes spent concentrating on the words you are hearing will pay big dividends all week.

### Avoiding Difficult or Demanding Material

This problem is akin to an earlier one we talked about — it's just as bad to say that a subject is difficult as it is to say it's dull or uninteresting. By staying with subjects and material you know and are already comfortable with, you limit your ability to grow intellectually. Any debate or forensics coach will tell you that listening is a skill, just like putting in golf or a free throw in basketball. If you are unwilling to work at it, you are unlikely to get any better.

### Rationalizing Poor Listening

We all can point to various people or circumstances to blame poor listening habits on: "No one taught me how to do this." "This office is filled with noise and distractions." "I've never paid much attention to listening as a skill." Don't give up. And don't accept that 25 percent efficiency rate as something you can't do anything about. Effective, active listening is important and you can improve.

### Criticizing the Speaker's Delivery

Rather than focus on the speaker's accent, pacing or phrasing, concentrate instead on the message they carry. Look for both cognitive and emotional content, but give the speaker a break. Most people haven't had much formal training in public speaking and, in the course of casual conversation, directional changes and fluency breaks are common. Concentrate on *what's* being said rather than *how* it's said.

### Jumping to Conclusions

Formulating a response prematurely may disrupt the speaker's thoughts, may take the conversation in an unintended direction or may reveal that you do not understand what the speaker has been trying to say. Rather than predicting the direction or outcome of a conversation, give your partner an opportunity to get to the point. Relax and let him or her talk for a little while.

### Getting Overstimulated

If you're more concerned about your response than about what's being said to you, chances are good that you will miss much of what you are hearing. "There's the old joke," says communications consultant Wicke Chambers. "The opposite of talking isn't listening. It's waiting to talk. That's what a lot of people do," she says. "They just wait to talk." The advice? Take it all in, think about it, then formulate a response. Go one step at a time.

### Assigning the Wrong Meaning to Words

This habit sounds remarkably simple, but we do it every day, at home, at work and at school. Some words have specific meaning and you can, in fact, look them up. (*Enormity* meaning "excessive wickedness" or "beyond all moral bounds," rather than "largeness" or "big.") Others require interpretation. ("The customer says he needs this right away." Does that mean 20 minutes from now? By the close of business? Or will sometime this week be okay? You'd better ask.)

### Listening Only for the Facts

On the face of it, this habit doesn't sound like such a bad idea. ("I wish he'd get to the point.") The problem, however, is that if we listen *only* for the facts, all we'll have is facts. We won't have any real understanding of why the issue is important, how it's linked to other issues or what the implications or outcomes may be. Along the way, you have to listen for context, connections and those rhetorical ligatures that link facts to human experience.

### Trying to Make an Outline of Everything We Hear

Because so little of what we'll hear from one day to the next is organized in any systematic way, forcing it into an outline is not a good idea. Not many extemporaneous speeches and few impromptu conversations are based on any sort of organized outline. Don't force what you hear into artificial patterns. Just take it in, sort it out as you go along and try as best you can to make sense of what the speaker is saying.

### Faking Attention to the Speaker

This skill, learned in high school and college classrooms all over the country, later develops as a high art form in business meetings everywhere. You don't want to seem impolite, so you smile and nod. The speaker thinks you not only understand but also agree! The fact is, you haven't heard a word that's been said, but you've given the impression that you have. As a direct result, the speaker is unlikely to repeat any information, offer additional examples or illustrations, or seek questions from those who might appear confused or curious.

### Letting Emotion-Laden Words Throw Us off the Track

Most intelligent speakers know well enough to avoid racist, sexist or profane language precisely because it is offensive to so many people. But what about words or phrases that have some emotional attachment for you that a speaker would have no clue about? Sometimes the attachment is personal (a date or a song title, for example); more often, it's a topic or subject reference that can set you off (taxes, for instance). It's easier said than done, but stay in control of your emotions and pay attention, at least until the conversation or speech is finished.

### Resisting the Temptation to Interrupt

One of the by-products of the imbalance between talkers and listeners is interruption, with three or four people talking and no one listening. "We have become a nation of interrupters," says Professor Kathy Thompson. It's as true at home as it is in business, where several people may be vying for the boss's attention, and none much cares what his or her competitors are saying. According to Sam Nelson, director of debate at the University of Rochester, "People want to take credit for things. If you're the first person to get it out, it's yours. So you go into the meeting thinking, 'I'm going to get this out if it kills me.'" That also helps explain the disappearance of the pause from many people's speech. Many experts see the value of pausing, however, saying that it signals a sense of confidence. If you are confident in your ideas, confident in your position, it will probably pay for you to wait your turn and avoid interrupting others.

### Wasting the Differential between the Rate at Which We Speak and the Rate at Which We Think

If all this weren't bad enough, biology also works against attentive listening. Most people speak at a rate of 120 to 150 words a minute, but the human brain can easily process more than 500 words a minute, leaving plenty of time for what Cynthia Crossen calls *mental fidgeting*. "If the speaker also happens to be slow, monotonal and wordy," she adds, "it requires a heroic effort to stay tuned instead of simply faking it."[20]

## DEVELOPING GOOD LISTENING HABITS

Researchers at UNISYS Corporation identified ways in which you can review your ineffective habits, identify those you should replace and substitute more effective strategies for listening, learning and remembering. In fact, they described more than a dozen habits you may wish to consider for your own inventory of communication skills:

### Stop Talking

This approach does not occur to many people, but it *is* effective.

### One Conversation at a Time

You can't talk on the phone and have a conversation with someone in the room at the same time. Choose the conversation you most want to have and tell the other person you'll be available in a few minutes.

### Empathize with the Person Speaking

Put yourself in his or her shoes; try as best you can to see it from the other person's point of view. It's not easy to listen empathetically, but it's important to try.

### Ask Questions

If you are confused, lost or need information, ask for clarification. Simple questions that seek data, positions or intentions can be especially helpful.

### Don't Interrupt

Asking questions may be useful, but initially at least it may be more helpful simply to let your conversation partner talk for a bit. If the conversation has any substance at all, it won't be long before you have an opportunity to react.

### Show Interest

Demonstrate complete interest in what's being said to you. Look the talker in the eyes, show interest with your facial expression and maintain an open and nonthreatening posture. Show that you care.

### Give Your Undivided Attention

If you can, close the door, hold your calls and give all of your attention to whomever is speaking. If privacy isn't possible, at least put aside what you're working on, reading or doing. If you really need some conversational privacy and your office isn't set up for that sort of thing, you might consider going for a walk. Low tones and a steady pace will usually provide you with an opportunity to speak in confidence.

### Evaluate Facts and Evidence

Listen critically. Ask yourself (and, perhaps, your conversation partner) how you know this information is true. What's the source of your confidence in the data? Ask whether the evidence is recent, reliable, accurate and relevant to the subject.

### React to Ideas, Not to the Speaker

It's tough to separate the message from the messenger, but give it a try. We often choose to believe what we hear based on who we hear it from. Wherever possible, look beyond your assessment of the speaker to the ideas contained in the speech.

### Wishing Doesn't Make It So

Just because you want to hear it doesn't mean it is what the speaker is saying. Shakespeare's phrase, "The wish is father to the thought" means simply that we don't listen carefully because we're often engaged in a great deal of wishful thinking.[21]

### Listen for What is Not Said

If you expect to hear something and don't, perhaps it's time to ask why you haven't. Match your expectations of the speaker's content against what you actually hear, and think carefully about what hasn't been said.

### Listen to How Something is Said

We told you earlier not to criticize the speaker's delivery and that's still a useful rule. You should consider listening, however, for the emotional content, for hints of sarcasm, cynicism or irony in what you hear. Often a speaker will downplay criticism or make light of a key point simply with a shift in his or her tone of voice. Tune in to the speaker's mood and intention, as well as the content of the speech.

### Share the Responsibility for Communication

It's not entirely the speaker's responsibility to make sure you understand what's being said. You have an obligation to seek out information that's useful or important to you. Focus, concentrate, ask questions, pay attention to what's going on.[22]

## THE FIVE ESSENTIAL SKILLS OF ACTIVE LISTENING

To become an effective, empathetic and skilled listener, you must participate in the dialogue. This process is much more active than the one you use when listening to speeches, lectures or in meetings. The dialogue process involves you and one or two other people engaged in direct conversation. To increase your probability of success, here are five skills you should practice and master:

### Paraphrase Others as They Speak

From time-to-time in a conversation, it will be useful for you to summarize what others are saying. It's helpful to use your own words to do this, but you must do it to their satisfaction in order to convince them you are really listening. Such summaries often begin with a phrase similar to this: "If I understand you correctly, what you're saying is . . . ," or "In other words, you're telling me that. . . . "

### Reflect Feelings

Some managers will look intently for the meaning in a spoken sentence without paying much attention to the emotional load attached to it. Try, as best you can, to grasp the affective intent of the speaker. Summaries that reflect feeling might sound like this: "You're not very confident about this, are you?" or "You seem determined to see this through."

### Reflect Meaning

It's always helpful for a manager to focus on the cognitive or logical content of a discussion – the facts at hand, how they're organized and how they bear on the topic being discussed. Consider this reflection of a conversation's meaning: "When you say you will need help with this project, am I correct in assuming you mean you will require additional support staff, particularly in the start-up phase?"

### Reflect Conclusions

Discussions can ramble far and wide and can include a great deal of information that may not be directly relevant. It's often useful to review what you have agreed to or concluded, particularly as a conversation is drawing to a conclusion. A summary reflecting the conclusion of a conversation might sound like this: "So, considering the cost of the upgrade and our other immediate needs, am I right in assuming you are not in favor of the purchase?"

### Follow Through

Important as listening is, follow-through is even more so. Calvin Morrill, a professor of sociology at the University of Arizona, cautions that once you have asked for feedback, "unless you take steps that show your employees that you've listened to them and intend to take action, they will never speak again. In cases like those," he says, "the manager would have been better off never having asked at all."[23]

## A SYSTEM FOR IMPROVING YOUR LISTENING HABITS

The time you spend preparing for your quarterly or semiannual performance review might be a good time to review your communication habits in general and your listening habits in particular. If you're serious about becoming a better listener, consider this four-step process:

1. **Review your listening inventory.** Make a few notes about those habits and behaviors that dominate your communication from day to day. Think, in particular, about those that you most often use and which seem to work best or work least for you.
2. **Recognize your undesirable listening habits.** If you display, even occasionally, any of those habits we have listed as undesirable, make a note of them: which ones, how often and under what circumstances (i.e., one-on-one conversations with employees, during meetings with colleagues and coworkers, and so on).
3. **Refuse to tolerate undesirable habits.** Even if the undesirable habits you list are infrequent and don't seem particularly serious, refuse to tolerate them as a part of your communication skill inventory. Tag them for removal and get to work on them.
4. **Replace undesirable habits with effective ones.** For every unproductive, undesirable or negative listening habit you have, identify a positive habit or skill to replace it. Don't simply tell yourself you won't daydream during a lecture; work out a system to use the spare time effectively.[24]

Becoming a good listener carries some risks. Talkers can attach themselves to you like barnacles to a boat, and detaching them isn't easy. Good listeners can also find themselves on the receiving end of other people's problems, even when they may have little to offer in the way of support or counsel. But the rewards can be enormous for developing this skill, both for you as an individual and for the organization that employs you. Remember: Putting other people's needs ahead of your own may seem counterintuitive, but doing so will help both you and others achieve your goals sooner, more efficiently and less stressfully. It's in your best interest to care about how well you listen.

Child psychologist Robert Coles, who teaches psychiatry and medical humanities at Harvard Medical School, cautions that listening is more than a set of cognitive skills – it's an approach to life and other people that involves the whole person. "I think real listening is something you do with your whole self," he says. "You have to hear what people are really saying beneath all the words. You have to pick up the messages that have a certain urgency and then respond to these nuances with further questions. Over the years," he notes:

I've learned that really attentive listening requires conversational responsiveness. You have to try to listen in such a way that you can respond with your own ideas and feelings and aspirations—so that you can show the speaker you've truly been paying attention.[25]

## GIVING AND RECEIVING FEEDBACK

When he was mayor of New York City, Ed Koch frequently walked the streets of his hometown asking his constituents, "How am I doing?" The question wasn't simply rhetorical; nor was it a ritualistic greeting for his faithful supporters. He asked the question of friend and foe alike. He cared about the responses he received because his ability to perform as that city's mayor depended on *feedback* – direct, honest, current, unfiltered feedback. If he wasn't doing well, New Yorkers let him know about it. When he performed to their satisfaction, they told him. For a public official, honest feedback is almost as important as campaign contributions. It is no less important to a manager in the private sector.

Kent Thiry is a prime example of an executive trying to avoid one of the most common and dangerous traps of corporate leadership: the higher an executive climbs, the easier it is for him to distance himself from problems. Top company officials are often surrounded by people who filter out bad news. They then convince themselves their strategies are working, even when they're not.

Mr. Thiry is the chief executive of DaVita of El Segundo, California, a large dialysis-treatment operator, who starts worrying that he is out of touch when all he hears is good news. He recently mingled with employees at an annual staff gathering, learning all he could about the company's buyout of Gambro Healthcare. When several people told him they thought it was "a fun process," he realized people were just telling him what he wanted to hear, rather than the truth. His efforts to build a truth-telling culture that provides honest feedback for executives is beginning to pay off: The company has reduced turnover by 50 percent and grown revenues by more than $5 billion. How do top executives know they're getting accurate feedback? Some comes from worker surveys, but much of it is culled at town hall meetings. Mr. Thiry holds about 20 a year and tells each of his vice presidents to convene one whenever they are with at least seven "teammates" or employees. "Most important," says Mr. Thiry, "is for executives who seek frank feedback to be candid about their own shortcomings."[26]

Good feedback doesn't just happen. It's the product of careful, deliberate communication strategies, coupled with good interpersonal communication skills. You can significantly increase the probability of communication success if you understand the role of feedback in both personal and professional communication.[27]

## GUIDELINES FOR CONSTRUCTIVE FEEDBACK

Now that you have improved your listening skills, it may be time to focus on how and when to provide feedback to others. Here are a few suggestions.

### Acknowledge the Need for Feedback

The first thing we each must recognize as communicators is the value of giving and receiving feedback, both positive and negative. Feedback is vital to any organization committed to improving itself, because it is the only way for managers and executives to know what needs to be improved. Giving and receiving feedback should be more than just a part of an employee's behavior; it should be a part of the whole organization's culture.

You will need high-level feedback skills to improve your organizational meetings and, more generally, interactions between employees. These skills will also help you communicate more effectively with customers and suppliers. In fact, you will find many opportunities to apply these skills across your working environment.

### Give Both Positive and Negative Feedback

Many people take good work for granted and give feedback only when they encounter problems. This policy is counterproductive; people will more likely pay attention to your complaints if they have also received your compliments. It is important to remember to tell people when they have done something well.

### Understand the Context

The most important characteristic of feedback is that it always has a context: where it happened, why it happened, what led up to an event. You should never simply walk up to a person, deliver a feedback statement and then leave. Before you give feedback, review the actions and decisions that led up to the moment. Every communication event exists in a context and if you don't understand the context to the events you're thinking of criticizing, your comments are unlikely to have a positive effect on others.

### *Provide Definitions*

Don't assume that the person you are counseling or offering feedback to will understand the words, phrases or terms you're using. Make certain that the language you use is both acceptable to the person you're speaking with and appropriate for the circumstances. More to the point, make sure you're using words whose meaning you both clearly understand and agree on. A simple example may help: *The American Heritage Dictionary of the English Language* lists 93 separate and distinct meanings for the word *get*. When you use that word in conversation, what do you mean? Some scholars now say the 500 most commonly used words in our language have more than 14,000 dictionary definitions. The fact is, the more meanings assigned to a word, the less it means. Make sure people understand you by providing definitions, examples and illustrations. You may even need to provide exceptions and limits. Make sure people understand the language you're using as you provide feedback to them.[28]

### *Use a Common Language*

Don't speak in a language that your conversation partner is likely to misunderstand, misconstrue or misinterpret. Use words, phrases, terms and ideas that are in line with what you know about that person. If you are sure he understands an acronym or company jargon, it's probably okay to use it, but if you're dealing with someone who doesn't share the same frame of reference you do, avoid language that will cause confusion.

### *Don't Assume*

Making assumptions invariably gets you into trouble. During interpersonal communications, it is dangerous to make the assumption that the other person either thinks or feels as you do at that moment. Communication consultant Tony Alessandra says:

> The other person may have a frame of reference that is totally different from your own. She reacts and perceives according to what she knows and believes to be true, and that may be different from your own reactions, perceptions and beliefs.[29]

To avoid the problems inherent in assumptions, ask for direct feedback, check on facts, examine underlying assumptions and use a healthy dose of skepticism before you say, "I know exactly what you mean."

### *Focus on Behavior Rather Than People*

When people receive feedback, especially feedback from a supervisor or superior, they are often defensive, fearful and likely to take anything you say as a personal assault. Defuse the hostility, minimize the fear and depersonalize the conversation by focusing your comments on the behavior involved and not the people. Saying "These trip reports need additional information," is substantially less threatening than saying, "Why can't you fill out a trip report correctly?"

### *Know When to Give Feedback*

Before deciding to offer feedback, determine whether the moment is right. You must consider more than your own need to give feedback. Constructive feedback can happen only within a context of listening to and caring about the other person. If the time isn't right, if the moment isn't appropriate, you can always delay briefly before offering your thoughts. Don't wait too long or you'll find that feedback won't be helpful, but choose your moments wisely.

Deborah Lake is a manager at SC Johnson who moved from a traditional office to a cubicle last year at the company's Commercial Markets headquarters. She quickly figured out that she had to unlearn advice on speaking forcefully in business conversations. Everyone, in fact, had to lower their voices in the open space to preserve their privacy and avoid disturbing the person in the adjacent cubicle. She doesn't hesitate to speak loudly, however, when giving positive feedback. "I want others to hear if I tell someone they've done a wonderful job, because I want that person to be recognized," she says. But if it's negative feedback, she speaks quietly.[30]

### Know How to Give Feedback

Providing constructive, useful feedback involves more than simply responding to people as they speak to you. Effective feedback involves an understanding of the language, people's intentions as they speak (or choose not to speak), the context in which the communication takes place and your objectives as a manager.

## KNOWING WHEN NOT TO GIVE FEEDBACK

You shouldn't attempt to give feedback to another person when:

- you don't know much about the circumstances of the behavior;
- you don't care about the person or will not be around long enough to follow up on the aftermath of your feedback – hit-and-run feedback is not fair;
- the feedback, positive or negative, is about something the person has no power to change;
- the other person seems low in self-esteem;
- you are low in self-esteem;
- your purpose is not really improvement but to put someone on the spot ("gotcha!") or demonstrate how smart or how much more responsible you are;
- the time, place or circumstances are inappropriate (e.g., in the presence of a customer or other employees).

## KNOWING HOW TO GIVE EFFECTIVE FEEDBACK

Most of us would prefer a trip to the dentist than a performance review session with an employee who isn't performing up to company standards. The irony is that while many managers will do all they can to avoid giving face-to-face feedback to an employee, they'll gladly complain about it in detail to their colleagues and peers.

Jamie Resker, the founder and president of Employee Performance Solutions, says we often steer clear of challenging feedback sessions with employees because we don't know what to say. "The employee is due to retire in two years anyway . . . I'm worried about the employee's reaction . . . What if I make things worse?" she says. Resker offers three steps to reducing defensive reactions to feedback: first, identify the performance issue. "It's clear that the key reason managers avoid giving feedback is not because they don't understand the problem, but rather because they don't know how to craft a message that is 'sayable' and 'hearable.'"

The second step is to be specific about the desired change. The more detailed and precise the description of what you want, the greater the chance your employee will understand you and begin to visualize the behavior you're asking for. Finally, Resker advises managers to detail the benefits of making the change. Show your employees the value of what you're asking for and explain how their lives and the company's performance will improve.[31]

The following suggestions should make it easier for you to provide feedback that works for another person:

### Be Descriptive

Relate, as objectively as possible, what you saw the other person do or what you heard the other person say. Give specific examples, the more recent, the better. Examples from the distant past are more likely to lead to disagreement over the facts.

### Be Objective

Objectivity may not be possible, but it's worth trying anyway. Do what you can to remove subjectivity from your discussions with others when you're providing feedback, at least at the beginning of the discussion. When it's time to offer personal opinions or subjective observations, identify them as such and explain that "it's only my view." Wherever possible, stick to the facts and focus on what you know for sure.

### Don't Use Labels

Be clear, specific and unambiguous. Words such as *immature, unprofessional, irresponsible* and *prejudiced* are labels we attach to a set of behaviors. Describe the behavior and drop the labels. For example, say "You missed the deadline we had all agreed to meet," rather than "You're being irresponsible and I want to know what you're going to do about it."

### Don't Exaggerate

Be exact. To say "You're always returning late from your lunch break" is probably untrue and, therefore, unfair. It invites the feedback receiver to argue with the exaggeration rather than respond to the real issue.

### Don't be Judgmental

Or at least don't use the rhetoric of judgment. Words such as *good, better, bad, worst* and *should* place you in the role of a controlling parent. This approach invites the person receiving your comments to respond as a child. When that happens, and it will most of the time, the possibility of constructive feedback is lost.

### Speak For Yourself

Don't refer to absent, anonymous people; don't attempt to speak for your supervisor or for people much higher up the line. Avoid such references as "A lot of people here don't like it when you. . . . " Don't allow yourself to be a conduit for other people's complaints. Instead, encourage others to speak for themselves. You must take responsibility for your own job, but don't attempt to speak on others' behalf.

### Talk First About Yourself, Not About the Other Person

Use a statement with either the word *I* or the word *we* as the subject, not the word *you*. This guideline is one of the most important and one of the most surprising. Consider the following examples regarding lateness:

1. "You are frequently late for meetings."
2. "You are not very prompt for meetings."
3. "I feel annoyed when you are late for meetings."
4. "We appreciate your coming to meetings on time."

The first two statements begin with second-person pronouns. People can become defensive when criticism begins with *you* and may be less likely to hear what you say when feedback is phrased as direct criticism. The last two statements begin with first-person pronouns and can help to create an adult/peer relationship. People are more likely to remain open to your message when the criticism does not appear to be aimed directly at them. Even if your rank is higher than the feedback recipient's, strive for an adult/peer relationship. Try using first-person statements (*I* or *we*) so the effectiveness of your comments is not lost in the accusation.

### Phrase the Issue as a Statement, Not as a Question

Contrast "When are you going to stop being late for meetings?" with "We can't begin the meeting on time when you are late." The question is controlling and manipulative because it implies "You, the responder, are expected to adjust your behavior to accommodate me, the questioner." Most people become defensive and angry when spoken to in this way. On the other hand, *I* or *we* statements imply, "I think we have an issue we must resolve together." The *I* statement allows the receiver to see what effect the behavior had on you.

## Encourage People to Change

Feedback must focus on things the recipient has the power to change. Most people can't change such basic personality preferences as shyness or a preference for openness over closure. But they can change the behavioral outcomes that affect the workplace. Leaving a set of sensitive documents scattered across a desktop is an outcome that a manager can focus on regardless of personality preferences. Focus on those issues that are both important to improvement and well within the power of the other person to change.

## Restrict Your Feedback to Things You Know for Certain

Don't present your opinions as facts. Speak only of what you saw and heard and what you feel or think. If you're not sure or can't say so with certainty, hold your comments. Feedback based on speculation or second-hand information may be far more destructive than you imagine. Make sure of what you know and then act on it.

## Build Trust

Although people occasionally learn valuable lessons from those they don't get along with, feedback is always more readily accepted if it comes from a trusted source. The psychological research on trust has shown that persuasive messages from a trusted source always produce greater impact and longer-lasting results. Skillful managers will use each opportunity for feedback to establish useful working relationships and build long-term trust.

## Help People Hear and Accept Your Compliments When Giving Positive Feedback

Many people feel awkward when told good things about themselves and will fend off the compliment ("Oh, it wasn't that big a deal. I just helped another manager put together a proposal.") Sometimes they will change the subject. It may be important to reinforce the positive feedback and help the person hear it, acknowledge it and accept it.[32]

# KNOWING HOW TO RECEIVE FEEDBACK

At times you may receive feedback from someone who does not know feedback guidelines. In these cases, *help your critic refashion the criticism* so that it conforms to the rules for constructive feedback ("Tell me what we can do to improve the conditions in your department."). When reacting to feedback:

## Breathe

Our bodies are conditioned to react to stressful situations as though they were physical assaults. Our muscles tense. We start breathing rapidly and shallowly. We need to follow some simple advice: Take full, deep breaths to force our bodies to relax and allow our brains to maintain greater alertness.

## Listen Carefully

Don't interrupt. Don't discourage the feedback-giver. You can't benefit from feedback you don't hear.

## Ask Questions for Clarity

You have a right to receive clear feedback. Ask for specific examples. ("Can you describe what I do or say that makes me appear hostile to you?") If you don't understand terminology or references, request an explanation.

## Acknowledge the Feedback

Paraphrase the message in your own words to let the person know you have heard and understood what was said. Don't simply sit there silently. Provide the other person with both verbal and nonverbal indicators that you've heard and understand what's been said. Remember, this situation isn't any easier for the other person than it is for you.

## Acknowledge Valid Points

Agree with what is true. Agree with what is possible. Acknowledge the other person's point of view ("I understand how you might get that impression") and try to understand their reaction. Agreeing with what's true or possible does not mean you agree to change your behavior. You can agree, for instance, that you sometimes jump too quickly to a conclusion without implying that you will slow down your conclusion-making process. Agreeing with what's true or possible also does not mean agreeing with any value judgment about you. You can agree that your work has been slow lately without agreeing that you are irresponsible.

## Don't be Defensive

Most of us don't take direct criticism well. We often spend part of the conversation planning our response (or defense), rather than listening carefully to what's being said. Don't listen *passively*; ask questions, inquire about issues that you don't understand or that aren't clear to you. But avoid the temptation to draw your sword and do battle then and there. Most feedback provided to you by a superior is carefully thought out in advance and is designed with your best interests and improvement in mind. Take it for what it's worth: an opportunity to improve your performance and chances for success.

## Try to Understand the Other Person's Objectives

Whether you're listening to your subordinates or to your own boss, you'll never fully understand what they're saying unless you set aside your own goals and objectives and focus on theirs. Try to see the world from their viewpoint and appreciate what motivates their comments.

## Take Time Out to Sort Out What You Heard

You may need time for sorting out or checking with others before responding to the feedback. It is reasonable to ask the feedback-giver for time to think about what was said and how you feel about it. Make a specific appointment for getting back to him or her. Don't use this time as an excuse to avoid the issue.

Communication is clearly a two-way process. People who serve in management positions must accept the responsibility for both providing and seeking out information that will be useful in correcting and improving the processes involved. The place to begin is with the recognition that feedback is both a useful and productive part of communication. With careful application of productive listening skills as you interact with others in the workplace, your chances for success are greater.[33]

## FOR FURTHER READING

Adler, R. and N. Towne. *Looking Out, Looking In.* Fort Worth, TX: Harcourt Brace, 1999.

Barker, L. L. and K. Watson. "The Role of Listening in Managing Interpersonal and Group Conflict," in D. Borisoff and M. Purdy (eds.), *Listening in Everyday Life.* New York: University Press of America, 1991, pp. 139–162.

Collins, S. and J. S. O'Rourke. (eds.). *Interpersonal Communication: Listening and Responding*, 2/e. Mason, OH: Cengage South-Western, 2008.

Crossen, C. "Blah, Blah, Blah," *The Wall Street Journal*, July 10, 1997, pp. A1, A6.

Fuhrmans, V. "Bedside Manner: An Insurer Tries a New Strategy: Listen to Patients," *The Wall Street Journal*, April 11, 2006, p. A1.

Jackman, J. M. and M. H. Strober. "Fear of Feedback," *Harvard Business Review*, April 2003, pp. 101–107.

Morse, G. "Feedback Backlash," *Harvard Business Review*, October 2004, p. 28.

Nichols, M. P. *The Lost Art of Listening: How Learning to Listen Can Improve Relationships*. New York: The Guilford Press, 2009.

Prospero. M. "Leading Listener," *Fast Company*, October 2005, p. 53.

Wilson, G. L. *Let's Talk It Over*, 5/e. Needham Heights, MA: Pearson, 2000.

Wolvin, A. and C. Coakley (eds.). *Perspectives on Listening*. Norwood, NJ: Ablex, 1993.

## NOTES

1   Goldsmith, M. "The One Skill That Separates," *Fast Company*, July 2005, p. 86. Reprinted by permission.

2   Ibid.

3   Nichols, R. G. and L. A. Stevens. *Are You Listening?* New York: McGraw-Hill, 1957.

4   Floyd, J. J. *Listening: A Practical Approach*. Glenview, IL: Scott, Foresman, 1985, pp. 2–3.

5   Nichols, R. G. "Listening Is a 10-Part Skill," in Huseman R. C., et al. (eds.), *Readings in Interpersonal and Organizational Communication*. Boston, MA: Holbrook Press, 1969, pp. 472–479.

6   Crossen, C. "The Crucial Question for These Noisy Times May Just Be: 'Huh?'" *The Wall Street Journal*, July 10, 1997, p. A1. Reprinted by permission of *The Wall Street Journal*. Copyright © 1997 Dow Jones & Company, Inc. All rights reserved worldwide.

7   Wolvin, A. D. and C. G. Coakley. *Listening*. Dubuque, IA: Wm. C. Brown, 1982.

8   Crossen. "The Crucial Question," p. A1.

9   Ibid.

10  Ibid.

11  Ibid.

12  Ibid.

13  Goleman, D. *Emotional Intelligence*. New York: Bantam Books, 1995, p. 145.

14  Floyd. *Listening: A Practical Approach*, pp. 2–8.

15  Sperry Corporation. *Your Personal Listening Profile*, 1981.

16  Nichols and Stevens. *Are You Listening?* p. 15.

17  Landry, D. L. "The Neglect of Listening," *Elementary English* 46 (1969): 599–605.

18  Nichols, R. G. and Stevens, L. A. "Listening to People," *Harvard Business Review*, September 1957. Online at https://hbr.org/1957/09/listening-to-people. Accessed Thursday, July 5, 2018 at 2:06 p.m. EST.

19  Hymowitz, C. "If the Walls Had Ears, You Wouldn't Have Any Less Privacy," *The Wall Street Journal*, May 19, 1998, p. B-1. Reprinted by permission of *The Wall Street Journal*. Copyright © 1998 Dow Jones & Company, Inc. All rights reserved worldwide.

20  This collection of ineffective listening habits was assembled from ideas presented in Nichols and Stevens, *Are You Listening?* "Listening is a 10-Part Skill," pp. 472–479; and Floyd, *Listening: A Practical Approach*, pp. 2–3. See also Alessandra, A. and P. Hunsaker. *Communicating at Work*. New York: Simon & Schuster, 1993, pp. 54–68.

21  Shakespeare, W. *King Henry IV, Part 2*, 1597.

22  This collection of effective listening habits was assembled from ideas presented in Sperry Corporation, *Your Personal Listening Profile*. See also Floyd, *Listening: A Practical Approach*; and Alessandra and Hunsaker, *Communicating at Work*, pp. 54–68.

23  Carvell, T. "By the Way . . . Your Staff Hates You," *Fortune*, September 28, 1998, pp. 200–212.

24  Floyd. *Listening: A Practical Approach*, pp. 34–43.

25  Reprinted by permission of *Harvard Business Review* from "Different Voice: The Inner Life of Executive Kids," *Harvard Business Review*, November 2001, pp. 63–68. Copyright © 2001 by the Harvard Business School Publishing Corporation; all rights reserved.

26  Hymowitz, C. "Executives Who Build Truth-Telling Cultures Learn Fast What Works," *The Wall Street Journal*, June 12, 2006, p. B1.

27  For a discussion of the role feedback plays in theoretical communication models, see: Rogers, Everett M. *A History of Communication Study*. New York: The Free Press, 1997, pp. 396–399.

28  Claiborne, R. *Our Marvelous Native Tongue: The Life and Times of the English Language*. New York: Times Books, 1983, pp. 3–24.

29  Tony Allesandra, *People Smart: Powerful Techniques for Turning Every Encounter into a Mutual Win*. Carlsbad, CA: Keynote Publishing Company, 1989.

30  Hymowitz. "If the Walls Had Ears," p. B1.

31  Resker, J. "3 Keys to Reducing Defensive Reactions to Feedback," *HR.com*, July 4, 2008. Online at www.hr.com. Accessed July 15, 2008 at 1:31 p.m.
32  For an extended discussion of feedback technique and applications, see Wolvin and Coakley, *Listening*, pp. 97–99, 214–219 and 223–238.
33  For a discussion of feedback applications in the workplace, see Alessandra and Hunsaker, *Communicating at Work*, pp. 79–90.

# Case 8.1: Earl's Family Restaurants (A)

## *The Role of the Regional Sales Manager*

Among the more difficult to master, yet less obvious, of human communication skills is that of listening. For many managers, listening often seems more of a luxury than a necessity. Time is short, pressures to accomplish work goals are substantial and communication often takes on a one-way character: It's my job to speak, it's your job to listen.

As managers rise from junior to more senior positions in an organization, they gradually discover that more and more of their time is spent in interpersonal communication, face-to-face with subordinates, peers and superiors. They are less task oriented, more process oriented. Gathering information is far less difficult than figuring out what it means.

The key to many management problems often lies in another's perspective. Finding out what others think of an issue, how they view the matter at hand, is frequently useful to a manager. The danger lies in wasted time or misspent effort in such conversations. Somehow learning to make listening a more structured, productive activity becomes increasingly important to managers who have the talent and the will to succeed.

Listening and hearing are not the same thing. Surprisingly, most North American adults listen at an efficiency rate of no more than 25 percent. Yet much of what we need to make decisions, to understand our circumstances and to solve the problems we face comes to us in an aural form.

Becoming an active listener, a reflective, skilled communicator is not easy, but it's certainly within reach for the average manager. Acknowledging bad listening habits is a good way to begin the process, systematically replacing such habits with productive, useful listening skills. Knowing that it's possible to become more skilled in this process makes listening one of the central talents that managers must concentrate on early in their careers.

## THE CASE AT HAND

The case of Earl's Family Restaurants involves two roles, each played from a different perspective. One is the regional sales manager for a foodservice manufacturing firm in the Midwestern U.S.; the other is the chief buyer for a mid-size chain of restaurants, also in the Midwest.

The facts of this case are the same for both participants. As is usual, though, both people see the facts through slightly different eyes. Each has a perspective unique to the position he or she occupies, and each has a set of objectives and goals that accompany the job. As you read the relevant facts in this case and assume your role, keep in mind that you are evaluated by your supervisor on the extent to which you can achieve those job-related goals. Keep in mind, as well, that communication may be one of the tools you can use to reach your objectives.

## YOUR TASK

Please read and familiarize yourself with the information in this case. You have been selected to participate in a role-playing exercise designed to demonstrate the importance of communication skills in practical everyday human interaction. Your portion of this exercise involves *only* the role of the regional sales manager for Exceptional Food Products, Inc.

Make whatever assumptions you need to in order to play your role, but be convincing as you create your character. The other person involved in this exercise knows many of the same facts about the incident, but may have a different perspective on those facts. Do your best to communicate effectively.

## THE FACTS OF THE CASE

You are the regional sales manager for Exceptional Food Products, Inc. of Chicago. You have seven territorial sales representatives who work directly for you, covering a five-state area in the Midwestern U.S. Your region includes Illinois, Wisconsin, Iowa, Michigan and Indiana. Your seven-person team handles more than 200 accounts; you have reserved several, special accounts for yourself and you handle those customers personally.

Among your more important accounts, both in dollar volume and in years of service, is Earl's Family Restaurants. Your grandfather, who established Exceptional Food Products, Inc., was a personal friend of Mr. Earl Tolliver of Indianapolis, the founder of Earl's Family Restaurants. Your two families have been doing business together for many years.

About six weeks ago, because of the growing volume of work in your office, you felt it safe to assign the account to your most successful territorial sales representative. This individual is relatively new to restaurant food sales, but seems bright, energetic and eager to succeed. He took the account gladly and, for the moment at least, appears to be doing well with it.

Exceptional Food Products, Inc. provides a full range of packaged goods to restaurants, clubs, schools, institutions and military installations throughout the country. Your region is one of the more important to the firm and, occasionally, your team leads the nation in sales volume. Your team regularly leads in market penetration. In recent months, however, problems have begun to arise. Customers have complained to delivery people, to your territorial sales representatives and, lately, to you.

Institutional complaints have not been as frequent or as great as restaurant complaints, but they're growing. Among the more routine complaints is one that alleges customers aren't getting what they ordered. On occasion, delivery people will leave a substitute product or two without notifying the restaurant or seeking permission to do so.

Deliveries have been late in recent days to a number of customers; your boss tells you a Teamsters job action (a work-to-rule slowdown) in the transportation division and some maintenance problems have slowed things down. That should improve soon, though, he says.

You have lost some customers in recent months to several new market entrants. They seem strongly customer oriented and are working hard to take away your business. One of the top people in finance at Exceptional Food Products, Inc. tells you that your top new competitor is now a subsidiary of a very large firm, Cub Foods, Inc., that is engaging in a deliberate policy of undercutting you on price. They are willing to lose money for an unspecified period of time in order to push you out of several lucrative markets. Frankly, this is a worrisome development.

The chief buyer for Earl's Family Restaurants has called and asked to meet with you. He is concerned about a number of things that have happened recently and he concludes the phone conversation with this: "Look, if you guys can't do any better than you've done over the past six weeks, we may just have to look somewhere else for a supplier."

Your objective in meeting with the buyer from Earl's is to save that account for Exceptional Food Products and, if possible, convince him that you'll be able to beat the competition on both price and service before long. You simply cannot afford to lose this account – it means nearly 15 percent of total sales for the region.

From your perspective, the problems in this case are primarily – though not entirely – about cost. You are under pressure to cut costs yet deliver the most competitively priced products possible to restaurants that face narrow margins and tough competition.

## ACKNOWLEDGMENTS

This case was prepared from public sources by James S. O'Rourke, Teaching Associate Professor of Management, as the basis for class discussion rather than to illustrate either effective or ineffective handling of an administrative situation. Personal and corporate identities have been disguised. Copyright © 1992.

# Case 8.1: Earl's Family Restaurants (B)

## *The Role of the Chief Buyer*

Among the more difficult to master, yet less obvious, of human communication skills is that of listening. For many managers, listening often seems more of a luxury than a necessity. Time is short, pressures to accomplish work goals are substantial and communication often takes on a one-way character: It's my job to speak, it's your job to listen.

As managers rise from junior to more senior positions in an organization, they gradually discover that more and more of their time is spent in interpersonal communication, face-to-face with subordinates, peers and superiors. They are less task oriented, more process oriented. Gathering information is far less difficult than figuring out what it means.

The key to many management problems often lies in another's perspective. Finding out what others think of an issue, how they view the matter at hand, is frequently useful to a manager. The danger lies in wasted time or misspent effort in such conversations. Somehow learning to make listening a more structured, productive activity becomes increasingly important to managers who have the talent and the will to succeed.

Listening and hearing are not the same thing. Surprisingly, most North American adults listen at an efficiency rate of no more than 25 percent. Yet much of what we need to make decisions, to understand our circumstances, and to solve the problems we face comes to us in an aural form.

Becoming an active listener, a reflective, skilled communicator is not easy, but it's certainly within reach for the average manager. Acknowledging bad listening habits is a good way to begin the process, systematically replacing such habits with productive, useful listening skills. Knowing that it's possible to become more skilled in this process makes listening one of the central talents that managers must concentrate on early in their careers.

## THE CASE AT HAND

The case of Earl's Family Restaurants involves two roles, each played from a different perspective. One is the regional sales manager for a foodservice manufacturing firm in the Midwestern U.S.; the other is the chief buyer for a mid-size chain of restaurants, also in the Midwest.

The facts of this case are the same for both participants. As is usual, though, both people see the facts through slightly different eyes. Each has a perspective unique to the position he or she occupies, and each has a set of objectives and goals that accompany the job. As you read the relevant facts in this case and assume your role, keep in mind that you are evaluated by your supervisor on the extent to which you can achieve those job-related goals. Keep in mind, as well, that communication may be one of the tools you can use to reach your objectives.

## YOUR TASK

Please read and familiarize yourself with the information in this case. You have been selected to participate in a role-playing exercise designed to demonstrate the importance of communication skills in practical everyday human interaction. Your portion of this exercise involves *only* the role of the chief buyer for Earl's Family Restaurants.

Make whatever assumptions you need to in order to play your role, but be convincing as you create your character. The other person involved in this exercise knows many of the same facts about the incident, but may have a different perspective on those facts. Do your best to communicate effectively.

## THE FACTS OF THE CASE

You are the chief buyer for Earl's Family Restaurants of Indianapolis. Your 54-restaurant chain extends throughout the Midwestern U.S., with most of your establishments concentrated in Illinois, Indiana, Michigan and Wisconsin. You have a few restaurants in Kentucky and Ohio. Your firm is publicly held, but the majority shareholder is Earl Tolliver, III, grandson of the restaurant chain's founder. You have been closely associated with the family for many years and have been employed with the firm since you left business school.

Exceptional Food Products, Inc. of Chicago is one of your principal suppliers of packaged goods. You buy most of your condiments, table supplies, canned and packaged restaurant supplies from them. They have done well for you and your firm for many years. Lately, though, you've had some trouble with Exceptional Food Products.

For one thing, your account was assigned about six weeks ago by the regional sales manager at Exceptional Food Products to a territorial sales representative. This person is loud, obnoxious, rarely available and doesn't seem to know your business particularly well. This sales rep is new to the area and has been in the food business for just three years.

You could put up with this new salesperson if it were just the personality that seemed to get in the way of a good working relationship. After all, there is no interaction with your customers; the only contact is with you and your central buying office. Lately though, other, more serious problems have arisen. Shipments have been late. Often, Exceptional Food Products will show up late on Fridays at your restaurants in Northern Indiana and Southwest Lower Michigan, just in the nick of time to re-stock for the weekends. Friday nights, Saturdays and Sunday breakfasts are typically your busiest times, both in volume and cash flow.

On several occasions, Friday deliveries in South Bend, Benton Harbor, Grand Rapids and Fort Wayne have simply been postponed until Monday. Last weekend, your Benton Harbor restaurant ran out of several crucial condiments and had to telephone the South Bend restaurant and ask for an emergency transfer by automobile.

Lately, Exceptional Food Products has pulled another clever stunt on you by leaving substitute brands that you didn't order. When your restaurant managers confront the delivery driver, he simply says: "Look, here's what's on the invoice. I got no control over what the invoice says or what they load on my truck. I'm just here to deliver what they tell me to deliver."

Your restaurant managers have been stuck with generic labels and off-brands when they clearly specified the national brand of several products. Worse, you've been billed for the national brand. You regard that as a kind of double-whammy: inferior products at name-brand prices.

Your contacts with the new territorial sales representative have been entirely unsatisfactory. You'd really like to do business with the regional sales manager once again, but have had trouble getting together. You have called Exceptional Food Products, Inc. and asked for a meeting with the regional sales manager from Chicago.

Your objective is to let these people know, in no uncertain terms, that their behavior has been unacceptable. You've spent far too much time and money straightening out the account with them and you want them to know that Exceptional Foods is causing more grief than your restaurant managers need.

From your perspective, the problems are entirely about the relationship between the supplier and your company, and are focused on deficiencies in service.

Exceptional Foods' task, in your view, is to make life easier for your managers, not harder. If things don't turn around soon, you're considering taking your business to another supplier. The fact that you have been doing business with Exceptional Foods for longer than anyone can remember makes no difference to you or to the Tolliver family. Business is business.

One last item: Don't let the sales manager go until you get an apology from their firm for their behavior. You want their service (and their prices) to improve, but you really want them to recognize what they've done to your business and an apology is in order.

## ACKNOWLEDGMENTS

This case was prepared from public sources by James S. O'Rourke, Teaching Professor of Management, as the basis for class discussion rather than to illustrate either effective or ineffective handling of an administrative situation. Personal and corporate identities have been disguised.

# Case 8.1: Earl's Family Restaurants (C)

## *The Role of the Observer*

Among the more difficult to master, yet less obvious, of human communication skills is that of listening. For many managers, listening often seems more of a luxury than a necessity. Time is short, pressures to accomplish work goals are substantial and communication often takes on a one-way character: It's my job to speak, it's your job to listen.

As managers rise from junior to more senior positions in an organization, they gradually discover that more and more of their time is spent in interpersonal communication, face-to-face with subordinates, peers and superiors. They are less task oriented, more process oriented. Gathering information is far less difficult than figuring out what it means.

The key to many management problems often lies in another's perspective. Finding out what others think of an issue, how they view the matter at hand, is frequently useful to a manager. The danger lies in wasted time or misspent effort in such conversations. Somehow learning to make listening a more structured, productive activity becomes increasingly important to managers who have the talent and the will to succeed.

Listening and hearing are not the same thing. Surprisingly, most North American adults listen at an efficiency rate of no more than 25 percent. Yet much of what we need to make decisions, to understand our circumstances, and to solve the problems we face comes to us in an aural form.

Becoming an active listener, a reflective, skilled communicator is not easy, but it's certainly within reach for the average manager. Acknowledging bad listening habits is a good way to begin the process, systematically replacing such habits with productive, useful listening skills. Knowing that it's possible to become more skilled in this process makes listening one of the central talents that managers must concentrate on early in their careers.

## THE CASE AT HAND

The case of Earl's Family Restaurants involves two roles, each played from a different perspective. One is the regional sales manager for a foodservice manufacturing firm in the Midwestern U.S.; the other is the chief buyer for a mid-size chain of restaurants, also in the Midwest.

The facts of this case are the same for both participants. As is usual, though, both people see the facts through slightly different eyes. Each has a perspective unique to the position he or she occupies, and each has a set of objectives and goals that accompany the job. As you read the relevant facts in this case and assume your role, keep in mind that you are evaluated by your supervisor on the extent to which you can achieve those job-related goals. Keep in mind, as well, that communication may be one of the tools you can use to reach your objectives.

## YOUR TASK

Please read and familiarize yourself with the information in this case. You have been selected to observe a role-playing exercise that is designed to demonstrate the importance of communication skills in practical everyday human interaction. Your task is to observe what happens during the conversation between two people playing the roles of the chief buyer for Earl's Family Restaurants and the regional sales manager for Exceptional Food Products, Inc.

Observe and take note of as much as you can during the conversation. Pay particular attention to both verbal and nonverbal communication issues. Note the direction and pace of the conversation. Who takes the lead in speaking? Who responds? What's the general tone of the exchange? Is this a conversation among friends? Are these people colleagues or business partners in a successful enterprise? What's the nature of the relationship between these two people? Does either participant emerge from the conversation having achieved the goals they had set for themselves in advance? Does this exchange between two people involve winners and losers, or are they able to accommodate each other's needs to reach a satisfactory compromise?

## THE PERSPECTIVE OF THE REGIONAL SALES MANAGER

The regional sales manager for Exceptional Food Products manages the work of seven territorial sales representatives over a five-state area in the Midwestern U.S. That seven-person team handles more than 200 accounts. Among the more important of those accounts, both in dollar volume and in years of service, is Earl's Family Restaurants.

About six weeks ago, because of growing volume, the regional sales manager assigned the Earl's Family Restaurant account to a successful territorial sales representative. This individual is new to restaurant food sales, but seems bright, energetic and eager to succeed. From the sales manager's perspective, the new rep seems to be doing well with the account.

Exceptional Food Products, Inc. provides a full range of packaged goods to restaurants, clubs, schools, institutions and military installations throughout the country. The Midwestern region is one of the more important to the firm and, occasionally, leads the nation in sales volume. This sales team, in fact, regularly leads in market penetration. In recent months, however, problems have begun to arise. Customers have complained to delivery people, to sales reps and, lately, to the sales manager.

Institutional complaints have not been as frequent or as great as restaurant complaints, but they're growing. Among the more routine complaints is one that alleges customers aren't getting what they ordered. On occasion, delivery people will leave a substitute product or two without notifying the restaurant or seeking permission to do so. Delivery truck drivers seem to feel that an occasional substitution is preferable to not delivering a much-needed product.

Deliveries have been late in recent days to a number of customers; the regional sales manager has been told by the national sales manager that a Teamsters job action (a work-to-rule slowdown) in the transportation division, along with some maintenance problems, have slowed things down. According to company officials, that should improve soon. The company has lost some customers in recent months to new market entrants. They seem strongly customer oriented and are working hard to take away business. A top new competitor is a subsidiary of a very large firm, Cub Foods, Inc., and they're engaging in a deliberate policy of undercutting Exceptional Food Products, Inc. on price. They're willing to lose money for an unspecified period of time in order to push Exceptional Foods out of several lucrative markets. This is a worrisome development.

The chief buyer for Earl's Family Restaurants has called and asked to meet directly with the regional sales manager for Exceptional Food Products. He is concerned about a number of things that have happened recently and he concludes the conversation with this: "Look, if you guys can't do any better than you've done over the past six weeks, we may just have to look somewhere else for a supplier."

From the regional sales manager's perspective, the problems are entirely about cost. The sales manager is under pressure to cut costs yet deliver the lowest-priced products possible to restaurants that face narrow margins and tough competition.

## THE PERSPECTIVE OF THE CHIEF BUYER

The chief buyer for Earl's Family Restaurants resides in Indianapolis and supervises purchasing for a 54-restaurant chain located throughout the Midwestern U.S. The firm is publicly held, but the majority shareholder is Earl Tolliver, III, grandson of the company's founder. The chief buyer, incidentally, is married to a member of the Tolliver family and has been with the company since graduating from college.

Exceptional Food Products, Inc. of Chicago is one of the company's principal suppliers of packaged goods. The company buys most of its condiments, table supplies, canned and packaged restaurant supplies from them. They've done well for Earl's Family Restaurants for many years. Lately, though, the company has experienced trouble with Exceptional Foods.

One bone of contention is the assignment of a new sales representative at Exceptional Foods to the account. For many years, the regional sales manager had personally overseen the Earl's account. And, from the perspective of Earl's chief buyer, the new sales rep is loud, obnoxious, never available when needed and doesn't seem to know the restaurant business particularly well. The new sales rep, in fact, has been in this business for just three years.

Lately, more serious problems have arisen. Shipments have been late. Often, Exceptional Food Products will show up late on Fridays at Earl's restaurants, just in the nick of time to re-stock for the weekends. Friday nights, Saturdays and Sunday breakfasts are typically the company's busiest times, both in volume and cash flow. On several occasions, deliveries have been postponed until Monday.

One other contentious issue is the delivery of generic labels and off-brands when the customer clearly specified the national brand of several products. Worse, Earl's has been billed for the national brand. The chief buyer has heard and seen enough and has asked for a personal meeting with the regional sales manager for Exceptional Foods. From the chief buyer's perspective, the problems are entirely about the relationship between the supplier and the restaurant chain, and are focused on deficiencies in service.

## ACKNOWLEDGMENTS

This case was prepared from public sources by James S. O'Rourke, Concurrent Associate Professor of Management, as the basis for class discussion rather than to illustrate either effective or ineffective handling of an administrative situation. Personal and corporate identities have been disguised.

# Case 8.2: The Kroger Company (A)

## *The Role of the Store Manager*

Among the more difficult to master, yet less obvious, of human communication skills is that of providing feedback to others in the workplace. For many managers, feedback must often wait for specified, formal counseling occasions, such as a performance review. Time is short, pressures to accomplish work goals are substantial and communication often takes on a one-way character: Feedback is used, not to improve communication, but to correct job-related performance issues.

As managers rise from junior to more senior positions in an organization, they gradually discover that more and more of their time is spent in interpersonal communication, face-to-face with subordinates, peers and superiors. They are less task oriented, more process oriented. Gathering information is far less difficult than figuring out what it means.

The key to many management problems often lies in another's perspective. Finding out what others think of an issue, how they view the matter at hand, is frequently useful to a manager. The danger lies in wasted time or misspent effort in such conversations. Somehow learning to make feedback a more structured, productive activity becomes increasingly important to managers who have the talent and the will to succeed.

Feedback is more than simply sending messages or issuing orders. Often, the process involves soliciting information from others so that you can first understand their perspective or point of view. Then, under planned and carefully controlled conditions, information regarding both performance and communication can assist both managers and subordinates in achieving organizational goals.

Knowing that it's possible to become more skilled in this process is the first step. Recognizing that, managers must concentrate early and often on improving their ability to both solicit from and provide feedback to others.

## THE ROLE OF THE STORE MANAGER

This case involves two roles, each played from a different perspective. One is the manager of a mid-size Kroger store in the Louisville Kroger Marketing Area. The other is the sales manager for a local Pepsi-Cola bottler.

The facts in this case are the same for both participants. As is usual, though, both people see the facts through slightly different eyes. Each has a perspective unique to the position he or she occupies, and each has a set of objectives and goals that accompany the job. As you read the relevant facts in this case and assume your role, keep in mind that you are evaluated by your supervisor on the extent to which you can achieve those job-related goals. Keep in mind, as well, that communication may be one of the tools you can use to reach your objectives.

## YOUR TASK

Please read and familiarize yourself with the information contained in this case. You have been selected to participate in a role-playing exercise designed to demonstrate the importance of communication skills in practical everyday human interaction. Make whatever assumptions you need to in order to play your role, but be convincing as you create your character. The other person involved in this exercise knows many of the same facts about the incident, but may have a different perspective on those facts. Do your best to communicate effectively.

## THE FACTS OF THE CASE

You are the manager of the Rosewater, Kentucky Kroger store, a mid-size store that's been in operation for seven years. The store is profitable and has shown strong sales growth over the past three years, despite competition from two other regional chains, one of which opened a year ago, and another which has been in place for five years.

You have been in the retail food business for 11 years, serving as manager of the Rosewater store for the past three months. This is your first store manager's job and you are determined to show the Louisville marketing director that you have management potential. Soft drink vendors have long been difficult to deal with for several reasons: first, they supply you with high-turn items that are nationally advertised and very popular with your customers; second, they are in constant competition with their rivals for display and shelf space; and, finally, soft drink vendors are often under great pressure from their distributors to push the product.

The local Pepsi-Cola sales manager is a fellow named Roger Willis. He works for a company called Southland Beverages, Inc., and is well-known within the company for moving high volumes of product; but also for his temper. His drivers rarely speak back to him and are under considerable pressure to comply with his tight schedules, large delivery loads and nearly impossible quotas. You have spoken with Mr. Willis several times on the telephone but have not yet met him in person.

You can deal with the drivers; after all, they have to earn a living, too, and most of them do a fine job of keeping your store stocked with fresh products at regular intervals. The local Pepsi vendor, however, is another story. Over the past six months his drivers have routinely dropped products you don't want on your loading dock, they're often late with deliveries, they have left quantities you can't sell and they have been entirely uncooperative with your receiving staff on the dock. Often, they're just rude.

As you ask one of your department heads what happened last Friday, he tells a story that other Kroger employees regard as familiar. "We had a new route man for Pepsi last week and this guy just wouldn't listen to us."

"How so?" you ask. "What'd he do?"

"Well," your employee replies, "in the first place, he dropped nine flats, instead of the three that we asked for. Most of the order was 12-packs, and we're running low on 6-packs. And he arrived right at a shift change, so nobody was really able to spend much time with him."

"What did you say?"

"When I saw nine flats, I asked him 'Why so many?' He just said, 'I'm stocking you up for the weekend.' Man, I'm tellin' you, we couldn't sell nine flats in a week, much less by Monday."

You pause for a moment, then ask, "Did you ask him to re-load six of those flats on the truck?"

Your department head replies, "I sure did, but he said 'Look, here's what's on the invoice. I got no control over what the invoice says or what they load in my truck. I'm just here to deliver what they tell me to deliver. Besides, it'd take me half the night to re-slot all this stuff back in the warehouse.'"

"Well," you say, "I think we can fix this."

"That's not all," your employee adds. "He installed that new Pepsi endcap display a week early. The Coke guy saw it this morning and had a fit. He's upset and wants to talk with you about it."

"A couple more phone calls to make," you think to yourself. "I think its time I met Roger Willis."

## YOUR MEETING WITH MR. WILLIS

Your objective is to let Mr. Willis know, in no uncertain terms, that their behavior has been unacceptable. You have spent too much time already dealing with the antics of his drivers. You really want three things from him: first, you want his unconditional assurance that his employees will quit delivering more product than you order, and will begin complying with your request for an appropriate product mix.

Second, you want him to arrange for a Southland Beverages, Inc. employee to disassemble the endcap display *today*. Their special promotion isn't scheduled for another week and the display space belongs to another vendor just now. Finally, you want an apology from them for the way they have behaved. Being an assertive business person is one thing, being rude and arrogant is another. You want his service to improve, but you also want him to recognize what he is doing to your store and an apology is in order

## ACKNOWLEDGMENTS

This case was prepared from public sources and personal interviews by James S. O'Rourke, Teaching Professor of Management, as the basis for class discussion rather than to illustrate either effective or ineffective handling of an administrative situation. Personal identities have been disguised.

# Case 8.2: The Kroger Company (B)

## *The Role of the Pepsi-Cola Sales Manager*

Among the more difficult to master, yet less obvious, of human communication skills is that of providing feedback to others in the workplace. For many managers, feedback must often wait for specified, formal counseling occasions, such as a performance review. Time is short, pressures to accomplish work goals are substantial, and communication often takes on a one-way character: Feedback is used, not to improve communication, but to correct job-related performance issues.

As managers rise from junior to more senior positions in an organization, they gradually discover that more and more of their time is spent in interpersonal communication, face-to-face with subordinates, peers and superiors. They are less task oriented, more process oriented. Gathering information is far less difficult than figuring out what it means.

The key to many management problems often lies in another's perspective. Finding out what others think of an issue, how they view the matter at hand, is frequently useful to a manager. The danger lies in wasted time or misspent effort in such conversations. Somehow learning to make feedback a more structured, productive activity becomes increasingly important to managers who have the talent and the will to succeed.

Feedback is more than simply sending messages or issuing orders. Often, the process involves soliciting information from others so that you can first understand their perspective or point of view. Then, under planned and carefully controlled conditions, information regarding both performance and communication can assist both managers and subordinates in achieving organizational goals.

Knowing that it's possible to become more skilled in this process is the first step. Recognizing that, managers must concentrate early and often on improving their ability to both solicit from and provide feedback to others.

## THE ROLE OF THE PEPSI-COLA SALES MANAGER

You are the territorial sales manager for Southland Beverages, Inc., a non-union regional Pepsi-Cola bottler. While your firm handles other products – including Mountain Dew and Dr. Pepper – Pepsi-Cola, Diet Pepsi and Pepsi One are clearly your most important products and account for nearly two-thirds of your company's revenues.

The soft drink business isn't easy. After all, you're in constant competition with the local Coca-Cola bottler, the RC Cola vendor, and another beer and soft drink distributor who sells Seven-Up products. Your margins are narrow, largely because of your cost structure. Most of your expenses come from delivery operations: ownership, maintenance and operation of your delivery fleet, and your wage structure. To cut your fixed costs just a bit, you have convinced your general manager to let you implement a program of driver incentives. Their hourly wages are lower by one-third, but they get a percentage of every product "flat" (a term used to describe a shipping container) they deliver.

Your general manager likes the idea of driver incentives and is pushing you to lower your costs even further with less frequent deliveries. Fewer stops at each retail outlet, combined with longer stock leads will mean lower costs and more profit for Southland. In general, the drivers are happy with the scheme, but they have encountered some resistance from store managers with limited storeroom and loading dock space.

"Keep it up, Roger," says your boss. "You're doin' a great job. I'm really pleased with the way we've been able to get control of our delivery costs."

"Thanks," you say. "I was pretty sure this system would work. Not everybody's happy, but – hey – that's life. Right?" Just as your general manager departs and closes the door to your office, the intercom beeps. It's your assistant, Darleen.

"Mr. Willis? It's Pat Hanson from Kroger on line two."

"Thanks," you say. "Hello. This is Roger Willis."

"Mr. Willis," says the voice on the other end, "this is Pat Hanson in the Rosewater Kroger Store. If you have a few minutes today, I'd really like to meet with you about some problems we've been having. I'd also like to show you something in your Pepsi display area. Can we get together today?"

"I suppose," you say. "How does four o'clock sound? I can be there by four, but I don't have much time."

"This won't take long," Hanson replies. "I'll see you at four."

## ACKNOWLEDGMENTS

This case was prepared from public sources by James S. O'Rourke, Concurrent Professor of Management, as the basis for class discussion rather than to illustrate either effective or ineffective handling of an administrative situation. Personal and corporate identities have been disguised.

# Case 8.2: The Kroger Company (C)

## The Role of the Instructional Facilitator

This case involves two roles, each played from a different perspective. One is the manager of a mid-size Kroger store in the Louisville Kroger Marketing Area. The other is the sales manager for a local Pepsi-Cola bottler.

Please read and familiarize yourself with the issues addressed in the background note, as well as the facts contained in both roles. The facts in this case are the same for both participants. As is usual, though, both people see the facts through slightly different eyes. Each has a perspective unique to the position he or she occupies, and each has a set of objectives and goals that accompany the job. As you read the relevant facts in this case and assume your role, keep in mind that you are evaluated by your supervisor on the extent to which you can achieve those job-related goals. Keep in mind, as well, that communication may be one of the tools you can use to reach your objectives.

### YOUR TASK

Your task is to facilitate a role-playing exercise designed to demonstrate the importance of communication skills in practical everyday human interaction. Make whatever assumptions you need to in order to assist the role-players, but be flexible as they create their characters and play out the details of the case. Each person involved in this exercise knows basically the same facts about the incident, but each has a slightly different perspective on those facts.

### Before the Role-Play Begins

Select two members of the class who would be willing to participate in a role-playing exercise. You can either ask the class as a whole for volunteers, or you can select two people based on your knowledge of their personality, cooperativeness and communication skills.

Give one copy of the store manager's role to one person and one copy of the Pepsi-Cola sales manager's role to the other. Have each person read their roles separately. If possible, give out the roles the day before you plan to conduct this exercise.

Please ask the two students who have agreed to participate in this exercise *not to read the other role-player's role.* Ask that they confine their reading only to the role they've been assigned, and to play the role with sincerity and conviction. Please ask them, as well, not to collaborate or to share information with each other. The success of this exercise depends, in part, on each person seeing the communication situation from his or her own perspective.

### As the Role-Play Begins

Tell all members of the class that two of their classmates have volunteered (or were selected) to participate in a communication exercise. Ask them all to observe carefully and, if they care to, take notes on what they see and hear. Then, tell the two role-players to simulate the first meeting between the Kroger store manager and the Pepsi-Cola sales manager, beginning with introductions.

As the two role-players begin, step back and observe the interaction carefully. They shouldn't be reading from their case instructions, but should assume the manners and actions of their character directly. Let the interaction go on for as long as you think it is productive. Most volunteers will play the character roles with enthusiasm and conviction and will carry the meeting through to some logical conclusion. If your players become frustrated, angry or confused, *step in and stop the role-play.*

### When the Role-Play Concludes

Take control of the classroom once again and, before you do anything else, thank the players for their time, effort and talent. A small round of applause usually makes each of them feel better about the experience. Then, ask the class as a whole about several issues:

* **Cognitive listening.** What *facts* arose during the discussion? Did either of the players come to the meeting with differing *assumptions*? Where did the discussions begin? Did either player ask the other to back up and review any details?
* **Affective listening.** What *emotions* arose during the discussion? Were either of the players angry, frustrated or upset? Did each maintain a professional manner? Were they courteous to one another? Did either player change his or her emotional tone as a result of the meeting?
* **Nonverbal listening.** What was the *body posture* and *gesturing* like during the interaction? Did both players exhibit open posture with arms unfolded, palms open or uplifted? Was the nonverbal communication essentially negative: arms folded, body posture at an angle, head down? What happened with *eye contact* during the meeting? Did both players look directly at each other, or did one search the ceiling or floor during the conversation? How close were they to one another? Did one of them back away from the other at some point? Did one interrupt the other at any point?
* **Listening for meaning.** Did each player understand the other? Did they work from the same set of intentions? Did both players reach some sort of mutually satisfactory agreement by the end of the meeting? What could each of them have done to make the meeting more successful? Give each member of the class an opportunity to comment and then observe that, while no two conversations are ever the same (different people, different subjects, different moments), a number of basic considerations can make each of us more effective listeners and, ultimately, communicators.
* **Quality of feedback.** Look for the quality of feedback provided by each participant in the exercise. Is the information exchange of any real value to the other participant in the conversation? Does emotion contribute to success in the exercise or hinder success? Is each participant saying and doing those things which will most likely lead to a successful resolution of the dispute?

## ACKNOWLEDGMENTS

This case was prepared from public sources and personal interviews by James S. O'Rourke, Teaching Professor of Management, as the basis for class discussion rather than to illustrate either effective or ineffective handling of an administrative situation. Personal identities have been disguised. Copyright © 1995. Revised: 2018.

# Case 8.3: Three Feedback Exercises

Organize the class into groups of three people each. Two people in each group will play roles defined for them in the exercises. The third person in each group will serve as the observer and recorder. The instructor should take three-to-four minutes to explain the role-playing exercise and assign roles to each of the participants.

Participants should take 10 to 12 minutes to read the exercise requirements and play their respective roles. Group observers should then take two to three minutes to brief their observations to the entire class.

## FEEDBACK EXERCISE #1: THE DISGRUNTLED ANALYST

*Relationship:* A supervisor and an employee who reports directly to him or her.

*Context:* You are an employee who joined the company 18 months ago as an entry-level analyst. You have a bachelor's degree in finance and some prior work experience in sales. You had other job offers but accepted this one because you thought it would offer the greatest challenge and most opportunity for growth and advancement. You are now no longer the most junior employee in the organization; others with similar education but less experience are assigned to your division.

*The Analyst:* You feel that you are stuck doing all of the most basic grunt work in the division: gathering and organizing data sets that everyone uses, dealing with ground-level maintenance problems and producing report documents that newer employees can claim credit for but contribute less to.

*The Supervisor:* You think the analyst is doing acceptable work, but it's far from top-level performance. During the past 30 days, you have had to counsel this individual twice about late "after market" reports and misrouted reports. You think this person might eventually make a good trader, but first must "grow up" and begin accepting responsibility on the job.

## FEEDBACK EXERCISE #2: THE WITHHOLDING COWORKER

*Relationship:* Two coworkers who both report to the same supervisor.

*Context:* You and a coworker are members of the same marketing department in a *Fortune* 500 firm. You have worked closely with this other person for the past eight months and have developed a casual relationship outside of working hours. You both enjoy your work, seem to like the company and the industry, and are dedicated to seeing your organization succeed. One of the reasons you like the work is that others who have preceded you in these positions have quickly moved on to "bigger and better things" within the company.

*Issue:* You feel that your coworker does not share information with you that is essential for you to be an effective department member. You suspect, in fact, that your coworker may occasionally withhold information (e.g., changes in team meeting times and locations, scheduling details, feedback from field visits) so that you don't look as good in the eyes of your supervisor. You have asked to meet with your coworker to talk about this.

## FEEDBACK EXERCISE #3: THE IMPERILED LINE EXTENSION

*Relationship:* Two coworkers who report to different supervisors.

*Context:* You and another employee who is about your age work in different divisions of a large packaged-goods firm. You have been assigned to work on a product line extension together. Your target launch date is eight months from now. Needless to say, a considerable amount of time, effort and money are being devoted to the success of this project.

*Issue:* You feel that your coworker (from another division) has simply not cooperated with you in gathering the information you'll need to make your launch window. Unless you can secure the cooperation of this person, key issues, including packaging, transportation, advertising and promotion, and retailer incentives, may be in jeopardy. You have asked to meet with your coworker to talk it over.

## ACKNOWLEDGMENTS

These exercises were prepared from public sources and personal interviews by James S. O'Rourke, Teaching Professor of Management, as the basis for class discussion rather than to illustrate either effective or ineffective handling of an administrative situation. Personal and corporate identities have been disguised.

CHAPTER 9

# Nonverbal Communication

Getting dressed for work used to be a snap for executive Ron Demczak. Then his company went casual – every day. With 30 suits and little else in his closet, Demczak spent several thousand dollars buying a new, sporty wardrobe. He learned to call ahead to clients to make sure he didn't wear khakis when they were wearing suits. And he dreaded the mornings.

"I hated it because every morning I had to have my wife match new outfits to wear," said Demczak. He is the liaison for U.S. customers of drugmaker Warner-Lambert. "Now," he adds, "I'm getting a little better at it."[1]

He's not alone. Robert Park is a manager at Ernst & Young, LLP, in northern California. For his firm, the switch to full-time casual dress was spurred by a desire to blend in. In that region, the accounting firm's clients were mostly from Silicon Valley, where software engineers and other young techies practically invented casual office wear. "We used to stick out like sore thumbs, being the only ones in suits and ties," he said. "Everybody knew we had to be the accountants or the bankers."

Still, Park keeps a traditional wardrobe for use when meeting outsiders who expect suits and ties. Some managers even stow suits in their cars so they won't be uncomfortably surprised. "That's when it gets complicated," said Wendy Liebmann, President of WSL Strategic Retail consultants. "Do I go by my code or theirs?"[2] Managers who are accustomed to wearing more formal business attire may be comforted by recent studies that indicate suits and ties are making a comeback.[3] Still, many of them struggle each day with the uncertainty of knowing exactly what to expect.

Why would managers feel uncomfortable in casual clothes? What's so complicated or difficult about being dressed differently from others you're doing business with? The answers to these and thousands of other questions about how humans interact with one another are related directly to how we communicate. For Ms. Liebmann, Mr. Park and everyone else in the workplace, the questions they are asking have little to do with language and a great deal to do with *nonverbal communication*.

If I look you directly in the eyes while we're speaking, is that a sign of respect or defiance? If you stare at a new employee while she's eating lunch, is that a sign of affection or harassment?

When you speak with a friend, how far apart should you stand? How close should you be when the boss asks you a question? If the boss reaches out to pat you on the shoulder, would it be acceptable for you to reciprocate?

Some workplaces, like the commodities exchange, encourage people to speak up and raise their voices. Others demand quiet. Some offices provide private space with doors that close, while others simply push desks together in huge, open rooms. In many instances, understanding what coworkers mean when they speak depends on your ability to understand whether they're being serious, sarcastic or humorous.

How can so much information be conveyed without using language? And, perhaps more importantly, how can one person possibly understand all the rules? What means one thing here may very well mean something else there, and what's seen as harmless in one company may be strictly forbidden in another. Clearly, understanding nonverbal communication is not simply useful for a manager. It's essential.

## A FEW BASIC CONSIDERATIONS

Communication experts have established the fact that less than a third of the meaning transferred from one person to another in a personal conversation comes from the words that are spoken. The majority of meaning comes from nonverbal sources, including body movement; eye contact; gestures; posture; and vocal tone, pitch, pacing and phrasing. Other messages come from our clothing, our use of time, and literally dozens of other nonverbal categories. Learning how to read and understand such wordless messages isn't easy, but may be essential to understanding everyone from your customers to your supervisor to your spouse.

Nonverbal communication is widely regarded as the transfer of meaning without the use of verbal symbols. That is, *nonverbal* refers in a literal sense to those actions, objects and contexts that either communicate directly or facilitate communication without using words.[4] As communication professionals and casual observers alike will testify, though, separating the effects of verbal and nonverbal behavior is never easy, largely because they tend to reinforce each other, contradict each other or are in some way *about* each other.

It's also important to note that, with the exception of emotional displays and certain facial expressions, virtually all nonverbal communication is culturally based. That is, we learn to behave and communicate in certain ways, and to interpret the meanings of those behaviors, as we grow up in our culture. Being *enculturated*, as we will see in the next chapter, means acquiring values, beliefs, possessions, behaviors and ways of thinking that are acceptable to others and, in fact, expected of us as members of our society. So what may be strictly forbidden in one culture – exposing an adult woman's face to strangers in public – may be perfectly normal in another. As members of a global community, we must not only learn and abide by the rules of the society we grew up in but also come to understand and appreciate the rules of other societies.

## NONVERBAL CATEGORIES

In a series of early studies of nonverbal communication,[5] communication researchers outlined three basic categories of nonverbal language:

### Sign Language

Gestures as simple as the extended thumb of the hitchhiker or as complex as the complete system of sign language for the deaf are all part of sign language.

### Action Language

Movements that are not used exclusively for communicating are part of action language. Walking, for example, serves the functional purpose of moving us from one place to another, but it can also communicate, as when we decide to get up and walk out of a meeting.

### Object Language

All objects, materials, artifacts and things – ranging from jewelry, clothing and makeup to automobiles, furniture and artwork – that we use in our daily lives are considered object language. Such things, including our own bodies, can communicate, whether we intend them to or not.

## THE NONVERBAL PROCESS

Nonverbal communication is really a three-step process involving a cue, our own expectations and an inference.

### Cue

We look first for a wordless cue – a motion, perhaps, or an object. On arriving at work, you notice a coworker who is glum, sullen and withdrawn. You say "Good morning," but he doesn't reply.

### Expectation

We then match the cue against our expectations, asking what seems reasonable or what seems obvious, based on our prior experiences. If your coworker is normally cheerful, talkative and outgoing, are your expectations at odds with the cue you've just perceived?

### Inference

Having picked up the cue and measured its importance and meaning against our expectations, we *infer* meaning. Because we can't see an attitude or intention directly, we must draw an inference based on the nonverbal cue and our own expectations. Given the cue and our expectations of this particular coworker, we conclude that he's unhappy, upset or depressed for some reason. Note that this conclusion is based on observation alone and not an exchange of verbal information between two people. If we are careful and observant, we can learn a great deal without the use of language. We should be careful, though, because our confidence often exceeds our ability when it comes to accurately interpreting nonverbal cues.

## READING AND MISREADING NONVERBAL CUES

"The great majority of us are easily misled," says Dr. Paul Ekman, a psychologist at the University of California at San Francisco. "It's very difficult, and most people just don't know what cues to rely on." To be sure, research shows that people can usually read someone else's feelings from the facial expression. "Most of us are fairly accurate in the rough judgments we make based on nonverbal cues," says Dr. Miles Patterson, editor of the *Journal of Nonverbal Behavior* and a psychologist at the University of Missouri at St. Louis.[6]

The new research, however, points to areas where people's confidence in reading nonverbal cues outstrips their accuracy. Recently, Dr. Robert Gifford reported finding specific nonverbal clues to such traits as aloofness, gregariousness and submissiveness. His report, which appeared in the *Journal of Personality and Social Psychology*, also found that even though reliable clues about character are present, "people read much into nonverbal cues that just isn't there, while missing much that is," says Dr. Gifford.[7]

People are right about their reading of character some of the time, especially for more obvious traits like gregariousness; the problem, according to Dr. Gifford, is that they are overly confident and assume that they are equally adept at reading more subtle aspects of character when they are actually misjudging. For example, in a recent study of people applying for a job, Dr. Gifford asked 18 seasoned interviewers, most of them Human Resource officers, to evaluate videos of the applicants.

Before going for their interviews, each applicant had taken tests that gauged their degree of social skills and how highly motivated for work they were. The test for motivation, for instance, asked such questions as how willing they would be to work unusual hours if it were necessary. The interviewers were far more accurate about the applicants' self-evident social skills than about their motivation, a more subtle trait important in employment decisions.

The nonverbal cues that made the interviewers decide whether an applicant had high motivation included smiling, gesturing and talking more than other applicants. In fact, though, none of those nonverbal patterns was a true indicator of motivation. The practical result of such mistakes is that many people are hired on a misreading of their personality traits, only to disappoint their employers. "Social skills are far more visible than motivation, but coming across well in your job interview is no guarantee of other traits that might matter in your day-to-day job performance," Dr. Gilford said. "People are being hired for some of the wrong reasons." A clever applicant might make a point of smiling, gesturing and talking a lot during a job interview, but a savvy interviewer would be cautious about reading too much into that show of outgoingness.[8]

## FUNCTIONS OF NONVERBAL COMMUNICATION

Nonverbal communication can serve any number of important functions in our lives, but researchers identify the following six major functions:

### Accenting

Nonverbal communication often highlights or emphasizes some part of a verbal message. A raised eyebrow might accompany an expression of surprise; a wagging finger might underscore an expression of disapproval.

### Complementing

Nonverbal communication also reinforces the general tone or attitude of our verbal communication. A downcast expression and slumping posture might accompany words of discouragement or depression; upright posture, a smile and animated movement might reinforce a verbal story about winning a recent promotion.

### Contradicting

Nonverbal communication, on the other hand, can contradict the verbal messages we send, sometimes deliberately, sometimes unintentionally. Tears in our eyes and a quiver in our voices might involuntarily contradict a verbal message telling friends and family that we're doing all right. A wink and a nod might deliberately send the nonverbal message that what we're saying just isn't so. The fact is, when verbal and nonverbal messages contradict, we tend – for a number of reasons – to believe the nonverbal. In the last analysis, it's simply much easier to lie than it is to control a range of nonverbal reactions: our facial expression, pupil dilation, tension in our vocal cords, pulse rate, sweating, muscle tone, and many others. Control of such things is, for most of us, well beyond our voluntary reach.

### Regulating

Certain nonverbal movements and gestures are used to regulate the flow, the pace and the back-and-forth nature of verbal communication. When I want you to speak to me, I'll face you, open my eyes, open my arms with hands extended and palms facing upward, and look expectantly into your eyes. When I want you to stop speaking so I can either talk or think of what I'm about to say, I will turn slightly away from you, fold my arms, put one hand out with palm facing forward and either close my eyes or turn them away from yours.

### Repeating

Nonverbal messages can also repeat what verbal messages convey. With car keys in hand, coat and hat on, I can announce: "I'm leaving now," as I walk toward the door. On another occasion, you might choose to hold up three fingers as you ask: "Is that the best you can do? I've gotta buy three of them."

### Substituting

Nonverbal communication can also substitute for, or take the place of, verbal messages, particularly if they're simple or monosyllabic. As a youngster looks toward a parent on the sidelines during an athletic contest, a quick "thumbs up" can substitute for words of praise or encouragement that might not be heard from a distance or in a noisy crowd.[9]

## PRINCIPLES OF NONVERBAL COMMUNICATION

After nearly a hundred years of research and 5,000 years of human experience with nonverbal communication, we have identified six principles that are thought to be universally true:

1. **Nonverbal communication occurs in a context.** Just as context is important to the meaning of verbal messages, so is context important to our understanding of nonverbal messages. Folded arms and laid-back posture may mean disinterest or boredom on one occasion, but may signify introspective thought on another. Professor Joseph DeVito of Hunter College says, in fact, that:

   > Divorced from the context, it is impossible to tell what any given bit of nonverbal behavior may mean. . . . In attempting to understand and analyze nonverbal communication . . . it is essential that full recognition be taken of the context.[10]

2. **Nonverbal behaviors are usually packaged.** Nonverbal behavior, according to most researchers, occurs in *packages* or *clusters* in which the various verbal and nonverbal messages occur more or less simultaneously. Body posture, eye contact, arm and leg movement, facial expression, vocal tone, pacing and phrasing of vocal expressions, muscle tone and numerous other elements of nonverbal communication happen at once. It's difficult to isolate one element of the cluster from another without taking all of them into account.

3. **Nonverbal behavior always communicates.** All behavior communicates, and because it is literally impossible not to behave in some way, we are always communicating, even when we aren't speaking with or listening to others. Even the least significant of your behaviors, such as your posture, the position of your mouth or the way you've tucked (or failed to tuck) in your shirt say something about your professionalism to others around you. Other people may not interpret those behaviors in the same way, or in the way you might want them to, but like it or not, you're always communicating, even if you're just sitting there "doing nothing." Doing nothing, in fact, may communicate volumes about your attitude.

4. **Nonverbal behavior is governed by rules.** The field of linguistics is devoted to studying and explaining the rules of language. And just as spoken and written language follow specific rules, so does nonverbal communication. A few forms of nonverbal behavior, such as facial expressions conveying sadness, joy, contentment, astonishment or grief, are nearly universal. That is, the expressions are basically the same for all mankind, regardless of where you were born, raised, educated or encultured. Most of our nonverbal behavior, however, is learned and is a product of the cultures in which we are raised. A motion or hand gesture that means one thing in my culture may well mean another in yours. Touching the thumb and forefinger to form a circle is often raised in North America to signify everything is "A-Okay." In Latin America and the Middle East, that same gesture is used to illustrate the anal sphincter muscle and is employed as a powerful insult.

5. **Nonverbal behavior is highly believable.** Researchers have discovered what we have known individually for quite some time: We are quick to believe nonverbal behaviors, even when they contradict verbal messages. When an employee's eyes dart away quickly, or search the floor as he thinks of an answer to a supervisor's question, most of us would suspect the employee is not telling the truth. Try as we might, there are many nonverbal behaviors we cannot fake. We might convincingly write or speak words that are untrue, but it's much more difficult to behave nonverbally in ways that are false or deceptive.

6. **Nonverbal behavior is metacommunicational.** The word *meta* is borrowed from Greek and means "along with, about or among." Thus, metacommunication is really communication about communication. The behaviors we exhibit while communicating are really about communication itself, and nonverbal communication occurs in reference to the process of communicating. Your facial expression reveals how you feel about the meal you've just been served; your handshake, vocal tone and eye contact tell us what you think about the person you've just been introduced to.[11]

## DIMENSIONS OF THE NONVERBAL CODE

When we talk about nonverbal communication, we're really talking about the codes we use to encrypt our messages and the signals that contain them. The code we use in verbal communication is language, and through thousands of years of human interaction, we've established rules to guide us and a structure for employing and interpreting the messages that language permits us to send and receive. With nonverbal communication, however, the code is neither as clear nor is it as precise, primarily because the meaning of our messages must be inferred without the benefit of feedback.

The code itself is divided into more than a dozen dimensions, each with the power to encode and carry messages from one person to another. Each has different characteristics: Some appeal to just one sense, while others appeal to several; some have a limited range of possible meanings, while others have a huge span of subtleties for encoding human intentions; some belong to the environment – both its physical and psychological aspects – of the communication event, while others belong to the participants in those events.

## THE COMMUNICATION ENVIRONMENT

The communication environment refers to that collection of nonhuman factors that can, and often do, influence human transactions. People often change environments in order to accomplish their communication goals: the choice of a restaurant for a business meeting or a resort hotel to conduct a conference. Often, people will simply say, "Let's go somewhere quiet where we can talk." This category concerns those factors that can influence a human relationship but are not, in Professor Mark Knapp's words, "directly a part of it," and includes elements such as the furniture, architectural style, interior decorating, lighting conditions, colors, temperature, background noise or music. It may be something as small as a dish left on a table you plan to use or something as grand as the city in which you are meeting.[12]

## BODY MOVEMENT

The study of human motion in communication, often referred to as kinesics or kinesiology, is concerned primarily with movement and posture. The way we walk, sit, stand, move our arms, hands, head, feet and legs tells other people something about us. This dimension also includes such areas of interest as facial expression, eye contact and posture. The five basic categories of human movement include:

1. **Emblems.** These nonverbal acts have a direct verbal translation or dictionary definition, sometimes a word or two or a brief phrase. The thumbs-up sign, the extended middle finger and the hitchhiker's thumb are three well-known examples.
2. **Illustrators.** These gestures often complement our verbal signals, helping to illustrate what's being said verbally. We can count off the number of items we want on our fingers or measure distance with the space between our hands.
3. **Affect displays.** These behaviors indicate the type and intensity of the various emotions we feel. Facial expressions, as well as hand and arm movements, are commonly used to communicate emotional or affective states of mind.
4. **Regulators.** These body movements help to control the flow of communication. Hand movement, arm positioning and eye contact can easily maintain or regulate the back-and-forth nature of personal conversation, for example.
5. **Adaptors.** These movements or behaviors involve personal habits and self-expressions. They are methods of adapting or accommodating ourselves to the demands of the world in which we live. We usually engage in these behaviors in private, but sometimes under pressure we will resort to twisting our hair, scratching, adjusting our glasses or, perhaps, picking our noses if we think no one's looking.

From a workplace perspective, a trend toward incivility is fostering a backlash, especially in response to unwelcome or rude nonverbal behavior. During tense talks in Chicago courts, now-retired Southwest Airlines Chief Executive Herb Kelleher crouched and slowly flipped his middle finger toward a pilots' union lawyer. "It was a joke," he explained. But other companies are cracking down on crude nonverbal behavior. Cleveland-based American Greetings Corporation has banned obscene talk and gestures. And an official of Roadway Services, an Akron, Ohio, freight hauler, says truckers are told to practice restraint.[13]

## EYE CONTACT

This human behavior is really a part of kinesics, but often deserves separate attention because of the importance it plays in human interaction. Direction, duration and intensity of gaze are often seen as indicators of interest, attention or involvement between two people. Keep in mind, however, that nonverbal mannerisms are culturally based, and eye contact is just one example of a human behavior that can vary from one society to another.

In Japan, for instance, looking a supervisor directly in the eyes is a sign of defiance, even insubordination. In the U.S. and Canada, supervisors expect direct and frequent eye contact as a sign of respect. A senior leader in a large organization once remarked, "I won't hire a person who won't look me in the eye." Why would he feel that way? Largely because in this culture we draw inferences about honesty and integrity from eye contact; if people look down or look away when we're speaking to them, we assume they are ashamed or being untruthful. Honesty and eye contact are, of course, unrelated behaviors, but people in our society make judgments about them, nonetheless.[14]

## A COMMUNICATOR'S PHYSICAL APPEARANCE

This area is not concerned with movement, as kinesics is, but with aspects of our bodies and appearance that remain relatively unchanged during the period of interaction. Such things as body type (ectomorph, mesomorph or endomorph), height, weight, hair and skin color or tone are included. Some researchers also focus on physical attractiveness and people's reaction to personal appearance. A number of studies, in fact, show that people readily attribute greater intelligence, wit, charm and sociability to those people whom they judge to be very attractive.[15]

Another new study found that good looks can yield substantial rewards. Economists Daniel Hamermesh of the University of Texas and Jeff Biddle of Michigan State University found that education, experience and other characteristics being equal, people who are perceived as good looking earn, on average, about 10 percent more than those viewed as homely.[16] Being overweight can hurt your income as well, particularly if you're a highly educated woman. A study conducted a few years ago in Finland has shown that obese women with good educations earn about 30 percent less than normal-weight or even plump women. Obesity had little or no effect on pay if women were poorly educated, manual workers or self-employed and, surprisingly, no significant effect at all on men's pay.[17]

Naomi Wolf, author of *The Beauty Myth*, agrees with Hamermesh and Biddle's conclusions but argues that women often face greater discrimination when it comes to appearance. One recent study looked at earnings of MBA graduates over their first ten post-degree years. Ratings of beauty based on school photographs correlated positively with starting and subsequent salaries for men. No relationship was evident between the starting salaries of women and their beauty, but attractive women experienced faster salary growth. Dr. Hamermesh suggests that better-looking people may have high self-esteem – from years of compliments – that translates into better performance on the job.[18]

Independent of such studies, conventional wisdom tells us that others make judgments about us based on our appearance, including everything from hairstyle to body weight, clothing style to skin tone. How you perform on the job may well be the most important aspect of your behavior in the workplace, but if you don't make a favorable first impression, you may not be given the chance to show what you can do. On the other side of that coin, judging a coworker or prospective employee by appearance may seem intuitive and useful but may also prove inaccurate. Even though you can make some judgments about a book by its cover, you may wish to withhold judgment until you have an opportunity to gather more information.

## ARTIFACTS

Artifacts are objects that are human-made or modified. The number and kind of things we might call *artifacts* is enormous, ranging from clothing, jewelry and eyeglasses to the objects we own and decorate our offices with. Certainly the way we dress denotes how we feel about an occasion or those we're with. Every family, for instance, has at least one cousin who will show up at a wedding wearing a t-shirt and corduroy sport coat. It's not that he can't afford dinner clothes or a tuxedo; it's just that he's thumbing his nose at the rest of the family.

People in the business world make judgments about those they deal with as a result of the artifacts they see in their offices and in the communication environment. A friend once asked if I would trust a stockbroker who drove an '03 Toyota to work each day. The implication was that a "successful" broker would have enough money to buy and drive a newer or more expensive automobile. And even though investment success and taste in motor cars are not necessarily related, the majority of adults in the marketplace make such judgment links with great regularity.

## TOUCH

Among the more widely discussed and, perhaps, least understood aspects of human behavior is touch. Numerous studies have shown that physical contact is essential to human existence. Adults need it for social and psychological balance; children need it for stimulation, security and reassurance. Many infants, in fact, will fail to thrive if they're not regularly offered the reassuring warmth of human touch. Needless to say, touch is conducted on many levels and for many reasons by each of us, with functional, professional, social and sexual implications for each kind of touch. Perhaps more than any other dimension of the nonverbal code, touching is a culturally determined, learned behavior. The relationship between the two people touching and the norms of the society in which they live – or were enculturated – will determine the length, location, intensity, frequency, acceptability and publicness of their haptic behavior.

A recent study in the *Journal of Personality and Social Psychology* revealed that a number of important aspects of your personality can easily and accurately be detected during a handshake.

Characteristics of a handshake, such as strength, vigor, completeness of grip and accompanying eye contact can determine whether a person makes a favorable first impression. More surprisingly, evaluators could surmise a number of other key traits, such as confidence, shyness or neuroticism. Lead researcher William Chaplin said that women should not worry about seeming too aggressive, because the firmer their handshake, the more favorably they are judged. Men, on the other hand, should have some concerns about creating bad impressions with weaker grips and lack of eye contact.[19]

The *rules* regarding touch in the North American workplace have changed in recent years from liberal to conservative – from frequent touch to little or no touch. Backslapping, arm-grabbing and other forms of behavior that ranged from affectionate friendship to adolescent horseplay are now widely banned in most businesses, largely from a fear of lawsuits. A colleague who returned to work following a maternity leave was cheerfully welcomed by friends and coworkers in her office, but no one would touch her until she spoke up, "It's alright to give me a hug. I would appreciate that."

The best advice regarding touch is to assume that if people extend their hand, it's probably alright to shake it. Touching any other parts of their bodies would be considered inappropriate unless you're specifically given permission to do so. These developments are largely the result of abusive behavior in the workplace, mostly aimed at women. Such developments are particularly unfortunate in view of numerous recent studies presented to the Society for Neuroscience finding that touch, or direct human contact, can have a positive influence on the production of a hormone affecting the body's reaction to stress. Subnormal levels of the hormone, in fact, have been linked to changes in a part of the brain involved with learning and memory.[20] The value of human touch is undisputed. The issue for managers is one of exhibiting good sense and good manners when touching others.

## PARALANGUAGE

The term *paralanguage* refers, very simply, to *how* something is said and not to *what* is said. It deals with the whole range of nonverbal vocal cues involved in speech behavior, including voice qualities, vocal characterizers, vocal qualifiers and speech segregates, and sometimes referred to as *vocalics*.[21]

Often, the only real clues we have to a person's actual intent as we listen to him or her speak are found in paralanguage. If your supervisor approaches you just before lunch one day and says, "Lisa, we need to talk about the LaSalle account," your reaction to those words may depend on a number of factors, including the communication environment and context, as well as your expectations. But your sense of urgency – how quickly you offer to set up a meeting, whether you postpone a lunch date to talk about the account – may well depend on *how* those words were spoken. Your cue is often contained in your interpretation not of the words themselves but of the pacing, phrasing, tone, pitch and intensity of your supervisor's delivery.

Vocal qualifiers are contained in the speech of every human and are an integral part of every spoken word. They are, in fact, our principal cue to identifying and interpreting sarcasm and cynicism. When you ask a coworker in a meeting if he thinks a new cost-control measure will work and the response is, "Oh yeah, you bet, no problem with *that* plan," you're faced with a brief dilemma. Was your coworker being sarcastic just then, or does he genuinely believe that plan will succeed? Your reaction to his words will depend entirely on how you interpret the tone of his voice.

Paralanguage not only serves to help listeners identify emotional states in the speaker but also plays an important role in conversational turn-taking. People often signal others in a conversation that it's their turn to talk or that they would like a turn to speak or that they aren't yet done speaking. Much of the signaling is done nonverbally through vocalics: rate, pacing, pitch, tone and other vocal, subverbal cues.[22]

## SPACE

The study of how humans use space, including the areas in which we work, live, socialize and conduct our lives, is often referred to in the research literature as *proxemics*. We know intuitively that space communicates in many ways in the business world, especially when we examine the subject of office space. Professor Joseph DeVito says:

> We know, for example, that in a large organization, status is the basis for determining how large an office one receives, whether that office has a window or not, what floor of the building the office is on, and how close one's office is to the head of the company.[23]

Workers in large organizations have faced two interesting, sometimes discouraging, trends in the allocation of office space: shrinking cubicles and disappearing personal space. With office space becoming more expensive per square foot, facility managers have looked for increasingly creative ways of dealing with the demand for workspace and privacy. The trend over the past 30 years away from huge office spaces with many desks and no privacy brought portable wall dividers known as *cubicles* into the workspace. The arrangement provided for a minimum of privacy, or in some cases, an illusion of privacy.[24]

Every couple of weeks, Michael McKay, a 33-year-old business analyst with a Santa Clara, California, Internet services company, finds his concentration totally disrupted when three colleagues who sit near his workstation hop onto the same conference call – all on speakerphones. "You get this stereophonic effect of hearing one person's voice live, and then hearing it coming out of someone else's speakerphone two or three cubes over," he says. The obvious solution to incessant phone-ringing, very personal conversations and rising noise levels would seem to be private offices. Don't count on it, says Jane Smith, a Manhattan office architect. "The open plan is here to stay."[25]

Julie Nemetz, a writer for a popular teen magazine, planned her wedding recently from under her desk. "It's quieter down there," she says. Nearly three-quarters of all U.S. and Canadian workers now do business in open plan or bullpen office space. And the average office space per person has shrunk steadily since the late 1990s, down by about 13 percent according to the International Facility Management Association. Do workers have a right to expect private space at their employers' expense? Legally no, it's a "fringe benefit," says Robert Ellis Smith, publisher of *Privacy Journal*. But given that more employees are putting in 60-plus hour weeks, he adds, "It's in employers' interests to make these accommodations for personal housekeeping."[26]

A second trend has developed in recent years, known as *hoteling*, to provide office space on demand for workers who have an infrequent need for private or semiprivate space. Greg Bednar is an audit partner in the accounting firm of Ernst & Young, LLP in Chicago. "We began 'hoteling' several years ago," Bednar said, "but expanded the program dramatically." The entire Chicago office of Ernst & Young, according to Bednar, including more than 3,000 people and 500,000 square feet of office space between the 11th and 17th floors were affected.[27]

"It seemed like a great idea at first," he said:

> because we were able to save so much money. We got an instant economic benefit from giving up 100,000 square feet of workspace. We also wanted a more technology-literate workforce. People had to be plugged into the system and into our clients. Additionally, we were hoping to develop a more flexible workforce.

What Ernst & Young got was a huge, temporary saving on office space rental but a workforce that felt disenfranchised from the company.[28]

Each morning, Ernst & Young employees report to work by checking in at the concierge desk in the outer lobby. Once properly identified, they receive access to a cubicle, known as a "four pod," so called, because four workers occupy one workspace about 20 feet square. They each have a desk and chair, a telephone and a network connection for their laptop computers. The cubicle offers no overnight storage space, no opportunity to put up pictures, bookshelves, or personal items, and virtually zero privacy.[29]

"It's become a morale issue," said Bednar:

What we've gained in revenue by renting less floorspace, we've lost in teaming, mentoring, and social interaction. We have no 'water cooler chats,' and very little informal interaction with each other. Frankly, no one knows where anyone else is on any given day.

Wayne Ebersberger, also a partner in Ernst & Young's Chicago office, says, "The loss of this personal space is an important matter. It isn't just a workspace or productivity issue any longer. We're losing some of the fabric of our culture."[30]

## The Effect of Space on Communication

Not long ago, Tom Allen, a professor at MIT, did a study determining the relationship between communication and distance in the workplace. For six months, he examined the communication patterns among 512 employees in seven organizations. He found that at a distance of 30 feet or less, the quality of communication is five times better than it is at a distance of 100 feet. Allen's research also showed that beyond 100 feet, distance is immaterial because communication is simply ineffective. In other words, ease of communication is largely dependent on physical location.[31]

## Categories of Personal Space

Cultural anthropologist Edward T. Hall observed and classified four categories of distance, each of which helps to define the relationship between the communicators:

- *Intimate.* This ranges from actual touching to a distance of about 18 inches. At this distance, the presence of other individuals is unmistakable: Each individual experiences the sound, smell, even the other's breath. To be given permission to position yourself so closely to another implies a personal relationship involving considerable trust. Often, though, we're forced to stand or sit next to someone, perhaps actually touching them, without really wanting to do so – in an elevator, a subway car or an airline seat. Most North Americans feel some level of discomfort at such closeness when they don't really know the other person. People try to avoid eye contact at this distance, focusing instead on distant or nearby objects.[32] Although most people feel uncomfortable at this distance from strangers or casual acquaintances, most are willing to briefly tolerate such closeness in order to get what they need – a trip to the top floor in an elevator, transportation to the next subway stop or lunch in a crowded café.
- *Personal.* Each of us, according to Dr. Hall, carries a protective bubble defining our personal distance, which allows us to stay protected and untouched by others. In the close phase of personal distance, about 18 to 30 inches, we can still hold or grasp each other but only by extending our arms. In the far phase (about 30 inches to 4 feet), two people can touch each other only if they both extend their arms. This far phase, according to Professor DeVito, is "the extent to which we can physically get our hands on things; hence, it defines, in one sense, the limits of our physical control over others."[33] The common business phrase "arm's-length relationship" comes from the definition of this distance, meaning that a proper relationship with customers, suppliers or business partners might be one in which we are not so close as to be controlled or unduly influenced by them.
- *Social.* At a distance of about 4 to 12 feet, we lose the visual detail we could see in the personal distance, yet we clearly are aware of another's presence and can easily make eye contact. You would have to step forward, however, in order to shake hands. Note that during most business introductions, people do just that: step forward, make

eye contact, shake hands, then step back. The near phase of social distance (4 to 7 feet) is the range at which most business conversations and interactions are conducted. In the far phase (7 to 12 feet), business transactions have a more formal tone and voices are raised just slightly. Many office furniture arrangements assure this distance for senior managers and executives, while still providing the opportunity for closer contact if participants decide it's necessary.[34]

- **Public.** In the close phase of public distance, about 12 to 15 feet, we feel more protected by space. We can still see people, observing their actions and movements, but we lose much of the detail visible at closer distances. We can move quickly enough to avoid someone and are not forced to make eye contact with people we do not know. In the far phase, more than 25 feet, we see people not as separate individuals but as part of the landscape or scene in the room. Communication at this distance is difficult, if not impossible, without shouting or exaggerated body movement.[35]

Our use of space varies greatly, depending on where we live and how we were raised, but it varies even more from one culture to another and is a frequent source of difficulty for people who move to another culture as adults. The next chapter, which deals with international and intercultural communication, will explain more about how U.S. business managers adapt to changes in such important nonverbal behaviors as proxemics.

## TIME

Our use of time and how we view its role in our personal and professional lives speaks volumes about who we are and how we regard others. This concept, too, is culturally determined to a large extent because the use of time involves extensive interaction with other people in our societies.

In North America, we place considerable importance on punctuality and promptness, announcing to anyone who'll listen that "time is money." U.S. and Canadian, and to a lesser extent European, society see time as a commodity that can be saved, wasted, spent or invested wisely. Mediterranean, Latin and Polynesian cultures, on the other hand, see time in a much more seamless fashion, moving past them in an inexorable stream. Lateness in South American nations is not only acceptable but often fashionable – a view that regularly frustrates North American businesspeople who experience it for the first time.[36]

Anthropologists have demonstrated how people from various parts of the world view time in different ways. Edward T. Hall has written at length about people who see the world in monochronic ways, that is, with one kind of time for everyone, while others see the world in polychronic ways, with many kinds and uses of time. U.S. and Canadian citizens, as well as those who live in Germany, Switzerland and the industrialized nations of the G7, tend to work in precise, accountable ways with an emphasis on "saving time" and being "on time" for appointments and meetings.

People who live and work along the Mediterranean, in Latin America and the Middle East, and in more traditional, developing economies often view time from a multifaced or polychronic perspective. Although being on time for a business meeting may be important in Latin America, it's probably not *more important* than a conversation with a friend who has been ill or whom you haven't seen in some time. Additionally, the pace of life as well as business in such societies can vary considerably but is invariably slower than the pace of activity in Western Europe or North America.[37]

## COLOR

Color, shading and hue as subtle and powerful message-senders have a long and, well, colorful history. We signal our intentions ("This project has the green light"); reveal our reactions ("That move prompted red flags throughout the organization"); underscore our moods ("I'm feeling a little blue today"); and call our emotions to the surface ("She was green with envy"). We coordinate and carefully select (for the most part) the colors we use in our offices, our homes, our automobiles, our clothing and even our hair. We even use color to stereotype and categorize others ("She's that blonde from marketing," and "He's one of the original graybeards in this company").

New marketing research has shown what we have suspected for some time: that color plays an important role in our perceptions of food purchase decisions and food packaging. According to psychological research, the use of red (and often the pairing of red and yellow) on restaurant signs makes you hungry. A trip downtown will confirm these findings: Many successful restaurants, from McDonald's to In-N-Out Burger and Pizza Hut to Ruth's Chris Steakhouse, use red or yellow signage. Often labeled the Ketchup and Mustard theory, it claims that the color red makes us feel warm and comforted while yellow grabs our attention (and even can, according to some research, speed up our metabolism).[38] Throughout much of the twenty-first century, green has also been used in advertising and political discourse to reflect an "environmentally friendly" approach to everything from marketing to public policy. This is certainly true for food packaging as well, usually indicating eco-friendly, organic or GMO-free food products.

"Color serves as a cue," according to Dr. Russell Ferstandig, a psychiatrist whose company, Competitive Advantage Consulting, advises marketers about the hearts and minds of consumers. "It's a condensed message that has all sorts of meanings." Some are no more than fads, such as clear drinks like Crystal Pepsi or Coors' Zima (do you even remember these?), while others are more enduring, including everything from raspberry Jell-O to traditional school colors.[39]

Food companies are usually aware of the meanings they send and tend to rely on certain colors until circumstances require a change. According to color researchers, no colors are inherently good or bad; the context affects the meaning. White, for instance, is seen as a good color but no longer in bread, where brown is becoming preferred because of its more healthful and natural connotations. In packaging and food advertising, again, the most popular colors have been red and yellow. According to John Lister, a partner in the New York design firm of Lister Butler, "People tend to be attracted to the warmth of these colors. They are cheery and friendly."[40]

## SMELL

A primitive perceptive capability, smell is a powerful communicator reaching far and wide throughout human emotion and experience. Though it is less understood and more subtle than most other dimensions of the nonverbal code, our sense of smell plays an important part in our ability to communicate. According to the Sense of Smell Institute, the average human being is able to recognize approximately 10,000 different odors. What's more, people can recall smells with 65 percent accuracy after a year, whereas the visual recall of photos sinks to about 50 percent after only three months.[41]

We wear perfume, cologne and after-shave lotions to signal others that we are freshly scrubbed and desirable. We use deodorants and antiperspirants to mask natural body odors. We use breath mints to cover the smell of bacteria growing in our mouths, and we use room fresheners to disguise the odors of everyday living trapped in our homes, cars and offices. Smells can be highly evocative and emotional, in part because they're associated with one of our most primitive and least-developed sense organs. Everything from the aroma of mom's pot roast or apple pie cooking in the kitchen to the scent of leather seats in a new Mercedes can have an emotional effect on each of us.[42]

From a marketing perspective, human response to aromas is personal and highly emotional. According to Dr. Trygg Engen, a professor at Brown University, "Aromas are learned in association with a moment and remain inextricably linked to the mood of that moment."[43] Researchers found that a whiff of baking bread is enough to transport many people back to an idealized childhood. Others are perked up by the smell of lemon or lulled by jasmine. Still others report allergic reactions to smells.

During a recent weekend in New York, shoppers on the prowl for digital electronics unwittingly stumbled into a research project related to olfaction. Riding up the escalator to the third floor of the Shops at Columbus Circle, they encountered a scent like that of a young man or woman primed for a night on the town – a unisex, modern fragrance along the lines of Calvin Klein's CK One. The scent wasn't emanating from one of the many tourists cruising the shops, however. Nor was it escaping from a promotional event at the nearby Aveda store. It was the seductive smell of consumer electronics. Samsung, the Korean electronics giant was conducting a test of its new signature fragrance in its *Samsung Experience* concept store. Researchers stopped shoppers leaving the store to ask them about whether they thought the scent was "stylish," "innovative," "cool," "passionate" or "cold," and – more important – whether the scent made them feel like hanging around the shop a little longer. According to Dr. Alan R. Hirsh, founder and neurological director of the Smell & Taste Treatment and Research Foundation in Chicago, "If a company can associate a mood state with a smell, it can transfer that happy feeling to the product." Those who don't lock in that connection risk being left behind, he warns.[44]

Aromatic mood manipulation is an area of increasing interest among productivity consultants, moving well beyond mom's spice jar and the romantically scented candle. Junichi Yagi, a senior vice president of Shimizu Technology, says,

"If you have a high-stress office environment, you want to soothe and stimulate alertness. In a hotel, you might want to create a relaxed mood." To perk people up, Mr. Yagi has experimented with central air circulation systems to alter or enhance the moods of everyone from office workers to shopping mall customers. Peppermint, lemon, rosemary, eucalyptus and pine have been shown to increase alertness, while lavender, clove, floral and woodlands scents create a relaxing effect. Experiment participants described feeling refreshed in the presence of a light citrus mixture.[45]

From a workspace perspective, most personal scents are deemed acceptable if they are insufficiently powerful to extend beyond intimate distance. Employees, customers and others have complained – and in some cases succeeded in court – about being exposed to various odors including food, perfumes, tobacco smoke and unvented product odors. To protect themselves against unwanted and expensive litigation, many business organizations have published policies asking employees to be respectful of others with whom they must share the workspace, keeping colognes, perfumes and other personal scents to a minimum.

## TASTE

Closely related to our sense of smell is our ability to taste. It's limited to a small grouping of sensations that include salty, sweet, bitter and other tastes located in a collection of small, flask-shaped sensors in the epithelium of the tongue. It's a complex response system that involves our abilities to see and smell as well, and one – much like color and touch – that is highly subjective in nature. What is "bitter" to some is "rich and full bodied" to others. For still others, such things as espresso coffee, broiled asparagus and scotch whiskey are "acquired tastes." Our appreciation for the taste of various food and drink is a function of both age and enculturation and, like our use of space, can pose problems when we move from one culture to another.

As the demographic makeup of our society changes, it's important to note that our taste in food is changing along with it. Various exotic sauces now outsell ketchup, and commercially prepared food ranging from fine dining to take-out is available in cuisines ranging from Mexican to Italian, Greek to French, and Thai to Szechuan.[46]

## SOUND

The study of acoustics and its effects on communication is now an important part of nonverbal research. Public speakers are particularly conscious of whether they can be heard by everyone in the room, and those who use amplification and public address systems are involved in a constant struggle with audio system feedback, acoustical bounce and other peculiarities of microphones, amplifiers and speakers.

Sound comes in other forms, too, including the melodic ranges of the human voice, the sounds produced by nature as well as mankind and our machines (e.g., jets, trucks and jackhammers), and, of course, there is music. Culture and, more often, subculture can determine our reaction to musical compositions and performances. The melodies of a big band or an orchestra may be attractive to some but sappy and dull to their grandchildren, whose tastes in music may run to indie pop, EDM or hip-hop.

## SILENCE

The absence of speech or sound may be used to communicate as powerfully and directly as any verbal code. Some researchers liken silence to acoustics in the same way that facial expressions are related to kinesics. Silence can be used both positively and negatively: to affect, to reveal, to judge or to activate. Asian cultures, in particular, make extensive use of silence during business meetings and contract negotiations.

Research in interpersonal communication has revealed that silence may serve a number of important functions:

- *To provide thinking time.* Silence can offer an opportunity for you to gather your thoughts together, to assess what's just been said by others or to weigh the impact of what you might say next. U.S. Ambassador Mike Mansfield once observed that he carried his pipe and tobacco with him for so many years because they gave him something to do while the room grew quiet. "I was never at a loss for words," he said. "I was just reluctant to say the first few that came to mind."[47] Somehow guests or colleagues were more willing to tolerate the tobacco smoke than the silence.

- **To hurt.** Some people use silence as a weapon to hurt others. Giving someone the silent treatment can be particularly powerful, especially if they expect to hear from you and speak with you. In many business organizations, a drop-off in communication can be an early indication of trouble; often, the recipient of the silent treatment is being eased out of the decision-making processes and, perhaps, the company itself.

- **To isolate oneself.** Sometimes silence is used as a response to personal anxiety, shyness or threats. If you feel anxious or uncertain about yourself or your role in an organization, particularly if you are new to the company or are junior in rank to others in the group, silence is a common response. Eventually, even the most junior or introverted of managers will be asked to speak up on important issues. The key is knowing when to speak and how much to say.

- **To prevent communication.** Silence may be used to prevent the verbal communication of certain messages. An executive may impose a "gag order" on employees to prevent them from discussing sensitive information with others inside or outside an organization. In other circumstances, silence may allow members of a negotiating team or collective bargaining group time to "cool off." If words have the power to inspire, soothe, provoke or enrage, then silence can prevent those effects from occurring.

- **To communicate feelings.** Like the eyes, face or hands, silence can also be used to communicate emotional responses. According to Professor DeVito, silence can sometimes communicate a determination to be uncooperative or defiant. "By refusing to engage in verbal communication," he says, "we defy the authority or legitimacy of the other person's position." In more pleasant situations, silence might be used to express affection or agreement.[48]

- **To communicate nothing.** Although it remains true that you "cannot *not* communicate," it is equally true that what you wish to communicate on occasion is that you have nothing to say. Keep in mind that receivers in the communication process will interpret silence, just as they interpret words, motion and other forms of communication, in their own way. They, not you, will assign meaning to what you are not saying, to whom you are not saying it and the occasion on which you are not saying anything. From a manager's perspective, it may be a good idea to call someone and say, "I don't have an answer for you yet, but I'll find one and get back in touch with you before the end of the week." That statement might be preferable to no contact at all. A customer might think you don't care about him or her; a supplier might think you have lost interest in doing business; an investment analyst might believe you have something to hide if you're not talking.

## The Effects of Nonverbal Communication

The following six general outcomes are important for every manager to know:

- **Nonverbal cues are often difficult to read.** During the 1970s, a number of popular books introduced the general public to nonverbal communication. One popular volume, *Body Language*, written by a journalist, described the nonverbal studies of several researchers.[49] That bestseller was followed by others that simplified and popularized research in this area; many of them, however, oversimplified the behavioral science behind the findings in the interest of making a sale, detecting a liar, attracting members of the opposite sex, and so on.
  According to Professor Mark Knapp:

  Although such books aroused the public's interest in nonverbal communication . . . readers too often were left with the idea that reading nonverbal cues as *the* key to success in any human encounter; some of these books implied that single cues represent single meanings. Not only is it important to look at nonverbal *clusters* of behavior but also to recognize that nonverbal meaning, like verbal, rarely is limited to a single denotative meaning.[50]

- **Nonverbal cues are often difficult to interpret.** What may mean one thing in one context, culture or circumstance may mean something entirely different in another. Professor Knapp goes on to say:

  Some of these popularized accounts do not sufficiently remind us that the meaning of a particular behavior is often understood by looking at the context in which the behavior occurs; for example, looking into someone's eyes may reflect affection in one situation and aggression in another.[51]

  The importance of reading context, just as we would with verbal expression, is especially critical. The meaning of all communication, after all, is context driven.

- *Nonverbal behaviors are often contradictory.* Our posture and vocal tone may say one thing, but our eyes may say another. We try to stand up straight and portray a dominant, confident posture, but our hands fidgeting with a pen may say something entirely different. Nonverbal behaviors do come "packaged" together, and we must often examine several behaviors before we begin to discern a coherent picture of the person before us. The problem with such packages or clusters of behaviors is that they're not always consistent and not always complementary. Which one should we believe?

- *Some nonverbal cues are more important than others.* As we examine several behaviors clustered together – vocal pace, tone and pitch; body posture; pupil dilation; arm and hand movement – it often becomes clear to careful observers that some cues are more important than others. For the most part, the relative importance of a given cue is dependent on habits and usual behaviors of the speaker. In other words, are the behaviors I'm observing usual or unusual for this person? If they're unusual, do they contradict verbal portions of the message? And, finally, it is important to note that some portions of our anatomy are simply easier to control than others: Even a nervous person can sit still if she makes a determined effort to do so, but few among us can control the dilation of our pupils. Many can control facial expression, but few can determine when tears will flow or when our voices will choke with emotion.

- *We often read into some cues much that isn't there and fail to read some cues that are clearly present.* We often look for cues that seem most important to us personally: whether a person will look us directly in the eyes as we speak or which direction they've crossed their legs. Such cues may be meaningless. We can also misread cues if we have insufficient information on which to base a judgment. Business leaders seen nodding off in a conference may be judged as indifferent by their hosts; in reality, it may be jet lag that's caught up with them.

- *We're not as skilled at reading nonverbal cues as we think we are; our confidence often exceeds our ability.* Caution is the byword in dealing with nonverbal communication. Even though a substantial portion of what we learn from a human transaction (between two-thirds and three-quarters of all meaning) comes from nonverbal cues, we simply aren't as skilled at this as we'd like to be. It's easy to misinterpret, misread or misunderstand someone. It's equally easy to jump to conclusions from just a few bits of evidence. The best advice for any manager would be to withhold judgment as long as possible, gather as much verbal as well as nonverbal information as possible, and then reconfirm what you think you know as frequently as possible. The stakes are high in business transactions, almost as high as the chances for error in decoding nonverbal cues.

## FOR FURTHER READING

Archer, D. and R. Akert. "Words and Everything Else: Verbal and Nonverbal Cues in Social Interaction," *Journal of Personality and Social Psychology* 35 (1978): 443–449.

Argyle, M. *Bodily Communication*, 2/e. London, U.K.: Methuen, 1998.

Buck, R. "A Test of Nonverbal Receiving Ability: Preliminary Studies," *Human Communication Research* 2 (1976): 162–171.

Christensen, D., A. Farina and L. Boudreau. "Sensitivity to Nonverbal Cues as a Function of Social Competence," *Journal of Nonverbal Behavior* 4 (1980): 146–156.

McConnon, A. "You Are Where You Sit: How to Decode the Psychology of the Morning Meeting," *BusinessWeek*, July 23, 2007, pp. 66–67.

Morris, D. *Bodytalk: The Meaning of Human Gestures*. New York: Random House, Inc., 1994.

Morris, D. *The Naked Ape: A Zoologist's Study of the Human Animal*. New York: Delta Publishing, 1999.

Remland, M. S. *Nonverbal Communication in Everyday Life*, 4/e. Thousand Oaks, CA: Sage Publications, Inc., 2016.

Rogers, E. M. (ed.). *A History of Communication Study: A Biographical Approach*. New York: The Free Press, 1994.

## NOTES

1 Jackson, M. "Some Workers Uncomfortable with Trend Toward Casual Clothes," *South Bend Tribune*, January 8, 1998, p. C7. See also Lee, L. "Some Employees Just Aren't Suited for Dressing Down," *The Wall Street Journal*, February 3, 1995, pp. A1, A6.

2 Jackson, "Some Workers Uncomfortable," p. C7. See also Berger, Joseph. "Black Jeans Invade Big Blue: First Day of a Relaxed IBM," *The Wall Street Journal*, February 7, 1995, pp. A1, B4; and Bounds, W. and J. Lublin. "Will the Client Wear a Tie or a T-Shirt?" *The Wall Street Journal*, July 24, 1998, pp. B1, B8. Reprinted by permission of *The Wall Street Journal*, Copyright © 1998 Dow Jones & Company, Inc. All rights reserved worldwide.

3  Critchell, S. "Men Move Toward More Dressy Clothes," *South Bend Tribune*, Sunday, April 28, 2002, p. F4. See also Jenkins, H. "Uptight Is Back in Style," *The Wall Street Journal*, Wednesday, November 21, 2001, p. A15; Kaufman, L. "Return of the Suit Tentatively: Some Men Are Dressing Up Again, but Casual Still Lives," *The New York Times*, Tuesday, April 2, 2002, pp. B1, B11; and Kaufman, L. "Casual Dress on the Way Out?" *Office Professional*, July 2002, p. 6.

4  Knapp, M. and J. Hall. *Nonverbal Communication in Human Interaction*, 3/e. Fort Worth, TX: Holt Rinehart and Winston, 1992, pp. 5–6.

5  Ruesch, J. and W. Kees. *Nonverbal Communication: Notes on the Visual Perception of Human Relations*. Los Angeles, CA: University of California Press, 1956.

6  Goleman, D. "Non-Verbal Cues Are Easy to Misinterpret," *The New York Times*, September 17, 1991, p. B5. Copyright © 1991 by The New York Times Company. Reprinted with permission.

7  Ibid.

8  Ibid., pp. B5–6. See also, "Dated Suit, Dirty Nails Can Tip the Balance if You're Job Hunting," *The Wall Street Journal*, Tuesday, June 1, 2004, p. B1. Reprinted by permission of *The Wall Street Journal*, Copyright © 2004 Dow Jones & Company, Inc. All rights reserved worldwide.

9  Eckman, P. "Communication Through Nonverbal Behavior: A Source of Information About an Interpersonal Relationship," in S. S. Tomkins and C. E. Izard (eds.), *Affect, Cognition and Personality*. New York: Springer and Co., Publishers, 1965.

10  DeVito, J. *The Interpersonal Communication Book*, 12/e. Boston, MA: Allyn & Bacon, 2009, p. 215.

11  Ibid., pp. 214–226.

12  Knapp and Hall. *Nonverbal Communication*, pp. 13–16.

13  "Be Civil: There Is a Clampdown on Obscene Gestures in the Office and on the Field," *The Wall Street Journal*, July 5, 1994, p. A1. Reprinted by permission of *The Wall Street Journal*, Copyright © 1994 Dow Jones & Company, Inc. All rights reserved worldwide.

14  Rubinkam, M. "'Voice Stress' May Betray Suspects' Lies," *South Bend Tribune*, February 11, 2002, p. B7.

15  Varian, H. R. "A Beautiful Mind Is Not Enough When It Comes to Evaluating Teachers," *The New York Times*, Thursday, August 28, 2003, p. C2. Copyright © 2003 by The New York Times Company. Reprinted with permission.

16  Harper, L. "Good Looks Can Mean a Pretty Penny on the Job, and 'Ugly' Men Are Affected More Than Women," *The Wall Street Journal*, November 23, 1993, p. B1. See also Brody, J. "Ideals of Beauty Are Seen as Innate: The Ideal Face Transcends Culture, Study Says," *The New York Times*, March 21, 1994, p. A6; Schoenberger, C. "Study Says the Handsome Turn Handsome Profits for Their Firms," *The Wall Street Journal*, Thursday, August 12, 1997, p. B1; and Coy, P. "Thinner Paychecks for Obese Women?" *Business Week*, October 30, 2000, p. 16.

17  "Fat Can Hit Women in the Wallet," *CBS News*. Online at www.cbsnews.com/stories/2004/03/03/health/main603825.shtml. Accessed July 28, 2008.

18  Ibid., p. B1. See also Newin, T. "Workplace Bias Ties to Obesity Is Ruled Illegal. Federal Judges Back a 320-Pound Woman," *The New York Times*, November 24, 1993, p. A10. Copyright © 1993 by The New York Times Company. Reprinted with permission.

19  Brown, A. "Get a Grip – A Firm One: Handshakes Tell All," *U.S. News & World Report*, July 17, 2000, p. 48.

20  Rubin, R. "The Biochemistry of Touch," *U.S. News & World Report*, November 10, 1997, p. 62.

21  Knapp and Hall. *Nonverbal Communication*, p. 16.

22  DeVito. *Interpersonal Communication*, p. 265.

23  Ibid., p. 247.

24  Hymowitz, C. "If the Walls Had Ears, You Wouldn't Have Any Less Privacy," *The Wall Street Journal*, May 19, 1998, p. B1. Reprinted by permission of *The Wall Street Journal*, Copyright © 1998 Dow Jones & Company, Inc. All rights reserved worldwide.

25  Rich, M. "Shut Up So We Can Do Our Jobs! Fed-Up Workers Try to Muffle Chitchat, Conference Calls and Other Open-Office Din," *The Wall Street Journal*, Wednesday, August 29, 2001, pp. B1, B8. Reprinted by permission of *The Wall Street Journal*, Copyright © 2001 Dow Jones & Company, Inc. All rights reserved worldwide.

26  Bounds, G. "I Can't Really Talk, I'm Here in the Office. But Did You Know . . . ?" *The Wall Street Journal*, Wednesday, July 10, 2002, p. B1. Reprinted by permission of *The Wall Street Journal*, Copyright © 2002 Dow Jones & Company, Inc. All rights reserved worldwide.

27  Bednar, G., partner, Ernst & Young, LLP, Chicago, in a telephone interview with the author, August 17, 1998.

28  Ibid.

29  Ibid.

30  Ebersberger, W., partner, Ernst & Young, LLP, Chicago, in a telephone interview with the author, August 17, 1998. See also Pristin, T. "A New Office Can Mean Making Do with Less," *The New York Times*, Wednesday, May 26, 2004, pp. Cl, C6.

31  Allen, T. J. *Managing the Flow of Technology*. Cambridge MA: The MIT Press, 1977, pp. 234–265.

32  For an excellent extended discussion of the role of space in social interaction, see Hall, E. T. *The Hidden Dimension*. New York: Doubleday, 1982.

33  DeVito. *Interpersonal Communication*, p. 248.

34  Ibid., p. 249.

35    Ibid., pp. 249–250.

36    Ferraro, G. *The Cultural Dimension of International Business*, 3/e. Upper Saddle River, NJ: Prentice-Hall, 1998, pp. 93–95.

37    For an excellent discussion of the role of time in human affairs, see Hall, E.T. *The Dance of Life*. New York: Doubleday, 1989.

38    Newbold, Curtis. "Red and Yellow Make Us Eat: How Restaurants Suck Us In," *The VCG*, October 13, 2013. Online at http://thevisualcommunicationguy.com/2013/10/13/red-and-yellow-how-restaurants-suck-us-in/. Accessed July 3, 2018 at 11:05 a.m.

39    Hall, T. "The Quest for Colors That Make Lips Smack," *The New York Times*, November 4, 1992, p. A13. See also Fountain, H. "Proof Positive that People See Colors with the Tongue," *The New York Times*, March 30, 1999, p. D5.

40    Hall. "The Quest for Colors That Make Lips Smack," p. A19.

41    Tischler, L. "Smells Like Brand Spirit," *Fast Company*, August 2005, pp. 52–59. See also Laurent, G. "Olfaction: A Window into the Brain," *Engineering & Science*, California Institute of Technology, 68, no. 1–2 (2005).

42    Hall. *The Hidden Dimension*, pp. 45–50.

43    Tischler. "Smells Like Brand Spirit," p. 52.

44    Engen, T. *Odor Sensation and Memory*. New York: Praeger, 1991.

45    O'Neill, M. "Taming the Frontier of the Senses: Using Aroma to Manipulate Moods," *The New York Times*, April 4, 1993, pp. B2, B6. Copyright © 1993 by The New York Times Company. Reprinted with permission.

46    Willoughby, J. "The Tip of Your Tongue Knows the Bitter Truth: Flavor Can Be Painful," *The New York Times*, April 27, 1994, pp. B1, B5. Copyright © 1994 by The New York Times Company. Reprinted with permission.

47    Mansfield, M. U.S. Ambassador to Japan, in a personal interview with the author in the U.S. Embassy in Tokyo, May 1983.

48    DeVito. *Interpersonal Communication*, pp. 258–261.

49    Fast, J. *Body Language*. New York: M. Evans, 1970.

50    Knapp and Hall. *Nonverbal Communication*, p. 27.

51    Ibid.

# Case 9.1: L'Oreal USA

## Do Looks Really Matter in the Cosmetic Industry?

The cosmetic and fragrance floor of the Macy's in San Jose was bustling with shoppers as Elysa Yanowitz, regional sales manager for L'Oreal, and John (Jack) Wiswall, general manager of L'Oreal's designer fragrance division, to whom Yanowitz reported, walked together through the store on a routine visit in the fall of 1997. As the two walked past the Polo Ralph Lauren counter, which is licensed to L'Oreal, Wiswall noticed a woman of Middle Eastern decent selling fragrances behind the counter. He instructed Yanowitz to "get [him] someone hot" and fire the Middle Eastern employee. Passing by a young good-looking blonde, Wiswall pulled Yanowitz aside and said, "Get me one that looks like that."

A few weeks later Wiswall visited the store again and was upset to discover that Yanowitz had not dismissed the saleswoman as instructed. Visibly frustrated with her refusal to follow his order, he asked Yanowitz upon leaving the store, "Didn't I tell you to get rid of her?"[1] Despite repeated inquiries from Wiswall, Yanowitz refused to fire the sales associate, claiming later that she could not dismiss the woman without adequate justification. Additionally, the employee was one of the top-selling sales associates in the region.

Wiswall became frustrated and with the help of Richard Roderick, vice president of designer fragrances and Yanowitz's immediate supervisor, he began to solicit complaints from Yanowitz's subordinates. In their quest for negative feedback on Yanowitz, they claimed that she maintained a dictatorial style of leadership and was disliked by her subordinates. Wiswall and Roderick also performed audits on Yanowitz's expense reports and prepared memos about problems with her performance. They told her she had become a liability and was making too many mistakes. Ironically, only one year prior, she had been awarded "L'Oreal's Regional Sales Manager of the Year."[2]

Yanowitz, typically a first-rate manager, became distressed and preoccupied to the extent that it affected her job performance. As a result, her sales numbers began to slip and in July 1998 she was forced to take a medical leave of absence. She cited job-related stress as the cause of her departure.[3] After three months, L'Oreal replaced her.

## ELYSA YANOWITZ

Elysa Yanowitz started as a sales representative with L'Oreal in 1981 when the company name was licensed by Cosmair, Inc. Yanowitz rose through the ranks to become a sales manager in 1986. She was responsible for managing L'Oreal's sales force and dealing with the department and specialty stores that sold L'Oreal's fragrances. Yanowitz's performance was consistently rated as "Above Expectations" or just short of "Outstanding." During her career she received multiple awards for her sales performance.[4] In 1997, L'Oreal restructured to merge its European Designer Fragrances division (where Yanowitz worked), with its Polo Ralph Lauren fragrances division. At this time, Yanowitz received the additional responsibilities of marketing Polo Ralph Lauren fragrances in her region.

## L'OREAL

L'Oreal S.A. Paris is the world's #1 cosmetic company specializing in the development and manufacturing process of hair care, hair color, skincare, color cosmetics and fragrances for the consumer and professional markets.

The history of L'Oreal began in 1907 when Eugene Schueller, a young French chemist, developed an innovative hair color formula and sold it to Parisian hairdressers. Mr. Schueller started a small company that would later be L'Oreal and put in place the guiding principles of the company: research and innovation in the interest of beauty. By 1912, Schueller was exporting his hair color products to Holland, Austria and Italy. A few years later, he was selling products to the U.S., Russia, South America and the Far East. While L'Oreal got its start in the hair color business, it soon expanded its operations to include other cleansing and beauty products. Today, L'Oreal is the world's largest cosmetic company marketing 500 brands and more than 2,000 products in all areas of the beauty business. In 2002, L'Oreal recorded over €14 billion in consolidated sales.[5]

L'Oreal USA, a wholly owned subsidiary of L'Oreal S.A. Paris, was founded in 1953 (by exclusive licensee Cosmair, Inc.). Since its foundation, the company has acquired a host of big-name consumer product brands, including Maybelline, Garnier and Softsheen Carson. The company also owns several salon product lines including Redken, Matrix, Kérastase and Mizani, as well as fragrance brands Ralph Lauren and Georgio Armani. L'Oreal USA's upscale Lancôme, Shu Uemura and Biotherm cosmetic and skincare lines are also sold in department stores nation-wide. With a broad distribution network of salons, mass-market, specialty and department stores, L'Oreal USA is the most comprehensive beauty company in the U.S.

## THE POLO RALPH LAUREN BRAND

In 1967, Ralph Lauren began the Polo Ralph Lauren company with 26 boxes of ties. Interested in promoting a lifestyle with his ties, Ralph Lauren named his line after Polo, a sport of discreet elegance and classic style. Today, 35 years later, the company is a $10 billion global business of menswear, womenswear, childrenswear, home collections, accessories and fragrances.

Polo Ralph Lauren's brand and distinctive image have been consistently developed across an expanding number of products, brands and international markets. Defined by its all-American style and combination of classic taste, quality and integrity, Polo Ralph Lauren is a leader in the fashion industry. The company's products are distributed through upscale department stores such as Macy's, Nordstrom's and Neiman Marcus.[6]

Polo Ralph Lauren's brand names, which include *Polo, Polo by Ralph Lauren, Ralph Lauren Purple Label, Polo Sport, Ralph Lauren, RALPH, Lauren, Polo Jeans Co., RL, Chaps* and *Club Monaco*, among others, constitute one of the world's most recognized families of consumer brands. Through an exclusive partnership with Polo Ralph Lauren, L'Oreal USA markets and manages the Polo Ralph Lauren fragrance line. However, not all of the company's brands products are licensed through L'Oreal, just the fragrance line. In 1997, L'Oreal's European Designer Fragrance Division merged with its Polo Ralph Lauren Fragrance Division.

## THE COSMETIC INDUSTRY

Cosmetic products are generally grouped into six main categories: perfumes, fragrances, decorative cosmetics, skincare, hair care and toiletries. The marketing of these products represents an important part of building cosmetic brands. The cosmetic industry typically markets its products using creative packaging and superior formulations. Employees in the cosmetic industry must have the ability to monitor and interpret fashion and consumer trends both locally and internationally in order to offer the latest in product innovation and packaging technology. They also must work closely with clients while creating products and developing marketing strategies to maximize the sales potential within specific market segments.[7]

The cosmetic industry is fortunate to operate in markets that are less sensitive to economic cycles than others.[8] When the economy is difficult, customers who delay purchase of a consumer durable will continue to buy cosmetics products because they provide a sense of well-being at a reasonable price. However, Lindsey Owen-Jones, Chairman and CEO of L'Oreal, recently warned investors that the current cosmetic market is "one of the worst we've seen for years."[9]

The target consumers for the cosmetic market are primarily working, college-educated women over the age of 20 who have an active lifestyle. However, there is an emergence of teenagers as a market segment as they wish to assert their identity and personality. Another consumer trend is the spread of skincare products and cosmetics for men. Although the market for men is in its infancy, it constitutes another promising opportunity for the cosmetics industry.

## APPEARANCE-BASED DISCRIMINATION: HUMAN RESOURCES/LEGAL IMPLICATIONS

Appearance in the fashion and cosmetic industries is very important because beauty products are tied directly to the brand's image. Companies in these industries depend on their sales associates to be "brand ambassadors" and project the qualities of the brand to the customer. In today's competitive environment and particularly in the fashion and beauty industries, it is critical that beauty-based companies create an experience that is appealing to the target customer. For example, at some Abercrombie stores, applicants are required to submit a professional head shot with their application to ensure that they are a good match with the "Abercrombie style."[10] This trend of hiring attractive employees is occurring in other industries as well. Hotels, bars and other businesses also are beginning to recruit only the best-looking employees to attract customers and charge premium prices.

Hiring someone who is attractive isn't illegal, per se. In recent years, however, several cases have emerged disputing whether employers can base employment decisions solely on physical appearance. In a 1981 case, *Wilson v. Southwest Airlines Co.*,[11] Southwest defended its then-existing policy that only attractive women could be hired as flight attendants and ticket agents. Southwest argued that female sex appeal was a bona fide occupational qualification (BFOQ) under Title VII because the airline wanted to project "a sexy image and fulfill its public promise to take passengers skyward with love."[12] However, since Southwest is not in the business of providing "vicarious sex entertainment," the district court rejected its defense.

What is and is not discrimination? Employers may fire their best employee; they may also fire a woman, a person who practices a certain faith, a pregnant woman, a disabled person, a gay or lesbian, or a foreigner. However, they cannot terminate them *because* they are a woman, of a certain religion, pregnant, disabled, gay or lesbian, or from a foreign country. The motive for the termination is the single governing factor in a lawsuit for discrimination when an employee falls within a protected category.[13]

Employees are protected under Title VII of the Civil Rights Act from discrimination based on sex, race, religion, color or national origin, but height, weight and physical appearance discrimination are not included.[14] Part of the problem is the fact that attractiveness is subjective; people have different opinions on what is appealing. To protect themselves, some companies have created policies that state that employees must be "well-groomed and attractive," but these companies run into difficulty when the policy is not consistently enforced across sexes and races.[15]

The Court of Appeal ruled that the L'Oreal case was one of sex discrimination: A male executive cannot insist that a female subordinate be terminated because she is not sexually appealing to him, when no similar orders are issued with respect to male employees. Just as an employer may not enforce rules that regulate men and women differently based on their appearance or sexual desirability, an employer may also not discriminate against employees on these bases.

The L'Oreal case also raises the question of wrongful termination. The state of California operates under an "at will" employment model. This means that employees work at the will of their employer – subject to two exceptions, discrimination and contract – and an employer may terminate without reason or notice. Employers cannot discriminate against employees on the basis of age, race, sex, national origin and several other criteria. Employers also cannot fire contracted employees who are hired to work for the company for a specified time period or purpose but are not directly employed by the company.

## WORKING AT L'OREAL

L'Oreal's sales team includes employees with different educational backgrounds and work experiences. For some positions, the company requires sales associates to have a cosmetology license, previous experience and specific knowledge. L'Oreal is particularly interested in employees who are enthusiastic about fashion and beauty, possess customer service abilities, are analytical, have excellent negotiation skills, are willing to travel and relocate, and are computer literate.[16]

L'Oreal describes itself as a fast-paced, energetic company that employs smart, focused individuals who enjoy their work. The company boasts that it is not a "cookie-cutter corporation." In fact, L'Oreal claims that its workforce diversity "will amaze and inspire you." Since the company strives for diversity, would it seem reasonable to terminate a sales associate on the basis of her appearance and background?

## YANOWITZ VS. L'OREAL

In 1999, Elysa Yanowitz filed a sexual discrimination suit against L'Oreal. During a four-year court battle, Yanowitz insisted that Wiswall had violated California's fair employment law barring sexual discrimination, when he sought to fire the saleswoman. She further argued that it was illegal for L'Oreal to retaliate against her for not carrying out an order she believed violated the law. L'Oreal's legal representatives argued that Wiswall and other company officials did nothing wrong and took action to reprimand Yanowitz for her errors and oversights.[17]

On March 7, 2003, a three-judge panel of the Court of Appeals for the First Appellate District in San Francisco reinstated her claim of retaliation which was dismissed previously by the trial court. The panel wrote: "An explicit order to fire a female employee for failing to meet a male executive's personal standards for sexual desirability is sex discrimination." The panel also said, "A lower-level manager's refusal to carry out that order is protected activity, and an employer may not retaliate against her for that refusal." On June 11, 2003, the California Supreme Court voted 6-to-1 to review the appellate court's ruling.[18]

## REBECCA CARUSO

On August 4, 2003, L'Oreal USA named Rebecca Caruso as its Executive Vice President of Corporate Communications. She replaced John Wendt, Executive Vice President, Corporate and Public Affairs, who retired in December after 23 years with L'Oreal USA. Prior to joining L'Oreal USA, Caruso worked in communications and public relations for Toys "R" Us, Inc., McDonald's Corporation, and Chrysler Corporation of America.

Caruso must decide the best way for her department to handle L'Oreal's communication response concerning Yanowitz's lawsuit. Because she joined the L'Oreal team in August 2003, she faces an interesting challenge of dealing with this case after all the major events have occurred. In her new capacity, Caruso is responsible for the management of all internal and external communications and diversity initiatives for L'Oreal USA. She must work closely with Mr. Jean-Paul Agon, President and CEO of L'Oreal USA, to deal with this lawsuit and prevent it from developing into a public relations disaster. With the upcoming trial date and the media heavily covering the case, she must determine how to retain L'Oreal's strong brand identity and reputation.

## QUESTIONS

- How should L'Oreal handle the negative press surrounding this lawsuit?
- Would an outside consulting firm be useful? How?
- Who should handle the communication with the public, stakeholders and the media?
- What should the message be and how should it be delivered?
- What actions should L'Oreal take to protect itself in the future?
- What are the critical issues and who are the major stakeholders in this case?
- What options does L'Oreal have regarding the lawsuit and is battling the case with Yanowitz in court the best decision?

## ACKNOWLEDGMENTS

This case was prepared by Research Assistants Allison A. Petty, Cynthia G. Reimer, and Ross R. Swanes under the direction of James S. O'Rourke, Concurrent Professor of Management, as the basis for class discussion rather than to illustrate either effective or ineffective handling of an administrative situation.

## NOTES

1  "Refusal to Fire Unattractive Saleswomen Led to Dismissal, Suit Contends," *The New York Times*, April 11, 2003, p. A10.
2  Ibid.
3  Leff, Lisa. "Woman Who Wouldn't Fire Cosmetics Clerk Over Looks Can Sue," *Associated Press*, April 12, 2003, 12:07 a.m.
4  Ofgang, Kenneth. "Firing Woman for Lack of Attractiveness Violates Anti-Bias Law," *Metropolitan New-Enterprise*, Monday, March 10, 2003.
5  L'Oreal website, www.loreal.com.
6  Ralph Lauren website, www.polo.com.
7  Cosmetic, Toiletry and Perfumery Association, www.ctpa.org.uk.
8  Ibid.
9  L'Oreal Finance website, www.loreal-finance.com.
10  Houston, David. "Abercrombie & Fitch Ads Offend Critics, Who Say Company Shuns Minority Workers," *Daily Journal*, June 23, 2003.
11  *Wilson v. Southwest Airlines Co.* N.D. Texas (1981) 517 F.Supp. 292 (Wilson).
12  Ibid.
13  www.discriminationattorney.com.
14  Kranke, Bell, Iyer & Hoffman, University of Northern Colorado. "Appearance Discrimination and Small Business." Online at www.eeoc.gov/laws/vii.html. Accessed December 16, 2003 at 11:53 a.m.
15  Ibid.
16  L'Oreal website, www.loreal.com.
17  "US Judge Lets L'Oreal Sex Discrimination Suit Proceed," *Associated Press*, April 11, 2003, 6:33 EST (Morning Star).
18  *Yanowitz vs. L'Oreal USA, Inc.* Legal Brief, California Court of Appeal. 7 March 2003.

# Case 9.2: Maria Sharapova

## Banishment from WTA Tour and a Loss of Sponsorship

You are running a $30-million-a-year sole proprietorship, and it depends on you remaining eligible . . . what was she thinking? Either she or her team really screwed up.[1]

~ Richard W. Pound, former president of WADA (World Anti-Doping Agency)

## INTRODUCTION

On March 7, 2016, Maria Sharapova walked to the podium at a press conference in a downtown Los Angeles hotel to make a "major announcement."[2] The press was gathered to hear from the tennis superstar, who had been ranked as the world's richest female athlete for 11 years straight due to her lucrative endorsement deals.[3] The common belief was that Sharapova was there to announce she had made the decision to retire at age 28 following several injuries. However, Maria made an even more shocking announcement, she had failed a drug test at the Australian Open in January (see Exhibit 9.1 at the end of this case study).

Following her loss to Serena Williams in the quarterfinals of the Australian Open on January 26, 2016, Sharapova tested positive for the banned substance Meldonium. Sharapova admitted to haven taken Meldonium and accepted responsibility for the failed drug test, but maintained she did not know that Meldonium was a prohibited substance. The International Tennis Federation subsequently announced that she was being provisionally banned and faced a potential two-year suspension following a review of the case.[4]

What followed was a flurry of reactions on social media and from her sponsors, including Nike, Tag Heuer, Porsche and Head. While Sharapova's sponsors were being pressured to end their substantial contracts with her, Sharapova was left to defend herself and her reputation.

## BACKGROUND

Maria Yuryevna Sharapova was born on April 19, 1987, in Nyagan, Siberia, Russia. Her parents, Yuri and Yelena, were both avid athletes who enjoyed playing tennis, and wanted to teach their young daughter the sport. Since they could not afford to buy a child-size racket, they sawed off a portion of the handle of an adult-size racket and gave that for her to use as a toddler.[5] Tennis great Martina Navratilova noticed her at a youth tennis clinic in Moscow at age 6 and suggested she attend the Nick Bollettieri Tennis Academy in Florida, a tennis-focused boarding school with notable alums including Andre Agassi, Pete Sampras and Monica Seles.[6]

Sharapova and her father went to Florida the following year, borrowing money from Sharapova's grandparents to afford the trip. Unfortunately, she was too young to enroll at that time, so her father took a job as a waiter and she worked with a private tennis coach until the age of 9, when she was old enough for a tryout. She performed so well during her tryout that they offered her a full-scholarship to the school, which cost $46,000 per year at that time.[7]

The Bollettieri Academy was part of the International Management Group (IMG), a sports and talent management company.[8] At age 11, Sharapova signed with IMG, which led to her first partnership with athletic shoe and apparel maker Nike. After showing immense potential, she turned professional on her 14th birthday, the youngest eligible age to join the women's professional tennis organization – the Women's Tennis Association (WTA).[9]

## FROM TENNIS PLAYER TO INTERNATIONAL BRAND

Sharapova became a household name after winning the Wimbledon singles title in 2004 at just 17 years old, the third youngest winner in history. She became the first Russian woman to win Wimbledon, and would subsequently became the first Russian woman to hold the coveted world's No. 1 ranking the following year.[10] Several injuries plagued her over the course of the next few years, but she lived up to her enormous potential, going on to win every major tournament. After winning the 2012 French Open, she became just the tenth woman to complete a career Grand Slam – having won the US Open, Australian Open, Wimbledon and the French Open over the course of her career. Later that year, she won a silver medal at the 2012 Summer Olympics in London.

Even amongst great triumphs on the court, Sharapova found even greater success off the court. Following her win at Wimbledon in 2004, she amassed numerous endorsement deals from leading companies and could command up to $500,000 per exhibition match.[11] *Fortune* estimates that over the course of her career she earned $285 million[12], of which approximately $35 million was in prize money from tournament wins. The remaining $250 million was through deals with Nike ($70 million over eight years), Head ($2 million per year to play using Head rackets)[13], and others such as Tag Heuer, Evian and Avon, totaling approximately $20 to $30 million per year.

## THE WORLD ANTI-DOPING AGENCY, PERFORMANCE ENHANCING DRUGS, AND BANNED SUBSTANCES

The World Anti-Doping Agency (WADA) was formed in 1999 through an initiative led by the International Olympic Committee to monitor and fight the use of drugs in sports. The World Anti-Doping Code "harmonizes anti-doping policies, rules and regulations within sport organizations and among public authorities around the world"[14], and WADA maintains a list of banned substances. WADA's Prohibited List Expert Group annually determines which drugs should be banned, and considers three criteria: whether the drug can enhance performance, whether taking the drug could harm the health of the athlete and whether taking the drug goes against the spirit of sport. Two of the three criteria must be satisfied for the drug to be prohibited. If an athlete has a legitimate medical need for a banned substance, they can apply for a therapeutic use exemption, which would be considered by WADA.[15]

Meldonium was being monitored by WADA for one year before becoming banned. At that time, WADA felt they had enough information to conclude there was a clear pattern of abuse relating to Meldonium and scientific evidence that it had performance-enhancing benefits.[16]

Meldonium, brand name Mildronate, is developed by Grindex, a Latvian pharmaceutical company, and is used to treat lack of blood flow to parts of the body due to heart failure. Other uses for the drug include treating infections of the lungs and upper respiratory tract and treating stomach ulcers. A licensed drug used widely throughout Eastern Europe and Central Asia, Meldonium is not approved by the Food and Drug Administration (FDA) for use in the U.S. The drug has become one of Latvia's biggest medical exports with sales reaching €56 million in 2013.[17]

According to the drug's designer, Ivar Kalvins, Meldonium was created to increase the body's oxygen-carrying capacity. It was used for a decade by Soviet troops in Afghanistan to increase their endurance while hiking throughout the mountainous terrain. A 2005 study found that taking Meldonium, in combination with an enzyme called Lisinopril, improved exercise capability and circulation in patients with chronic heart failure.[18] This ability to increase endurance and exercise capacity perked the interest of athletes. A 2015 study of Russian athletes found that 17 percent of those tested had Meldonium in their systems, and another study found that 8 percent of all athletes tested at the 2015 European Games tested positive for Meldonium.[19]

Sharapova was prescribed Meldonium by her family doctor in 2006 after irregular EKG results and was given the drug to treat a variety of problems including a magnesium deficiency and due to a family history of diabetes.[20] She regularly took the drug for the next ten years.

In the fall of 2015, WADA announced that Meldonium would be banned beginning on January 1, 2016.[21] The International Tennis Federation warned its players five times during the month of December regarding the impending ban.[22] However, Sharapova said she failed to click on the link to the updated banned substance list that was sent to her via e-mail.[23] She also insists that she only knew the drug by the brand name, Mildronate, and was unaware that it was the same drug being added to the banned substance list.[24]

## THE WOMEN'S TENNIS ASSOCIATION, GRAND SLAMS AND PRIZE MONEY

The Women's Tennis Association (WTA) is the organizing body for women's professional tennis. Its counterpart for men's professional tennis is the Association of Tennis Professionals (ATP). The WTA organizes 50-plus competitive events and the four Grand Slam tournaments each year.[25] The Grand Slam tournaments rely on sponsors and fan attendance to earn revenue. Wimbledon advertises that for nearly $40,000 a fan can reserve a guaranteed seat for the first ten days of the tournament over the next five years.[26] In 2015, the Australian Open reported revenue of nearly $175 million, the French Open just over $200 million, Wimbledon $240 million and the US Open over $250 million. Wimbledon was the most profitable event, netting nearly $80 million in profits.[27]

The WTA was formed in 1973 by legendary tennis great Billie Jean King. In 1980, the tour offered a total of $7.2 million in prize money, before reaching $23 million in 1990, and $50 million in 2001. After a decades-long campaign for equal pay in the sport, all four Grand Slam tournaments offered equal prizes to men and women for the first time in 2007. In 2009 the WTA created a shorter season and a more fan-friendly structure, and by 2013, overall prize money had skyrocketed to $118 million as tennis became increasingly popular with fans around the world.[28]

In 2016, the WTA included more than 2,500 players representing nearly 100 nations. More than 400 million fans watched WTA tennis on television and other digital channels, and total prize money reached a record $139 million.[29]

## CELEBRITY SPONSORSHIPS AND ENDORSEMENTS: THE GOOD AND THE BAD

Celebrity endorsements can be a great way to build awareness and excitement regarding a company or product. According to MarketWatch, research indicates that, on average, sales increase by 4 percent after signing a celebrity endorser.[30] Successful endorsements can provide substantial revenues, such as Nike's sponsorship of Michael Jordan and the creation of the Jordan shoe brand. Generating significant profits for Nike, the shoe brand now holds 75 percent market share in basketball shoes and nearly 11 percent market share in the overall shoe market.[31]

However, celebrity endorsements can have severe potential downsides as well. While not only incredibly expensive to sponsor an international athlete or celebrity, the company also becomes intricately linked to that individual and his or her every action. Restaurant-chain Subway benefited from rapid growth after launching an extensive campaign around Jared Fogle, who was prominently featured in advertisements after attributing his weight loss to eating Subway sandwiches. Fogle was the face of Subway for nearly 15 years and was estimated to be worth $15 million until he was arrested on child pornography charges.[32] After news broke, Subway immediately cut ties with Fogle, but saw a 3.4 percent revenue decline over the next year and faced harsh criticisms about its involvement with Fogle.[33]

The sports world has also been rocked by celebrity athlete scandals, most notably Tiger Woods and Lance Armstrong. Tiger Woods was propelled into the spotlight by news of his infidelity to his wife, Elin. As a result, he lost

$22 million of endorsement deals in 2010.[34] Sponsors such as Gatorade, AT&T and Accenture all chose to cut ties with Woods as a result of his actions. Other sponsors, most notably Nike, chose to stick by Woods. Lance Armstrong, a seven-time Tour de France winner, was another sports star plagued by scandal. After testing positive for performance-enhancing drugs, he was stripped of his titles and lost many sponsors. It is estimated he lost $150 million in potential earnings after being dropped by numerous sponsors, including Nike.[35]

## STATEMENTS FROM SHARAPOVA'S SPONSORS

The reaction from three of Sharapova's most prominent sponsors following her announcement was swift and unfavorable. The day after the press conference, her largest sponsor, Nike, said they were "saddened and surprised by the news" and that they had "decided to suspend our relationship with Maria while the investigation continues."[36] Luxury Swiss watch-maker Tag Heuer suspended ongoing negotiations with Sharapova to renew her contract that had expired in December of 2015. Automaker Porsche, owned by Volkswagen, said it was postponing all planned sponsorship activities with Sharapova.[37] Most of her other sponsors did not release statements and were monitoring the investigation before making any decisions (see Figure 9.1).

One notable exception was her racket sponsor, Head, which pledged its support for Sharapova, saying "the honesty and courage she displayed in announcing and acknowledging her mistake was admirable. Head is proud to stand behind Maria, now and into the future, and we intend to extend her contract."[38] Head would later face scrutiny on social media and in the mainstream press for its decision.[39]

Additionally, Sharapova has her own candy line, Sugarpova. This line could also be adversely affected by Sharapova's scandal if her fans decide not to support her. With the availability of close substitutes in the market, such as Dylan's Candy Bar, the main differentiator for Sharapova's company was its founder's name and celebrity status. If her public perception is negatively affected by the scandal, revenues may also drop for Sugarpova.

**FIGURE 9.1** Reactions from Sharapova's Sponsors

*Source*: Brown, Andy. "Sponsors Ditch Sharapova Over Anti-Doping Rule Violation," *The Sports Integrity Initiative*, March 8, 2016. Online at www.sportsintegrityinitiative.com/sponsors-ditch-sharapova-over-anti-doping-rule-violation.

## SOCIAL MEDIA REACTIONS

The continued growth and prevalence of social media makes social media responses a real-time hazard during a time of scandal. When news of Sharapova's failed drug test broke, there was a flurry of social media responses both in support of Sharapova as well as angry outbursts toward her. Retired tennis players Martina Navratilova, James Blake and Jennifer Capriati all tweeted their reactions to the news.[40] While Navratilova and Blake showed support for Sharapova (see Figures 9.2 and 9.3), Capriati unleashed a Twitter rant toward Sharapova, calling her a cheat, questioning her need to take Meldonium, and saying it was all about the money (see Figure 9.4). Capriati's first two tweets have since been deleted, but her remaining rant was published on Twitter (see Figures 9.5, 9.6, 9.7 and 9.8).

**Martina Navratilova** ✓
@Martina
                         ✔ Follow

Sharapova Announces That She Failed Doping Test, -hope this gets cleared up as it seems 2 me to be an honest mistake
nytimes.com/2016/03/08/spo...
3:40 PM - 7 Mar 2016

**James Blake** ✓
@JRBlake
                         ✔ Follow

Wow. Classy of @MariaSharapova to hold a press conference for this and admit making a mistake. Definitely agree that have to be aware though
3:17 PM - 7 Mar 2016
↩ ⟲ 277 ♥ 402

**FIGURES 9.2 AND 9.3** Positive Twitter Reactions

*Source*: Hendricks, Maggie. "See Reaction to Maria Sharapova's Shocking Announcement That She Failed a Drug Test," *USA Today Sports*, March 7, 2016. Online at http://ftw.usatoday.com/2016/03/see-reaction-to-maria-sharapovas-shocking-announcement-that-she-failed-a-drug-test

---

Im extremely angry and disappointed. I had to lose my career and never opted to cheat no matter what.i had to throw in the towel and suffer

— Jennifer Capriati (@JenCapriati) March 7, 2016

i didn't have the high priced team of drs that found a way for me to cheat and get around the system and wait for science to catch up — Jennifer Capriati (@JenCapriati) March 7, 2016

---

**FIGURE 9.4** Capriati Rant

*Source*: Gaines, Cork. "Former US Tennis Phenom Rips Maria Sharapova Over Failed Drug Test," *Business Insider UK*, March 8, 2016. Online at www.businessinsider.com/jennifer-capriati-rips-maria-sharapova-for-failed-drug-test-2016-3.

**Jennifer Capriati** ✓ @JenCapriati · 7 Mar 2016
What's the point of someone taking a heart medicine that helps your heart recover faster unless you have a heart condition? Is thataccurate?
↩ 46 ⟲ 117 ♥ 146

**Jennifer Capriati** ✓ @JenCapriati · 7 Mar 2016
It's always about one thing that benefits everyone.#money
↩ 12 ⟲ 38 ♥ 85

**FIGURES 9.5, 9.6, 9.7 AND 9.8** Capriati Rant

*Source*: https://twitter.com/jencapriati?lang=en

Jennifer Capriati ● @JenCapriati · 7 Mar 2016
Maybe I should start taking it? Lol I might feel better

↩ 21    ↻ 11    ♥ 30

Jennifer Capriati ● @JenCapriati · 3 Mar 2016
So for 10 years you've been able to play with a now banned substance? That's a careers worth of time

↩ 55    ↻ 56    ♥ 83

**FIGURES 9.5, 9.6, 9.7 AND 9.8**   (Continued)

## THE SUSPENSION

A three-member tribunal appointed by the International Tennis Federation held a hearing in May 2016 to discuss Sharapova's failed drug test. On June 8, they suspended Sharapova for two years, acknowledging that the violation was not intentional. She could have been suspended for up to four years if the tribunal had found the violation was intentional. Sharapova said she would appeal the suspension through the Court of Arbitration for Sport.[41]

## DISCUSSION QUESTIONS

1. How should Sharapova communicate with both her sponsors and fans to protect her brand and reputation? What should she say to each and how can she ensure her messaging is aligned?
2. What should Sharapova's sponsors communicate to their customers? Should they cut ties with Sharapova? If so, should they part ways immediately or wait for the results of the investigation?
3. Should companies continue to use celebrity endorsers? What are the pros and cons?
4. Who is to blame for the failed drug test? Sharapova or members of her team? If her team is at fault, does that effect how her sponsors should react?
5. What is at stake for the WTA and the Grand Slam tournaments? How should they combat a star player being off the tour for two years?
6. Should the WTA release a statement regarding Sharapova's failed drug test? If so, what should they say?

## APPENDIX

### *Exhibit 9.1: Sharapova's Press Conference Statement*

*"I received a letter from the ITF that I failed a drugs test at the Australian Open. I take full responsibility for it.*

*"For the past 10 years I have been given a medicine called mildronate by my family doctor and a few days ago after I received the ITF letter I found out that it also has another name of meldonium which I did not know.*

*"It is very important for you to understand that for 10 years this medicine was not on Wada's banned list and I had legally been taking the medicine for the past 10 years.*

*"But on January 1st the rules had changed and meldonium became a prohibited substance which I had not known.*

*"I was given this medicine by my doctor for several health issues that I was having in 2006," Sharapova continued.*

*"Throughout my long career I have been very open and honest about many things and I take great responsibility and professionalism in my job every single day and I made a huge mistake.*

*"I let my fans down. I let the sport down I have been playing since the age of four and I love so deeply.*

*"I know with this I face consequences and I don't want to end my career this way and I really hope I will be given another chance to play this game.*

*"I know many of you thought I was retiring but if I was ever going to announce my retirement it would probably not be in a downtown Los Angeles hotel with this fairly ugly carpet."*

*Source*: de Menezes, Jack. "Maria Sharapova Fails Drug Test: Her Statement in Full After Admitting Testing Positive for Meldonium," *The Independent*, Monday March 7, 2016. Online at www.independent.co.uk/sport/tennis/maria-sharapova-fails-drug-test-her-statement-in-full-after-testing-positive-for-meldonium-a6917911.html.

## ACKNOWLEDGMENTS

This case was prepared by research assistants John Coughlin and Natasha Fritz under the direction of James O'Rourke, Teaching Professor of Management, as the basis for class discussion rather than to illustrate either effective or ineffective handling of an administrative situation. Information was gathered from corporate as well as public sources.

## NOTES

1 Clarey, Christopher. "More Than 60 Athletes Have Tested Positive for Meldonium," *The New York Times*, March 10, 2016. Online at www.nytimes.com/2016/03/11/sports/tennis/maria-sharapova-meldonium-positive-tests.html?_r=0.

2 de Menezes, Jack. "Maria Sharapova Retirement Rumours as Tennis Star Calls Press Conference to Make 'Major Announcement,'" *The Independent*, March 6, 2016. Online at www.independent.co.uk/sport/tennis/maria-sharapova-retirement-speculation-after-tennis-star-calls-press-conference-to-make-major-a6915341.html.

3 Leongsong, Randolph. "Maria Sharapova Highest Paid Female Athlete for 11th Straight Year," *The Inquirer*, August 13, 2015. Online at http://sports.inquirer.net/189552/maria-sharapova-highest-paid-female-athlete-for-11th-straight-year.

4 Ubha, Ravi. "Maria Sharapova Fails Drug Test," *CNN*, March 8, 2016. Online at http://edition.cnn.com/2016/03/07/tennis/maria-sharapova-tennis-injuries.

5 "Maria Sharapova Biography," *Encyclopedia of World Biography*. Online at www.notablebiographies.com/news/Ow-Sh/Sharapova-Maria.html.

6 Ibid.

7 Ibid.

8 Ibid.

9 Ibid.

10 "Maria Sharapova," *Biography.com*. Online at www.biography.com/people/maria-sharapova-13790853.

11 Badenhausen, Kurt. "How Maria Sharapova Earned $285 Million During Her Tennis Career," *Forbes*, March 8, 2016. Online at www.forbes.com/sites/kurtbadenhausen/2016/03/08/how-maria-sharapova-earned-285-mill-during-her-tennis-career/#74d6f9478e2f.

12 Ibid.

13 Long, Michael. "Sharapova Signs Multi-Million Head Racquet Deal," *SportsPro media*, January 12, 2011. Online at www.sportspromedia.com/news/sharapova_signs_multi-million_head_racquet_deal.

14 "The Code," World Anti-Doping Agency. Online at www.wada-ama.org/en/what-we-do/the-code.

15 Beans, Carolyn. "What Does It Take to Get a Drug Banned for Enhancing Athletes' Performance?" *NPR.org*, June 14, 2016. Online at www.npr.org/sections/health-shots/2016/06/14/482010754/what-does-it-take-to-get-a-drug-banned-for-enhancing-athletes-performance.

16 "What Is Meldonium and Why Did Maria Sharapova Take It?" *The Guardian*, June 8, 2016. Online at www.theguardian.com/sport/2016/mar/08/meldonium-maria-sharapova-failed-drugs-test.

17 Newman, Tim. "Meldonium (Mildronate): What Is It and What Does It Do?" *Medical News Today*, April 19, 2016. Online at www.medicalnewstoday.com/articles/309165.php.

18 Ibid.

19 "What Is Meldonium and Why Did Maria Sharapova Take It?" *The Guardian*.

20 Ibid.

21 Ibid.

22 "Report: Maria Sharapova Was Warned Multiple Times About Banned Drug," *Sports Illustrated*, March 9, 2016. Online at www.si.com/tennis/2016/03/09/maria-sharapova-warned-meldonium-banned-wada-itf-wta.

23 Clarey. "More Than 60 Athletes Have Tested Positive for Meldonium."

24 de Menezes, Jack. "Maria Sharapova Fails Drug Test: Her Statement in Full After Admitting Testing Positive for Meldonium," *The Independent*, March 7, 2016, Online at www.independent.co.uk/sport/tennis/maria-sharapova-fails-drug-test-her-statement-in-full-after-testing-positive-for-meldonium-a6917911.html.

25 "About the WTA," *Women's Tennis Association*. Online at www.wtatennis.com/scontent/article/2951989/title/about-the-wta.

26    Ahmed, Murad. "Wimbledon to Air-Condition Grass as Part of Modernisation," *Financial Times*, June 26, 2016. Online at www.ft.com/content/000ff1b8-3911-11e6-a780-b48ed7b6126f.

27    Carter, Aliko. "Grand Slam 2016: Tennis' Four Majors by the Numbers," *Forbes*. January 20, 2016. Online at www.forbes.com/sites/alikocarter/2016/01/20/grand-slam-2016-tennis-four-majors-by-the-numbers/#4024c01a7b0a.

28    Ibid.

29    Ibid.

30    Sager, Ryan. "Do Celebrity Endorsements Work?" *MarketWatch*, March 21, 2011. Online at www.marketwatch.com/story/do-celebrity-endorsements-work-1300481444531.

31    Ibid.

32    Peterson, Hayley. "FBI Raids Home of 'Subway Diet' Spokesman Jared Fogle," *Business Insider*. July 7, 2015. Online at www.businessinsider.com/fbi-raids-home-of-subway-diet-spokesman-jared-fogle-2015-7.

33    Hatic, Dana. "Subway's Sales Growth Has Been Sluggish Post-Jared Fogle Scandal," *Eater*, March 29, 2016. Online at www.eater.com/2016/3/29/11326278/subway-sales-down-in-2015.

34    Wei, Will. "Tiger Woods Lost $22 Million in Endorsements in 2010," *Business Insider*, July 21, 2010. Online at www.businessinsider.com/tiger-woods-lost-22-million-in-2010-endorsements-2010-7.

35    Rishe, Patrick. "Armstrong Will Lose $150 Million in Future Earnings After Nike and Other Sponsors Dump Him," *Forbes*, October 18, 2012. Online at www.forbes.com/sites/prishe/2012/10/18/nike-proves-deadlier-than-cancer-as-armstrong-will-lose-150-million-in-future-earnings/#7c4c95cb6298.

36    Mullen, Jethro. "Maria Sharapova Loses Endorsement Deals After Failing Drug Test," *CNN*, March 8, 2016. Online at http://money.cnn.com/2016/03/08/news/nike-maria-sharapova-nike-suspension-doping/.

37    Ibid.

38    "Sharapova Sponsor: We Will Work With "Courageous" Star for Many More Years," *Haymarket Media Group*, March 11, 2016. Online at www.prweek.com/article/1387021/sharapova-sponsor-will-work-courageous-star-years.

39    Lovett, Samuel. "Maria Sharapova: Sponsors Congratulate Convicted Russian with Controversial Tweets After Ban is Reduced to 15 Months," *The Independent*, October 4, 2016. Online at www.independent.co.uk/sport/tennis/maria-sharapova-russian-sponsors-ban-tweet-head-appeal-15-months-two-years-a7344591.html.

40    Hendricks, Maggie. "See Reaction to Maria Sharapova's Shocking Announcement That She Failed a Drug Test," *USA TODAY*, March 7, 2016. Online at http://ftw.usatoday.com/2016/03/see-reaction-to-maria-sharapovas-shocking-announcement-that-she-failed-a-drug-test.

41    Meyers, Naila-Jean and Ben Rothenberg. "Maria Sharapova Is Suspended from Tennis for Two Years," *The New York Times*, June 8, 2016. Online at www.nytimes.com/2016/06/09/sports/tennis/maria-sharapova-doping-suspension.html.

# CHAPTER 10

# Intercultural Communication

The world you inhabit in the twenty-first century is becoming a vastly different place from the one your parents knew as children of the twentieth century. The industrialized nations of the world are experiencing change of an unprecedented sort, and the U.S. is gradually but inevitably becoming different from the nation your parents and grandparents lived and worked in. What will be different in the days ahead? Almost everything, from the food you eat to the climate you know to the technology you use as you work. The organizations that will employ you are changing, restructuring and transforming themselves. The products and services they provide are changing, as are the skills needed to produce them. The community in which you live will change, as will the people who live there.

The people who inhabit our society, in fact, will change more profoundly and more quickly than at any previous time in our history, bringing with them fundamental cultural shifts that will redefine what it means to be an American, what *work* is, what *business* means and what we mean by a *family*. In sum, life in the twenty-first century will not be "business as usual."

Let's look first at some areas we know will change dramatically in the years just ahead and then examine what we mean by culture and diversity. If you understand the circumstances you are likely to face as you tackle the task of managing a business in a highly competitive, global environment, your chances for success are greater. And more than anything else – more than technology, science, law, the environment or systems of government – the social norms and new rules of our society will affect how your business will operate and the challenges you will face as a manager.

## INTERCULTURAL CHALLENGES AT HOME

### Ethnicity

According to the U.S. Census Bureau, profound shifts in the next few decades will leave this country older and far more ethnically diverse than ever before. By 2045, the U.S. will no longer have a "majority" race, but instead will be a nation of multiple ethnic groups. Non-Hispanic whites will account for just under half of our population. Hispanics will comprise about one-quarter of this country's people, and African Americans will grow slowly to just over 13 percent. Asian Americans are projected to become about 8 percent of the nation's citizens while other ethnic minorities will comprise around 4 percent.[1]

### Population Growth

The current U.S. population of 325 million is projected to reach about 335 million in 2020 and more than 400 million by mid-century. That increase may sound huge, but it will actually reflect an all-time *low growth rate* after the year 2025. Put simply, the large group of aging baby boomers – those 76 million Americans born between 1946 and 1964 – will begin dying faster than new Americans are born, reducing net population increases.[2]

### Immigration

Offsetting some of that decline is a surge in immigration that has brought the number of foreign-born residents to the highest level in this nation's history. The most recent census figures available show that the number of foreign-born residents and their children will grow from 34 million in the 1970s to more than 69 million in 2060. A comprehensive study of the census data shows that, on average, foreign-born residents are much more likely to live in or around a handful of large cities than are people born in the U.S. That same study also shows the near impossibility of generalizing about immigrants and their experience here. For example, while just one-third of those residents over 25 who were born in Mexico had completed high school, more than 95 percent of those born in Africa had. And although median household income for those born in Latin America was well under $25,000 annually, it was more than $50,000 for those from Asia, just below that of the native U.S. population.[3]

Census Bureau figures show that the immigrant population is becoming younger, a shift likely to foster more tolerance for diversity and perhaps accelerate assimilation. Those figures also show that immigration trends are forming a unique generational divide: those immigrants over 40 are largely white, whereas those under 40 are increasingly Hispanic, Asian and from other minority groups. By the second decade of this century, half of all Hispanics were under age 27, and one of every five children under age 18 in the U.S. was Hispanic. Most impressive, Hispanics account for about half of the overall population growth in the U.S. since the turn of the century.[4]

### Age

In the next decade alone, the number of people in the U.S. over the age of 50 will increase by half. In July 1983, the number of Americans over the age of 65 surpassed the number of teenagers. And with continuing improvements in lifestyle and medical technology, the over-65 population in this country is likely to be more than 86.7 million by the year 2050 – a figure that represents between one-fourth and one-fifth of our population. From 2010 through 2030, some 78 million "baby boomers" in the U.S. will turn 65 at the rate of 7,000 a day.[5] Today, in fact, more than 72,000 Americans are over the age of 100. And by the middle of the twenty-first century, that number may be more than 800,000.[6]

At the same time that the average ages of the population and the workforce are rising, the pool of young workers entering the labor market is shrinking. The average worker's age in the U.S. in 1987 was 36. By 2014, that average would be nearly 42. And workers in the 16-to-24-year-old age group will shrink by several million, or nearly 8 percent of the population.[7]

### Families

The shape, size and even the definition of American families have changed over the past 30 years. Since 1970, they have become smaller; more of them are led by just one parent; and more have mothers who work outside the home. According to Ken Bryson of the U.S. Census Bureau, "In the 1970s and 1980s, we had a big shift from married couples with children to one-parent families and people living alone." A 2017 study found that the number of married couples with children under 18 shrank from 40 percent of all households to 16 percent.[8] Divorce rates have soared, and the number of single-person households has climbed from 17 to 25 percent.[9]

## Women in the Workforce

More women are entering the workforce than at any time since the end of World War II. Since 1998, two-thirds of all new workers in the U.S. have been female. And by 2010, nearly two-thirds of all working-age women were employed. Today, the U.S. has a workforce that is about 47 percent female, compared with smaller figures in Japan and Mexico but larger percentages in Sweden and Denmark. A U.S. Labor Department study shows that women hold 43 percent of all executive, administrative and managerial jobs in the U.S. By comparison, women hold just 17 percent of all managerial positions in Sweden and less than 10 percent in Japan.[10]

Noteworthy as well is that even though working women in the U.S. are doing better in terms of opportunity and advancement than the vast majority of their counterparts in other nations, they still bear a disproportionate share of the burden of child care and household duties. Some 42 percent of working moms, in fact, have children under seven years of age.[11]

# CULTURAL CHALLENGES ABROAD

## A New World Order

Among the more important events of the twentieth century was the fall of the Berlin Wall in 1988. In the decades that followed the collapse of communism and the disintegration of the Soviet Union, we have witnessed a flowering of freedom in Eastern Europe, the establishment of a single European currency and a lowering of restrictions on the movement of capital, labor and finished goods. The world has seen its exchanges and bourses integrate into a seamless, global marketplace for money. Jobs flow to areas with lower-priced, competent labor. Capital flows to investment opportunities that best balance risk with return. And the definition of "made in America" now depends on which part of the product or process you examine. In the early decades of the twenty-first century, the market never sleeps. The manager who plans to participate only in a domestic economy will have few places left to work.

International business is a fact of life today as never before. And in order to succeed, whether as a manager in a transnational corporation, or as an entrepreneur in a small business hoping to sell goods and services to people in other nations, you will need a thorough understanding of the people in your company, your industry and the global marketplace. The key to understanding them is an understanding of their culture.

## Customs and Culture Abroad

In Hungary, men customarily walk on the left side of women or anyone of greater status, like a boss. It's considered intrusive to ask a man from the Middle East about his wife or female members of his family. It's also considered impolite for a woman to serve wine on social occasions in Italy. Why? Well, as you will discover, different cultures promote different ways of thinking and behaving. What's considered customary for you at home may well be unacceptable overseas. And, of course, what's perfectly natural for people – even professional businesspeople – in other countries may be considered peculiar or offensive here.

Some mistakes can be worse than embarrassing. Anthropologist Margaret Nydell tells of an American woman in Saudi Arabia who slid into the front passenger seat of a car and planted a friendly kiss on the cheek of the man at the wheel. Public displays of affection don't play well there. The gesture was spotted by a captain of the Saudi National Guard who demanded to know if the couple was married. They were, but not to each other. As a result, the woman was expelled from the country and the man, who argued with the guardsman, spent some time in jail.[12]

Nonverbal communication can be as much a source of misunderstanding as verbal, according to American business consultant, Elizabeth Ulrich. "The classic example is the 'A-OK' gesture which is positive in the United States," she says, "but obscene in much of the rest of the world." That same gesture in France means "worthless." It is impolite to point to people in Japan or to give the split-fingered "victory" sign knuckles out in England. It is offensive to use the "thumbs-up" sign in Nigeria or to eat with your left hand in most Arab countries.[13]

Mary Murray Bosrock, author of a series of international etiquette books, says showing up on time for a dinner party in South America could be a disaster – no one expects anyone to be less than half-an-hour to an hour late. She says you are liable to find your host or hostess still getting dressed if you actually arrive at the hour printed on the invitation.[14]

In many Asian cultures, particularly Japan, saying no is considered very impolite. In fact, it's unusual to the point of being rare, particularly in business negotiations. According to Philip R. Harris, an international business consultant, and Robert T. Moran, a professor of international management, indirect and vague approaches are more acceptable than direct and specific references. "Sentences are frequently left unfinished so that the other person may conclude them in his or her own mind. Conversation often transpires within an ill-defined and shadowy context, never quite definite so as not to preclude personal interpretation."[15]

Japanese businesspeople are reluctant in the extreme to say no to a direct question, even when the answer is, in fact, no. Instead, you may hear, "These things often take much time," "Issues of this sort, as you understand, are sometimes difficult" or "We are sorry that things have developed in such a fashion." Often, a Japanese businessperson will simply change the subject or direct an unrelated question back to you. In the most extreme conditions, if you ask for a yes or no response, you will receive only silence, usually accompanied by head nods, tightened lips and a break in eye contact with you. A senior, experienced Japanese trade negotiator puts it this way: "It is true that we Japanese try diligently to prevent any situation from becoming what we call *tairitsu*, a confrontation, whether in our personal lives or in business and politics."[16]

Being culturally sensitive is essential to your success. In Japan, for example, the presentation of a business card is done with reverence, almost like an intricate dance. Cards, which represent the person's importance to the company and personal identity within the community, are gently presented with two hands and accomplished with a bow. Businesspeople exchanging cards always face each other, holding their cards on the upper two corners. The recipient is expected to take the card and, with studied seriousness, examine it thoroughly before carefully and respectfully putting it in a cardholder. During business meetings, cards are often kept out in the open and used respectfully as a reference point during conversations.[17]

In the U.S., according to Roger E. Axtell, former marketing vice president for Parker Pen Co., "We just stuff them in our pockets or even write on them." During a business trip to Japan, Axtell saw an American businessman picking his teeth with a business card. "I thought, 'Hey, that's my personal identity there!'"[18]

One further caution regarding business cards: Bring enough for everyone. You'll find that not only do the principals in a meeting want your card – everyone in the room expects one. Americans traveling in Asia should expect to hand out 200 cards a week. You'll get bonus points if your card is translated into the local language on the reverse side. To make absolutely certain the translation is precise and correct, ask your U.S. Chamber of Commerce contact for advice on having your cards printed on the backside before you arrive.

You've undoubtedly heard or read about the elaborate rituals of gift giving in Japan, where just about every business occasion demands an exchange of gifts. You know some numbers are unlucky in China or that some colors are inappropriate for gifts or flowers in the Middle East. But the rules are many and varied, so if you are traveling to a new part of the world to try to make money – or even as a tourist – you are well advised to learn something of the culture and the local customs.

## BUSINESS AND CULTURE

Whether you are dealing with issues of marketing, management, finance or even the details of accounting for a firm's assets and business activities, the success or failure of your company abroad will depend on how effectively your employees can exercise their skills in a new location. That ability will depend on both their job-related expertise and each individual's sensitivity and responsiveness to a new cultural environment. Among the most common factors contributing to failure in international business assignments, according to Professor Gary P. Ferraro of the University of North Carolina, "is the erroneous assumption that if a person is successful in the home environment, he or she will be equally successful in applying technical expertise in a different culture."[19]

Research has shown that failures in an overseas business setting most frequently result from an inability to understand and adapt to foreign ways of thinking and acting, rather than from technical or professional incompetence. At home, U.S. businesspeople equip themselves with vast amounts of knowledge about their employees, customers and business partners. Market research provides detailed information on values, attitudes and buying preferences of U.S. consumers. Middle- and upper-level managers are well versed in the intricacies of their organization's culture, and labor negotiators must be highly sensitive to what motivates those on the other side of the table. Yet when North Americans begin doing business abroad, they frequently are willing to work with customers, employees, suppliers and others about whom they know and understand very little.[20]

In the last few years, a growing number of Americans in their 20s and 30s have been heading to China for employment, lured by its faster-growing economy and lower jobless rate. Their Chinese coworkers are often around the same age. But the two groups were raised differently. The Americans have had more exposure to free-market principles. "Young Americans were brought up in a commercial environment, said Neng Zhao, 28, a senior associate at Blue Oak Capital in Beijing. We weren't. So the workplace is a unique learning process for my generation."[21]

It is imperative for Americans working in China to adjust, according to Michael Normal, senior vice president at Sibson Consulting. "In the West, there is such a premium on getting things done quickly, but when you come to work in China, you need to work on listening and being more patient and understanding local ways of doing business." The Chinese now rising in the workforce were raised and educated in a system that tended to prize obedience and rote learning. Their American counterparts may have had more leeway to question authority and speak their minds, and this can affect workplace communication.[22]

Communication styles, according to Professor Vas Taras of the University of North Carolina at Greensboro, can create workplace challenges. "Americans often perceive the Chinese as indecisive, less confident and not tough enough, whereas the Chinese may see Americans as rude or inconsiderate."[23]

## DEFINITIONS OF CULTURE

So what exactly is culture and how does it affect the way we do business? *Culture is everything that people have, think and do as members of their society.* Culture affects and is a central part of our society, our economy and the organizations that employ us. Culture is, thus, composed of material objects; ideas, values and attitudes; and expected patterns of behavior.

### Material Objects

Everything you own, lease, borrow or use is defined as a part of your culture, from the automobile you drive to the clothing you wear. We make judgments each day, often without even being aware we are doing so, about the people we meet and do business with. Many, if not most, of those judgments depend on what we think about the way people are dressed, whether their shoes are polished, how their offices are furnished, the sort of wristwatch they wear or briefcase they carry, and so on. People, in turn, judge us by the material objects we use and surround ourselves with.

### Ideas, Values and Attitudes

We also tend to categorize people according to the ways they think, the ideas they believe or the basic values they hold to be true. Sometimes the categories are easily described, such as *liberal* or *conservative*. Other ideas, including religious beliefs, or fundamental ideas about family, society and self are not so easy to categorize.

### Expected Patterns of Behavior

Every society has certain cultural norms regarding behavior. In the U.S., women expect equal treatment under the law, but in many Middle Eastern nations, such as Saudi Arabia, women do not have voting privileges, may not travel independently and have only recently been permitted to drive an automobile. Cultural norms in that part of the world are very closely tied to Islamic religious doctrine and prescribe a wide span of expected behaviors ranging from what clothing is permissible to when and with whom a woman might be away from her home.

In many ways, culture defines how we look at life in general, and it guides how we respond to characteristics such as race, ethnicity, physical attributes, age, social class, education and many other factors. It also shapes our responses to these qualities, both within ourselves and in other people.[24] At the broad social level, culture tells us who we are (what groups we belong to), tells us how we should behave and "gives us attitudes about 'them,' the people who are different from us. It tells us what should be important as well as how to act in various situations."[25]

Culture surrounds us so completely, and from such an early point in life, that we are often unaware of other ways of dealing with the world, that others may have a different outlook on life, a different logic or a different way of responding to people and situations.[26]

## SOME PRINCIPLES OF CULTURE

Here, then, are a few ideas about culture that have been shown to be true across time and across both national and cultural boundaries:

### Culture Is Learned

In 1861, Giuseppe Garibaldi played a pivotal role in uniting a collection of feudal kingdoms and principalities into the modern nation-state of Italy. As the populace of southern Italy acclaimed Garibaldi as their ruler, he told the cheering throngs, "Now that we have founded the nation of Italy, we must all learn to be Italian."[27] Few of us would give a moment's thought to *learning* how to be American, Italian, Mexican or any other culture. If you were born into a culture, you learn from the moment you begin to see, hear and breathe. Our first culture is so closely defined with each of us that we're barely aware we *have* one. Learning a second culture, though, is clearly more difficult. The older we become, the closer to impossible the task becomes.

### Culture Is Universal to Human Society

Everyone has a culture, regardless of where they were born, raised, educated and civilized. For some among us, the idea of a *specific* culture is not as easy as it may look. My college roommate was born and raised in Syracuse, New York. His wife, Mary, was born and raised in northern California. Following their marriage in the 1970s, they moved overseas and have lived in the Philippines, Kenya, Greece, Italy and England.

No matter where they move, however, and no matter how many different cultures they're exposed to, they'll always be thoroughly American. Their vocabulary and preferences in food have changed a bit, but not their basic culture. For their two boys, Jim and John, culture is a different matter. Even though they grew up with U.S. passports and American parents, they lived in societies different from those their parents grew up in. They were educated in British schools and, for all intents and purposes, they've really become British by culture and "citizens of the world" by experience.

All societies exhibit an interest in passing along cultural values and norms to their children. It's really the similarity of those values and norms that collectively creates and defines a culture. Thus, no matter where you travel, you'll find people with cultures of their own that are interesting, diverse and rich, but different from the one in which you grew up.

### Culture Is Constantly Undergoing Change

Among the basic truths about culture is that none is ever static. The clothing people wear, the transportation they use, the books they read, the topics they talk about, the food they eat, the music they listen and dance to, all will change over time. Compare the lives your grandparents led to the life you are leading, and you'll get some sense of how your own grandchildren will look at you. Change is the constant in every culture. Some will insist that whatever is new in a culture (what sort of music is your little brother listening to?) is inferior to whatever came before. True or not (and, usually, it's a matter of opinion about whether change is an improvement), the elements that make us who we are will constantly remain in flux.

Cultures change because of *internal forces*, such as discovery, invention and innovation. They also change because of *external forces*, including the diffusion of innovation across space and time, and borrowing the traits, habits or customs of another culture.

### Some Cultures Change More Quickly Than Others

Some societies are isolated by geography, such as vast oceans or tall mountain ranges. Others are isolated by preference. The more keenly tuned-in a society is to the interests and preferences of other cultures, the more quickly change will come. If fashions change quickly in Paris or Milan each spring, can New York and Los Angeles be far behind in producing copies? Life in parts of the American Midwest and South change more slowly, in part because of geography and in part because of preference. Some people prefer things as they are and try to preserve life as they know it; others prefer change and will move to cities or other nations in search of that change.

Los Angeles, California, is nearly 3,000 miles from New York City, but culturally the two cities are not vastly different. Residents will point to a faster pace in New York and a more laid-back style in Los Angeles, but they are both metropolitan centers of business, politics, media, publishing, fashion, food and much more. Needles, California, is just over 400 miles from Los Angeles, but culturally it's light years away. The pace of life, the food available in local restaurants, the clothing worn there, and everything else from entertainment to commerce are vastly different. The people of Needles proudly point to the fact that not much has changed in their little town over the past 50 years, and they like it that way. Life in Los Angeles can, and probably will, change in significant ways before you have lunch tomorrow.

Five factors influence the *rate* of change as well as the *kind* of change a culture may experience. These factors include:

- **Relative advantage.** Is it superior to what already exists? If the change isn't superior in some way to existing habits, the innovation is unlikely to catch on (think: 3-D television).
- **Compatibility.** Is it consistent with existing cultural patterns? Some changes are superior to current practices but they may be at odds with existing culture patterns. If what's new is not compatible with the ways in which the majority of people think and behave, change may be slow to occur.
- **Complexity.** Is it easily understood? Desktop computers represent a clearly superior means of communicating and processing both text and data, but their general complexity held back widespread adoption for the better part of a decade in our society.
- **Trialability.** Is it testable? Can we try it out experimentally? The difference between hair dye and a tattoo is that while one is temporary, the other is permanent. Cultural change comes more quickly when people can experiment a bit without making irrevocable decisions.
- **Observability.** Are the benefits clearly visible to those affected by change? If you can't see its value, you may be unwilling to try it.[28]

## Culture Is Not Value-Neutral

The diversity movement in this country, for all the good and positive change it has brought to American business and higher education, has passed along one subtle *untruth* that is frequently repeated: "We must respect all other cultures because our culture is really no better than theirs. Ours is simply different."

Our culture certainly *is* different from others, but that's not the same as saying that all cultures are equally moral, equally fair or equally humane. Amnesty International annually publishes a list of cultures in which people are denied basic human rights. And Transparency International develops a list of nations each year that are rank-ordered according to level of corruption. The U.S., by the way, is among the least corrupt nations on earth but is still some distance from the top of the list. In 2018, New Zealand was listed as the least corrupt among nations.[29]

With human rights and corrupt behavior as basic considerations, we must also understand that many factors from ancient tradition to religious belief can produce human behavior that you and I may well regard as offensive or outrageous. Well into the twenty-first century, women are still not allowed to vote or own property in many nations, and in other nations they are often ritualistically mutilated or sold into slavery. The fact that such practices are accepted in those societies and simultaneously shock us is a sign that our values and theirs aren't the same. Our cultures may well be quite different from one another, but they are neither equal nor interchangeable in all respects. Culture, in fact, is *not* value-neutral.

## Not All Cultures Are Equally Complex

Because of size, geography, distance from great population centers and other factors, some cultures are simpler in their patterns of organization, behavior and belief than others. Vast sections of sub-Saharan Africa, the Polynesian islands of the South Pacific, the dense interior of South America's jungles and rain forests, and the frozen tundra of the Arctic have developed cultures that are both ancient and rich in their heritage but not terribly complex. Many still depend on barter to survive and small councils of elders for adjudicating legal problems. The modern G-7 nations have legal systems and tax codes so complex that no lawyer or accountant could claim expertise in all of them.

### Virtually All Cultures Permit the Development of Subcultures

Within each culture, small groups of people inevitably develop separate and specialized interests: hikers, bikers, baseball fans, gourmet cooks, Bible readers, bird-watchers and volunteer firefighters. The list is potentially endless as people gather together in the same room, on the telephone or on the Internet to pursue their common interests. The tolerance of some societies is not endless, however. Highly repressive cultures permit little in the way of deviation from doctrine. Cuba, for example, banned the celebration of Christmas from 1959 until 1998. Even the U.S. officially bans certain activities by hate groups even though the U.S. Constitution protects their right to exist. The more complex the culture, the greater the likelihood that subcultures will flourish, and the greater their number is likely to be.

### Culture Can Influence Biology and Biology Can Influence Culture

This concept may not seem self-evident at first, but culture can, and does, have an enormous influence on human biology. The most striking example can be seen in the dramatic increase in average height and body weight of the Japanese people during the past 70 years of the twentieth century. Men in their third decade of life now weigh substantially more than their grandfathers did and are, on average, several inches taller. The gains in women's physiognomy are equally impressive.

Other illustrations abound, from facial scars and body adornment in West Africa to breast implants and plastic facial surgery in the U.S. Even such issues as caloric and fat content in our diets can affect how big we grow and how fit we are. The U.S., to counterbalance a culture that had grown soft and averse to exercise, has actively portrayed exercise and fitness as desirable and worthwhile. Not only have many people worked themselves into generally better physical condition, several new industries have grown up around them, offering sportswear, exercise machines, high-tech shoes and high-energy diets.

## FUNCTIONS OF CULTURE

Cultures universally respond to human problems and challenges by developing systems to deal with them. Most successful cultures develop economic systems, marriage and family systems, educational systems, and supernatural belief systems. These systems are more complex and intricate in some cultures than in others, but for the most part, people collectively establish rules for economic value and trade, systems for assigning responsibility, for establishing and raising families, for educating children, and for a belief in God or an afterlife. Individual beliefs may vary somewhat, but it is the culture itself that establishes how most people in a society think, believe and behave.[30]

## ETHNOCENTRISM

All cultures, to one degree or another, display *ethnocentrism*, or the tendency to evaluate a foreigner's behavior by the standards of one's own culture and to believe that one's own culture is superior to all others. We take our culture for granted. We're born into it, live with its rules and assumptions, day in and day out. We quickly come to believe that the way we live is simply "the way things should be." As a result, we see our behavior as correct and others' as wrong. Keep in mind what we've said about culture *not* being value-neutral. We have good reasons for believing and behaving as we do, but that doesn't necessarily mean that others are "wrong."

All cultures are ethnocentric, some more so than others. Ethnocentrism, in fact, can enhance group solidarity within a society and is often used by corrupt national or ethnic leaders as a means of building or consolidating power and excluding outsiders. Clearly, ethnocentrism can foster prejudice, contempt, stereotypes and conflict.[31]

## CROSS-CULTURAL COMMUNICATION SKILLS

One set of skills essential to success in a global economy, then, is the ability to communicate across cultures. According to a number of authors on this subject, the skill set you need involves several personal capacities:

- *The capacity to accept the relativity of your own knowledge and perceptions.* We each tend to judge people, events and ideas against our own education, background and beliefs. Simply recognizing that some of these are bound to be different from those of other cultures is a useful starting point.
- *The capacity to be nonjudgmental.* Make personal judgments, if you wish. Just keep them to yourself.
- *A tolerance for ambiguity.* Accept the fact that you'll never understand everything about another culture; you can still appreciate and function within that culture satisfactorily. This skill set, then, involves the capacity to communicate respect for other people's ways, their country and their values without adopting or internalizing them. These skills also include the capacity to display empathy, to be flexible (particularly under conditions of high ambiguity or uncertainty), to take turns (or wait your turn, if you're uncertain of the protocol) and the humility to acknowledge what you do not know or understand.

Clearly, understanding what motivates the people you hope to do business with will be crucial to your success. Technical competence in your line of work is important, but so is an understanding of the culture, customs, norms and beliefs of others, whether domestically or internationally. Curiously, as we find the world's economy becoming more global and interdependent, we also find our own nation undergoing similar changes. The only constant in the years ahead, it seems, will be change itself.

## FOR FURTHER READING

Beamer, L. and I. Varner. *Intercultural Communication in the Global Workplace*, 4/e. Boston, MA: McGraw Hill Irwin, 2007.

Binns, C. "American Can't Step Into Shoes of Others; Individualism Stops People from Seeing Others' Viewpoints, Study Suggests," *MSNBC.com*. Updated: 1:48 p.m. ET July 18, 2007. Online at www.msnbc.msn.com/id/19832287/from/ET/.

Brinkley, C. "Where Yellow's a Faux Pas and White Is Death," *The Wall Street Journal*, December 6, 2007, pp. D1, D8.

Ely, R. J., D. E. Meyerson and M. N. Davidson. "Rethinking Political Correctness," *Harvard Business Review*, September 2006, pp. 79–87.

Ferraro, G. P. *Global Brains: Knowledge and Competencies for the 21st Century*. Charlotte, NC: Intercultural Associates, Inc., 2001.

Harrison, L. E. and S. P. Huntington. *Culture Matters: How Values Shape Human Progress*. New York: Basic Books, 2000.

Jandt, F. E. *An Introduction to Intercultural Communication: Identities in a Global Community*. Thousand Oaks, CA: Sage, 2003.

Javidan, M. "Forward-Thinking Cultures," *Harvard Business Review*, July–August 2007, p. 20.

Nagourney, E. "East and West Part Ways in Test of Facial Expressions," *The New York Times*, March 18, 2008, p. D5.

Neuliep, J. W. *Intercultural Communication: A Contextual Approach*, 7/e. Thousand Oaks, CA: Sage Publications, 2017.

Tierney, J. "As Barriers Disappear, Some Gender Gaps Widen," *The New York Times*, Tuesday, September 9, 2008, pp. D1, D4.

Tuleja, E. A. *Global Business: How Leaders Communicate for Success*. London, U.K.: Routledge (Taylor & Francis), 2016.

Walker, D. M., T. Walker and J. Schmitz. *Doing Business Internationally: The Guide to Cross-Cultural Success*, 2/e. New York: McGraw Hill Trade, 2002.

Zimmer, C. "What Is the Limit of Our Life Span?" *The New York Times*, Tuesday, July 3, 2018, p. D3.

# NOTES

1 Frey, William H., "The US Will Become 'Minority White' in 2045, Census Projects," *Brookings*, March 14, 2018. Online at www.brookings.edu/blog/the-avenue/2018/03/14/the-us-will-become-minority-white-in-2045-census-projects/.

2 "Population Projections for the United States from 2015 to 2060 (in Millions)," *Statista*. Online at www.statista.com/statistics/183481/united-states-population-projection/. Accessed July 2, 2018 at 10:31 a.m. See also U.S. Census Bureau. "National Population Projection (Summary Files)," Retrieved on January 6, 2011 at 12:03 p.m.

3 Vespa, Jonathan, "Demographic Turning Points for the United States: Population Projections for 2020 to 2060," *U.S. Census Bureau*, March 2018. Online at www.census.gov/content/dam/Census/library/publications/2018/demo/P25_1144.pdf. Accessed July 2, 2018 at 11:02 a.m. See also Swarns, R. L. "Hispanics Resist Racial Grouping by Census," *The New York Times*, October 24, 2005, pp. 1, 18; and Scott, J. "Foreign Born in U.S. at Record High: Census Puts Number at 56 Million, with Mexico Chief Supplier," *The New York Times*, February 7, 2002, p. A18.

4 Files, J. "Report Describes Immigrants as Younger and More Diverse," *The New York Times*, June 10, 2005, p. A11. Copyright 2005 © by The New York Times Company. Reprinted with permission.

5 Marshall, Barbara. "With Boomers Turning 65, Retirement Turns from Slo-Mo to Go-Go," *The Austin Statesman*, December 31, 2010. Online at www.statesmancom/news/nation/with-boomers-turning-65-retirement-turns-from-slow-1156635.html. Accessed January 6, 2011 at 12:15 p.m. Eastern Time.

6 Xu, J., M.D. "Mortality Among Centenarians in the United States, 2000 to 2014," *NCHS Data Brief*, No. 233, January 2016. U.S. Department of Health and Human Services, Centers for Disease Control and Prevention, National Center for Health. Online at www.cdc.gov/nchs/data/databriefs/db233.pdf. Accessed Tuesday, July 3, 2018 at 12:04 p.m.

7 The Los Angeles Gerontology Research Group. "Official Tables," updated July 15, 2008. Online at www.grg.org/calment.html. For additional current figures and trends, see www.census.gov. See also Soergel, Andrew. "Pretty Soon, Old People Will Have All the Jobs," *U.S. News*. Online at www.usnews.com/news/articles/2015-12-24/older-workers-to-dominate-labor-market-by-2024. Accessed July 2, 2018 at 11:08 a.m.

8 "Percentages of Family Households With Own Children Under 18 Years in the United States from 1970 to 2017, By Type of Family," *Statista*. Online at www.statista.com/statistics/242074/percentages-of-us-family-households-with-children-by-type/#0. Accessed July 2, 2018 at 11:19 a.m.

9 Kilborn, P. T. "Shifts in Families Reach a Plateau, Study Says," *The New York Times*, November 27, 1996, p. B1. Copyright 1996 © by The New York Times Company. Reprinted with permission.

10 Thomas, P., V. Reitman, D. Solis and D. Milbank. "Women in Business: A Global Report Card," *The Wall Street Journal*, July 26, 1995, p. B1. Reprinted by permission of *The Wall Street Journal*. Copyright © 1995 Dow Jones & Company, Inc. All rights reserved worldwide. See also "Women in the Labor Force in 2010," *U.S. Department of Labor*. Online at www.dol.gov/wb/factsheets/qf-laborforce-10.htm. Accessed July 2, 2018 at 11:28 a.m.

11 Ibid.

12 Maxa, R. "How to Avoid Cultural Blunders: For Business Travelers, a Few Rules Can Go a Long Way," *MSNBC*. Online at www.msnbc.com/news/224480/asp. Accessed December, 23, 1998.

13 Adams, D. "Don't Get Upset If Foreign Executive Holds Your Hand," *South Bend Tribune*, December 20, 1998, p. B5.

14 Bosrock, M. M. *Put Your Best Foot Forward*. Minneapolis, MN: International Educational Systems, 1995.

15 Harris, P. R. and R. T. Moran. "Doing Business with Asians – Japan, China, Pacific Basin, and India," in *Managing Cultural Differences: High Performance Strategies for a New World of Business*, 6/e. Houston, TX: Gulf Publishing Company, 2004, pp. 393–406.

16 Barnlund, D. *Communicative Styles of Japanese and Americans: Images and Realities*. Belmont, CA: Wadsworth Publishing Company, 1989, pp. 156–157.

17 Adams. "Don't Get Upset," p. B5.

18 Ferraro, G. P. *The Cultural Dimension of International Business*, 5/e. Upper Saddle River, NJ: Prentice-Hall, Inc., 2005, p. 7.

19 Seligson, H. "For American Workers in China, a Culture Clash," *The New York Times*, Thursday, December 24, 2009, pp. B1, B2.

20 Ibid., p. B2.

21 Ibid., p. B2.

22 McCartney, S. "Teaching Americans How to Behave Abroad," *The Wall Street Journal*, April 11, 2006, p. D1.

23 Harvey, C. and M. J. Allard. *Understanding Diversity: Readings, Cases, and Exercises*. New York: HarperCollins, 1995, p. 7.

24 Simons, G. *Working Together: How to Become More Effective in a Multicultural Organization*. Los Altos, CA: Crisp Publications, 1989, p. 5.

25 Harvey and Allard. *Understanding Diversity*, p. 7.

26 Ferraro. *The Cultural Dimension*, pp. 25–30.

27 See Harris, W. H. and J. S. Levey. *The New Columbia Encyclopedia*. New York: Columbia University Press, 1975, p. 1046. See also Trevelyan, G. M. *Garibaldi and the Making of Modern Italy*, 1911, reprinted 1948.

28 Ferraro. *The Cultural Dimension*, pp. 22–25.

29  Ma, A. "These Are the 31 Least Corrupt Countries on Earth," *Business Insider*, February 25, 2018. Online at www.businessin
    sider.com/the-least-corrupt-nations-according-to-transparency-international-2018-2. Accessed Tuesday, July 3, 2018 at 1:03
    p.m. EST.
30  Lustig, M. and J. Koester. *Intercultural Competence: Interpersonal Communication Across Cultures*, 4/e. New York: Addison Wesley
    Longman, 2002, pp. 146–149.
31  Ibid.

# Case 10.1: Oak Brook Medical Systems, Inc.

Jacqueline Harris has been an employee of Oak Brook Medical Systems for about 12 years. For the past 24 months, she has been Director of Strategic Planning for the Hospital Supply Division, a segment of Oak Brook Medical Systems that has grown at the phenomenal rate of nearly 35 percent per year over the past three years.

The division is relatively new, having been formed just seven years ago as a result of changes in the healthcare marketplace. The division's growth has been the direct result of good products, solid customer service and the quality-focused people the company has managed to attract. The people working for the Hospital Supply Division are, for the most part, self-starters – entrepreneurial, competitive types who are dedicated and hard-working. The people in Jackie's division and the corporate leadership pride themselves on making things happen for their customers.

Jackie is considered a very valuable asset to her division and is widely credited with developing the strategy that resulted in a $40 million business for the company. She is also considered a no-nonsense, results-oriented manager with a history of being able to get things done. Jackie is also known for her directness and, on several occasions, has had problems interacting with her colleagues. According to friends and coworkers, she is known to be curt with colleagues as well as subordinates.

Others in the division see her as being defensive and, at times, overwhelming. They say she overwhelms people with data when presenting an idea or making a point. Another person has been quoted as saying that "I feel like I am being talked down to when I have a conversation with her." As a result of these perceptions, some feel that she is unapproachable and tough to work with. In the last couple of years, her difficulty in communicating with colleagues has been a greater concern during discussions of her future in the division. To date, however, no one has brought this to her attention directly.

Jackie has experienced the difficulty of communicating with her colleagues, but she considers this simply to be a part of getting the job done. In fact, she thinks she is behaving in a manner comparable to the successful people who have preceded her. Jackie has grown increasingly frustrated, though, because of a lack of attention from senior management.

Despite her highly successful performance with the strategic plan, no one seems to be talking with her about a promotion, and she cannot understand why she is being overlooked. Increasingly, she thinks it is a result of her manager (a division vice president) and the president of the division not wanting to promote her because she is black. She won't say it aloud, but she is beginning to suspect that subtle forms of racism are holding her back.

This frustration has grown more acute, at least to her thinking, because she has always known success. She graduated in the top 10 percent of her engineering class at a large, well-known Midwestern university. She was in the top 5 percent of her MBA class in the Sloan School of Management at MIT. Jackie has always taken pride in her work and has always worked toward excellence in whatever tasks she took on. She selected this division of Oak Brook Medical Systems, in fact, because it was fast paced, results oriented, and the market was growing dramatically for its products and services. This was an industry and a company, Jackie thought, that could provide job opportunities for people who could do good work and produce results.

This division, however, has had very little representation of women and people of color in its management ranks. At first, Jackie thought this would work to her advantage, creating opportunities for her to move up quickly. Now she was beginning to suspect that there were few women and no people of color in division upper management because those in power didn't want them.

Both Jackie and other senior management officials recognized the shifting demographics in their customer base and the positive implications of having someone in the division who could identify with such customers and bring a different perspective to the business. With this in mind, she decided to remain with the division. Before long, though, it became plain to those around her that she was not happy.

As her manager, how would you approach Jackie with your concerns about her problems in communicating with others? How would you help her with her professional development and career growth within the division? In assisting her, you may wish to consider these questions:

## DISCUSSION QUESTIONS

1. What are the assumptions being made about Jackie by her colleagues and managers?
2. What growth opportunities do you see for Jackie which could address the issue of communication with other employees?
3. What do you see as obstacles that could get in the way of Jackie's growth and development in the Hospital Supply Division? How do you think the environment in the division may have contributed to the difficulties she is experiencing?
4. What should you as her manager do to provide support and communicate that support to her? How would you go about challenging your assumptions about her? What would you do to confront her assumptions about others in the division?
5. If you would find it helpful, describe some examples of the sort of feedback you might provide for Jackie regarding her work and her interactions with others in the division.

## WRITING ASSIGNMENT

This assignment requires two documents: a professional business memo and a professional business letter. Please assume that you are Vice President of the Hospital Supply Division and were promoted to that position 90 days ago from another division in the company. Please cast your reply to the issues addressed in this case in the form of a **proposal memo to your division president**. At a *minimum*, in your response to this case, please identify:

- business and management issues;
- legal issues;
- cultural issues.

In your response to this case, you *must* also answer two additional questions:

- What must I do *right now* to solve the problem? What actions do I take immediately?
- What advice would I offer to senior management about this matter? Have any company policies (or lack of policies) contributed to the events described earlier? Please address your business letter to all employees in the Hospital Supply Division, explaining what's happened and what you and the company's leadership have decided to do about it.

## ACKNOWLEDGMENTS

This case was prepared by Ms. Kay Wigton with the assistance of James S. O'Rourke, Teaching Professor of Management, as the basis for class discussion rather than to illustrate either effective or ineffective handling of an administrative situation. Personal and corporate identities have been disguised.

# Case 10.2: Barneys New York

## A Case of "Shop and Frisk"

> We are not going to live in a town where our money is considered suspect and everyone else's money is respected.
>
> Reverend Al Sharpton, political activist, founder of the National Action Network

## INTRODUCTION

As the 2013 holiday season approached, Barneys New York (Barneys) quickly found itself embroiled in controversy. Within the span of a few days, Barneys CEO Mark Lee's attention shifted from ensuring record-breaking holiday sales to a lawsuit, an Attorney General's investigation, a potential boycott and his company's biggest holiday contract hanging in the balance. News media and political activists labeled Barneys a "racist culture."[1] Lee needed to find a way to regain the trust of customers and the public at large; the Barneys brand, and likely his job, depended on it.

## THE INCIDENTS

On the evening of April 29, 2013, Trayon Christian, a black, 19-year-old college student, entered the Barneys flagship store on Madison Avenue in New York City and purchased a $350 Salvatore Ferragamo belt with money he had earned from a work-study program.[2] Shortly after leaving the store, Christian was stopped by New York Police Department (NYPD) detectives and was questioned, handcuffed and taken to a local police precinct.[3] According to Michael Palillo, Christian's attorney, his client was "told [by police] that his identification was false and that he could not afford to make such an expensive purchase."[4] Christian also maintained that officers told him that someone at Barneys had called the police to report that his debit card was fake.[5]

Accounts of the incident differ regarding how long Christian was detained by police. An NYPD spokesperson claimed that he was detained for only 42 minutes, while Christian said that he was kept in a holding cell for approximately two hours before being released.[6] On October 21, 2013, nearly six months later, Trayon Christian filed a lawsuit against Barneys and the NYPD in state court seeking unspecified damages and alleging, among other things, unlawful racial profiling.[7] The lawsuit quickly grabbed media attention.

Media coverage surrounding Christian's lawsuit prompted Kayla Phillips, a black, 21-year-old nursing student, to come forward with her own racial discrimination grievances against Barneys and the NYPD. Phillips claimed that on the evening of February 28, 2013, she used a temporary ATM card to buy a $2,500 Céline bag at the same Barneys flagship store on Madison Avenue that Christian claimed illegally profiled him.[8] Phillips asserted that after she left the store with her new bag, four plain-clothed officers swarmed and "manhandled" her at a nearby subway station,[9] blocking the turnstile in front of her, pushing her up against a wall and demanding to see her identification.[10] She also maintained that detectives "kept asking how [she] could afford this expensive bag and why had [she] paid for it with a card with no name on it."[11] Although never charged with a crime, Phillips expressed her intent to sue both Barneys and the NYPD over the encounter. In fact, less than 24 hours after Trayon Christian filed his lawsuit, Phillips filed a $5 million notice of claim with New York City, formally conveying her intent to sue the NYPD.[12]

## BARNEYS

Barneys is among the oldest and most prestigious of luxury department stores in the U.S. Barney Pressman opened the first Barneys New York store in 1923 at 17th Street and Seventh Avenue in Manhattan with $500 obtained from pawning his wife's engagement ring.[13] His philosophy was to offer the lowest price possible on the most popular brands. Barneys sold clothing at discounted prices by purchasing showroom samples, retail overstocks and manufacturers' closeouts at auctions and bankruptcy sales. It also offered free alterations and free parking to attract customers.

Barney's son, Fred Pressman, took over the company in 1958, and in the 1970s changed the direction of the company from bargain store to boutique. He slowly transformed the store from a discount house to a purveyor of fine Italian designers, but continued to offer the same amenities, such as free alterations, that initially gave Barneys its reputation.[14]

In 1993, Barneys abandoned its Seventh Avenue flagship, moving to the current 226,040-square-foot, nine-story, Kohn Pederson Fox-designed Manhattan store on Madison Avenue at East 61st Street. When it opened, it was the largest store built in New York City since the Great Depression. The store is currently located in a 22-story building with 14 floors of offices above it. With its marble mosaics and gold-leaf ceilings, its value is estimated at $270 million.[15]

Headquartered in New York, Barneys owns flagship stores in New York City, Beverly Hills, Chicago and approximately 40 other locations throughout the U.S. and Japan. The company filed for Chapter 11 bankruptcy in 1996 and was forced to close many of its boutique stores. In 2004, the Pressman family sold its less-than-2 percent remaining ownership interest to the Jones Apparel Group, which in turn sold the company in 2007 to Dubai-based private equity firm Istithmar PJSC. In 2012, a majority of the company was acquired by Perry Capital.[16] Barneys is a privately held company.

## DEPARTMENT STORES

Department stores retail a broad range of general merchandise, such as apparel, jewelry, cosmetics, home furnishings, general household products, toys, appliances and sporting goods. The origins of the modern-day department store can be traced back to the Industrial Revolution at the turn of the nineteenth century. This period was characterized by a rapidly expanding economy and a resulting increase in the size and wealth of the middle class. The rise in prosperity and social mobility increased the number of people with disposable income and transformed shopping into a leisure activity enjoyed by the masses rather than a chore performed by the lower class. Department stores were established to serve this new market.[17]

Consumer spending and fashion trends drive demand in the department store industry. By the early 2000s, department stores had lost their cutting-edge appeal to specialty shops and brand-specific stores that could move in and out of fashion trends quicker and more efficiently. In addition, competition from e-commerce and discounters accelerated their decline. During the five years leading up to 2013, industry revenue fell an average of 4 percent per year; revenue was expected to continue falling over the next five years, though at a slower rate.[18]

Today, the industry is highly concentrated with the top eight companies generating about 95 percent of industry revenue.[19] However, there appears to be a sharp divide between department store chains that are ready to embrace change, and those unwilling or unable to reinvent themselves. The latter retailers will likely disappear from the industry, either through consolidation or bankruptcy.

## RETAIL LOSS PREVENTION

Retail loss prevention is a set of policies and procedures employed by retail companies to preserve profit by preventing the loss of inventory or monies due to theft. U.S. retailers lose an average of 1.3 percent of sales through preventable business losses caused by deliberate or inadvertent human action, commonly known as "shrink." In 2013, shrink cost U.S. retailers approximately $42 billion. Of that $42 billion, 37 percent, or $15.5 billion, was lost to shoplifting.[20]

Retail theft is even more of a problem in struggling economies. As a growing share of the population struggles to meet its financial obligations, the occurrence of retail theft rises. Shoplifters generally target expensive and popularly branded items. These items include perfume, cosmetics and small leather products, all of which are sold in department stores.[21] Traditional approaches to retail loss prevention include visible security measures coupled with various forms of technology, such as closed-circuit television (CCTV) and radio-frequency identification (RFID) sensors. Most department stores have a department dedicated to retail loss prevention, which is staffed with investigators sometimes referred to as Loss Prevention Officers (LPOs). It is also common for a department store to have policies and procedures in place to deter and identify retail theft.

## SIMILAR SCANDAL AT MACY'S

On October 25, 2013, just days after Trayon Christian and Kayla Phillips publicized their experiences at Barneys, Robert Brown, a black actor who was at the time playing a role as a musician on the HBO series "Treme," filed a lawsuit in state court against Macy's. He alleged that staff and police officers in the Macy's flagship store in Herald Square, New York City, had racially profiled him. Brown claimed that on June 8, 2013, he was "paraded" through that store in handcuffs and placed in a holding cell after purchasing a $1,350 gold Movado watch as a gift for his mother.[22] Officers reported suspicion that Brown's credit card was fake and that the identification he had provided to them was false.

According to Brown, officers gave him conflicting reasons for their involvement. One officer allegedly told Brown that a suspicious Macy's employee had called the police, while another officer told him that the NYPD was already conducting a sting operation in the store in pursuit of a crooked clerk at the time of his apprehension.[23] After being released with no charges, Brown voiced his frustration on his Twitter account, tweeting statements that criticized both Macy's and Barneys. For example, one tweet read: "If anyone knows Trayon Christian's email please DM me. #Barneys #falsearrest."[24]

On October 27, yet another black shopper came forward with racial profiling allegations against Macy's. Art Palmer, a 56-year-old fitness trainer from Brooklyn, told the media that after he had purchased $320 worth of Polo dress shirts, he was surrounded and questioned by police officers only a few blocks from the Macy's store in Herald Square.[25]

Allegations of racial profiling are nothing new for Macy's. In 2005, the company paid $600,000 to settle claims that a number of its New York locations had profiled blacks and Latinos, unlawfully targeting those groups as a strategy to prevent shoplifting.[26]

## BARNEYS RESPONDS

On October 23, 2013, two days after Trayon Christian filed his lawsuit against the company, Barneys posted the following statement on its Facebook page:

The following statement can be attributed to a Barneys New York spokesperson:
Barneys New York typically does not comment on pending litigation. In this instance, we feel compelled to note that after carefully reviewing the incident of last April, it is clear that no employee of Barneys New York

was involved in the pursuit of any action with the individual other than the sale. Barneys New York has zero tolerance for any form of discrimination, and we stand by our long history in support of all human rights.[27]

This initial statement, which received over 1,500 comments from Facebook users within the next few days, was met with outrage and disappointment. Many users criticized the statement for its lack of an apology, and a substantial number of comments vowed to never shop at Barneys again.

One day later, Barneys posted a statement signed by CEO Mark Lee on the company's Facebook page (see Exhibit 10.1 at the end of this case). In that post, Lee apologized to customers and announced that Barneys had retained civil rights expert Michael Yaki, a member of the United States Commission on Civil Rights, to assist in a review of company practices and procedures. Lee also noted that Barneys had reached out to community leaders to discuss the issue. This second post received a similar negative reaction from Facebook users. It received over 800 comments, with users voicing much of the same criticism that was directed at the company's initial statement.

## THE NYPD COUNTERS

In response to these allegations of racial profiling, both Barneys and Macy's initially, either directly or indirectly, took the stance that NYPD officers had acted without the direction of store employees. However, NYPD spokesman John McCarthy countered those accusations by saying that in three of the four incidents, officers were acting on information that was provided to them by store employees.[28] McCarthy also confirmed that, "in both instances, NYPD were conducting unrelated investigations" within the stores.[29]

## THE ATTORNEY GENERAL STEPS IN

The high level of public attention given to these possible examples of racial profiling by local department stores prompted the New York State Attorney General's Office to launch an investigation. On October 28, 2013, Kristen Clarke, Bureau Chief of the office's Civil Rights Bureau, sent a letter to Barneys CEO Mark Lee requesting, among other things, that Barneys provide: (1) its policies and procedures for stopping, detaining and questioning customers; (2) the number of stops and detentions of customers of each race within the past year; (3) its policies and procedures for contacting law enforcement regarding customers; and (4) any training materials concerning the aforementioned policies and procedures (see Figures 10.1 and 10.2). A similar letter was sent to Peter Sachse, Chief Store Officer of Macy's, that same day. Both letters requested that the recipient contact the New York State Attorney General's Office within the next two days to schedule a meeting in order to further discuss a potential pattern of racial profiling.

## THE GRAND LARCENY PROBLEM

Grand larceny, which in New York is theft of property valued over $1,000 or theft of a debit or credit card,[30] is a major problem in New York City, accounting for more than 75 percent of the crime in the precincts that have jurisdiction over the Barneys and Macy's stores at issue.[31] Two years prior to these incidents, grand larceny rose 31.6 percent in the NYPD's Midtown North precinct, an area that includes the Macy's flagship store in Herald Square; grand larceny also increased nearly 4 percent in the NYPD's Upper East Side 19th precinct, which houses the Barneys flagship store on Madison Avenue.[32] Furthermore, at the time of the Trayon Christian allegations, NYPD officials claimed they had received 53 grand larceny complaints within the last year for credit card fraud from the Barneys store on Madison Avenue, leading to 47 arrests.[33]

## STOP AND FRISK IN NEW YORK CITY

In 1968, the Supreme Court of the U.S. endorsed the use of brief seizures by police officers, commonly known as the "Terry Stop." Pursuant to the Court's decision in *Terry v. Ohio*,[34] officers may lawfully initiate a "stop" if they have "reasonable, articulable suspicion that criminal activity is afoot." In making such a stop an officer may frisk, or conduct a cursory search of the person, if there is reasonable suspicion that the person is armed and dangerous. Reasonable suspicion is a lower standard than probable cause, which is the standard required to make a lawful arrest.[35]

STATE OF NEW YORK
OFFICE OF THE ATTORNEY GENERAL

ERIC T. SCHNEIDERMAN
ATTORNEY GENERAL

DIVISION OF SOCIAL JUSTICE
CIVIL RIGHTS BUREAU

October 28, 2013

**VIA FACSIMILE AND OVERNIGHT MAIL**

Mr. Mark Lee
Chief Executive Officer
Barneys New York
575 Fifth Avenue, 11th Fl.
New York, NY 10017

Re: Investigation of Racial Profiling of Customers

Dear Mr. Lee:

I am writing to address recent reports that Barneys profiles its customers on the basis of race. It is our understanding that, in two separate incidents earlier this year, Barneys may have falsely accused at least two African American customers of committing credit card fraud. These recent reports, as well as additional information reviewed by the Office of the Attorney General ("OAG"), suggest that Barneys may be engaging in a potential pattern of unlawful racial profiling of customers.

Under state and local civil rights law, "racial discrimination in places of public accommodation," including retail stores such as Barneys, is prohibited. Customers must be afforded the full and equal enjoyment of a public accommodation's goods, services, and facilities, regardless of race. *See* New York State Human Rights Law, N.Y. Executive Law § 296 and New York Civil Rights Law § 40.

Attorney General Schneiderman is committed to ensuring that all New York residents are afforded equal protection under the law. The alleged repeated behavior of your employees raises troubling questions about your company's commitment to that ideal. For that reason, we ask that Barneys provide the following information to the OAG by November 1, 2013: (1) Barneys' policies and procedures for stopping, detaining and questioning its customers; (2) the total number of stops and detentions of customers between October 15, 2012 and October 15, 2013, by race; (3) all documents concerning stops and detentions identified in response to Request No. 2; (4) Barneys' policies and procedures for contacting law enforcement regarding its customers; (5) copies of all contracts or agreements with private security firms, law enforcement agencies or other entities that provide store security, including copies of all related security protocols and

**FIGURES 10.1 AND 10.2** Letter to Barneys CEO Mark Lee from the New York Attorney General's Office

*Source*: Lovett, Kenneth. "New York Attorney General Targeting Barneys, Macy's Over Racial Profiling Claims," *Daily News*, October 29, 2013. Online at www.nydailynews.com/new-york/lattorney-general-probe-barneys-macy-incidentslretailers-accused-repeated-troubling-behavior-shopping-black-state-involvedlay-law-article-. Accessed February 21, 2015.

policies; (6) anti-discrimination policies in effect as of October 1, 2013; (7) training materials for store personnel concerning the aforementioned policies and procedures; and (8) customer complaints received within the last year relating to discrimination on the basis of race, and stops, detentions, and/or questioning of customers by or at the request of store personnel.

Please contact my office by Wednesday, October 30, 2013 to schedule a meeting to discuss this matter further. You can reach my office by contacting me at 212-416-8250, or Assistant Attorney General Dariely Rodriguez at 212-416-8253.

Sincerely,

Kristen Clarke
Bureau Chief, Civil Rights Bureau
Office of the Attorney General of the State of New York

**FIGURES 10.1 AND 10.2** (Continued)

In the mid-1990s, the NYPD began using stop and frisks intensively, sparking a heated debate over its reliance on that crime prevention strategy. Consequently, in 1999, the New York State Attorney General's Office ordered the first comprehensive empirical analysis of the NYPD's stop and frisk practices. Since that initial analysis was conducted, stop and frisks by the NYPD have steadily increased over the years, with city officers conducting 97,000 stop and frisks in 2002.[36] That number rose to nearly 700,000 stops in 2011. All of these stops were part of the city's strategy to stop and frisk suspicious persons, primarily with the aim of locating illegal firearms and deterring their possession and use. Of those stops initiated in 2011, only 12 percent uncovered evidence of wrongdoing. In addition, an overwhelming majority (90 percent) of the stops recorded that year were minority males.[37] Approximately 83 percent of the stops between 2004 and 2012 targeted blacks and Hispanics, despite those populations making up approximately 50 percent of the city's residents.[38]

The disproportionate racial impact of these stops led to public and political scrutiny, ultimately prompting the filing of a federal class action lawsuit in United States District Court against New York City and the NYPD as the city's agent.[39] The suit alleged violations of the Fourth and Fourteenth Amendments of the Constitution. Following a two-month bench trial, on August 12, 2013, Judge Shira A. Scheindlin ruled in a 195-page decision that the stop and frisk tactics of the NYPD had violated the constitutional rights of minorities. Judge Scheindlin ordered various remedies, including, but not limited to, an immediate change to certain policies and activities of the NYPD, a trial program requiring the use of body-worn cameras in one precinct per borough, and the appointment of an independent monitor to ensure that the NYPD's use of stop and frisks be carried out in accordance with the Constitution as well as the court's opinion.[40]

## PUBLIC REACTION

Concurrently, as Trayon Christian's lawsuit was filed, Reverend Al Sharpton, a prominent political activist and founder of the National Action Network, conducted a rally at National Action Network headquarters in Harlem, New York City, where he announced that he would be meeting with Barneys officials the following Tuesday. At that rally, Sharpton also threatened a boycott if the store's response to racial profiling allegations were to be inadequate.[41]

Also, on October 30, 2013, a group of protestors gathered outside of the Barneys storefront on Madison Avenue to express their outrage over the shop and frisk scandal. Although only consisting of a few dozen demonstrators, these sign-toting activists purportedly wanted to deliver a message to Barneys CEO Mark Lee, giving him two days to respond.[42]

## JAY Z CONTRACT

In late September of 2013, Barneys announced that it had partnered with hip-hop artist Shawn "Jay Z" Carter for a collection of limited-edition products. The partnership was called "A New York Holiday," and it was the latest in a series of high-profile holiday promotions undertaken by Barneys. The line of products would be named BNY SCC (short for Barneys New York and Shawn Corey Carter, respectively) and would feature holiday pieces created in collaboration with Jay Z and luxury labels such as Balmain, Lanvin and Balenciaga. Barneys announced that 25 percent of the sales from the project would go toward the Shawn Carter Scholarship Foundation, a charity providing educational opportunities to disadvantaged youth.[43] Similar projects had led to record-breaking December sales at Barneys, and the BNY SCC contract was estimated to be worth millions of dollars. The collection was scheduled to hit stores on November 20, 2013.[44]

Shortly after the "shop and frisk" allegations attracted media attention in October, Jay Z faced pressure from his fans and civil rights leaders to end his upcoming holiday partnership with Barneys. In following weeks, more than 50,000 people signed a petition that called on Jay Z to end his partnership with the department store.[45] On October 26, Jay Z released a statement in which he said that he was reserving judgment on Barneys until he learned more about the allegations, while also emphasizing the good cause to which a portion of the partnership's proceeds would be directed.[46]

## DISCUSSION QUESTIONS

1. Many are calling for Jay Z to walk away from his holiday partnership with Barneys. What, if anything, should Barneys do to entice the rapper to remain with the brand? If Barneys loses the contract, what remedial measures should the company take?
2. What other steps, if any, should Barneys take to address public outrage over the racial profiling allegations? How should the company communicate any policy changes it chooses to make?
3. Barneys opted to respond to Trayon Christian's lawsuit through two Facebook posts on its company page. Both posts gained a negative response from Facebook users. Why do you believe Barneys chose to communicate through that medium? Would you have done the same?
4. Grand larceny is a major problem in New York City. How should Barneys tailor its loss prevention policy in a way that adequately addresses that crime problem as well as racial profiling concerns?
5. Macy's, a competitor within the department store industry, is facing similar racial profiling allegations. Should Barneys and Macy's address the issue of racial profiling jointly? Why, or why not?

## WRITING ASSIGNMENT

Please respond in writing to the issues presented in this case by preparing two documents: a communication strategy memo and a professional business letter.

In preparing these documents, you may assume one of two roles: you may identify yourself as a Barney's New York senior manager who has been asked to provide advice to CEO Mark Lee regarding the issues he and his company are facing. Or, you may identify yourself as an external management consultant who has been asked by the company to provide advice to Mr. Lee.

Either way, you must prepare a strategy memo addressed to Mark Lee, Chief Executive Officer of the company, that summarizes the details of the case, identifies critical issues, discusses their implications (what they mean and why they matter), offers specific recommendations for action (assigning ownership and suspense dates for each) and shows how to communicate the solution to all who are affected by the recommendations.

You must also prepare a professional business letter for Mr. Lee's signature. That document should be addressed to all Barney's employees, explaining the actions the company is taking. If you have questions about either of these documents, please consult your instructor.

## APPENDIX

### *Exhibit 10.1 Barneys CEO Mark Lee's Facebook Post*

**Barneys New York**

October 24, 2013

Barneys New York believes that no customer should have the unacceptable experience described in recent media reports, and we offer our sincere regret and deepest apologies.

Further to our statement of yesterday, we want to reinforce that Barneys New York has zero tolerance for any form of discrimination. We are a strong proponent of equal rights and equal treatment for all human beings. Our mission is to ensure that all customers receive the highest-quality service—without exception.

To this end, we are conducting a thorough review of our practices and procedures as they relate to these matters to ensure that they reflect our continued commitment to fairness and equality. To lead this review, we have retained a civil rights expert, Michael Yaki, who also serves on the U.S. Commission on Civil Rights. The Commission has been the nation's watchdog for civil rights for more than 50 years. Mr. Yaki will be provided with unrestricted access to all aspects of our store operations.

In addition, Barneys New York has reached out to community leaders to begin a dialogue on this important issue.

Sincerely,
Mark Lee
CEO of Barneys New York

*Source*: Barneys New York Facebook Page, October 24, 2014. Online at www.facebook.com/BarneysNY/posts/10151940354699244.

## ACKNOWLEDGMENTS

This case was prepared by research assistants Christopher Cellante and Timothy Kelly under the direction of James O'Rourke, Teaching Professor of Management, as the basis for class discussion rather than to illustrate either effective or ineffective handling of an administrative situation. Information was gathered from corporate as well as public sources. Editorial assistance: Judy Bradford and Jennifer Cronin.

## NOTES

1   Bhasin, Kim and Julee Wilson. "Barneys Racist Culture Deeply Ingrained in Store, Insiders Say," *The Huffington Post*, November 7, 2013. Online at www.huffingtonpost.com/2013/11/07/barneys-racist_n _4225710.html. Accessed April 7, 2015.

2   Robbins, Christopher. "Teen Sues Barneys & NYPD After Cops Arrest Him for Buying $350 Belt," *Gothamist*, October 23, 2013. Online at http://gothamist.com/2013/10/23/teen_sues_barneys_for.php. Accessed February 21, 2015.

3   Green, Treye. "Who Is Trayon Christian? All About the NYC Teen Arrested for Buying Designer Belt at Barneys," *International Business Times*, October 23, 2013. Online at www.ibtimes.com/who-trayon-christian-all-about-nyc-teen-arrested-buying-designer-belt-barneys-1439142. Accessed February 21, 2015.

4   Wilson, Julee. "Black College Student Arrested for Buying a Designer Belt, Barneys & NYPD Slapped With Lawsuit (UPDATE)," *Huffington Post*. October 23, 2013. Online at www.huffingtonpost.com/2013/10/23/trayon-christian-lawsuit-barneys-new-york-nypd_n_4148490.html. Accessed February 21, 2015.

5   Robbins. "Teen Sues Barneys & NYPD."

6   Green. "Who Is Trayon Christian?"

7   Winsor, Morgan. "Student Sues Barneys Department Store, NYPD, Alleges Racial Profiling," *CNN*, October 25, 2013. Online at www.cnn.com/2013/10/23/justice/new-york-profiling-lawsuit/. Accessed February 21, 2015.

8   Mukherjee, Aparna. "Jay Z, Barneys, and the Shop-and-Frisk Problem," *The New Yorker*, December 16, 2013. Online at www.newyorker.com/business/currency/jay-z-barneys-and-the-shop-and-frisk-problem. Accessed February 21, 2015.

9   O'Connor, Clare. "New York AG To Barneys, Macy's: Turn Over 'Shop and Frisk' Racial Profiling Policies by Friday," *Forbes*, October 29, 2013. Online at www.forbes.com/sites/clareoconnor/2013/10/29/new-york-ag-to-barneys-macys-turn-over-shop-and-frisk-racial-profiling-policies-by-Friday/. Accessed February 21, 2015.

10  Moore, Tina, and Ginger Adams Otis. "Another Black Barneys Shopper Accused of Credit Card Fraud After Buying $2,500 Purse: Claim," *Daily News*, October 24, 2013. Online at www.nydailynews.com/new-york/black-barneys-shopper-accused-buying-2g-purse-article-1.1494855. Accessed February 21, 2015.

11  Ibid.

12  Wilson, Julee. "Another Black Shopper Accuses Barneys and NYPD of Racism (UPDATE)," *Huffington Post*, October 24, 2013. Online at www.huffingtonpost.com/2013/10/24/barneys-racism- kayla-phillips_n_4155176.html. Accessed February 21, 2015.

13  "Barneys' Fred Pressman, 73," *SunSentinel*, July 15, 1996. Online at http://articles.sun-sentinel.com/1996-07-15/news/9607140212_1_barney-pressman-fred-pressman-barneys-new-york. Accessed February 21, 1996.

14  Ibid.

15  "New York's Fashion Palace," *Modern Wearing*, April 10, 2013. Online at www.modernwearing.com/trends-news/new-yorks-fashion-palace/. Accessed February 21, 2015.

16  Timberlake, Cotton and Katherine Burton. "Barneys New York Taken Over by Perry Capital in Debt Swap," *Bloomberg-Business*, May 8, 2013. Online at www.bloomberg.com/news/articles/2012-05-07/barneys-new-york-taken-over-by-perry-capital-in-debt-swap. Accessed March 12, 2015.

17  Grant, Linda. "Balm for the Soul," *The Guardian*, February 26, 2009. Online at www.theguardian.com/lifeandstyle/2009/feb/27/shopping-trips-fashion. Accessed February 21, 2015.

18  "Industry at a Glance," Department Stores in the US, *IBISWorld*, November, 2014. Online at www.ibisworld.com/industry/default.aspx?indid=1090. Accessed February 21, 2015.

19  "Department Stores Industry Profile," *First Research*, November 24, 2014. Online at www.firstresearch.com/Industry-Research/Department-Stores.html. Accessed February 21, 2015.

20  Wilson, Marianne. "Study: Shrink Costs U.S. Retailers $42 Billion; Employee Theft Tops Shoplifting," *Chain Store Age*, November 6, 2014. Online at www.chainstoreage.com/article/study-shrink-costs-us-retailers-42-billion-employee-theft-tops-shoplifting. Accessed February 21, 2015.

21  Kavilanz, Parija. "Store Theft Cost to Your Family: $435," *CNN Money*, November 11, 2009. Online at http://money.cnn.com/2009/11/10/news/economy/retail_recession_theft/. Accessed February 21, 2015.

22  Burke, Kerry, Ginger Adams Otis and Dareh Gregorian. "Rob Brown, Star of 'Treme,' Says He Was Arrested at Macy's After Buying Mom Watch," *Daily News*, October 25, 2013. Online at www.nydailynews.com/new-york/black-man-sues-macy-cuffed-making-legit-purchase-article-1.1496735. Accessed February 21, 2015.

23  Ibid.

24  Ibid.

25   Moore, Tina and Reuven Blau. "Fourth New York Shopper, Pointing at Macy's, Makes Racial Profiling Allegations," *Daily News*, October 27, 2013. Online at www.nydailynews.com/new-york/4th-nyc-shopper-accusing-macy-race-profil ing-claims-article-1.1498427. Accessed February 21, 2015.

26   Skinner, Curtis. "Boycott Threatened After Racial Profiling Claims at Macy's, Barneys," *Reuters*, November 4, 2013. Online at www.reuters.com/article/2013/11/04/us-usa-newyork-barneys-macys-idUSBRE9A313Q20131104. Accessed February 21, 2015.

27   Barneys New York Facebook Page, October 23, 2013. Online at www.facebook.com/BarneysNY/posts/10151 937662404244.

28   Skinner. "Boycott Threatened After Racial Profiling Claims at Macy's, Barneys."

29   Francescani, Chris and Curtis Skinner. "New York Retailers, Police Trade Blame on 'Shop and Frisk,'" *Reuters*, October 29, 2013. Online at www.reuters.com/article/2013/10/29/us-usa-newyork-barneys-macys-idUSBRE99S0P920131029. Accessed February 21, 2015.

30   *Onecle*. New York Penal Law § 155.30 (McKinney 2010). Online at http://law.onecle.com/new-york/penal/PEN0155.30_ 155.30.html.

31   O'Donnell, Noreen. "Macy's Joins Barneys in Brewing NYC 'Shop-and-Frisk' Scandal," *Reuters*, October 26, 2013. Online at www.reuters.com/article/2013/10/26/us-usa-newyork-barneys-macys-idUSBRE99P08420131026. Accessed February 21, 2015.

32   Ibid.

33   Burke, Kerry, Mark Morales, Barbara Ross and Ginger Adams Otis. "Barneys Accused Teen of Using Fake Debit Card for $349 Belt Because He's a 'Young Black American Male': Lawsuit," *Daily News*, October 22, 2013. Online at www.nydaily news.com/new-york/barneys-accused-stealing-black-teen-article-1.1493101. Accessed February 21, 2015.

34   Justia, US Supreme Court. 392 U.S. 1 (1968). *Terry v. Ohio*, U.S. Supreme Court. Argued Dec. 12, 1967. Decided June 10, 1968. Online at https://supreme.justia.com/cases/federal/us/392/1/case.html.

35   Bellin, Jeffrey. "The Inverse Relationship Between the Constitutionality and Effectiveness of New York City 'Stop and Frisk,'" *Boston University Law Review* 94 (2014): 1502. Online at www.bu.edu/bulawreview/files/2014/10/ BELLIN.pdf.

36   Harris, David. "Across the Hudson: Taking the Stop and Frisk Debate Beyond New York City," *NYU Journal of Legislation and Public Policy* 16 (2013): 854. Online at www.nyujlpp.org/wp-content/uploads/2014/01/Harris-Across-the-Hudson-16nyu jlpp853.pdf.

37   Bellin. "The Inverse Relationship," 1498.

38   Goldstein, Joseph. "Judge Rejects New York's Stop-and-Frisk Policy," *The New York Times*, August 12, 2013. Online at www. nytimes.com/2013/08/13/nyregion/stop-and-frisk-practice-violated-rights-judge-rules.html?pagewanted=all&_r=2&. Accessed February 21, 2015.

39   Center for Constitutional Rights (2008). *Floyd, et. al v. City of New York, et. al*. Online at http://ccrjustice.org/floyd.

40   *Floyd v. City of New York*, 959 F. Supp. 2d 540, 563 (S.D.N.Y. 2013), *appeal dismissed* (Sept. 25, 2013)

41   Eversley, Malanie. "Sharpton Threatens NYC Store Boycott Over Profiling Claims," *USA Today*, October 26, 2013. Online at www.usatoday.com/story/news/nation/2013/10/26/new-york-racial-profiling-barneys-macys/3247097/. Accessed February 21, 2015.

42   Francescani, Chris and Curtis Skinner. "New York Protesters Target Barneys After Black Shoppers Claim Bias," *Reuters*, October 30, 2013. Online at www.reuters.com/article/2013/10/31/us-usa-newyork-barneys-macys-idUSBRE99S0P920131031. Accessed February 21, 2015.

43   Lipke, David. "Get Carter: Barneys Jay Z Holiday." *Women's Wear Daily*. September 25, 2013. Accessed February 21, 2015, through Business Insights Essentials.

44   "Jay Z & Barneys New York Partner for a 'A New York Holiday,'" *The Fashionisto*, September 25, 2013. Online at www.the fashionisto.com/jay-z-barneys-new-york-partner-new-york-holiday/. Accessed February 21, 2015.

45   Bowers, Derick. "End All Partnerships with Barneys New York; Barneys New Slaves," *Change.org*. Online at www.change. org/p/shawn-carter-aka-jay-z-end-all-partnerships-with-barneys-new-york. Accessed February 21, 2015.

46   Carter, Shawn. "A Statement From Shawn 'Jay Z' Carter," *Life and Times*, October 26, 2013. Online at http://lifeandtimes. com/a-statement-from-shawn-jay-z-carter. Accessed February 21, 2015.

CHAPTER 11

# Managing Conflict

The workplace of the twenty-first century is filled with tension and strife. Over the past 20 years, incivility has risen noticeably in the American workplace. Nearly half of those surveyed on this subject in 1998 reported that they were treated rudely at least once a month, a figure which rose to 55 percent in 2011 and 62 percent in 2016.[1] Georgetown University management professor Christine Porath argues that civility in the workplace matters. Among other things, she says, "it helps dampen potential tensions and furthers information sharing and team building."[2]

Despite the obvious advantages to getting along in the workplace, incivility is rampant and on the rise. "The accumulation of thoughtless actions," says Professor Porath, "leaving employees feeling disrespected – intentionally ignored, undermined by colleagues, or publicly belittled by an insensitive manager – can create lasting damage that should worry every organization."[3]

Conflicts unsurprisingly arise under pressure-cooker deadlines, increased workloads, fear of layoffs and the unrelenting demand for higher productivity. Under such stress, workplace violence has been increasing. And even in calm settings, routine business negotiations often turn ugly.[4]

## COSTS OF WORKPLACE CONFLICT

A study by Consulting Psychologists Press reveals that employees in the U.S. spend just over two hours each week involved in some form of conflict. This amounts to around $359 billion in hours paid that are filled with – and focused on – conflict instead of positive productivity. That's the equivalent of 385 million days on the job devoted to arguing, rather than collaborating.[5]

According to Pollock Peacebuilding Systems, a conflict resolution consulting firm in California, some 60 percent of employees they surveyed have never received basic conflict management classes or lessons. Of those who did, 95 percent said the training helped them navigate workplace conflict positively and seek mutually beneficial outcomes.[6]

A recent Columbia University study revealed that companies with a healthy corporate culture report, on average, a turnover rate of just 13.9 percent annually, compared with 48.9 percent at companies with a conflict-prone culture.[7] Typically those who quit in response to an experience of bad behavior don't tell their employers, but costs can add up quickly. Most companies spend about twice an employee's annual salary trying to replace that person. In Professor Porath's survey, about 12 percent of those treated poorly said they had left their jobs because of uncivil treatment.[8]

The documented toll of workplace conflict and incivility goes further. University of Arizona professor Allison Gabriel and her colleagues found that 80 percent of employees indicated that they lost time at work because they were worried about or experienced incivility, with about two-thirds of them saying that their performance had declined. More than three-quarters of the people they studied said they had lowered their commitment to the organization at a monetary cost of about $14,000 per employee.[9]

Another related cost of such behavior affects companies through the legal system. Pollack Peacebuilding Systems reports an annual cost of $482 million in settlement damages for victims of employment-related abuse. The average cost to a company is $125,000 per case, taking some 275 days to resolve. And, while most employment conflict matters don't end up in court, those that do will be even costlier. The median judgment is now approximately $200,000, in addition to the cost of defense. About a quarter of all cases result in a judgment of $500,000 or more.[10]

The final, and perhaps most important cost to a business, is a decline in customer experience. Research by Christine Porath of Georgetown, and Valerie Folkes and Debbie MacInnis at the University of Southern California shows that many "consumers are less likely to buy anything from a company they perceive as uncivil, whether the rudeness is directed at them or other employees."[11]

## CAUSES OF WORKPLACE CONFLICT

Conflict can arise from a variety of sources, but many experts see it as a function of such workplace variables as personality, personal and professional relationships, cultural differences, working environments, demands of the marketplace and of course, competition. "Workers today compete for schedules and projects, for money and training," says Marilyn Moats Kennedy, a career coach in Wilmette, Illinois.[12]

And as organizations move increasingly to teams and teamwork to accomplish specific objectives, differences among team members can lead to conflict. "A lot of people are in workplaces where they are being emotionally abused and bullied and that can take a toll," says Paul Spector, a professor of industrial and organizational psychology at the University of South Florida in Tampa. "It's becoming much more socially acceptable to be mean and nasty to others." Anna Maravelas, a psychologist in St. Paul, Minnesota, says she regularly sees anger, hostility, rudeness and general inhumanity in the workplaces where she consults. A corporate vice president, for example, told her, "I pay my people well; I don't have to appreciate them, too." And a bank employee said, "Being nice here is seen as a weakness."[13] Spector said his research has found that 2 to 3 percent of people admit to pushing, slapping or hitting someone at work. With roughly 100 million in the U.S. workforce, he said, that's as many as 3 million people.[14]

"Conflict in any endeavor that requires the input of two or more people is a real possibility," says Jeanne Gulbranson, President of Key Performance International in Las Vegas, Nevada:

As the scope of a project increases, the likelihood of differences in opinion and approach increases as a function of the number of tasks involved and the amount of time spent by the staff in the resolution of the project.

These conflicts, according to Gulbranson, may arise because of people's natural resistance to change, scheduling pressures, perceived difficulties in reporting procedures or simply because things aren't working well.[15]

Not all conflict within an organization is unhealthy, but conflict between and among people within an organization can quickly become counterproductive, divisive and destructive if not properly managed. In some quarters, most notably high-tech companies, conflict is actually encouraged as a catalyst for creativity. An idea is turned loose on the company's intranet, and other employees begin to examine it for flaws. In the best of circumstances, a good idea can be turned into a great idea with creative input and reflective critical thinking from those who must take ownership of the project. At its worst, such conflict can encourage predators in the electronic jungle to "flame" the idea's creator with derisive e-mail messages, and the struggle for idea supremacy begins.[16]

In its most basic form, conflict driven by stress can be unsettling and even dangerous to an organization and its employees. Office workers, frazzled by long hours, excessive e-mail, unrealistic deadlines and demanding supervisors, feel the effects directly. In a pair of recent surveys, Integra, a New York-based property valuation firm, discovered that

**TABLE 11.1** "Desk Rage" in the Workplace

| | |
|---|---|
| Witnessed yelling or other forms of verbal abuse | 42% |
| Yelled at coworkers themselves | 29% |
| Cried over work-related issues | 23% |
| Seen someone purposely damage machines or furniture | 14% |
| Seen physical violence in the workplace | 10% |
| Struck a coworker | 2% |

*Source*: Integra Realty Resources, 2000/2001 survey of 1,305 adults 18 and older. Online at www.irr.com.

an increasing number of people have witnessed workplace violence, abuse or emotional outbursts. Labeling the phenomenon "desk rage," the studies cite a number of sources for the behavior, including office layout and managerial insensitivity to the problem (see Table 11.1).

## A DEFINITION OF CONFLICT

Not surprisingly, we have even seen conflict over how to define conflict.[17] Most experts agree, however, that while opposition, incompatibility and interaction are important ingredients in conflict, a perception of conflict is essential. In other words, if no one thinks a conflict exists, there probably isn't one.[18]

We can define conflict, then, as a process that begins when someone perceives that someone else has negatively affected, or is about to negatively affect, something that the first person cares about. In practical terms, says Erik Van Slyke of HR Alliance, a Greensboro, North Carolina, consulting firm, "conflict is any time we disagree to the point where we can't go forward." Unchecked, he thinks, small matters can quickly mutate from a business conflict to a personality issue.[19] And from there, everything from productivity to working relationships to share price can suffer.

## CONFLICT IN ORGANIZATIONS

### The Traditional View

This perspective assumed that all conflict was bad. Conflict in an organizational setting was viewed negatively and was often used synonymously with words such as *violence, destruction* and *irrationality* to reinforce the negative image. Conflict was assumed to be the result of poor communication, a lack of openness and trust between workers and management, and a failure on the part of managers to be responsive to the needs and aspirations of their employees.[20] Naturally, good managers would do all in their power to avoid conflict. A workplace without conflict was assumed to be a happy, productive workplace.

### The Human Relations View

Popular from the 1940s to the 1970s, this viewpoint assumed that conflict was a natural occurrence in all groups and organizations. Because conflict was inevitable, industrial and labor psychologists argued in favor of simply accepting conflict. They rationalized its existence: It can't be eliminated; it may even be beneficial. Embrace it, they said. It's a natural part of every organization.

### The Interactionist View

This perspective, which emerged in the social science literature during the 1980s and 1990s, was a bit more radical than its predecessors. The interactionist approach actually *encourages* conflict on the grounds that a harmonious, peaceful, tranquil and cooperative group may become static, apathetic and unresponsive to a need for change and innovation. Without a minimum level of conflict, they reason, no organization can change, adapt and survive the rigors of the marketplace.[21]

In theory, the idea of ongoing minor conflict as a stimulus to creativity sounds good. But does it work in practice? Is it really a good idea to have people at each other's throats just for the sake of a few new market initiatives? "Never underestimate the power of a good idea," says business journalist Michael Warshaw. "Most people in most companies want to do the right thing. Give them an opportunity to make a positive contribution and chances are that they will." Warshaw, who writes for *Fast Company* magazine, also thinks people will work hard in order to leave their mark on a project or an organization. But, "most new-idea champions aren't in a position to order people to participate in their projects," he says.[22] Often, resources are scarce, values compete and colleagues are looking for visibility in the company. The result is conflict. Properly managed, however, conflict *can* have a beneficial effect on a business. The important questions concern *why* conflict arises and *how* the process should be managed.

## SOURCES OF CONFLICT IN ORGANIZATIONS

Conflict may develop over any number of issues or factors, but these five appear regularly in the social psychology literature:

### Limited Resources

People in organizations large and small often confront one another over resources that are either scarce or dwindling. These issues might include managerial responsibility, supervision of other employees, office or storage space, budget, tools and equipment, training, and access to superiors. If one person thinks another has some advantage (fair or not), conflict may arise over that perception. It may be something as simple as whose copier budget is bigger or as complex as who will lead the organization in a new, high-visibility product launch.

### Values, Goals and Priorities

Confrontation often occurs because of differences in specialty, training or beliefs. Karen A. Jehn of Pennsylvania's Wharton School demonstrated in a series of experimental field studies that if people share the same basic values, they're less likely to experience conflict, regardless of task or working conditions.[23]

### Poorly Defined Responsibilities

Conflict may result from differences between formal position descriptions and informal expectations on the job. "The book" says one thing, but "the job" demands another. In many instances, job design problems arise from ill-defined, vague or imprecise descriptions that are linked to everything from scheduling to compensation to performance review systems.

### Change

Among the few constants in organizational life is change itself. Everything, including annual budgets, organizational priorities, lines of authority, limits of responsibility, restructuring, mergers, divestitures, and layoffs can induce anxiety, uncertainty and conflict in a business.

### Human Drives for Success

Conflict may also be a by-product of the natural sense of goal orientation that every human experiences. Virtually every organization, even those in the not-for-profit sector, produces competition among its members by employing many competitors striving for very few rewards. The greater the imbalance between competitors and rewards, the greater the potential for conflict. In a retail establishment, access to walk-in customers may produce significant conflict if compensation schemes are linked directly to sales. In a military organization, where salaries are determined by rank and seniority, competition develops for fewer and fewer available promotions as competitors move up the chain of command.

## SENSING CONFLICT

It doesn't take a social psychologist to find conflict in a business. Conflict takes many forms and manifests itself in a number of ways – most of them easily visible, others not. Each manager in a business must assume responsibility for identifying conflict, both potential and actual, within the work environment and using appropriate means for managing or resolving differences that are unhealthy to the life of the organization.

As we have seen, conflict can be potentially healthy or destructive to a business. Social psychologists draw a distinction between *functional* and *dysfunctional* conflict. A healthy disagreement about when to act, how much to spend, whom to hire or which path to take is essential to the survival of a business. Conflict becomes dysfunctional, however, when it impedes or prevents managers and their employees from achieving the organization's business objectives. Here are some ways to sense day-to-day conflict in the workplace:

### Visualize

Try to visualize or imagine how your actions or those of others might cause, or are causing, conflict. Ask yourself the sort of questions a journalist might ask in reporting a news story: *Who? What? When? How? Why?* Sometimes those self-inquiries begin with if: "*If* I were to change the production schedule to assist the folks in shipping, how would *my* crew react?" You can't always know the answers, but knowing what questions to ask can help prevent serious conflict before it begins.

### Give Feedback

The amount, accuracy and timeliness of information that you can provide to an employee will help you to understand his or her point of view. Sharing your thoughts and feelings first, in a nonthreatening way, often encourages others to tell you what's on their minds. Your employees may not like a particular set of circumstances, but they are likely to be more accepting if they think they know the whole story.

### Get Feedback

Take the time to find out what your associates are thinking and feeling. Don't wait until the last moment to discover that you have trouble. Probe for more information by asking questions such as: How so? In what way? Why? Can you tell me more? The quality of the feedback you receive, particularly from subordinates and those who are not in your reporting chain, will be a direct function of the level of mutual trust you are able to establish. Harvard professor Linda Hill concludes that balancing advocacy with inquiry is essential. "Managers are trained to be advocates," she says:

> They are rewarded for being problem solvers – for figuring out what should be done, putting forth plans for action, and influencing others to adopt them. By contrast, inquiry skills – the ability to ask questions – have gone relatively undeveloped and unrecognized. But as managers rise in their organizations and the issues they confront become more complex and divergent from their personal experiences, inquiry skills become essential. Managers need to access and embrace the diverse expertise and perspectives of other people. They need to learn how to balance advocacy and inquiry to promote mutual learning.[24]

### Define Expectations

Meet regularly with your associates to determine priorities for the day ahead or the coming week. Any major discrepancies or misunderstanding between your expectations and theirs will alert you to potential conflict. Managers often discover that, as they define their expectations for employees in clear, easily understood terms, they will receive information in return about what team members and associates expect. Such conversations may be among the few opportunities for supervisors and subordinates to exchange both objective and subjective views of the workplace and the tasks at hand.

## *Review Performance Regularly*

When supervisors and employees communicate openly about how they are (or are not) working together, they reduce the opportunity for serious conflict and help to build stronger working relationships. Most businesses require annual performance reviews for managerial employees and more frequent reviews – semiannual or quarterly – for hourly employees. Experts say that when such reviews are seen by all participants as fair, objective and professional, morale and workplace satisfaction are likely to be high.

## THE BENEFITS OF DEALING WITH CONFLICT

Both you and the organization you work for will benefit if you deal directly with conflict. For you, personally, the benefits are important.

- *Stronger relationships.* You will be able to build stronger interpersonal relationships as a result of being comfortable expressing your true thoughts and feelings.
- *Increased self-respect.* You will be able to feel good about yourself and learn not to take every small bit of criticism personally. A key element in the definition of a professional is that he or she is able to accept feedback and handle criticism in a professional, rather than personal, manner. It's not about *you*. It's about the organization, the task at hand, and serving those who depend on you.
- *Personal growth and development.* When you break down some of your own invisible barriers and become more assertive in resolving or preventing conflict, you will invariably learn more and gain support from others. And if others in the organization come to know that they can depend on you when it really counts, team bonds are strengthened and success is that much easier to realize.

Dealing professionally with conflict in the workplace benefits not only you but the organization that employs you. Those benefits might include the following:

- *Improved efficiency and effectiveness.* Employees will be able to do their jobs more effectively, and probably with greater levels of efficiency and productivity, by focusing their efforts where they will produce the greatest results. Rather than wasting time and energy on workplace conflict, they can do what they were hired to do in the first place.
- *Creative thinking.* By encouraging people to share and learn from their mistakes, the organization will reap the benefits of creative thinking and a dramatically improved learning curve. By confronting potential conflict before it has an opportunity to paralyze the organization, managers can lower the level of apprehension and fear in the workplace, as well. An important consideration for any employee who is thinking about looking for work elsewhere is whether his work is valued over the long term by management. Advertising the fact that your organization is not a "one-mistake outfit" can help people become less fearful of making mistakes and more confident in trying new ideas and new ways of thinking.
- *Synergy and teamwork.* Managers and associates will be able to focus on serving customers and clients by helping each other. We often hear in the U.S. that "the customer is number one." In many Asian societies, however, executives have come to realize that "the employee is number one." By taking care of your employees, developing a sense of teamwork and organizational loyalty, you can be assured that they, in turn, will take care of your customers. And those customers, whose loyalty and business you've worked so hard to earn, will take care of your shareholders.

## STYLES OF CONFLICT MANAGEMENT

Not everyone approaches conflict in quite the same way. Some welcome the opportunity for a good dust-up. Others duck into the shadows and do their best to avoid confrontation. The style you adopt should reflect a deliberate, thoughtful view of the reasons why people may be in conflict, the culture of your organization and the personalities

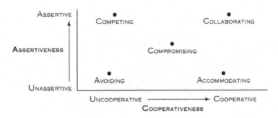

**FIGURE 11.1** Five Styles of Conflict Management

*Source*: Adapted from Thomas, K. "Conflict and Negotiation Processes in Organizations," in M. D. Dunnette and L. M. Hough (eds.), *Handbook of Industrial and Organizational Psychology*, 2/e, Vol. 3. Palo Alto, CA: Consulting Psychologists Press, 1994.

of those involved. Figure 11.1 represents author Kenneth Thomas's view of conflict management arrayed along two separate dimensions: *cooperativeness* and *assertiveness*. Thomas defines cooperativeness as the degree to which one person tries to satisfy another person's concerns, whereas assertiveness is seen as the degree to which one person tries to satisfy his/her own concerns.

With cooperativeness arrayed from low to high along the horizontal axis and assertiveness arrayed from low to high along the vertical axis, these two dimensions form a matrix that can be used to plot a manager's conflict response style. The "conflict-handling intentions," as he calls them, are *competing, collaborating, avoiding, accommodating* and *compromising*.[25]

## Competing

This style of conflict management involves people who are both assertive and uncooperative. People who try to satisfy their own interests at the expense of others involved are regarded as competitive. It's a strategy that works when dealing with other participants in the marketplace, but it's often seen as counterproductive inside an organization. Internal competition often produces impressive results, but it certainly does not promote teamwork or the cooperative behaviors required of teammates. This approach clearly produces winners and losers.

## Collaborating

This style involves people who are assertive but cooperative. If those involved in a situation with the potential for conflict express a desire to fully satisfy the concerns of all others, we're likely to see cooperation and a search for mutually beneficial outcomes. In collaborating, the intention is to solve the problem by clarifying differences rather than by accommodating various points of view. This approach seeks win–win solutions that incorporate the viewpoints of all those involved.

## Avoiding

This conflict management style involves people who are both unassertive and uncooperative. When a manager chooses to withdraw from a discussion or a situation in which conflict is likely, his choice is based on a desire to avoid a fight as well as those with whom he may disagree.

## Accommodating

This style involves people who are unassertive but cooperative. A manager seeking to appease an opponent or an employee may be willing to place that other person's interests above her own, usually for the sake of maintaining a good working relationship. In spite of personal misgivings or doubts, accommodators are willing to "give in" and "get along," either to promote the goals of the other person or for the sake of group harmony. Consistent accommodation to the needs and interests of others is sometimes seen as another form of conflict avoidance.

## Compromising

This approach involves people who are at the midpoint on both assertiveness and cooperativeness. Compromise occurs when each party to a conflict demonstrates a willingness to give up something in order to promote a solution. When sharing of this sort occurs, there are no clear winners or losers. Rather, there is "a willingness to ration the object of the conflict and accept a solution that provides incomplete satisfaction of both parties' concerns."[26]

# SO, WHAT SHOULD YOU DO?

In approaching the challenge posed by conflict in your organization (or any organization, for that matter), it seems clear that a single approach simply won't work. To succeed – that is, to achieve many different goals and balance the tug among opposing values – you may have to demonstrate skill at each of the five styles of conflict management we've just discussed. In some situations, you may need to accommodate to keep a valued employee. In other circumstances, you wish to compromise on an issue that's not especially important to you in order to get what you want. On other occasions, you may be faced with situations that involve many competitors and few rewards; to stay in the game, your approach may be thoroughly competitive. On still other occasions, you may decide to pack up your armor and avoid a fight altogether.

As you gather information and assess the situation, however, negotiation and conflict experts have identified a number of additional important considerations and suggestions.

## Listen, Listen and Then Listen Some More

That helped Los Angeles attorney Alan Liker navigate the sensitive negotiations for the purchase of Budget Rent-a-Car from Ford Motor Company by a group of licensees he represented. In such deals, he says, you have to find out what people are sensitive about, and you can do that only by listening carefully. Then you can adjust negotiation terms "so that it's perceived as a win-win situation." It takes a great deal of discipline to be a good listener, according to William P. Dunk, a management consultant in Chapel Hill, North Carolina. "You're tempted to start speaking and intervening," he says, unwisely taking ownership of the problem. "By talking too much, even if you're not posing a solution, you're not pushing the employee into self-awareness."[27]

## Separate the People from the Problem

Having clarified the mutual benefits to be gained by successfully concluding a negotiation, it may be useful to focus attention on the real issue at hand – solving the problem. Negotiations are more likely to conclude satisfactorily if the parties involved depersonalize the discussions. You're much more likely to get what you want if "one-upmanship" or revenge isn't part of your agenda. How can you do that? Begin to see the other party as an advocate for a point of view rather than an adversary or a rival. It's far better to say, "I can't support that solution," than it is to say, "I can't support you."[28]

## Focus on Interests, Not Positions

A demand that a negotiator makes is also known as a position. Interests are the real reasons behind the demands. Experience shows that it is easier to establish agreement on interests, given that they tend to be broader and multifaceted. You should also recognize that a negotiating position may be driven more by emotion than logic. It may be useful to inquire about that: "Can you tell me why you feel that way?" Or perhaps a simple declarative statement will prompt the response you're looking for: "Help me understand why you are advocating that position."[29]

## Recognize and Accept the Feelings of the Individuals Involved

Irrational feelings are often generated in the midst of controversy, even though the participants don't always want to recognize this fact. Each wants to believe that she is examining the problem objectively. Recognizing and accepting feelings such as fear, jealousy, anger or anxiety may make it possible for the participants to accept their own true feelings. Effective managers don't adopt a critical attitude, saying, "You have no right to feel angry." Rather, they accept those feelings for what they are and work to communicate empathy for those people involved.[30]

### Keep Your Own Emotions in Neutral

When John Day headed the transition team that closed down pharmaceutical manufacturer Sterling Winthrop in New York after its parts were sold to four different companies, he was faced with the anger of employees who were losing their jobs. "You've got to keep your cool and keep busy and focus on the positive side," he says. "After they got their point across, I'd say, 'I'm in the same situation. Here's what I'm trying to do.'" All the parties involved in a conflict have to focus on what they're going to do next to begin solving the dilemma, says Mr. Day, who is now an executive with Ingersoll Rand. "That defuses the situation."[31]

### Track the Conflict to Its Source

Conflicts may arise from a manager's personality or style. Outside influences may also contribute. "Maybe an employee's got a sick parent in Georgia or a horrible two-hour commute," says William Dunk. "An effective executive at any level must realize both the drain on productivity and the incremental amount of conflict coming from forces outside the workplace." Then, he says, you can get the employee some help in dealing with them.[32]

### Communicate Continually and Frankly

In the Sterling Winthrop negotiations, the transition team communicated as much as possible. "We had constant meetings and newsletters, even if there wasn't much to tell them," says John Day. That communication made employees feel involved and helped lessen the tension of the company's difficult, final days. Day's team was also brutally honest, telling employees it was unlikely they would be hired by the acquirers. That sort of honesty brought them credibility when other conflicts arose. "On reflection," Mr. Day says, "that was a big thing."[33]

### Get People Together on the Small Stuff First

When disagreements crop up, get the parties together and decide on three or four small measures that everyone can agree on and work on those. If people can agree on at least a few things, experts say, the big issues won't be quite as difficult. Moreover, if you establish a harmonious negotiating environment, a little goodwill can help to carry difficult conversations on other, larger issues.[34]

### Devise Options for Mutual Gain

This approach will involve some creativity on your part as a manager. By focusing your collective attention on brainstorming alternative mutually agreeable solutions, the conversational dynamic shifts from competitive to collaborative. This effort can demonstrate to others that you are a person of goodwill whose perspective does not necessarily require winners and losers. Additionally, the more options, alternatives and combinations you have to explore, the greater the probability of reaching a solution that will please everyone involved.[35]

### Define Success in Terms of Gains Rather Than Losses

If a manager seeking a 10 percent raise receives only 6 percent, that outcome can be seen as either a 6 percent improvement (over current income) or a 40 percent shortfall (over desired outcome). The first interpretation focuses on gains, while the second focuses on losses (in this case, unrealized expectations). The outcome is the same, but the manager's satisfaction with it varies substantially. It is important to recognize that our satisfaction with an outcome is affected by the standards we use to judge it. A sensible manager might ask, "Is this a meaningful improvement over current conditions?"[36]

### Follow Up to Ensure Success

Review all of the issues, definitions, discussions, data and details with everyone involved. Make sure that you're in agreement on the solution you plan to implement and the ways in which you plan to go about it. Establish some means of determining whether your solution is working. If possible, quantify outcomes. Agree to revisit the problem at a specific point in the future if the solution you have chosen doesn't seem to work.

### Know When to Cut Your Losses

Sometimes the conflict has simply gone too far and you have to decide where and when to start cutting. "All conflicts don't get resolved," says management consultant William Dunk, "and all people aren't worth saving."[37]

## WHAT IF YOU'RE THE PROBLEM?

"The fact is, people get angry an average of 10 to 14 times a day," says Hendrie Weisinger, a clinical psychologist and anger-management specialist. "But anger is especially endemic to work. If you have a job, you're guaranteed to get angry."[38] The worst cases of workplace anger can explode into violence that makes banner headlines. But according to most professionals who deal with such issues, anger rarely rises to such extremes. Most people deal with life's disappointments in a calm, evenhanded way. "Keep in mind," writes business journalist Jane Brody, "that even if your anger is fully justified, blowing your top can still cost you; you may lose your job, your spouse, or your health."[39]

Anger has become widely accepted as a part of contemporary culture, according to Phil D'Agostino, a therapist based in Raleigh, North Carolina. He cites popular television shows displaying a hard, angry edge. "In an office," he recalls, "a man calls a female co-worker 'honey' and another woman tells her, 'You have a right to get angry.' No one has a right to be angry," he says, "and it's delusional to think that anger can be productive. If you're passed over for a promotion, you can do three things: accept it, leave it, or change it."[40] Other psychologists would disagree with D'Agostino, noting that while anger may be perfectly justified in such situations, hostile behavior in response would not.

In the case of the coworker's offense, a generation gap may be more to blame than a lack of respect. "Often, when we feel hurt by someone else, we're mixing up impact and intent," explains Mark Gordon of the Boston-based Vantage Partners, a consulting firm specializing in negotiation and relationship management. "In other words, we are attributing to them the intent to hurt us because we feel hurt, when in reality, there can be a negative impact on us even though they had a perfectly benign, if not positive intent."[41]

Anger management experts, such as Mitchell Messer of Chicago's Anger Institute, and Albert Mehrabian, a psychologist at the University of California at Los Angeles, offer a number of guidelines to help in controlling your emotions. These suggestions appear frequently in the anger-management literature:

- *Acknowledge your anger.* Left unmanaged, anger festers. Don't ignore it in the hope that it will go away or pretend it isn't there because it seems unjustified.
- *Don't look for slights.* A colleague who seems to snub you as you meet in the hallway may simply be headed for the bathroom.
- *Know what's provoking you.* If you're upset with your spouse or a jammed photocopier, don't take it out on your colleagues.
- *Don't become infected by coworkers' gripes.* The fact that they're angry doesn't mean you should join them in their rage.
- *Check your own anger signals.* Anger often reveals itself through physical and emotional responses: a racing pulse, shortness of breath, pacing. Learn to read these signs before your anger gets out of hand.
- *Take a breather.* Find ways to cool off before your anger consumes you. Try deep breathing, a brisk walk or even busy work.
- *Write a letter.* If someone has enraged you, write him or her a letter. Pour out your feelings; be candid and direct. Just don't mail it. You will still feel better.
- *Confide in a friend.* If it seems unwise to direct your anger toward its source, discuss the problem with someone you trust.[42]

Having read these suggestions, keep two important things in mind: First, many – if not most – conflicts resolve themselves before they become generalized workplace dilemmas. Most people of goodwill are willing to work with one another for the benefit of the organization, as long as they can see their own best interests linked in some way with those of the organization. And second, managers get paid to listen to their employees, gather useful information, resolve disputes and make tough decisions. The more of it you do, the better you'll get.

If all else fails, consider the advice of Canadian Zen master Albert Low. "Zen teaches that fundamental conflicts exist in every being and that striving to reconcile them is the cause of all suffering, and all life," Low explains. "Conflict abounds in business, too – in the turf wars between departments and in the competing demands of shareholders, employees, customers, and community. The conventional approach to settling the strife with trades-offs actually kills the only sources of growth." The director of the Montreal Zen Centre and author of *Zen and Creative Management* says, "Managers are always choosing between two or more equally desirable resolutions, but all of them are in conflict. The real management charter," he says, "is to harness the energy of opposing forces. And that requires a really creative act. Responding is about trying to catch up. Acting takes you to the future."[43]

## FOR FURTHER READING

Borisoff, D. and D. A. Victor. *Conflict Management: A Communication Skills Approach*, 2/e. Boston: Allyn & Bacon, 1997.

Collins, S. D. *Managing Conflict and Workplace Relationships*, 2/e. Mason, OH: Cengage South-Western, 2008.

De Dreu, C. K. W. "Productive Conflict: The Importance of Conflict Management and Conflict Issue," in C. K. W. De Dreu and E. Van de Vliert, *Using Conflict in Organizations*. London: Sage Publications, 1997.

Drory, A. and I. Ritov. "Effects of Work Experience and Opponent's Power on Conflict Management Styles," *International Journal of Conflict Management* 8.2 (April 1997): 148–161.

Gordon, J. *The Pfeiffer Book of Successful Conflict Management Tools*. Hoboken, NJ: Pfeiffer Publishing, Inc., 2007.

Janssen, O. and E. Van de Vliert. "Concern for the Other's Goals: Key to (De)escalation of Conflict," *International Journal of Conflict Management* 7.2 (April 1996): 99–120.

Parker-Pope, T. "When the Bully Sits in the Next Cubicle," *The New York Times*, March 25, 2008, p. D5.

Rahim, M. A. and R. T. Golembiewski (eds). *Styles of Managing Organizational Conflict: A Critical Review and Synthesis of Theory and Research*. Greenwich, CT: JAI Press, 1997.

Ritov, I. and A. Drory. "Ambiguity and Conflict Management Strategy," *International Journal of Conflict Management* 7.2 (April 1996): 139–155.

Stone, D., B. Patton and S. Heen. *Difficult Conversations: How to Discuss What Matters Most*. New York, NY: Penguin Books, 2010.

Withers, B. *The Conflict Management Skills Workshop: A Trainer's Guide*. New York: American Management Association, 2002.

"Workplace Anger Viewed Differently by Gender: Antagonistic Men Admired, While Women Seen 'Out of Control.'" *Reuters/MSNBC.com*. Updated: 11:53 a.m. ET, August 3, 2007. Online at www.msnbc.mns.com/20108425.

## NOTES

1 Porath, C. *Cycle to Civility*, Georgetown University working paper, 2016.
2 Porath, C. "The Hidden Toll of Workplace Incivility," *McKinsey Quarterly*, 2016. Online at www.mckinsey.com/business-functions/organization/our-insights/the-hidden-toll-of-workplace-incivility. Accessed Saturday, July 14, 2018 at 12:31 p.m. (EDT).
3 Ibid.
4 Lancaster, H. "Solving Conflicts in the Workplace Without Making Losers," *The Wall Street Journal*, May 27, 1997, p. B1. Reprinted by permission of *The Wall Street Journal*. Copyright © 1997 Dow Jones & Company, Inc. All rights reserved worldwide.
5 Thompson, Rich. "New Study Details Both Crippling and Beneficial Effects of Workplace Conflict on Businesses," Consulting Psychologists Press, 2008. Online at https://shop.cpp.com/PRESS/Workplace_Conflict_Study.aspx. Accessed Saturday, July 14, 2018 at 12:57 p.m. (EDT).
6 Pollock Peacebuilding Systems, "Workplace Conflict Statistics." Online at https://pollackpeacebuilding.com/workplace-conflict-statistics/. Accessed Saturday, July 14, 2018 at 1:03 p.m. (EDT).

7   Medina, E. "Job Satisfaction and Employee Turnover Intention: What Does Organizational Culture Have to Do with It?" Columbia University, Fall 2012. Online at http://static1.1.sqspcdn.com/static/f/1528810/23319899/1376576545493/medina+elizabeth.pdf?token=fkutsVuiRC/GspEXW6RG6PPvkAY. Accessed Saturday, July 14, 2018 at 1:10 p.m. (EDT).

8   Porath. "The Hidden Toll of Workplace Incivility."

9   Gabriel, A., M. Butts and M. Sliter. "Women Experience More Incivility at Work – Especially from Other Women," *Harvard Business Review*, March 28, 2018. Online at https://hbr.org/2018/03/women-experience-more-incivility-at-work-especially-from-other-women. Accessed Saturday, July 14, 2018 at 1:23 p.m. (EDT).

10  Pollock Peacebuilding Systems, "Workplace Conflict Statistics."

11  Porath. "The Hidden Toll of Workplace Incivility."

12  Warshaw, M. "The Good Guy's (and Gal's) Guide to Office Politics," *Fast Company*, April 1998, p. 156.

13  Stenson, J. "Desk Rage: Workers Gone Wild," MSNBC.com. Updated: November 27, 2006, 6:54 a.m. ET. Online at www.nbcnews.com/id/15814840/ns/health-mental_health/t/desk-rage-workers-gone-wild/#.W0o12TpKipo. Accessed Saturday, July 14, 2018 at 1:42 p.m. EDT.

14  Wulfhorst, E. "Get Out of the Way, Road Rage. Here Comes Desk Rage," *Reuters*, Thursday, July 10, 2008. Online at www.reuters.com/article/idUSN0947145320080710. Accessed January 6, 2011 at 2:38 p.m. EDT.

15  Gulbranson, J. E. "The Ground Rules of Conflict Resolution," *Industrial Management* 30.3 (May–June 1998): 4.

16  Lancaster. "Solving Conflicts."

17  See Fink, C. F. "Some Conceptual Difficulties in the Theory of Social Conflict," *Journal of Conflict Resolution* (December 1968): 412–460.

18  Robbins, S. P. *Organizational Behavior: Concepts, Controversies, and Applications*, 11/e. Upper Saddle River, NJ: Prentice Hall, 2004, p. 445.

19  Thomas, K. W. "Conflict and Negotiation Processes in Organizations," in Dunnette, M. D., and L. M. Hough (eds), *Handbook of Industrial and Organizational Psychology*, 2/e., Vol. 3. Palo Alto, CA: Consulting Psychologists Press, 1994.

20  Robbins. *Organizational Behavior*, p. 445.

21  Ibid., pp. 446–447.

22  Warshaw. "The Good Guy's (and Gal's) Guide to Office Politics," p. 156.

23  Jehn, Karen A. "Enhancing Effectiveness: An Investigation of Advantages and Disadvantages of Value-Based Intragroup Conflict," *International Journal of Conflict Management* 5.3 (July 1994): 223–238.

24  Ibid., p. 4.

25  Thomas. *Handbook of Industrial and Organizational Psychology*.

26  Robbins. *Organizational Behavior*, pp. 451–453.

27  Lancaster. "Solving Conflicts," p. B1.

28  Whetten, D. A. and K. S. Cameron. *Developing Management Skills: Managing Conflict*. New York: HarperCollins, 1993, p. 35.

29  Ibid.

30  Schmidt, W. H. and R. Tannenbaum. "Management of Differences," in *Harvard Business Review on Negotiation and Conflict Resolution*. Boston: Harvard Business School Press, 2000, pp. 18–19. Copyright © 2000 by the Harvard Business School Publishing Corporation. All rights reserved.

31  Lancaster, "Solving Conflicts," p. B1. See also Brody, J. E. "Why Angry People Can't Control the Short Fuse," *The New York Times*, May 28, 2002, p. D7. Copyright © 2002 by The New York Times Company. Reprinted with permission.

32  Ibid.

33  Ibid.

34  Ibid.

35  Whetten and Cameron. *Developing Management Skills*, p. 35.

36  Ibid., p. 36.

37  Lancaster. "Solving Conflicts," p. B1.

38  Felton, B. "Earning It; When Rage Is All the Rage," *The New York Times*, March 15, 1998, p. 12.

39  Brody. "Why Angry People Can't Control the Short Fuse."

40  Ibid.

41  Felton. "Earning It; When Rage Is All the Rage," p. 12.

42  Gordon, M. Telephone interview, Vantage Partners/Boston, November 25, 2002.

43  Green, W. "Zen and the Art of Managerial Maintenance," *Fast Company*, June 1996, p. 50.

# Case 11.1: Hayward Healthcare Systems, Inc.

Bob Jackson is the new operations manager of the distribution center for Hayward Healthcare Systems, Inc., a mid-size, non-union company located in California. The distribution center is a $80-million-dollar-a-year operation that has 50 employees, including 15 minorities and 18 females in the workforce.

Jackson was transferred from another operations position in the company to fill this position because of some serious performance problems in the distribution center that had resisted all attempts at improvement. The center had experienced a very high level of defects (140 per month) and an unacceptable rate of errors in the orders taken from client hospitals. Jackson accepted the assignment knowing that top management would expect him to improve the performance of the distribution center in a relatively short period of time.

Jackson's first few weeks on the job were revealing, to say the least. He discovered that the five supervisors that his predecessor had selected to lead the center's workforce had little credibility with the employees. They had each been selected on the basis of their job seniority or their friendship with the previous manager.

The workforce was organized into three categories. *Pickers* identify supplies by code numbers in the storage area, remove packaged items from the shelves and sort them into baskets. *Drivers* operate forklifts and electric trucks, moving baskets and boxes of supplies to different locations within the distribution center. *Loaders* transfer supplies onto and off of the forklifts and delivery trucks.

## THE SITUATION MR. JACKSON ENCOUNTERED

Jackson found that his employees were either demoralized or had tough, belligerent attitudes toward management and other employees. Part of the problem, he soon learned, was a lax approach to background checks and prior job references. Seven employees were convicted felons who had been imprisoned for violent assaults on their victims. The previous manager had made all of the hiring decisions by himself without bothering to check on the applicants' references or backgrounds.

Jackson soon discovered that it was not unusual for employees to settle their differences with their fists or to use verbally abusive language to berate people who had offended them. His predecessor had unintentionally encouraged these disruptive activities by staying in his office and not being available to the other workers. He had relied largely on his discredited supervisors to handle their own disciplinary problems. Before long, the center employees felt they could handle their own affairs in any way they wanted, without any interference from management.

## THE LOADING DOCK INCIDENT

While sitting in his office, planning to make several policy changes to improve the efficiency of the distribution center, one of Jackson's supervisors entered and reported that two of the loaders had just gotten into a heated dispute, and the situation on the loading dock was tense.

The dispute was between Ed Williams, an African-American, male employee, and Buddy Jones, a white, male employee, and focused on which radio station to play on the loading dock sound system. Williams is the only black employee who works on the loading dock. The company's policy permits employees to listen to music while they work and, in recent years, workers have considered listening to music to be a benefit that improves their working conditions.

Williams insisted that he couldn't stand to listen to the country music that Jones preferred to play. For his part, Jones claimed that Williams' choice of rap and hip-hop music was offensive to him and made working conditions difficult. An emotional and angry argument developed between the two men over their choices in music, and each yelled racial slurs at the other. Neither the company nor the division have a policy governing the choice of music permitted in the workplace. Apparently, whoever gets to work first chooses the music for the day.

Both Jones and Williams were known as tough employees who had previous disciplinary problems at Hayward Hospital Supply. Jones had been incarcerated for 18 months prior to being hired by the company. Jackson knew that he should take immediate action to resolve this problem and to avoid a potentially volatile escalation of the conflict. His supervisors told Jackson that, in the past, the previous manager would simply have hollered at the two antagonists in the conflict and then departed with no further action.

Jackson's objectives in resolving the conflict included the establishment of his own control in the workplace. He knew that he would have to change "business as usual" in the distribution center so that employees would respect his authority and would refrain from any further unprofessional conduct.

## RESOLVING THE PROBLEM

In determining the most appropriate solution to the dispute between Jackson's employees, you should consider the following questions:

1. What seems to be the cause of the conflict?
2. What style of conflict management are the distribution center's employees using?
3. What style of conflict management have these managers used in the past?
4. What should Mr. Jackson do to settle the conflict? Should either or both of the employees be punished for their behavior?
5. What can Mr. Jackson do over the long term to ensure that incidents such as the one described in this case are less likely to occur?
6. What can Mr. Jackson do to develop a group of supervisors who can provide the support he requires and who can properly direct the work of the employees in the distribution center?
7. How important is communication in this case? What should Mr. Jackson do to improve the quality of communication in the distribution center?

## WRITING ASSIGNMENT

This assignment requires two documents: a professional business memo and a professional business letter. Please assume the role of Mr. Jackson, the distribution center operations manager. Cast your reply to the issues in this case in the form of a **proposal memo to the distribution center director**.

At a *minimum*, in your response, please identify the business and management issues, the legal issues, and the cultural issues present in this case. Please consider two additional questions:

- What must I do *right now* to solve the problem? What actions do I take immediately?
- What advice would I offer to senior management about this matter? Have any company policies (or lack of policies) contributed to the events described?

Please address your business letter to all employees in the distribution center, explaining what's happened and what you and the company's leadership have decided to do about it.

## ACKNOWLEDGMENTS

This case was prepared by Ms. Kay Wigton with the assistance of James S. O'Rourke, Teaching Professor of Management, as the basis for class discussion rather than to illustrate either effective or ineffective handling of an administrative situation. Personal and corporate identities have been disguised.

# Case 11.2: Dixie Industries, Inc.

Middle managers are frequently called upon to draft documents, including letters, memoranda, position papers, background reports and briefing documents for senior people in their organizations. Sometimes, senior managers will ask subordinates not only to prepare a document for signature, but to gather the relevant supporting information, as well.

Often, the preparation of such documents requires no more than a quick referral to a balance sheet, database or filing system to gather the information needed. Sometimes, though, a management response requires that the company – often in the person of the chief executive or president – take a position on an issue. It is in such circumstances that middle managers can reveal who among them is most perceptive, thoughtful and insightful.

Some management problems are easily resolved. The issues are clear, the resources are available and implementation is not difficult. Other problems are more difficult. Resources may be limited, intentions and agenda may not be clear and more than one audience may be paying attention to the response.

The issue at hand deals with corporate policy, corporate actions in regard to that policy and with the public perceptions of both. This case requires two documents: a brief (two-or-three-page) communication strategy memorandum, and a letter to an employee. The strategy memo should be directed to the President of Dixie Industries, Inc. and should describe in detail how you plan to handle the case and why. The letter will help to implement the strategy.

Assume that you are the Vice President for Human Resources and report directly to the President of the firm. Dixie Industries, Inc. is a mid-size, non-union textile company located in the American south. The author of the study referred to by your president is a loom operator with ten years' experience and six years of job tenure with the firm. Your memorandum to the president and letter to Ms. Feldman should be in finished form and ready to transmit.

# DIXIE INDUSTRIES, INC.

## 3128 Northeast Industrial Park Road
## Meridian, Mississippi 39201

**DATE:**     [Today's Date]

**TO:**     Vice President, Human Resources

**FROM:**     Keith Harkins

President, Dixie Industries, Inc.

**SUBJECT:**     Dixie Industries Women's Group Study of Company Promotion Practices.

This memo asks for your assistance in gathering the advice of key staff officers in response to accusations of bias in our personnel policies from an unofficial employees' group.

## BACKGROUND

As you know, Dixie Industries, Inc. has recently been accused by an ad-hoc committee of employees of "a continuing and pervasive bias in promotions in favor of men." You may recall that Ms. Linda Feldman, founder and chairperson of the Dixie Industries Women's Group, has produced a so-called study of this problem and has demanded that we respond. The DI Executive Committee has read her study (such as it is) and asked for my response. I have attached a copy of her letter.

As far as I can determine, we now have four women in positions *above* that of Assistant Department Head. None of the senior executive positions, other than your own, has ever been filled by a female, but we're certainly open to hiring some as positions come open.

Now you know, of course, that more than 40 percent of our 1,800 employees are female – all of them industrious and hard-working. Many of them are quite loyal to the company, but many others (Ms. Feldman included) come and go with some frequency. We have experienced 23 maternity leave requests in the past 12 months. Others have poor attendance records (sick children, school problems, etc.).

## OUR OFFICIAL POSITION

My position, and the position of Dixie Industries, Inc., is this: we'll promote the most deserving individual who is available to fill a particular vacancy. We'll certainly consider any qualified woman (or any qualified man, for that matter) when a job in the executive ranks comes open. Our long-standing policy of promoting from within remains firm.

We go outside the company only when no fully qualified applicants are available in-house. Ms. Feldman's complaint ignores a number of important points, including the fact that few, if any, of our loom operators and plant floor personnel have the education and background to become managers. Also, a number of the figures she cites in the study are simply wrong. She does have a point, however, in that we have *very few* women in management or executive positions.

The other issue she ignores is the fact that we haven't had much turnover in management or executive positions in the past five years. In 25 positions, we've had one retirement and one resignation. The retirement resulted in an internal promotion (to VP, Finance from Comptroller), and the resignation resulted in an external hire. We have such low turnover, in my view, because of employee loyalty. And, as you know, we're well ahead of the industry in this regard.

## ISSUES TO BE RESOLVED

I'm concerned about several issues here:

- ***Unionization***. If Ms. Feldman manages to get enough of our hourly wage employees excited about this issue, we could be looking at a petition for establishment of a collective bargaining unit – probably with the ILGWU. That's a distraction that would be costly and counterproductive.

- **Publicity.** This is just the sort of thing that could hurt our image in the local community and, ultimately, drive our stock price down even further. We just cannot afford to have employees airing their grievances in the newspapers. We could use a little positive publicity for a change.
- **Job Action.** We've had a difficult time over the past 18 months in recruiting and retaining dependable loom operators. I'm concerned that Ms. Feldman and her group may instigate a slowdown, a walkout or some other job action that will harm this company's ability to respond to customer orders and remain competitive. As you know, margins in this industry are shrinking every year because of foreign competition.
- **Productivity.** We're below industry standards in productivity. Again, we cannot afford to spend more time worrying about issues like this. Instead, we must work on absenteeism, turnover and unit productivity.
- **The Right Thing to Do:** I am also concerned about more than simple appearance here. I want this company to do "the right thing," whatever that may be.

The problem, of course, is that I'm not at all certain what the "right thing" might be. We can't promote high-school educated loom operators to management positions simply because we don't have many women in management.

Give me your best thoughts on this. What should we do? Shall we confront Ms. Feldman and her group? Or, should we try to work with her to resolve the issues we face?

I'm ready to move on this issue. Please prepare a plan for me that will respond to Ms. Feldman, address her concerns, and do what you can to help us calm this situation. Please let me know whether or not you think we should meet with this women's group. Involve whichever members of the staff you think are appropriate and copy them on your memo. Make it confidential but don't leave our key players in the dark.

Additionally, I'd like you to prepare a letter for my signature to Ms. Feldman. I don't want any publicity about this matter, and I certainly don't want any lawsuits. Let me see your draft within 48 hours.

[Dated One Week Ago]
310 Azalea Lane
Meridian, MS 39203

Mr. Keith Harkins
President
Dixie Industries
3128 Northeast Industrial Park Road
Meridian, MS 39201

Dear Mr. Harkins:

The Dixie Industries Women's Group has asked me to write to you on behalf of the women of our company. We have some questions and concerns that we would like to share with you.

The first concerns promotion opportunities for women at Dixie Industries. According to Mr. Darryl Robbins of the DI Human Resources Department, this company employs approximately 1,798 employees in various jobs. Mr. Robbins also says that about 720 of them are women. That seems to be about 40 percent of the Dixie Industries workers who are female.

At the same time, Mr. Robbins told me that the company has about two dozen upper management positions here, but only four are staffed by women. That's not much better than 16 percent. This company has, according to its own HR Department, 54 managers and 25 senior managers. Of those, just seven women are managers and only two are senior managers. In addition to that, one of just two female executives, Mrs. Dorothy Wyatt, left the company last year. Some of her close friends say she left because of the general working environment here and the lack of opportunity for women.

An informal survey of other firms in the textile industry (see table below) shows that Dixie Industries is below average in promotion opportunities for women employees. West Point Pepperell in Georgia has told a member of our group that 35 percent of their senior managers are women. That's twice the average of Dixie Industries. Berkshire Mills of Alabama told us more or less the same thing. On top of that, both of those firms offer college tuition and specialized training to their employees which Dixie does not.

The fact of the matter, Mr. Harkins, remains that Dixie Industries has not promoted a woman to a management position in over two years. Dixie does nothing to encourage and retain good women in management. And Dixie has done nothing to show current women employees that they have any future with this company. The only conclusion our group can draw is that the company is demonstrating a continuing and pervasive bias in promotions in favor of men.

The second significant issue that I have been asked to bring to your attention concerns training opportunities. Most of the promotions to supervisory positions on the plant floor have gone to people with advanced training in textile production and automated loom operations. Those people, with very few exceptions, have been men. We

**TABLE 11.2** Women Managers in Regional Textile Mills, 2018–2019: Mississippi, Alabama, Georgia

| Mill Name | Location | Employees | Managers | Sr. Mgrs. | Women Mgrs. |
|-----------|----------|-----------|----------|-----------|-------------|
| Pepperell | West Point, GA | 2,650 | 78 | 33 | 36 (32%) |
| Berkshire | Prattville, AL | 2,245 | 72 | 30 | 19 (19%) |
| Hoover | Anniston, AL | 1,277 | 36 | 21 | 16 (28%) |
| Cannon | Columbus, GA | 2,130 | 65 | 29 | 28 (30%) |
| Dixie | Meridian, MS | 1,798 | 54 | 25 | 11 (14%) |

would like to know when the company plans to establish a fair and equitable means for selecting employees for training, especially training that is likely to lead to better employment opportunities.

Mr. Harkins, I have personally been employed here over six years and am certified as a master loom technician. My reason for writing to you is to explain that a number of women employees of Dixie Industries are upset about these facts and concerned that no opportunity for a better future exists for them here. On their behalf, I respectfully ask that you explain what the company plans to do.

Sincerely,

Mrs. Linda S. Feldman

## WRITING ASSIGNMENT

Please respond in writing to the issues presented in this case by preparing two documents: a communication strategy memo and a professional business letter.

In preparing these documents, you may assume the role of the Vice President for Human Resources for Dixie Industries. Your task is to provide advice to Mr. Keith Harkins regarding the issues he and the company are facing. Or, you may identify yourself as an external management consultant who has been asked by the company to provide advice to Mr. Harkins.

Either way, you must prepare a strategy memo addressed to Keith Harkins, Chairman and Chief Executive Officer of the company, that summarizes the details of the case, rank-orders critical issues, discusses their implications (what they mean and why they matter), offers specific recommendations for action (assigning ownership and suspense dates for each) and shows how to communicate the solution to all who are affected by the recommendations.

You must also prepare a professional business letter for Mr. Harkins' signature. That document should be addressed to Mrs. Linda Feldman. If you have questions about either of these documents, please consult your instructor.

## ACKNOWLEDGMENTS

This case was prepared from field interviews by James S. O'Rourke, IV, Teaching Professor of Management, as the basis for class discussion rather than to illustrate either effective or ineffective handling of an administrative situation. Personal and corporate identities have been disguised.

# Case 11.3: The National Football League

## Tackling Difficult Positions

I am not going to stand up to show pride in a flag for a country that oppresses black people and people of color. To me, this is bigger than football and it would be selfish on my part to look the other way.

~ Colin Kaepernick, former San Francisco 49ers quarterback[1]

## INTRODUCTION

Just before the 2017 football season began, the National Football League (NFL) found itself facing a serious threat to its viewership. NFL Commissioner Roger Goodell realized that football fans were shifting their attention from the game itself to a controversial player protest movement occurring before each game even started. Some fans were filled with rage and demanded to know how Goodell could allow such behavior while others sympathized with the protests.[2] Goodell's office would need to take action before some football viewers decided enough was enough and abandoned the NFL forever.

## THE INCIDENT

At the beginning of the 2016 preseason, the San Francisco 49ers' quarterback, Colin Kaepernick, remained seated on the team bench as the national anthem played. Although few noticed it at the time, this was the beginning of a sweeping movement that brought the attention of national news coverage. Kaepernick chose not to stand for the national anthem, in protest of police brutality and social injustice.

One of Kaepernick's, teammates, Eric Reid, recalled that he, "didn't notice at the time, and neither did the news media. It wasn't until after [their] third preseason game on Aug. 26, 2016, that his protest gained national attention, and the backlash against him began."[3] Before the next game, Reid approached Kaepernick, wanting to affect the social justice movement in a positive manner. The two decided that they would kneel for the national anthem, a more humble and powerful gesture than simply sitting on the bench. Reid noted that their posture in kneeling reminded him of a "flag flown at half-mast to mark a tragedy."[4]

Critics of Kaepernick's actions rebuked him for not showing respect to the Star-Spangled Banner, which honors the brave Americans who serve the country. On the other side, many individuals praised Kaepernick for bringing attention to social issues, such as police brutality. The debate continued, and each game, viewers attentively watched the national anthem in anticipation of what he would do. This situation quickly grew, as teammates, competitors, other sports players and even celebrities began to take their own stances on the national anthem.

The divisiveness and widespread coverage of the national anthem protest created a difficult business problem for the NFL. The league office, and commissioner Goodell, had to respond. Some fans praised what Kaepernick had started, while others called for fines and suspensions for his actions before each game.

## THE NATIONAL FOOTBALL LEAGUE

Rebranded from the American Professional Football Association (APFA) in 1920, the NFL slowly built professional American football from an unpopular game that paled in comparison to college football into the country's most watched sport. With only 18 teams in 1920, the NFL grew steadily to 32 franchised teams throughout metropolitan areas in the U.S. Each team competes each year to win the NFL championship game, the Super Bowl.[5] The league activities, rules and functions are overseen by Commissioner Roger Goodell. The commissioner is appointed by a majority vote from the 32 team owners and can only be removed by a vote of more than three-fourths.[6]

Today, the NFL is the undisputed king of American sports leagues, leading the industry in the U.S. in revenue year over year, but it was not always so.[7] The NFL hardly competed with Major League Baseball (MLB), affectionately known as "America's Pastime" since the 1850s.[8] The National Hockey League (NHL) also offered alternatives for sports fans. Furthermore, with the inception of the National Basketball Association (NBA) in 1949, the NFL became classified as just one of four major American professional sports leagues.

The 1990s were the pivotal decade for disruption in American professional sports. MLB had dominated the American sports market since its inception in 1903, but was overtaken by the NBA in the 1990s. With immensely popular superstars, including Larry Bird, Magic Johnson and Michael Jordan, the NBA enjoyed massive popularity as America watched the Chicago Bulls become a dynasty much like the New York Yankees. The dynamic Jordan began to decline in the late 1990s, however, and the NBA's brief burst of success was soon overshadowed by the NFL.

As the 1990s came to a close, the NFL began to seize more market share from MLB, the NBA and the NHL to become America's most popular sport. The most significant factor allowing the NFL to overtake the other leagues was nothing strategic on the league's part. It was simply massive fan dissatisfaction with the other sports. The MLB, NBA and NHL were all plagued by strikes or lockouts in the 1990s over negotiations with player unions. Baseball even cancelled its World Series Championship in 1994. Fans, fed up with cancelled games and player drama, devoted more attention to the strike-free NFL.[9]

The other major factor contributing to the rapid increase in popularity for the NFL was a phenomenon known as fantasy football. The virtual competition traced its origins to the early 1960s, but it was not widespread until Yahoo! Sports offered free online fantasy football leagues in 2001. With ready access to free leagues, fantasy players began to obsessively research player statistics, check injury statuses, and watch games that did not even feature their favorite teams, just to keep track of their fantasy teams.[10] Other leagues tried to catch up but by 2018, fantasy football was still by far the most played fantasy sport.[11]

## REVENUE GENERATION

The NFL is a trade association with 32 franchises that distributes its profits among the teams.[12] The NFL's revenue is derived from numerous sources, with the major cash streams being corporate sponsorships; broadcasting service contracts from television, satellite, Internet and radio; and merchandise sales.[13] The NFL is a private organization and does not release earnings, but was thought to have generated some $14 billion in revenue in 2017.[14] Commissioner Goodell has publicly stated his goal of increasing revenue to $25 billion by 2027.[15]

## THE NATIONAL ANTHEM IN THE NFL

The NFL heavily focuses on game day organization and cherishes consistency among its pregame routines. The NFL game operations manual gives instructions on how games should be run in order to ensure that everything runs smoothly and improve viewer experience. Regarding the U.S. National Anthem, the game operations manual states:

> The National Anthem must be played prior to every NFL game, and all players must be on the sideline for the National Anthem. During the National Anthem, players on the field and bench area should stand at attention, face the flag, hold helmets in their left hand, and refrain from talking. The home team should ensure that the American flag is in good condition. It should be pointed out to players and coaches that we continue to be judged by the public in this area of respect for the flag and our country. Failure to be on the field by the start of the National Anthem may result in discipline, such as fines, suspensions, and/or the forfeiture of draft choice(s) for violations of the above, including first offenses.

Punishments "may" result from noncompliance with these rules. Whether or not punishment is issued from the league office is determined solely by Commissioner Goodell. Individual owners additionally have the right to punish or discipline their players as they see fit.[16]

## THE FIRST AMENDMENT

The First Amendment to the U.S. Constitution, adopted in 1791, reads:

> Congress shall make no law respecting an establishment of religion, or prohibiting the free exercise thereof; or abridging the freedom of speech, or of the press; or the right of the people peaceably to assemble, and to petition the Government for a redress of grievances.[17]

Players participating in the anthem protests claim that their right to peaceably assemble and protest stems from the First Amendment. The NFL, as a private organization, has the legal right to set its own cultural standards and can punish players for protesting, since the First Amendment was intended to apply only when the U.S. government tries to restrict freedoms.[18]

## HISTORICAL COMMITMENT TO DIVERSITY

The NFL was a segregated sports league for the first 26 years of its history. Although black athletes competed in earlier football leagues comprising athletic clubs, the big business of the NFL did not welcome blacks into their ranks until Bill Willis, Marion Motley, Kenny Washington and Woody Strode signed their first NFL contracts in 1946.[19] This was one year before the NFL's biggest competitor, Major League Baseball (MLB), famously broke the color barrier with the signing of Jackie Robinson by the Brooklyn Dodgers in 1947.

## NFL COMMISSIONER ROGER GOODELL

As commissioner, Roger Goodell oversees negotiations with media partners, players, owners, refs, and he oversees the quality of the league. Part of this duty involves overseeing and implementing the rules. If league rules are broken, Goodell can employ suspensions, fines and other penal tools. Though the league does not require players to stand for the national anthem, it does suggest it.[20]

In September of 2016, Commissioner Goodell commented on the national anthem situation and Kaepernick, according to the NFL Network:

> Well my personal thoughts are . . . I support our players when they want to see change in society, and we don't live in a perfect society. We live in an imperfect society. On the other hand, we believe very strongly in patriotism in the NFL. I personally believe very strongly in that. I think it's important to have respect for our country, for our flag, for the people who make our country better; for law enforcement, and for our military who are out fighting for our freedoms and our ideals.
>
> These are all important things for us, and that moment is a very important moment. So, I don't necessarily agree with what he is doing. We encourage our players to be respectful in that time and I like to think of it as a moment where we can unite as a country. And that's what we need more, and that's what I think football does – it unites our country. So, I would like to see us focusing on our similarities and trying to bring people together.
>
> Players have a platform, and it's his right to do that. We encourage them to be respectful and it's important for them to do that.[21]

Following Goddell's comments, players including Kaepernick continued to kneel during the national anthem during the rest of the 2016 season. The issue continued on into the 2017 season, with each game bringing more coverage of the protests. However, the protests had moved beyond Kaepernick

## REACTIONS

Kaepernick ended up opting out of the final year of his contract in March 2017, in order to enter unrestricted free agency. Kaepernick's on-field performance had been declining since 2015, when he suffered an injury. The 49ers posted two wins and 14 losses in the 2016 season, Kaepernick's final season with the franchise. Although he posted a 90.7 quarterback rating, Kaepernick was never picked up in the offseason, and remained undrafted through the 2017 season.[22] Off the field, Colin Kaepernick was named "Citizen of the Year" for 2017 by *GQ Magazine*, for his social justice stance.[23]

## PITTSBURGH STEELERS

On September 24, 2017, the Pittsburgh Steelers took on Chicago Bears. Like every game that season, people paid attention to what teams did during the national anthem. The Pittsburgh Steelers, under coach Mike Tomlin, opted to stay in the tunnel as a team for the national anthem. Outside the entrance of the tunnel stood a sole Steelers offensive lineman, Alejandro Villanueva. The left tackle was an Army ranger and served three tours in Afghanistan.[24]

The next day, Steelers' quarterback Ben Roethlisberger issued a statement, wishing his team had approached the situation in a different manner. He explained that the choice was meant to show unity, and that everyone was supposed to be in the tunnel. The idea was to be unified inside the tunnel, and not out on the field where any choice, whether it be sit, stand or kneel, brought scrutiny by the media.[25]

Immediately, news reports portrayed Villanueva as an American hero, juxtaposed by an absent team. Unfortunately, this was not what the players intended. Villanueva explained that he wanted to be with his team but was separated from the rest of the group shortly before the national anthem began. As a result, he was the only one still on the field, and he did not want to be walking off the field into the tunnel as the anthem began playing.[26] So, he stopped where he was, arm over chest, and faced the flag.

## JERRY JONES

One of the first owners to react to the protest movement was Jerry Jones of the Dallas Cowboys, an NFL franchise with an estimated value of $4.2 billion.[27] Jones made it clear what would happen if his players took a knee, saying, "If there's anything that is disrespectful to the flag, then we will not play. Understand? If we are disrespecting the flag, then we will not play."[28] After several weeks had passed and the tension had increased between NFL players and fans, Jones had a change of heart, and he decided to try to unite both groups. On September 25, 2017, the Dallas Cowboys played the Arizona Cardinals.

Before the national anthem was played, every member of the Dallas Cowboys, including Jones, took a knee in support of the protests, yet as soon as the national anthem began to play, every member of the Dallas cowboys stood up out of respect for the flag. Newscasters and analysts viewed this act as appropriate because it brought attention to the racial equality issue while also respecting the flag.[29] Through Jones's leadership, players were able to both stand up for social justice through the act of taking a knee before the national anthem, as well as honor the flag during the national anthem.

## PRESIDENT TRUMP

The 45th President of the United States, Donald J. Trump, made a number of public remarks about the players' kneeling protests. Mr. Trump said he believes that kneeling for the national anthem does not have to do with race but, rather, everything to do with disrespecting the country. He called attention to the situation via Twitter by posting:

> The NFL should've suspended some of these players for one game. Not fire them. Suspended them for one game and then if they did it again, it could be one game then two games then three games and then for the season. You wouldn't have people disrespecting our country right now.[30]

Several weeks later, the President discussed how the American people were upset with the kneeling incidents, causing decline of the viewership over the course of the 2017 season. In addition, the President referred to the players who kneeled during the national anthem as "sons of bitches."[31] Outraged, the players fired back at the President. One player, Julius Thomas, spoke out about the President's words as if they were an attack on justice, saying, "The President is not concerned with the people who feel less privileged in this country."[32] Unable to reach middle ground, both sides continued to feel disrespected and tensions grew.

## VICE PRESIDENT PENCE LEAVES GAME

Vice President Michael Pence attended an NFL game between the Indianapolis Colts and the San Francisco 49ers on October 8, 2017. This game was a high-profile event for the NFL because it featured the retirement of Peyton Manning's jersey by the Colts. Manning was a quarterback famous for winning a record five Most Valuable Player awards. While the national anthem was playing, some of the players on both sides kneeled, as was then common in NFL games. Pence noticed players kneeling, left the game and flew back to a scheduled event in Las Vegas in protest of the players' disrespect. Pence later posted via Twitter his response to the NFL players who were kneeling:

> I left today's Colts game because President Trump and I will not dignify any event that disrespects our soldiers, our Flag, or our National Anthem. At a time when so many Americans are inspiring our nation with their courage, resolve, and resilience, now, more than ever, we should rally around our Flag and everything that unites us. While everyone is entitled to their own options, I don't think it's too much to ask NFL players to respect the flag and our National Anthem. I stand with President Trump, I stand with our soldiers, and I will always stand for our Flag and National Anthem.[33]

Later that evening, Mr. Trump reached out to the media and told reporters that he asked Vice President Pence to leave the game in the event of players taking a knee during the anthem. Some of the players expressed their disdain for the Vice President's actions, calling his departure a publicity stunt.[34] After the incident, President Trump even threatened to call for boycotts of NFL games.[35]

## NFL LOSING MONEY FROM PROTESTS

In the first eight weeks of 2017, studies revealed that the kneeling movement caused a 5 percent decline in NFL game viewership in comparison to the previous season.[36] On the other hand, a higher than average rate of injury among league's top players could also have caused declining viewership. Some of the NFL stars injured included Andrew Luck, J.J. Watt, Richard Sherman, Odell Beckham Jr., David Johnson and Joe Thomas.[37] Either way, a substantial number of viewers stopped watching professional football. Another study surveyed individuals on whether the kneeling protests would cause them to become more likely, less likely or indifferent to watching an NFL game. The results demonstrated that 32 percent were less likely to watch the game, while 13 percent of individuals were more likely to watch the game, with the remaining 55 percent indifferent.[38]

In the face of the controversy, Under Armour and Nike have continued to sponsor protesting athletes. The two companies differed slightly in their support, however, with Under Armour issuing a public statement illuminating its loyalty to the American Flag in addition to athletes' freedoms, while Nike mentioned only athlete's rights:

> UNDER ARMOUR: The company "stands for the flag and by our athletes for free speech, expression and a unified America."[39]
>
> NIKE: "Nike supports athletes and their right to freedom of expression on issues that are of great importance to our society."[40]

Some sponsors did choose to end their relationships with the NFL. Check Into Cash decided to pull the company's advertisement during the games for the remainder of the season. The founder and CEO of Check Into Cash, Allen Jones, said "Our companies will not condone unpatriotic behavior!"[41] With the NFL being a private company and not reporting revenues, the effect of sponsorship loss is unclear, but some sponsors have made their support of the players very clear.

## ACKNOWLEDGMENTS

This case was prepared by research assistants Kevin Bradley, Matthew Morcio and Alec Sims under the direction of James O'Rourke, Teaching Professor of Management, as the basis for class discussion rather than to illustrate either effective or ineffective handling of an administrative situation. Information was gathered from corporate as well as public sources.

## NOTES

1  Curtis, Charles. "Colin Kaepernick: I Won't Stand 'to Show Pride in a Flag for a Country That Oppresses Black People'," *USA Today*, Gannett Satellite Information Network, August 27, 2016. Online at ftw.usatoday.com/2016/08/col in-kaepernick-49ers-national-anthem-sit-explains.

2  Arthur, Kenneth. "Why Fan Reaction to NFL Protests is About Racism, Not Patriotism," *Rolling Stone*, September 26, 2017. Online at www.rollingstone.com/sports/news/fan-reaction-to-nfl-national-anthem-protests-about-racism-w505387.

3  Reid, Eric. "Eric Reid: Why Colin Kaepernick and I Decided to Take a Knee," *The New York Times*, September 25, 2017. Online at www.nytimes.com/2017/09/25/opinion/colin-kaepernick-football-protests.html.

4  Ibid.

5  Smith, Brandon J. "Football Origins, Growth and History of the Game," *The People History*. Online at www.thepeoplehistory.com/footballhistory.html.

6  Jhabvala, Nicki. "What Would It Take to Remove Roger Goodell as NFL Commissioner?" *The Denver Post*, Digital First Media, September 9, 2014. Online at blogs.denverpost.com/broncos/2014/09/09/take-remove-roger-goodell-nfl-commissioner/29392/.

7  Kutz, Steven. "NFL Took in $13 Billion in Revenue Last Season," *MarketWatch*, July 2, 2016. Online at www.market watch.com/story/the-nfl-made-13-billion-last-season-see-how-it-stacks-up-against-other-leagues-2016–07–01.

8   Curtis, Bryan. "Debating America's Pastime(s)," *The New York Times*, February 1, 2009. Online at www.nytimes. com/2009/02/01/sports/01iht-01curtis.19835372.html.

9   Schottey, Michael. "How the NFL Became America's Sport," *Bleacher Report*, July 3, 2013. Online at bleacherreport.com/ articles/1691465-how-the-nfl-became-americas-sport.

10  Ibid.

11  Gillies, Trent. "The $26B Market Nobody Can Agree Is Legal," *CNBC*, February 7, 2016. Online at www.cnbc. com/2016/02/05/fantasy-sports-the-lucrative-market-that-may-be-legal.html.

12  Lee, Angela. "NFL: Non-Profit or Corporation? Which Team Are You on?" *Rocket Lawyer*, January 29, 2015. Online at www. rocketlawyer.com/blog/nfl-non-profit-or-corporation-which-team-are-you-on-916494.

13  Ejiochi, Ike. "How the NFL Makes the Most Money of Any Pro Sport," *CNBC*, September 4, 2014. Online at www.cnbc. com/2014/09/04/how-the-nfl-makes-the-most-money-of-any-pro-sport.html.

14  Kaplan, Daniel. "NFL Revenue Reaches $14B, Fueled by Media," *Sports Business Journal*, March 6, 2017. Online at www. sportsbusinessdaily.com/Journal/Issues/2017/03/06/Leagues-and-Governing-Bodies/NFL-revenue.aspx.

15  Kaplan, Daniel. "Goodell Sets Revenue Goal of $25 Billion by 2027 for NFL," *Sporting News*, April 5, 2010. Online at www. sportingnews.com/nfl/news/151602-sbj-goodell-sets-revenue-goal-25-billion-2027-for-nfl.

16  Fitzpatrick, Alex. "Here's What NFL Rules Say About Standing for the National Anthem," *Sports Illustrated*, September 25, 2017. Online at www.si.com/nfl/2017/09/25/does-nfl-require-players-stand-national-anthem.

17  "First Amendment – U.S. Constitution," *Findlaw*. Online at constitution.findlaw.com/amendment1.html.

18  Bussing, Heather. "Is There Free Speech at Work?" *HR Examiner*, October 15, 2012. Online at www.hrexaminer.com/ is-there-free-speech-at-work.

19  Patmas, Michael. "Who Broke the NFL Pro Football Color Barrier?" *Bleacher Report*, February 18, 2013. Online at bleacher-report.com/articles/1533593-nfl-pro-football-the-men-who-broke-the-nfl-color-barrier.

20  "Roger Goodell on Colin Kaepernick: 'We Believe Very Strongly in Patriotism in the NFL'." *USA TODAY*, September 7, 2016. Online at www.usatoday.com/story/sports/nfl/2016/09/07/goodell-doesnt-agree-with-kaepernicks-actions/89958636/.

21  Ibid.

22  "Division Standings," *National Football League*. Online at www.nfl.com/standings/division/2016/REG.

23  "Colin Kaepernick Is GQ's 2017 Citizen of the Year," *GQ*, November 13, 2017. Online at www.gq.com/story/colin-kaeper nick-cover-men-of-the-year.

24  Rapaport, Daniel. "Ben Roethlisberger on Steelers Sitting Out Anthem: 'I Wish We Approached it Differently'," *Sports Illus-trated*, September 25, 2017. Online at www.si.com/nfl/2017/09/25/ben-roethlisberger-pittsburgh-steelers-national-an them-protest.

25  Ibid.

26  Wilson, Ryan. "Alejandro Villanueva to Media: I Won't Be Used As a Tool to Push Political Agendas," *CBS Sports*, October 1, 2017. Online at www.cbssports.com/nfl/news/alejandro-villanueva-to-media-i-wont-be-used-as-a-tool-to-push-political-agendas/.

27  "Dallas Cowboys on the Forbes NFL Team Valuations List," *Forbes Magazine*. Online at www.forbes.com/teams/dallas-cow boys/.

28  Rosenberg, Michael. "Will Jerry Jones Really Not Play His Stars If They Kneel During the Anthem, or Is It Just a Show?" *Sports Illustrated*, October 9, 2017. Online at www.si.com/nfl/2017/10/09/jerry-jones-dallas-cowboys-kneeling-nation al-anthem-protests.

29  Ibid.

30  Chavez, Chris. "President Trump: People of Our Country Are Very Angry at the NFL," *SI.com*, October 16, 2017. Online at www.si.com/nfl/2017/10/16/donald-trump-nfl-national-anthem-protests-kneeling-hillary-clinton-comments.

31  Kurtz, Jason. "Trump Remark Moves NFL Player to Kneel during Anthem," *CNN*, December 21, 2017. Online at www.cnn. com/2017/09/25/politics/dolphins-tight-end-julius-thomas-national-anthem-kneel-erin-burnett-outfront-cnntv/index. html.

32  Ibid.

33  Watkins, Eli. "Pence Leaves Colts Game after Protest during Anthem," *CNN*, October 9, 2017. Online at www.cnn. com/2017/10/08/politics/vice-president-mike-pence-nfl-protest/index.html.

34  Ibid.

35  Ibid.

36  Haring, Bruce. "NFL Anthem Protests Week 9: Vin Scully Speaks Out as Finger-Pointing Continues," *Deadline*, November 5, 2017. Online at www.deadline.com/2017/11/nfl-anthem-protests-week-9-vin-scully-speaks-out-1202202265.

37  CNN Wire. "NFL's TV Ratings Drop Following a Season of Injuries, Anthem Protests," *WGNO*, January 8, 2018. Online at wgno.com/2018/01/08/nfls-tv-ratings-drop-following-a-season-of-injuries-anthem-protests.

38  Ozanian, Mike. "Confirmed: NFL Losing Millions of TV Viewers Because of National Anthem Protests," *Forbes Maga-zine*, October 13, 2016. Online at www.forbes.com/sites/mikeozanian/2016/10/05/confirmed-nfl-losing-millions-of-tv-viewers-because-of-national-anthem-protests/#6920484226c2.

39   Astor, Maggie. "How N.F.L. Sponsors Have Reacted to 'Take a Knee' Protests," *The New York Times*, September 27, 2017. Online at www.nytimes.com/2017/09/27/business/nfl-sponsors-anthem-protests.html.

40   Ibid.

41   Prestigiacomo, Amanda. "BACKLASH: NFL Loses First Sponsor Over National Anthem Protest," *The Daily Wire*, September 28, 2017. Online at www.dailywire.com/news/21660/backlash-nfl-loses-first-sponsor-over-national-amanda-prestigiacomo.

# CHAPTER 12

# Business Meetings That Work

Say the word in a small group of your colleagues. Go ahead, say it. *Meeting.* Suggest that your group schedule a meeting; tell them that you think they can resolve the issue they're discussing by setting up a meeting. Now watch the nonverbal reactions: eyes roll, noses scrunch up, people begin hyperventilating. Eyes that don't roll begin to glaze over.

You know the reason: No one likes meetings. "Too many of them are a waste of time," says Marge Boberschmidt. "Too many people walk out of too many meetings feeling that they didn't accomplish anything." Boberschmidt is a former public relations executive at AT&T who now runs her own consulting firm – planning meetings. "My greatest fear is that people will leave a meeting I've planned – having spent time, money, energy, and all sorts of lost opportunity – and come to the conclusion that it just wasn't worthwhile."[1]

Boberschmidt's reactions are common among managers who know that people and productivity are at the top of their list of current concerns. "People are my most important asset," says Bill Mountford, founder of a chain of Midwestern restaurants called *Studebagels.* "And I know that, even though I have information to share with them and they have information to share with me, I'm almost certain that having a meeting is among the least productive things I can do."[2]

Meetings are the most universal – and universally despised – part of business life. But bad meetings do more than ruin an otherwise pleasant day. William R. Daniels, senior consultant at American Consulting & Training in Mill Valley, California, is adamant about the real stakes: Bad meetings make bad companies. "Meetings matter because that's where an organization's culture perpetuates itself," he says:

> Meetings are how an organization says, "You are a member." So if every day we go to boring meetings full of boring people, then we can't help but think that this is a boring company. Bad meetings are a source of negative messages about our company and ourselves.[3]

Bad meetings waste time and money, but they may also harm employee health. Professors in the U.S. and Britain recently surveyed 676 employees, who said they spend an average of 5.6 hours a week in meetings. The more time they spent in meetings they considered ineffective, says Steven Rogelberg, a principal researcher, the more gloomy and anxious they became about their jobs.[4]

It's not supposed to be this way. In a business world that is faster, tougher, leaner and more downsized than ever, you might expect the sheer demands of competition (not to mention the impact of e-mail, texting and groupware) to curb our appetite for meetings. In reality, according to author Eric Matson, the *opposite* may be true. As more work becomes teamwork and fewer people remain to do the work that exists, the number of meetings is likely to increase rather than decrease.[5]

Roger Mosvick, a communications professor at Macalester College in St. Paul, Minnesota, says meetings are on the upswing. The average number of meetings jumped from seven to about ten a week, based on surveys of business professionals done over a 15-year period. Many participants, says Mosvick, reported that they don't even know why they're attending some meetings. "It's an alarming statistic," he says. "Many meetings are just mind-numbing."[6]

Teresa Taylor, chief operating officer of Quest, begins each of her meetings by saying, "Do we all know why we're here?" When asked if she really does that, she replied, "Yes, because so many people say, 'No, I don't know why I was invited.' It's usually the bigger meetings – not so much my direct report team." Her motivation is to get everyone on the same page:

> I get invited to a lot of meetings where someone wants to brief me, or bring me up to speed on something. So I open with 'Do we all know why we're here? Are you going to ask me for something at the end?' I try to get that out right away. It's amazing, there will be eight people in the room and they all have a different answer of what's going on there.[7]

Meetings are also a time drain. Business professionals spend about half of their time in meetings, according to the 3M Meeting Network, an online resource covering meeting issues. As much as 50 percent of that time is unproductive, and up to 25 percent of meeting time covers irrelevant issues, according to professionals surveyed by 3M. "People just have a tendency to ramble," says J. Doug Batchelor, owner of Dalcom Systems, a software firm in Fort Worth, Texas. "There's entirely too much time spent on meetings." And meetings can trigger stress. Workers asked to rank emotionally charged situations on the job listed people taking up more time than necessary with meetings as a top problem, according to a survey by the American Management Association. "So often people get into a meeting and talk around an issue," says Beryl Loeb, a consultant and executive training specialist in Needham, Massachusetts. "Then they have to meet again."[8]

A recent survey of 613 workers by Office Team, a temporary-staffing agency in Menlo Park, California, indicated what most workers think about the subject. On a list of workplace timewasters, "meetings that last too long" came in first, chosen by 27 percent of the respondents. According to Patti Hathaway, an author and change management consultant, "Nobody can afford to waste time anymore, sitting in a meeting that isn't productive. And the reality is, most corporate meetings are a colossal waste of time."[9]

## WHAT'S THE MOTIVATION FOR MEETING?

So why do people hold meetings? Most management experts tell us that there are really three reasons: First, because they're scheduled and attendance is not optional; second, because participants have ulterior or non-meeting-related motives for attending (those meetings are usually in nice hotels located far from the company headquarters); and third, because they have no other options for achieving their goals. There is one other reason for meeting, and that's the potential for human contact. "The drive for social connection is a very strong one," says Nicholas Epley, a professor of behavioral science at the University of Chicago's Booth School of Business. "Sitting in a cubicle is stupefying and isolating," he says, "only intensifying a social need."[10]

In some industries where product development and marketing programs rely heavily on teamwork across departments, meetings are simply unavoidable. Survey results published by the Annenberg School of Communications at the University of Southern California and the University of Minnesota's Training and Development Research Center confirm what the people at 3M found: Executives, on average, spend 40 to 50 percent of their working hours in meetings. Further evidence of the pervasiveness of meetings comes from facility consultant Jon Ryburg, who says he advises corporate clients to provide twice as much meeting space as they did 20 years ago.[11]

According to a recent survey by a large telecommunication company, managers now attend an average of 60 meetings a month, more than a third of which are difficult or unproductive.[12] In some professions, that percentage is much higher. "I must spend three-quarters of my working day in meetings," says Nancy Hobor. "I meet with our CFO regularly. I meet with my staff, with investment analysts, with mutual fund managers, with dozens of different people during the day." Hobor is the vice president for corporate communications and investor relations at W. W. Grainger and Company in Lake Forest, Illinois. "Time to myself is a luxury, so I have to use it wisely. I also have to use my meeting time wisely, as well as the time I take from other people."[13]

## SO, WHY MEET?

An unspoken but widely accepted rule of business meetings is this: You should never, ever call a meeting – especially one that involves the time, energy and budget of a considerable number of people – unless you have no other choice. A formal meeting is a communication alternative available when you cannot accomplish your goals or objectives in any other way. It is, in other words, the communication tool of last resort, after you have considered and discarded other forms of information exchange. Professional meeting consultants see six legitimate reasons for taking people's time, spending their company's money and devoting both energy and effort into a meeting:

- *To motivate.* A sales force, for instance, may get the jump start it needs to begin a highly competitive new season by meeting with people who can provide both motivation and methods for successful selling.
- *To educate.* An investor relations manager may meet with analysts or fund managers to brief them on new earnings growth projections, an update to the company's strategic plans, or a proposed product line.
- *To recreate.* Team building exercises often take place off-site in a hotel or conference center or, perhaps, in a wooded, outdoors setting designed to build confidence and unity.
- *To initiate.* Gathering employees together prior to a new product launch or brand line extension might help to explain product features and the market position management is hoping to sell to customers.
- *To network.* Members of professional societies and trade associations often gather to meet and speak with each other as much as they do to hear scheduled speakers or participate in carefully planned panel discussions or breakout sessions.
- *To reward.* Management can show employees that they genuinely care about them by offering a trip – often with family members accompanying them – to a company meeting in a desirable location (think warm in the winter, cool in the summer). A resort hotel or theme park can combine the professional and social goals of meeting, as long as costs are kept within reason and recreational goals are specified as an important part of the meeting agenda.[14]

## WHAT IS A BUSINESS MEETING?

A business meeting is a gathering in which a purposeful exchange or transaction occurs among two or more people with a common interest, purpose or problem. Many meetings, of course, turn out to be neither purposeful nor productive, but the best of them can help to solve problems, build consensus, provide training, gather opinion and move an organization forward. Many, in fact, are not only productive but actually fun.

## WHEN SHOULD I CALL A MEETING?

As we've already noted, people meet for a variety of reasons. Generally, they gather together to move group actions forward, often referred to as a *task focus*. To meet this goal, participants usually do two things in meetings: They present information to others and they collaborate. That is, they review, evaluate, discuss, solve problems and decide what to do next. When any of these actions is essential to your business, consider a meeting.

As we've also noted, people want to meet for social reasons. Numerous studies show that people gather in meetings because they feel a need to belong, a need to achieve or make a difference of some sort or because of a desire to communicate, to build and share a common reality.[15] A particularly interesting study by Professor Vanessa Bohns of Cornell University has found that people tend to overestimate the power of their persuasiveness via text-based communication, and underestimate the power of their persuasiveness via face-to-face communication.

According to Professor Bohns, "Participants who made requests over e-mail felt essentially just as confident about the effectiveness of their requests as those who made their requests face-to-face, even though *face-to-face requests were 34 times more effective* than e-mailed ones."[16]

Why else should you consider meeting? Here are ten more reasons why a meeting may be your best communication option:

| | |
|---|---|
| Talk about goals. | Build morale. |
| Listen to reports. | Reach a consensus. |
| Train people. | Discover or solve problems. |
| Explain plans and programs. | Gather opinions. |
| Tell people what they're supposed to do and how they're to do it. | Keep things moving. |

## WHEN SHOULD I NOT CALL A MEETING?

You should consider some other communication alternative when a phone call, a memo or an e-mail message would do just as well. Frequently, managers think they must meet with people – usually their employees and coworkers – in order to simply pass along information. If the flow of information is entirely one-way, you certainly should consider alternative routes for it. Unless the information is highly sensitive or personal – the death of a colleague or the sale of the company – a face-to-face meeting is usually not necessary.

You should also not plan a meeting when:

- *A key person is not available*. Often, a substitute can fill in for a colleague, but in some instances, it simply makes no sense to meet without a particular person in the room.
- *Participants don't have time to prepare*. If the group needs certain data or information to guide its discussion, make sure you have time to gather and distribute it. If preliminary reading or small group discussions must take place first, don't short-circuit your intentions by scheduling a meeting before all of that can happen.
- *Personality conflicts or the plans of higher management might make the meeting a waste of time*. If the issue you plan to discuss has become highly polarized in your organization, gathering people on opposite sides of the issue may provoke conflict rather than discussion. Preliminary, one-on-one meetings may be necessary to smooth the way for larger discussions to follow. Of course, if you know (or think you know) that organizational executives have other plans, a meeting to discuss the issue *may* be unproductive. Planning a rebuttal or response might be a good reason for meeting, but if the issue has already been resolved higher up in the organization, save your time and energy. Cancel the meeting.

## WHAT SHOULD I CONSIDER AS I PLAN FOR A MEETING?

Three issues – the *objective*, the *agenda* and the *participants* – are essential to the success of any meeting, regardless of size, length or purpose.

### The Objective

Your foremost consideration should be your purpose in getting together. What is the meeting's objective? Why is this important? If participants aren't clear on your purpose for meeting, they'll make up one of their own. When that happens, it's easy to lose control and watch your participants wander off in a dozen different directions.

How can you build clarity into your purpose for meeting? Christopher Avery, a communications consultant who owns Partnerwerks in Austin, Texas, thinks the following steps may help. First, consider why you want people to meet. Ask yourself what you will accomplish face-to-face (or via conference call) that you wouldn't accomplish otherwise. Are you meeting to share information, build relationships, make decisions, design something or solve a problem? After you know the objective of the meeting, think about the outcomes you're hoping for and write down at least two of them: What is the *perfect* outcome for this meeting? What is your *minimum acceptable* outcome?

Next, validate the objective and outcomes to the best of your ability. Can you reasonably expect this group to produce your outcome in the time allotted? What can they achieve? What sort of preparation will they need? Include others whom you trust in this process if it will help you achieve clarity. Finally, start the meeting by clearly stating the objective and outcomes. Make sure all of the participants understand the objective and are willing to work toward it.[17]

## The Agenda

Create a solid agenda. It's nothing more than an outline of things to be discussed at the meeting, along with a time budget for each item. To create an effective agenda, ask three questions: To achieve our objectives, what do we need to do in this meeting? What conversations will be important to the people who attend? What information will we need to begin?

Two additional important considerations: First, prioritize your agenda items. Make sure you don't spend most of your time on more immediate but less important issues. Leaving the most crucial or urgent items until last runs the risk of running out of time and not considering them at all. Second, assign realistic amounts of time to each agenda item. When you have exhausted the time allocated for discussion of a particular item, the meeting chair must gently nudge the group: "Any other thoughts on this? It's time to move on."

What's the most effective use of your agenda? Conventional wisdom says that agendas should be created and distributed in advance. For formal meetings and meetings requiring preparation, that approach makes considerable sense. For informal meetings or for those called in the midst of change, however, you can easily build an agenda as you begin. Simply poll the participants on topics they think should be covered, establish a set of priorities and budget the meeting time.[18]

The most important thing you can do with your agenda, once it's written, is to stick to it. In too many meetings, too many participants wander off topic, spending too much time discussing issues irrelevant to the reason they are in the room. Michael Schrage, a consultant on collaborative technologies, acknowledges that most meetings in most companies are decidedly agenda-free. "In the real world," he says, "agendas are about as rare as the white rhino. If they do exist, they're about as useful. Who hasn't been in meetings where someone tries to prove that the agenda isn't appropriate?"[19]

Agendas are worth taking seriously, however. Intel Corporation, the Silicon Valley semiconductor manufacturer, is fanatical about them. They've developed an agenda template that everyone in the company uses. A typical Intel agenda, which circulates several days before a meeting to let participants react to and modify it, lists the meeting's key topics, who will lead which parts of the discussion, how long each segment will take and what the expected outcomes will be.

Of course, even the best of agendas can't ensure the success of a meeting. The challenge, according to Kimberly Thomas, a former director of small business services for a telecommunication firm in Chicago, is to keep meetings focused without stifling creativity or insulting participants who stray. "When comments come up that aren't related to the issue at hand," she says, "we record them on a flip chart labeled 'The Parking Lot.' We always track the issue and the person responsible for it," she adds. "We use this technique throughout the company."[20]

## The Participants

The people on your participant list should be only those people who are directly related to the goals for the meeting. Failing to invite key decision makers or influencers invites frustration and failure. Including people either because they're interesting or simply to fill up chairs in the room is a waste of your time and theirs. So, who should you include? Think carefully about inviting people who:

- will have to carry out or implement what's been decided;
- have valuable information or good ideas;
- can approve the results;
- can act as an advocate on behalf of the group's ideas at a higher level;
- represent divergent views or traditionally excluded viewpoints;
- are indispensable to the success of the decision.

In many companies, it's bad form to not invite lots of people to a meeting. What managers don't realize is that every additional attendee adds cost. Unnecessary attendees also get in the way. Bain & Company consultant Michael Mankins recommends the *Rule of 7*, which states that every attendee over seven reduces the likelihood of making a good, quick, executable decision by 10 percent. "Once you hit 16 or 17," he says, "your decision effectiveness is close to zero."[21]

When you know whose input is needed, as well as those whose buy-in will be necessary to move forward, you're ready to secure the facilities and issue invitations.

## HOW DO I PREPARE FOR A SUCCESSFUL MEETING?

We mentioned three essential considerations as you plan for a meeting – the objectives, the agenda and the participants – but there's more. Here are some additional steps you should think about carefully.

### Arrange for a Meeting Time, Date and Place

Think carefully about what times and dates would be most convenient for everyone concerned. In the absence of convenience, when can people be there? Although it may not be possible to accommodate literally *everyone's* schedule as you plan for a meeting, be as flexible as possible in trying to arrange a time that the largest number of participants will find workable. Mealtimes are often used as an opportunity to get an otherwise difficult-to-assemble group together. Most people have at least something to eat at breakfast and lunch each day, and if you offer to buy, they may be willing to join you.

Keep in mind that it's generally a bad idea to convene a meeting outside of normal business hours. Sometimes you must, but the editors of the *Harvard Management Communication Letter* say such occasions should be reserved for real emergencies:

> People who schedule meetings for evenings and weekends are merely advertising the embarrassing fact
> that they have no life – and they're expecting others to give up theirs. That kind of person should not be
> allowed to run anything, much less part of a modern corporation, because they lack the basic humanity to do
> a good job.[22]

Selecting a location for your meeting can be just as important as drafting your objectives and drawing up a participant list. "If people are meeting for recreational reasons or are being rewarded in some way by the company, think very carefully about where you want to meet," says meeting consultant Marge Boberschmidt. "A world-class hotel or even a nice corporate conference center can often compensate for an otherwise uninspired panel of speakers or weak agenda."[23]

### Coordinate Details at the Meeting Site

"The small stuff will always come back to bite you," says Boberschmidt. "Pay attention to the size of the room, the quality and comfort levels of the seating, the conference table, projection equipment, lighting, temperature controls, refreshments, and anything else that will influence a participant's frame of mind."[24] Everything from parking to pencils and pads will affect how people feel about the experience of being in a meeting room, she says, and all of it is worth considering.

Consider, as well, all of those issues related to travel requirements, location and cost. Make absolutely certain that every participant knows how to find the meeting location. Anticipate commonly asked questions, then provide a telephone number for last-minute questions or unanticipated problems. Having a real human being to talk with can be comforting as a busy manager tries to pull his act together at the last minute before an important business meeting.

If you're responsible for planning the meeting, talk to or meet with those responsible for supporting or carrying out your plans, including audio-visual technicians, caterers, front-desk managers, and banquet and meeting managers. Make certain they know how to find you – no matter what the hour – and be explicit about what you want. Be pleasant to them, though. Keep in mind that they are probably overworked and underpaid, and the success of your meeting is in their hands. A generous tip at the right moment wouldn't hurt, either.

## Announce the Agenda

Unless secrecy is essential, your meeting is more likely to succeed with a published agenda that everyone has had an opportunity to examine and think about in advance. State your objectives and explain the outcomes you're hoping for. Be sure to include all relevant detail in the announcement, including themes, topics, speakers, times, dates, places, directions and the specific responsibilities of the participants. If you e-mail the agenda, ask for a return receipt to make sure everyone received and displayed the document. If you are at all nervous about getting everyone on the same page, follow up with paper copies and, perhaps, a phone call to confirm that the event is a high priority.

## Assign Roles

An important part of the planning process involves the assignment of roles. Any well-run meeting will involve at least four important roles:

- facilitator
- recorder
- leader
- participant.

Some meeting planners like to add a fifth role, the timekeeper, so that each agenda item gets its fair share of attention and the discussion stays on track. Different people can play each of these roles, or one person can play them all, but they all have to be accounted for if the meeting is to flow well and produce results. Determining role assignments at the beginning engages everybody in the process and, if done properly, validates each participant's expectations and contributions.[25]

---

### A Weekly Meeting at Wal-Mart Becomes a Competitive Advantage

The idea of it is very simple. Nothing very constructive happens in the office. Everybody else had gone to regional offices – Sears, Kmart, everybody – but we decided to send everybody from Bentonville out to the stores Monday through Thursday and bring them back Thursday night.

On Friday morning, we'd have our merchandise meetings. But on Saturday morning we'd have the sales for the week. And we'd have all the other information from people who'd been out in the field. They're telling us what the competitors are doing, and we get reports from people in the regions who had been traveling through the week. So we decide then what corrective action we want to take. And before noon on Saturday, the regional manager was required to be hooked up by phone with all his district managers, giving them direction as to what we were going to do or change.

By noon on Saturday we had all our corrections in place. Our competitors, for the most part, got their sales results on Monday for the week prior. Now they're ten days behind, and we've already made the corrections.

David Glass

CEO, Wal-Mart Stores, Inc.
1988–2000

*Source*: Gilman, H. "The Most Underrated CEO Ever," *Fortune*, April 5, 2004, pp. 244–246.

---

# WHAT FORM OR MEETING STYLE WILL WORK BEST?

Each organization has its own style that is based in part on the personalities of both the leadership and participants, as well as the organizational culture. The style you select has to fit the preferences of those who will participate as well as the business needs of the organization. Here are three styles or meeting forms that are well suited to smaller business-oriented meetings:

## *The Staff Conference*

This military-style meeting often works well if you clearly outrank everyone else in the room. In this format, each team member reports to you on how his or her project is going, answers your questions and makes recommendations. The two of you then discuss strategy, usually with little input from other team members.

This style keeps everyone informed of what each team member is doing, forces all team members to be ready with reports and to be accountable in front of their peers, and lets you control the flow of the meeting. Disadvantages include a limited exchange of ideas, an autocratic management style and the potential for conflict if participants' responsibilities overlap.

## *The "Congressional" System*

If you're chairing an association meeting, where officers are elected and all members are of equal standing, your role in the chair will be that of a presiding officer rather than an executive. In this case, a parliamentary format is almost always the right choice. In this style of meeting, people don't just talk when they please: It's hands up, like in school, and when everyone's had their say, they vote.

This system is useful if you have particularly argumentative members or if the issues to be discussed are especially contentious. As chair of a parliamentary meeting, you must be careful not to take sides publicly. If you want something specific to happen, you'll have to ensure that other members bring the matter up and get it passed with very little help from you. You can't let participants think that you're forcing your own agenda through.

This meeting style allows input from whoever wants to give it; it encourages people to think before speaking; and agreed-upon rules of order make it easier to maintain decorum. To prevent interruptions or side-tracking, the chair simply says, "Hold that thought, Jeff. Carolyn has the floor." An obvious disadvantage is that the chair has severely limited power, and it does encourage a certain amount of intrigue and power-brokering in advance of the meeting.

## *The "House of Commons" System*

In the British House of Commons, the prime minister is the head of government, but that person sits on the floor of the House like any other member; the prime minister does not preside. If you're clearly the ranking person present but want to make the meeting as democratic as possible, appoint (or elect) another member to chair the meeting. Remind the presiding officer beforehand that you are subject to the same rules as every other member and to treat you accordingly.

One obvious advantage to this approach is that you will spend less time planning the meeting. It also provides leadership experience to other members and encourages subordinates to speak frankly. If the newly elected (or appointed) meeting leader isn't careful, however, this approach can create the impression that no one is in charge.[26]

# HOW DO I KEEP A MEETING ON TRACK?

Meetings don't actually go off-topic, people do. It usually takes at least two people adrift to take the meeting off course. Sometimes, a participant with ulterior motives can try to hijack a meeting and use it for his or her own purposes, but that's a less common threat than these three:

## *Topic Drift*

Almost any meeting can attract comments or observations from participants who will take the discussion in an unintended direction. Sometimes a brief discussion of non-agenda items can lighten the mood in the room and may, in fact, be helpful in getting certain people to speak, but you can tolerate such diversions for just so long. When this drifting off course happens, the meeting chair has a couple of choices: Call the group back on topic, "OK, let's see if we can focus on the problem we need to solve . . . " Or, the chair can ask if the group would like to consider the new topic separately: "This discussion seems to be outside the scope of the agenda. Can we table it for now or do we need to add it as a separate discussion item?"[27]

## *Breaking Time Agreements*

A meeting that doesn't start or end at the times advertised in the agenda or doesn't honor the time budgeted for a given agenda item breaks the meeting time agreement. This issue can become a serious problem that prevents the group from reaching its goals. Dealing with the agenda time budget is generally easier; the chair can either continue the discussion and reschedule other agenda items or limit the discussion and move on to the next item.

What happens if people don't show up on time, leave early or fail to show up at all? Improving the "crispness" of meetings means getting participants to take them seriously. How often have you heard someone declare at the end of a gathering, "Well, meeting's over. Let's get back to work." The mind-set at Intel Corporation is that meetings *are* work. They're an important part of the job and each participant has to take them seriously. Other companies punish latecomers with a penalty fee or reprimand them in the minutes of the meeting for being late or absent.

One other important consideration is the "default time" for a meeting. Not long ago, most companies called 30-minute meetings. Now the typical default time has grown to 60-minutes, even though every additional minute adds cost and often yields little additional benefit. Bain & Company consultant Michael Mankins points out that one company established a rule: if a meeting were to last more than 90 minutes, it required approval by an executive two layers up from the convener. That rule quickly cut meeting time.[28]

## *Subgroup Focus*

Sometimes agenda items will spawn dialogue among members of a small group who have important views and ideas to share with each other. When other participants have no interest in that conversation, however, they become bystanders at their own meeting. How should the meeting handle such conversations? The chair has two choices: First, ask subgroup participants to rejoin the main discussion, or if that approach is unsuccessful, ask those involved in the spontaneous breakout session if the topic they're exploring is something that would interest the entire group. Either way, the leader must reassert control or risk losing the direction and commitment of the larger group.[29]

## WHAT SHOULD I LISTEN FOR?

Some people have such a deep-seated need to be right that they simply can't stand evidence to the contrary. They are the ones who work overtime to prove others are wrong and disparage anyone who offers a different point of view. These folks make meetings difficult because, for them, meetings become a win/lose occasion, an opportunity to show other people just how wrong they really are. If they can't argue the evidence, they'll debate the procedure. If that doesn't work, they'll attack or threaten others in the room. They'll bluff, bluster, pull rank and – if all else fails – they'll get up and leave.

How do you get people to listen? Well, that's not an easy question to answer. The key is showing them how cooperating with others is in their own best interest. At a minimum, you can lead by example, trying to improve your own listening behavior in meetings.

- *Consider all of your knowledge, ideas and opinions as functions of your unique perspective*. Consider each other person's knowledge, ideas and opinions as functions of their perspective. Each person is entitled to his or her own point of view, though they are not entitled to their own set of facts.

- *Pay attention to your own point of view, especially as it relates to others.* Such deliberate reflection will help you discern your own beliefs and values and be more comfortable with them.
- *Remember that considering an issue from many different viewpoints is what makes a team smart.* Value the opportunity to meet with people who see things differently than you do.
- *Practice what collaboration consultant Christopher Avery calls "playback listening."* Pay careful attention to what others say so that you can play back their words to them exactly. This powerful practice will help you develop the capacity to acknowledge others' points of view and help them to be heard.
- *Hear others with the intention of integrating your point of view with as many others as you can.* This goal means you must be willing to hear and validate all other points of view consistently over time, not just when you agree with them.
- *Try not to think in terms of right and wrong, but rather in terms of what works and doesn't work.* Think about outcomes for the group and achieving the group's goals, not merely your own goals of contributing to the process.[30]

## WHAT SHOULD I LOOK FOR?

Have you ever been to a meeting where, even though the leader said she wanted high participation, she stood at the end of the table and "talked at" the participants, each of whom was seated silently down both sides? It's not all that uncommon. Leaders who don't plan for participation in a meeting won't get it, no matter what they say they want. Standing at the end of a long table sends a strong nonverbal message: Don't talk, just listen. It's a great setup for discouraging participation.

As you saw in Chapter 9, actions not only speak louder than words but often speak in ways that words simply cannot. Think about what that means as you look around your meeting room and where people will sit. In his book *Silent Messages*, Albert Mehrabian tells us the words we say account for just 7 percent of total message communication. Our tone of voice accounts for another 38 percent. More than half (55 percent) of received message communication in an interpersonal setting comes from body language, including such issues as eye contact, posture, gestures, hand movement and position in the room.[31]

Deliberately conveying nonverbal messages is not all that difficult. When you are the leader and you need to maintain control of a meeting, run the meeting yourself to signal that you have both authority and control. Stand while others are sitting to signal that you have the floor. And, of course, sit at the head of the table to show that you are in charge.

On the other hand, if you want a more participative or collaborative meeting, ask a team member or facilitator to run the meeting to signal shared control. Sit while others are sitting to signal that your views are equally important. And consider taking a seat along the side of the conference table to demonstrate that you're one of them, rather than in charge of them.[32]

You can even defuse confrontation by changing the furniture in the room. A living room atmosphere with sofas, upholstered chairs and low-rise coffee tables is likely to encourage people to speak up in a more participative way. Conference tables clearly denote authority and who outranks whom.

To minimize participation and interruptions:

- set up a long, narrow table for a smaller meeting, placing the leader at the end;
- choose a seating arrangement that minimizes eye contact between participants (classroom style seating), where one presenter faces the audience;
- create an expectation that speech only comes from the front of the room.

To maximize participation and collaboration:

- choose a round or square table, with the leader seated as a member of the group;
- for longer meetings, set up chairs in a U-shape, instead of using classroom-style row seating, so that participants face each other;
- for large groups, arrange banquet-style seating to accommodate five to eight people, using as many round tables as necessary.[33]

## WHAT SHOULD I WRITE DOWN?

In every meeting, someone should be designated to take notes. At the very least, the names and titles of those present, the agenda items discussed, the participant comments and the ideas generated should find their way onto paper. If the group leader is to follow up on decisions, new ideas or opportunities discussed during the meeting, a simplified, streamlined method of recording and sharing the minutes of each meeting must be a priority.

Increasingly, technology has begun to play a role in note-taking during meetings. 3M Corporation has developed a digital whiteboard that's as simple to write on and erase as a traditional whiteboard. The difference? The board captures a complete record of the evolution of ideas during a meeting. Every board full of information can be saved as a page on your iPad or PC, ready to edit, print, e-mail, and cut and paste into other applications.

In too many organizations, discussions are held and ideas are written onto flip charts, chalk boards and white boards, but somehow, nothing happens. Decisions don't get turned into actions. According to Michael Schrage, a consultant on collaborative technologies, the best way to avoid that is to convert from *meeting* to *doing* – where the doing focuses on the creation of shared documents that lead to action. At most computer-enabled meetings, the most powerful role for technology is also the simplest: recording comments, outlining ideas, generating written proposals, projecting them for the entire group to see and printing them so people leave with real-time minutes.

"You're not just having a meeting," says Schrage:

you're creating a document. I can't emphasize enough the importance of that distinction. It is the fundamental difference between ordinary meetings and computer-augmented collaborations. Comments, questions, criticisms, insights should enhance the quality of the document. That should be the group's mission.[34]

## END YOUR MEETINGS PROPERLY

A common complaint among managers is that the conversations they have with employees aren't producing results. "We keep talking about the same issue over and over, but nothing seems to happen." That's because most managers haven't developed the ability to properly close a conversation.

Meetings are really just a series of conversations – to clarify issues, set direction, sharpen focus and to move projects forward. Corporate trainer Paul Axtell recommends that managers consider five essential tasks as a meeting draws to a close:

- *Check for completion.* "Is there anything else we need to say or review before we move on to the next agenda item? Anything we've forgotten?"
- *Check for alignment.* "Are we in agreement, then, on what we'll do? Any last objections we haven't heard?"
- *Agree on next steps.* "What, specifically, will each of us do between now and our next meeting? Let's review the action list now."
- *Acknowledge the value of what you've accomplished.* "Alright then, here's what we've done today. Here is a brief list of what I think we've accomplished this morning."
- *Thank participants for their contributions.* Don't just say, "Thanks everyone." That's simply a cue that the meeting is adjourned. Specifically acknowledge important contributions, "Sandra, thanks very much for your insights on the procurement process. And, Amanda, your analysis of the budget impact made all the difference this morning."[35]

## HOW CAN I MAKE MY MEETINGS MORE PRODUCTIVE?

Technology may be one answer. Gordon Mangione, a product-unit manager at Microsoft Exchange Group, uses video technology to improve the experience for his team in Redmond, Washington. "Daily meetings are a valuable tool for keeping projects on track," he says. "But as the number of participants grows – our team includes about 60 key managers – we face a dilemma: How do we ensure real-time interaction, keep everyone informed, and maintain cohesiveness – without tying up the whole team?"

Team meetings are critical at Microsoft. "Teams come together, review daily builds, and identify any developments from the past 24 hours. We haven't found an 'enabling technology' that works better than face-to-face conversation," he observes. "But when meetings turn into standing room only affairs, the disadvantages are overwhelming."

Mangione's answer is a hybrid meeting, part physical and part virtual. "We still hold the daily meeting in our conference room, but now just 20 people sit in the room. The other 40 'attend' from their offices." Three technicians make the meetings work. Video cameras and microphones in the conference room and on everyone's computer screen allow "virtual" and "physical" participants to see and hear one another. A large-screen TV captures presentations that are broadcast to the desktops, and people pass notes to one another via instant messaging technology.[36] Microsoft isn't alone in embracing new technology to improve meetings. WebEx of San Jose, California, now offers software that plugs into your browser, permitting people in different physical locations to look at the same document and discuss changes as they are being made.

They can talk on the phone, even though the calls are being sent via the Web.[37] Technology, of course, can do more than just bring people in different locations together. It can also increase productivity – that is, help generate more ideas and decisions per minute. One of the main benefits of "meetingware" is that it allows participants to violate the first rule of good behavior in most other circumstances: *Wait your turn to speak*. With Ventana Corporation's *GroupSystems V*, a powerful meeting software program, participants enter their comments and ideas into workstations which, in turn, organize the comments and project them onto a monitor for the whole group to see. Nearly everyone who has studied or participated in computer-enabled meetings agrees that this capacity for simultaneity produces dramatic gains in the number of ideas and the speed with which they are generated.[38]

Other companies have tried different methods for making meetings more productive and more interesting. Kaufman and Broad Home Corporation, one of the top home builders in the U.S., recognized that the grind of workday pressures made group meetings especially difficult. Their solution? The "After Five" meeting. Jeff Charney, a senior vice president of marketing and communications, began gathering his team for freewheeling brainstorming sessions after 5:00 p.m., when the workday normally concludes. "Without all the day-to-day pressures," says Charney, "it's much easier to engage our imaginations and let them run wild."

Keep in mind that we explicitly warned you a few pages back against holding meetings after 5:00 p.m. Kaufman and Broad, however, think the culture of their organization is appropriate for such late-afternoon gatherings. During one of their After Five sessions not long ago, the team devised a major promotional campaign that used a full-scale replica of the home of Marge and Homer Simpson – a marketing gambit that got worldwide media attention. "Nine-to-five," says Charney, "we're in a taking-care-of-business mode. By holding the meeting at the day's end, we can switch gears and leave behind phones and pagers. Those things just kill creativity."[39]

Still others have tried an updated version of an old military stand-by: the "7:30 a.m. Stand-Up." Researchers at the University of Missouri wanted to test the notion that one way to make better, certainly shorter, meetings was to take away the chairs. And sure enough, after comparing outcomes for 111 meetings, they found that those conducted while the participants were seated lasted an average of 34 percent longer than meetings in which the participants remained standing. More importantly, they discovered the quality of decision making was the same for both formats. Dr. Mary Waller, a professor who specializes in organizational behavior at the University of Illinois, and who was not involved with the study, added: "I think it's a pretty important finding. If I were consulting with an organization, I would probably suggest that they combine sit-down and standing-up meetings."[40]

The Ritz-Carlton hotel chain – the only hotel company ever to receive a Malcolm Baldrige National Quality Award – uses the same idea with considerable success. Every day at precisely 9:00 a.m., about 80 of the company's top executives gather for a ten-minute stand-up meeting in the hallway outside the office of President and COO Horst Schulze. Just as important, within 24 hours, every hotel from Boston to Bali, along with the rest of the company's 16,000 employees, gets the same concentrated dose of the Ritz credo at their daily shift meetings. "We prepare a monthly calendar of lineup topics," says Leonardo Inghilleri, a senior vice president for human resources, "ranging from the opening of a new hotel in Dubai to meeting-planner programs – and e-mail them weekly to each hotel. For one critical moment each day," he says, "the entire organization is aligned behind the same issue."[41]

## CAN BUSINESS MEETINGS EVER IMPROVE?

Bernard DeKoven, founder of the Institute for Better Meetings in Palo Alto, California, remains hopeful about the improvement of meetings:

People don't have good meetings because they don't know what good meetings are like. Good meetings aren't just about work. They're about fun – keeping people charged up. It's more than collaboration. It's 'coliberation' – people freeing each other up to think more creatively.[42]

## FOR FURTHER READING

Bohns, V. K. "A Face-to-Face Request Is 34 Times More Successful than an E-mail," *Harvard Business Review*, April 11, 2017. Online at https://hbr.org/2017/04/a-face-to-face-request-is-34-times-more-successful-than-an-email. Accessed Monday July 18, 2018 at 4:24 p.m. EDT.

Crockett, R. "The 21st Century Meeting: The Latest Gear May Finally Deliver on the Promise of Videoconferencing," *BusinessWeek*, February 26, 2007, pp. 72–79.

Dvorak, P. "Corporate Meetings Go Through a Makeover," *The Wall Street Journal*, March 6, 2006, p. B3.

Farivar, C. "How to Run an Effective Meeting," *Bnet.com*. Online at www.bnet.com. Accessed April 10, 2007 at 11:28 A.M.

Fricks, H. "The Five W's: Tips for Planning Your Company Meeting," *Indiana Business Magazine*, July 1998, pp. 34–37.

Goldberg, M. "The Meeting I Never Miss," *Fast Company*, February 1997, pp. 28–30.

Grenny, J. "How to Save a Meeting That's Gotten Tense," *Harvard Business Review*, December 29, 2017.

Knight, R. "How to Refocus a Meeting After Someone Interrupts," *Harvard Business Review*, April 16, 2015.

Kopytoff, V. G. "The Necessary Art of the Impromptu Meeting," *The New York Times*, August 24, 1997, p. A11.

Korkki, P. "Another Meeting? Say It Isn't So," *The New York Times*, July 20, 2008, p. BU-8.

Lohr, S. "Face Time That Relies on Screens," *The New York Times*, July 22, 2008, pp. C1, C8.

McAdams, S. "Engage Employees in Nine Minutes? Yes, It's Possible," *Ragan.com*. Online at www.ragan.com. Accessed February 4, 2008, at 1:44 p.m.

McGarvey, R. "Making Meetings Work: The Benchmark Hospitality Formula for Successful Conferences," *Harvard Business Review*, March 2003, pp. 51–58.

Mosvick, R. K. and R. B. Nelson. *We've Got to Start Meeting Like This: A Guide to Successful Meeting Management*. Indianapolis, IN: Jist Works, 1996.

Yeaney, J. "The Top Ten Meeting Personalities," *Fast Company*, November 18, 2009. Online at www.fastcompany.com/node/1460895.

Zimmerman, E. "Staying Professional in Virtual Meetings," *The New York Times*, September 29, 2010. Online at www.nytimes.com/2010/09/26/jobs/26career.html.

## NOTES

1   Boberschmidt, M. Personal communication, July 25–26, 2005.

2   Mountford, W. Personal communication, September 19, 1999.

3   Matson, E. "The Seven Sins of Deadly Meetings," *Fast Company*, April 1996, pp. 122–128.

4   Dvorak, P. "Corporate Meetings Go Through a Makeover: Better Productivity Is Goal as Methods Differ to Boost Effectiveness of Employees," *The Wall Street Journal*, March 6, 2006, p. B3.

5   Ibid.

6   Armour, S. "Business' Black Hole: Spiraling Number of Meetings Consume Time and Productivity," *USA Today*, December 8, 1997, pp. Al, A2.

7   Bryant, A. "Everything on One Calendar, Please," *The New York Times*, Sunday, December 27, 2009, p. D7.

8   Ibid.

9   Ligos, M. "Cutting Meetings Down to Size," *The New York Times*, January 11, 2004, p. 10. Copyright © 2004 by The New York Times Company. Reprinted with permission.

10  Sandberg, J. "Another Meeting? Good. Another Chance to Hear Myself Talk," *The Wall Street Journal*, March 11, 2008, p. B1.

11  "Making Meetings Work," *The 3M Meeting Guides*. Online at www.3M.com/meetings/. Accessed August 2, 2005.

12  "Men and Women Fall Back into Kids' Roles at Corporate Meetings," *The Wall Street Journal*, December 15, 1998, p. B1. Reprinted by permission of *The Wall Street Journal*. Copyright © 1998 Dow Jones & Company, Inc. All rights reserved worldwide.

13  Hobor, N. Personal communication, January 7, 2000.

14  Boberschmidt. Personal communication.

15  "Anatomy of Great Meetings," *The 3M Meeting Guides*. Online at: www.3M.com/meetings/. Accessed August 2, 2005.

16  Roghanizad, M. M. and V. K. Bohns. "Ask in Person: You're Less Persuasive Than You Think Over E-mail," *Journal of Experimental Social Psychology*, 69 (March 2017): 223–226.

17  Avery, C. M. "Clear Objectives Make Powerful Meetings," *The 3M Meeting Guides*. Online at www.3M.com/meetings/. Accessed August 2, 2005.

18  "Building Great Agendas," *The 3M Meeting Guides*. Online at www.3M.com/meetings/. Accessed August 2, 2005.

19  Matson. "The Seven Sins of Deadly Meetings."

20  Ibid.

21  Mankins, M. "Yes, You Can Make Meetings More Productive," *Harvard Business Review*. June 9, 2014. Online at https://hbr.org/2014/06/yes-you-can-make-meetings-more-productive. Accessed Tuesday, July 17, 2018 at 10:54 a.m. EDT. See also Nazarali, R. "Meeting Efficiency and Decision Making: The Rule of 7," *Ridiculously Efficient*. September 5, 2014. Online at https://ridiculouslyefficient.com/blog/meeting-efficiency-decision-making-rule-7. Accessed Tuesday, July 17, 2018 at 10:58 a.m. EDT.

22  *Harvard Management Communication Letter*, 2, no. 11 (November 1999), pp. 1–3.

23  Boberschmidt. Personal communication.

24  Ibid.

25  "Anatomy of Great Meetings," *The 3M Meeting Guides*.

26  "Chairing a Meeting: To Keep Order, Be True to Form," *The New York Times*, September 22, 1999, p. C25. Copyright © 1999 by The New York Times Company. Reprinted with permission.

27  Mann, Merlin. "9 Tips for Running More Productive Meetings." Online at www.43folders.com/2006/02/21/meetings. Accessed July 21, 2008 at 11:41 a.m.

28  Mankins, M., C. Brahm and G. Caimi. "Your Scarcest Resource," *Harvard Business Review*, May 2014. Online at https://hbr.org/2014/05/your-scarcest-resource. Accessed Tuesday, July 17, 2018 at 11:10 a.m. EDT.

29  "Keeping a Meeting on Track," *The 3M Meeting Guides*. Online at www.3M.com/meetings/. Accessed August 2, 2005.

30  Avery, C. M. "Listening to Others in Meetings," *The 3M Meeting Guides*. Online at www.3M.com/meetings/. Accessed August 2, 2005.

31  Mehrabian, A. *Silent Messages: Implicit Communication of Emotions and Attitudes*. Belmont, CA: Wadsworth Publishing, 1981.

32  "Nonverbal Messages in Meetings," *The 3M Meeting Guides*. Online at www.3M.com/meetings/. Accessed August 2, 2005.

33  Ibid.

34  Matson. "The Seven Sins of Deadly Meetings."

35  Axtell, P. "The Right Way to End a Meeting," *Harvard Business Review*, March 11, 2005. Online at https://hbr.org/2015/03/the-right-way-to-end-a-meeting?utm_source=newsletter_weekly_hotlist&utm_medium=email&utm_campaign=hotlist112612&cm_lm=&cm_mmc=email-_-newsletter-_-weekly_hotlist-_-hotlist112612&referral=00202&cm_ven=spop-email&cm_ite=weeklyhotlist-0316 15%20(1). Accessed Tuesday July 17, 2018 at 11:26 a.m. EDT.

36  Olofson, C. "So Many Meetings, So Little Time," *Fast Company*, January–February 2000, p. 48.

37  Mardesich, J. "Putting the Drag in WebEx's Ad Campaign," *Fortune*, January 10, 2000, p. 174.

38  Matson. "The Seven Sins of Deadly Meetings."

39  Olofson, C. "Open Minds After Closing Time: Meetings I Never Miss," *Fast Company*, June 1999, p. 72.

40  Berger, A. "The All-Rise Method for Faster Meetings," *The New York Times*, June 22, 1999, p. D7. See also Germer, E. "Meeting I Never Miss: Huddle Up!" *Fast Company*, December 2000, p. 86.

41  Olofson, C. "The Ritz Puts on Stand-Up Meetings," *Fast Company*, September 1998, p. 62. See also Farivar, C. "Shake It Up: Alternative Meeting Strategies," *BNET*, April 9, 2007. Online at www.bnet.com/article/shake-it-up-alternative-meeting-strategies/61204. Accessed January 7, 2011 at 1:00 p.m.

42  Matson. "The Seven Sins of Deadly Meetings."

# Case 12.1: Yahoo!

## *A Female CEO and New Mother Forbids Working from Home*

On September 28, 2012, Yahoo General Counsel Ron Bell warned, "We will fire employees who leak company confidential information and we will avail ourselves of all other legal remedies to protect those confidences." Ironically, Kara Swisher of *All Things Digital* posted Bell's confidential warning hours later on her popular technology website, http://allthingsd.com.[1] Just six months later, Swisher again posted a brand-new leaked Yahoo memo that informs "work-from-home" employees to begin daily commutes to Yahoo offices. She credits a "plethora of irked Yahoo employees" as her source for the memo that has quickly spread throughout the media over the last week.[2]

Yahoo CEO Marissa Mayer now conspicuously keeps a low profile as a storm of media scrutiny descends on the content of yet another "leaked" memo. Her company, whose business it is to connect people over the Internet, now unintentionally finds itself at the center of a nation-wide debate on workplace flexibility. Thousands of passionate social media posts interpret Mayer's move as everything from an archaic management decision to a statement on feminism.

Anne Espiritu, Yahoo Corporate Communications Director, knows that Mayer never intended to make a broad industry statement on working from home.[3] But, it is difficult to ignore public perception considering Yahoo's already declining reputation in the technology industry.

She must now advise Mayer on how to react to the leaked memo before Yahoo's reputation of being an Internet dinosaur further solidifies.

## THE E-MAIL

---

**YAHOO! PROPRIETARY AND CONFIDENTIAL INFORMATION — DO NOT FORWARD**

Yahoos,

Over the past few months, we have introduced a number of great benefits and tools to make us more productive, efficient and fun. With the introduction of initiatives like FYI, Goals and PB&J, we want

---

everyone to participate in our culture and contribute to the positive momentum. From Sunnyvale to Santa Monica, Bangalore to Beijing — I think we can all feel the energy and buzz in our offices.

To become the absolute best place to work, communication and collaboration will be important, so we need to be working side-by-side. That is why it is critical that we are all present in our offices. Some of the best decisions and insights come from hallway and cafeteria discussions, meeting new people, and impromptu team meetings. Speed and quality are often sacrificed when we work from home. We need to be one Yahoo!, and that starts with physically being together.

Beginning in June, we're asking all employees with work-from-home arrangements to work in Yahoo! offices. If this impacts you, your management has already been in touch with next steps. And, for the rest of us who occasionally have to stay home for the cable guy, please use your best judgment in the spirit of collaboration. Being a Yahoo isn't just about your day-to-day job, it is about the inter-actions and experiences that are only possible in our offices.

Thanks to all of you, we've already made remarkable progress as a company — and the best is yet to come.

Jackie

*Source*: www.allthingsdigital.com[4]

## YAHOO!

Started by two Stanford Ph.D. students in 1994, Yahoo grew to be massively influential by 2000. However, Yahoo's Internet search engine prominence waned substantially throughout the next decade. While competitors continued to innovate and change their business model after the dot-com bust, Yahoo stuck to its old methods. As a result, Google and others remained steps ahead of Yahoo in paid-search-advertising, advanced search algorithms, social media, and app development for mobile devices.[5] At its peak, Yahoo traded at $118.75 a share, but the stock by the spring of 2013 was trading somewhere in the $20s. Google's stock, on the other hand, was trading at that time in the $800s.[6]

Yahoo employs 11,500 people in more than 20 countries across the globe; however, a declining reputation in the technology industry continues to hamper their ability to retain and recruit the top talent needed to return to prominence. Yahoo is currently struggling to fill 900 open positions, 8 percent of its total payroll. "We don't typically run into Yahoo," said Alan Shapiro, the owner of San Jose-based software engineer search firm, Technology Search International. He says, "When we represent a candidate, we'll ask who else they're talking to. Yahoo is not a name that's frequently mentioned."[7]

After rotating through five new CEOs in five years, Yahoo set its sight on one of Google's most famous leaders, Marissa Mayer. Analysts initially hailed the hire as a step in the right direction. Mayer was instrumental in Google's success and is a well-known leader in the technology community. Although Yahoo missed opportunities for growth, and sales continue to fall, Yahoo still has influence and hope. Many original Yahoo users never bothered to change their e-mail or search engine habits.[8] As a result, Yahoo has the third largest mobile reach in the U.S. with 68 million users. Moreover, Yahoo owns successful web-based and mobile application offerings such as Flickr, Yahoo! Finance and Yahoo! Sports.[9]

## MARISSA MAYER

Marissa Mayer developed a passion for computers after learning how to operate a mouse for the first time during her freshman year at Stanford University. She went on to earn both a Bachelor of Science degree in symbolic systems and a Master of Science degree in computer science and artificial intelligence. Mayer joined Google in 1999 as the company's 20th employee and first female engineer. Over the course of 13 years, she moved up the ranks, eventually running 25 percent of the tech giant.

As one of the most highly visible women in business and a celebrity in the tech community, Mayer is not new to headlines and controversy. She made a splash in the summer of 2012 when she took over as President and CEO of Yahoo at age 37, becoming not only one of 20 female *Fortune* 500 CEOs, but also the youngest. Additionally, hours after her move to Yahoo was announced, Mayer revealed that she was six months pregnant, becoming the first ever pregnant *Fortune* 500 CEO.

Mayer admits that she had to get comfortable with taking risks. "I always did something I was a little not ready to do," she says of her best decisions. "That feeling at the end of the day, where you're like, 'what have I gotten myself into?' I realized that sometimes when you have that feeling and you push through it, something really great happens." As a result, Mayer has developed a reputation over her 14-year career for defying stereotypes. "I refuse to be stereotyped. I think it's very comforting for people to put me in a box. 'Oh, she's a fluffy girlie girl who likes clothes and cupcakes. Oh, but wait, she is spending her weekends doing hardware electronics.'"

Mayer's barrier-breaking career has caused many to hold her up as role model for a new generation of women business leaders. But, Mayer plays down the role of gender in obtaining success in the computer sciences, asserting instead, "I'm not a woman at Google, I'm a geek at Google." She believes that passion is a "gender neutralizing force" that opens doors for everyone, regardless of whether you are a man or woman. Mayer also shies away from the phrase "feminism," stating that the word has a negative connotation. She says, "There are amazing opportunities all over the world for women, and I think that there's more good that comes out of positive energy around that than negative energy."[10]

## TELECOMMUTING: IN GENERAL

Modern technology makes working from home a very real and practical option for many employers. Workers can use real-time data, video and voice telecommunications to operate from remote locations in the same manner as they would a traditional business office. While companies continuously look to fill full-time and part-time jobs with telecommuters, the practice has not matched the pace of the overall technological evolution. According to the U.S. Census Bureau, U.S. employees who worked remotely for at least one day a week increased only to 9.5 percent in 2010 from 7 percent in 1997.[11]

Most work-from-home proponents advance four main professional and societal benefits of telecommuting. First, working from home eliminates wasted time in the car and reduces stress caused by a daily commute, improving overall worker productivity and morale. Second, a reduction in traffic results in less pollution and energy consumption, helping the environment and saving money. Third, the company saves money with lower overhead and real estate costs. Fourth, the opportunity to work from home provides a better work–life balance and increased opportunities for otherwise would-be high-performing employees, especially the disabled, elderly, stay-at-home parents and rural residents.[12]

Others, however, believe that telecommuting has yet to gain considerable momentum for good reason. Critics insist that innovation, direction and culture rely on employees sharing the same physical space. First, they argue that the innovation necessary for modern companies to thrive relies on ideas that often come from everyday conversations that start over lunch or in the hallway.

Additionally, these conversations provide employees with a better overall understanding of the company's direction and mission, enabling them to execute superior and more effective business strategies. Further, critics suggest that positive corporate culture develops when teams work and socialize together side-by-side, increasing morale and organizational loyalty. Moreover, this personal familiarity allows managers to better identify high performers and weed out shirkers.

Finally, instead of facilitating work–life balance, many argue that telecommuter technology is actually creating more conflict and less balance in society. *The Hard Truth About Telecommuting*, by Noonan and Glass, states:

> telecommuting appears, instead, to have become instrumental in the general expansion of work hours, facilitating workers' needs for additional work time beyond the standard workweek and/or the ability of employers to increase or intensify work demands among their salaried employees.[13]

## SILICON VALLEY TELECOMMUTING

Mayer's outright ban is a first in the region considered to be the birthplace of telecommuting. Other Silicon Valley companies quickly responded to *All Things Digital* with their more progressive work-from-home guidelines. A Google spokesperson said, "We do not have a formal policy and leave Googlers to use good judgment." Facebook responded similarly, confirming a "policy to provide flexibility as work permits." Business networking site LinkedIn says that they also allow for employees to work from home, but have "no formal policy at present." A Hewlett-Packard spokesperson responded:

> We do not ban [work from home] and many HP people do it . . . it is not at all an issue at HP and hasn't been for years. Some folks have a regular schedule, while others can do it from time-to-time with the okay of their supervisors.

A Netflix spokesperson elaborated on their flexible work policy, "We don't measure people by how many hours they work or how much they are in the office. We do care about accomplishing great work." AOL, IBM, Microsoft and Twitter all responded similarly, offering their employees the ability to work from home.[14]

## YAHOO: BACKLASH

Yahoo's surprising hard line stance came as a shock to many and continues to fuel a flurry of mainstream and social media exposure. Although reaction is decidedly mixed, those who oppose Mayer's decision are particularly incensed. News websites, blogs and social media outlets are reporting a wide range of disapproving views from impacted employees, business leaders, tech experts and women's rights advocates.

Swisher reports that many affected employees feel betrayed because they took their Yahoo job with an understanding that they would enjoy a more flexible work arrangement. Others believe Mayer should have handled the situation better. One employee wrote to *All Things Digital*, "Even if that was what was previously agreed to with managers and HR, or was a part of the package to take a position, tough . . . It's outrageous and a morale killer."[15]

Much of the widespread media exposure focuses on women's rights and work–life balance issues. So-called "mommy bloggers," a large and influential online community of mothers, already scorned Mayer earlier this year when she returned to work from maternity leave after only two weeks claiming, "The baby's been way easier than everyone made it out to be."[16]

The new telecommuting policy expands the rift, especially because Mayer constructed a private nursery inside of her Yahoo office. Kara Baskin, a work–life blogger for *Boston.com*, wrote, "While she might have the luxury of making such an arrangement somehow workable, she's thoroughly out of touch with the majority of her employees . . . With her draconian, snobbish decree, she's robbed women *and* men of their freedom."[17]

Ruth Rosen, historian of gender and society, told *The New York Times*, "The irony is that (Mayer) has broken the glass ceiling . . . but seems unwilling for other women to lead a balanced life in which they care for their families and still concentrate on developing their skills and career."[18] Bonnie Erbe, host of the PBS show *To The Contrary*, writes that "Mayer was six months' pregnant when she started work and was widely expected to be family-friendly, instead of decidedly family-unfriendly."[19]

Many in the business community claim Mayer's decision is out of touch and destructive.

*Forbes* contributor Adam Hartung contends that ultimately, "Bringing these employees into offices will hurt morale, increase real estate costs and push out several valuable workers who have been diligently keeping afloat a severely damaged Yahoo ship. And (in the) short-term hurt productivity of everyone."[20] Several high-powered technology leaders agree. Richard Branson, founder of Virgin Group, criticized Mayer in his blog stating:

> We like to give people the freedom to work where they want, safe in the knowledge that they have the drive and expertise to perform excellently, whether they are at their desk or in their kitchen. Yours truly has never worked out of an office, and never will.[21]

Bill Gates also disagrees with Mayer's strategy. "If you've got development centers all over the world," he said, "you've got a sales force out with the customers, the fact that tools like Skype, digital collaboration are letting people work better at a distance, that is a wonderful thing."[22]

Matt Mullenburg, CEO of prominent blog company WordPress, used the media attention to recruit in the *All Things Digital* comment section: "For anyone who enjoys working from wherever they like in the world . . . [we are] 100% committed to being distributed. 130 of our 150 people are outside of San Francisco."[23]

The tech blog community is also immersed in the conversation. *Venture Beat*, a top technology blog, posted, "Must we go back to limiting ourselves to the talent that happens to reside within 25 miles of the office and the people who sit in a cubicle during traditional business hours?"[24] *Slate's* Farhad Manjoo predicts that Mayer is going to regret her decision. He writes, "It's myopic, unfriendly, and so boneheaded that I worry it's the product of spending too much time at the office. (She did, after all, build a nursery next to her office to house her new baby)."[25] Tech blog readers are also weighing in on the debate. In a survey, 93 percent of *Mashable* blog readers overwhelmingly favored the benefits of telecommuting.[26]

## SILICON VALLEY: COLLABORATION

Some in Silicon Valley believe the debate is misguided. Although working from home is common in the Valley, that work is usually in addition to the 40-plus hours spent in the office. Sarah McBride, San Francisco-based blogger, explains, "Despite the area's image as a freewheeling space that makes much of the technology that allows people to work remotely, Bay Area workers tend to head into the office, especially at start-ups."[27]

Research published in the *MIT Sloan Review* shows that telecommuters are less likely than those who work in the office to receive promotions.[28] Surprisingly, this result held true even for California tech companies that encouraged employees to work from home.[29] Jack and Suzy Welch offer an explanation:

Companies rarely promote people into leadership roles who haven't been consistently seen and measured. It's a familiarity thing, and it's a trust thing. We're not saying that the people who get promoted are stars during every "crucible" moment at the office, but at least they're present and accounted for. And their presence says: Work is my top priority. I'm committed to this company. I want to lead. And I can.[30]

*Harvard Business Review* research shows that innovation happens faster and culture is easier to control when companies use "daily huddles" and "roundings" as ways to bring everyone together to share physical space.[31] Sahil Lavingia, founder of Silicon Valley start-up Gumroad, says of his company, "Every idea we have is a result of more than two people sitting in a room, riffing on or trying to think up a clever solution to a certain problem," he said. "Things like that you can't do over any Internet protocol."[32]

While Yahoo's direct approach is a first in Silicon Valley, other area companies indirectly encourage employees to share physical space. Even though Google employees can officially work wherever they want, CFO Patrick Pichette says about their work-from-home culture:

The surprising question we get is: "How many people telecommute at Google?" And our answer is: "As few as possible" . . . There is something magical about sharing meals. There is something magical about spending the time together, about noodling on ideas, about asking at the computer "What do you think of this?" These are [the] magical moments that we think at Google are immensely important in the development of your company, of your own personal development and [of] building much stronger communities.[33]

In fact, Google employs "people analytics" managers in order to "create the happiest, most productive workplace in the world." *The New York Times* reporter James Stewart describes his tour of Google's campus as a:

dizzying excursion through a labyrinth of play areas; cafes, coffee bars and open kitchens; sunny outdoor terraces with chaises; gourmet cafeterias that serve free breakfast, lunch and dinner; Broadway-theme conference rooms with velvet drapes; and conversation areas designed to look like vintage subway cars.[34]

Data storage giant NetApp constructed a $4 million fitness complex on the first floor of its headquarters building which includes basketball courts, massage rooms and exercise rooms that accommodate 34 weekly exercise classes. Eventbrite, an online event planning firm voted best workplace by *SF Business Times* best workplaces, provides its employees a "never ending snack supply," access to Legos and a "Bring your pet to work day." The company also facilitates outside social breakfasts, bike rides and team trips to the trampoline park.[35]

## YAHOO: SUPPORT

Yahoo so firmly embraced telecommuting that "WFH" (work-from-home) refrigerator magnets were sold in the company store. Former Yahoo executives speculate that Mayer's move is likely an effort to change the Yahoo corporate culture and reduce unproductive, dispassionate employees. Despite Swisher's "many irked" Yahoo contacts, not everyone at Yahoo disapproves of the change. One source close to the company reports to *businessinsider.com*, "There isn't a massive uprising. The truth is, they've all been [upset] that people haven't been working." *Gawker*'s Maggie Lange reports that many former Yahoo workers experienced a significant amount of abuse of the Yahoo's former work-from-home policy.[36]

One Yahoo employee wrote anonymously on *Quora*:

I have been at Yahoo for four years and let's just say the house needed and still needs a lot of cleaning up and Marissa is doing just that. So I am glad that the change in policy was made.[37]

While the majority of *Mashable* readers strongly believe that Yahoo should not eliminate the work-from-home option, many agree that year-long losses are a good reason for Mayer to do something different.[38] *Forbes* contributor Peter Cochran describes Yahoo's productivity problem:

Google's 53,861 employees generate $931,657 in revenue per worker, 170% higher than Yahoo's $344,758 worth of revenue per employee. Google is heavily populated by super-smart engineers who invent new businesses that help it to boost its top line. And new business ideas get better when smart people from different disciplines randomly bump into each other in the same building to discuss and refine those ideas.[39]

*Harvard Business Review*'s Michael Schrage writes:

I'm pretty confident this reflects a data-driven decision more than a cavalier command. In all likelihood, Mayer has taken good, hard looks at Yahoo's top 250 performers and top 20 projects and come to her own conclusions about who's creating real value – and how – in her company.[40]

Reaction from the tech blog community is widespread. Kelly Faircloth of *Beta Beat* defends Mayer's move as an attempt to simply make it less of a "complete bummer" to work at Yahoo.[41] *The New York Times* technology section describes Yahoo's work environment:

Parking lots and entire floors of cubicles were nearly empty because some employees were working as little as possible and leaving early. Then there were the 200 or so people who had work-at-home arrangements. Although they collected Yahoo paychecks, some did little work for the company and a few had even begun their own start-ups on the side.[42]

*The Verge* tech blogger Elizabeth Spiers believes that a male would have been applauded in the tech community for his tough love approach. She writes, "That's the sad reality for women at the highest rungs of the executive ranks in corporate America. Everyone applauds when they shatter that glass ceiling. Then they pick up the shards, and start cutting away."[43]

## DISCUSSION QUESTIONS

1. What are the critical issues in the case and who are the stakeholders?
2. Is there a need for Yahoo to defend or further explain its new work-from-home policy? If so, what should the content of the message be, to whom should it be delivered, who should send the message and what would the best delivery medium be?

3. Should Yahoo adjust its new policy? If so, what changes should be made and why should they be made?
4. Should Yahoo change the way it disseminates company-wide confidential information? If so, what is a better alternative to their current practice?
5. Should Marissa Mayer be concerned about reactions from individuals, special interest groups, the media or experts who are not associated with Yahoo?
6. Should Marissa Mayer be concerned about reactions from Wall Street, particularly among institutional investors?


## WRITING ASSIGNMENT

Please respond in writing to the issues presented in this case by preparing two documents: a communication strategy memo and a professional business letter.

In preparing these documents, you may assume one of two roles: you may identify yourself as a senior communications manager for Yahoo who has been asked to provide advice to the company regarding the issues it is facing. Or, you may identify yourself as an external management consultant who has been asked by the company to provide advice to Ms. Espititu and her executive team.

Either way, you must prepare a strategy addressed to Ms. Ann Espiritu, Corporate Communications Director, that summarizes the details of the case, identifies critical issues and discusses their implications (what they mean and why they matter), offers specific recommendations for action (assigning ownership and suspense dates for each) and provides advice on how to communicate the solution to all who are affected by the recommendations. Please include a digital media component to your recommendations.

You must also prepare a professional business letter for Ms. Mayer's signature. That document should be addressed to Yahoo employees, explaining the actions she intends to take, why those are important, and the effect her new policies and directives will have on key stakeholders (including investors, customers, suppliers, creditors and others). If you have questions about either of these two documents, please consult your instructor.


## ACKNOWLEDGMENTS

This case was prepared by research assistant R. H. Heatherman under the direction of James S. O'Rourke, Teaching Professor of Management, as the basis for class discussion rather than to illustrate either effective or ineffective handling of an administrative situation. Information was gathered from corporate as well as public sources.

## NOTES

1 Swisher, K. "Yahoo's Top Lawyer Says Leaked Memos Are 'Uncool' (According to Oops — A Cool Leaked Internal Memo)," *AllThingsD*, September 24, 2012. Online at http://allthingsd.com/20120924/yahoos-top-lawyer-says-leaked-internal-memos-are-uncool-according-to-oops-a-cool-leaked-internal-memo/. Accessed April 12, 2013.

2 Swisher, K. "Physically Together: Here's the Internal Yahoo No-Work-From-Home Memo for Remote Workers and Maybe More," *AllThingsD*, February 22, 2013. Online at http://allthingsd.com/20130222/physically-together-heres-the-internal-yahoo-no-work-from-home-memo-which-extends-beyond-remote-workers/. Accessed April 12, 2013.

3 Bailey, B. "Yahoo Responds to Outcry, Says Work-from-Home Ban is Not An 'Industry View'," *The Mercury News*, February 26, 2013. Online at www.mercurynews.com/business/ci_22673297/yahoo-says-its-work-from-home-ban-isnt. Accessed April 12, 2013.

4 Swisher. "Physically Together."

5 Ulanoff, L. "Yahoo Then and Now: Diagnosing a Sad Decline," *Mashable*, April 5, 2012. Online at http://mashable.com/2012/04/05/yahoo-then-and-now/. Accessed April 12, 2013.

6 Dunbar, L. "In Defense of Marissa Mayer: Hello, People! It's a Turnaround!" *CommPRO.biz*, March 18, 2013. Online at www.commpro.biz/corporate-communications/leadership-careers/in-defense-of-marissa-mayer-hello-people-its-a-turnaround/. Accessed April 12, 2013.

7 Oreskovic, A. "Yahoo's Mayer Gets Internal Flak for More Rigorous Hiring," *Reuters*, March 12, 2013. Online at www.reuters.com/article/2013/03/12/us-yahoo-hiring-idUSBRE92B06R20130312. Accessed April 12, 2013.

8    Miller, C. C. and N. Perlroth. (2013). "Yahoo Says New Policy Is Meant to Raise Morale," *The New York Times*, March 5, 2013. Online at www.nytimes.com/2013/03/06/technology/yahoos-in-office-policy-aims-to-bolster-morale.html?pagewanted=all&_r=0. Accessed April 12, 2013.

9    Carlson, N. "Marissa Mayer Announces a New Yahoo Mail – And It's by Far the Most Important Move She's Made Yet," *Business Insider*, December 11, 2012. Online at www.businessinsider.com/marissa-mayer-announces-a-new-yahoo-mail-and-its-by-far-the-most-important-move-shes-made-yet-2012-12. Accessed April 12, 2013.

10   Hare, B. "How Marissa Mayer Writes Her Own Rules," *CNN Tech*, March 13, 2013. Online at www.cnn.com/2013/03/12/tech/web/marissa-mayer-yahoo-profile. Accessed April 12, 2013.

11   Garling, C. "Yahoo Decree Reignites Work-from-Home Debate," *The Denver Post*, March 3, 2013. Online at www.denverpost.com/business/ci_22701823/yahoo-decree-reignites-work-from-home-debate. Accessed March 29, 2013, 2013.

12   Kotkin, J. "Marissa Mayer's Misstep and the Unstoppable Rise of Telecommuting," *Forbes*, March 26, 2013. Online at www.forbes.com/sites/joelkotkin/2013/03/26/marissa-mayers-misstep-and-the-unstoppable-rise-of-telecommuting/. Accessed March 29, 2013.

13   Noonan, M. and J. Glass. "The Hard Truth About Telecommuting," *Monthly Labor Review* (June 2012), p. 39. Online at www.bls.gov/opub/mlr/2012/06/art3full.pdf. Accessed March 29, 2013.

14   Swisher, K. "Survey Says: Despite Yahoo Ban, Most Tech Companies Support Work-From-Home for Employees," *AllThingsD*, February 25, 2013. Online at http://allthingsd.com/20130225/survey-says-despite-yahoo-ban-most-tech-companies-support-work-from-home-for-employees/. Accessed March 29, 2013.

15   Swisher. "Physically Together."

16   Beck, K. "Marissa Mayer Says You Made Motherhood Out to be Way Harder Than it Actually Is," *Mommyish*, November 28, 2012. Online at www.mommyish.com/2012/11/28/marissa-mayer-yahoo/. Accessed April 2, 2013.

17   Baskin, K. "Marissa Mayer Is Snobbish, One-Dimensional, and Out of Touch," *Boston.com*, February 26, 2013. Online at www.boston.com/community/moms/blogs/24_hour_workday/2013/02/marissa-mayer-working-from-home.html. Accessed 2013.

18   Miller, C. C. and C. Rampell. "Yahoo Orders Home Workers Back to the Office," *The New York Times*, February 26, 2013. Online at www.nytimes.com/2013/02/26/technology/yahoo-orders-home-workers-back-to-the-office.html?pagewanted=all. Accessed 2013.

19   Erbe, B. "Erbe: Marissa Mayer's Telecommuting Bomb Hurts Many," Newsday OpEd, *Scripps Howard News Service*, February 27, 2013. Online at www.newsday.com/opinion/oped/erbe-marissa-mayer-s-telecommuting-bomb-hurts-many-1.4722870. Accessed April 12, 2013.

20   Hartung, A. "Yahoo Investors Need to Worry About Marissa Mayer," *Forbes*, March 1, 2013. Online at www.forbes.com/sites/adamhartung/2013/03/01/why-yahoo-investors-need-to-worry-about-marissa-mayer/2/. Accessed April 11, 2013.

21   Groth, A. "Richard Branson Says That Marissa Mayer Got It Wrong About Remote Employees," *Business Insider*, February 25, 2013. Online at www.businessinsider.com/richard-branson-says-that-marissa-mayer-got-it-wrong-about-remote-employees-2013-2. Accessed April 12, 2013.

22   Bort, J. "Bill Gates on Marissa Mayer's Telecommuting Ban: Ever hear of Skype?" *Business Insider*, March 10, 2013. Online at www.businessinsider.com/gates-to-meyers-ever-hear-of-skype-2013-3. Accessed April 13, 2013.

23   Swisher. "Physically Together."

24   Bisharat, J. "Yahoo and Best Buy Are Wrong: Great Work Can Happen from Anywhere," *VentureBeat*, March 6, 2013. Online at http://venturebeat.com/2013/03/06/yahoo-and-best-buy-are-wrong-great-work-can-happen-from-anywhere/. Accessed April 13, 2013.

25   Manjoo, F. "Marissa Mayer Has Made a Terrible Mistake; Working from Home Is Great for Employees – and Employers," *Slate*, February 26, 2013. Online at http://mobile.dev.slate.com/articles/technology/technology/2013/02/yahoo_working_at_home_marissa_mayer_has_made_a_terrible_mistake_working.html. Accessed April 13, 2013.

26   Akalp, N. "Why I Dropped the Work-From-Home Policy Long Before Yahoo," *Mashable*, March 1, 2013. Online at http://mashable.com/2013/03/01/work-from-home-policy/. Accessed April 13, 2013.

27   McBride, S. "Valley Workers On Yahoo Dustup: I Work from Office AND Home, Who Cares?" *Silicon Valley Mercury News*, February 28, 2013. Online at www.siliconvalley.com/the-valley/ci_22689482/valley-workers-yahoo-dustup-I-work-from-office?source=pkg. Accessed April 13, 2013.

28   "Working from Home: Out of Sight, Out of Mind," *The Economist*, October 13, 2012. Online at www.economist.com/node/21564581. Accessed April 1, 2013.

29   Ibid.

30   Cable, D. and K. Elsbach. "Why Showing Your Face at Work Matters," *MIT Sloan Management Review*, June 19, 2012. Online at http://sloanreview.mit.edu/article/why-showing-your-face-at-work-matters/. Accessed April 13, 2013.

31   Power, B. "In Praise of Face Time," HBR Blog Network. *Harvard Business Review*, December 21, 2012. Online at http://blogs.hbr.org/cs/2012/12/physical_teams_in_an_increasin.html. Accessed March 29, 2013.

32   McBride. "Valley Workers On Yahoo Dustup."

33   Swisher. "Survey Says."

34  Stewart, J. B. "Looking for Lesson in Google's Perks," *The New York Times*, March 15, 2013. Online at www.nytimes.com/2013/03/16/business/at-google-a-place-to-work-and-play.html?hp&_r=0. Accessed March 29, 2013.

35  "12 Tech Companies That Offer Their Employees the Coolest Perks," *The Next Web*, April 9, 2012. Online at http://thenextweb.com/insider/2012/04/09/12-startups-that-offer-their-employees-the-coolest-perks/.

36  Lange, M. "Yahoo CEO Marissa Mayer Installed a Nursery in Her Office," *Gawker.com*, February 26, 2013. Online at http://gawker.com/5987043/yahoo-ceo-marissa-mayer-installed-a-nursery-in-her-office. Accessed April 13, 2013.

37  "Marissa Mayer Ends WFH (February 2013): What Has Been the Internal Reaction at Yahoo to Marissa Mayer's No-Work-from-Home Policy?" *Quora*. Online at www.quora.com/Marissa-Mayer-Ends-WFH-February-2013/What-has-been-the-internal-reaction-at-Yahoo-to-Marissa-Mayers-no-work-from-home-policy.

38  Fee, J. "The Reaction to Yahoo's Ban on Working from Home," *Mashable*, March 2, 2013. Online at http://mashable.com/2013/03/02/working-from-home-2/. Accessed April 13, 2013, 2013.

39  Cohan, P. "4 Reasons Marrisa Mayer's No-Work-At-Home Policy Is an Epic Fail," *Forbes*, February 26, 2013. Online at http://www.forbes.com/sites/petercohan/2013/02/26/4-reasons-marissa-mayers-no-at-home-work-policy-is-an-epic-fail/. Accessed April 12, 2013.

40  Schrage, M. "Marissa Mayer Is No Fool," HBR Blog Network, *Harvard Business Review*, February 26, 2013. Online at http://blogs.hbr.org/schrage/2013/02/marissa-mayer-is-no-fool.html. Accessed March 31, 2013.

41  Miller and Perlroth. "Yahoo Says New Policy Is Meant to Raise Morale," as cited in: Faircloth, K. "Report: Marissa Mayer Was Just Trying to Make Working at Yahoo Less of a Complete Bummer," *Beta Beat*, February 26, 2013. Online at http://betabeat.com/2013/03/report-marissa-mayer-was-just-trying-to-make-working-at-yahoo-less-of-a-complete-bummer/. Accessed April 9, 2013.

42  Miller and Perlroth. "Yahoo Says New Policy Is Meant to Raise Morale."

43  Spiers, E. "Beware of Broken Glass: The Media's Double Standard for Women at the Top," *The Verge*, March 6, 2013. Online at www.theverge.com/2013/3/6/4070338/beware-of-broken-glass-the-medias-double-standard-for-women-at-the-top. Accessed April 12, 2013.

# Case 12.2: Zappos

## An Experiment in Holacracy

### THE OFFER: TONY'S E-MAIL TO EMPLOYEES

Imagine going to the office on a Monday morning having no idea what you will be doing at work that day. What if this happens every other day? You have no clearly defined set of responsibilities and are supposed to pitch in and make yourself useful according to the tasks assigned to different teams. Welcome to Zappos! For better or worse, Tony Hsieh, CEO of Zappos, has introduced a new self-management system known as Holacracy in the organization.

The concept of Holacracy was created in 2007 by Brian Robertson and Tom Thomison. It is now governed by HolacracyOne. According to Holacracy's official website holacracy.org, *Holacracy is a complete, packaged system for self-management in organizations. Holacracy replaces the traditional management hierarchy with a new peer-to-peer "operating system" that increases transparency, accountability, and organizational agility.* Under this system, there are no job descriptions for any employee. Employees will have roles, which can be multiple, that are defined around the work. The traditional hierarchical system is discouraged and, instead, transparent rules are set so that each employee in the organization knows exactly what the others are doing. Teams are entrusted to make their own decisions, as there is no delegated authority to influence them.

According to Tony Hsieh, he implemented Holacracy to prevent the formation of a bureaucratic system due to Zappos's rapid expansion. He wanted to keep the start-up spirit alive and empower employees. However, critics of Holacracy point out that it does not take human emotion into account and is, hence, an inefficient system. Moreover, there are rigid meeting formats which govern when a participant can speak up during a meeting. Unsurprisingly, not everyone was on board with the new self-management system. On March 24, 2015, Tony Hsieh sent a 4,700-word e-mail to employees reaffirming the company's commitment to Holacracy.[1] In it, he gave employees until April 30 to decide if they wanted to remain with the company or leave. If they chose to leave, they would receive a generous severance package worth nearly half their annual salary.[2] By the deadline, 18 percent of the staff took the offer. This is in addition to the 11 percent who left the company for other reasons throughout the year. Ultimately, 29 percent of the 1,500 Zappos employees left the company in 2015.[3] One year after its implementation, we look back at how the new management style is functioning, the benefits of the implementation and the challenges it faces going forward.

## ZAPPOS: HISTORY AND CULTURE

Zappos.com is an online shoe and clothing store. The company was founded in 1999 by young, soft-spoken entrepreneur Nick Swinmurn. The website was initially named "Shoesite" with the idea of selling footwear online and was later renamed to "Zappos," derived from the Spanish word Zapatos, meaning shoes. Swinmurn took pictures of shoes in local stores and published them on his website. When an order was placed on the website, he would buy the shoe from the store and ship it to the customer. Before approaching Tony Hsieh of Venture Frog for seed funding, Swinmurn had already been rejected by almost every other Venture Capital firm.[4]

One year earlier, Hsieh sold LinkExchange for $295 million to Microsoft and was investing in a number of projects.[5] Describing his first meeting with Swinmurn, Hsieh says in his book *Delivering Happiness*, "We didn't know if the shoe idea would work or not, but they (Nick and Fred, Nordstrom employees who had risked their jobs to join Zappos) were clearly passionate and willing to place big bets." Initially, the idea was to invest enough money for Zappos to grow in the first year and seek further funding at the end of the year.[6]

With the burst of the Internet bubble, Zappos was unable to generate another round of funding after the first year. Short of cash and desperate for survival, Hsieh sent out an e-mail to Zappos employees with a nine-month plan and the decision of laying off some staff. Some employees voluntarily left, while others offered to take a pay cut. In his book, he describes the time saying:

> We realized that we had laid off the underperformers and the nonbelievers, but because everyone remaining was so passionate about the company and believed in what we were doing, we could still accomplish just as much work as we had before.

The need for survival had brought the team together. The tough times had also forced Tony to sell 11 of his properties in San Francisco to keep Zappos open.[7]

Over time, Zappos started keeping inventory. Although the sales were continuously increasing: $70 million in 2003, $184 million in 2004 to $370 million in 2005, the company was still not profitable.[8] Struggling to keep up with the expenses and in order to hire cheaper labor, the company moved from San Francisco to Las Vegas in 2004. Even during the struggling times, Hsieh made sure that customer service was not affected. His goal was to be the number one e-commerce company, larger even than Amazon.[9]

Also, in 2004, the idea of the Zappos culture book was born. The book meant new hires were to read what the Zappos culture means to its employees. According to Hsieh, the final print on the book was unedited. While most of the entries were positive, there were some employees who were unhappy with the additional processes and procedures at Zappos. For him and his senior management, these criticisms were also important. In fact, they led to the launch of a monthly newsletter *Ask Anything*, where employees could ask any question and have it answered in a company-wide e-mail. Later, Zappos also started offering company tours to the general public.[10]

Hsieh always emphasized building the company culture. He believed that a company's culture and brand are closely tied. Being technically competent is not enough to get you a job at Zappos; cultural fit is a very important factor, as well. Every new employee, irrespective of the role, is asked to take customer calls for the first few weeks after the training to imbibe the belief in customer service. At the end of training, everyone is given an option to leave the company along with a severance package of $2,000 if they do not believe in the culture of the company.[11] All employees of the company were involved in forming the ten core values of the firm.[12]

## AMAZON ACQUIRES ZAPPOS

Until 2007, the company was growing at a fast pace and was exceeding the revenue expectations it set for itself each year. The 2008 recession slowed growth, however, and Zappos laid off 8 percent of its workforce.[13] Zappos offered generous severance packages to those employees affected by the layoffs.

Amazon had an eye on Zappos for a long time. Jeff Bezos was convinced that Amazon was not the right platform to sell shoes because of the complexity involved. Bezos, Chief Executive Officer of Amazon, had first approached Zappos in 2005, but Zappos wanted to remain independent. After the initial Zappos–Amazon deal failed, Bezos launched an online marketplace for shoes called Endless.com. The new website offered numerous discounts but failed to dent the growth of Zappos.[14]

Meanwhile, Amazon kept monitoring Zappos's progress and, as its growth stagnated in 2008–2009, Hsieh looked for outside investors. Amazon approached Zappos again and on July 22, 2009, Zappos announced that Amazon had acquired it in an all-stock deal. Amazon would purchase Zappos for 10 million shares of Amazon.[15] By the time the deal was closed in 2009, it was worth $1.2 billion. As a result of the acquisition, the shares paid for Zappos represented 2.31 percent of the 433 million shares of the combined company.[16] The deal was beneficial for both the parties. Zappos received the much-needed cash, retained all its employees, and was allowed to protect its culture by working independently.

For Amazon, Bezos said: "Zappos is a customer focused company. We see great opportunities for both companies to learn from each other and create even better experiences for our customers."[17]

Zappos has a customer obsession which is so easy for me to admire. It is the starting point for Zappos. It is the place where Zappos begins and ends. And that is a very key factor for me. I get all weak-kneed when I see a customer-obsessed company, and Zappos certainly is that. Zappos also has a totally unique culture. I've seen a lot of companies, and I have never seen a company with a culture like Zappos's. And I think that kind of unique culture is a very significant asset.[18]

Zappos continued to grow steadily under Amazon and earned an operating profit of $54.5 million in 2014, which was expected to reach $97 million in 2015.[19] In 2008, Zappos had reported net income of $10.8 million.[20] According to Hsieh, the relationship between Zappos and Amazon was "governed by a document that formally recognizes the uniqueness of Zappos's culture and Amazon's duty to protect it."[21] Zappos continues to operate as an independent unit within Amazon and is free to set its own organizational structure; however, Amazon has influenced some key aspects of Zappos operations. In September 2012, Zappos handed over its two Kentucky distribution and fulfillment warehouses to Amazon to improve operational efficiency.[22] This change meant 2,000 Zappos employees became Amazon employees and Hsieh described the change as "bittersweet."[23]

| In Traditional Companies | With Holacracy |
| --- | --- |
| **Job descriptions** | **Roles** |
| Each person has exactly one job. Job descriptions are imprecise, rarely updated, and often irrelevant. | Roles are defined around the work, not people, and are updated regularly. People fill several roles. |
| **Delegated Authority** | **Distributed Authority** |
| Managers loosely delegate authority. Ultimately, their decision always trumps others. | Authority is truly distributed to teams and roles. Decisions are made locally. |
| **Big Re-Orgs** | **Rapid Iterations** |
| The org structure is rarely revised, mandated from the top. | The org structure is regularly updated via small iterations. Every team self-organizes. |
| **Office Politics** | **Transparent Rules** |
| Implicit rules slow down change and favor people "in the know". | Everyone is bound by the same rules, CEO included. Rules are visible to all. |

**FIGURE 12.1**  Holacracy vs Traditional

*Source*: "What is Holacracy," *Holacracy*. Online at www.holacracy.org/how-it-works/.

## HOLACRACY

Brian Robertson and Tom Thomison founded Holacracy, a self-governing management system in 2007. Under his consultancy, HolacracyOne, his team advises companies on how to implement the new management style. Holacracy also features a constitution that governs how meetings are run. According to the Holacracy website, Holacracy "increases transparency, accountability, and organizational agility."

The following is an extract from the Holacracy Constitution which directs instructions on how to convene a meeting:[24]

## MEETING PROCESS

The Facilitator must use the following process for Governance Meetings:

- **(a) Check-in Round:** The Facilitator allows each participant in turn to share their current state or thoughts, or offer another type of opening comment for the meeting. Responses are not allowed.
- **(b) Administrative Concerns:** The Facilitator allows space to discuss and resolve any administrative or logistical matters the Facilitator deems worthy of attention.
- **(c) Agenda Building & Processing:** The Facilitator builds an agenda of Tensions to process, then processes each agenda item in turn.
- **(d) Closing Round:** The Facilitator allows each participant in turn to share a closing reflection or other thought triggered by the meeting. Responses are not allowed.

A Policy of the Circle may add to this process, but may not conflict with any of the steps or other rules defined in this Article of the Constitution.

## PRINCIPAL FEATURES OF HOLACRACY

1. **No Job titles or managers**. Every employee has a clearly defined role of his or her choice which aligns with the company's goals and the employee's skills. A person having multiple skills can choose to be part of multiple-issue-based circles (or teams). Every circle has a Lead Link, who is primarily responsible for driving that task to closure and is also responsible for other administrative work.
2. **No hierarchy of managers**. Compared to traditional management structures, Holacracy is a relatively "flat" structure. Since an employee can have multiple roles in different circles, he/she may have authority over his/her colleague in one circle, while the colleague might have similar authority in another circle.
3. **Every role is clearly accountable** according to the Holacracy constitution. That constitution has in-built mechanisms to address situations when two roles may conflict.[25]

Other organizations using Holacracy:[26]

- Accord Immobilier, Reunion Island – Real estate
- Adscale Laboratories, New Zealand – Online advertising
- ARCA, Mebane, NC – Cash automation
- arTerre, Reunion Island – Agroecology
- David Allen & Co, Ojai, CA – GTD method
- Conscious Capitalism
- Dev Bootcamp, San Francisco, CA – Information technology and services
- Kahler Financial Group, Rapid City, SD – Financial services
- MaestroConference, Oakland, CA – Social conferencing
- Pantheon Enterprises, Phoenix, AZ – Chemical industry

- Precision Nutrition, Toronto, ON – Fitness and nutrition industry
- SOPRODI, Clermont-Ferrand, France – Metallurgical Industry
- Springest, Amsterdam, Netherlands – Training programs and courses
- Waking Up the Workplace
- Office of the Chief Information Officer of Washington State, Washington State, USA

According to reports, Bezos has spoken to Hsieh about Holacracy and he's observing Zappos's deployment of it with interest.[27]

## HOLACRACY FAILURES AT OTHER ORGANIZATIONS

Online publishing platform, Medium, implemented the Holacratic management style for a few years until it was abandoned in 2016. After Medium stopped using Holacracy, Andy Doyle, Head of Operations, complemented Holacracy for its decentralized management approach and the HolacracyOne team for their innovative work. He acknowledged, however, a few challenges the system presented. In his blog,[28] Doyle admits that implementing Holacracy for large initiatives can become "time consuming and divisive to gain alignment." Record-keeping and focus on governance are among the other problems associated with the holacratic management structure. He further adds that the process to recruit experienced candidates had become difficult in a "bossless company." The following excerpt from his blog sums up his argument:

> We are moving beyond it because we as a company have changed and want to make fundamental changes
> to reflect this. Many of the principles we value most about Holacracy are already embedded in the organization
> through how we approach our work, collaborate, and instigate change. Beyond that, the system had begun to
> exert a small but persistent tax on both our effectiveness, and our sense of connection to each other.

Another technology start-up that tested Holacracy for a few years before abandoning it was GitHub.[29] Even Tony Hsieh's pet, the downtown Vegas project, an initiative to revitalize the district, had to exit Holacracy after a few months.[30]

## ONLINE SHOE BUSINESS: INDUSTRY OVERVIEW

In 2015, total global footwear sales grew by 6 percent and reached $340 billion.[31] Of this, online sales from all sources represented about 12 percent or $41 billion and a growth rate of 22 percent over the previous year. Several factors have contributed to the growth of the online shoe and apparel industry, including changing demographics, increased customizability, operational efficiencies and larger selection. Millennial shoppers are more likely to shop online and are a key driver for the growth in global online shoe and apparel sales. Millennials are also driving the trend toward customization and personalization in an effort to obtain a distinct product that differentiates them in the marketplace. Nike, for example, offers online bespoke models which allow customers to customize the print, color and stitching for up to $1,000. Customers can also add their names or other text to the design to further personalize the shoe. This type of customization is more practical for online retailers and is another source of growth for the e-commerce shoe market.

The athleisure trend has driven growth in the shoe and apparel industry as a whole; as a result, the athletic shoe market grew by 14 percent in 2015 globally. This growth is also reflected in the increased sales for online shoe retailers but is not a point of differentiation between brick-and-mortar retailers. Larger selections and operational efficiencies, on the other hand, do represent a point of differentiation for online footwear retailers relative to traditional retailers. Online retailers can continuously update their inventory to match consumer trends whereas traditional retailers may only update inventory once per season. This helps online retailers attract fashion-conscious shoppers.[32] Additionally, the larger selection and greater sizing options of online retailers have contributed to sales growth. Online retailers are better equipped to stock rare or unique products that may command a premium than are traditional retailers.

## KEY COMPETITORS AND THEIR ORGANIZATIONAL STRUCTURE

The online shoe retail industry has low barriers to entry but several well-established competitors exist. They may be grouped based on their available distribution channels into categories of pure-play or mixed-channel competitors. Pure-play competitors such as Zappos have only an online distribution channel, while mixed-channel competitors such as DSW and Nike have physical stores as well as an online presence. The largest domestic competitor for Zappos is Foot Locker. However, the low concentration for the industry has led to a large number of small competitors.[33] International competitors include Shoes.com (Canada), Zalando (Germany), Sarenza (France) and Spartoo (France). Additionally, Amazon itself continues to compete in the online footwear industry.

In 2015, all of Zappos's competitors in the online shoe industry had traditional management structures. Additionally, none of the competitors changed their corporate structure in response to Zappos. The impetus for the organizational change at Zappos was not driven by distinctive market pressure and has not spread throughout the online shoe retail industry. Instead, the idea for Holacracy at Zappos sprang from Tony Hsieh's vision for the company moving forward.

## HOLACRACY AT ZAPPOS

Tony Hsieh is an avid book reader and he was inspired by *Triumph of the City* by Harvard Professor Edward Glaeser. According to the book, as the size of the city doubles, innovation and productivity per citizen increases by about 50 percent. Hence, Hsieh wanted Zappos to grow more like a city rather than a typical bureaucratic organization that resisted growth as the number of employees increased. Motivated by this vision, Hsieh began the transition to Holacracy from 2013 in the form of a small pilot program in the Human Resources department. By early 2015, Hsieh decided to expand the program to the entire organization.[34] Ensuing frustration and confusion on the part of employees provided the impetus for him to write "The Offer" e-mail. At that point, Zappos became the largest organization ever to implement Holacracy.

Each Zappos employee has 100 total people points to use in the circles they join. Both their badges and their people points constrain which roles they are allowed to take within the company. A senior manager named John Bunch was the implementation lead for the Holacracy transition at Zappos.[35] He oversaw the introduction of a system of badges to signify the capabilities and expertise employees possess over a wide range of work-related functions.[36] Performance reviews are handled by each circle individually. Some circles may choose to conduct performance reviews, while others do not.[37]

Holacracy doesn't clearly define any process governing compensation for employees. At Zappos, however, every employee is assigned a badge according to the roles and skills the employee possesses. Salaries may be linked to the badges in the future. Hence, an employee qualifying for multiple badges may receive a higher salary. For now, employees are required to submit their application to the Zappos Compensation Circle. There are other circles tasked with hiring and firing decisions.[38] These badges are necessary to qualify for different project roles which are listed on the Role Marketplace.[39] For example, an employee can get a "writer" badge to answer customer e-mails or a "GlassFrog" badge to work on the Holacracy software.[40]

Employee response to the implementation of Holacracy at Zappos has been generally, though not entirely, positive. Jordan Sams from the Holacracy implementation team said that ideas previously rejected have now been implemented and people no longer have to wait for promotions to demonstrate their abilities to handle more complex and challenging roles.[41]

Holacracy empowers employees to collectively make important decisions, as evidenced by the reversal of a decision made by the CEO. Tony Hsieh closed the bridge connecting the parking garage to the Zappos office before the transition to Holacracy because he felt employees would be more collaborative if they all entered the building through the same entrance. Some employees felt this was unsafe when they worked late at night because it forced them to walk through the streets of Downtown Las Vegas. After implementing Holacracy, the organization made the decision to reopen the bridge.[42]

Dogs were not allowed in the Zappos office prior to Holacracy. After the transition, employees organized to implement a viable plan to allow dogs into the office that addressed the most common objections. Now, dogs are allowed in the office, provided they pass a behavioral test and do not enter the "allergy zones" designated for people sensitive to dander. Zappos chief of staff Jamie Naughton said this change would not have been possible without Holacracy.[43]

Not everyone embraced the change to Holacracy. Nox Voortella worked for Zappos as a sales planner before deciding to leave because of the new self-management system. She initially thought Holacracy was great but eventually felt the insecurities of some former managers led them to attempt to reconstruct their power within the new system.[44] She went on to say that the managers who stayed had less to offer than the ones who left. Tyler Williams, who is lead link of a marketing circle, echoes that sentiment but says the problem is getting better:

> Now we are getting back to that place where we are being kind and forgiving to people, and people that used holacracy as a weapon are finding themselves getting smaller and smaller islands to work from. We're more policed now as a company based on peer pressure rather than on micromanagement.[45]

Charles Kim is another Zapponian who left the organization in 2015 after ten years of service. When asked if he left because of Holacracy, he said "Personally, no. I had other reasons for leaving Zappos. Others I know, yes." When asked if Holacracy affected company culture, he said, "Yes, the culture became obsolete. Although they encouraged an emphasis on upholding the culture, Holacracy was the root cause for it to diminish."[46]

In addition to the loss of staff, the implementation of Holacracy was associated with some notable changes in performance metrics for the company. Because Amazon prepares consolidated financial statements, they do not have to publicly disclose profit forecasts specifically for Zappos. However, according to a 2016 *Fortune* article, "the company achieved its 2015 profit goals, but several employees say that it has lowered its 2016 targets."[47] Additionally, Zappos was present on the *Fortune* "100 Best Companies to Work For" list from 2008 to 2015; they were dropped from the list for 2016, however, largely due to the implementation of Holacracy.[48] As a measure of comparison, Glassdoor employee reviews exist for the company as early as 2009. Employee review ratings increased slightly from 3.6 out of 5 in March to 3.8 out of 5 in December 2015.[49]

Responding to the additional turnover in 2015, the company's official statement says it "was mostly due to us giving long-time employees the opportunity to pursue their dreams (average severance paid out was about 5.5 months' pay when we last analyzed the data)." The statement also said:

> We have always felt like however many people took the offer was the right amount of people to take the offer, because what we really want is a group of Zapponians who are aligned, committed, and excited to push forward the purpose and vision of Zappos.[50]

Industry experts give Holacracy mixed reviews. Ethan Bernstein, a Harvard Business School professor, says Holacracy isn't the answer to self-management but is a useful framework for conflict resolution. "Holacracy replaces that [traditional] structure with a structuring process, at least for particularly frequent kinds of conflicts, to resolve conflicts in a potentially less-hierarchical, more self-organized, and more adaptive fashion."[51] Similarly, David Ulrich from the University of Michigan Ross School of Business says the principles of Holacracy aren't necessarily new: "The basic insight is that employees should be more engaged in decision making – through teams or individual involvement – when they are able to make good decisions and willing to work hard on the right things."[52] Stanford Professor of Organizational Behavior Jeffrey Pfeffer in his 2013 article, "You're Still the Same: Why Theories of Power Hold Over Time and Across Contexts" believes hierarchy to be the fundamental principle of all organizational systems. According to the tweet from his official account on July 18, 2015, "The idea that employee empowerment is imposed from the top is a logical contradiction. Plus, people prefer hierarchy."[53]

## HOW SHOULD ZAPPOS PROCEED?

In late December of 2015, Zappos employees working in their downtown Las Vegas office contemplate the Holacracy experiment. Eighteen percent of their colleagues have left the company due to Holacracy and it was an open question whether this restructuring will succeed with those that remained. They have recently learned the company has been dropped from the *Fortune* "100 Best Companies to Work For" list and they have had to reduce profit estimates for the upcoming year.

Great companies have tried and failed with non-traditional management systems. Tech giant Google, in 2002, attempted to implement a flat organization structure by eliminating the need for managers. Founders Larry Page and Sergey Brin soon realized the importance of managers. As of 2013, Google had over 37,000 employees, with 5,000 managers, 1,000 directors and 100 vice-presidents.[54] Where others have failed, will Holacracy work for Zappos?

## DISCUSSION QUESTIONS

1. What should the organization do moving forward?
2. Was moving to Holacracy the right decision? How long should they wait to find out?
3. Who are the key stakeholders affected by the departing employees? How should Zappos respond?
4. To which audience(s) should Zappos communicate regarding the reduction in workforce?
5. What actions, if any, should Zappos take to minimize the effect of the departing employees?
6. What lessons can Zappos learn from previous organizations implementing Holacracy?

## ACKNOWLEDGMENTS

This case was prepared by research assistants Bryan Golden and Anusheel Pandey under the direction of James O'Rourke, Teaching Professor of Management, as the basis for class discussion rather than to illustrate either effective or ineffective handling of an administrative situation. Information was gathered from corporate as well as public sources.

## NOTES

1 Groth, A. "Internal Memo: Zappos is Offering Severance to Employees Who Aren't All in with Holacracy," *Quartz*, March 26, 2015. Online at https://qz.com/370616/internal-memo-zappos-is-offering-severance-to-employees-who-arent-all-in-with-holacracy/.
2 Lam, B. "Why Are So Many Zappos Employees Leaving?" *The Atlantic*, January 15, 2016. Online at www.theatlantic.com/business/archive/2016/01/zappos-holacracy-hierarchy/424173/.
3 Reingold, J. "How a Radical Shift Left Zappos Reeling," *Fortune*, March 4, 2016. Online at http://fortune.com/zappos-tony-hsieh-holacracy/.
4 Yarrow, J. "The Zappos Founder Just Told Us All Kinds of Crazy Stories – Here's the Surprisingly Candid Interview," *Business Insider*, November 28, 2011. Online at www.businessinsider.com/nick-swinmurn-zappos-rnkd-2011-11.
5 Hsieh, Tony. *Delivering Happiness: A Path to Profits, Passion, and Purpose*, 1/e. New York, NY: Grand Central Publishing, June 2010.
6 Ibid.
7 Ibid.
8 Ibid.
9 Ibid.
10 "Zappos Tours," *Zappos Insights*. Online at www.zapposinsights.com/tours.
11 Lam. "Why Are So Many Zappos Employees Leaving?"
12 Hsieh. *Delivering Happiness*.
13 Ibid.
14 Stone, Brad. *The Everything Store: Jeff Bezos and the Age of Amazon*, 1/e. New York, NY: Little, Brown and Company, October 2013.

15  "Amazon Closes Zappos Deal, Ends Up Paying $1.2 Billion," *Tech Crunch*. Online at https://techcrunch.com/2009/11/02/amazon-closes-zappos-deal-ends-up-paying-1-2-billion/.

16  "Amazon Shares Outstanding," *Macro Axis*. Online at www.macroaxis.com/invest/ratio/AMZN—Shares-Outstanding.

17  "Amazon.com to Acquire Zappos.com," *BusinessWire*. Online at www.businesswire.com/news/home/20090722006145/en/Amazon.com-Acquire-Zappos.com

18  "Video from Jeff Bezos About Amazon and Zappos," *YouTube*, July 22, 2009. Online at www.youtube.com/watch?v=-hxX_Q5CnaA.

19  Snel, Alan. "Zappos Predicts Massive Profit Growth for 2015," *Las Vegas Review-Journal*, February 11, 2015.

20  Evans, Katie. "Zappos Posted Strong Profits in 2008," *Digital Commerce 360*, Digital Commerce 360 | Internet Retailer, November 2, 2016. Online at www.digitalcommerce360.com/2009/07/28/zappos-posted-strong-profits-in-2008/.

21  Lashinsky, A. "Why Amazon Tolerates Zappos' Extreme Management Experiment," *Fortune*, March 4, 2016. Online at http://fortune.com/2016/03/04/amazon-zappos-holacracy/.22. Ibid.

22  Ibid.

23  McGarry, Caitlin. "Zappos Sheds Its Kentucky Warehouses," *Las Vegas Review-Journal*, June 7, 2012. Online at www.review-journal.com/business/zappos-sheds-its-kentucky-warehouses.

24  Holacracy website. Online at www.holacracy.org.

25  Ibid.

26  "How Holacracy Works," *Wiki*. Online at http://wiki.holacracy.org/index.php?title=FAQ.

27  Groth, A. "Holacracy at Zappos: It's Either the Future of Management or a Social Experiment Gone Awry," *Quartz*, January 14, 2015. Online at https://qz.com/317918/holacracy-at-zappos-its-either-the-future-of-management-or-a-social-experiment-gone-awry/.

28  Doyle, A. "Management and Organization at Medium," *Medium*, March 4, 2016. Online at https://blog.medium.com/management-and-organization-at-medium-2228cc9d93e9.

29  Mittelman, M. "Why GitHub Finally Abandoned Its Bossless Workplace," *Bloomberg*, September 6, 2016. Online at www.bloomberg.com/news/articles/2016-09-06/why-github-finally-abandoned-its-bossless-workplace.

30  Carr, P. B. "Staff at Tony Hsieh's Downtown Project Decided to Abandon Holacracy Nine Months Ago," *Pando*, July 8, 2015. Online at https://pando.com/2015/07/08/staff-tony-hsiehs-downtown-project-voted-abandon-holacracy-nine-months-ago/.

31  Weinswig, Deborah. "Deep Dive: Global Footwear E-Commerce: Growing by Leaps and Bounds," *Fung Global Retail & Technology*, October 25, 2016. Online at www.deborahweinswig.com/wp-content/uploads/2016/10/Global-Footwear-E-Commerce-October-25-2016-1.pdf .

32  Carney, M. "Why Shoes Have Dominated This Generation of Ecommerce," *Pando*, February 18, 2013. Online at https://pando.com/2013/02/18/why-shoes-have-dominated-fashion-ecommerce/.

33  "Online Shoe Sales Industry in the US," Industry Market Research Report, *IBISWorld*, February 2018. Online at www.ibisworld.com/industry/online-shoe-sales.html.

34  Zander, R. P. "Alexis Gonzales-Black: Zappos, Holacracy, and How We Work in the 21st Century," *Robin Peter Zander Blog*, January 7, 2017. Online at www.robinpzander.com/alexis-gonzales-black-zappos-holacracy-and-how-we-work-in-the-21st-century.

35  Bernstein, E., J. Bunch, N. Canner and M. Lee. "Beyond the Holacracy Hype," *Harvard Business Review*, July–August 2016. Online at https://hbr.org/2016/07/beyond-the-holacracy-hype.

36  Ibid.

37  White, Sarah K. "What Is Holacracy and Why Does It Work for Zappos?" *CIO*, August 5, 2015. Online at www.cio.com/article/2956721/staff-management/what-is-holacracy-and-why-does-it-work-for-zappos.html.

38  Ibid.

39  Ibid.

40  Bernstein, Bunch, Canner and Lee. "Beyond the Holacracy Hype."

41  White. "What Is Holacracy and Why Does It Work for Zappos?"

42  Gelles, D. "At Zappos, Pushing Shoes and a Vision," *The New York Times*, July 17, 2015. Online at www.nytimes.com/2015/07/19/business/at-zappos-selling-shoes-and-a-vision.html.

43  Reingold. "How a Radical Shift Left Zappos Reeling."

44  Ibid.

45  Ibid.

46  Personal correspondence with the author, February 26, 2017.

47  Reingold. "How a Radical Shift Left Zappos Reeling."

48  Ibid.

49  "The Zappos Family Reviews," *Glassdoor*, updated November 5, 2018. Online at www.glassdoor.com/Reviews/The-Zappos-Family-Reviews-E19906.htm.

50  Lam. "Why Are So Many Zappos Employees Leaving?"

51  Groth. "Holacracy at Zappos."

52  McGraw, Mark. "Goodbye Hierarchy, Hello Holacracy?" *Righting the Ship*, LRP Publications, June 1, 2015. Online at hrearchive.lrp.com/HRE/print.jhtml?id=534358778.

53  Schumpeter. "The Holes in Holacracy," *The Economist*, July 5, 2014. Online at www.economist.com/news/business/21606267-latest-big-idea-management-deserves-some-scepticism-holes-holacracy.

54  Garvin, D. A. "How Google Sold Its Engineers on Management," *Harvard Business Review*, December 2013. Online at https://hbr.org/2013/12/how-google-sold-its-engineers-on-management.

# CHAPTER 13

# Dealing with the News Media

Some people are simply better than others at saying what they mean and sounding sincere in the process. When a Starbucks manager called the police to evict two men who had entered a Philadelphia coffee shop to discuss a real estate deal, the cops didn't just tell them to move along. They handcuffed the men and took them into custody. Of course, the two men were black, feeding a continuing narrative about American business and police harboring a long-standing bias against people of color. Upon viewing bystanders' videos of the incident, Starbucks' CEO Kevin Johnson described the scene as "very hard to watch."

He and Howard Schultz, former CEO and executive chairman of Starbucks, stepped forward almost immediately with a contrite, heartfelt apology. They assured the nation that they were, " . . . personally committed to act on several fronts to ensure it never happens again." But they did more, asking the entire company to stand down for a day to discuss race relations and for employees to receive racial-bias training. Additionally, he ran full-page ads in *The New York Times*, *The Wall Street Journal* and other papers.[1]

Apparently it worked. In the months following the incident, in spite of their expectations, Starbucks reported better-than-average sales and a 0.2 percent greater world-wide growth than projected at the beginning of the quarter.[2]

On the other side of the coin, during the massive oil spill in the Gulf of Mexico, BP chief executive Tony Hayward famously said, "I think the environmental impact of this disaster is likely to be very, very modest." That same day, when asked about whether he was able to sleep at night in light of the oil spill's effects, he replied, "Of course I can." Just two weeks later, in a televised interview in Louisiana, he addressed the people of the Gulf region, saying, "We're sorry for the massive disruption it's caused to their lives. There's no one who wants this thing over more than I do. I'd like my life back." Those words, played over and over again on evening newscasts, came to haunt Mr. Hayward until he was relieved of his duties weeks later by BP's chairman.[3]

## INTRODUCTION

Maintaining a positive, honest, accessible relationship with the news media who report on your industry and your company will never be easy, but it will be essential. Few managers and virtually no executives will make it through a career successfully without responding to the media – in good times and in bad.

More than 40 years ago, consultant and former president of CBS News, Chester Burger said:

> A corporate president is not chosen for his outstanding ability to articulate corporate problems. He is selected by his board of directors because of his management know-how, or his financial expertise, or his legal proficiency, or whatever particular combination of these talents may be required by the immediate problems facing the company. In utilizing his own skills, he is usually very good indeed.[4]

But the skills of management are not the same as those required to deal with the news media. Reporters, whether they are employed by television (where most people still get most of their news these days), newspapers, magazines, radio or an Internet blog, are trained in their ability to talk with someone and unearth a newsworthy story, one that will stimulate their viewers or readers. This ability is why they were selected; it is their surpassing talent; and it is precisely what unnerves corporate managers who choose to face their questions.[5] Most media relations and corporate communication experts will acknowledge that reporters are not only well-trained in their profession, but most are also quite good at the process of asking good questions in pursuit of a newsworthy story. What few outsiders understand, however, is that managers and executives have faced others – many of them better informed and better prepared to ask tough questions – whom they respect but do not fear.

"There's little in this world tougher than a bond road show," says Jordan Industries President and COO Tom Quinn. "The people in that audience have money to invest and plenty of tough questions about what you're planning to do with it." In many respects, investors in the debt market are sharper than equities investors:

> People who manage mutual funds, retirement plans, or insurance companies know dozens of tough questions to ask and they take their measure of you as you sit there on a stool or stand in front of them with nothing but your wits and charm to defend yourself.[6]

The fact is, managers get paid to answer difficult questions every day from people who know the facts, understand the business and are familiar with the products and services involved. Everyone from worried or irate shareholders to curious government regulators have posed questions that managers must answer – many of them on the spot, without reference to files, databases or conversations with others in the organization.

The relationship between the media and business is essentially adversarial, which is simply part of doing business in a democratic society. NBC reporter and later ABC News commentator David Brinkley once said, "When a reporter asks questions, he is not working for the person being questioned, whether businessman, politician, or bureaucrat, but he is working for the readers and listeners."[7] He also once said, "News is what you don't want to tell me. Everything else is public relations."

Can you do it? Are you equal to the challenge of facing a reporter and straightforwardly answering questions about your business? Sure you are. It won't be easy, but you certainly have the talent and the motivation to do the job. What you need is the preparation.

This chapter looks at why it will be in your best interest to cooperate with reporters and editors who wish to interview you and suggests a number of ways to prepare yourself. Specifically, we examine six issues that confront any manager who faces the prospect of a press interview, whether for good news or bad:

- Why interviews are important
- Should I or shouldn't I?
- A look at the media
- Getting ready
- Making it happen
- Follow-up

## WHY INTERVIEWS ARE IMPORTANT

### They Are a Chance to Reach a Large Audience

An interview with a reporter is an unparalleled opportunity to reach a large audience. You simply cannot attend enough Kiwanis Club breakfasts or Rotary Club luncheons to tell your story directly. Those events, by the way, are wonderful opportunities, and you should take advantage of every invitation you receive to speak before such groups. They represent a chance to network, to meet community leaders and to put your message forward in a direct and unfiltered fashion. The disadvantage is that they offer a limited audience for your message.

If you must reach thousands or millions of people with your message in a short period of time, you have very few choices. One choice is to take out newspaper and magazine advertisements (television advertisements are usually too expensive and inappropriate for most corporate information campaigns). People usually look at such ad campaigns as one-sided and biased and pay little attention to the content of the message.

Social media and a digital component to your strategy will be helpful, but it won't be enough. Not enough people follow you or your company on Twitter or will receive push-notices from your Facebook account. That digital approach is necessary but not sufficient.

If you need to speak to a metropolitan, state-wide or national audience, the mass media are – or should be – among your first few choices. Arranging for dinner or luncheon speeches will be helpful, as will the information you plan to post on your company's website or share with selected bloggers. But there is simply no substitute for speaking directly to a newspaper, wire service or television reporter. Their reach is global; their speed is near-instantaneous; and their reputation for objectivity is your guarantee that "informed attenders" in the public (those who read newspapers and watch national television newscasts) will see, hear or read your message. It may not be pleasant, but you have few other choices.

## They Represent an Opportunity to Tell Your Story

For better or worse, most people in your target audience really don't know much about you. If your company is typical, many people will recognize the company's name; some will know of your products and services; a few will understand issues related to ownership, organization or the industry in which you compete; and no one will seem to understand much about the issues that worry you the most. Like it or not, most people are basically ignorant about your people, your mission and your goals as an organization.

Is this all bad? Not necessarily. Anonymity can have its rewards. The owner of a small bookshop near campus once remarked, "Whenever some stink about book publishing, censorship, or objectionable publications hits the news, reporters in this town always go over to interview the manager at Barnes & Noble. Good," she said. "I don't want to answer those kinds of questions." Being anonymous, however, often means you must fight to be noticed when it's important for the public to know who you are.

## They Are an Opportunity to Inform

Talking to a reporter is a chance for you, as a manager, to establish yourself as an expert on certain subjects, or at least as a specialist who knows something about the market, the product category or the industry. Being friendly with those who are in search of information to support a newsworthy story can buy some goodwill for you when times are more difficult and the story is about you rather than someone else.

If you make it a regular practice to offer information to the news media about your company and your industry, chances are much greater that the readers and viewers of those news outlets will associate your name, your company's name and your product or service line with such important attributes as quality, currency, value and desirability. You can't afford to be shy when the media come looking for a comment on a story related to your business, even if it doesn't involve you directly.

## They Offer an Opportunity to Address Public Concerns

The public at large are worried about any number of things, including the environment, the economy, job opportunity, working conditions, security, and product safety. Where does your company fit into those concerns? Do you know what concerns are most important to people across the nation or in your own community? If not, you should because those issues are most likely to become the motivating factors that frame a reporter's questions.

You should be ready with little or no notice to address questions that concern how your company treats the environment. Do you produce hazardous waste or non-biodegradable by-products? How do you dispose of that waste?

How does your company treat its workers? What are the wages, conditions of employment or benefits for those who make your products or deliver your services? If a company across town or somewhere else in the country makes an unsafe product and you happen to compete in the same industry, are you ready to answer detailed, direct questions in an honest and believable manner?

When people watch television news interviews – particularly in a crisis or during a breaking news story – they tend to ask one question of themselves as they observe a businessperson responding to a reporter: "Is anyone smart in charge here?" If so, they go on about their own business and don't think much about yours. They're confident in the knowledge that some smart young man or woman is taking care of that messy business they saw on television. If the answer is "no," then the viewers tend to think less of the company involved, and may decide that company shouldn't be permitted to do business in their community any longer.

Keep in mind that just because you may have a license to do business – to assemble things, to transform raw materials into finished goods or to store or process various materials – doesn't mean you'll be in business forever. Your real license to continue what you're doing depends directly on the goodwill and permission of the people who live in your community, who work in your facilities and who buy your products and services. If they lose confidence in you, you're done. It's up to you to convince them that someone smart is in charge. AT&T vice president Arthur W. Page may have said it best when he wrote: "All business in a democratic country begins with public permission and exists by public approval. Real success," he said, "both for big business and the public, lies in large enterprise conducting itself in the public interest and in such a way that the public will give it sufficient freedom to serve effectively."[8]

## They Give You an Opportunity to Set the Record Straight

Although many people know little (and some want to know even less) about your company and its business practices, much of what some people know just isn't true. American humorist Artemus Ward once said, "It isn't what we know that gives us trouble, it's what we know that ain't so."[9]

You'd be surprised, indeed, if you were to speak directly with many people about your business or your industry. Misconceptions, stereotypes, distortions and often some disinformation will form the bulk of what they "know for sure." A news media interview is an opportunity to set the facts straight, to offer your own perspective, to refute allegations or stories that are simply untrue.

## They Offer an Opportunity to Apologize

Investors have lost trillions in recent business scandals; popular anger with corporate executives is at its highest level since the Great Depression; and foreign allies are questioning the vitality of American capitalism. So how do the executives responsible for these improprieties, illegalities and bad judgment respond? Jeffrey K. Skilling says he is "immensely proud" of what he accomplished at Enron. Marc Shapiro, vice-chairman of J. P. Morgan Chase, insists his bank's transactions with the Houston energy company were "entirely appropriate." Duke Energy's round-trip power trades were "well within the market rules," says CEO James Donnell, while Martha Stewart called insider-trading allegations "ridiculous."

The first reaction of many executives is to hunker down; deny everything; hire tough, expensive lawyers; and try to wait out the mess, hoping the headlines, animosity and bad feelings will eventually pass. A more productive approach to such problems might involve a sincere, unrestrained and heartfelt apology. New academic research indicates that goodwill generated by such *mea culpa* could more than make up for the legal costs involved. State legislatures, meanwhile, are quietly passing laws that encourage contrition by making apologies inadmissible as evidence against those making them.[10]

Professor Lamar Reinsch of Georgetown University's McDonough School of Management has studied the effects of public apologies and their effect on liability. After reviewing hundreds of recent cases, he concludes:

The risk of litigation is one that corporations balance against public backlash and loss of consumer base. In the end, judges and juries have demonstrated an understanding that expression of remorse and apology are not necessarily admissions of responsibility or liability, as evidenced by protections enacted by federal and state bodies. When a plaintiff goes to court armed with naught but an apology, courts are likely to find that the apology is useless in fulfilling the legal elements necessary to impose liability.

Liability is not admitted when a corporation publicly pronounces regret that its customers have been injured, and that the corporation is willing to use its power to cure problems faced by its customers ... Well-timed apologies and promises to investigate the root of the injury can often diffuse a potential crisis, or at least lessen its intensity.

In sum, corporations must carefully weigh the factors of their particular situation when contemplating a public apology and decide whether the risk of potential liability is worth the possible alleviation of public censure and legally mitigating effects of public contrition on rulings of judge and jury. In other words, executives are advised to seek advice both from public relations professionals and from attorneys who are familiar with the details of the specific circumstances.[11]

According to business journalist Mike France, companies may be overestimating the costs of apologies and underestimating their benefits. "For one thing," he writes, "juries weigh the fact that a company has faced up to its problems when assessing punitive damages. More important, apologies can defuse victims' anger." Some evidence suggests that people may be just as interested in apologies as they are in money. In one recent study of British medical malpractice patients, 37 percent said they wouldn't have brought suit if the doctor had provided them with an explanation and an apology.[12]

The details differ, but the laws generally prevent expressions of sympathy from being used as evidence of fault after an accident. They do not, however, apply to expressions of guilt. So the statement "I'm sorry your son died in the crash" would not be admissible as evidence of guilt, whereas "I'm sorry your son died because of the faulty brakes in the automobile we made," probably would be.

Apologies can have surprising power when they are delivered well. Not long ago, for instance, Joette Schmidt, a vice president for customer service at America West Airlines Inc., appeared on NBC television's *Today* show to ask the forgiveness of Sheryl Cole, a passenger who had been thrown off a flight for joking about the company's recent drunken-pilot episode. Ignoring interviewer Matt Lauer's invitation to defend the airlines' conduct, Schmidt declared: "I'm here primarily to apologize to Ms. Cole. We overreacted." The victim, who had spent the first minute of the segment tearing into America West, was caught off guard. "I appreciate the apology," Cole responded. "I'm sympathetic to America West right now. I know they're going through a tough time."[13]

### They Are an Opportunity to Reinforce Credibility

When the public stops believing in you, you're finished. An important part of your task as a manager is to reinforce public belief in what you do, what you make or provide, and in who you are as an organization. How do you do that? One easy way for a manager to find credibility for his or her statements to the press is to cite the speeches, public pronouncements or public statements of the company's executive team. Where will you find such statements? In your company's advertising brochures, on your corporate website, in the annual report or in the company's 10-K and 10-Q filings with the Securities and Exchange Commission. You needn't spend a great deal of time inventing clever things to say about your organization; people have already done that for you, including public relations and advertising firms, the corporate communication staff and the company's senior team. Read those documents; look for ideas, phrases and concepts that you can easily include in a conversation with a reporter. Remember, the more often you say it, the more likely it is a reporter will eventually use it in a story.

## SHOULD YOU OR SHOULDN'T YOU?

In deciding whether to respond to a reporter's request for an interview or whether to call a press conference to attract attention to your message, here are a few basic considerations.

### Follow the Few Blanket Rules That Apply

One of the most important rules is "Never talk to strangers." If your mother passed along that bit of wisdom to you as a child, consider yourself well-raised. Your mother was wise, indeed. Dealing with strangers is a high-risk proposition, especially in the news media.

If you are approached by a reporter and asked to respond to a series of questions about your company, your products or services, or the industry, do what you can to gather some basic information first: Who is the reporter? Which organization does he or she work for? What sort of deadline is the reporter working against? Then ask for some time to gather information, consult with others and formulate a decision about participating.

Public relations expert Vic Gold once said, "There are no blanket rules in this business, except one: If Mike Wallace calls, hang up."[14] Did the venerable CBS journalist do something to anger or upset Mr. Gold? Probably not, but the advice is useful, anyway. His point is simple: *60 Minutes*, the program for which Mr. Wallace was a reporter for so many years, is not a news program. It's owned and operated by the News Division of the CBS Television Network. The program employs journalists and former reporters – Anderson Cooper, Lara Logan, Scott Pelley, Steve Kroft and others – to report the stories you see on air. Executive producer Jeff Fager and his staff are long-experienced in the business of television news. So why isn't *60 Minutes* a news program? What makes it different?

*60 Minutes* is merely the longest-running and most successful of a television genre that includes such programs as NBC's *Dateline*, ABC's *20/20*, *PrimeTime Live* and a host of equally profitable but less reputable programs such as *Hard Copy*, *Inside Edition*, *American Journal*, *E!*, *Access Hollywood* and many others. These programs are clearly not news programs. They are entertainment programs. Often, they are dressed up to look like news: Well-known news reporters are hired to speak into the camera; news editing techniques are employed to create movement and tension in their stories; and studio sets as well as field reporting techniques create the impression of a news program. Nothing could be further from the truth.

The objective standards and search for the truth that characterize legitimate news operations are frequently strangers to these programs and those who produce them. Stories on such programs are usually chosen more for their emotional value or audience appeal than their news value. Producers have been known to accept an assignment or begin reporting on a story because of preconceived views or an ideologically driven perspective.

The truth about such programs as *60 Minutes* and others is that they are wonderfully entertaining. But as you smile or nod when Scott Pelley disassembles some poor soul on camera, think to yourself: "That could be me." Few people have the skills or abilities to present themselves and their argument in a fashion that a producer could not edit to suit his or her own taste. Even experienced politicians, long skilled in the arts of dealing with the press, have been eaten alive by the interviewers and producers of these "magazine format" shows. Former Alaska Governor Sarah Palin fumbled for an answer when Katie Couric asked her what newspapers and magazines she regularly reads.

Some businesspeople have agreed to *60 Minutes* interviews and have lived to tell of it. Others have emerged successfully: They've told their stories to a large audience; they were treated fairly; the facts were presented in an evenhanded and professional manner. Joseph and William Coors of Coors Brewing Company made the deliberate decision to be interviewed by CBS's *60 Minutes* in the midst of an ongoing labor dispute and emerged looking like conscientious, caring, responsible businesspeople. Keep in mind, they are an exception to the rule.

The same general considerations we've discussed here also apply to print publications that pass themselves off as newspapers. They include *The National Enquirer*, *The Globe*, *Midnight*, *Weekly World News* and other supermarket tabloids. Even their most loyal readers admit that they don't buy those publications for serious news; they see them for what they are: entertainment. Some focus on celebrities, others on the bizarre and still others on the near-believable. It would be difficult, indeed, to see how you and your company could benefit from being quoted or featured in an edition of one of these papers.

## Ask Your Public Affairs or Corporate Communication Office for Help

Unless you work in a small company, chances are good that the firm employs people with public relations skills. Your organization, no doubt, will have people who are experienced professionals, able to advise you in making your decision to participate in an interview.

"Why doesn't the public affairs person do the interview?" you ask. The reason is simple enough: No self-respecting reporter wants to talk to a public affairs specialist. They know full well that the public affairs office or corporate communication media specialists have an agenda to discuss. Reporters understand that experienced public affairs and public relations people will say only what they want a reporter to hear and report.

Should that make you cautious? It should, primarily because a reporter will feel more comfortable with you, hoping for more candid and revealing statements. In a reporter's eyes, you will have more credibility because you're closer to the action in the organization; you are on the front lines where business decisions are made and the essence of the business happens each day. Your public affairs or corporate communication office can still be of great help to you, though, as you search for information, bring yourself up-to-date on the story and gather details that will be useful in determining whether to participate in the interview. Ask them for assistance – they won't say no.

### Get Some Background Before Committing

Among the many things you'll want to know before agreeing to a press interview is whether this story is primarily about you and your business or whether it's simply an industry trend story that you're being asked to comment on. It will be especially useful for you to know the background of the story before saying yes to an interview. Simply ask the reporter, "What's the backdrop here? How did this story develop?" You should also consider asking who else is participating in this interview. What sources has the reporter consulted? If you know a competitor is talking to him or her, your awareness may influence your decision to participate. If you know that a well-recognized industry critic or media gadfly is being quoted, that knowledge may influence your decision, as well.

### Pay Attention to Gut Feelings

If the story is sufficiently negative, or if you think the news organization you are dealing with won't give you an opportunity to tell your story accurately, fairly and completely, you may well decide not to participate. If a reporter has deceived you about his or her identity, affiliation or intentions, you might not want to cooperate. If the news organization that this reporter works for has an unsavory reputation, that may influence your feelings.

You have to trust your instincts. They have taken you a long way in life and have served you well. They have helped you get through college, find a job and get into business school. They usually won't fail you if you simply let them work on your behalf. Don't agree to participate if:

- you don't trust the reporter;
- you aren't clear on the direction or intent of the story;
- a reporter tries to high-pressure or blackmail you into cooperation;
- a reporter says, "I'm on deadline and need an answer now";
- the nature of the story is so strongly negative that you do not want your name or your company's name associated with the report.

Remember, if you don't participate, you won't have an opportunity to tell your side of the story, from your perspective, or to set the record straight on issues that are most important to your firm. On the other hand, if you honestly think you won't get a fair shake from the reporter or the news organization, you're perfectly within your rights as a citizen and an employee to back off and think about it. The advantage is that your remarks won't be misquoted or taken out of context, and you won't be a part of a story you consider unseemly. The disadvantage may be that others set the tone and direction of the story, and you may be running to catch up.

## A LOOK AT THE NEWS MEDIA

In order to know what you're getting into, we should examine a few basics about the news media.

### It's a Business

First and foremost, news is a business; it is not a philanthropic enterprise. Newspapers, magazines, television stations and networks, and radio broadcasters make money not by selling news but by selling airtime and space to commercial advertisers. It's a straightforward exchange of audience for money. The greater the audience for commercial advertisements, the more the publisher or broadcaster can charge for the time or space.

One interesting aspect of this arrangement is that many businesspeople sign contracts with broadcasters without knowing exactly how much the ads they run will cost them. They know what the rate per thousand households will be, but they won't know until the rating estimates have come in just how much they will pay for the privilege of airing their commercial announcement. Again, the greater the audience, the larger the invoice.

If broadcasters want greater revenues for the airtime they sell, the easiest way to obtain it is to increase the size of the audience that watches their programming. In the case of news broadcasts, that may mean anything from a new hairdo for the news anchor to new graphics or a dramatic new set design. It may also mean more controversial news stories – stories designed to pique the interest of the audience and draw in more viewers. Newspapers and news websites do it with dramatic headlines ("Mom Locks Tot in Trunk at JFK"), more stories about celebrities ("Lindsay Lohan Checks into Rehab . . . Again!"), sports figures (O. J. Simpson, Barry Bonds, Marv Albert) and other people (Kim Kardashian, Paris Hilton) who – in the greater scheme of things – really don't matter.

Journalist and newspaper editor Pete Hamill recently wrote:

True accomplishment is marginal to the recognition factor. There is seldom any attention paid to scientists, poets, educators, or archaeologists. Citizens who work, love their spouses and children, pay taxes, give to charities, and break no laws are never in a newspaper unless they die in some grisly murder. Even solid politicians, those who do the work of the people without ambitions for immense power, and do so without scandal, are ignored. The focus of most media attention, almost to the exclusion of all other subjects, is those big names.[15]

Does this mean you can't get into the news unless you're famous? No, although it certainly helps to be famous if you want attention. Chrysler Corporation's Jim Tolley said: "[Lee] Iacocca's prominence and personality put us in an unusual and enviable situation. Other professionals spend their careers trying to get publicity for their company or client; at Chrysler, we get paid to cope with it."[16]

News organizations are also eager to boost ratings by searching for bad guys, wrongdoers and companies whose products bring people to grief. Of course, that's good. You would expect that the media would perform a public watchdog function, looking out for our best interests. But what if they get the story wrong? What if someone feeds a reporter some details about your company or your products that are simply not true? To keep from becoming a ratings booster for a news program or a local paper out to do good for the community and its readers, you should consider taking the initiative, demonstrating both good citizenship and good sense by helping a reporter see your company's perspective.

## *Markets and Sophistication*

Most market areas are served by broadcasters and newspaper publishers who are loath to mistreat businesspeople, and for good reason. Those same businesspeople are the lifeblood of their advertising program. If word gets around that the local paper has misquoted, misrepresented or mishandled a business or its management, the publisher will hear about it. And, in turn, so will the editors and reporters.

News gathering and advertising are supposed to be separate but rarely ever are, which doesn't mean that reporters will spike a legitimate investigation or important news story just because an advertiser is involved. Nor does it mean that a businessperson can buy his or her way off the front page with a healthy advertising account. It does mean that in a small to medium-sized market of 50,000 to 750,000 people, you can generally expect courteous, fair and professional treatment most of the time. In large markets of 1 million or more people, life is a bit different. For one thing, it's tougher to get your story into the news when you want exposure for your company or your products. Announcing good news is difficult in a large market because it's usually a much bigger deal to those who generate it than it is to those who report it. And in a large market there's simply a lot more news, good and bad.

Reporters in large markets are also much less sensitive to the relationship between advertising and profits. When they smell a good story, they'll go after it with little regard for the names involved. Big cities also produce a certain amount of "hit-and-run" journalism in which reporters will do just about anything to get the details or the pictures of a story, including climbing the fence to your property, bribing the gate guards or hassling your employees until they've found one who's disgruntled enough to talk. Once the story is done, they don't need you any more, and you have little leverage with them. If you're located in a metropolitan area and become involved in an important breaking news event, you should seek professional help from your corporate communication office or a professional public relations firm at once. Even a few hours' delay can be disastrous.

Another aspect of market size and sophistication is that media outlets in smaller markets can rarely afford to develop reporters who are genuine specialists. In New York, financial and economics reporters often know more about the market and the issues than the people they are interviewing. In Detroit, dozens of reporters focus exclusively on the automotive industry and have a professional lifetime's experience in writing about cars and auto-making. In San Francisco, literally hundreds of journalists specialize in the information technology industry; many of them have advanced degrees and are highly sophisticated in their approach to the issues they write about.

You get the picture. If you live and work in a big city, you can and should expect the journalists you deal with to know a great deal about your business. Be careful: They know the issues in your industry; they understand the vocabulary; and they know the questions to ask. The real danger here is not that you will be misquoted. The danger is that you'll say something dumb and they will get it right. Worse yet, a broadcast journalist will save the video.

In a smaller market – say Syracuse, New York; Montgomery, Alabama; or South Bend, Indiana – the danger is just as great for a manager, but it's danger of a different type. The risk in small to medium-sized markets is that a general assignment reporter will know little or nothing of your business or industry. So, if she gets it wrong in the story that appears on tonight's six o'clock news or in tomorrow's newspaper, it's probably your fault.

In such cases, you're dealing with a bright, curious, capable journalist but one who is probably overworked and underpaid, and ends up covering a car wreck and a cat show later that same day. Your story is just one stop along the way. It's up to you to explain the story in simple, everyday terms the audience will understand. It's your job to make complex issues simple, to make difficult terms clear and to turn a confusing story into one that's easy to understand. You can do so by offering your company's perspective early and often in the interview and by flagging the interview with easy-to-follow cues: "The key issue here, Maureen, is . . . " or "If there's one thing I think is more important for your viewers to understand than any other, Mark, it's this . . . "

## They Do Make Mistakes

Daily newspapers contain literally thousands of facts and dozens of opinions. Occasionally, a reporter will simply get it wrong by copying down the wrong fact, transposing numbers or worse, speaking with someone who doesn't know anything.

This sort of thing happens from time to time, even in large markets with sophisticated and highly regarded news operations. The reporters who make such mistakes rarely ever do so because of malice or bad feelings about the source. Mistakes most often occur because of naiveté or pressure to get a story done before deadline. Occasionally, reporters feel a kind of internal pressure to sensationalize a story when neither hype nor hyperbole are called for.[17]

If it happens to you, if you are misquoted or your words are taken out of context, if the facts in the story about your company are distorted or just plain wrong, you should respond, but do so carefully. Deal first with the reporter. On the telephone or in person, ask if he misunderstood you or if you weren't clear in your response to his questions. Try to begin such conversations with this phrase: "I know you don't want your readers to be misinformed, so . . . " Complete the thought with words such as these: "I thought you should know that some of what appears in your story on page three this morning is inaccurate."

## Demanding a Retraction

You should never, ever, under any circumstances, demand a retraction or threaten a reporter. For one thing, it won't work. For another, it puts you in a position of obligation to a reporter who's just misquoted you. In exchange for retracting the incorrect story, you now "owe her one." In addition, reporters are threatened all the time; they have grown accustomed to hearing threats from news sources. Your best bet is to appeal to a reporter's sense of integrity and credibility. Without credibility, a reporter has nothing. Stories about journalists making up details of a story or inventing sources for feature reports invariably end with the notation that the reporter has been fired by the paper or the television station. Once you have a reporter's full attention, give him the details or the perspective you hope to reach the public with and conclude the conversation with the phrase, "Thanks. I know you'll do the right thing."

If dealing directly with the reporter who wrote or broadcast your story doesn't work, your next step is the news director (in broadcasting) or the managing editor (in newspapers). The approach should be exactly the same: "I know you don't want your viewers to be misinformed, so. . . ." Editors and news directors are seasoned professionals who know their business and who want to make sure that the sources and subjects of their news stories are treated fairly.

Your last resort is the publisher or station manager, but it's unlikely they will be of much help. Such executives are reluctant to back a version of the truth other than the one presented to them by their news managers. Only in rare circumstances of willful misconduct will publishers or general managers back down, apologize or retract a story. If all else fails, you can threaten to sue, but that's a lengthy and expensive process that often ends in disappointment. Only in the most egregious cases do publishers or broadcasters end up losing in court.

## Facts Versus Opinions

If the mistake is an error in fact, editors and news directors will be quick to correct it and will usually do so with a sincere and direct apology to the person or organization who was misrepresented. If the mistake, however, is a matter of opinion, perspective or viewpoint, it will be much more difficult – if not downright impossible – to get a correction or response from the paper or broadcaster. Editors and news directors feel strongly that they are entitled to report opinion, even if it's a minority viewpoint, and as long as it's labeled as such, they owe an irate reader or viewer little in the way of an apology. Bill Moyers of CBS News once said, "Our business is truth as much as news."[18] Even though facts can be easy to produce and easy to correct, truth can be highly subjective. One man's "ecological calamity" can be another man's "routine clean-up."

## Few Reporters Are Decision Makers

Although you want to deal directly with and try to make friends of the reporters who cover your business and your industry, it's important to note that few reporters are influential enough to make key decisions about the stories they cover. Lester Holt can decide whether a story is big enough for him to be there personally, but Anne Thompson cannot. Reporters, even big-name anchors, are responsive to the decisions made by their managing editors and news directors. Some stories become big enough, fast enough for general assignment reporters to be bumped aside in favor of a bigger name on the byline. On other occasions, reporters know they are in the doghouse with their bosses because of the insignificance or remoteness of the stories they have been assigned to cover.

Business executives find it useful to cultivate the friendship and favor of certain reporters. In fact, unless they involve breaking news or a crisis of some sort, most news stories rarely get any attention when they're first suggested to a media outlet. Corporate communication professionals will tell you it may take six months to a year to convince someone at *Fortune, Barron's* or *Bloomberg BusinessWeek* to cover a soft feature. But you should know that reporters rarely make the decisions that lead to extensive reporting, the investment of photography or research talent, or the assignment of airtime or print space to a story. Those decisions are made by news management professionals, and regardless of what you do for a living, you should make it your job to get to know them.

## Get to Know Local Management

If you work in a metropolitan market, the professionals in your corporate communication department will help you and others in the organization tell your story through the media. Follow their lead. If you work in a smaller market, you may need to take the initiative to meet and speak with news professionals on your own.

You should systematically set about, with the assistance of your corporate communication people, meeting radio and television news directors, newspaper managing editors and – if your community has a business news weekly – the editors of that publication. Meeting with them may take no more than 20 minutes, and you may do little more than offer them your business card, a brief overview of your business and its products and services, and an offer to help if a story should ever develop on a subject related to your business. Conclude the conversation by asking for an opportunity to comment on any story, whether it deals directly with your company or not. "Call me," you should say. "Give me a chance to help you tell the story accurately, fairly and completely."

If you maintain a regular, steady dialogue and keep open lines of communication with local editors and news directors, you're unlikely to be surprised by bad news. You're also unlikely to have serious disagreements with them about how a story should be covered. Do your part and respond each time you are asked for a comment. Be there ahead of their deadline and respect their rules; you won't get to edit your own comments, nor will you get to look over a story before it goes to press. But you certainly can get a news organization into the habit of calling you back to check a quote or ask for additional details if you treat them as intelligent professionals and respect the work they do.

## GETTING READY

Preparing to meet with a reporter or to be interviewed by a journalist will involve some homework on your part, beginning with your strategy. If you don't have a strategy, it means that you don't know what your objectives are; if you have no specific objectives, you shouldn't agree to the interview.

### Develop a Strategy

Both your supervisor and your public affairs office should know of your interest in meeting with and working with local news managers, and you should go about cultivating a good working relationship with a strategy in mind. That strategy should specify the following in clear terms:

- The goals you hope to achieve by working with local news professionals
- The general content of your message
- The intended audience for your message
- The visuals or photo opportunities you intend to offer
- The timing and sequence of events involved in your story
- What makes this story different from others
- What makes your story newsworthy
- The media you plan to work with to tell your story.

Your strategy should be committed to paper as soon as you have a story to tell. Keep in mind that a strategy on paper is not a commitment to one course of action; it should be a living, changing document as you discover new ways to tell the story, new ideas for promoting your message and new opportunities to use the news media to your advantage. Review it and revise it as often as you need to.

### Research the Reporter

Make a point of getting to know the reporter you've agreed to interview with. Find out as much as you can: writing and reporting style, story types, experience, general reputation in the community. The best place to start is with the media relations staff of your corporate communications office. They'll know something about nearly every reporter who takes an interest in your company and can help prepare you.

If you have the time, look at some of this reporter's previous stories. Read some clips from the company archives and get a sense of the reporter's style. Does she frequently use direct quotes? Is the style friendly, professional or aggressive? Should you prepare background information on your company and its products or services to take with you to an interview? Would this reporter welcome a tour of your facilities?

The same is true of television reporters. If time permits, look for online video clips of your reporter's work. If you've been invited to a regularly scheduled local program for an interview, make certain you watch at least one episode of the program in advance to get some idea of the style the interviewer uses with his or her guests.

## Refine and Practice Your Message

Even the most experienced of professionals can benefit from practice occasionally. CEOs, board chairmen and senior managers will often draft a message they want to convey during a press interview, edit it carefully, review it and rehearse it. Most important, they will work on sound bites, those 10-to-12-second memorable phrases that they hope will appear again and again on television and in the newspaper.

Do you know the *central theme* of your message – the one nugget of truth that you really want a reporter to record or write down? Begin with your central theme and work from there to develop *examples, illustrations* and *anecdotes* to support that message. Make sure all of the evidence you plan to use is *accurate, current* and *easy to understand.* Speak in terms of the public's interest, not the company's. Don't talk about what the company wants or needs, but speak instead of how the company will benefit the community, the consumer, your customers and others, including your employees. Speak in personal terms, showing how you and your coworkers are involved in making better products, providing better services, building a better community.

Rehearse the words you actually plan to use during a press interview. Don't assume that you'll be able to ad lib the content of your interview when the pressure is on. You won't. You'll rely on what you know, what you have rehearsed and what you feel most comfortable with. Practice your message until you know it so thoroughly you would feel comfortable conducting the interview in the middle of the night.

And when all else fails: Go to the mission statement. Make sure you know your company's mission statement, because when you really can't think of another thing to say, you can always offer the mission statement and then show how the subject at hand is related to the company's basic goals. It'll give you time to think and an opportunity to link the basic vision, values and beliefs of your firm to the subject of the interview.

## Confirm the Details and Ground Rules

Double-check the time, day, date and location of the interview. If it's a studio interview and you've never been to that location, you might consider driving by that location *before* you actually need to be there. Can you find the studio or offices you've agreed to meet in? Do you know where you can park? Do you know how long it will take you to get there? Will traffic patterns be different at the time of day you've agreed to meet?

If you've arranged for a telephone interview, make sure you tell the reporter up front how much time you can devote to the conversation. Make certain you know whether the interview is being recorded. In a face-to-face interview, it's not a bad idea for you to bring along a digital recorder so that you'll have your own copy of what you were asked and what you said in response. The presence of the recorder will keep a reporter honest. A reporter who knows you have a copy of the conversation will feel little temptation to get inventive with a direct quote, a fact or figure, or some important element of the story. If you're using a telephone and plan to record the interview, both parties must know of and agree to the recording. Otherwise, you may be in violation of one or more wiretap laws. As you double-check the rules, ask if you can stop or correct quotes as you speak. Almost all reporters will allow such corrections. Also inquire about what the reporter's interests are one more time. What in particular would he like to talk about?

## Review the News of the Day

Even if your interview is scheduled early in the day, make sure you check the morning paper, watch the headlines on CNN and briefly tune into the local news. If you have the time and network access, you may want to check the Internet news sites to see whether any stories regarding your company or your industry are on the Net. You never want to be surprised.

If a reporter offers a story or a headline to you that you haven't seen or heard before, you aren't obligated to respond. You can never be certain that the report is accurate, or that you've been told the whole story. Journalists sometimes ask you to respond to a quote from someone else. If you haven't seen or heard that quote before, say so. "I'm sorry, Erin, I haven't seen that story yet. I'd rather read the full story before I respond." Don't be goaded into responding to a quote or a story you haven't read and haven't had an opportunity to think about.

## Remember, You Are the Expert

Often lost in all of the anxiety and rush to prepare for an interview is the idea that you know more about the subject than the reporter does. Granted, some financial and business press journalists know a great deal about the subject, but it's rare that they would know your company, your projects, your products, your services, your strategy and your plans for the future as well as you. Rely on the confidence and detailed preparation that got you this far to take you one step further.

## MAKING IT HAPPEN

When the moment of the interview arrives, here's a final checklist to consider:

## A Prepared Pocket Card May Help

Many executives carry a small 3" x 5" (or slightly larger) index card to record and review important details. A manufacturing facility manager in Michigan carries a card in his jacket pocket that contains the number of acres inside the perimeter fence, the square footage on the plant floor, the number of employees per shift, the hourly output in each division, production goals for the week and other important, quantifiable information.

What's most important about your work? Can you jot down a few things that are unlikely to change in the next few days and keep them on hand? What about those issues related directly to the reason you're being interviewed? Write down one or two main points you hope to impress the reporter with. Include supporting details, numbers and examples, if you can. Think about jotting down several key points you could talk about if the interview runs long. What *good news subjects* would you like to talk about if time permits?

## Arrive Early, Check Out the Setting

Again, if you're being interviewed at a studio, the offices of a newspaper or magazine, or at some neutral location, plan to arrive early. Even if your schedule is busy that day, squeeze out a few extra minutes so that when the interviewer arrives or it's your turn to go on, you're calm, relaxed and familiar with the surroundings.

## Appearance and Makeup Are Important

Television is a visual medium and it's one that favors close-up shots. If a production assistant offers you an opportunity to apply makeup, take it. Men: Swallow your pride and let the makeup artist improve your looks. A little light powder will help to reduce glare produced by perspiration under the studio lights and, most importantly, it will help to prevent dark shadows from forming under and around your eyes. Women: If you routinely wear makeup, don't do anything differently for a television appearance. If you don't routinely wear makeup, follow the same rules offered for men.

One reminder: Make sure you stop in the rest room on your way out and remove the makeup. If you show up at work wearing makeup, the staff may not understand.

## Get Your Points in Early

Most interviews, especially in broadcasting, will move quickly. Lead with your main point. Rephrase it in the next sentence. Then, mention your key issues or principal concerns again before a minute has elapsed. Don't assume that a reporter will get around to asking you what you want to say. He may never get around to asking you about those subjects you would most like to talk about. Raise your principal concerns early and often.

## Take the Mother-in-Law Test

This simple test asks whether your mother-in-law would understand the explanation you've just given. Does your response to a question or does your prepared statement for the press contain acronyms, technical terms and industry lingo? Is it filled with insider jargon?

Remember that those people watching your interview or reading the report of your conversation with a journalist are generally pretty smart, but they probably don't know much about your business. Use everyday terminology, simple explanations and direct, declarative sentences. Draw pictures for them, tell stories, use anecdotes. Do what you can to make the subject both real and interesting for them. And if you don't have a mother-in-law, borrow mine. She's a lovely woman named Edna who'd be more than happy to tell you if she understands what you have just said.

### Be Yourself

Unless you're the Boston strangler or someone with a personality no one would want to meet, you're much better off simply being yourself. Don't pretend, don't posture and don't try to be someone you're not. A great reservoir of goodwill exists in this country for ordinary people who look and act like they're honest. The audience will give you the benefit of the doubt, as long as you act like yourself and play it straight.

## STAYING IN CONTROL OF AN INTERVIEW

Among the worst things that could happen is for you to lose control of an interview. It's no different from managing a project or a business event. If you lose control, you cannot determine the outcome; other people will do that for you.

### The Importance of Staying in Control

Simply focus on your goals for the interview and offer responses that are directed toward those goals. Keep your objective in mind, get your key points in early and repeat them as often as you can. Don't let a reporter take the interview in a direction that is negative, counterproductive or off-topic.

Say what you want to say. If they don't use it, you're only out the time and effort you spent preparing. If you say something in response to a question that you hadn't planned on or didn't intend to say, you're asking for trouble. If a reporter asks you a question you don't want to answer, answer a question you wish he had asked. If a journalist asks you a question you can't answer, say why it is you can't offer an answer ("That information is confidential," "We don't yet know what caused the accident" or "Those details are protected by the Privacy Act").

Avoid responding with simple yes or no responses, even if the questions are posed in that way. Use the opportunity to seize control of the interview and get your key points across. It's free airtime or print space that's at stake here. Use it to your best advantage.

### You Don't Have to Accept a Reporter's Premise

If a reporter begins a question with the phrase, "Isn't it true . . . ," watch out. What usually follows is often not true and is usually designed to put you on the spot. Don't accept what a reporter says as gospel truth, even if the reporter seems especially well informed. Stick to what you know and repeat your most important contentions. If a reporter uses words you wouldn't use or phrases you wouldn't say, don't repeat them, even to deny the accusation.

### Tell the Truth

Being completely truthful is a novel idea for some managers, but it's one that usually works. If you've done what you are accused of doing – unless your attorney advises otherwise – admit it, but explain in the next breath what you are doing to correct the problem or improve the issue. Don't invent, embellish, stretch or puff up the facts. Reporters are exceedingly good at finding the truth in most stories; they're trained professionals in research and investigation. If they smell a liar, they'll come after you like a pack of dogs. You needn't reveal everything, of course, but what you do say should be honest, accurate and truthful.

## Avoid Arguments

Don't pick a fight. Journalists are trained in the techniques of combative interviews, and you are unlikely to win. If you get angry and lash out at a reporter, he or she will likely remain quiet and let you look foolish. Stay calm, under control and professional. You'll win the respect of the reporter and the audience in the process.

## You are Always on the Record

People who watch television shows about reporters often think they can go *off the record* to tell an interviewer something confidential, hoping that it won't make it into the story. People who tell reporters something off the record usually have an ulterior motive: "You can use this information any way you want, just don't attach my name to it." Reporters are suspicious of sources who pass along information that is off the record.

Bob Franken, who was assistant managing editor of the *Arizona Republic* for many years, once said, "If you don't want it to appear in the paper, don't ever say it to a reporter."[19] He meant simply that saying something to a reporter will somehow, someday eventually work its way to the surface and appear in print, on the air or in public. If you're concerned about keeping something secret, don't say it. You can't fault a reporter for using something you've said, even though you tried to preface (or backpedal) with the words, "off the record." Every successful manager's career steers clear of off-the-record comments to a reporter.

## Use Examples, Illustrations, Brief Anecdotes

People respond to stories, especially those with circumstances they can easily envision or identify with. Illustrate your response or press statement with tales that will capture the hearts and imagination of those listening or reading. Rather than talk about how many metric tons of snow were removed from your company's property during last week's blizzard, relate a story that involves one of your employees; talk about how long she worked and what the experience was like. Examples and stories will work much better than dry facts, figures and statistics.

## If You Can't Speak to the Questions, Speak to the Issue

Individual questions may be phrased in a way that makes them tough to answer. More important, your response to this particular question may be of little help in assisting the audience to understand the larger issue. You may need to deflect the question slightly: "That would be interesting to know, Jay, but the more important issue at the moment is . . . " Or you may simply need to refocus the question: "The number of units involved in this recall is much less important than the overall issue of product safety . . . "

A number of experts cite New York City mayor Rudolph W. Giuliani and his remarkable performance before the cameras during the autumn of 2001. His daily press conferences dealing with the city's exposure to anthrax provide a model for how to handle a crisis effectively. Most observers said the mayor had consistently done the right thing by appealing to people's most rational selves. While literally millions of people were afraid they might be exposed to a terrifying and unpredictable microbe that could attack without warning, Giuliani offered perspective on the issue and reminded them that just one person had died. Dr. Arieh Shalev of Hadassah University Hospital in Jerusalem cautions senior officials to be sensible in their approach, especially to bad news. "Information," he says, "always has to be seen as accurate and reliable and not contaminated by efforts to encourage people."[20]

## Above All Else, Stay Likeable

If the audience doesn't like you, you're dead meat. A great reservoir of goodwill and understanding is available out there for people who work hard, play by the rules and respond honestly to a question. If the audience decides that they like the reporter better than they like you, it will be all but impossible to win any friends for your company or your cause. Use humor, be self-effacing, stay humble. You've got a lot to lose if you don't.

# FOLLOW-UP

After it's over, you shouldn't simply put the experience behind you. Each press interview should be an opportunity to learn, grow and improve your abilities. Another event, another product rollout, another small crisis may be just around the corner.

## Review the Article or Video

Read what's been written about you, watch the videotape and look carefully at the way the story came together. Did the reporter get it right? Are the key facts there? If most of it is right and if your company is cast in a generally favorable light, be glad. That's the most you can ask. Few reporters will get every detail exactly right; even fewer will say things the way you'd have said them if you had written the story yourself.

## Inform the Chain of Command

No surprises. Keep your boss informed about every interview you do. Tell the people in corporate communication how it went; they may wish to pass along information to others in the company who may be contacted for an interview. No one expects perfection from each encounter with the media, but no one in higher management wants to be blindsided by employee quotes or statements in the press.

## Provide Feedback

It's not a bad idea to pick up the phone and call the reporter who interviewed you. He or she will likely enjoy hearing from you, especially if the experience was a good one. If it didn't work out the way you had planned or hoped, talk with the reporter and see what went wrong. If it did work, consider a follow-up opportunity. Perhaps there's another story in your organization that would be of interest to that reporter or another opportunity to show what your company can do.

## Leave a Record for Your Successor

Don't walk away from an encounter with the Fourth Estate and simply press on with business as usual. Take a few minutes to draft a memo for the record, explaining how the request for an interview developed, what the key issues were, who was involved, where the interview took place and what your impressions were. Include a copy of the newspaper or magazine clipping or a copy of the videotape. The more information your successor has to work with, the greater the chances for success if the same reporter or news outlet should call again.

# FOR FURTHER READING

Bland, M., A. Theaker and D. Wragg. *Effective Media Relations: How to Get Results.* Sterling, VA: Kogan Page, 2005.

Cutlip, S. M., A. H. Center and G. M. Broom. *Effective Public Relations*, 9/e. Upper Saddle River, NJ: Prentice Hall, 2005.

Evans, F. J. *Managing the Media: Proactive Strategies for Better Business-Press Relations.* Westport, CT: Quorum Books, 1997.

Harmon, J. F. *Feeding Frenzy: Crisis Management in the Spotlight.* New York: AEG Publishing Group, 2009.

Henderson, D. *Making News: A Straight-Shooting Guide to Media Relations.* Lincoln, NE: iUniverse, 2006.

Hoover, J. D. *Corporate Advocacy: Rhetoric in the Information Age.* Westport, CT: Greenwood Publishing Group, 1997.

Howard, C. M. and W. K. Matthews. *On Deadline: Managing Media Relations*, 3/e. Prospect Heights, IL: Waveland Press, 2000.

Johnson, J. *Media Relations: Issues and Strategies.* Crows Nest NSW, Australia: Allen & Unwin, 2007.

Mathis, M. E. *Feeding the Media Beast: An Easy Recipe for Great Publicity.* West Lafayette, IN: Purdue University Press, 2002.

Matthews, W. *How to Create a Media Relations Program.* International Association of Business Communicators, 1997.

Mayhew, L. H. *The New Public: Professional Communication and the Means of Social Influence.* Cambridge, U.K.: Cambridge University Press, 1997.

Moore, S. *An Invitation to Public Relations.* London, U.K.: Cassell, 1996.

Overholt, A. "Are You Ready for Your Close-Up?" *Fast Company*, November 2002, p. 53.

Stewart, S. *Media Training 101: A Guide to Meeting the Press.* New York: Wiley & Sons, 2003.

Wilcox, D. L., P. H. Ault, G. T. Cameron and W. K. Agee. *Public Relations: Strategies and Tactics*, 7/e. Boston, MA: Allyn & Bacon, 2002.

Yale, D. R. *Publicity and Media Relations Checklists.* New York: NTC Business Books, 1995.

## NOTES

1   Stevens, Matt. "Starbucks C.E.O. Apologizes After Arrests of 2 Black Men," *The New York Times*, April 15, 2018.

2   "Starbucks' Philadelphia Incident Hasn't Affected Sales, CEO Says," *CBS News*, April 26, 2018.

3   Durando, J. "BP's Tony Hayward: 'I'd Like My Life Back'," *USA Today*, June 1, 2010., Online at http://content.usatoday.com/communities/greenhouse/post/2010/06/bp-tonyhayward-apology/1.

4   Reprinted by permission of *Harvard Business Review* from Burger, C. "How to Meet the Press," *Harvard Business Review*, July–August 1975, p. 63. Copyright © 1975 by the Harvard Business School Publishing Corporation. All rights reserved.

5   Ibid.

6   Quinn, T. President and Chief Operating Officer, Jordan Industries, Inc., Chicago, Illinois, in a personal interview, November 20, 1997, Notre Dame, Indiana.

7   Burger. "How to Meet the Press," p. 62.

8   "The Arthur W. Page Society: Background and History," *The Page Philosophy*. Online at www.awpagesociety.com/site/about/page_philosophy/. Accessed July 21, 2008 at 3:00 p.m.

9   White, B. "Bloopers: Quote Didn't Really Originate with Will Rogers," *The Morning Call*, July 5, 2018. Online at www.mcall.com/opinion/white/mc-bw-bloopers-20160627-column.html#. Accessed Thursday, July 5, 2018 at 4:17 p.m. EST.

10  France, M. "The Mea Culpa Defense," *BusinessWeek Online*, p. 2. Online at: www.businessweek.com/magazine/content/02_34/b3796604.htm. Accessed November 21, 2002.

11  Patel, A. and L. Reinsch. "Companies Can Apologize: Corporate Apologies and Legal Liability," *Business Communication Quarterly*, 66.1 (2003): 9–25. See also Cooper, D. A. "CEO Must Weigh Legal and Public Relations Approaches," *Public Relations Journal* (January 1992): 39–40; and Fitzpatrick, K. R. and M. S. Rubin. "Public Relations vs. Legal Strategies in Organizational Crisis Decisions," *Public Relations Review*, 21 (1995): 21–33.

12  France. "The Mea Culpa Defense," pp. 2–3.

13  Ibid., p. 3.

14  Gold, V. "If Mike Wallace Calls, Hang Up: Ten Rules for Dealing with Today's Journalists," *The Washingtonian*, September 1984, pp. 87–89.

15  Hamill, P. *News Is a Verb: Journalism at the End of the Twentieth Century.* New York: The Ballantine Publishing Group, 1998, p. 80.

16  Tolley, J. L. "Iacocca Still Charms the Media," *ABC Communication World*, September 1987, p. 21.

17  Hamill. *News Is a Verb*, pp. 79–94.

18  Lichter, S. R., S. Rothman and L. S. Lichter. *The Media Elite: America's New Powerbrokers.* Bethesda, MD: Adler & Adler, 1986, p. 132.

19  Franken, R. Personal interview, May 19, 2005. Notre Dame, Indiana.

20  Goode, E. "Anthrax Offers Lessons in How to Handle Bad News," *The New York Times*, October 23, 2001, pp. D1, D6. Copyright © 2001 by The New York Times Company. Reprinted with permission.

# Case 13.1: The United States Olympic Committee

## Protecting Their Girls or The Gold?

### THE CONVICTION

On January 24, 2018, Ingham County Circuit Court Judge Rosemarie Aquilina sentenced former Michigan State University and USA Gymnastics doctor Larry Nassar to 40 to 175 years in prison for seven counts of first-degree sexual misconduct.[1] During the hearing, more than 150 girls, including gymnasts, Olympians, dancers, rowers and runners shared accounts of their abuse when they were supposed to be receiving medical treatment at the hands of Nassar.[2]

Twelve days later, Eaton County Circuit Judge Janice Cunningham sentenced Nassar to 40 to 125 years in prison for the three counts of criminal sexual assault to which he had pleaded guilty in November 2017. The sentence will run concurrently with the Ingham County sentence. Both sentences will begin after the 60 years he will already have served for child pornography.[3]

### THE U.S. OLYMPIC COMMITTEE AND AFFILIATED ORGANIZATIONS

The International Olympic Committee (IOC) is an international organization that holds final authority on the national Olympic Movement. It owns the rights to the Olympic symbols, flag, motto and anthem. Its Executive Board performs legislative functions and enacts all necessary regulations to implement the Olympic Charter.[4] President Thomas Bach leads the Board, along with four vice presidents and ten other members.[5] The Olympic Charter is the founding document of the Olympic Movement. The goal of the Olympic Movement is "to contribute to building a peaceful and better world by educating youth through sport practiced in accordance with Olympism and its values."[6]

The IOC is an international advocate for physical activity at all levels.[7] It provides free teaching resources to promote good citizenship and emphasizes the benefits of physical activity for individual health, enjoyment and social interaction. It also promotes the simultaneous development of the body and mind through values including excellence, respect and friendship.[8]

The IOC also advances women's rights through athletic activity at all levels. It states on its website, "The goal of gender equality is enshrined in the Olympic Charter."[9] On November 15, 2017, the IOC partnered with UN Women to affirm women's rights through a Memorandum of Understanding (MoU). Both institutions renewed their commitment to empowering women and girls through sports. They also vowed to advance women's leadership and gender equality.[10]

The IOC oversees national Olympic committees. The United States Olympic Committee (USOC) is the national Olympic committee of the U.S., which establishes and develops amateur athletic activity in the U.S. in order to meet national athletic goals while, at the same time, furthering the values of the IOC.[11] Its responsibility includes all matters related to the U.S. participation in the Olympic Games and represents the U.S. to the IOC.[12]

The USOC oversees 47 national governing bodies that administer the various athletic disciplines of the Olympic Games.[13] USA Gymnastics (USAG) holds the accreditation of national governing body for gymnastics in the U.S., and a 21-person Board of Directors governs the organization. This board consists of two representatives from both the men's and women's programs, one each from rhythmic gymnastics, acrobatic gymnastics and trampoline/tumbling, three representatives from the newly created Advisory Council, five athletes (one per discipline), four public sector members, and the chairman of the board.

The USOC and the International Gymnastics Federation designate the USAG as the authoritative national governing body of gymnastic sports in the U.S. The USAG's responsibilities include selecting and training the U.S. Gymnastics Teams for the Olympics. The men's, women's, rhythmic and acrobatic gymnastics and trampoline and tumbling programs each have a junior and senior national team. Both teams compete in the Olympic Games. The USAG also has a Junior Olympic and elite development program, which starts training promising young athletes between ages 7 and 12.[14]

The USOC created the U.S. Center for SafeSport in March 2017. This center "seeks to enable every athlete to thrive by fostering a national sport culture of respect and safety, on and off the playing field."[15] Additionally, the center's nine-member Board of Directors includes experts in abuse prevention and investigation, ethics compliance and sports administration. The center has a 24/7 reporting hotline for sexual misconduct.[16] The USOC created the center after 80 victims brought complaints against Nassar in February 2017. During that time, he faced first-degree criminal sexual misconduct charges related to his work at Michigan State University's sports medicine clinic and Twistars Gymnastics Club.[17]

## U.S. OLYMPIC COMMITTEE FUNDING AND PARTNERSHIPS

The USOC receives most of its revenue from television broadcast rights, sponsorships and gifts from individuals. The U.S. government, the city of Colorado Springs, where U.S. Olympics and Paralympics are based, and the U.S. Olympic Foundation provides additional funding. The USOC also asks for contributions through public service announcements or similar direct solicitations. The USOC also receives proceeds from sales in its online store.[18] Its online store sells merchandise including clothing for men, women and children, jewelry and other accessories, and autographed photos.[19]

Two primary types of Olympic corporate sponsorship fund the USOC and IOC: world-wide and domestic. Tiers of sponsorship grant companies various marketing rights and offer exclusive use of Olympic and Team USA images and marks. The USOC also has special partnerships with various licensees, suppliers and outfitters that provide services and products to support Team USA through its domestic sponsorship program.[20] The USOC publishes a list of its world-wide and domestic sponsors and licensees, but it does not disclose individual donors.[21] Sponsorships provided about 45 percent of revenues for the IOC as of February 2018.[22]

Kellogg Company renewed its corporate partnership with USOC in September 2016. It pledged its sponsorship and support by supplying breakfast products to Team USA for the 2018 and 2020 Olympics and Paralympics.[23] Due to the Nassar scandal's rising prominence, both Kellogg and Procter & Gamble (P&G) dropped their partnerships with USAG on December 14, 2017.[24] Spokespeople from P&G stated,

We will evaluate whether to renew our partnership next spring, in light of our longer term priorities and continued actions on their part. . . . We want to ensure all voices who have been affected by abuse have been heard and that USAG takes all measures necessary to address such vitally important issues.[25]

More companies joined Kellogg and P&G in dropping their partnerships and sponsorships with USAG in January 2018. These companies include AT&T, Hershey, Chobani and KT Tape. Industry analysts estimate these deals are worth single-digit millions of dollars, and constitute 20 to 33 percent of the federation's annual revenues.[26] After these sponsors removed their support, Rachael Denhollander, the first woman to file a police report against Nassar, said, "I am deeply grateful for the sponsors of USAG like AT&T who have heard the voices of the victims and say no more."[27]

## HISTORY OF U.S. OLYMPIC PARTICIPATION

The first modern Olympic Games occurred in April of 1896 in Athens, Greece. The U.S. sent 14 athletes and finished with 11 Olympic championships. These humble beginnings prompted an international Olympic movement.[28] Since then, the Olympic Games have represented international unity while simultaneously celebrating a diversity of cultures, but they have not been a stranger to political controversy.

The 1900 Games dealt with women's rights as the first Olympic Games to feature female athletes. Women did not compete again until 1924, when the IOC voted to admit them permanently. Numerous boycotts against the hosting country served as large-scale political protests. For example, during the Cold War, Russia refused to participate in the 1984 Los Angeles Games for "security reasons." The Games also have provided individuals the opportunity to express their opinions about timely political issues. Jesse Owens, an African-American athlete, dominated in the 1936 Olympics and issued a powerful message opposing Aryan supremacy.[29]

The Olympic Games currently occur every two years and alternate between summer and winter Games. Nations select their best athletes to represent them in the Games. Each set of Games showcases a variety of athletic disciplines spanning from diving to alpine skiing. Athletes must meet minimum qualifying standards based on international competitions in order to compete.[30] However, meeting the minimum standards does not guarantee an athlete will participate in the Olympic Games. Athletes must receive approval from their sport's national governing body, national Olympic committee and the International Olympic Committee in order to compete.[31] Ninety-three countries and 2,925 athletes[32] competed in the 2018 Winter Games in PyeongChang, Korea.[33] Some 207 countries and 11,238 athletes competed in the 2016 Summer Games in Rio de Janeiro, Brazil.[34] Each contest awards victors in first, second and third place a gold, silver or bronze medal.

Olympic Games occur in different cities across the globe. The IOC determines which city will host each set of Games many years in advance. Hosting the Olympic Games endures as both a lucrative and prestigious honor, so nations vie for the glory.[35] National Olympic Committees from various nations and cities officially commit to the Olympic Candidature Process. The process spans two years and concludes with the Host City Election by the IOC.[36]

## DR. LARRY NASSAR

Dr. Larry Nassar began working with gymnasts in the 1970s as a student athletic trainer. He graduated from the University of Michigan in 1985 with a degree in Kinesiology. In 1986, Nassar joined the medical staff of USA Gymnastics as an athletic trainer and volunteered as a trainer in 1988 with youth gymnastics coach John Geddert.[37] Geddert continually recommended Nassar as a trainer to girls he coached.

In 1993, Nassar received an osteopathic medical degree from Michigan State University and began to perform osteopathic manipulation. This discipline requires that a doctor uses his or her hands to move a patient's muscles and joints to stretch, apply gentle pressure and seek resistance.[38] In 1997, he became the gymnastics team physician and assistant professor at Michigan State University.

In 1996, Nassar was named the national medical coordinator for USA Gymnastics before the 1996 Olympic Games in Atlanta. At the 2000 Olympic Games in Sydney and at the 2008 Olympic Games in Beijing, Nassar was the U.S. women's artistic gymnastics team physician. Nassar also attended all Summer Olympic Games with USA Gymnastics from 1996 to 2008.[39]

## SEXUAL MISCONDUCT IN THE MEDICAL PROFESSION

A national investigation in 2016 identified more than 2,400 confirmed cases of sexual abuse by doctors.[40] The doctors retained their white coats and continued practicing medicine despite their confirmed abuse. The victims spanned across all ages. Some abuses were obvious while others were under the guise of legitimate medical examinations.[41]

Sexual abuse by a medical practitioner persists as a widespread problem. Some victims are too embarrassed or confused to report their abuse, colleagues and nurses remain silent, and healthcare organizations brush off allegations or deal with them quietly. Even medical boards, prosecutors and communities soften their treatment toward abusive doctors.[42]

The American Medical Association (AMA) does not favor the mandatory revocation of medical licenses of doctors who commit sexual abuse against their patients.[43] The association has not independently researched the pervasiveness of sexual abuse in clinical settings. It has fought to retain the confidentiality of a federal database delineating doctors disciplined for sexual misconduct. While it does identify sexual misconduct as a breach of medical ethics, it has done little to ensure sexual predators are removed from medical practice.[44]

The AMA is reluctant to institute a universal protocol for dealing with sexual misconduct within the medical practice because it believes in redemption. It also recognizes that all circumstances are different, according to former AMA president Steven Stack. He stated, "[Doctors] are humans like anybody else, and there are a lot of complexities in some of these cases."[45]

The AMA has not provided universal guidelines because it does not want to risk ruining a doctor's career on the basis of unsubstantiated allegations. However, the AMA does not license or discipline doctors. Those are the responsibilities of state medical authorities. AMA endures as a voice of the profession and as a powerful lobbyist at the state and national level.[46]

Dr. John Zdor, PT, PDT, expressed the importance of accountability for both the patient and doctor. He stated:

As a [doctor of physical therapy], concern for false sexual harassment accusations are very real. In speaking with co-workers and an MD friend, overall rates of false accusations are very rapidly increasing. [While] it's important to think of it from the patient's point of view, medical providers need protection from false accusations, as well. The system is extremely biased toward the potential victim. [In] the vast majority of cases, their word trumps all. Better physician/provider protection is just as important as patient protection.[47]

He also described accountability protocols in his own practice. He chooses only to perform manual work on a patient of the opposite gender when a coworker or friend of the therapist is present. He also said that simply having a friend or parent of a patient increases the likelihood of false accusations. At his clinic in Washington, all treatment rooms have one-half height Dutch doors so that "the door is always at least partially open." He also said that he is not aware of a set of standardized "best practices" for medical practitioners.[48]

## SEXUAL ASSAULT VICTIMS OF DR. LARRY NASSAR

Judge Rosemarie Aquilina of Ingham County Circuit Court, near East Lansing, Michigan, extended Nassar's 2018 hearing from January 16 through to January 24 to allow more than 150 girls and women to come forward and provide Victim Impact Statements. She addressed them all as survivors and said publicly that she believes in life and rehabilitation.[49] The judge did not sense Nassar's remorse or foresee a possible future life in which he would not be a danger, so she sentenced him to 40 to 175 years on top of his 60-year sentence for child pornography.[50]

On August 29, 2016, Rachael Denhollander filed the first police report against Larry Nassar with the Michigan State University (MSU) police department. Her Victim Impact Statement concluded the Ingham County hearing.

Rachael Denhollander was a 15-year-old gymnast who received treatment from Nassar for chronic lower back pain in 2000. Larry Nassar obstructed her mother's view while he deliberately and calculatedly sexually assaulted Rachael for over a year. With ungloved hands, he groped, fondled and penetrated her without her consent or permission. She assumed that he often performed similar actions on other patients. She also thought officials must have known about his conduct and "not stopped him." These facts effectively silenced her. She thought it must have been legitimate medical treatment and the problem must have been hers.[51]

In her Victim Impact Statement on the final day of the hearing, Denhollander stated:

I did not know that at the same time Larry was penetrating me, USAG was systematically burying reports of sexual assault against member coaches in a file cabinet instead of reporting them, creating a culture where predators like Larry and so many others in the organization up to the highest-level coaches were able to sexually abuse children, including our Olympians, without any fear of being caught. . . . This is what it looks like when institutions create a culture where a predator can flourish unafraid and unabated and this is what it looks like when people in authority refuse to listen, put friendships in front of the truth, fail to create or enforce proper policy and fail to hold enablers accountable.[52]

The earliest reported sexual assault involved a 12-year-old in 1992, while Nassar was a medical student at MSU. The assaults occurred under the guise of medical research at a gymnastics facility near Lansing and at Nassar's apartment.[53]

The youngest reported sexual assault involved 6-year-old Kyle Stephens, now a young woman and the first to give her testimony at the hearings. Nassar was a close friend of the Stephens family. He began assaulting her when she was only in kindergarten. When Stephens eventually understood that she was being molested, she told her parents. They did not believe her.[54]

The most recently reported sexual assault involved 15-year-old Emma Ann Miller, who had been seeing Nassar for treatment each month since she was 10 years old. Miller testified in court that Nassar assaulted her one week before Michigan State University fired him. She claimed that the MSU Sports Clinic was still attempting to bill her family for the appointment.[55]

Overall, more than 250 women and girls told law enforcement that former MSU and USA Gymnastics doctor Larry Nassar sexually assaulted them.[56]

## U.S. OLYMPICS WOMEN'S GYMNASTICS TEAM

The women that have competed at recent U.S. Olympics events have been outspoken in their grievances with the U.S. Olympic Committee. These are currently the most influential women giving their testimonies and statements, and have received the most media attention for their words. Their popularity in the eyes of the general public distinguishes them from the other Nassar victims, and makes their voices all the more powerful.

### Aly Raisman

Aly Raisman has been in gymnastics since 1996, when she was just 2 years old. She started winning competitions for USA Gymnastics nationally and internationally in 2009, and participated in the Olympics with Team USA in 2012 and 2016, medaling in multiple categories.[57]

Raisman has been noticeably outspoken about her perceived lack of support from the USOC. In one statement, she said, "Why has the U.S. Olympic Committee been silent? Why isn't the USOC here right now?"[58]

She also called out USAG for its lack of support, with statements such as:

It seemed like [USAG] threatened me to be quiet. You know, their biggest priority from the beginning and still today is their reputation, the medals they win and the money they make off of us. I don't think that they care.[59]

### McKayla Maroney

McKayla Maroney's parents put her in gymnastics in 1997, at the age of 2, because she had so much energy. She started competing with Team USA nationally in 2009 and internationally in 2010 and won a gold and silver medal at the 2012 Olympics.[60]

In her Victim Impact Statement, Maroney shared:

The scariest night of my life . . . I had flown all day and night with the team to get to Tokyo. [Nassar] had given me a sleeping pill for the flight, and the next thing I know, I was all alone with him in his hotel room getting "treatment." I thought I was going to die that night.[61]

She ended her statement saying:

If Michigan State University, USA Gymnastics and the United States Olympic Committee had paid attention to any of the red flags in Larry Nassar's behavior I never would have met him, I never would have been "treated" by him, and I never would have been abused by him.[62]

### Jordyn Wieber

Jordyn Wieber's parents put her in recreational gymnastics in 1999, when she was 4 years old. She began competing with Team USA nationally in 2006 and internationally in 2007, eventually going to the Olympic Games in 2012, where she won a gold medal.[63]

In her Victim Impact Statement, Wieber wrote:

Nobody was protecting us from being taken advantage of. Nobody was even concerned whether or not we were being sexually abused. I was not protected, and neither were my teammates . . . And now the lack of accountability from USAG, USOC and Michigan State have caused me and many other girls to remain shameful, confused and disappointed.[64]

### Simone Biles

At age 5, Simone Biles attended Bannon's [Gymnastix] on a daycare field trip and started imitating the gymnasts as she watched. The coach noticed, and the gym sent home a letter requesting that she join tumbling or gymnastics. She started competing with Team USA nationally in 2010, and internationally in 2013. She has been named USOC Athlete of the Month and Athlete of the Year, and her four 2016 Olympic gold medals tied the Olympic record for a female gymnast in a single Games.[65]

Although Biles did not give a statement at Nassar's hearing, she came forward on Instagram to share that she, too, experienced Nassar's abuse and said that she no longer blamed herself for being a victim. She stated that the blame belongs to Nassar, USAG and others. She used the #MeToo hashtag in her post as a reference to the contemporary cultural movement about sexual abuse.[66]

### Jamie Dantzscher

Jamie Dantzscher competed for Team USA from 1994 to 2001, and won bronze in the 2000 Olympics.[67] She said that Nassar's abuse began during treatment for lower back pain when she was 12 years old, and that the abuse continued for six years.[68]

## CULTURAL MOVEMENT OF HIGH-PROFILE SEXUAL ABUSE SCANDALS

In October 2017, *The New York Times* published an article chronicling movie producer Harvey Weinstein's serial sexual misconduct and paying off victims. The abuse spanned nearly three decades and involved a multitude of women, many of whom were celebrities.[69] While he issued an apology in response to the allegations, he denied many of them as "patently false." The board of his production firm, the Weinstein Company, dismissed him in October of 2017 in response to the onslaught of allegations of misconduct.[70] High-profile celebrities including George Clooney and Meryl Streep decried Weinstein's alleged actions as "indefensible."[71] The Academy of Motion Pictures Arts and Sciences expelled Weinstein later that month.[72]

A bombardment of sexual assault allegations against powerful men from many industries followed the allegations against Weinstein. These include Kevin Spacey, star of the smash hit *House of Cards*; actor Ben Affleck; NPR editor Michael Oreskes; Lockhart Steele, editorial director for Vox Media;[73] and Matt Lauer, host of the NBC Television *Today* show.[74]

#MeToo became a battle cry of women reporting their stories or a statement of solidarity with the victims across social media.[75] The hashtag surfaced the weekend after the Weinstein story broke. It provided a simple yet efficient way to communicate their concerns that "sexual abuse is a common experience in women's lives."[76] Users of the hashtag lamented what they described as a culture of silence and shaming related to sexual misconduct. A women's studies professor at Wellesley College, Leigh Gilmore, said the high-profile nature of the Weinstein scandal directed attention to the problem of sexual abuse, but said it was not enough. She hoped for a "transformation in daily life about sexual abuse and sexual harassment."[77]

*Time* Magazine named the 2017 Person of the Year the "Silence Breakers" in response to the Weinstein scandal and the "reckoning . . . [that had] been simmering for years, decades, centuries." It intended to capture the frustration of many women who had previously feared expressing their allegations who were finally bravely calling out their abusers. It featured celebrities including Ashley Judd and Taylor Swift.[78]

## MICHIGAN STATE UNIVERSITY INVOLVEMENT

Michigan State University (MSU) is a public research university located in East Lansing, Michigan. The university had approximately 50,019 enrolled students in Fall 2017. It has more than 200 programs of undergraduate, graduate and professional study. Its external research funding totaled $596 million in 2016–2017.[79]

Dr. Larry Nassar served as an associate professor of osteopathic medicine and a sports medicine doctor for MSU for over two decades. Trainers and athletic assistants reported allegations of his sexual misconduct to at least 14 Michigan State officials during the decades before his arrest. No fewer than eight women reported his inappropriate actions. The notified officials included Dr. Lou Anna Simon, who resigned from her position as president of the university during the firestorm that followed the conviction of Dr. Larry Nassar.[80] The university apparently missed numerous opportunities to stop Nassar, a graduate of its osteopathic medical school.[81]

Dr. William Strampel, dean of the Michigan State University College of Osteopathic Medicine, imposed protocols on Nassar, including wearing gloves and requiring a chaperone. However, he failed to enforce these requirements.[82] John Engler, the University's interim president following Dr. Simon's resignation, said on February 9, 2018, that he planned to fire Dr. Strampel and sought the revocation of his tenure at MSU.[83]

In an official statement issued in February 2018, MSU spokesperson Kent Cassella wrote:

> Now we must support the courageous survivors of Nassar's abuse and provide them with the help they deserve. MSU is committed to making sure that we are doing what we must to provide a healthy and safe environment for all members of our community. President Engler has called for a culture change at MSU and we will be taking all necessary steps to begin a new day and improve the environment at the university.[84]

Michigan State trustees have denied wrongdoing on the University's behalf. They wrote, "We have worked diligently with outside counsel, who are providing the board with regular direct briefings. . . . The evidence will show that no MSU official believed that Nassar committed sexual abuse prior to newspaper reports in the summer of 2016."[85]

MSU has been under U.S. Department of Education oversight since 2014 because of its mishandling of sexual assault and gender discrimination cases.[86] It requested to end this governance in Fall 2017 because it had gone "above and beyond" in meeting official federal standards.[87] In light of the university's treatment toward Dr. Larry Nassar, such cessation will most likely occur far in the future.[88]

## DECISION POINT

How should the USOC respond in order to regain trust both with the victims and the general public? What should their communication goal be? What communication channels should it use?

## DISCUSSION QUESTIONS

1. Who are the relevant stakeholders in the case?
2. What practical steps can the USOC take to ensure long-standing abuse does not happen again within its organization?
3. How should the USOC communicate those actions to various stakeholders?
4. Is the USOC protected from negative perception because of its position as the sole Olympic committee in the U.S.?

5. Does the infrequency of the Olympic Games decrease the importance of the USOC's response since the relevance of the Nassar conviction will diminish over time?
6. What is the impact of the recent cultural movement on the perception of Nassar's conviction?
7. How should the USOC Board communicate the results of the investigation to its stakeholders?
8. How should the USOC interface its professed values with its proposed actions?
9. How should the USOC attempt to regain trust with Nassar's victims?
10. How should the USOC measure the success of its response?
11. Was this a failure of USA Gymnastics, Michigan State University or does the USOC bear greater responsibility?

## ACKNOWLEDGMENTS

This case was prepared by research assistants Erica Levy and Rebeckah Wellen under the direction of James O'Rourke, Teaching Professor of Management, as the basis for class discussion rather than to illustrate either effective or ineffective handling of an administrative situation. Information was gathered from corporate as well as public sources.

## NOTES

1 Hauser, Christine and Maya Salam. "Women Confront Larry Nassar in Court: 'I Was So Brainwashed Then'," *The New York Times*, January 22, 2018. Online at www.nytimes.com/2018/01/22/sports/larry-nassar-abuse-victims-statements.html.

2 Dator, James. "A Comprehensive Timeline of the Larry Nassar Case," *SBNation.com*, January 19, 2018. Online at www.sbnation.com/2018/1/19/16900674/larry-nassar-abuse-timeline-usa-gymnastics-michigan-state.

3 "Larry Nassar: Disgraced US Olympics Doctor Jailed for 175 Years," *BBC.com*, January 25, 2018. Online at www.bbc.com/news/world-us-canada-42811304.

4 "Olympics and International Sports Law Research Guide," Guides.ll.georgetown.edu, Georgetown University Law Library, February 9, 2018. Online at guides.ll.georgetown.edu/c.php?g=364665&p=2463479.

5 "IOC Executive Board," *Olympic.org*, International Olympic Committee, February 24, 2018. Online at www.olympic.org/executive-board.

6 "Leading the Olympic Movement," *Olympic.org*, International Olympic Committee. Online at www.olympic.org/the-ioc/leading-the-olympic-movement.

7 "Sport and Active Society," *Olympic.org*, International Olympic Committee. Online at www.olympic.org/sport-and-active-society.

8 "Olympic Values and Education Program," *Olympic.org*, International Olympic Committee. Online at www.olympic.org/olympic-values-and-education-program+.

9 "Women in Sport," *Olympic.org*, International Olympic Committee. Online at www.olympic.org/women-in-sport.

10 "Mainstreaming of Sport as a Tool for Girls' and Women's Empowerment," *Olympic.org*, November 15, 2017. Online at www.olympic.org/news/mainstreaming-of-sport-as-a-tool-for-girls-and-women-s-empowerment.

11 "The Organisation," *Olympic.org*, International Olympic Committee, August 29, 2017. Online at www.olympic.org/about-ioc-institution.

12 "Rating for United States Olympic Committee," *Charity Navigator*, February 1, 2018. Online at www.charitynavigator.org/index.cfm?bay=search.summary&orgid=4621.

13 "Structure," *TeamUSA.org*, United States Olympic Committee. Online at www.teamusa.org/About-the-USOC/Inside-the-USOC/Olympic-Movement/Structure.

14 "About USA Gymnastics," *USA Gymnastics*. Online at usagym.org/pages/aboutus/pages/about_usag.html.

15 "U.S. Center for SafeSport," *USA Gymnastics*. Online at usagym.org/pages/education/safesport/center.html.

16 Ibid.

17 Dator. "A Comprehensive Timeline of the Larry Nassar Case."

18 "Team USA Fund," *TeamUSA.org*, United States Olympic Committee. Online at www.teamusa.org/us-olympic-and-paralympic-foundation/team-usa-fund.

19 TeamUSAShop.com, Fanatics, Inc. Online at www.teamusashop.com+.

20 "Team USA Fund."

21 "Sponsors," *TeamUSA.org*, United States Olympic Committee. Online at www.teamusa.org/sponsors+.

22 "Revenue Sources and Distribution," *Olympic.org*, International Olympic Committee, January 16, 2018. Online at www.olympic.org/ioc-financing-revenue-sources-distribution.

23 "Kellogg Company Renews Partnership with U.S. Olympic Committee," *Kellogg Company*, September 27, 2016. Online at investor.kelloggs.com/news-and-events/press-releases/2016/09-27-2016-180044944.

24 Reid, Scott. "Procter & Gamble, Kellogg's Drop USA Gymnastics Sponsorship after Sex Abuse Scandal," *Ocregister.com, The Orange Country Register*, December 14, 2017. Online at www.ocregister.com/2017/12/14/procter-gamble-kelloggs-drop-usa-gymnastics-sponsorship-after-sex-abuse-scandal/.

25 Ibid.

26 Klayman, Ben. "'Stench' of Nassar Scandal Will Dog USA Gymnastics for Years: Experts," *Reuters*, January 25, 2018. Online at www.reuters.com/article/us-gymnastics-usa-nassar-sponsors/stench-of-nassar-scandal-will-dog-usa-gymnastics-for-years-experts-idUSKBN1FE2X6+.

27 Ibid.

28 History Staff. "Remembering the First U.S. Olympic Team," *History.com*, A&E Networks, July 20, 2012. Online at www.history.com/news/remembering-the-first-u-s-olympic-team.

29 Blackburn-Dwyer, Brandon and Andrew McMaster. "18 Times Politics Trumped Sport in Olympic Games' History," *Global Citizen*, February 7, 2018. Online at www.globalcitizen.org/en/content/history-political-activism-olympics-rio/.

30 Fears, Shannon. "How Do Athletes Qualify for the Winter Olympics?" *Seattle Pi*, February 1, 2018. Online at www.seattlepi.com/olympics/article/How-athletes-qualify-for-the-Winter-Olympics-12496600.php.

31 Ibid.

32 Ibid.

33 "NOCs List," *Olympic.org*, International Olympic Committee. Online at www.olympic.org/pyeongchang-2018/results/en/general/nocs-list.htm.

34 "Rio 2016," *Olympic.org*, International Olympic Committee, January 22, 2018. Online at www.olympic.org/rio-2016.

35 Chang, Andrew. "How an Olympic Host City Is Determined," *ABC News Network*, July 11, 2008. Online at abcnews.go.com/International/story?id=80796.

36 "Olympic Games Candidature Process," *Olympic.org*, International Olympic Committee, January 26, 2018. Online at www.olympic.org/all-about-the-candidature-process.

37 Adams, Dwight. "Victims Share What Larry Nassar Did to Them under the Guise of Medical Treatment," *Indianapolis Star*, February 3, 2018. Online at www.indystar.com/story/news/2018/01/25/heres-what-larry-nassar-actually-did-his-patients/1065165001/.

38 Ibid.

39 Dator. "A Comprehensive Timeline of the Larry Nassar Case."

40 Journal-Constitution, The Atlanta. "A Broken System Forgives Sexually Abusive Doctors in Every State, Investigation Finds." *Doctors & Sex Abuse*. Online at doctors.ajc.com/doctors_sex_abuse/?ecmp=doctorssexabuse_microsite_nav.

41 Ibid.

42 Ibid.

43 "The Organisation," *Olympic.org*, International Olympic Committee.

44 Judd, Alan. "Medical Profession Condemns Sexual Abuse by Doctors but Resists Solutions." *Doctors & Sex Abuse*. Online at doctors.ajc.com/ama_sex_abuse_doctors/?ecmp=doctorssexabuse_microsite_stories.

45 Ibid.

46 Ibid.

47 Wellen, Rebeckah and John Zdor. Interview with Dr. John Zdor. February 12, 2018.

48 Ibid.

49 Saul, Stephanie. "Calls Grow for Michigan State University President to Resign Over Nassar Case," *The New York Times*, January 19, 2018. Online at www.nytimes.com/2018/01/19/us/michigan-state-nassar.html.

50 Dator. "A Comprehensive Timeline of the Larry Nassar Case."

51 "Read Rachael Denhollander's Full Victim Impact Statement about Larry Nassar," *CNN*, January 30, 2018. Online at www.cnn.com/2018/01/24/us/rachael-denhollander-full-statement/index.html.

52 Ibid.

53 Dator. "A Comprehensive Timeline of the Larry Nassar Case."

54 Swenson, Kyle. "Abuse Survivor Confronts Gymnastics Doctor: 'I Have Been Coming for You for a Long Time'," *The Washington Post*, January 17, 2018. Online at www.washingtonpost.com/news/morning-mix/wp/2018/01/17/ive-been-coming-for-you-for-a-long-time-abuse-survivor-confronts-gymnastics-doctor/?utm_term=.e19a84abeb95.

55 Hauser and Salam. "Women Confront Larry Nassar in Court."

56 Mencarini, Matt. "Some 256 Women and Girls Have Come Forward as Larry Nassar Victims," *Lansing State Journal*, January 31, 2018. Online at www.lansingstatejournal.com/story/news/2018/01/31/judge-265-have-come-forward-larry-nassar-victims/1082707001/.

57 "Athletes." *USA Gymnastics | Alexandra Raisman*. Online at usagym.org/pages/athletes/athleteListDetail.html?id=97680.

58 Longman, Jeré. "Will Larry Nassar Take Down the U.S. Olympic Committee?" *The New York Times*, January 25, 2018. Online at www.nytimes.com/2018/01/25/sports/olympics/larry-nassar-usoc.html?hp&action=click&pgtype=Homepage&clickSource=story-heading&module=photo-spot-region®ion=top-news&WT.nav=top-news.

59    "Aly Raisman: USA Gymnastics 'Ignoring Us, Not Creating Change'." *ESPN*, Internet Ventures, January 17, 2018. Online at www.espn.com/espn/otl/story/_/id/22122752/aly-raisman-says-usa-gymnastics-threatened-quiet-larry-nassar-accusations.

60    "Athletes." *USA Gymnastics | McKayla Maroney*. Online at usagym.org/pages/athletes/athleteListDetail.html?id=135334.

61    Levenson, Eric. "Read McKayla Maroney's Full Victim Impact Statement in Larry Nassar Case," *CNN*, January 18, 2018. Online at www.cnn.com/2018/01/18/us/mckayla-maroney-nassar-letter/index.html.

62    Ibid.

63    "Athletes." *USA Gymnastics | Jordyn Wieber*. Online at usagym.org/pages/athletes/athleteListDetail.html?id=80263.

64    Trabka, Laura. "Read Jordyn Wieber's Full Statement at Larry Nassar Sentencing Hearing," *Lansing State Journal*, January 19, 2018. Online at www.lansingstatejournal.com/story/news/2018/01/19/full-statement-olympian-jordyn-wieber-nassar-sentencing/1048530001/.

65    "Athletes." *USA Gymnastics | Simone Biles*. Online at usagym.org/pages/athletes/athleteListDetail.html?id=164887.

66    "Jamie Dantzscher," *USA Gymnastics Official Biography: Jamie Dantzscher*. Online at usagym.org/pages/athletes/archived bios/d/jdantzscher.html.

67    Dator. "A Comprehensive Timeline of the Larry Nassar Case."

68    Ibid.

69    Kantor, Jodi and Megan Twohey. "Harvey Weinstein Paid Off Sexual Harassment Accusers for Decades," *The New York Times*, October 5, 2017. Online at www.nytimes.com/2017/10/05/us/harvey-weinstein-harassment-allegations.html.

70    "Harvey Weinstein Sacked after Sexual Harassment Claims," *BBC News*, October 9, 2017. Online at www.bbc.com/news/business-41546694.

71    "Harvey Weinstein: George Clooney Says Alleged Behaviour Is 'Indefensible'," *BBC News*, October 10, 2017. Online at www.bbc.com/news/entertainment-arts-41567216.

72    Ulaby, Neda. "Harvey Weinstein Expelled From the Academy of Motion Pictures Arts and Sciences," *NPR*, October 14, 2017. Online at www.npr.org/sections/thetwo-way/2017/10/14/557790894/weinstein-expelled-from-the-academy-of-motion-pictures-arts-and-sciences.

73    Criss, Doug. "The (Incomplete) List of Powerful Men Accused of Sexual Harassment after Harvey Weinstein," *CNN*, November 1, 2017. Online at www.cnn.com/2017/10/25/us/list-of-accused-after-weinstein-scandal-trnd/index.html.

74    "TIME Person of the Year 2017: The Silence Breakers," *Time*. Online at time.com/time-person-of-the-year-2017-silence-breakers/.

75    Criss. "The (Incomplete) List of Powerful Men Accused of Sexual Harassment."

76    McCammon, Sarah. "In the Wake of Harvey Weinstein Scandal, Women Say #MeToo," *NPR*, October 16, 2017. Online at www.npr.org/2017/10/16/558165331/in-the-wake-of-harvey-weinstein-scandal-women-say-metoo.

77    Ibid.

78    "TIME Person of the Year 2017: The Silence Breakers."

79    "MSU Facts," University, Michigan State. Online at msu.edu/about/thisismsu/facts.html.

80    Kozlowski, Kim. "What MSU Knew: 14 Were Warned of Nassar Abuse," *The Detroit News*, January 19, 2018. Online at www.detroitnews.com/story/tech/2018/01/18/msu-president-told-nassar-complaint-2014/1042071001/.

81    Ibid.

82    Saadi, Altaf. "The Medical Profession Needs to Do More to Stop Sexual Abuse of Patients," *STAT*, February 4, 2018. Online at www.statnews.com/2018/02/05/larry-nassar-doctors-sexual-assault/.

83    Associated Press. "Michigan State University Plans to Fire Dean in Fallout from Nassar Scandal," *Los Angeles Times*, February 9, 2018. Online at www.latimes.com/sports/la-sp-michigan-state-nassar-20180209-story.html.

84    Cassella, Kent. "Statement on Nassar's Eaton County Sentencing," *News & Info*, Michigan State University, February 5, 2018. Online at msu.edu/ourcommitment/news-information/2018–02–05-Eaton-Sentencing-Statement.html.

85    Saul. "Calls Grow for Michigan State University President to Resign Over Nassar Case."

86    Lavigne, Paula. "Michigan State Sought to End Federal Oversight, Delayed Sending Nassar Files," *ESPN*, ESPN Internet Ventures, January, 2018. Online at www.espn.com/espn/otl/story/_/id/22211140/michigan-state-sought-end-federal-oversight-delayed-sending-feds-files-larry-nassar-espn.

87    Ibid.

88    Ibid.

# Case 13.2: Whole Foods Market, Inc.

## *Damage Control Over Product Mislabeling (A)*

Our inspectors tell me this is the worst case of mislabeling they have seen in their careers, which DCA and New Yorkers will not tolerate.[1]

~ Julie Menin, Consumer Affairs Commissioner, New York City

On the morning of Wednesday, June 24, 2015, New York City's Department of Consumer Affairs (NYDCA) issued a press release announcing the findings of a recent investigation of eight Whole Foods Market (Whole Foods) locations in the city. Inspectors at the NYDCA claimed to have uncovered a " . . . systematic problem with how products packaged for sale at Whole Foods are weighed and labeled" through a thorough audit process lasting months. Of the 80 sample pre-packaged food items purchased and weighed by the NYDCA, every single one had been mislabeled, resulting in overcharges to customers ranging from 80 cents to $14.84 for an individual product.[2]

At Whole Foods' headquarters in Austin, Texas, founder and co-CEO John Mackey knew that a long day was ahead of him. The "E Team," as Whole Foods employees referred to the five most senior leaders of the company, would not be able to meet until early afternoon, by which point media coverage would have descended upon the story. "Defending" Whole Foods from public scrutiny was Mackey's least favorite part of leading the company, but the E Team's response to the NYDCA's charges was especially important to get right.[3]

Though Mackey was no stranger to controversy, the scrutiny from the NYDCA was unprecedented. Overnight, customer perception plummeted to an all-time low.[4] E-mails were pouring in; stakeholders wanted to know if the allegations were true, how this happened and what the company would do to fix the problem. Worse yet, the allegations of "price gouging" caught fire through the media and were compounded by the public image as an overpriced grocer which earned Whole Foods the nickname, "Whole Paycheck."

In the year leading up to this incident, Whole Foods experienced a slow but steady decline in market share and growth. The customers' message seemed clear: we will no longer pay more for identical products.

John Mackey knew that Whole Foods could not afford to remain quiet. News of the investigation into the New York City stores was going to seriously damage trust among customers throughout the nation. With the company's key financial metrics in peril, and Whole Foods' stock price along with it, Mackey knew that the decisions he had to make in the coming days would dramatically affect the company he built.

## BACKGROUND OF WHOLE FOODS

John Mackey and then-girlfriend Renee Lawson borrowed $45,000 to open SaferWay, a natural foods grocery store in Austin, Texas, in 1978. Mackey changed the name to Whole Foods Market after merging with another natural grocer in 1980.[5] After several years of success and modest expansion, Whole Foods went public in 1992,[6] followed by explosive nation-wide growth. Much of Whole Foods' growth over the next 20 years was due to mergers with and acquisitions of other health-food and all-natural grocery chains, and the company entered the *Fortune* 500 list in 2005.[7] By 2014, Whole Foods was the 30th largest retailer in the U.S. based on revenue.[8]

Throughout 2015, Whole Foods' stores boasted a wide range of offerings including produce, meat, seafood, baked goods, prepared foods, catering, nutritional supplements, vitamins and body care products, as well as lifestyle products, including books, pet products and household products. The company operated 431 stores and employed 91,000 people in the U.S., Canada and the U.K.[9]

By 2015, the Whole Foods brand had become as much a lifestyle choice as a grocery store. Known for charging premium prices, the company leveraged high-quality standards and a wholesome brand to attract customers. By highlighting an emphasis on quality standards and prepared and pre-packaged food offerings (accounting for 19 percent of total revenue from 2012 to 2014) as key differentiators, Whole Foods maintained a competitive advantage while still marking up prices by an average of 35 percent compared to an industry average product markup of 25 percent.[10]

## WHOLE FOODS, WHOLE PEOPLE, WHOLE PLANET

Whole Foods has always touted itself as a progressive company with an emphasis on social responsibility. Every year since opening its first store, Whole Foods has donated 5 percent of its annual net profit to charitable causes. Over the years, it has earned many awards for its social and environmental initiatives such as the Whole Trade Guarantee launched in April 2007.[11]

Whole Foods' emphasis on giving back extends to its employees. According to *Glassdoor* in 2015, the average Whole Foods cashier was paid $11.16 per hour making them the highest paid in the industry, compared to a national average of $8.69.[12] Favorite employee benefits include a 20-percent-off employee discount and paid time off for all workers. In an industry with notoriously high turnover rates and low employee morale, Whole Foods made the *Fortune*'s "100 Best Companies to Work For" list every year since its inception in 1998 and ranked #55 by 2015.[13]

## THE RETAIL GROCERY AND NATURAL FOODS MARKETS

The Supermarket and Grocery Store Industry, the largest food retail channel in the U.S., brought in $638.3 billion in 2014 alone.[14] Profit margins have historically been very slim in this industry due to high overhead costs and the fragmented and highly competitive nature of this market, which drives prices down. Average operating margin for retail grocery stores in 2014 was just 1.5 percent.[15]

Even with Whole Foods' leading margins of 3.5 percent, volume is crucial to profitability in the industry. As this industry has matured, a substantial number of mergers and acquisitions has taken place, 37 of them in 2014 alone, which have helped retailers reach economies of scale.[16]

However, retailers have also benefited from a growing demand for all-natural and organic products for which they can charge a much higher premium, compared to traditional foods. A *Consumer Reports* analysis found that on average, the prices on organic foods were 47 percent higher than those of their conventional counterparts.[17]

Natural Foods stores have been around since 1869 when the Thomas Martindale Company opened in Pennsylvania.[18] In the 1920s, the term "health food" was first coined and similar stores with a focus on "food consciousness" began sprouting up throughout the U.S. The counterculture movement of the 1960s also increased consumer awareness for eating foods free of harmful pesticides grown through sustainable farming practices. Whole Foods had very little direct competition when they first opened their doors in 1980. They marketed themselves as "America's Healthiest Grocery Store," and led the trend for "fresh format" stores that emphasized locally grown products as well as high-quality gourmet and ethnic food options.

The decade from 2005 to 2015 saw a boom in the organic food industry as it became increasingly mainstream. According to research conducted by the Organic Trade Association, "about 75% of consumers purchase organic food because they believe it is healthier for them than non-organic food."[19] While the rest of the retail grocery industry was largely static, organic and natural food sales increased 12 percent in 2013 alone, according to research firm IRI.[20]

As seen by the improvements made in the Healthy Eating Index produced by USDA, consumers became more health-conscious and purchased a greater variety of all-natural and organic products during this decade.[21] Consequently, as consumers demanded a greater variety of premium products, such as organic produce, industry revenue increased. In 2016, the Healthy Eating Index experienced substantial growth.[22] Traditional supermarkets recognized the opportunity that selling these natural foods at premium prices had on their bottom line and many, such as Kroger, continued to extend their organic product offerings to their customers.

Whole Foods' market share has also been encroached on by "limited assortment" stores such as Trader Joe's and Aldi, which experienced rapid growth during the same time period. These stores, often located in populated urban areas, are much more compact and efficient than traditional grocery stores. Rather than offer dozens of brands of the same product, these stores provide a more selective offering. Unlike their larger counterparts, limited assortment stores sell primarily private label products, which are both less expensive for consumers and more profitable for the stores. Private label goods account for over 80 percent of sales for Trader Joe's, the leading supermarket in sales-per-square-foot.[23] The company's products are also free of GMOs, artificial coloring, trans-fat and high fructose corn syrup.

While private label brands are traditionally perceived as inferior, stores such as Trader Joe's have positioned their store brands as premium products without charging the premium prices seen at Whole Foods. These limited assortment stores are particularly popular among millennials who are typically more driven by price than brand. According to data from Mintel, 42 percent of millennial grocery shoppers find private label foods more innovative than branded products, and 70 percent believe that the quality of these store brand products has increased.[24]

In an attempt to compete with Trader Joe's and Aldi, Whole Foods announced plans in 2015 to open a line of stores aimed toward millennials in the coming year. These locations, called "365 by Whole Foods," are smaller in size and exclusively offer private label items. With so many suppliers in the organic foods market, customers now have myriad cheaper options to meet their demand. According to equity research by Jeffries, Trader Joe's prices comparable products 30 percent lower than Whole Foods, Sprouts products are 18 percent lower and Kroger's comparable goods are 13 percent lower.[25]

To combat their "Whole Paycheck" image and compete in the new market in which they found themselves, Whole Foods reduced prices in 2015 of some goods up to 7.2 percent from the previous year.[26] Without a paid media campaign in place to promote these lowered prices, though, customers remained unaware and 70 percent had not noticed any price changes in a national Suntrust survey.[27] Whole Foods' share of the retail grocery market dropped from 2.4 percent in 2014 to just 1.4 percent in 2015, and Kroger was expected to overtake them as the largest seller of organic goods by 2016.[28]

## PAST CONTROVERSIES

Unfortunately, Whole Foods was no stranger to problems beyond the financial statements. At the time that the NYDCA announced the investigation, Whole Foods had already struggled with negative media attention. Between 2007 and 2015, multiple incidents had thrust the company directly into the public awareness, including:

1. In July 2007, CEO John Mackey was found to have been posting disparaging comments under a pseudonym about Wild Oats, a Whole Foods acquisition target, on the message boards of Yahoo! Finance. Some of the posts were used as evidence in a Federal Trade Commission suit to block the acquisition.[29]
2. In August 2009, Mackey wrote an opinion piece in *The Wall Street Journal* taking a strong stance against the proposed Affordable Care Act, asserting that "many of our health-care problems are self-inflicted."[30]
3. In January 2013, Mackey responded to the passage of the Affordable Care Act by equating it to "fascism" in an NPR interview. He recanted the next day, calling his comments "a bad choice of words on my part."[31]

4. In June 2013, two WFM employees were suspended from working at a store in Albuquerque after filing a complaint about the company's policy prohibiting employees from speaking Spanish while on the clock.[32]

5. In August 2015, a customer in a Los Angeles store posted a picture to Instagram of an incorrectly labeled bottle of "asparagus water" priced at $5.99. The posting went viral and attracted national media attention.[33]

These events, and others like them, have followed one of two patterns. First, the anti-healthcare outbursts and other employee relations incidents juxtapose the company's image as a socially progressive force against the outspoken libertarian views of its CEO and the free-market pressures on a publicly traded enterprise. For a company whose core values include "[supporting] team member excellence and happiness," standing against the Affordable Care Act was seen as hypocritical by many of Whole Foods' target demographic.[34]

Second, the public has been increasingly willing to mock Whole Foods as an archetypical overpriced luxury goods peddler. Incidents such as the "asparagus water" post, which was ridiculed in a satirical segment by late night host John Oliver, have continued to reinforce the brand's image of inaccessibility.[35] Whole Foods' reputation as a predator of customers who choose a healthy lifestyle is only strengthened by incidents of overcharging or exorbitant pricing. In fact, the NYDCA's investigation came only a year after a remarkably similar incident in California.

## OVERCHARGING IN CALIFORNIA, 2014

On June 24, 2014, the City Attorney of Los Angeles, California, announced that Whole Foods agreed to pay $800,000 in penalties for violating consumer protection laws regarding false advertising and unfair competition.[36] A year-long investigation found that the company charged more than the advertised price for a wide variety of food items. Specifically, the investigation discovered that Whole Foods:

1. failed to subtract the weight of containers when charging for the self-serve salad bar and hot bar;
2. overstated the weight of packaged items sold by the pound;
3. prepared deli items, such as kebabs, that were sold by unit instead of by weight, as required by law.

As a result, Whole Foods was subjected to a five-year court injunction requiring the company to conduct random audits, charge accurate prices and appoint employees to oversee pricing accuracy state-wide. Whole Foods responded with an open letter via their newsroom about the settlement, saying:

> You may have heard about the now settled California case regarding weights and measures in our stores. We're disappointed that some customers who purchased weighed and measured items in our stores may have been slightly overcharged unintentionally. In some cases, customers were also *under*charged. While close to 99% of the millions of transactions we processed during the evaluation period were found to be accurate, we are constantly committed to getting as close to 100-percent accuracy as possible.[37]

## THE INVESTIGATION AND ALLEGATIONS

The New York City Department of Consumer Affairs (NYDCA) is the largest municipal consumer protection agency in the U.S.[38] In addition to other regulatory activities surrounding consumer advocacy, the agency's responsibilities include inspecting city supermarket scales and scanners to verify their accuracy.[39] The current investigation began in late 2014 when routine inspections of the city's eight Whole Foods stores revealed unacceptable labeling and weighing errors. NYDCA personnel returned to these stores in early 2015 and found similar errors, leading to the agency's accusation of "systemic overcharging."[40]

Several examples of particular items found to be mislabeled were published by NYDCA, whose press release pointed to overcharges approaching $15 for a single pre-packaged item. Commissioner Julie Menin described "the worst case of mislabeling [the inspectors] have seen in their careers, which DCA and New Yorkers will not tolerate."[41] Menin also noted that maximum fines for false labeling were $1,700 for each of the "thousands" of violations documented in Whole Foods stores across the city.[42]

## GROCERY STORES OVERCHARGING ACROSS THE COUNTRY

While Whole Foods might have been the worst case of overcharging the NYDCA has ever seen, mispricing of grocery and other retail items is not uncommon. In the same Fall 2015 sweep of 120 stores in New York City, dozens of other grocery stores had at least one product type with a mislabeled package.[43] The problem of overcharging customers also extends outside New York City. In 2012, a Los Angeles court fined Ralphs Grocery Company $1.1 million for overcharging deli customers in addition to other weighed food products, and for failing to subtract the weight of packaging.[44]

In the Fall of 2015 in North Carolina, where businesses were allowed a 2 percent error discrepancy in overcharges, nine stores were fined for price scanning errors, including Dollar General, Target and Walgreens.[45] These discrepancies typically occur when a sale sign is not taken down after the advertised sale period is concluded, or there is a delay between an item's price being changed in the store's system and the new price being posted at the shelf.

## THE E TEAM CONVENES

The fines would hurt, and it would take time for lawyers to negotiate a reasonable settlement with the NYDCA. But taking losses of even a few million dollars seemed like a negligible setback compared to the larger image concerns that loomed ahead for Whole Foods. Efforts to combat the "Whole Paycheck" perception of the company shared by many consumers would be undercut. The repeat of a nearly identical violation to the one in California a year earlier would call into question the competence and trustworthiness of management. Perhaps worst of all, consumer protection groups across the country might detect a trend within Whole Foods' operations, and similar investigations could follow.

The first half of 2015 had been hard for Whole Foods' financial performance, and the introduction of a public crisis would not help. Looking around the room, John Mackey knew that the people he saw would be busy in the coming weeks responding to the NYDCA press release and public attention that was sure to follow. But somewhere in the back of his mind, Mackey wondered if there was a way for Whole Foods to break free of the cycle of public incidents.

## DISCUSSION QUESTIONS

*Retrospective Questions:*

1.  Who within Whole Foods' management team should take responsibility for responding to the investigation?
2.  Which stakeholders are affected by the NYDCA investigation?
3.  What are the key points that Whole Foods must emphasize when developing its messaging for a public response?
4.  What medium (or media) will be most effective for the communications team (earned, paid or owned media, or a combination of these)?

*Prospective Questions:*

1.  Should Whole Foods take steps to increase the company's capacity to respond to controversies and crises? If so, what can they do?
2.  Whole Foods has received much more negative attention than many other retailers facing similar mislabeling investigations and charges. Why is this, and should they choose to draw attention to it?
3.  What steps should Whole Foods take to respond internally to the NYDCA investigation? What messages should be communicated throughout the organization and how should they be delivered?

## WRITING ASSIGNMENT

Please respond in writing to the issues presented in this case by preparing two documents: a communication strategy memo and a professional business letter.

In preparing these documents, you may assume one of two roles: you may identify yourself as a Whole Foods Market senior manager who has been asked to provide advice to CEO John Mackey regarding the issues he and his company are facing. Or, you may identify yourself as an external management consultant who has been asked by the company to provide advice to him.

Either way, you must prepare a strategy memo addressed to Mr. Mackey that summarizes the details of the case, identifies critical issues, discusses their implications (what they mean and why they matter), offers specific recommendations for action (assigning ownership and suspense dates for each) and shows how to communicate the solution to all who are affected by the recommendations.

You must also prepare a professional business letter for Mr. Mackey's signature. That document should be addressed to all Whole Foods Market employees, explaining what happened and the actions the company is taking. If you have questions about either of these documents, please consult your instructor.

## APPENDIX

Department of Consumer Affairs (DCA) Commissioner Julie Menin today announced an ongoing investigation into Whole Foods after finding that the company's New York City stores routinely overstated the weights of its pre-packaged products – including meats, dairy and baked goods – resulting in customers being overcharged. DCA tested packages of 80 different types of pre-packaged products and found all of the products had packages with mislabeled weights. Additionally, 89 percent of the packages tested did not meet the federal standard for the maximum amount that an individual package can deviate from the actual weight, which is set by the U.S. Department of Commerce. The overcharges ranged from $0.80 for a package of pecan panko to $14.84 for a package of coconut shrimp.

DCA's findings point to a systematic problem with how products packaged for sale at Whole Foods are weighed and labeled. The snapshot suggests that individual packages are routinely not weighed or are inaccurately weighed, resulting in overcharges for consumers. The overcharges were especially prevalent in packages that had been labeled with exactly the same weight when it would be practically impossible for all of the packages to weigh the same amount. These products included nuts and other snack products (flavored almonds, pecan panko and corn nuts), berries, vegetables, and seafood. In some cases, this issue was found for the same exact products at multiple stores.

Several examples of overcharges include:

DCA inspected eight packages of vegetable platters, which were priced at $20/package. Consumers who purchased these packages would have been, on average, overcharged by $2.50—a profit of $20 for the eight packages. One package was overpriced by $6.15.

DCA inspected eight packages of chicken tenders, which were priced at $9.99/pound. Consumers who purchased these packages would have been, on average, overcharged by $4.13—a profit of $33.04 for the eight packages. One package was overpriced by $4.85.

DCA inspected four packages of berries, which were priced at $8.58/package. Consumers who purchased these packages would have been, on average, overcharged by $1.15—a profit of $4.60 for the four packages. One package was overpriced by $1.84.

---

FOR IMMEDIATE RELEASE: Wednesday, June 24, 2015
MEDIA CONTACT: Connie Ress/Abigail Lootens
Department of Consumer Affairs (212) 436–0042 press@dca.nyc.gov

**Department of Consumer Affairs Investigation Uncovers Systemic Overcharging for Pre-packaged Foods at City's Whole Foods**

*Expanded Investigation to Examine the Extent of the Chain's Overcharging for Pre-Packaged Foods*

---

**FIGURE 13.1** Press Release issued by New York Department of Consumer Affairs

"It is unacceptable that New Yorkers shopping for a summer BBQ or who grab something to eat from the self-service aisles at New York City's Whole Foods stores have a good chance of being overcharged," said DCA Commissioner Menin. "Our inspectors tell me this is the worst case of mislabeling they have seen in their careers, which DCA and New Yorkers will not tolerate. As a large chain grocery store, Whole Foods has the money and resources to ensure greater accuracy and to correct what appears to be a widespread problem—the city's shoppers deserve to be correctly charged."

DCA regularly inspects all of the city's supermarkets for scanner and scale accuracy, pricing, and charging tax on non-taxable items. Last fall, DCA conducted in-depth inspections into how Whole Foods was weighing and labeling its pre-packaged foods and discovered troubling issues with their labeling of the weight of pre-packaged foods. This winter, DCA revisited several stores and found products continued to be mislabeled. DCA's expanded investigation will further evaluate the company's compliance with City and state laws. To date, DCA's inspections have focused on the eight stores that were open during the time of inspections. There are currently nine Whole Foods stores in New York City and they reportedly have plans to open an additional location in Harlem. Nationally, the chain is rapidly expanding and also recently announced that it plans to open a lower-priced chain called 365 by Whole Foods Market.

The fine for falsely labeling a package is as much as $950 for the first violation and up to $1,700 for a subsequent violation. The potential number of violations that Whole Foods faces for all pre-packaged goods in the NYC stores is in the thousands.

An investigation in California, which began in 2012, also found pricing irregularities in the state's Whole Foods stores. City Attorneys for Santa Monica, Los Angeles, and San Diego brought a civil consumer protection case on behalf of the people of the State of California. As a result of that case, Whole Foods agreed to pay close to $800,000 in penalties and initiate a stringent in-house pricing accuracy effort that included a state-wide compliance coordinator, a designated employee at each location for pricing accuracy, and random audits.

*Source:* "Department of Consumer Affairs Investigation Uncovers Systemic Overcharging for Pre-packaged Foods at City's Whole Foods," *Department of Consumer Affairs*, News release, June 24, 2015. Online at www1.nyc.gov/site/dca/media/pr062415.page. Accessed January 31, 2016.

**FIGURE 13.2** YouGov BrandIndex 2015 Ratings, Whole Foods and Trader Joe's

*Source:* "Whole Foods 'Love' Delivers Modest Perception Recovery," YouGov – BrandIndex, September 30, 2015. Online at www.brandindex.com/article/whole-foods-new-love-campaign-delivers-modest-perception-recovery.

**FIGURE 13.3** Whole Foods Monthly Closing Stock Price and Select Events

*Source*: Yahoo! Finance, various (see endnotes 15-18)

## ACKNOWLEDGMENTS

This case was prepared by research assistants Dylan Koehler, Stephanie Rearick and Dustin Schoedel under the direction of James O'Rourke, Teaching Professor of Management, as the basis for class discussion rather than to illustrate either effective or ineffective handling of an administrative situation. Information was gathered from corporate as well as public sources. Editorial assistance: Judy Bradford.

## NOTES

1 "Department of Consumer Affairs Investigation Uncovers Systemic Overcharging for Pre-packaged Foods at City's Whole Foods," *New York Consumer Affairs*. Press Release dated June 24, 2015. Online at www1.nyc.gov/site/dca/media/pr062415. page. Accessed January 31, 2016.

2 Ibid.

3 Mackey, John. "Keeping Our Executive Team Together For 10 More Years," *John Mackey's Blog, Whole Foods*, May 12, 2010. Online at www.wholefoodsmarket.com/blog/john-mackeys-blog/keeping-our-executive-team-together-10-more-years. Accessed February 21, 2016.

4 Marzilli, Ted. "Whole Foods 'Love' Delivers Modest Perception Recovery," *YouGov – BrandIndex*. September 30, 2015. Online at www.brandindex.com/article/whole-foods-new-love-campaign-delivers-modest-perception-recovery.

5 "Whole Foods Market History," *Whole Foods* website. Online at www.wholefoodsmarket.com/company-info/whole-foods-market-history#wholefoodsmarket. Accessed May 18, 2016.

6 "Whole Foods Market, Inc. History," *Funding Universe*. Online at www.fundinguniverse.com/company-histories/whole-foods-market-inc-history/. Accessed May 18, 2016.

7 "Whole Foods Market Newsroom. History and Timeline," *Whole Foods* website. Online at http://media.wholefoodsmarket.com/history/. Accessed May 18, 2016.

8 "The Highest Standards Weren't Available, So We Created Them. *2014 Annual Report*," *Whole Foods* website. Online at https://assets.wholefoodsmarket.com/www/company-info/investor-relations/annual-reports/2014-WFM_Annual_Report.pdf. Accessed May 18, 2016.

9   "Whole Foods Market," *CrunchBase*. Online at www.crunchbase.com/organization/whole-foods-market#/entity. Accessed May 18, 2016.

10  *Annual Stakeholders' Report 2015*. Financial report, November 13, 2015. Online at http://assets.wholefoodsmarket.com/www/company-info/investor-relations/annual-reports/2015-WFM-Annual-Report.pdf.

11  Kannel, Charlie. "Corporate Responsibility Spotlight: Whole Foods Market," *Fool.com*, September 14, 2012. Online at www.fool.com/investing/general/2012/09/14/corporate-responsibility-spotlight-whole-foods-ma.aspx. Accessed February 22, 2016.

12  "Whole Foods Market Overview," *Glassdoor*. Online at www.glassdoor.com/Overview/Working-at-Whole-Foods-Market-EI_IE422.11,29.htm. Accessed February 20, 2016.

13  "Whole Foods Market Celebrates 18 Consecutive Years on FORTUNE's '100 Best Companies to Work For' List," *Whole Foods Market Newsroom*, March 5, 2015. Online at http://media.wholefoodsmarket.com/news/whole-foods-market-celebrates-18-consecutive-years-on-fortunes-100-best-com. Accessed February 23, 2016.

14  "Supermarkets & Grocery Stores in the US Market Research," *Ibisworld.com*, 2016. Online at ibisworld.com/reports/us/industry/currentperformance.aspx?entid=1040. Accessed February 20, 2016.

15  "FMI – Food Marketing Institute – Supermarket Facts," *Fmi.org*, 2016. Online at www.fmi.org/research-resources/supermarket-facts. Accessed February 22, 2016.

16  Popovec, Jennifer. "Supermarket M&A Activity Creates Ripples for Shopping Center Owners," *National Real Estate Investor*, 2016. Online at http://nreionline.com/retail/supermarket-ma-activity-creates-ripples-shopping-center-owners. Accessed February 22, 2016.

17  "Cost of Organic Food," *Consumer Reports*, 2016. Online at consumerreports.org/cro/news/2015/03/cost-of-organic-food/index.htm. Accessed February 20, 2016.

18  "Brief History of Possibly the 1st Health Food Store in U.S.," *Martindalesnutrition.com*, 2016. Online at Martindalesnutrition.com/about/history/. Accessed February 22, 2016.

19  "Supermarkets & Grocery Stores in the US Market Research," *Ibisworld.com*.

20  Ibid.

21  "Healthy Eating Index, Center for Nutrition Policy and Promotion," *Cnpp.usda.gov*, 2016. Online at www.cnpp.usda.gov/healthyeatingindex. Accessed February 20, 2016.

22  Ibid.

23  "Supermarkets & Grocery Stores in the US Market Research," *Ibisworld.com*.

24  "Nearly Half of US Millennials Find Store Brand Products More Innovative than Name Brands," *Mintel*, March 10, 2015. Online at www.mintel.com/press-centre/retail-press-centre/nearly-half-of-us-millennials-find-store-brand-food-products-more-innovative-than-name-brands.

25  Clark, Meagan. "Whole Foods Confronts Its 'Whole Paycheck' Image Amid Growing Competition," *International Business Times*, 2014. Online at www.ibtimes.com/whole-foods-confronts-its-whole-paycheck-image-amid-growing-competition-1718641. Accessed February 20, 2016.

26  "Whole Foods Prices Drop, But Sluggish Sales Likely to Continue," *Austin Business Journal*, 2016. Online at www.bizjournals.com/austin/news/2014/09/22/whole-foods-prices-drop-but-sluggish-sales-likely.html. Accessed February 23, 2016.

27  Clark. "Whole Foods Confronts Its 'Whole Paycheck' Image Amid Growing Competition."

28  Lutz, Ashley. "Whole Foods is Falling to Competitors Because of One Mistake," *Business Insider*, 2016. Online at www.businessinsider.com/whole-foods-biggest-problem-2015-5. Accessed February 20, 2016.

29  Kesmodel, David and John Wilke. "Whole Foods Is Hot, Wild Oats a Dud – So Said 'Rahodeb'," *The Wall Street Journal* (New York), July 7, 2007. Online at www.wsj.com/articles/SB118418782959963745. Accessed February 8, 2016.

30  Mackey, John. "The Whole Foods Alternative to ObamaCare," *The Wall Street Journal* (New York), August 11, 2009. Online at www.wsj.com/articles/SB10001424052970204251404574342170072865070. Accessed February 2, 2009.

31  Kavoussi, Bonnie. "Whole Foods CEO: Obamacare Is 'Like Fascism'," *Huffington Post*, January 16, 2013. Online at www.huffingtonpost.com/2013/01/16/whole-foods-ceo-obamacare-fascism_n_2488029.html. See also "Whole Foods CEO John Mackey Takes Back Fascism Comment," *Morning Edition*, National Public Radio, January 18, 2013. Online at www.npr.org/2013/01/18/169684978/whole-foods-ceo-john-mackey-takes-back-fascism-comment.

32  "Whole Foods Workers Allegedly Suspended Over Spanish-Speaking Ban," *HuffPost Live*, Week Ending May 13. Video. Online at http://live.huffingtonpost.com/r/highlight/51b1283578c90a03cd000261.

33  "Whole Foods to Pay Hefty Price to Settle Overcharging Allegations," *CBS Money Watch*, December 28, 2015. Online at www.cbsnews.com/news/whole-foods-to-pay-hefty-price-to-settle-overcharging-allegations/.

34  "Our Core Values," *Whole Foods*. Online at www.wholefoodsmarket.com/mission-values/core-values. Accessed February 16, 2016.

35  "Whole Foods," *Last Week Tonight* with John Oliver, HBO, August 10, 2015. Online at www.youtube.com/watch?v=R9gGL1cnnhg.

36  From the Office of the City Attorney Mike Feuer. "Whole Foods Agrees to Pay $800,000 and Adhere to Sweeping Court Injunction in Statewide Pricing Inaccuracy Case." News release, June 24, 2014. Online at http://freepdfhosting.com/95ed 8feabe.pdf.

37  "An Open Letter to Whole Foods Market Shoppers in California and Beyond," *Whole Foods Market Newsroom*, June 26, 2014. Online at http://media.wholefoodsmarket.com/news/an-open-letter-to-whole-foods-market-shoppers. Accessed February 23, 2016.

38  "Consumer Affairs is Here to Help You," *NYC Consumer Affairs*. Last updated February, 2016. Online at www1.nyc.gov/site/dca/about/overview.page.

39  "Department of Consumer Affairs," *New York Consumer Affairs*. Press Release.

40  Ibid.

41  Ibid.

42  Ibid.

43  Kim, Susanna. "Grocery Stores Overcharging Across the Country," *ABC News*. 2016. Online at http://abcnews.go.com/Business/grocery-stores-overcharging-country/story?id=32025735. Accessed February 20, 2016.

44  Ibid.

45  Ibid.

# Case 13.3: Mars, Incorporated

## Skittles Becomes Part of a Controversial Shooting

On February 26, 2012, George Zimmerman, a 28-year-old mixed-race Hispanic neighborhood watch captain, shot and killed Trayvon Martin, a 17-year-old African-American student, near Zimmerman's home in Sanford, Florida. The night of the shooting, Zimmerman sustained wounds to his nose and the back of his neck, and he told authorities that he shot Martin in self-defense. Charges were not initially filed against Zimmerman because no evidence was found refuting Zimmerman's story.[1]

Nearly a week and a half later, the shooting gained national media attention because of two key facts: first, Trayvon Martin was African American and George Zimmerman was not; and second, Trayvon Martin was unarmed at the time of the shooting. In an interview published by Reuters, Ben Crump, the lawyer for Trayvon Martin's family, said that on the night of the shooting police found "a can of Arizona ice tea in [Trayvon Martin's] jacket pocket and Skittles in his front pocket. . . . "[2]

## MARS, INC.

In 1911, Frank C. Mars began making and selling butter cream candy from his home in Tacoma, Washington. From its modest beginnings, Mars, Incorporated grew steadily until 1923, when the business rapidly expanded after the introduction of the Milky Way candy bar. By 1932, Mars had moved its operations to Chicago, Illinois, and introduced the iconic brands Milky Way, Snickers and 3 Musketeers. That same year, Forest E. Mars, Sr., Frank's son, began operations in the U.K., thus making Mars an international company.[3]

The privately held company continued to grow through the 1900s and early 2000s, both organically and through acquisitions. In 2009, Mars acquired the William Wrigley Jr. Company for $23 billion, greatly expanding its gum and confectionery portfolios. At the time of the acquisition, Wrigley had $5.4 billion in sales.[4]

In 2012, Mars was headquartered in McLean, Virginia, and operated in six segments – petcare, chocolate, Wrigley, food, drinks and symbioscience (the global health and life sciences segment of Mars) – with more than 90 percent of revenues generated by pet care, chocolate and Wrigley.[5] Mars consisted of seven candy and gum brands including M&Ms (worth $3.49 billion), Snickers ($3.57 billion), Dove/Galaxy ($2.60 billion), Mars/Milky Way ($2.38 billion),

Twix ($1.51 billion), Extra ($2.23 billion) and Orbit ($2.50 billion).[6] With more than $33 billion of total net sales and a 35.2 percent share in the candy production industry, Mars was the largest confectionery company in the U.S.[7]

## MARS CORPORATE SOCIAL RESPONSIBILITY INITIATIVES

Mars, Inc. remains dedicated to the goal Forrest E. Mars, Sr., laid out in 1947: "a 'mutuality of benefits' for all stakeholders."[8] To this end, Mars strives to use its business to make a positive difference in the communities in which it operates. Each year, the company outlines these corporate social responsibility initiatives in its "Principles in Action Summary." The 2011 issue of the document highlighted efforts to make an impact on health and nutrition, develop environmentally sustainable business operations and empower its associates to volunteer in their local communities.[9]

Mars believes that it can exercise the greatest control over its environmental impact by making changes for sustainability in its operations and supply chain. The company set lofty goals such as reducing direct fossil-fuel energy use and greenhouse gas emissions by 25 percent and achieving zero waste to landfill by 2015.[10] In addition, the company is taking steps to "secure safe, reliable, sustainable supplies of high-quality raw materials" in an effort to help "farmers and suppliers boost their incomes by selling more product."[11]

Mars also lays out two programs through which it creates opportunities for its associates to benefit communities around the world:

In addition to making a difference through their work, Associates have opportunities to make a difference in their communities through two signature initiatives: the Mars Ambassador Program . . . and the Mars Volunteer Program (MVP).

Through MVP, Mars Associates receive paid time off to support our three community engagement priorities: health and prosperity for people, a better world for pets, and a greener planet. Over 9,600 Associates volunteered more than 37,000 hours with 290+ organizations through MVP. In 2011, 80 Associates representing every business segment and region participated in MAP assignments with 16 partner organizations to make a tangible difference in communities.[12]

As a family-owned private company, Mars's vision and goals seek to set the company up for success for generations to come. Mars believes that its CSR initiatives on sustainability and local volunteer work are crucial to the company's long-term prosperity.

## SKITTLES

Skittles were first introduced in the U.K. in 1974 and first sold in the U.S. in 1979 in their original flavor combination: orange, lemon, lime, grape and strawberry. Skittles' candy shells are imprinted with a small "S," and a combination of sugar, corn syrup and hydrogenated palm oil give Skittles their sweet flavor and chewy texture.[13] Skittles' sweet flavors, bright red packaging and "Taste the Rainbow" slogan have made the candy a favorite among children and adults alike.

*Bloomberg BusinessWeek* named Skittles America's No.14 Favorite Candy in 2009 based on retail sales[14] and the brand surpassed 10 million Facebook fans in 2010.[15] Skittles has been managed under Mars's Wrigley segment since 2009. Since 2012, Skittles have been available in several different flavor combinations including tropical, wild berry and sour, and the brand has annual net sales greater than $200 million.[16]

## THE NATIONAL SPOTLIGHT

During the first few days following Trayvon Martin's death, the story was covered at a local level and received only minor national attention. That changed soon after a Reuters article published more details about the shooting, and news spread quickly across various blogs and social media websites. The public instantly became outraged that a teenager carrying only Skittles and iced tea was killed, but no charges had been brought against the adult who pulled the trigger.

Media outlets began discussing the role that racial profiling may have played in the initial shooting. The issue of racial profiling was amplified because Zimmerman had called the police to report "a suspicious person" prior to shooting the unarmed teenager. By March 22, 2012, a Change.org petition started by Trayvon Martin's parents that called for the arrest of George Zimmerman had passed 1.3 million signatures.[17] The next day, President Barack Obama released a statement calling the shooting a "tragedy" and stated, "If I had a son, he'd look like Trayvon Martin."[18]

In addition to the outrage pervading social media websites and national television, rallies calling for the indictment of Zimmerman and memorializing Martin rose throughout the country. Rally attendees were often seen wearing hoodies and waving bags of Skittles to symbolize the circumstances surrounding Martin's death. One such rally, referred to as the Million Hoodie March, attracted hundreds of people to New York City to protest for the arrest of George Zimmerman.[19]

## SKITTLES AS A PROTEST ICON

On March 8, 2012, the day after Reuters published its article, the story began to appear on popular gossip blogs such as Gawker.com and news blogs such as Huffingtonpost.com. These articles and numerous social media posts repeatedly claimed that Martin had been carrying Skittles, rather than a firearm.[20,21] #Skittles was trending and became one of the top 15 Trayvon Martin-related hashtags on Twitter.[22] In April 2012, Skittles was mentioned in approximately 1,600 tweets, an increase of 1,200 percent compared to the 133 mentions the brand received in April 2011.[23]

The mere presence of the candy on the night of the shooting, however, was not the only factor that made Skittles a central symbol of the tragedy and subsequent public outrage. Trayvon Martin was also carrying Arizona iced tea at the time, but Arizona did not receive the same recognition as Skittles. The candy's bright colors and slogan, "Taste the Rainbow," gave Skittles a natural connection to youth and innocence. The association became important because many supporters believed that Trayvon Martin was an innocent child killed while walking home from the gas station.[24]

In addition to becoming a flag at protests for George Zimmerman's arrest, Skittles were used in other ways to call attention to the case and to offer support to Trayvon Martin's family. Filmmaker Spike Lee used Twitter to encourage his followers to send bags of Skittles to the Sanford Police Department to protest the lack of arrest.[25] On Facebook, many supporters posted pictures of themselves on the ground pretending to be shot while lying next to a bag of Skittles. Spelman College, a historically black women's college in Atlanta, began buying Skittles in bulk and reselling the candy individually for 50 cents a pack to raise money for the Martin family.[26] Some people even used the association between Skittles and Trayvon Martin for their own gain, selling unlicensed merchandise with the images of Martin and Skittles.

In light of all the attention and exposure the Skittles brand received, Mars remained silent. Although Mars is not a publicly traded company, sources close to the company acknowledged a spike in Skittles sales in the months following the shooting, which continued to grow as the conversations surrounding the incident escalated.[27] Many people began to wonder if Mars was deliberately profiting from the tragedy, and they demanded that the company speak up and get involved.

## INITIAL RESPONSE FROM MARS

The theory that Mars was profiting from a tragedy created significant public backlash for the company. Mars initially attempted to abstain from any response regarding the tragedy; however, as calls for its involvement grew louder, the company was forced to comment. On March 22, 2012, Jennifer Jackson-Luth, a spokeswoman for Mars, released a statement:

> We are deeply saddened by the news of Trayvon Martin's death and express our sincere condolences to his family and friends. . . . We also respect their privacy and feel it inappropriate to get involved or comment further, as we would never wish for our actions to be perceived as an attempt of commercial gain following this tragedy.[28,29]

Mars Inc.'s response was met with pragmatic acceptance by industry peers and experts. Amy Stern, president of Bender Hammerling Group, a public relations firm that works with food companies, said that Mars acted exactly as they should. Stephanie Child, former crisis manager for ConAgra Foods, implied that there was not a right move for Mars, noting that any misstep could lead to further backlash. Beth Gallant, a marketing professor at Lehigh University and former brand manager for Nabisco, Kraft, Pfizer and Crayola, also acknowledged that this was a unique and very difficult situation for any company.[30]

Others, however, were not satisfied with the response, calling Mars "tone deaf" and oblivious to the reality of the outside world. Even before Mars responded, many were calling for the company to donate its excess profits. This sentiment only intensified after the company released a formal response. A petition posted on Change.org requested that excess profits be donated to a non-profit organization of Trayvon Martin's parents' choice.[31]

Many threatened a boycott if Mars did not agree to the donation of profits. Rashad Moore, a student at Morehouse College, suggested donating to underprivileged communities. Weldon McWilliams, professor of African-American studies at Cheyney University of Pennsylvania, also called for a boycott if Mars did not donate to less fortunate communities.[32] Some even suggested a boycott due to the association Mars had with the American Legislative Exchange Council, a non-profit organization that assisted with the legislation behind Florida's "stand your ground" law.[33] These views caught on with the general public who echoed them via social media websites.

## PAST CONTROVERSIES

Controversial news stories following homicides that involved food and beverage brands as nationally recognized as Skittles have troubled several companies in the last half-century. Even Mars itself has experienced an attempt to sour its brand image. In 2007, the People for the Ethical Treatment of Animals (PETA) organization attempted to spread the claim that Mars funded unethical testing of its candy products on small animals.

### Don't Drink the Kool-Aid

On November 18, 1978, Rev. Jim Jones, founder of the racially integrated People's Temple, and more than 900 of his followers committed mass suicide by drinking Flavor Aid poisoned with cyanide in the Jonestown establishment located in the Guyana jungle.[34] Although it is unclear whether Flavor Aid's leading competitor, Kool-Aid, was also used, the colloquial phrase, "Don't drink the Kool-Aid," has become a common way to express the idea that people should not blindly follow a leader without considering the consequences of their actions.

Kraft Foods Group, Inc., owner of the Kool-Aid brand, has not sought to mute the phrase. A senior manager for beverages in the U.S. at Kraft, Bridgett MacConnell, "cringes when she hears the words 'drink the Kool-Aid'" but acknowledges that it has "become ubiquitous [. . .]" and "the idea of trying to fight it is not worth it."[35]

### The Twinkie Defense

On November 27, 1978, Dan White, a former police officer and member of the San Francisco Board of Supervisors who resigned from his position only 17 days earlier, fatally shot and killed George Moscone, mayor of San Francisco at the time, and Harvey Milk, a fellow Board of Supervisors member and civil rights activist, in City Hall. At the trial, White's defense lawyer argued that White had fallen into a depression prior to the shooting, which inhibited his ability to determine right from wrong. To provide evidence of White's mental instability, the defense highlighted his recent change in eating habits. After resigning from the San Francisco Board of Supervisors, White ditched his usual healthy diet for one of junk food, a symptom that supported the notion of his depression. The jury was swayed by White's "diminished capacity plea" and on May 21, 1979, returned two verdicts of voluntary manslaughter rather than murder.[36]

The case became known as the "Twinkie Defense," a term coined by journalists explaining White's defense argument. The term itself is "so ingrained in our culture that it appears in law dictionaries, in sociology textbooks, in college exams and in more than 2,800 references on Google."[37] Although the case sparked a change in California Law, the effect on the Twinkies brand appears to have been limited. In 2005, Theresa Cogswell, a vice president for research and development at Interstate Bakeries Corporation, which owned Hostess and the Twinkie brand, proclaimed the resiliency of the Twinkie brand when she said, "[Twinkies] are a constant in your life. They always come back around. . . . The way we look at it, sometimes you just need a sugar fix."[38]

### Mars Response to 2007 PETA Campaign

The People for the Ethical Treatment of Animals organization chastised Mars in 2007 with claims that the company funded animal testing that killed mice and rabbits. In August and September of 2007, PETA sent two letters to Mars President Paul Michaels demanding that the company "discontinue funding of all animal" tests while making the following statement:

> Mars is currently funding a cruel cardiac experiment on rodents at the University of California, San Francisco, as well as sponsoring nutrition research chairs held by known animal experimenters at the University of California, Davis, and the University of Illinois–Urbana Champaign. Mars also funded a deadly experiment on mice that was published in a 2007 issue of the *Journal of Neuroscience* in which animals were fed flavanols and forced to swim in a pool of water filled with white paint. The mice had to find a platform to try to avoid drowning, only to be later killed and dissected.[39]

PETA also posted a video to their website titled, "Mars' Ghoulish Secret: Candy-maker Kills Animals," and developed a separate site with the domain name marscandykills.com to raise awareness for the issue.[40] On December 7, 2007, Reuters reported that PETA was calling for a boycott of Mars and its products including M&Ms, Snickers and Twix. The article claimed that Mars spokeswoman Alice Nathanson said, "I can't speak to any information that PETA may or may not have. I can't speak to any experiments," but Mars "would never issue or post a statement that we were not 100 percent confident in."[41]

It does not appear that Mars endured significant financial setbacks as a result of the animal testing claims. In 2007, annual revenue for Mars was approximately $25 billion.[42] In 2008, the yearly revenue grew to $30 billion.[43]

## CONCLUSION/DECISION POINT

The presence of social media and the momentum with which it carried the Skittles story into the national spotlight added an unprecedented amount of widespread attention and urgency. Mars, Inc., would have to develop a strategy to appropriately manage the Skittles brand that was rapidly becoming recognized as a symbol of racial injustice, tragedy, youth and innocence. The company also faced the critical question regarding what it should do with the additional profits.

## DISCUSSION QUESTIONS

1. Did Mars make the right decision when it initially released the short statement expressing the company's condolences and declining to comment further?
2. Should Mars have been more transparent about the increased sales of Skittles following the shooting? Should they have disclosed specific sales figures?
3. Did the presence of Skittles as a key symbol and the increase in profits for the brand give Mars a responsibility to become actively involved in supporting the tragedy?
4. Should Mars issue another public statement or take additional action?
5. How can Mars (or similar companies) protect brand image and corporate reputation when consumers have the power to influence company brands via social media?
6. How can Mars be proactive in minimizing the backlash from possible future situations like the one they faced after the death of Trayvon Martin?
7. Should Mars consider expanding its corporate social responsibility portfolio? If so, how?

## ACKNOWLEDGMENTS

This case was prepared by research assistants Matthew Boylan, Joseph Gibilisco and Douglas McCallum under the direction of James O'Rourke, Teaching Professor of Management, as the basis for class discussion rather than to illustrate either effective or ineffective handling of an administrative situation. Information was gathered from corporate as well as public sources. Editorial assistance: Judy Bradford and Jennifer Cronin.

## NOTES

1 "Trayvon Martin Shooting Fast Facts," *CNN*, Turner Broadcasting System. Online at www.cnn.com/2013/06/05/us/trayvon-martin-shooting-fast-facts/. Accessed February 11, 2015.

2 Liston, Barbara. "Family of Florida Boy Killed by Neighborhood Watch Seeks Arrest," *Reuters*, March 7, 2012. Online at http://reuters.com/article/idUSBRE82709M 20120308?irpc=932. Accessed February 7, 2015.

3 "History Timeline," *Mars.com*. Online at www.mars.com/global/about-mars/history.aspx. Accessed February 7, 2015.

4 Sorkin, Andrew Ross. "Mars to Acquire Wrigley for $23 Billion," *The New York Times*, April 27, 2008. Online at www.nytimes.com/2008/04/28/business/28gum-web.html?r=0. Accessed February 6, 2015.

5 "Our Principles in Action Summary 2012," *McLean: Mars, Incorporated*, 2012. Online at www.mars.com/global/assets/doc/pia_exec_2012/Mars_PIA_Highlights_2012_EN_report.pdf. Accessed February 6, 2015.

6 Kaplan, David A. "Mars Incorporated: A Pretty Sweet Place To Work," *Fortune*. Time Inc. Network, January 17, 2013. Online at http://fortune.com/2013/01/17/mars-incorporated-a-pretty-sweet-place-to-work/. Accessed February 14, 2015.

7 Ahmad, Amal. "Candy Production in the US," *IBISWorld*, September 2014. Online at www.ibisworld.com/industry/default.aspx?indid=234. Accessed February 7, 2015.

8 "People, Planet and Performance," *McLean: Mars, Incorporated*, 2011. Online at www.mars.com/global/about-mars/people-planet-performance.aspx. Accessed February 12, 2015.

9 "Principles in Action Highlights 2011," *McLean: Mars, Incorporated*, 2012. Print. Online at www.wrigley.com.cn/pia/pdf/2011_Mars_en_simplify.pdf.

10 Ibid., p. 4.

11 Ibid., p. 9.

12 Ibid., pp. 16–17.

13 "Skittles®," *Wrigley.com*. Mars, Inc., 2012. Online at www.wrigley.com/global/brands/skittles.aspx. Accessed February 7, 2015.

14 Arndt, Michael. "America's 25 Favorite Candies: Top Selling Sweets," *Bloomberg.com*. Online at www.bloomberg.com/ss/09/10/1021_americas_25_top_selling_ candies/ 13.htm. Accessed February 18, 2015.

15 "Skittles®," *Wrigley.com*.

16 Choi, Candice. "In Trayvon Martin Killing, Skittles Joins Food Brands at Center of Tragedy," *MassLive.com*. The Associated Press, April 12, 2012. Online at www.masslive.com/talk/index.ssf/2012/04/in_trayvon_martin_killing_skit.html. Accessed January 20, 2015.

17 "Trayvon Martin Shooting Fast Facts," *CNN*.

18 Condon, Stephanie. "Obama: 'If I Had a Son, He'd Look like Trayvon'," *CBSNews*, CBS Interactive, March 23, 2012. Online at www.cbsnews.com/news/obama-if-I-had-a-son-hed-look-like-trayvon/. Accessed February 14, 2015.

19 Hajela, Deepti. "Trayvon Martin 'Million Hoodie March' March Draws Hundreds In New York City," *Huffington Post*, March 21, 2012. Online at www.huffingtonpost.com/2012/03/21/trayvon-martin-million-hoodie-march_n_1371403.html. Accessed February 14, 2015.

20 Lee, Trymaine. "Trayvon Martin's Family Calls for Arrest of Man Who Police Say Confessed to Shooting," *Huffington Post*, March 8, 2012. Online at www.huffingtonpost.com/2012/03/08/family-of-trayvon-martin-_n_1332756.html. Accessed February 6, 2015.

21 Gold, Danny. "Unarmed Black Teen Gunned Down by Neighborhood Watch Leader After Being Deemed Suspicious," *Gawker*, March 8, 2012. Online at http://gawker.com/5891805/unarmed-black-teen-gunned-down-by-neighborhood-watch-leader-after-being-deemed-suspicious. Accessed February 6, 2015.

22 "Trending Zimmerman-Trayvon Martin Hashtags and Tweets on Twitter," *Tweeting.com*, March 27, 2012. Online at http://tweeting.com/trending-zimmerman-trayvon-martin-hashtags-and-tweets-on-twitter. Accessed February 6, 2015.

23 Crain's Chicago Business Twitter account, *Twitter*, April 27, 2012. Online at https://twitter.com/crainschicago/status/195946764933664768. Accessed February 6, 2015.

24    Severson, Kim. "For Skittles, Death Brings Both Profit and Risk," *The New York Times*, March 28, 2012. Online at www. nytimes.com/2012/03/29/us/skittles-sales-up-after-trayvon-martin-shooting.html?_r=0. Accessed February 1, 2015.

25    Johnson, Craig. "Skittles, Arizona Iced Tea Speak Out About Shooting," *HLNtv.com*, March 29, 2012. Online at www.hlntv. com/article/2012/03/22/skittles-speak-out-trayvon-martin-deeply-saddened. Accessed February 10, 2015.

26    Alexander, Blayne. "Spelman Students Sell Skittles for Trayvon Martin," *11Alive News*, NBC Atlanta, March 30, 2012. Online at www.11alive.com/news/article/235856/3/Spelman-students-sell-Skittles-for-Trayvon-Martin. Accessed February 6, 2015.

27    Severson. "For Skittles, Death Brings Both Profit and Risk."

28    "Skittles Releases Statement on Trayvon Martin's Murder," *NewsOne*, Interactive One, March 22, 2013. Online at http:// newsone.com/1951455/skittles-releases-statement-on-trayvon-martins-murder/. Accessed February 6, 2015.

29    Johnson. "Skittles, Arizona Iced Tea Speak Out About Shooting."

30    Severson. "For Skittles, Death Brings Both Profit and Risk."

31    Caldwell, Emily. "Donate Excess Profits Since Trayvon Martin's Death," *Change.org*. Online at www.change.org/p/makers-of-skittles-and-arizona-iced-tea-donate-excess-profits-sincetrayvon-martin-s-death. Accessed February 6, 2015.

32    Ghosh, Palash. "Trayvon Martin's Death and Skittles: A Peculiar Marketing Dilemma," *International Business Times*, July 15, 2013. Online at www.ibtimes.com/trayvon-martins-death-skittles-peculiar-marketing-dilemma-1346469. Accessed February 6, 2015.

33    "Stupid Is as Stupid Does: People Who Flocked to Buy Skittles Helped Fund Law that Gave George Zimmerman Excuse to Remain Free For 46 Days," *Axiom Amnesia*, The Axiom Amnesia Theory, April 14, 2012. Online at http://axiomamnesia. com/2012/04/14/people-flocked-buy-skittles-helped-fund-law-george-zimmerman-remain-free-46-days/. Accessed February 6, 2015.

34    Rothenberg Gritz, Jennie. "Drinking the Kool-Aid: A Survivor Remembers Jim Jones," *The Atlantic*, November 18, 2011. Online at www.theatlantic.com/national/archive/2011/11/drinking-the-kool-aid-a-survivor-remembers-jim-jones/248723/. Accessed February 11, 2015.

35    Kislingbury, Graham. "Setting the Record Straight on 'Drink the Kool-Aid™'," *Corvallis Gazette Times*, June 13, 2010. Online at www.gazettetimes.com/blogs/graham-kislingbury/setting-the-record-straight-on-drink-the-kool-aid/article_fac6fe07-1d90-532f-9174-2c57c0b7a107.html. Accessed February 11, 2015.

36    Ernst, Cindi. "The Dan White (Harvey Milk Murder) Trial (1979): Selected Links & Bibliography," *The Dan White (Harvey Milk Murder) Trial (1979): Selected Links & Bibliography*, n.d. Online at http://law2.umkc.edu/faculty/projects/ftrials/milk/danwhitelinks.html. Accessed February 11, 2015.

37    Pogash, Carol. "Myth of the 'Twinkie Defense'/The Verdict in the Dan White Case Wasn't Based on His Ingestion of Junk Food," *SFGate*, November 23, 2003. Online at www.sfgate.com/ health/article/Myth-of-the-Twinkie-defense-The-verdict-in-2511152.php. Accessed February 11, 2015.

38    Sagon, Candy. "Twinkies, 75 Years and Counting," *The Washington Post*, April 13, 2005. Online at www.washingtonpost.com/wp-dyn/articles/A46062-2005Apr12.html. Accessed February 11, 2015.

39    Gala, Shalin G. "Food and Beverage Company Statement Regarding Animal Testing," Letter to Paul S. Michaels, *Marscandykills.com*. People for the Ethical Treatment of Animals, August 31, 2007. Online at www.marscandykills.com/pdf/Mars_Paul_Michaels_letter.pdf. Accessed February 12, 2015.

40    "Mars' Ghoulish Secret: Candy-maker Kills Animals," *People for the Ethical Treatment of Animals*, n.d. Online at www.peta.org/videos/mars-ghoulish-secret-candy-maker-kills-animals/. Accessed February 12, 2015.

41    Bartz, Diane. "PETA Boycotting Mars Candy Co. Over Animal Cruelty," *Reuters*, December 7, 2007. Online at http://uk.reuters.com/article/2007/12/08/science-mars-peta-boycott-dc-idUKN073174 8320071208. Accessed February 12, 2015.

42    "The 35 Largest U.S. Private Companies," *Fortune*, May 28, 2008. Online at http://archive.fortune.com/galleries/2008/fortune/0805/gallery.private_companies.fortune/10.html. Accessed February 23, 2015.

43    "America's Largest Private Companies," *Forbes*, October 28, 2009. Online at www.forbes.com/lists/2009/21/private-companies-09_Mars_L600.html. Accessed February 23, 2015.

# APPENDIX A

## Analyzing a Case Study

Among the many tools available to business educators, the case study has become increasingly popular. Professors use it to teach the complexities of many different, modern business problems. That's not a surprising development. Beyond the fundamentals, memorization and description will take you just so far. The real test of whether you are ready to manage a business will come when you are asked to assume the role of a manager, step into an authentic business situation, make sense of the circumstances you see, draft a plan and take action.

### WHY STUDY CASES?

Schools of law have studied cases for many years as a means of exploring legal concepts and understanding the practices of the courts. Harvard Business School began inviting executives and managers into their classrooms after World War I, hoping to provide students with some insight into the thinking of successful businesspeople. Not long afterward, professors of business began writing down the narratives of these business managers in an effort to capture the ambiguities and complexities involved in the day-to-day practice of commerce and administration.

The idea spread to other schools of business and migrated from graduate to undergraduate programs. Today, many business educators use case studies because their narratives are so valuable in developing analytic and critical thinking abilities, as well as organizational and communication skills. You can memorize lists, procedures and attributes. You can occasionally guess successfully at the answer to a multiple-choice question. But you cannot memorize the answer to a problem you have never encountered, nor can you guess at the options available to a manager who must resolve a complex, difficult, often ambiguous situation.

### TYPES OF CASES

Although each case is different, you are likely to encounter three basic types of case studies, depending on the subject you are studying: field cases, library cases (sometimes referred to as *public record cases*) and armchair cases.

#### Field Cases

Field cases are written by professors and students of business with the cooperation of managers and executives who experienced the events and problems described in the case. They involve extensive interviews with people who are often identified by name as the narrative unfolds. Information contained in these cases is known best – and sometimes only – to insiders in a business. Newspaper accounts and descriptions of events contained in the business press may play a role in establishing key facts, but the sequence of events – what was said to whom, what each manager knew at the time and which managerial options were open to the principals of the case – are often a mystery to the public-at-large.

Extensive interviews with employees, managers and executives will often reveal more. Careful examination of business records and databases can provide background and context for the events. And, frequently, the active cooperation of a company is the only way a case author will ever know exactly what happened with any measure of certainty.

Field cases are often more extensive and thorough than other case types but present a dilemma for the case writer: What does the company have to gain by granting access to its premises, its records and its employees? Is this merely an attempt to make executives look good after the fact? Are such cases an attempt at public relations when things go wrong in a business? Often, to gain access to a business, a case writer must have some special relationship with those who own or manage it and must have a reputation for reporting on events in an accurate and fair manner. One disadvantage of such cases is that, once they are published, they are difficult to modify and may quickly become dated.

## Library Cases

Unlike a field case, library or public record cases do not involve special access to the businesses being studied. They do not involve interview material or direct quotes that are unavailable elsewhere. And they most often do not include figures, data or information that are not somehow a part of the public record, available to anyone with a library card, Internet access and basic research skills.

Companies that have failed somehow – blown a great opportunity, overlooked the obvious, chosen the wrong path or failed to act when they should have – are understandably reluctant to permit case writers to speak with their employees or look at the evidence. If they've done something terribly wrong – committed a crime or imperiled the public welfare – a company may do all it can to withhold, obscure or cover up what has happened. That is precisely the challenge facing most business reporters as they gather information for publication each day.

Writers who produce library cases, however, have a wealth of information available to them. In addition to stories produced for broadcast, print and online news organizations, business case writers can look to numerous government documents and other sources, particularly for publicly held firms. Annual filings with the Securities and Exchange Commission, such as forms 10-Q, 10-K and 8-K, can be very helpful as well.

When one company declares its intention to acquire another or is sued in federal court, numerous documents relevant to the issues at hand may become a part of the public record. When a company prepares to launch an IPO or float a bond offering, numerous public disclosures are required. Case writers have a high degree of confidence in the accuracy of such records, because the penalty for falsifying them may involve heavy fines or jail time.

## Armchair Cases

Armchair cases are fictional documents about companies that don't really exist and events that have never really occurred. Although they bear some resemblance to authentic cases, they are often lacking in the richness of detail and complexity that accompany real events. They may be useful, however, in introducing basic concepts to students or in provoking a discussion about key issues confronting businesses.

Business educators produce armchair cases when they are denied access to the people and data of real businesses or when they wish to reduce complex events to a series of simple decision opportunities. Armchair cases are often useful to begin a discussion about change management, the introduction of technology or a rapidly unfolding set of events in other cultures. A principal advantage of these cases is that they can be modified and updated at will without securing the permission of the fictional companies and managers they describe.

# PRODUCING A CASE SOLUTION

Producing a case solution that demonstrates you are ready for management-level responsibility will involve the following steps:

## *Read the Case*

The first step to a successful case solution is to read the case, carefully and with an eye for detail, more than once. Personality theorists tell us that some people are eager to get to the end of a story quickly. "Don't bother me with details," they say. "Just tell me what happened." Such people, often dependent on *Cliff's Notes* and executive summaries, will bypass the details of a case in order to reach a conclusion about what happened in the story. They are often reluctant to read the case attachments and will frequently avoid tables of numbers altogether. Many arrive at conclusions quickly and begin formulating responses before they have all the facts. The less clever in this crowd see the details of a case as a nuisance; reading the facts will only interfere with their preparation of a response.

After you have read and thought about the issues in a case, if you are uncertain about what to do, read it again. As you mature in the experiences of business school, you will get better at this, but at first, your best defense against being surprised or frustrated by a case is to read it thoroughly.

## *Take Notes*

College students typically want to either underline or highlight much of what is contained in a book chapter, reprint or essay. Case studies, however, are constructed a bit differently. Textbook chapters are typically organized in a hierarchical fashion, with key points and sub-points listed in order of importance, carefully illustrated and summarized. Not so with case studies, which are often simply arranged in chronological order. Textbooks usually proceed in logical fashion, with one concept building on others that came before it. Case studies, on the other hand, are seemingly chaotic: Many events happen at once, order and discipline are sometimes missing, and key issues are not always self-evident.

Case studies may also contain substantial amounts of information in tabular form: annual revenues, product shipment rates, tons of raw materials processed or cost data organized by business units. To know what such data mean, you will have to read the tables and apply what you have learned about reading a balance sheet, or about activity-based costing. You may find crucial information contained in a sequence of events or a direct quote from a unit manager. Sometimes you will discover that the most important issues are never mentioned by the principals in the case – they are simply ideas or tools that they weren't clever enough to think of, or didn't think were important at the time.

Your notes should focus on the details you will need to identify the business problems involved in the case, the issues critical to solving those problems, as well as the resources available to the managers in the case. Those notes will be helpful in producing a case solution.

## *Identify the Business Problem*

In each case, at least one fundamental business problem is present. It may be a small, tactical issue, such as how this company will collect money from a delinquent customer. But the issue may be broader in nature: "How can they reduce accounts receivable ageing to 30 days or less?" Larger, more strategic problems might involve the company's chronic, critical cash-flow difficulties. "If this company were no longer cash-starved, what longer-term opportunities might open up?"

You may identify more than one problem in a case. Complex cases often involve several such problems simultaneously. They may be technical in nature and involve accounting or cost control systems. They may involve the use of technology. You might see supply-chain problems in the business you are studying. You may identify marketing deficiencies. Or, you might see human problems that involve supervision, communication, motivation or training.

## Specify an Objective for the Managers Involved

Once you have identified one or more business problems present in the case, think about the outcome(s) you would most hope to see for the company and people you have read about. If you were asked to consult on this company's problems – and that is the role most business students are playing as they read a case study – what results would you hope for? Don't limit your thinking to what the company should *do*, but what the most *successful outcome* would look like. Be specific about how the company will know whether it has succeeded. Quantify the desired results whenever you can.

## Identify and Rank-Order the Critical Issues

These issues are at the heart of the case. If you miss a critical issue, you may not be able to solve the case to the satisfaction of your professor.

- *Some issues are interdependent.* That is, a solution to one issue might necessarily precede or depend on another. In a product-contamination case, for example, a media relations team can't draft a press release until the production or packaging team knows what's wrong with the product. The team responsible for a new product launch can't make final advertising and promotion decisions until issues related to packaging, transportation and distribution have been solved.
- *Some issues are more important than others.* A company may have a great opportunity to launch a product line extension but not have sufficient market research data to support the idea. More to the point, they may not have the talent on staff to understand and properly use such data. Thus, hiring a market research chief might be more important than simply contracting with an outside firm to find the data.
- *Each issue has a time dimension.* Even though two problems may be equally important to the success of a company, one may be near term in nature while the other is long term. Upgrading a corporate website may be important, but it won't solve the longer-term issue of marketing strategy: Should we sell directly over the Web or use retail partners to market our products?

    Specify which problems must be addressed first, but think, as well, about the duration of the solutions – how long will it take to fix this?
- *Some issues are merely symptoms of larger or deeper problems.* Two managers in open warfare with each other about budget or resource issues may be symptomatic of more serious, long-term budget problems, inadequate communication among the management team or perhaps a corporate culture that encourages confrontation over minor issues. When Sears Roebuck & Co. discovered that auto service managers in California were charging customers to replace parts that were not yet worn out, the problem was deeper than a few overzealous managers. After analyzing the complaints brought by the California Attorney General, Sears realized that their compensation system rewarded managers for selling more parts, and not for simply servicing customers' vehicles.

## Consider Relevant Information and Underlying Assumptions

Accept the fact that much of the information contained in the case will not be useful to your analysis. You should also accept the fact that you will never know all that you would like in order to produce a solution. Life is like that. So are case studies. Identify the relevant facts contained in the case and think carefully about them. Identify additional information you might like to have – that might be part of your solution – but don't dwell on it.

Separate facts from assumptions. Recognize that there are some things you will know for sure and others that you will not. Recognize further that you may be required to subjectively interpret some evidence and to assume other evidence not directly stated in the case. The more suppositions you make, however, the weaker your analysis becomes.

## List Possible Solutions to the Problem

Just about every problem lends itself to more than one solution. Keep looking for good ideas, even when you have already thought of one that will solve the problem. Listing possible solutions is a form of brainstorming that will later permit you to assign values or weights to those ideas: Is one solution less expensive than another? Will one be more effective than another? Will one idea work more quickly? Will one of these ideas have a more enduring effect?

### Select a Solution

After assigning weights and values to the various solutions you have thought about, select the one you like best and prepare to defend it. Show why the ideas you have thought about are superior and how they will work. If you have rejected other, more obvious ideas, you may want to explain why.

### Decide How to Implement the Best Solution

Having good ideas is insufficient. You must be able to put them to work. Graduate students of business are often praised by executives for being theoretically well grounded but criticized for lacking practical application. "A team of young MBAs told me that we needed to sell this division of my company," said an executive in the chemical industry. "But they couldn't tell me what to do or how to go about it. All they knew was that we should try to find a buyer. Interesting," he concluded, "but not very helpful."

### Explain How to Communicate the Solution

In a management communication case study, you will be asked to identify key audiences for your message. That means identifying which groups you want to communicate with and the means you will use to reach them. Think carefully about the broad range of *stakeholders* in the case: employees, customers, shareholders, business partners, suppliers, regulators and the marketplace at large. Identify exactly how you would plan to transmit your message, assure that it has been received and understood, and think about how you would analyze feedback from those audiences. You should think, as well, about timing and sequencing of messages. Who should you speak with first? Who should send the message? How should this particular audience hear about this particular message?

### Write It Up

Different professors will have different expectations about what they want from you in a written case solution. They will probably not provide you with specific, detailed instructions regarding their expectations, but they will certainly tell you if you've missed the boat or have produced a solid response. Some will ask for wide-ranging responses that cover many issues, while others will expect a more focused response. Just provide your professor with your best thinking and be as detailed as you think you can within the page limits you've been given.

## WHAT YOU SHOULD EXPECT

If you have read the case thoroughly, identified the business problems, rank-ordered the critical issues, proposed various solutions and then identified how you will implement and communicate them, you can expect to be relatively well prepared for classroom case discussion. Here's what else you should expect:

- *An occasional cold call.* Be prepared for your professor to ask you to provide key details from the case, sometimes referred to as a "shred." Simply explain what happened in the case, identifying the business and its principles, and give your best thinking on critical issues in two minutes or less. Don't worry about providing a solution just yet. Your professor is likely to want a more thorough discussion of the issues first. If you are feeling especially confident, you may wish to volunteer.
- *A logical, step-by-step approach.* If classmates offer information that is useful but not relevant or in line with the question the professor asks, wait for the discussion to return to the issues the professor thinks are most important before you move on.
- *Different approaches from different professors.* No two professors are exactly the same in their approach or preferences. Virtually all of them, however, appreciate a bold, "do something" approach over hedging, caution and a reluctance to act.

## WHAT YOU SHOULD *NOT* EXPECT

- *More information.* From time to time, your professor will present you with a "B" case that offers new or subsequent information. Such cases represent an extension of the facts in the "A" case and usually provide another managerial decision opportunity. For the most part, though, the information given in the "A" case is all you will have and you must make do with that.
- A *"right answer."* Because case studies are most often based on real events, no one can say for certain what would have happened if your ideas or other, "better" ideas had been implemented.

    Some solutions are clearly better than others, but many ideas will work. Some of the very best ideas may not yet have been thought of or spoken aloud.
- *An explanation of what "actually happened."* Many professors either don't know what happened to the managers and the businesses described in your case studies or they don't think that your having that information will be useful or productive in the learning process. Your own thinking may be limited or skewed if you focus on actual outcomes.
- *A single discipline focus to each case.* Although some cases are principally about accounting, they may contain issues related to finance, operations management, human resources or communication. Authentic business problems are rarely, if ever, unidimensional. The more you are willing to think about other dimensions of business and their interdependency, the more you will learn about how real businesses work.
- *That your response will solve all of the problems in the case.* Focus on the most important, most urgent and most relevant problems first. You may wish to identify issues for further thought or investigation by the management team described in the case, but you cannot and should not try to solve all the problems in the case.

In summary, your task is to read, identify and understand the business problems in the case. By identifying, rank-ordering and exploring the critical issues it contains, you should be able to propose a workable solution, identifying how to implement and communicate it. From that point forward, you must explain your choices in writing and be ready to defend them in the classroom.

## FOR FURTHER READING

Barnes, L. B., C. R. Christensen and A. J. Hansen. *Teaching and the Case Method*, 3/e. Boston, MA: Harvard Business School Press, 1994.

Bouton, C. and R. Garth. (ed.). *Learning in Groups.* San Francisco, CA: Jossey-Bass, 1983.

Corey, R. "The Use of Cases in Management Education," Harvard Business School Case No. 376–240.

Erskine, J., M. R. Leenders and L. A. Mauffette-Leenders. *Teaching with Cases.* London, Ontario: School of Business, University of Western Ontario, 1981.

Gragg, C. J. "Because Wisdom Can't Be Told," *The Case Method at the Harvard Business School.* New York: McGraw-Hill, 1954, p. 6.

McNair, M. P. "The Genesis of the Case Method in Business Administration," *The Case Method at the Harvard Business School.* New York: McGraw-Hill, 1954, pp. 25–33.

Penrose, J. M., R. W. Raspberry and R. J. Myers. "Analyzing and Writing a Case Report," *Advanced Business Communication*, 3/e. Cincinnati, OH: South-Western College Publishing, 1997.

Wasserman, S. *Put Some Thinking in Your Classroom.* Chicago, IL: Benefic Press, 1978.

## ACKNOWLEDGMENTS

This teaching note was prepared from personal interviews and public sources by James S. O'Rourke, Teaching Professor of Management, as the basis for class discussion.

# APPENDIX B
## Writing a Case Study

For the better part of a century now, business schools world-wide have used the case study as a principal learning tool in business education. Schools in North America, such as Harvard, Wharton, Darden, Mendoza, Ivey, Tuck and others, have made the case study method a central part of the way they prepare managers to step into authentic business situations, analyze the circumstances they have encountered and take action.

### WHAT IS A BUSINESS CASE STUDY?

A business case study is, essentially, a story. It's a narrative tale about a problem, challenge or opportunity faced by a manager or executive that students are asked to read, think about and respond to. The contents of a case study – including narrative details, direct quotations from those involved in the events of the case, and attachments – will form the basis for an analytic discussion. Those discussions are often conducted aloud in a classroom, while others are conducted on paper between professor and student.[1]

### THE CHARACTERISTICS OF A CASE STUDY

The stories offered up in a business case usually do not include either direct answers or disclosure of the resolution to the business problem. The point of such documents is to gather as much information as possible to explain what happened to the business as accurately, fairly and completely as possible, incorporating as many viewpoints as the author can reasonably accommodate. Such cases are never written for the purpose of identifying heroes and villains, but for the purpose of beginning a discussion about business problems.

Case studies are different from case histories in several important respects. First, as noted, a case study does not provide answers, outcomes, alternatives or resolution to the problems encountered by the managers depicted in the story. Instead, they provide enough detail for readers to understand the nature and scope of the problem, and they serve as a springboard for discussion and learning.

A case history, on the other hand, often summarizes events, describing not only what happened to create the problem, conditions or opportunity facing the manager, but frequently revealing the manager's response in detail.

Case histories are usually more focused on managerial responses and solutions than they are on the events leading to a decision point. And, by revealing what the company actually did in response to the crisis or events, such brief, historical summaries often limit student thinking and suppress the wide-ranging, open forms of imagination that case studies are designed to stimulate.

A business case study, then, is really a learning tool. It's an instrument that provides a discussion leader with an opportunity to explore issues that do not lend themselves to deduction or memorization. It is designed to promote analytic problem solving and teach critical thinking.

Case studies are not particularly well suited to training in which learners will be asked to memorize approved responses to carefully defined stimuli. They're really much better at promoting learning in situations that involve ambiguity, uncertainty and multiple outcomes. If an instructor aims at having all students arrive at a single, correct solution, a case study might not be the best tool to facilitate learning. On the other hand, if an instructor has learning objectives in mind that focus on the process of identifying and analyzing business problems, followed by a discussion in which various possible responses might be implemented, a case study may be a suitable tool.

## WHY STUDY BUSINESS CASES?

The principal difference between training and education, according to educational philosopher John Dewey, is that – however necessary it may be – training merely modifies external habits of action. Learners are presented with a menu of stimuli and taught to respond with an approved behavior. It's fairly easy to test for learning proficiency when a trainer can offer a stimulus or situation to a learner who can, in turn, exhibit the approved response.

Education, on the other hand, is designed to provide learners with the intellectual and analytic skills they will need to solve problems they've never seen, and to respond to stimuli they could not have imagined as students. Without out a comprehensive menu of stimuli and responses, students must rely on the values acquired during their education. Knowing what they value, what the hierarchy of those values is and why they have arranged them in that fashion will be enormously useful to a student later in life. Training and education are both essential to our success, of course, but only education can prepare us for circumstances we have yet to encounter.[2]

## TYPES OF CASES

Although each case is different, you are likely to encounter three basic types of case studies, depending on the subject you are studying: field cases, library cases (sometimes referred to as *public record cases*) and armchair cases. For a detailed description of each, please refer to Appendix A, "Analyzing a Case Study."

## SELECTING A SUBJECT

If you're interested in writing a business case study, you should begin by selecting a topic that is interesting both to you and to your prospective audience. If you have some passion for the subject, you'll be more likely to know what the issues are, who the key players may be and which sources would be most useful to consult. The subject must also be of interest to a significant number of people in your prospective audience. A case study – no matter how well researched, organized and expressed – that interests only a few people is unlikely to reach a wide audience and achieve the goals you've set for the project.

In choosing a topic to write about, you must understand the audience for whom you are writing. Will they have the intellectual and professional skills to understand the issues and events in the case? Will they have a working knowledge of the processes, structures and organizations you plan to describe? Will they understand the vocabulary of the industry or profession you're writing about? The more general knowledge your audience has about the subject, the better. If necessary, you may need to define terms, explain concepts and provide examples that will help your audience better understand the issues in the case.

It also helps if the events you plan to write about are not seriously out-of-date. If most events described in your case are more than five years old, you might consider switching to a more current topic. Finally, you must have access to accurate, reliable and current information about the events that you hope to describe. It's one thing to select an interesting subject. It's quite another to get informed sources to talk with you about it.

## BEGINNING YOUR RESEARCH

Once you've selected your subject, you must begin preliminary research to make certain you have a viable topic. This would include a review of newspaper files and online databases such as Factiva or NYTimes.com; broadcast websites, such as CNN.com or MSNBC.com; or other news-gathering sources such as Associated Press and Reuters. You may even wish to pick up the telephone and ask to speak with relatively low-ranking people who may know something about the topic you've chosen.

If you are not yet confident that you have access to enough information to write the case, you should set a firm "go/no-go" decision date, backed up by at least one or two alternative topic ideas. Knowing whether you have enough information is often very subjective but you'll quickly develop a sense of confidence about whether your principal problem is too much information and not enough perspective, or too little information and not enough cooperation.

### Make Some Choices

When you are confident that you have a viable topic, you must then select:

- *The perspective* from which the story is to be told. Who is the decision maker in this case? From whose perspective will the reader see the details of the case?
- *The start-and-stop dates* for the story. Each story begins at a moment in time and concludes with a decision point for the manager. You may choose to start at the beginning of the story, or you may select a relatively recent but crucial moment in the sequence of events, and then move back to the beginning to lay out other details. Either way, this decision is important for you as a writer.
- *The kind and level of detail* that you plan to include in the story. Some issues can be included as a passing reference in the dependent clause of just one sentence. Others will require their own boldface heading and several paragraphs (or pages) to describe in detail. Don't overwhelm your readers with detail that is unnecessary to understand the story and issues involved, but – on the other hand – don't assume that they already understand the finer points, or know who each of the principal characters is.

### Make Some Lists

The next step in your research will involve several issues that you may wish to include in your Teaching Notes.

- *Construct a timeline* with key events in chronological order. This timeline may run to several pages, but it will help you (and, perhaps, your readers) to keep people, issues and events straight. It's easy to forget what happened when, and in what sequence; a detailed timeline will be helpful.
- *Identify key players* in the story, by name and by role. Explain to the readers who they are, what their background is and why they're important to the case. Again, if more than just a few people are involved, an alphabetical list may be helpful to you as you begin writing.
- *Identify the critical issues* in the case, rank-ordering them by importance to the executive decision maker. You would not wish to directly reveal these issues to your readers, but you will want to include them in your Teaching Notes. This list would include, from most important to least important, those issues the executive or manager will need to think about and address, along with a brief explanation of why they are important. Remember, what seems crucial to one observer may not be important at all to another. This list will be the basis for an interesting and animated discussion.

### Consider a Spreadsheet

Although it's not essential, a two-axis matrix or text-based spreadsheet (Excel, Lotus, QuatroPro and others) may be useful in tracking the details of your case. Along the $x$-axis (horizontal), list the key events or issues as reported in the public record or documented in your interviews. Along the $y$-axis (vertical), list the source for each of those. Check off each item so that you'll know where you found it and how many sources have reported the same information.

You will, of course, have greater confidence in those facts that are reported by just about every source. You may wish to pay special attention to those items that are "one of a kind," or available to you from just one source. Ask yourself why that may be so. Is that one source particularly knowledgeable or well informed? Are you sure it's accurate? If you are unable to confirm (or corroborate) that information, you must decide whether you believe it. If you don't believe it, cross it off and do not include it in the case. If you do believe it, you are obligated to explain in your narrative that the information comes from just one source and, if possible, identify that source in the text.

## The Division of Labor

Once you're sure you have a viable case and enough information to begin, it may be useful to assign responsibility for various actions:

* Gathering financial data information about the firm.
* Doing historical research on the companies and people involved.
* Saving photos and screen-grabs for your PowerPoint presentation.
* Saving videotape of the evening news, if your case involves ongoing events or breaking news.
* Looking for streaming video of press conferences, interviews, commercials or other products that may be useful in framing a discussion of the case.
* Scheduling personal or telephone interviews with key figures in the case.

## TIME TO BEGIN WRITING

Once you're sure of your topic, your sources and your approach to the issues – and you have established the key decision maker's perspective, your timeline and the start/stop dates – and all team members are clear on their obligations, it's probably time to begin writing.

Your case need not be written in sequence, beginning with the opening paragraph, and it need not be written entirely by one person. But your writing style must be consistent throughout and must flow easily and effortlessly for the reader. You can certainly delegate different research and writing tasks to different members of the team, but one person – preferably the best writer – must be responsible for reading, integrating, editing and revising the final product.

As you begin, make absolutely certain that you have at least one reliable source (preferably more) for everything you plan to say or include in the case. Insert the footnotes or endnotes as you write, not later on. Don't create additional work for yourself by saying, "I'll come back later and figure out which sources each of these facts and quotes came from." The opportunity for error grows with each draft of the paper. You must be scrupulous about accurately documenting everything.

To make life easier as you write, make photocopies and keep detailed notes. Copy down dates, times, page numbers, volume and edition numbers, and anything else that will help to reveal to your readers where this information came from. Avoid any confusion about who said something or about the source of a fact important to your case.

## PREPARE A FIRST DRAFT

As you begin writing, it is important to grab the reader's attention directly with an anecdote, a quote, an event or a revealing fact of some sort. If you cannot convince your reader in the first few paragraphs that the case is worth reading, many of them may give up or simply skim through to pick up highlights. No matter how you begin, you must make the sequence of events clear from the first paragraph. Don't give your readers an opportunity to get lost or become confused.

Move next to an explanation of the company or organization's history, the industry in which it operates, the products or services it produces, and the annual revenues it generates. You should give some attention, as well, to the size of the company's employee base and market share.

Having established a big-picture overview of the company and industry, you should next introduce key characters in the case, along with various role players and decision makers. As readers move from paragraph to paragraph, they should develop a clear notion of who will be responsible for the decisions you will ask them to think about in the final few sentences.

Here are a few suggestions to keep in mind as you get your first draft down on disk and, later, on paper:

- Explain in plain English what happened, when and how.
- Identify all relevant assumptions.
- Reveal your sources in text, where necessary.
- Don't look for conclusions, causal factors or solutions just yet.
- Be specific. Quantify where possible.
- Use direct quotes, identifying and qualifying those whom you quote.
- Identify those issues you don't understand and those questions you cannot answer. Save them for the executive or managerial interviews you hope to schedule later.

## CONSULT MULTIPLE SOURCES

A one-source case is dangerous. Your principal or sole source could, quite simply, be mistaken about things. He or she could have a political point of view or an axe to grind that would skew or color the information you receive. The result could be a case study that is simply embarrassing as other important details emerge. Protect yourself and your teammates by consulting as many sources and viewpoints as you possibly can.

Consider frontline supervisors, hourly workers, as well as senior executives for telephone, e-mail or face-to-face interviews. Remember, though, that each has a point of view and a motive for talking with you. Your goal is accuracy, completeness and fairness in your presentation of the facts.

Read broadly. Consider out-of-town publications, even foreign publications for differing viewpoints. If you can't make sense of all the facts, consider calling a reporter who has written on or covered this story. Ask if he or she will speak with you. Many of them are more than happy to share what they know with sincere, well-mannered students.

Talk to various stakeholders, including customers, suppliers, shareholders, community and civic officials, regulatory agency officials, employees or competitors. You might even think about speaking with people who live in the neighborhood around the company or others who may have been affected by the events of the case.

If people won't talk with you, be polite and offer to show them the preliminary draft of your work. Offer to let them mark it up or suggest changes. Make them a partner in the process. Your work is, in some ways, like that of a journalist, but the rules of the game are different. A reporter would never let a source see the story before it's published. You have nothing to lose by showing your work to a source. If the reasons they offer for suggesting changes make sense to you, the case will be better for your having asked.

## PREPARE A SECOND DRAFT

Assemble what you've written. Read it for storyline flow as well as grammar and syntax. Your goal is to make it lively, tightly written, cogent and correct. It must be interesting to read, but it must – above all else – be right.

Consider including tables, figures, stock charts, diagrams, maps or other visual devices in the text to help explain the story to your reader. If you devise these yourself, you won't need the permission of a publisher or Internet site to use them. If you download a stock chart from Yahoo! Finance or CNN.com, you'll have to e-mail them and ask if you can use the graphic. Most news-gathering organizations will gladly let you use their work for free, as long as you acknowledge the source and indicate that it was used by permission. Some sources, particularly print magazines, will ask that you pay a royalty for the privilege of reprinting large portions of their work. You'll have to decide for yourself whether you are willing or able to do that.

Don't even think about publishing your second draft. Show it to a trusted colleague, an associate, your professor or someone whose professional opinions you value. Make certain it's as good as you can possibly make it, and as grammatically correct as you are able. Then, read it again, just to be sure.

## PREPARE YOUR TEACHING NOTE

Every good case study includes a Teaching Note. That's simply a document that explains what the case is about, what the issues and options may be, and how an instructor might go about leading a discussion of the case. Most Teaching

Notes are just a few pages in length but will contain valuable information about how to probe for student thinking, how to time the discussion and what to expect as students offer various viewpoints. At the least, a comprehensive Teaching Note should include:

- The purpose of the case study.
- A clear statement of the *business problem* – not the communication or public relations problem, but the central business problem in the case.
- A forecast of the most desirable outcome – If you could write a "Hollywood ending" for this case, what would it be? What do the various stakeholders most want or hope for?
- A statement and rank-ordering of the critical issues in the case – you might also briefly explain why each issue is important.
- A list of stakeholders and what's at stake for each of them.
- A list of definitions for specialized or unusual terms – you might also think about issues, concepts or ideas that students might have trouble with. What sort of things need additional explanation as the discussion moves along?
- A list of possible solutions to the problem.
- A plan for implementing and communicating the optimal solution.
- A plan for teaching the case, including what you believe the instructor should do prior to the discussion to prepare the class, and suggestions on how to spend class time during the first five to ten minutes, the next 30 minutes, and so on. Suggest ways to summarize and wrap up the discussion, as well.
- A timeline of events and a series of five or six discussion questions. You need not suggest a specific course of action in your Teaching Notes, if you'd rather not, but you should acknowledge various approaches that students may mention in discussion. You may also wish to reveal what actually happened in the case (if you know), but you would certainly not want to include any of those details in the case itself.

Complex cases may include not only a printed timeline, but also a glossary of specialized terms, and financial data, such as balance sheets, profit-and-loss statements or cash statements. You must have permission, of course, to use those documents unless they are made public as part of an annual report or SEC filing.

## PREPARE YOUR POWERPOINT

Think visually as you prepare your ideas for the big screen. Look for ways to show people what happened. Include visual images that will help carry your message:

- Photos of key characters or company officials.
- Company logotypes, symbols or trademarks.
- Products, people, events or other images that will generate visual interest.

Keep background templates clean, crisp, simple and uncluttered. The less visual distraction, the better. Keep animation to a minimum and avoid sound effects, except under the most unusual of circumstances. Be consistent and straightforward as you prepare those images. Think, as well, about hyperlinks, streaming video and VHS news clips from commercial television and cable networks. You're entitled to capture newscasts on videotape and use them in the classroom as long as the use is brief, and not for profit.

## PULLING IT ALL TOGETHER

Meet regularly as a team. Talk with one another about progress, deadlines and next steps. Much of your work can be done by telephone and e-mail, but occasional face-to-face sessions will prove helpful. As the process moves along, respect each other and offer to help whenever you can. Your teammates will appreciate that and, in return, give you their best effort.

Finally, as you prepare your publication draft of the case, admit that you may need to update or correct it, and then rehearse your presentation. Your task is to make it all look as sincere and professional as possible. If you've done it right, you'll be rewarded with the attention and approval of a number of important audiences.

## ACKNOWLEDGMENTS

This teaching note was prepared by James S. O'Rourke, Teaching Professor of Management, as the basis for class discussion.

## NOTES

1  Barnes, Louis B., C. Roland Christensen and Abby J. Hansen. *Teaching and the Case Method*, 3/e. Boston, MA: Harvard Business School Press, 1994.
2  Dewey, John. *Democracy and Education: An Introduction to the Philosophy of Education.* New York: Simon and Schuster, 1997. Originally published 1916.

# APPENDIX C

## Sample Business Letter

---

**BIG DOG SOFTWARE**

*Innovative Applications • Enterprise Software • Business Control Systems*

---

October 25, 2019

Mr. Ryan P. McCarthy
786 Elliott Street
Seattle, WA 91277–3022

Dear Mr. McCarthy:

*This is an example of the Full Block Letter style*, one of the most popular styles in business use today. The primary reason the Full Block style is so popular is its clean, efficient look. Typists favor this style, too, because it's easy to prepare and simple to compose.

Each element in this letter style begins at the left-hand margin. That includes the date, the inside address, the salutation, each body paragraph, the complimentary close and the signature block. There is no need to use additional keystrokes to center the date or to move the complimentary close and signature block to the other side of the page.

Please note that this letter style uses full punctuation, including the colon following the salutation and the comma following the complimentary close. The open, or ragged, right-hand margin gives the letter a slightly informal appearance, yet requires no additional work on the typist's part.

This is the most common variation of business letter format in use today. Some writers prefer other styles, especially if the letter extends beyond one page, because it's easy to tell where a paragraph begins if it's indented. In the Full Block Letter style, none of the paragraphs are indented. The letter is composed with a single space between lines within each paragraph and two spaces between paragraphs.

The vast majority of business correspondence in North America features the one-page letter. There are two reasons for this: First, most business letters are focused on just one subject and most writers can say what they must in three or four paragraphs. Second, the Full Block Letter style doesn't use indented paragraphs.

Mr. Ryan P. McCarthy
October 25, 2019

Page 2

There is another reason for the popularity of the one-page letter and it's cultural. Most North American business writers come directly to the point in the first – or at the very least – second paragraph. European, Asian and Latin American business writers will spend more time developing personal relationships, inquiring about the health and well-being of the readers, but most U.S. and Canadian writers prefer to put their main point up front and say what they mean, using fewer words.

If you choose to write a multi-page letter, the Full Block Letter style can easily accommodate that. You must simply be sure to enter a page heading in the upper left-hand corner of each succeeding page. That page heading should contain the name of the letter recipient, the page number and the date of the letter.

Remember, if you write a two-page letter, the second page must contain at least two lines of text. Most writers prefer to include at least a full paragraph. The final paragraph of the letter is followed by a complimentary close, a signature block and – if circumstances require – a copy line or an enclosure line, indicating that either others have received a copy of the letter or that the envelope contains other documents.

Sincerely,

Paul Magers General Manager
Enclosures
cc: Doug Hemphill

# APPENDIX D

## Sample Strategy Memo

---

The Eugene D. Fanning Center

University of Notre Dame • Mendoza College of Business

DATE:     October 25, 2019
TO:       Management Writing Students
COPY:     Interested People with a Need to Know But No Responsibility for Action
FROM:     J. S. O'Rourke (234 Mendoza College of Business; Phone 555–8397)
          Fanning Center for Business Communication

SUBJECT:   **STRATEGY MEMO: FORMAT AND CONTENTS**

This memo format recommends a communication plan in response to a specific event or circumstance facing a company or organization. It will briefly summarize the details of the event/circumstance; discuss their implications, importance or probable outcome; and will provide a specific list of actions taken and actions recommended.

## Background

In this portion of the memo, the writer briefly but completely reviews the *facts* of the case. This paragraph will contain historical data, information that is a matter of public record and facts that are relevant to the recommended communication strategy.

- Crisp, tightly expressed sentences set apart from the main paragraph by bullet points are often useful in highlighting factual information.

---

- This paragraph *does not* include assumptions, suppositions or speculative information. Nor does it include gratuitous references in the first-person singular, such as "I think . . . ," "In my opinion . . . ," or "I feel. . . . "
- If a specific source is available for each piece of information in this paragraph, the writer should consider embedding it directly in a sentence, that is, "2000 Census figures reveal that. . . ." Another approach is to list a source in parentheses following the information you provide, that is, "Mead Corporation's Stevenson, Alabama, mill has an annual production capacity of 400,000 tons of corrugated containerboard" (Source: *Mead Financial Fact Book*, Mead Corp., 2003, p. 5).

## Discussion

In this portion of the memo, the writer expands on the implications of the facts cited in the Background. This is where the writer explains to the reader what those facts mean and why they matter. The discussion paragraph often becomes the basis for the recommendations that follow. If the discussion is extended or complex, writers often use separate paragraphs, subheadings and bullet points to highlight various issues.

Strategy Memo: Format and Contents
October 25, 2019

Page 2 of 2

This section of the memo is frequently much longer than either the Background or Recommendation sections. It often contains a robust, detailed discussion of the issues and events present in the Background, followed by some sense of what they mean and why they matter.

## Recommendations

In this paragraph, the writer lays out each recommendation in specific terms. Where possible, recommendations lead with a verb, are separated from one another with white space, are underlined or printed in boldface type for emphasis and are either numbered (if the writer recommends more than three actions) or bullet-pointed. For example:

1. **Sign the attached letter of apology to the customer.** The letter not only apologizes for the flaw discovered in our shipment of July 1, but also offers a 2 percent discount on the shipment and a full replacement of all defective parts. (Action: President)

2. **Forward the defective parts to Quality Control for examination.** When the QC report is complete, copies of their findings should be shared with Sales & Marketing, Customer Service, and members of the Senior Management Team. (Action: Customer Service)

3. **Contact the retailer who sold the equipment to review return/refund procedures.** We must make certain that each retailer handling our products fully understands his/her obligation to accept customer returns and to provide full refunds, if appropriate. (Action: Sales Manager)

4. **Follow up with the customer to make sure he is satisfied with our actions on his behalf.** This is a particularly large account and, while each customer is important to this company, some customers are more important than others. Direct, personal contact to assure customer satisfaction, followed by an after-action report for company files, is essential. (Action: Customer Service)

## Other Issues

On occasion, the Recommendations paragraph will be labeled "Actions Recommended" and would be preceded by a paragraph labeled "Actions Taken." The difference is a matter of authority in the organization. The memo writer clearly has authority to take certain actions on his or her own and to *backbrief* the supervisor or manager by means of this memo. That same writer might propose actions for his superiors or for other divisions/agencies in the company that the reader is asked to agree to. It's always useful for the reader to know what tasks have already been done and what tasks he or she is being asked to approve.

Most memoranda *do not* include a signature block, nor do they feature salutation lines ("Dear . . .") or complimentary closing lines ("Sincerely yours,"). Rather than a full signature, most memos will include the initials of the writer next to the "FROM:" line.

Strategy Memo: Format and Contents
October 25, 2019

Page 3 of 3

Please note that this two-page memo requires a "second page header" that includes the subject line (exactly as written on page one), a date line and a page number.

To conclude, most memos will feature some distinctive typographical mark just beneath the last line of type. Some authors will use their initials; others simply use the pound sign or other mark of their choice.

# APPENDIX E

## Documentation

### Acknowledging the Sources of Your Research

### BACKGROUND

The idea is simple: When you borrow the words or ideas of others, your readers or listeners must know where they came from and who wrote them. In practice, it's not so easy. Who among us has had a *truly original* idea today? A few, perhaps, but not many. Most of what we know is derived from what we have read and heard from others. The more innovative among us might modify or adapt ideas that others have thought and put them to work in a new context, but few of us take the time to properly credit our sources.

Your Management Communication instructors look at this a bit differently. If you use the words, ideas or intellectual property of another, your instructors will insist that you scrupulously document all of it. If it's not common knowledge or your own original work, they'll expect to see a source note. If you use the words of another directly, they'll look for quotation marks.

It's a matter of fairness, honesty and candor. Showing your readers where you found a statistic or a quotation is simply being fair – with them and with the source of your information. In addition, it's a matter of credibility. If you insist that we believe you (and only you) as we examine the evidence in your argument, then you place yourself in a difficult position, indeed. It's much easier to let the evidence and the experts speak for themselves. Your own credibility is probably not as great as the source you've consulted, so why not explain who wrote those words? Why not use their title, position and accomplishments to help carry your argument?

Some folks think this just isn't that big a deal. Two notable (and once well-respected) historians might disagree. According to Martin Arnold of *The New York Times*:

> Recently Stephen E. Ambrose and Doris Kearns Goodwin, both best-selling authors of some admirable books, have been caught lifting material from other people's books, kidnapping the words of others. So far, they have gotten off easy, as nearly as can be determined. There has been some criticism. . . . [1]

More to the point, there's been trouble. Goodwin recently resigned from the prestigious Pulitzer Prize committee at Colombia University, and Ambrose promised to correct the problems in subsequent editions of his work. Mr. Arnold and others who follow these issues have stepped up their expressions of concern:

For Mr. Ambrose, with so much to do, naturally a careless slip occurs. People shrug. But they shouldn't: a writer of Mr. Ambrose's reputation should read every sentence before he ships a manuscript to this publisher and he certainly should be able to recognize his own sentences when sees them.[2]

"Those are professional historians," you say. "They're held to a higher standard than students." Perhaps, but not everyone thinks carelessness or intellectual theft should be quickly or easily forgiven in college and high school students. A tenth-grade botany project in Piper, Kansas, resulted in multiple teacher resignations – in protest over the local school board's refusal to back a teacher who uncovered plagiarism in her students' work.[3]

Christine Pelton concluded that 28 of her 118 students had plagiarized portions of a major project and gave them grades of zero for it. When the school board superintendent reversed her decision and gave passing grades to the students who had cheated, an uproar ensued that is still the subject of controversy to this day. Ms. Pelton resigned, as did her principal, Michael Adams. When Nick A. Tomasik, the Wyandotte County, Kansas, district attorney began looking into the case, he said, "So much is unknown. A large concern for teachers is that if this happens to one of us, one of our own, what's going to keep it from happening to me?"[4]

## WHAT IS PLAGIARISM?

As a college student, you will encounter the work of other people every day: you'll see their paintings, hear their music, read their words and work with their inventions. That's part of the magic of college: Learning directly from people who are considered to be gifted or insightful. To help measure your understanding and, from time to time, your achievement of learning objectives, your instructors will ask that you write or speak in class. They won't expect that everything you say or write will be your own ideas. They will, however, expect that you will tell your readers and listeners when and from where you found the ideas and words you're using.

"Plagiarism," in the view of Indiana University's writing center, "is using others' ideas and words without clearly acknowledging the source of that information."[5]

This appendix will examine your responsibilities as a writer and as a student. We'll show you the distinction between *informal documentation* and *formal documentation*. We'll also look at the difference between *paraphrasing* and *direct quotes*. We'll show you the value of an *attribution line* in the text of your work, as well. We will also look at *framing* both quotations and paraphrased material, and we'll show you how to properly set up a footnote or endnote so that your reader knows exactly where to find the source of the information in your paper.

## WHAT IS COPYRIGHT?

First though, a quick distinction between *plagiarism* and *copyright infringement*. A plagiarist is one who would have you believe the words and ideas in a paper are his own when, in reality, he's simply lifted them from someone else (usually a better writer who is both more famous and not around to object). Such papers are often submitted for credit in colleges and universities.

A copyright infringer, on the other hand, is trying to borrow the works of others for profit. It does not matter that she has properly credited the source of her material; she doesn't have the *right to copy* and sell it. That's what copyright means. If you copy someone else's poetry and include it in a book you plan to sell, you must first get permission from the copyright holder (usually the author or a publisher) and then you may be asked to pay for the right.

Brief passages or small portions of a copyrighted work may be used in a student paper, a newspaper review or even a textbook sold for profit. According to Richard Posner of the *Atlantic Monthly*:

The doctrine of "fair use" permits brief passages from a book to be quoted in a book review or critical essay; and the parodist of a copyrighted work is permitted to copy as much of that work as is necessary to enable readers to recognize the new work as a parody.[6]

How much of a work is considered suitable for "fair use"? According to Stanford University Professor and former U.S. Secretary of State, Condoleeza Rice:

The concept of fair use is necessarily somewhat vague when discussed in the abstract. Its application depends critically on the particular facts of the individual situation. Neither the case law nor the statutory law provides bright lines concerning which uses are fair and which are not.[7]

Like insider trading, the law is deliberately vague, but will permit educational institutions to copy small portions of a protected document for one-time use. It's also important to note that the courts take a dim view of copying work that is available for purchase in the campus bookstore.

Works that are no longer protected by copyright law are said to be "in the public domain" and may be used without obtaining permission or paying a fee. Even so, they may not be cited in a college paper without proper documentation (to do so would be plagiarism).

## WHEN SHOULD I DOCUMENT SOMETHING?

When it's clear that the words or ideas aren't your own. Documentation comes in two forms: informal and formal:

- *Informal documentation* includes an acknowledgment of the source as the information is revealed. For example, "Michelin has become a world leader in tire production and sales. Chairman Edouard Michelin once revealed the creation of a joint-stock company with the number one tire manufacturer in China, Shanghai Tire and Rubber Company." It's clear from this reference that the ideas came from Mr. Michelin and not from the student who wrote the paper.
- *Formal documentation* includes footnotes, endnotes or parenthetical documentation that clearly establishes exactly where the information, statistics, ideas or direct quotes came from. They follow one of several conventions and will permit the reader to find the same information for herself. For example, "Michelin demonstrated that they could remain profitable under difficult market conditions, achieving a 6.6% operating margin in 2001" (*Michelin 2001 Annual Report*, p. 3).

Formal documentation means that you will use a style that is consistent, widely accepted and useful to your reader. Three sources for documentation are commonly used by business writers:

- *The author–date method* (*Publication Manual of the American Psychological Association*).[8] The source is identified by the last name of the author(s) and the date of publication. Example:

  Professor Carolyn Boulger (2003, p. 2) says the transformation to integrated communications will begin when "businesses and large organizations train their people to recognize appropriate channels for communication within and among various audience groups."

  At the end of the paper, you would include a section entitled "Works Cited" or "References" and you would include the following entry: Boulger, C. *e-Technology and the Fourth Economy*. Cincinnati, OH: Thomson South-Western College Publishing, 2003.

  The APA manual encourages writers to be as specific as possible in directing readers to the original source material. So, if you're citing a specific passage as we've just done in the paragraph above, you should include the page number. If you're referring broadly to information contained in just one chapter of that book, you should cite the chapter number (Boulger, 2003, ch. 1). If you're simply referring to the author's findings in general but aren't focused on a particular page or chapter, you should cite just the author's name and the year of publication (Boulger, 2003).

  Be as helpful to your readers as you can. If you want them to pay attention to a particular passage or quote in your sources, tell them where to find it.
- *The author–page method* (*MLA Handbook for Writers of Research Papers*).[9] The source is identified by the last name of the author(s) and the page number in the source where the information can be found. Example:

  Work groups are an indisputable Twenty-First Century necessity for most of us, one likely to continue to dominate organizational life as industries, businesses, organizations, institutions, and communities adapt to a dramatically evolving global marketplace (Yarbrough 1).

At the end of the paper, you would include a section entitled "Works Cited" or "References" and you would include the following entry: Yarbrough, B. *Leading Groups and Teams.* Cincinnati, OH: Thomson South-Western College Publishing, 2008.

- **The numerical method** (*The Chicago Manual of Style*).[10] The source is identified by a raised (superscript) numeral in the text, with a corresponding numbered footnote or endnote that provides complete documentation for the source. Example:

> After more than a year of animosity, suspicion and distrust between Ford Motor Company and the Firestone division of Bridgestone, Inc., the gloves finally came off. Not only were the world-famous automaker and the global tire manufacturer no longer cooperating, but they had chosen to end their century-long relationship by blaming each other for a disastrous series of tire failures and auto wrecks that had injured thousands and taken more than 100 lives around the world.[11]

> At the end of the paper, you would include a section entitled "Works Cited" or "References" and you would include the following entry: 11. O'Rourke, J. "Bridgestone/Firestone, Inc. and Ford Motor Company: How a Product Safety Crisis Ended a Hundred-Year Relationship," *Corporate Reputation Review*, 4.3 (Autumn 2001): 255–264.

If you plan to be a college student for the next few years, you might consider having a copy of one of these reference books handy. Please consult your instructors to see what advice they might have or which system of documentation they prefer.

## PARAPHRASING

A paraphrase is the simple rephrasing of someone else's words. This approach is often helpful when you want to explain complex ideas simply and in your own words. Some years ago, investment executive Warren Buffet saw a mutual fund prospectus that read:

> Maturity and duration management decisions are made in the context of an intermediate maturity orientation. The maturity structure of the portfolio is adjusted in the anticipation of cyclical interest rate changes. Such adjustments are not made in an effort to capture short-term, day-to-day movements in the market, but instead are implemented in anticipation of longer term, secular shifts in the levels of interest rates (i.e., shifts transcending and/or not inherent to the business cycle). Adjustments made to shorten portfolio maturity and duration are made to limit capital losses during periods when interest rates are expected to rise. Conversely, adjustments made to lengthen maturity for the portfolio's maturity and duration strategy lies in analysis of the U.S. and global economies, focusing on levels of real interest rates, monetary and fiscal policy actions, and cyclical indicators.

He paraphrased that prospectus, putting the ideas into his own words:

> We will try to profit by correctly predicting future interest rates. When we have no strong opinion, we will generally hold intermediate-term bonds. But when we expect a major and sustained increase in rates, we will concentrate on short-term issues. And, conversely, if we expect a major shift to lower rates, we will buy long bonds. We will focus on the big picture and won't make moves based on short-term considerations.[12]

## ATTRIBUTION LINES

Another form of paraphrasing is the *attribution line*, in which you explain in the text of your paper or talk where the ideas came from:

> *According to authors Majken Schultz and Jo Hatch*, organizational identity refers to how people inside a company see and understand who they are and what they stand for.[13]

*Professor Cees B.M. van Riel of The Netherlands thinks of* a "sustainable corporate story" as a means of maintaining key relationships with customers and investors. While that's certainly true, a consistent, interesting corporate story is more than that. It's also a way to signal the marketplace about who you are and who you hope to become.[14]

In each of these paraphrases, the writer has taken the ideas of others and put them into his own words. At the same time, he's been careful to explain whose ideas they were and where they came from. (You wouldn't use *italics* to identify an attribution line or a paraphrase, but I've used them here to help you recognize them.)

## QUOTATIONS

If you use words written by someone else – and don't paraphrase them by putting the ideas into your own words – you must surround the words with *quotation marks.*

> "If you go to a good hotel and ask for something, you get it," says John Collins, the HR director. "If you go to a great hotel, you don't even have to ask."[15]

If you directly quote someone who is, in turn, quoting someone else, you have what's known as a quote within a quote, or an *indirect quote.* To identify an indirect quote, use *single quote marks.*

> "Today, the subject is Basic 14, which admonishes employees to use the right sort of language with guests and one another. For example, we are to say, 'Please accept my apologies,' rather than 'I'm sorry'; 'Certainly, my pleasure,' instead of 'Okay.'"[16]

Note that the period goes *inside* the quote mark and that single and double quote marks may be used to end a sentence.

## BRACKETS

Square brackets are used to indicate that the words are *yours* and not those of the author being quoted. For example:

> At the midpoint of the twentieth century, management philosopher Peter Drucker wrote, "Managers have to learn to know language, to understand what words are and what they mean. Perhaps most important, they have to acquire respect for language as [our] most precious gift and heritage."[17]

## ELLIPSES

Use ellipses (plural) or ellipsis periods to show that you've left words out of a quotation. Please note that a space follows the word preceding the ellipses and the next word of the quote. You must also insert a space between each of the periods. For example:

> No matter how much money your clothes cost, an omission or error in grooming can sabotage the entire effect. If you have trouble paying attention to small details, post a grooming checklist in your home . . . run down the list and check yourself, point by point, so that when people see you, they will see nothing out of place.[18]

## USING THE INTERNET FOR RESEARCH

The Internet has become the go-to research tool, both for businesspeople and for students studying to become one of them. Hundreds of millions of computers, linked together world-wide, have instantaneous (well, perhaps immediate) access to information by, from and about businesses across the globe.

The Internet, however, is not without its problems. For one thing, the information it contains is not organized. Stephen Hayes, a university business services librarian, has described the Internet as "a library with all the books on the floor."[19] It's no ordinary library, either. Literally anyone can set up a home page, buy an address and begin doing business on the Internet. The U.S. Supreme Court ruled in 1997 that government censorship of Internet content is unconstitutional. So, a student in search of information can – and often does – find inaccurate information alongside something of value on the Internet. "There's little we can do to verify the accuracy of the information contained in most sites on the World Wide Web," said Mr. Hayes. "Thus, each of us should approach what we find with appropriate caution and skepticism – just as we would a print source."[20]

The *World Wide Web* is organized broadly into four categories of sites: government, educational, commercial and not-for-profit. Internet addresses, known as URLs, reflect these categories in the letters they contain. Corporate home pages (usually ending in ".com") will tell you things about a company that they want you to know, such as where to buy their products, how their stock price is doing and how to apply for employment. In many ways, it's simply another form of advertising.

Government-sponsored websites (ending in ".gov") provide large categories of information, including census data, international trade and banking data, and regulatory information. These sites usually have a legal mandate to maintain the authority of the data. Educational institutions, such as colleges and universities, sponsor websites (ending in ".edu") that permit students, alumni and others to find out more about everything from academic curricula to how the varsity lacrosse team is doing.

Finally, websites sponsored by not-for-profit organizations (usually ending in ".org"), such as the American Red Cross, Goodwill Industries and National Public Radio, offer everything from program schedule and broadcast transcripts to detailed descriptions of current activities in their organizations.

*Search engines and directories* are among the most useful tools to someone looking for information on the Internet. Simply speaking, search engines and directories are programs that will search for information that you ask about. If you visit www.yahoo.com, you will find one of the most popular and widely used directories. Simply type in the keywords that best describe the product, service, company or industry that you want information about and the Yahoo! directory will produce numerous references with links to websites that may prove useful. *Directories* will search only the higher levels of a website, such as the title and author, while *search engines* will explore deeply for the data requested.

The more precisely or narrowly you define what you're looking for, the greater the chance that one of the more widely used search engines will find what you're seeking. Among the more popular search engines are google.com, bing.com, yahoo.com, ask.com and aol.com

## CITING INTERNET SOURCES

Search engines have made it so easy to find information on the Web that it takes little more than a phrase or question in the Google search to generate hundreds of sources for academic research papers, business proposals, reports, and business correspondence. In addition to heeding Stephen Hayes's comment about not believing everything you see on the Internet, two other issues become important. We've already talked about the first, that is, not plagiarizing the work of others. You must scrupulously document absolutely everything you borrow or quote from another source. And, of course, if you use a lot of it, you may have to obtain permission and pay a royalty fee.

For the vast majority of your work in college, however, your real challenge is twofold: First, figuring out whether the information you've found is accurate, current and reliable. Second, you must figure out how to cite the source of that information so that others will know where it came from. Complicating your task is the simple fact that home pages and websites on the Internet are constantly undergoing change each day. What was there last night won't necessarily be there tomorrow morning. And what's available today may be "down" or unavailable in a week.

Here are some examples that may prove helpful:

**How to cite a book in a bibliography:**
Dickens, C. *A Tale of Two Cities*. New York: Vintage Classics, 1990.

**How to cite an e-book in a bibliography:**
Dickens, C. *A Tale of Two Cities* [Internet]. Charlottesville, VA: University of Virginia Library, Electronic Text Center; 1994; © 1999 [updated 1996 May; cited 2002 June 24]. Available from www.etext.lib.virginia.edu/toc/modeng/public/DicTale.html.

## How to cite a newspaper article:

Stanley, A. and C. Hayes. "Martha Stewart's New Project Is Reconstructing Her Image," *The New York Times*, June 23, 2002, pp. A1, A24.

## How to cite the same article taken from a website:

Stanley, A. and C. Hayes. "Martha Stewart's To Do List May Include Image Polishing," *The New York Times* [Internet]. 2002 June 23 (cited 2002 June 23). Online at www.nytimes.com/2002/06/23/business/23MART.html?todaysheadlines.

## How to cite a website:

The Eugene D. Fanning Center for Business Communication [Internet]. Notre Dame, IN: Mendoza College of Business, University of Notre Dame; [updated 2002 May 14; cited 2002 Jun 23]. Online at www.nd.edu/~fanning.

## How to cite an e-mail:

Rodgers, Priscilla (University of Michigan.psr@umich.edu). Materials for ORA Nomination [Internet]. Message to: James S. O'Rourke, IV (jorourke@nd.edu). 2002 Jun 18, 13:22:28 (cited 2002 Jun 23).

According to Kathleen Sheedy of the American Psychological Association, the purpose of a bibliography is to identify an author's sources so a reader can look them up. The APA wants the bibliographies used in its journals to "get the user as close to the source as possible. You want to point him to the specific page."[21]

The problem with websites, of course, is they don't have page numbers or chapters. In addition, you may find that the article posted online is shorter or a bit different from the article printed in the paper version of the magazine or newspaper you're hoping to cite. If you've compared the two *New York Times* stories mentioned earlier, you'll note that they're the same story but with different headlines. And, according to June Kronholz of *The Wall Street Journal*, there is no single authority on bibliography style. Social scientists follow the style set by the APA. Historians follow *The Chicago Manual of Style*, and anyone writing about the humanities follows the Modern Language Association, or MLA style.[22]

Will any of those manuals help you in citing information taken from an Internet website? Well, the APA updated its manual last year, devoting 19 pages to the intricacies of citing electronic publications. And, according to Ms. Kronholz, the MLA has already updated its style manual twice to accommodate the Internet and is now working on another edition. So is the *Chicago Manual*. But, says Ms. Kronholz, "styles still differ: some manuals dictate square brackets around Web addresses. Some decree angle brackets instead. Punctuation and abbreviation are still thorny matters."[23]

If this is all a matter of heated debate among professional bibliographers – people who do this sort of thing for a living – then what should you do? The answer is relatively simple: Do your very best to show your reader where and when you found the work and, if you know, who wrote the work. With some luck, perhaps they'll be able to find it, as well.

Here's some additional advice from Ms. Kronholz and her sources at *The Wall Street Journal*:

*What should you do if you can't find a page number on a website?*
Answer: Use [about page 5] or [about screen 6].
*What should you do if you can't find the title of an article on a website?*
Answer: Make one up, using the first words on the screen.
*What should you do if you can't find an author's name on a website?*
Answer: Look. Look hard, make sure you really can't find it, then forget about it.[24]

Do everything you can to be fair, honest, and candid with your readers and the sources you've taken your information from. Double-check things, proofread your work carefully, then sleep well, knowing you've done your best.

## ACKNOWLEDGMENTS

Copyright © 2002. Revised: 2011. James S. O'Rourke, Teaching Professor of Management, Mendoza College of Business, University of Notre Dame. All rights reserved. No part of this publication may be reproduced, stored in a retrieval system, used in a spreadsheet, or transmitted in any form by any means – electronic, mechanical, photocopying, recording, or otherwise – without express written permission.

## NOTES

1 Arnold, M. "Historians Who Resort to Cutting and Pasting," *The New York Times*, February 28, 2002, p. B1.
2 Ibid.
3 Trotter, A. "Plagiarism Controversy Engulfs Kansas School," *Education Week*, April 2, 2002, 21, no. 9, p. 5.
4 Ibid.
5 "Plagiarism: What It Is and How to Recognize and Avoid It," *Writing Tutorial Services*, Indiana University, Bloomington, IN. Online at www.indiana.edu/~wts/wts/plagiarism.html. Accessed June 22, 2002.
6 Posner, R. A. "On Plagiarism," *Atlantic Monthly*, April 2002. Online at www.theatlantic.com/issues/2002/04/posner.htm. Accessed June 22, 2002.
7 Rice, C. "Copyright Reminder," A memo to members of the faculty, Hoover Institution fellows, academic staff, and library directors, Stanford University, October 30, 1998. Online at www.firuse.stanford.edu/rice.html. Accessed June 22, 2002.
8 *Publication Manual of the American Psychological Association*, 4/e. Washington, DC: American Psychological Association, 1994.
9 Gibaldi, J. and H. Lindenberger. *MLA Style Manual and Guide to Scholarly Publishing*, 2/e. New York: Modern Language Association of America, 1998.
10 *The Chicago Manual of Style: The Essential Guide for Writers, Editors, and Publishers*, 14/e. Chicago, IL: University of Chicago Press, 1993.
11 O'Rourke, J. "Bridgestone/Firestone, Inc. and Ford Motor Company: How a Product Safety Crisis Ended a Hundred-Year Relationship," *Corporate Reputation Review*, 4.3 (Autumn 2001): 255–264.
12 *USA Today*, October 14, 1994, p. C1.
13 Schultz, M. and J. Hatch. "Scaling the Tower of Babel: Relational Differences Between Identity, Image, and Culture in Organizations," in *The Expressive Organization: Linking Identity, Reputation, and the Corporate Brand*. Oxford, U.K.: Oxford University Press, 2000, p. 15.
14 Van Riel, C. "Corporate Communication Orchestrated by a Sustainable Corporate Story," in *The Expressive Organization: Linking Identity, Reputation, and the Corporate Brand*. Oxford, U.K.: Oxford University Press, 2000, pp. 157–181.
15 Hemp, P. "My Week as a Room-Service Waiter at the Ritz," *Harvard Business Review*, 80.6 (June 2002), p. 54.
16 Ibid.
17 Drucker, P. F. *The Practice of Management*. New York: Harper & Row, 1954.
18 Baldrige, L. *Letitia Baldrige's New Complete Guide to Executive Manners*. New York: Rawson Associates, 1993, p. 225.
19 Hayes, S. Mahaffey Center for Business Information, Mendoza College of Business, University of Notre Dame. Personal communication, April 2001.
20 Ibid.
21 Kronholz, J. "Bibliography Mess: The Internet Wreaks Havoc with the Form," *The Wall Street Journal*, May 2, 2002, p. A1.
22 Ibid.
23 Ibid.
24 Ibid.

# APPENDIX F

## Media Relations for Business Professionals

*How to Prepare for a Broadcast or Press Interview*

### INTRODUCTION

During the course of your career in business, it will be virtually impossible for you to avoid meeting and dealing with the news media. Inevitably, the media will want access to you as a functional expert when you are least prepared and willing to deal with them – often during a crisis of some sort. Even though they are not a surrogate for dealing with the public directly and their influence on public opinion formation is indirect and somewhat limited, the news media can provide a useful service and valuable opportunity to reach large numbers of people with a carefully prepared message. Those people who have been most successful in dealing with the news media have discovered that such encounters require careful preparation and some understanding of how media representatives operate.

### DISCUSSION

Have you ever done a media interview before? How did it go? What was your impression of the reporter? Did you have an opportunity to see the broadcast or read the interview after it was completed? Did the reporter treat you fairly in the interview and in the story to which it contributed?

A separate series of questions concerns the news media in general. What's your impression of the media? Of reporters in general? Do you think it's a good idea to cooperate when reporters or editors ask for your reaction to something?

Regardless of your initial experience, are you ready to do it again?

In general, most businesses and profit-making organizations take a positive stance regarding press interviews and public appearances by company officials, particularly those in positions of senior responsibility. Most not-for-profit institutions follow a policy that requires that you work with and through your public relations office to arrange and prepare for such interviews, but contact with reporters is not limited, by any means, simply to the public relations office. In fact, most news organizations would rather speak with a "newsmaker" or responsible official than an "official spokesperson."

If you are asked to do an interview, look on it as a positive experience, an opportunity to tell your company's story, a chance to get your point of view across to the public. It is, at the very least, an inexpensive means of communicating your message to a very large audience. It's an opportunity to show the flag and to talk about your agenda – regardless of what the interview was called for – with the public at large.

If you agree to an interview, though, remember that it's not without risk. You can fail – it's not common, but it can happen if you're unprepared for the occasion. Preparing yourself is not difficult if you keep a few basic suggestions in mind.

## ONE WEEK BEFORE THE INTERVIEW

Several things you may wish to consider at least a week before you're to be interviewed:

- Consult with your public relations director on his or her plan for the interview. When and where will it take place? What's the subject? Will we plan to limit the questions to a particular subject or will the reporter want to talk about many subjects? Remember, it's best to focus or limit the interview and prepare yourself well to answer a narrow range of questions than it is to let a reporter "go fishing." If your business does not have a public relations officer, prepare yourself by speaking with a knowledgeable, senior colleague whom you trust. Think about the questions you're most likely to be asked, and think about those you would most like to answer. Think, as well, about those you really hope you don't have to answer. After a thorough review session with a trusted colleague, if you still aren't confident, consider asking a professional media relations consultant for help. The time and money spent on such help will pay huge dividends down the road in protecting your company's reputation, share price, market share and public image.
- Read some of the reporter's work, or watch a video copy of the show you're to appear on. Get some idea of how the interviewer or reporter works, what his style may be, how she works.
- Begin to assemble information for and to define your "agenda." What's on your mind? What's your message? What three or four key issues do you want to talk about? Get the most current facts and figures together and focus your mind on how best to package that information. Practice expressing your point of view in 15-to-20-second segments that could stand alone if they were edited out of a longer interview. Say your message aloud until you are thoroughly familiar with the words, numbers and phrases you will use. Practice until you are confident, self-assured and professional in your approach to the subject.
- Prepare a pocket or purse card. Be sure to include the time, place of the interview, name of the interviewer and his or her media outlet. Include other key details, as well, such as how you will get there, who will accompany you, phone numbers and names. On the other side, write down your three or four key points, along with supporting detail, numbers or facts you want to talk about.

## ONE DAY BEFORE THE INTERVIEW

The day before you do the interview, check on a few final details:

- Have your corporate communication director confirm the time and place of the interview with the reporter or host. Who will you follow on the show? Who else is being interviewed? Who will ask the questions? You don't need any surprises at this point.
- Check your card to make sure it's complete and accurate and fully reflects your position on the issues to be discussed. Make sure that position also reflects institutional policy and current administration views. Remember, you represent not only your business, but its employees, shareholders and other stakeholders, as well.
- Check on transportation, parking and other elements in your schedule for tomorrow. How will you get there? Where will you park? How long will it take to get there? Will traffic or weather be a problem?
- Make sure your clothing is among the best you own. Dress conservatively so that your attire doesn't detract from your message. Consider getting a haircut.

## THE DAY OF THE INTERVIEW

On the day you're to be interviewed, you'll have a few, final details to attend to:

- Watch the news that morning; read the papers; search your favorite news-gathering sites on the Internet. Check the local news and have a look at the morning's latest stories. Is there anything late-breaking that could serve as a springboard for a reporter's question? Even though the issues in the morning's news may be well beyond your expertise or influence, they could still become part of a reporter's question. Prepare yourself to respond.

- If the interview is scheduled for late afternoon or later in the day, men may want to shave again, particularly if you have a heavier beard. Check your shirt, suit coat and shoes. You want to make the best impression possible.
- Plan to arrive early. Give yourself a few minutes to calm down, examine your surroundings and review your notes before you go on the air.
- Unbutton your suit jacket if it's a sit-down interview. To remove wrinkles and "collar creep," pull the jacket down from the rear. Button your jacket if it's a stand-up interview.
- Men: Wear over-the-calf socks. Choose complementary colors and plain patterns.
- Women: Wear plain, unpatterned hosiery. Keep jewelry simple. Those diamonds may look terrific at a dinner party, but on television, they will catch the light and distract the audience.
- Wear your glasses if you need them to see. They will make you more comfortable and, often, people will develop facial marks if they wear glasses all the time. You don't want those to show.
- Don't wear sunglasses, either indoors or outdoors if at all possible, or tinted photochromatic lenses while you're on camera. Studio lights will turn those lenses very dark and you don't want to hide your eyes from the audience.
- Men: Don't wear vests, wide stripes or checks. Solid colors, pinstripes or narrow chalkstripes are best.
- Women: Don't wear extremely light or exceptionally dark dresses. Extremely short skirts can be difficult during a sit-down interview, as well.

## BEFORE YOU GO ON CAMERA

As you arrive at the studio, there are a few things to think about:

- Look at the studio and set. Observe the cameras, mikes, lighting equipment and positions of the crew members. Talk with crew members if you have the opportunity – it will make you seem more human to them and it will dispel any nervousness you may be experiencing.
- Men: If they offer makeup, swallow your pride and take it. You will look better on-camera and it's easy to remove once you're done.
- Women: Don't do anything different or unusual about your makeup. If it's suitable for a business meeting, it's suitable for television.
- Check out the position of the studio floor monitor, then ignore it while you're on the air. Focus only on your host.
- Introduce yourself to people. The act of reaching out to someone, psychologically, will help you to feel friendly, generous and relaxed.
- Tell the program staff if you have a genuine physical reason for preferring one profile or side (e.g., a hearing disability).
- Sit on the front of the chair, turning your body 45 degrees to the camera lens, facing the interviewer. Hands on your knees or in your lap; don't slouch, sit up straight.
- Gestures are constructive communication. Hold your hands lightly, loosely on your legs so they're free to gesture when you need to. Gestures will also help dispel nervous energy.
- Plan to look at the person conducting the interview about 90 percent of the time. Look away infrequently, only to focus your thoughts as necessary. Try as best you can to maintain eye contact to heighten sincerity.
- About 7 percent of the meaning in our statements comes through in our words; some 38 percent is delivered in our voice and vocal quality, while about 55 percent of our total meaning is communicated in other, purely non-verbal ways, including muscle tone, facial expression, body posture, body movement and hand gestures. Some of this happens at the conscious level, but much of it goes on with little or no awareness on our part. Your goal is to project a relaxed, confident, professional image. People will listen to what you say, but they will take their measure of you by watching how you behave.
- Try to remember that your audience will remember less of what you say than they will of the way in which you've said it. How your message is packaged and delivered is important. That's unfortunate, but it's true – they'll come away with few facts from a television interview, but many impressions and images.
- Use the audio-level check, or "mike check" to identify yourself and make a positive point about your organization or your cause.

- Don't ever say anything into or near a microphone that you wouldn't want broadcast to the rest of the world. Assume that all cameras are "on" and all microphones are "live." Remember, you're always on the record and if you say or do something dumb, they will save the tape.

## GETTING YOUR CONVICTIONS ACROSS

- Your presentation must contain not only your thoughts, but also your feelings. Your emotions, energy and enthusiasm will account for much of your success in this interview – stress the affective more than the cognitive.
- You need to get your points across through your voice, your gestures, proxemics and body motion, as well as your words. Those words won't stand alone; they're accompanied by facial expressions, vocal tone and a host of other nonverbal mannerisms.

## THE KINDS OF QUESTIONS YOU ARE LIKELY TO FACE

In most interviews, you will find a number of different question types. Your success in handling those questions depends, in part, on your being able to identify what sort of question is being asked:

- *Focus Questions.* Those that give you an opportunity to expand on a point by going into further detail, or by giving an illustration.
- *Avoidance Questions.* Those that you would just as soon not have to answer, probably because they put you or your business in a bad light. Acknowledge the question by repeating the key part in a positive way and then bridge to the point you want to make.
- *Control Questions.* Those that seem relatively simple, but which you would like to pass back to the interviewer. You should respond to these questions by making a positive point about the thrust of the question, not by dealing with the question itself. You may even consider restating the question in a way you'd like to have it asked.
- *Factual Questions.* Those that seem very direct or straightforward. They ask for factual data. Don't stop with the facts or the numbers, though. Show how they're related to a positive point you want to make.
- *Hypothetical Questions.* Those that require you to speculate about the future or provide a response to a set of assumptions that may never prove to be true. Don't be drawn into speculation, assumptions or guessing. Deflect a hypothetical question by answering one you wish the interviewer had asked.
- *Forced Choice Questions.* Those that require you to adopt either of two unacceptable viewpoints put forward by the interviewer. Don't be drawn into accepting a reporter's terminology, choices, analysis or alternatives. Use your own words and avoid the trap of selecting one or another of the extremes presented in a question. Most issues are rarely black-and-white, this choice or that; most issues are sufficiently complex to have several points of view.
- *False Facts or False Assumption Questions.* Those that begin with an error in fact by the reporter or host, leading to a mistaken impression in the audience. Set the record straight directly and politely, but don't ever let a mistaken or erroneous statement of any significance go unchallenged in the course of answering a question.
- *Leading or Loaded Questions.* Those that are clearly headed in the direction of a predetermined conclusion on the part of the questioner. Don't be led down the garden path by a reporter who is looking for evidence to support a conclusion he or she has already reached; take control of the interview by raising the "more important issue" or by refocusing the discussion on the one point you think the audience most needs to understand.

## MAINTAINING CONTROL OF THE INTERVIEW

A few simple techniques will help you to control the interview, rather than the reporter or host. If you're in control, you get to focus on your agenda, say what you want and put your point of view forward. If you don't maintain control, the reporter or host takes the interview in whatever direction he or she wants and it's a lost opportunity for you, your company and your people.

- *Gaining Time to Think.* You can create a few moments of thinking or organizing time for yourself by asking the reporter to repeat the question or by asking for the question to be restated in another way. Don't overuse this technique, but once or twice in a long interview, it may buy you some time.
- *Set the Pace Yourself.* Don't let a reporter rush or badger you by picking up the pace of the interview. Just because a questioner jumps in at the end of a response with another question or interrupts you is no reason to change your pacing, timing or frame of mind. Stay cool, slow down and stay in charge.
- *Bridging.* If you're faced with a tough question that you simply can't duck, go ahead and acknowledge it. After acknowledging the factual aspect of what's been asked, bridge to a point you want to make.
- *Flagging.* In a long interview that may be subject to editing, you can help yourself, the interviewer and the editor by identifying the key points, the one thing to remember, the principal issue at hand.
- *Hooking.* You can draw the interviewer into asking a question that might not otherwise have occurred to him or her by addressing an issue at the end of a response to another question that leaves the area open for questioning.
- *Stay Positive.* Don't repeat negative words or phrases. Don't let the reporter put words in your mouth; don't use any emotionally loaded words or phrases just because that's the way the interviewer chose to describe things.
- *Don't Say More than You Intend.* Once you have answered a reporter or talk-show host's question fully and accurately, once you've said all you need to say on a given subject, it's perfectly all right to remain silent. After all, it is not your responsibility to "feed the microphone," it is the host or reporter's responsibility. If the adrenaline rush produced by standing or sitting before the camera and microphone leads you to talk more than you usually might, protect yourself by preparing and offering responses that are complete, accurate and thoughtful, but that don't lead you to continuous, nonstop talking. Don't ramble on and say things you might later wish you hadn't.

## OTHER THINGS TO KEEP IN MIND

- *Know your interviewer and your audience.* Who are you talking to? Who is watching, listening or tuning in?
- *Tell the truth.* Answer honestly. If you don't know the answer, say so, but don't ever say "no comment." That simply sounds like you're guilty and are afraid to talk about it.
- *Avoid an argument.* You can't win when you grow antagonistic with a professional journalist or talk-show host. They've been doing this sort of thing much longer than you have.
- *Protect the record.* You are *never* off the record.
- *Use your experience, ethos, authority and expertise.* You, after all, are the one they want to see, hear and talk to.

## IN CONCLUSION

An interview with a reporter or talk-show host can be a win-win situation for you both: He or she gets an interview, fills airtime or column inches, and you get an opportunity to get your agenda or point of view across. You must prepare yourself, though, stay confident, and maintain control. If you do, your company, your coworkers, shareholders and customers will be better for it.

## ACKNOWLEDGMENTS

This teaching note was prepared by James S. O'Rourke, Teaching Professor of Management, as the basis for class discussion.

# Index

Note: Information in figures and tables is indicated by page numbers in *italics* and **bold**, respectively.

accenting 304
action language 302
Adamson, Jim 42
adaptors 306
admired individuals 193
affect displays 306
Affleck, Ben 441
age: of audience 118; intercultural communication and 332
Aiello, Greg 86, 89
Airbnb 12–20, *14–16*
Alderfer, Clayton 190, 191
Alessandra, Tony 275
Allen, Elizabeth 137–139, 230
Allen, Tom 310
anecdote 124
apologies: in writing 151
appearance-based discrimination 320
Aquilina, Rosemarie 436, 439
Arison, Micky 170
Arison, Ted 167–168
armchair cases 464
Arnold, Chris 48
artifacts 307–308
attitudes *185*, 186, 187–188
attribution lines 486–487
audience: age of 118; attention of 189; attitude toward subject of 119; in communication 40; education of 118; ethnic origin of 119; expectations 40–41; gender of 119; income of

118; interest 126–128; motivation for 189–190, *190*; needs 128; occupation of 118; personal beliefs of 118; in persuasion 189, 196; resistance in, persuasion and 193–194; sex of 119; socioeconomic status of 118; in speaking 117–119; subject knowledge of 119; *see also* reader
author-date method 485
authority: persuasion and 189
author-page method 485–486
Avery, Christopher 388
Axtell, Roger E. 334

Bailes, Julian 88
Ballmer, Steve 157–160
Barneys New York 345–352, *349–350*, *352*
Barra, Mary 3
barriers, communication 38
Barsade, Sigal 257
Barton, Lawrence 42
Baskin, Kara 402
Batchelor, J. Doug 386
Batjer, Hunt 91
Baumhart, Raymond 67
Bednar, Greg 309, 310
Begeman, Michael 232
behaviorism 184
beliefs *185*, 185–186
Bell, Ron 399
belonging needs 190

Bem, Daryl 197n15
Bentley, Sheila 266
Bernstein, Ethan 414
Bezos, Jeff 3, 409, 410
Biddle, Jeff 307
Biersdorfer, J. D. 225
Big Data 98–104
Biles, Simone 441
Blau, Brian 259
Boberschmidt, Marge 385, 390
Bohns, Vanessa 387–388
bookmarking, social 219
Bosrock, Mary Murray 333
Boulger, Carolyn 218
Bowen, Michael G. 70
Branson, Richard 402
Brin, Sergey 415
Brinkley, David 420
Brody, Jane 364
Brown, Robert 347
Buffett, Warren 142
Burger, Chester 420
Burke, James 76
business ethics 67–68
business letters 149–150, 477–478
business memo 144–145
Byrne, John A. 66

Carnival Cruise Lines *167*, *168*, 168–174, *171*
Caruso, Rebecca 321

case studies: analysis of 463–468; armchair 464; characteristics of 469–470; conflict 367–381; critical issues in 466; defined 469; feedback 291–297; field 463–464; first draft for 472–473; intercultural communication 342–353, *349–350, 352*; library 464; listening 282–290; media 436–460, *452, 453*; meetings 399–415, *410*; multiple sources in 473; nonverbal communication 318–322, 323–329, *326–328*; persuasion 199–212; producing 465–467; reasons for 463, 470; research in 471–472; second draft for 473; solutions in 466–467; speaking 135–136, 137–139; subject selection in 470; teaching note for 473–474; technology 239–261, *240, 241, 243–245, 256, 257, 259, 260*; types of 463–464, 470; in writing 157–163, *158, 167, 168,* 168–174, *171, 176–180, 178*; writing of 469–474

cell phone etiquette 229
Cerner Corporation 176–180, *178*
Chambers, Wick 266
Chaplin, William 308
Chesky, Brian 12–13, 17, 18
Chipotle Mexican Grill 46–53, *47, 48, 49, 50, 52*
Christian, Trayon 345–346, 350
chronic traumatic encephalopathy (CTE) 84–92
Cialdini, Robert 188
citations 483–489
climactic moment 125
Clinton, Bill 126
clothing 301
Coben, Larry 91
Coca-Cola 42
Cochran, Peter 404
cognitivism 185
Colbert, Stephen 103
Coles, Robert 273
Collins, Sandra 230–231, 258
color: nonverbal communication and 311–312
communication: accountability and 41; action due to 40; audience and 40; audience expectations and 40–41; barriers to 38; channels 7–8; as circular 36; code in 39; as complex 37; as continuous 36; contrary 40; crisis 42–44; culture and 123; defining 35–36; as dynamic 36; elements of 36; ethics 65–77, **72**; evidence in 123–124; feedback and 39; feelings and 122; interpersonal 37; intrapersonal 37; as invention

8–9; as irreversible 37; language and 123; levels of 37; as manager 41–42; mass 37; medium in 39; message in 38, 39; motivation and 40; noise and 39; obstacles 122–123; organizational 37; organizational culture and 41; organizational dynamics and 41; organizational goals and 39; organization in 124–126; personality preferences and 41–42; physiological barriers to 38; prejudice and 122; principles of 36–37; psychological barriers to 38; public 37; receiver in 38; responsibility and 41; sender in 38; stereotypes and 122; strategic 38–39, 39–41; successful 39–41; technology and 218–219; terminology in 40; as unrepeatable 37; *see also* intercultural communication; nonverbal communication

complementing 304
conference reports 148
confidence: in speaking 131–132
conflict: accommodation in management of 361, *361*; avoidance in management of 361, *361*; benefits of dealing with 360; case examples 367–381; causes of 356–357, **357**; change and 358; collaboration in management of 361, *361*; communication and 363; competition in management of 361, *361*; compromise in management of *361*, 362; costs of 355–356; defined 357; emotions and 363; expectations and 359; feedback and 359; feelings and 362–363; goals and 358; in human relations view 357; in interactionist view 357; limited resources and 358; listening and 362; management styles 360–362, *361*; meetings and 388; oneself as source of 364–365; in organizations 357–358; performance reviews and 360; and poorly defined responsibilities 358; priorities and 358; sensing 359–360; separation and 362; sources of 358, 363; stress and 356–357; success and 358, 363; in traditional view 357; values and 358; visualization and 359

conformity 193
"congressional" system, for meetings 392
consistency 188, 192–193
Consumer Privacy Bill of Rights 101
context: meaning and 9
contradicting 304
conversations: one-on-one 6; telephone 7
Coors, Joseph 424
Coors, William 424

copyright 484–485
corporate social responsibility 68, 108–109
corporate values 75
cosmetic industry 318–322
*Costa Concordia* 167, *168*, 168–174, *171*
Couric, Katie 424
Cox Communications 43
creative outlets 191
Cribari, Lynne 199–200
crisis: communication 42–44; defined 42–43; preparation for 43–44; types of 42–43
crisis handler role 4
crisis management plan 43
Crossen, Cynthia 270
Crumpacker, Mark 51
CTE *see* chronic traumatic encephalopathy (CTE)
cue 303–304
culture: attitudes in 335; biology and 338; business and 334–335; change in, as constant 336; change in, speed of 336–337; compatibility and 337; complexity and 337; complexity of 337–338; definitions of 335; ethnocentrism and 338; functions of 338; ideas in 335; as learned 336; material objects in 335; as not value-neutral 337; observability and 337; organizational, communication and 41; and patterns of behavior 335; principles of 336–338; relative advantage and 337; speaking and 123; subculture and 338; trialability and 337; as universal 336; values in 335; *see also* intercultural communication
Cuomo, Mario 126

D'Agostino, Phil 364
Daniels, William R. 385
Dantzscher, Jamie 441
Dayton, George D. 102
decisional roles 4
decision making: ethics and 68–69, 71–72, **72**
defensiveness 279
DeKoven, Bernard 396–397
Demczak, Ron 301
Denhollander, Rachael 439–440
Denny's 42
"desk rage" **357**
Dickson, Randy 228
digital age 217–218
discrimination, appearance-based 320
disseminator role 4
Dixie Industries, Inc. 370–375, **373**
Dominos Pizza 27–32, *28, 29*
Donnell, James 422
Donnley, Dana 202–203

Dornacher, Nathan 239
Dorsett, Tony 92
Doyle, Andy 412
dramatic forecasts 124
Drucker, Peter 1
drug development 58
Duerson, David 84
Duhigg, Charles 101, 103
dunnhumbyUSA 99

Earl's Family Restaurants 282–290
Easterling, Ray 84, 91
Ebersberger, Wayne 310
Eccles, Robert 1
editing 8
education: of audience 118
efficiency: as core skill 5
ego gratification 191
Ekman, Paul 303
Electronic Communication Privacy Act 226
Ellenbogen, Richard G. 91
Ells, Steve 47, 52
Elop, Stephen 157, 162–163
Elwood, Mark 221
e-mail 220–224, 230
emblems 306
emotional security 191
employer ethics 67
Engen, Trygg 312
Enron 66
entrepreneur role 4, 5
Epley, Nicholas 116
Eppes, Francis 65
ERG theory of motivation 190–191, 191
Espiritu, Anne 399, 405
esteem needs 190
ethical conduct 73
ethical leadership 73–74
ethical principles 74
ethical reasoning 73
ethical sensibility 72
ethical statements 74–76
ethical values 75
ethics: business 67–68; communication 65–77, 72; decision making and 68–69, 71–72, 72; employer 67; integrated approach to 69–70; levels of inquiry in 68; moral principles and 70–71
ethnicity: intercultural communication and 331–332
ethnic origin: of audience 119
ethnocentrism 338
etiquette: technology 228–230
evidence: in communication 123–124
examples: in speaking 125
Excel Industries, Inc. 80–82
existence needs 190

expectation: nonverbal communication and 303
eye contact 307

Facebook 219–220, 254–261, 256, 257, 259, 260
Fager, Jeff 424
Faircloth, Kelly 404
Fast Casual (FC) 49
FC see Fast Casual (FC)
FedEx 44
feedback: acknowledgment of 279; behavior in 275; breathing and 278; case examples 291–297; clarity in 278; common language in 275; communication and 39; conflict and 359; constructive 274–276; context and 274; defensiveness and 279; definitions in 275; descriptive 276; effective 276–277; exaggeration in 277; exercises 298–299; judgmentalism and 277; labels in 277; listening and 278; need for 274; negative 274; objective 276; positive 274; quality of 297; receiving 278–279; timing of 275; when not to give 276
feelings: communication and 122
Feldman, Linda 371, 373–374
Fiedler, Edell 219
field cases 463–464
figurehead role 3
Finnessy, Joan 116
First Amendment 378
Flood, Amy 60, 61
Floyd, James J. 267
Flynn, Nancy 226
football 84–92, 376–381
Foschi, Luigi 170
France, Mike 423
"front page" test 77

Gabriel, Allison 356
Galaxy Note 7 239–245, 240, 241, 243–245
Gates, Bill 402
Gebbia, Joe 12–13
gender: of audience 119
Gidley, Dick 135
Gifford, Robert 303
Gilead Sciences 56–62, 57
Giles, Micaela 12
Gilmore, Leigh 441
Giuliani, Rudolph 433
Glass, David 391
Gold, Vic 424
Goldsmith, Marshall 265
Goleman, Daniel 266
Goodell, Roger 84, 88–89, 377, 378–379
Gordon, Darryl 115–116

Gordon, Mark 364
Green, Brian 239
growth: safety and 12–20, 14–16
growth needs 191
Guest, Robert H. 4
Guest ID systems 102–103
Gulbranson, Jeanne 356
Gulick, Alan 266
Guskiewicz, Kevin 90

habit formation 100
Hall, Edward T. 310, 311
Hamermesh, Daniel 307
Hamill, Pete 426
Hammond, Kristi 27–32, 28, 29
Harding, Jacqueline 228
Harkins, Keith 373–374
Harris, Jacqueline 342–343
Hartung, Adam 402
Hartung, Jack 52
Hayward, Tony 419
Hayward Healthcare Systems, Inc. 367–369
hepatitis C 58–60
Heraclitus 37
Hill, Kashmir 258
Hirsh, Alan R. 312
Hobor, Nancy 387
Hoff, Susan 183–184
Holacracy 408–415, 410
Holmes, Elizabeth 205–212
Holt, Lester 428
"House of Commons" system, for meetings 392
Hsieh, Tony 408, 409, 412, 413
humor 124
Humphrey, Judith 130

illustrators 306
IM see instant messaging (IM)
immigration: intercultural communication and 332
immortality 192
income: of audience 118
inference 303
informational roles 4; as socially constructed 9
informative memo 146–147
Inghilleri, Leonardo 396
instant messaging (IM) 228
interactionism 357
intercultural communication: abroad 333–334; age and 332; business and 334–335; case examples 342–353, 349–350, 352; ethnicity and 331–332; families and 332; immigration and 332; population growth and 332; women and 333; see also culture

Internet: online behavior and 219; in research 487–489
interpersonal roles 3–4
interviews, media 491–495; anecdotes in 433; appearance in 430; arguments in 433; audience and 420–421; communications office and 424–425; control of 432–433; decision to take 423–425; examples in 433; follow-up for 434; ground rules for 430; illustrations in 433; importance of 420–423; likability in 433; makeup in 430; messaging in 430; as opportunity to address public concerns 421–422; as opportunity to apologize 422–423; as opportunity to inform 421; as opportunity to reinforce credibility 423; as opportunity to set record straight 422; as opportunity to tell story 421; pocket cards for 430; public affairs office and 424–425; researching reporter in 429; strategy development for 429; see also media
intimate space 310
introduction: in speaking 124–125
Ivester, Doug 42

Jackson, Bob 367–369
Jackson-Luth, Jennifer 458
Jay Z 351
Jefferson, Thomas 65
Jensen, Dave 115
job characteristics, of manager 5
Jobs, Steve 131
Johnson, Belinda 19
Johnson, Kevin 419
Johnson & Johnson 248–252
Jones, Allen 381
Jones, Buddy 368
Jones, Jerry 379–380
Jones, Steve 219
journalism see interviews, media; media
judgments: moral 70, 72–74; value 72

Kaepernick, Colin 376–381
Kelleher, Herb 306
Kennedy, Marilyn Moats 356
Kim, Charles 414
Kissane, Erin 259
Koch, Ed 273–274
Kool-Aid 459
Kotter, John 2
Kraft, Robert 86
Kramer, Adam D. I. 257
Kravis, Henry 42
Kroger 99, 291–297

Lake, Deborah 275
Lange, Maggie 404

language: importance of 1–2
Larson-Green, Julie 158–159
Lashinsky, Adam 131
Lauer, Matt 441
Lavingia, Sahil 403
Lawson, Renee 447
layoff announcement 157–163, *158*
leader role 3, 5–6
leadership: ethical 73–74
Lee, Mark 345, 348
legalese 152
Leonard, Rob 135–136
letters, business 149–150, 477–478
Levitt, Arthur 127, 142
Lewandowsky, Stephan 195
liaison role 3–4
library cases 464
Liebmann, Wendy 301
liking 188
Ling, Rich 224
Liotta, Dennis 57
Lipovetsky, Gilles 75
listening: acceptance and 267; active 272–273; affective 297; benefits of 267; bias and 268; case examples 282–290; cognitive 297; distraction and 268–269; emotional collisions and 267; emotion-laden words and 270; empathy and 271; as essential skill 265–266; facts and 269–270; faking attention in 270; follow through and 273; habits 270–272; improvement of 273; ineffective 267–268; interruption and 270, 271; inventory 273; for meaning 297; nonverbal 297; oversimplification and 268; overstimulation and 269; paraphrasing and 272; prejudice and 268; preoccupation in 268; problem-solving and 267; rationalization of poor 269; reasons for 266; receptiveness and 267; reflecting conclusions in 272–273; reflecting feelings in 272; reflecting meaning in 272; self-centeredness and 267; self-consciousness and 267; self-esteem and 267; speaking and 120–122
lithium-ion batteries 239–245, *240*, *241*, *243–245*
local vision 6
Lohman, James J. 81
Long, Terry 91
Lopez, Jacob 12, 19
L'Oreal USA 318–322
Lorigan, Brian 135–136
Lovell, Mark R. 90
love needs 190
love objects 192
Low, Albert 365

MacConnell, Bridgett 459
Mackey, John 446–447, 448
Macy's 347
Madoff, Bernie 66
management skills: conceptual 6; technical 6
manager: crisis handler role of 4; decisional roles of 4; disseminator role of 4; entrepreneur role of 4, 5; figurehead role of 3; informational roles of 4; interpersonal roles of 3–4; job characteristics 5; leader role of 3, 5–6; liaison role of 3–4; monitor role of 4; negotiator role of 4; resource allocator role of 4; roles 3–4; spokesperson role of 4
Mangione, Gordon 395
Mankins, Michael 390
Maravelas, Anna 356
Maroney, McKayla 440
Mars, Incorporated 456–460
Martin, Trayvon 456–460
Maslow, Abraham 189, *190*
material objects: in culture 335
Mayer, Marissa 400–404
McBride, Sarah 403
McCarthy, John 348
McIntyre, Tim 27–28, 30
McKay, Michael 309
McKee, Ann 91
McMahon, Jim 92
McNealy, Scott 225
Meade, Dana 230
meaning: context and 9
media: as business 425–426; case examples 436–460, *452*, *453*; fact *vs.* opinion in 428; interviews 420–423; local management in 428–429; markets 426–427; mistakes by 427; retractions 427–428; sophistication 426–427; see also interviews, media
media relations 491–495
meeting reports 148
meetings: agenda for 389; case examples 399–415, *410*; conflict and 388; "Congressional" system for 392; defined 387; dislike of 385; for education 387; ending 395; forms of 392; "House of Commons" system for 392; improving 396–397; keeping on track 392–393; listening in 393–394; for motivation 387; motivation for 386–387; for networking 387; notes in 395; objective of 388–389; participants in 389–390; planning for 388–390; preparation for 390–391; productivity in 395–396; for recreation 387; as reward 387; roles in 391; site details

for 390–391; styles of 392; subgroup focus in 393; time agreements for 393; timing of 387–388; topic drift in 393; when not to have 388
Mehrabian, Albert 364, 394
memo: attractive 148–149; business 144–145; editing 149; formats 147–148; informative 146–147; inviting 148–149; persuasive 147; sample 479–482; *see also* writing
memory 195
Menin, Julie 446, 449, 452
Merck 44
Messer, Michael 364
#MeToo 441
Michaels, Paul 460
Microsoft Corporation 157–163, *158*
Milgram, Stanley 184
Miller, Emma Ann 440
Mintzberg, Harvey 2, 3
Monaghan, Tom 29
monitor role 4
Moore, Rashad 459
moral judgments 70, 72–74
moral principles 70–71
Mosvick, Roger 386
motivation: basic needs as 189; channeling 193; consistency and 192–193; ERG theory of 190–191, *191*; human needs as 189, *190*; providing, for audience 189–190, *190*; rationality and 192–193; security needs and 190
Motrin 248–252
Mulcahy, Anne 75
Mullenburg, Matt 403
Murphy, Patrick E. 74

Nadella, Satya 160–161
Nash, Laura 76
Nassar, Larry 436–442
national anthem 378
National Football League (NFL) 84–92, 376–381
National Football League Players' Association (NFLPA) 85–86
Naughton, Jamie 414
negotiator role 4
Negroponte, Nicholas 217–218
Nemetz, Julie 309
Nichols, Ralph 265–266, 267
Niehaus, Chris 228
Nohria, Nitin 1
noise: communication and 39
nonverbal communication: accenting in 304; action language in 302; adaptors in 306; affect displays in 306; artifacts in 307–308; basic considerations in 302; believability of 305; body movement in 306;

case example 318–322, 323–329, *326–328*; categories of 302; clothing as 301; color and 311–312; and communication environment 306; as communicative 305; complementing in 304; context and 305; contradicting in 304; cues and 303–304; dimensions of code 305–306; effects of 314–315; emblems in 306; expectations and 303; eye contact in 307; functions of 304; illustrators in 306; inference and 303; as metacommunication 305; object language in 302; packaging and 305; paralanguage in 308–309; physical appearance and 307; principles of 305; process of 303; regulating in 304; regulators in 306; repeating in 304; rules and 305; sign language in 302; silence and 313–315; smell and 312–313; sound and 313; space and 309–311; substituting in 304; taste and 313; time and 311; touch in 308
Nulty, Christopher 17
numerical method, for citations 486
Nydell, Margaret 333

Oak Brook Medical Systems, Inc. 342–343
object language 302
Olympic Committee 199–200, 436–442
one-on-one conversations 6
one-sided arguments 194
online behavior 219
opinions, persuasion and *185*, 186, 187
Oreskes, Michael 441
organizational culture: communication and 41
organizational dynamics: communication and 41
Osgood, Charles 115
overview paragraph 145–146

Packard, Vance 191
Page, Larry 415
Palillo, Michael 345
Palin, Sarah 424
Palmer, Art 347
Papas, Nick 19
paralanguage 308–309
paraphrasing 486
Park, Robert 301
Pash, Jeff 86
Patterson, Neal L. 176–177
Pavolv, Ivan P. 184
peer groups 193
Pelley, Scott 424
Pellman, Elliot 90
Pence, Michael 380

Perez, Andy 219
personality preferences: communication and 41–42
personal space 310–311
persuasion: attitudes and *185*, 186, 187–188; audience in 189, 196; audience motivation and 189–190, *190*; authority and 189; basic needs and 189; in behaviorism 184; beliefs and *185*, 185–186; case example 199–212; in cognitivism 185; consistency and 188; for creation of new attitudes 188; for crystallization of latent opinion 187; emotions in 197; hearts and minds in 195–196; human needs and 189, *190*; liking and 188; listening in 196; memory and 195; for modification of existing attitudes 188; for neutralization of hostile opinion 187; objects of 187; one-sided arguments in 194; opinions and *185*, 186, 187; reciprocity and 188; for reinforcement of existing attitudes 188; for reinforcement of positive opinion 187; scarcity and 189; schools of thought on 184–187, *185*; science of 188–189; simplicity in 196; social proof and 188; successful attempts at 189–194, *190*, *191*; two-sided arguments in 194–195
persuasive memo 147
Pfeffer, Jeffrey 414
Phillips, Kayla 346
photo sharing 219
physical appearance: nonverbal communication and 307
Pichette, Patrick 403
plagiarism 484
pocket cards 430
Pole, Andrew 102
Polet, Jacques 74–75
Polo Ralph Lauren 319
Porath, Christine 355, 356
Power, F. Clark 70
power needs 192
predictions: in speaking 124
predictive analytics 98–104
prejudice: communication and 122
presentations: to small groups 7
press conference 137–139
privacy 98–104, 225–228
problem-solving 267
Procter & Gamble 437
project lists 148
Proposition F 16–17
public distance 311
public speaking 7 *see* speaking
Putnam, J. Adaire 43

questions, listener 121–122
Quinn, Tom 420
quotations: in research 487; in speaking 125

Raisman, Aly 440
reader: needs 144; time of 143; *see also* audience
reciprocity 188
reflective statements 71
regulating 304
regulators 306
rehearsal: in speaking 131
Reid, Eric 376–377
Reinsch, Lamar 422
relatedness needs 191
repeating 304
research: in case studies 471–472; sources in 483–489
resource allocator role 4
retractions 427–428
Richardson, Jerry 42
Riordan, Michael 56–57
Ritz-Carlton 396
Robertson, Brian 408, 411
Rocci, Fulvio 166
Roderick, Richard 318
Rogelberg, Steven 385
Rokeach, Milton 185
roles, manager 3–4
roots 192
Rosen, Ruth 402
Rossman, Katherine 224
Rozakis, Bob 224
Ryburg, Jon 386

safety: growth and 12–20, *14–16*
Samsung Electronics Co., Ltd. 239–245, *240, 241, 243–245*
San Francisco Proposition F 16–17
scarcity: persuasion and 189
Scheindlin, Shira A. 350
Scherker, Amanda 258
Schettino, Francesco 169–170
Schinazi, Raymond 57
Schrage, Michael 389, 395, 404
Schultz, Howard 108, 419
Seau, Junior 84, 92
security needs 190
self-actualization needs 190
self-centeredness 267
self-consciousness 267
self-esteem 267
Setzer, Michael 27–32, *28, 29*
sex: of audience 119
Shalev, Areih 433
Shapiro, Alan 400
Shapiro, Marc 422
Sharapova, Maria 323–329, *326–328*

sharing economy 13
Sharpton, Al 350
Sherwood, Kaitlin 221
sign language 302
silence: nonverbal communication and 313–315
*60 Minutes* 424
Skilling, Jeffrey K. 422
skills: conceptual 6; relating 6; technical 6
Skinner, B. F. 184
Skittles 456–460
smell: nonverbal communication and 312–313
Smith, Brad 3
Smith, DeMaurice 85
Smith, Jane 309
social conformity 193
social construction: of information 9
social media 27–32, *28, 29,* 30–31, 219–220, 248–252, 254–261, *256, 257, 259, 260*
social networking 219
social news 219
social proof 188
societal norms 193
socioeconomic status: of audience 118
sound: nonverbal communication and 313
Sovaldi 56–62, *57*
space: nonverbal communication and 309–311
Spacey, Kevin 441
speaking: acoustics in 132; anecdotes in 124; audience in 117–119; audience interest in 126–128; audience needs in 128; brevity in 126; case example 135–136, 137–139; cause and effect in 125; chronological order in 125; clarity in 127; climactic moment in 125; communication obstacles in 122–123; conclusion in 126; confidence in 131–132; culture and 123; current events in 125; delivery approach in 128–129; descriptions in 125; dramatic forecasts in 124; evidence in 123–124; extemporaneous 129; fear allaying in 128; fear of 115; feelings and 122; geographic structure in 125; humor in 124; impromptu 129; introduction in 124–125; language and 123; lectern in 132; lights in 132; listening and 120–122; logic in 127; manuscripted 128–129; memorized 128; message delivery in 132–133; microphone in 132; negative styles of 120–121; notes in 131, 132; opinions in 125; organization in 124–126; plain 127; poise in 129; positive styles of 120; predictions in 124; prejudice

and 122; preparation for 117; problem solution in 125; questions and 121–122; quotations in 125; reasonableness in 127; reasons for 116, 119–129; rehearsal in 131; relaxation in 126; room layout in 132; simplicity in 125; spatial structure in 125; stage in 132; stereotypes and 122; strategy for 117; striking examples in 125; structure in 125; topical organization in 125; visual support in 129–131; in writing 153; writing *vs.* 116–117
Spector, Paul 356
Spiers, Elizabeth 404
spokesperson role 4
Sproull, Lee 2
staff conference 392
Staples, Inc. 137–139
Starbucks 107–111, 419
Steele, Lockhart 441
Steele, Shari 225
Stephens, Kyle 440
stereotypes 122
Stern, Amy 459
Stevens, Leonard 265–266
Stewart, James 403
Stewart, Martha 66, 422
Stewart, Rosemary 2–3, 4
stop and frisk 348–350
stress: conflict and 356–357
striking examples: in speaking 125
style: in writing 151–152
subculture 338
substituting 304
supply chain: in restaurant industry *50,* 50–51
Swinmurn, Nick 409
Swisher, Kara 399, 402

Tamer, Delly 229
Target Corporation 98–104
taste: nonverbal communication and 313
taxation, international 109–110
Taylor, Teresa 386
technology: case example 239–261, *240, 241, 243–245, 256, 257, 259, 260;* communication and 218–219; digital age and 217–218; email 220–224; ethics and 69; etiquette with 228–230; online behavior and 219; privacy and 225–228; social media and 219–220; text messaging 224–225; virtual work and 230–232; workplace monitoring and 225–228
telecommuting 401–402
teleconferencing, video 7, 232–234
telephone conversations 7
tennis 323–329, *326–328*
Terry Stop 348–350

text messaging 224–225, 228
Theranos, Inc. 205–212
Thiry, Kent 274
Thomas, Kimberly 389
Thomas, Landon 66–67
Thomison, Tom 408, 411
Thompson, John 160
Thompson, Kathy 266
time: nonverbal communication and 311
time fragmentation 5
Tobin, Glenn 177
Tolley, Jim 426
Tolliver, Earl, III 286
Tomlin, Mike 379
topic drift 393
touch: in nonverbal communication 308
traumatic brain injuries 84–92
Trevino, Linda Klebe 76
Trump, Donald 380
"Twinkie Defense" 459–460
Twitter 219–220
two-sided arguments 194–195
Tylenol 76

Ulrich, David 414
Ulrich, Elizabeth 333
United States Olympic Committee
    199–200, 436–442

value judgments 72
values: as in competition 5; conflict and
    358; corporate 75; ethical 75
Van Slyke, Erik 357
Vaughan-Nichols, Steven J. 259
video sharing 219
video teleconferencing 7
Villanueva, Alejandro 379

Vioxx 44
viral videos 27–32, *28, 29*
virtual work 230–232
vision, local 6
visual support: in speaking 129–131
voice mail etiquette 229–230
Voortella, Nox 414

Wahba, Phil 52
Wallace, Mike 424
Waller, Mary 396
Wal-Mart 391
Walters, Chad 89
Ward, Artemus 422
Warren, Nigel 18
Watson, John B. 184
webinars 232–234
Weiner, Sophie 259
Weinstein, Harvey 441
Weisinger, Hendrie 364
Welch, Jack 403
Welch, Suzy 403
West, Alfred P., Jr. 70
Whirlpool Corporation 202–203
White, Dan 459–460
Whole Foods Market, Inc. 446–453,
    *452, 453*
Wieber, Jordyn 441
wikis 219
Williams, David K. 3
Williams, Ed 368
Wiswall, John 318
Wolf, Naomi 307
women: intercultural communication and
    333
working virtually 230–232
workplace monitoring 225–228

World-Com 66
writing 8; apologies in 151; brevity in 145;
    business letters 149–150; business
    memo 144–145; case example
    157–163, *158, 167, 168*, 168–174,
    *171*, 176–180, *178*; clarity in 145,
    149; communication strategies
    in 145; conference reports 148;
    contractions in 153; development
    of 155; editing of 149; efficiency in
    152; encouragement of 155; errors
    in 144; explanations in 150–151;
    fact *vs.* opinion in 144; headings in
    155; informative memo 146–147;
    layoff announcement 157–163, *158*;
    legalese in 152; meeting reports 148;
    in meetings 395; overview paragraph
    in 145–146; passive verbs in 153–154;
    personal pronouns in 153; persuasive
    memo 147; project lists 148; reader
    needs and 144; reader time and 143;
    sentence length in 153; speaking in
    153; speaking *vs.* 116–117; specialized
    terms in 152; style in 151–152;
    subheadings in 155; technical terms
    in 151; as threshold skill 143; *see also*
    memo

Yahoo! 399–405
Yanowitz, Elysa 318–319, 321
Young, Misty 221

Zappos 408–415, *410*
Zdor, John 439
Zhao, Neng 335
Zimmerman, George 456–460
Zuckerberg, Mark 254–255